THE 'SMALL TOWNS' OF ROMAN BRITAIN

THE 'SMALL TOWNS' OF ROMAN BRITAIN

Barry C. Burnham and John Wacher

B.T. Batsford Ltd, London

© Barry C. Burnham and John Wacher 1990
First published 1990

All rights reserved. No part of this publication
may be reproduced, in any form or by any means,
without permission from the Publisher

Typeset by Servis Filmsetting Ltd, Manchester
and printed in Great Britain by
Butler & Tanner, Frome, Somerset

Published by B.T. Batsford Ltd
4 Fitzhardinge Street, London W1H 0AH

A CIP catalogue record for this book is
available from the British Library

ISBN 0 7134 6175 6

Crown Copyright/RAF Photographs
reproduced by permission of the Controller HMSO

For my Mum,
who, sadly, did not live to
see the end product.
(B. C. B.)

TABLE OF CONTENTS

ILLUSTRATIONS

NOTE

Numerals in square brackets, at the head of each page, refer to the page numbers on which the relevant notes can be located.

PREFACE

The 'small towns' of Roman Britain have for a long time been something of a Cinderella in urban studies, with pride of place going to the cities and civitas capitals of the province. This book is intended to help rectify this attitude. It follows very much the same pattern set by John Wacher's earlier book *The Towns of Roman Britain*. A number of chapters at both the beginning and the end are devoted to a general overview of the subject. The central core deals individually with 54 of the best-known sites, which are grouped together according to the similarity of their morphological features and their identifiable functions. Thus there are groups of what might be termed potential cities, minor towns, religious and industrial sites, fortified and unfortified settlements. In each case the genesis of the site and its functions are examined, followed by its physical development and decline; the major, and some minor, buildings,

and fortifications where they exist, are described individually. Each site is accompanied by a plan, showing, as far as possible, the most recent discoveries.

There are also collections of comparative plans of building types, such as winged-corridor buildings and *mansiones*. Plates have been restricted to aerial photographs, and these only where they add significantly to the archaeology; surprisingly, even now, not all small towns have been adequately recorded from the air. It was decided at an early stage not to have bibliographies for individual sites, since they would have led to a good deal of needless repetition; consequently there is a very comprehensive bibliography to which the reader is referred by means of notes related to each chapter.

B. C. B. and J. S. W.
June 1989

ACKNOWLEDGEMENTS

The writers are grateful for all the help that they have been given, without which the book could not have been written: to Helen Burnham for typing – and retyping – the entire manuscript; to Andy Clark and Adam Sharpe for preparing the town plans; to Susan Vaughan for compiling the index; to John Alexander, Ken Annable, Frank and Nancy Ball, Philip Barker, Richard Bartlett, D. Bestwick, David Bird, Tony Brown, Gilbert Burleigh, Tony Clark, Barry Cunliffe, Geoffrey Dannell, Brian Dix, Christopher Going, Michael Green, Dennis Harding, Richard Hingley, Derek Hurst, Phil Jones, Keith and Vivienne Knowles, Peter Leach, Don Mackreth, Alan McWhirr, Christine Mahany, Martin Millett, Nicholas Palmer, Jonathan Parkhouse, Clive Partridge, Joyce Pullinger, Warwick Rodwell, Trevor Rowley, Brian Simmons, C. Stanley, Ian Stead, Malcolm Todd, Graham Webster, John Peter Wild and David Wilson, many of whom read through and corrected sections of the text as well as providing vital unpublished information. Despite all this valuable help the writers reserve all errors of fact or interpretation to themselves.

ONE
INTRODUCTION AND PROBLEMS

This book is intended to cover the very wide range of sites which are euphemistically called 'small towns' in the literature on Roman Britain. Such sites have been a source of considerable argument among scholars, much of it directed at a fruitless semantic debate over what constitutes a 'town' and which sites can legitimately be included. Fortunately, for our purposes, almost all of them have been subject to some level of excavation and research in the past, while the last 30 years or so have seen a dramatic increase in the quality of the evidence from fieldwork, excavation and aerial archaeology. Thus the time is now ripe for a full assessment of their character and of the outstanding problems.

The earliest, and still perhaps the most useful, general synthesis of the small towns is the short article published by M. Todd in 1970.[1] This was followed by a longer and more disparate volume edited in 1975 by W. Rodwell and T. Rowley, which contained both general articles and syntheses of specific sites;[2] among them was an early attempt to subdivide the class as a whole into more manageable categories.[3] More recently, the west Midlands sites have been analysed in detail by J. Crickmore,[4] while roadside settlements in general have received attention from R. F. Smith.[5] Sadly, despite the recognition in this literature of an apparently discrete class of small towns, there is to date no commonly agreed list of sites covered by the term, witness the changing categories used by the successive editions of the Ordnance Survey's *Map of Roman Britain*.[6]

To some extent, such debate is hardly surprising for a number of reasons: (1) the time-span of Roman Britain and the internal changes within the empire ensured that individual sites often varied in importance and status; (2) the adoption of different 'concepts of urbanism' and the selection of subjective criteria by past and present scholars has operated against any level of consensus; (3) the limitations and biases of the archaeological record, especially when dealing with unwalled and isolated nucleated settlements and with those sites which are closest to the threshold between town and village; (4) the frequent recognition of new sites as work becomes more extensive (e.g. Frilford and Cowbridge).

As far as this book is concerned, there will be broadest agreement at the upper end of the small-town scale, where the major towns or cities are clearly distinguished in legal, functional and morphological terms;[7] though we should not forget that some of our small towns may have aspired to the rank of civitas capitals during the third and fourth centuries.[8] No such easily defined or comparably simple solution is available at the lower end of the scale. There is general agreement that sites which are primarily agricultural must be excluded and the position seems to be reasonably clear at an excavated village site like Catsgore or Fotheringhay;[9] but there remains a considerable grey area above this level between one man's 'small town' and another's 'village', largely because here the problems of conflicting terminology, subjective criteria, and, above all, the limitations of the archaeological record are at their most acute. Attempts to include sites because they had defences or because they were related to the communications network have not found much favour, while the suggestion that a dependence upon trade is essential has proved difficult to quantify in archaeological terms.

Given such problems and the likelihood that definitive proof will not be forthcoming, only the unwary would try to impose a strait-jacket definition upon the existing evidence. Instead, it has been found appropriate to include a wide range of sites which have at one time or another been called small towns, even though, for some,

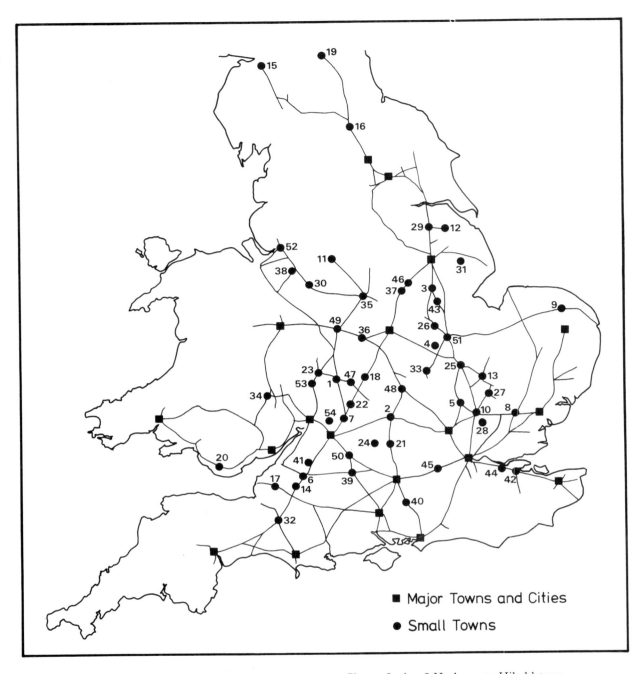

I Map of Small Towns discussed in Chs. 6–12.
1 Alcester; **2** Alchester; **3** Ancaster; **4** Ashton;
5 Baldock; **6** Bath; **7** Bourton-on-the-Water;
8 Braintree; **9** Brampton; **10** Braughing;
11 Buxton; **12** Caistor (Lincs); **13** Cambridge;
14 Camerton; **15** Carlisle; **16** Catterick;
17 Charterhouse; **18** Chesterton-on-Fosse;
19 Corbridge; **20** Cowbridge; **21** Dorchester-on-Thames; **22** Dorn; **23** Droitwich; **24** Frilford;
25 Godmanchester; **26** Great Casterton; **27** Great
Chesterford; **28** Harlow; **29** Hibaldstow;
30 Holditch; **31** Horncastle; **32** Ilchester;
33 Irchester; **34** Kenchester; **35** Little Chester;
36 Mancetter; **37** Margidunum; **38** Middlewich;
39 Mildenhall; **40** Neatham; **41** Nettleton;
42 Rochester; **43** Sapperton; **44** Springhead;
45 Staines; **46** Thorpe-by-Newark;
47 Tiddington; **48** Towcester; **49** Wall;
50 Wanborough; **51** Water Newton;
52 Wilderspool; **53** Worcester; **54** Wycomb

there is likely to be little agreement among archaeologists (fig. 1). This has allowed us to explore all the variations within the archaeological evidence and to propose identifiable subgroups within the general category. Whether a recognisable or acceptable urban or non-urban threshold is thereby defined will depend more on the personal prejudice of the reader than on any assertion made by the writers.

Any study of the small towns of Roman Britain relies almost entirely upon archaeological evidence, since there is almost no documentary or epigraphic material of any real value. This inevitably imposes limitations upon what we can study, not least because past excavations show a marked imbalance in the scope and extent of what has been achieved.[10] Before the twentieth century much of the work was dictated by the Antonine Itinerary, which acted as a convenient road map and guide to the location of Roman sites on the ground; exceptions to this include the pioneering work of Artis at Water Newton, Lawrence at Wycomb and May at Wilderspool. Within this century, the yearly 'Roman Britain in . . .' summaries contained in the *Journal of Roman Studies* (1921–69) and *Britannia* (since 1970) give a good impression of the level of research and its scope.

For the 1920s and 1930s work on the small towns was relatively limited and small scale, ranging from sections through the defences as at Alchester and Dorchester-on-Thames to internal structural complexes, as at Camerton, Kenchester and Margidunum.[11] The war years inevitably interrupted most excavation work, and even when it was resumed in the late 1940s and early 1950s, it remained small scale. Most excavations took the form of individual narrow trenches, providing in hindsight inadequate samples by modern requirements. Long-term campaigns were underway at Camerton and Margidunum, while in 1948–9 rescue work enabled trenching of the northern part of Great Chesterford in some detail. The later 1950s onwards saw an increasing number of excavations directed at small towns. Extended campaigns sampled the defences, notably at Great Casterton, Kenchester and Mildenhall, while larger-scale excavations signalled a growing interest in the internal layout; trenching at Holditch revealed much about a previously unknown site, while significant progress was made by the excavations in advance of roadworks at Catterick, in which about one-quarter of the site was examined. At sites like Godmanchester and Springhead, the earliest campaigns in what were to become extensive programmes were just beginning, while the seeds of the later regional interest in west Midlands small towns were being sown at Droitwich, Mancetter and Wall among others.

By comparison with preceding years, the 1960s and 1970s saw something of an explosion in the number of sites being excavated. Parallel with this, there has also been an important shift from small-scale trenching towards larger open-area excavations directed at examining internal features, often at the expense of the defences. Hence the explosion of information has been even more pronounced. It would be impossible to mention all the sites in detail here, but it is worth identifying at least the scope of recent work as an indicator to its variable character and intensity at individual sites. At some small towns, for instance, specific building complexes have been examined in detail, including the temple and bathing facilities at Bath, the Bays Meadow complex at Droitwich and the temples precinct at Springhead; at others, only limited rescue work has been undertaken, among them Ancaster, Braintree, Irchester and Thorpe; elsewhere a range of individual locations has been sampled over a number of years, most notably at Alcester, Cambridge, Godmanchester, Wall and Worcester; and at a growing number of sites, large-scale excavations have been undertaken, including Baldock, Hibaldstow, Ilchester and Wanborough. Together, these have all contributed abundant new information, much of which is now in the process of being published in detail.

At the regional level, however, there has been a considerable disparity in the interest given towards broader questions about small towns. One of the most progressive regions in this respect has been the west Midlands under the guidance of several individuals and urban units.[12] An equally important regional emphasis has been inspired in Essex,[13] but sadly such studies have not been followed in neighbouring areas.

Alongside this explosion in the amount of excavation at small towns, a further source of information, especially from the 1950s onwards, has been the growing importance of aerial archaeology. That by the Cambridge Committee for Aerial Photography, among others, has provided an invaluable source of new material,[14] not just as an obvious bonus to the excavated evidence, as at Kenchester, but also at those sites, like Brough-on-Fosse and Dorn, where it supplies virtually the only evidence currently available. The potential of this method when carried out season after season has recently been demonstrated by the composite plans drawn up for Water Newton and its suburbs.

Within this body of steadily increasing information, much of which is now being published in scattered local, regional and national sources, an attempt is long overdue to collate the available evidence and to identify its strengths and weaknesses. In the following chapters, not only will a selection of sites be described in detail, but their various functions and associations will also be examined in an attempt to explain the reasons which lay behind their foundation and continued existence.

Given the importance attached to the archaeological evidence for any study of the small towns, and a corresponding need to subdivide them into manageable sub-groups, it is clear that the questions of internal morphology and assumed functions are vital to our understanding. Together, they help to define also points of difference and similarity between the small towns under discussion and those which are more properly called major towns or cities.

When broad morphological comparisons are made, it rapidly becomes obvious that most small towns reveal little evidence of ordered planning, a point well illustrated by Water Newton and Irchester. Most of them originated as ribbon developments at route centres or along the main roads to which side-lanes or streets were added as need arose. There appears to be a distinction, however, between sites dependent entirely on the main roads and those where an internal street network represents a significant feature, a fact which may help to distinguish between different levels of importance within the settlement hierarchy. Only in one or two instances is there any evidence for some form of regulated street arrangement, as for instance at Catterick, where the initial layout conformed to the outlines of the fort.

The buildings were arranged within this framework of streets. Few small towns in Britain appear to possess any buildings planned in such a way as to be obviously associated with local government, such as a *forum-basilica* complex.

Many did, however, possess buildings, including fortifications, which are likely to reflect some function of the provincial government, most notably those associated with the *cursus publicus*. Even so, the more important of the small towns appear to have possessed some form of urban core, in the form of either official buildings (Water Newton and Corbridge), or a market-place (Godmanchester), while others had an obvious religious focus (Springhead, Harlow and Frilford).

Equally, most small towns appear not to have possessed much in the way of amenities, except the obvious spa towns like Bath and perhaps some of the religious sites like Frilford; admittedly, Catterick inherited a water supply system from the fort and *vicus*, while the mining town of Charterhouse may likewise have inherited its amphitheatre, but most had little such provision. Bath-houses are more common than might be expected, although even these are likely to have had some sort of official role in connection with *mansiones*, as at Chelmsford, Godmanchester and Wall. Just as markedly, few small towns possess large, comfortably appointed private houses to match those more frequently found in the chartered cities and civitas capitals. Some exceptions exist, apparently at Bath and Kenchester for instance, but generally where they do, they are few in number and are often in comparison lacking in the extremes of architectural sophistication. Individual examples, like that at Great Chesterford, are often very difficult to interpret in terms of potential domestic, agricultural or official functions. In contrast to these larger structures, most of the buildings in small towns are simpler in character, frequently taking the form of a strip building with combined shop and living quarters set end-on to the street frontage, as at Corbridge and Hibaldstow.

In common with their larger counterparts, fortifications were often provided at some stage for many small towns, though not every site seems to have been thus protected. Among those which were, a tentative distinction can be drawn between those, like Water Newton and Kenchester, where the defences enclosed a substantial urban core, and those, like Wall or Mancetter, where they seldom encompassed more than a small defended strongpoint at the heart of a straggling ribbon settlement.

At the functional level, interpretations are

subject to the limitations imposed by the quality of the archaeological evidence, but a general picture emerges even from that. Once established, for whatever reason, the small towns had to develop some economic or other factor to ensure their survival. Most of them, therefore, developed some sort of economic base in much the same way as their major counterparts. In reality, all settlements, regardless of their size, provided some level of manufacturing capacity not only for their own communities, but also frequently for the surrounding countryside. Small towns in turn were dependent upon larger towns both for administration and for those goods which they could not supply themselves, so that with time, a hierarchy of settlements would be built up, all to some extent interdependent upon each other and upon the rural areas they served. Excavations and surveys at the small towns have repeatedly shown that even the smallest had some servicing capacity, usually in the form of the characteristic shops and workshops fronting the main streets. Indeed almost all the chief manufacturing and service industries are represented in one form or another, such as the goldsmith at Norton, tanning at Alcester, the bakery at Springhead and the metal-working capacity at Wilderspool. It was for this reason that Rivet proposed dependence on trade as the key factor in defining towns,[15] but, as Fulford has recently demonstrated, the surviving archaeological evidence may not be adequate to quantify this fact independent of documentary sources.[16]

Occasionally, small towns display a concentration on particular industries; Water Newton and Mancetter for instance lay at the centres of huge potteries, while others were closely connected with large-scale extraction, including Charterhouse (Mendip lead), Weston-under-Penyard (Forest of Dean iron) and Droitwich (brine). At several small towns, a predominance of metal-working and associated industries apparently suggests a more specialized role, perhaps linked to the specific needs of the army, witness those sites on the fringes of the highland zone at Northwich, Middlewich, Wilderspool and Little Chester. Such apparently industrial specialization among the small towns can be matched in the sphere of religion as well, as several clearly developed around some sort of existing religious centre, such as the temple

complexes at Harlow and Frilford or the medicinal hot springs at Bath. This can sometimes be difficult to define, however, because temples and religious activity are generally well represented in all small towns.

Despite such enhanced economic and specialist roles, there is little doubt that most small towns were closely connected with agricultural production, even those with an apparent industrial bias, for even potters and smiths need to eat and drink and be clothed and shod. The evidence for contemporary field systems is a clear indicator of such activities. Many also acted as centres for groups of villas and peasant settlements, and it is possible that they provided a reservoir of agricultural labour, as well as their economic services, at special times in the agricultural year.

One further specialized function conferred upon small towns was that connected with provincial or local government. The *cursus publicus* signified by the existence at several sites of *mansiones* was one of the earliest; examples have been identified at Catterick, Wanborough and Wall. Provincial officials are also represented by inscriptions from Dorchester-on-Thames, Bath and Irchester. While certainty is impossible, the presence of such officials may help to explain the presence of some more sophisticated buildings in the small towns, as for example the massive masonry-built structure with good quality painted plaster just inside the north gate at Thorpe-by-Newark. Epigraphic evidence from several small towns might also be taken to indicate that they served within the framework of local government by acting as centres for the constituent *pagi* of the *civitates* or even as promoted civitas capitals in their own right, though what types of buildings are to be expected in consequence is still unknown in Britain.

Many of these official functions were imposed on their respective small towns, especially those along the major provincial roads. At a later date, in the later third, or more probably in the fourth, century, several existing sites were fortified as road stations or *burgi*, a class of sites well known in northern Gaul and Germany. One such sequence has been identified along Watling Street between Towcester and Wroxeter, but others suggest themselves, despite less consistent spacing, along the Fosse Way and Ermine Street. In addition, the two sites on the Lincolnshire Wolds fit logically into this late official sphere, perhaps in connection with coastal defence. Yet other sites may have operated partly as naval bases, at Caister-by-Yarmouth or Richborough, and to an even greater extent at Dover. Catterick for a short period in the late fourth century appears to have doubled as a garrison town for a unit of the field army, while Dorchester-on-Thames, with its extensive early Saxon associations, may well be another.

These morphological and functional criteria form the basis of the following chapters alongside a discussion of origins, development and decline. Individually, the morphological issues are covered by Chapter 3, while the functional dimension is split between Chapters 4 and 5. In combination, such criteria have also been used to subdivide the small towns conveniently into manageable categories (Chapters 6 to 12). For the purpose of this subdivision, the following criteria have proved to be the most useful in general terms: the existence of a developed internal street network in contrast to simple ribbon developments; the presence of some sort of central core or focus within the plan; the range and diversity of individual building types; the presence or absence of romanized buildings and their specific location and function; the urban-core or strong-point nature of the defences; the level of economic specialization visible in the evidence, especially shops and workshops, in contrast to agricultural preoccupations; the level of specialized functions; and the importance of officially inspired functions.

It is to be hoped that this subdivision of the umbrella term 'small towns' will help to clarify the current state of knowledge while also identifying where more research is needed.

TWO
ORIGINS AND DEVELOPMENT

The study of the origins and development of the small towns has often been considerably over-simplified in Romano-British literature. Most assessments have taken the form of specific case-studies of individual sites, as for example at Bath,[1] because excavation and research have been sufficiently prolonged. Otherwise, more genera-lized syntheses have been produced, often making use of some sort of theoretical frame-work, such as the application of geographical central-place theory.[2] Most discussion has also focused on the formative importance of military and related official factors in the developmental process, to the detriment of economic aspects, within a chronological framework commencing with the Claudian invasion in AD 43. This state of affairs has been conditioned partly by the nature of our evidence and partly by the all too widely accepted theory that most small towns had military origins.[3] This essentially monocausal explanation has now been complicated and chal-lenged, at least in the south and east, by the recognition of a significant number of nucleated settlements in the late Iron Age, with the result that new avenues of research have been opened up.[4] In particular, the broader time-scale involved makes it much less relevant to separate the question of origins from the wider issue of the Roman impact on existing systems, while also forcing us to see the official Roman dimension as just one of a series of causative factors behind the development of small towns.

The idea that Romano-British towns had military origins has a long pedigree and has received considerable support both in theory and in practice. It is a well-established fact that soldiers throughout the Roman world attracted a whole host of camp followers, drawn by the lure of their pay packets and their enhanced spending power. Such camp followers became established in extra-mural settlements immediately outside fort gates, and, in time, developed sufficient economic potential to be able to survive the departure of the garrison itself. Among these extra-mural settlers can be found several groups: some were craftsmen and shopkeepers, many of them probably local natives, providing a range of services; others were merchants involved in long-distance trade, perhaps in connection with army supply; yet more were the unofficial wives and families of the soldiers, as well as prostitutes. In the Romano-British period, such military *vici* appear to have possessed some sort of communal organization sufficiently independent of the fort to set up their own dedications and to make limited corporate decisions.[5] Such a military origin is well attested by the settlements outside the forts of Wales, north England and Scotland, where groups of houses, official buildings and temples cluster along the roads and streets outside the main gates. Examples include Caer-hun and Trawscoed in Wales;[6] Chesters, House-steads and Old Carlisle in the North;[7] and Croy Hill on the Antonine Wall.[8] Unfortunately, the exact chronology of their development is often very poorly known; in Wales, few sites have been examined in any real detail, while the situation on Hadrian's Wall is made more complicated by the presence of the *vallum*, which very probably restricted development immediately outside the Wall forts until the third century. Relatively early development is attested, however, outside the forts at Corbridge[9] and Carlisle,[10] both of which were later to become independent towns in the frontier district. At most sites, there is normally nothing to indicate that such military *vici* were anything but symbiotically tied to their respect-ive forts and therefore ultimately dependent upon them for their survival.

Such clear military origins in the frontier

districts have encouraged the belief that the argument can be transferred as a useful working model for what happened during the early stages of conquest elsewhere in the province before the army moved north and west. Here, indeed, the well-attested correlation between abandoned conquest forts and later small towns has only helped to make this a particularly attractive proposition. This line of argument was pioneered initially by Webster,[11] but it has been repeated by Frere among others,[12] who have thereby concluded that the overwhelming majority of small towns originated as military *vici*; apparent examples of this process are well known at Chelmsford, Godmanchester, Great Casterton, Northwich and Wall. Generally speaking our knowledge of these early military *vici* is extremely scanty because so few have been excavated in any detail if at all. At Wall, however, enough of a pattern emerges to begin to document the developmental sequence.[13] Here several timber buildings have been found to predate the first metalling of Watling Street and might well represent the *vicus* attached to the sequence of forts to the north, dated to the period *c*. AD 50–70; interestingly, when the known line of Watling Street was adopted, subsequent occupation took advantage of its frontages and abandoned the earlier alignments dictated by the military complexes. A similar new layout in the post-military phase has also been suggested at Godmanchester, though here the earlier *vicus* remains poorly known.[14]

Attractive though this developmental model appears for the civilian regions, there are several problems about its general application to the origin of every small town. Not least among them is the fact that several fort sites, such as Greensforge and Metchley,[15] are known to have failed to spawn later small towns, suggesting that the process was not always consistent. Perhaps in some cases this is because military occupation was too short-lived for its *vicus* to take root; hence what camp followers there were would naturally move forward with the troops. Elsewhere, however, it would seem that additional factors necessarily contributed to the survival of the settlement once the army departed. First among them must have been the site's potential within the existing socio-economic framework and the ease with which it could be incorporated into the main communications network. The latter might well explain why some small towns appear to be set

apart from their 'parent' installations, as for example at Alcester, Penkridge and Water Newton.[16] The situation in the south and east is further complicated by the existence of a significant number of nucleated settlements in the immediately pre-Roman Iron Age. This zone of 'urbanization' has been the subject of much discussion in recent years, and it is now widely recognized that this had some part to play in the subsequent growth of small towns.[17]

Within this zone, among the main coin-using tribes, most interest attaches to the large settlements, both open and enclosed, because here there are examples of direct continuity between Iron-Age and Romano-British sites. A particularly good example is Braughing, an important trade centre sited strategically at a junction of several routes.[18] Chance finds of Iron-Age coinage, Gallo-Belgic pottery, brooches and metalwork from the Gatesbury Wood enclosure have now been supplemented by the excavations at Skeleton Green, which located considerable structural remains and a large collection of Italic and Gallo-Belgic pottery from the last quarter of the first century BC onwards. In the early Roman period, the road junction was formalized and a link road connected this original focus of settlement to an apparently new development on Wickham Hill. A comparable nucleus at Rochester, though poorly known, appears to have been incorporated just as easily into the Roman framework.[19] At several sites where continuity seems likely, there appears to have been an original religious connection in the Iron Age which then flourished in the Roman period; this possibility exists at Bath,[20] though more concrete evidence occurs at Harlow[21] and Springhead.[22] Occasionally, too, conquest-period forts were constructed at or near such existing settlements as in the case of Ancaster.[23] Here an apparently large settlement of the last century before the invasion, located at a strategic site on the Jurassic Way, was in part overlain by the defences of a Claudian fort. Such actions must have involved a considerable level of interference at first, but the subsequent re-emergence of the site in the post-military phase must reflect the overriding socio-economic importance and attraction of the Iron-Age location.

Far less certain cases of continuity can be demonstrated in those areas dominated by large centralized hillforts, especially among the Durotriges and less certainly in parts of the Welsh Marches, though their potential as centres given the right circumstances is well attested by the rise of Dorchester (Dorset) near Maiden Castle.[24] Part of our problem in these areas is that we are not in a position to chart how many of the known hillforts were actually occupied in AD 43, so that apparent examples of continuity, such as the roadside settlements outside Badbury and Old Sarum, are too poorly known to form the basis of a convincing argument.[25] One case of local interaction, however, may be represented at Kenchester, only 2 km (1.25 miles) south of the fort at Credenhill;[26] here the small town which emerged at a convenient road junction, perhaps as a successor to a military *vicus*, would have been a logical successor to its Iron-Age counterpart, though the contemporary disturbances noted on the hillfort point to a less than peaceful transition. Such examples are insufficiently conclusive in themselves and it would seem that development in these regions was conditioned by a much more complex set of factors than simple continuity.

Not all small towns can be accommodated easily within the categories outlined so far. Of these, one broad group calls for more detailed attention because it includes sites where a predicted military origin has proved elusive but whose location upon the main roads points towards some degree of official stimulus in their early development. At Towcester, for instance, excavation has failed to locate an early base, and the earliest occupation appears to have begun in the AD 70s, suggesting that it was the road itself which acted like a magnet, perhaps reinforced by the establishment of a government post.[27] Such a function connected with communications is clearly an important factor in the continuity of other classes of site.

Obviously, in the light of the examples considered so far, there appears to be considerable regional diversity in the early development of small towns. Military origins appear to predominate in the originally heavily garrisoned civilian areas lying for the most part north and west of the Fosse Way; this trend is particularly well represented in the west Midlands, but even here the early pattern of development is in reality slightly more complex.[28] The evidence makes it clear that it was primarily those military *vici* which lay on the main roads and rivers which had the greatest ability to survive an army evacuation, either by

developing their capacity for supplying services and facilities to official and private travellers as for example at Wall, or in some cases by extending their existing industrial occupations as at Droitwich[29] and possibly Holditch.[30] A more complicated situation appears to have arisen in the more developed lowland regions of the province for the most part south and east of the Fosse Way, where the Romans had to contend with coin-using communities already sufficiently advanced to possess their own sophisticated nucleated traditions. It has recently been suggested that this lowland area, in particular, experienced a marked state of flux in the decades after AD 43 with two overlapping and competing systems in operation, each with its own dynamic and requirements, and each contributing in different ways to the specific evolution of the whole.[31]

One of them is represented by the existing framework of nucleated settlements of varying sizes which had clearly developed to meet the specific socio-economic and political requirements of the indigenous communities. Their general survival within the Roman province was not in doubt, as the evidence clearly indicates, but how they prospered depended on various factors, not least their continued economic viability and the ease with which they could be incorporated into the wider provincial framework. Some sites clearly benefited from becoming road centres on the new communications system, as for example Braughing and Ancaster; but others, being geared to specifically native needs, were often far less conveniently located for provincial requirements and so were often bypassed when the first main roads were constructed, a situation which clearly occurred for example at Dragonby and Old Sleaford in Lincolnshire.[32] Such inclusion or exclusion was often the vital developmental factor at individual sites.

The second system is represented by those new settlements which emerged in response to the developing military and political needs of the central government, based partly on the establishment of the fort network and partly on the development of a coherent province-wide system of communications which followed in the wake of the military advance. The importance of the roads as a significant catalyst has already been recognized in the regions north and west of the Fosse Way; here too, a comparable process is evident, with the roads being responsible either for encouraging the survival of existing military *vici*, as for example at Great Casterton and Chelmsford, or for fostering the later emergence of other roadside settlements providing facilities for travellers, as at Towcester and Cave's Inn. Such roads and new settlements formed an alternative framework for development in addition to the existing socio-economic system; sometimes the two systems coincided, as noted earlier, but more usually the new centres, being geared from the outset to meet wider provincial needs, had a much better chance of developing into more sophisticated urban sites. Such a process is well represented by the recognizable developments at Alcester, Ilchester and Water Newton, all of which appear to have had some sort of military origin.

Beyond such diverse provincial origins, the subsequent development of small towns was a complex process, only the bare outlines of which can be pieced together with any real certainty. This is partly a result of the known complexities of the changing local and provincial requirements within Britain during the Roman occupation, and partly because of the variable quality of the archaeological research at individual sites. It is clear, nevertheless, that various factors contributed to the overall process, once the initial disruptions caused by military annexation had been replaced by relative internal stability. The most important appear to have been economic expansion, the establishment of official functions, industrial expansion and religious and cultural attraction. Such factors clearly operated both independently and cumulatively in diverse ways at individual sites, being ultimately responsible for the distinctive pattern of continuity and dislocation which emerged during the course of the next three centuries.

All four factors were capable of operating independently as primary stimuli to the development of individual sites, as well as in a secondary or tertiary capacity alongside other aspects. Economic expansion, for instance, was largely responsible for the third- and fourth-century flowering at Camerton,[33] reflecting the increased regional prosperity of the south-west; the establishment of official functions, especially the *cursus publicus*, and the growth of related services at such sites as Chelmsford and Wall,[34] acted as a prime reason for their continuity consequent upon the evacuation of their respective forts; industrial expansion provided the basis for the first-century expansion of the lead-mining settlement at Charterhouse;[35] while religious and cultural factors inspired the very impressive first-century developments at Bath.[36] In several such cases, particularly where other factors did not subsequently come into play in force, the overall character and level of development was often constrained by the potential of these primary functions and the range of attendant services which they attracted. This is most clearly demonstrated by those specialist settlements in the west Midlands–Cheshire plain area where industrial-type occupations formed the basis of their second-century prosperity and, in many cases, for their subsequent demise (p. 12). A comparable situation seems likely for many roadside settlements which depended entirely for their survival on the presence of an official establishment and the market supplied by through traffic.

In the development of the more important towns, however, it would have been the cumulative interplay of a combination of such factors which ensured the enhanced expansion of the site's general functional role. Something of this interplay between official and economic factors can be seen at Godmanchester,[37] while at Water Newton, though the developmental picture is rather poorly known, enough strands are available to reconstruct the process at work.[38] Early growth was probably limited to the main frontages of Ermine Street, perhaps in connection with an official *mansio*, and yet by the late second century it was already one of the largest of the defended small towns with additional extra-mural suburbs. Various factors obviously contributed to this rise including both industrial and economic expansion, for the site lay at the centre of both a flourishing and widespread pottery industry, and a cluster of villas developing from the second century onwards. It also enjoyed the benefits of convenient road and river communications. The resulting intense economic symbiosis may have been enhanced also by the extension of the site's official functions, particularly the provision of defences and the possible rise in status to the rank of a civitas capital. Such a complex picture can be paralleled in other case-studies.

The broad development of the small towns during the later first and second centuries followed gradually in the wake of two inter-related processes: the changing military deployment within the province and the constitution of the new self-governing *civitates*. The first of these saw a gradual movement west into Wales and north into Scotland from the AD 50s onwards, culminating eventually after much trial and error in the establishment of a satisfactory frontier along the Tyne-Solway in the AD 160s.[39] The second, following in the wake of this, witnessed the designation of specific civitas capitals as administrative centres and their subsequent adornment with the relevant public buildings and amenities.[40] The broad outline of their date of constitution is now tolerably clear; the earliest were apparently established in the Claudio-Neronian period among those tribal units in the immediate south and east, followed by a major extension first in the Flavian-Trajanic era in a broad arc from Lincolnshire to Devon and then in parts of Wales and north England in the Hadrianic-Antonine period. While the speed of the military advance conditioned the date at which specific military *vici* emerged, it is no surprise to find that the earliest signs of small-town growth and prosperity appear to coincide with the Flavian-Trajanic stimulus to urbanization attested historically and archaeologically.[41]

Even so, the early evidence tells us much about the continuing state of flux within the province, involving as it does a surprising level of new development at pre-existing native settlements. Elsewhere, unless specialized factors came into operation, development at the new centres often appears to have lagged behind, in the interval between the evacuation of the military and the more formalized development of the communications network and the *cursus publicus*. The most spectacular example of this new development is provided by Bath, where the monumental complex comprising the main reservoir, the well-known classical temple and the suite of baths has been shown to have been under construction between AD 65 and 75.[42] This early development not only represents a considerable financial outlay, but it also appears to predate the main burst of building activity at most civitas capitals; at Cirencester and Verulamium, for instance, the *forum-basilica* complexes belong to the Flavian era,[43] while those at Leicester and Wroxeter were not even started until well into the second century.[44] Less spectacular but equally interest-

ing development can also be demonstrated at several other pre-Roman sites, where a religious centre was given a new temple or temple complex. At Harlow,[45] for example, the Romano-Celtic temple has been dated to the Flavian period, while at Springhead,[46] the earliest temple should also belong in a late first-century context prior to its replacement by Penn's Temple 1, probably c. AD 120.

Equally important developments appear to be visible at Braughing,[47] though these are not so well known and are less closely dated. Here, besides the early occupation centred on the main crossroads of Ermine Street and Stane Street, at least one new building was also constructed in the late first century on Wickham Hill; it has been variously identified as a temple or a market, but its real importance lies in the fact that it is clearly contemporary with one of the streets apparently forming a more or less regular layout on the hill. This perhaps hints at the existence of an early formalized nucleus at what had been an important pre-existing centre. A possible comparable arrangement at Baldock needs much closer elaboration before certainty is reached.[48] Such examples of early development reflect an important degree of continuity, particularly at sites with religious connections or where incorporation into the Roman framework proved both convenient and beneficial. Comparable incorporation is also evident in the civitas capitals at Canterbury, Silchester and Verulamium, and in the *colonia* at Colchester, even if minor relocations were necessary. Not all pre-existing sites featured in this early progress, however, as the evidence from Cambridge[49] and Dragonby[50] clearly attests; at both, the known layouts are dominated by simple domestic structures in fenced or ditched plots, all within an agricultural setting.

Most new centres within the province tended to develop less quickly, unless there were specific factors at work contributing to a faster, more specialized growth. Particularly interesting in this latter context are those small towns where early industrial functions loomed large. An obvious candidate here is likely to be Charterhouse, judging from the presence of the Claudio-Neronian fort nearby and the evidence of the early lead pigs,[51] though little is known of the actual mining site itself. The material from Weston-under-Penyard might also suggest an early interest, but again virtually nothing is known about the settlement.[52] Much more certainty, however, attaches to several specialized sites in the west Midlands-Cheshire plain area, where industrial activity appears to have developed at an early date in the later first century AD. At Holditch, for instance, excavation has revealed evidence for not only large-scale metalworking c. AD 80 but also a range of attendant services, which might have begun life within a military *vicus*, though its exact relationship to the Flavian fort at Chesterton to the north remains unclear.[53] Likewise at Middlewich, early brine extraction has been dated to c. AD 80–90 and was soon supported by pottery production, iron-smelting and smithing, bronze- and lead-working, glass-making, cobbling and weaving.[54] Early industrial activity is also attested by the evidence from Wilderspool,[55] Droitwich[56] and possibly Whitchurch,[57] though more detailed confirmation would be welcome at the last. Comparable evidence in the form of salt-working and iron-smelting has been recorded at Northwich, but it now seems likely that this activity was broadly contemporary with, and did not therefore outlast, the two phases of military occupation at the site.[58]

These apparently specialized industrial centres were not just confined to independent civilian settlements at this date, as a comparison with the contemporary development within the military *vici* at Little Chester and Manchester clearly demonstrates.[59] Excavation at both has revealed the growth of considerable industrial quarters from the later first century onwards, with evidence for much the same range of activities as their civilian counterparts. It would appear as if all these specialized sites emerged in the wake of the Roman advance and were then sustained by the operation of special factors, not least of which was probably the continuing demands of the army in an area straddling both the military and the civil zones of the province. Not all such early centres prospered, however; at Margidunum, for example, extensive iron-working was carried on in the period c. AD 50–75, presumably in connection with a fort or military depot, but this declined thereafter and its civilian successor lost momentum for a generation or so.[60]

The pattern of late first-century development at other new sites is considerably more varied, but on the whole it was much less spectacular than the examples discussed so far. Many sites provide some evidence for occupation during this period,

but it is all too frequently difficult to define either its character or its extent in the light of the existing information. A good example of the generally lower-key development is represented by the post-military re-planning at Godmanchester, in which a series of regular plots was laid out along the Ermine Street frontages, containing various buildings and features which were predominantly agricultural in character.[61] A slightly different arrangement occurs at Chelmsford, where the post-military road frontages gradually became occupied by narrow properties little more than 60 m (200 ft) deep, containing strip buildings.[62] This clearly invites comparison with Wall, where the roads have already been cited as the main factor in the post-military realignment of the site (p. 8), though too little has been excavated so far to determine its overall character. This evidence would seem to indicate that many new sites took the form of characteristic ribbon developments of varying size and density, strung out along the new provincial roads, often with only a rudimentary level of functional specialization. The speed with which such sites developed obviously varied: at Braintree it was initially confined to the route leading west from the central crossroads, but in the early second century it expanded along the route leading south-west as well;[63] at High Cross and Penkridge, late first-century pottery has been recovered from the roadside occupation;[64] while at Brough-on-Fosse and Willoughby, the pottery evidence would suggest only patchy occupation before AD 100.[65] Such variations in date and character clearly need exploring as more evidence becomes available, especially in the light of contemporary trends at neighbouring civitas capitals.

The process of late first- to early second-century development at the small towns was further influenced by the formalization of the provincial *cursus publicus*. This took the form of official *mansiones* and *mutationes* set at regular intervals along the main roads. Occasionally, pre-existing sites were conveniently located to house such establishments, as appears to have happened at Braughing,[66] but the more normal sequence saw their construction either at the sites of previously occupied forts or at the newly emerging roadside settlements, as for example at Chelmsford.[67] This had the effect of reinforcing the pattern of new centres and the process of settlement dislocation which they and the roads had initiated. Such buildings generally only become recognizable in the early second century, with the stone structures at Godmanchester,[68] Catterick[69] and Wall.[70] The presence elsewhere of bath-houses and other large romanized buildings hints at the original extent of the system.

In contrast to the rather variable trends considered so far, the second century witnessed a much more pronounced pattern of development at the small towns. Many now provide clear evidence for sustained growth along the roads and a greater level of organization in their internal street layouts. This was presumably the period when economic forces began to figure much more prominently, generating the need for convenient local markets and for an expanding range of craftsmen. Such forces also influenced the prosperity of the contemporary civitas capitals, witness the continued provision of new public buildings and amenities and the widespread appearance of wealthier town houses alongside an extended range of craftsmen and traders. Among the small towns, several examples can be cited as being representative of this broader pattern of second-century growth. At Alcester, for instance, the industrial quarter in the Birch Abbey area to the south of the likely centre of the settlement was already well established by the mid second century, and this must imply that much of the main street network was already well developed at this date;[71] likewise at Irchester, the construction of the Romano-Celtic temple and its attached precinct alongside one of the principal east-west streets, apparently in the early to mid second century, would also seem to indicate that the rest of the internal layout was in existence prior to the imposition of the earthwork defences.[72] At Godmanchester, the development of the site's official role represented by the *mansio*, was soon followed by an intensification of the occupation along the frontages of Ermine Street and by an increasing number of timber-framed buildings lying end-on to the roads;[73] several of these have been shown to house workshops, suggesting a growing emphasis here on service industries such as smithing. Much the same picture emerges at Ashton, where the main road leading south from the settlement was lined by a growing number of second-century strip buildings and their associated yards, several of them connected with iron-working and related indus-

tries.[74] Comparable growth can also be demonstrated at Ancaster, Great Chesterford, Tiddington, Wanborough and Whitchurch.

One of the most interesting features of this phase of expansion was the trend by which several small towns developed a more complex, if irregular, street layout at their centre, in contrast to those roadside settlements where straggling ribbon developments prevailed. The best example occurs at Water Newton, where numerous side-streets run both obliquely and at right angles to the line of Ermine Street south of the River Nene.[75] It is even possible that the two more regularly-shaped *insulae*, visible on the aerial photographs, originally extended beyond the line of the stone wall, suggesting that here at least the town was well built-up by the end of the second century. Comparable developments may be indicated by the shape of the defences at both Rochester and Towcester, though the internal layout is completely unknown. By far the most interesting case in this category, however, is the small town at Kenchester, though the nature of the early excavations makes conclusive dating very difficult.[76] Early developments here took the form of ribbon development, but it has recently been suggested that the central area was remodelled at some time in the later part of the second century, perhaps, but not certainly, contemporary with the construction of the earthwork defences. Such a deliberate 'modernization' of the layout is as yet unparalleled elsewhere and clearly requires further elaboration.

Interestingly, many of these apparently more-developed sites were chosen by the central government for defensive provision,[77] either in the last quarter of the second century, or as part of the third-century programme of stone wall construction; these defences clearly aimed to enclose the viable urban core in line with the cities, as well as any official installations they might have contained. Most of these towns were also new sites in terms of their origins.

In the north of the province, too, the second century saw urban expansion in the course of which the military *vici* at Corbridge and Carlisle developed into independent small towns. At the former,[78] the layout following the evacuation of the fort was dominated on either side of the main east-west road by a planned central core, whose construction despite interruptions spanned the late second and early third centuries; south of the road lay two walled compounds serving military functions, as well as several temples, while to the north lay two granaries, an aqueduct and a large open area fronted by a range of shops (though originally it had been designed to house a much larger, almost square, building). At Carlisle, where a continued military enclave is also attested, excavation at several points has revealed intensified occupation along all the main second-century frontages.[79] Further south at Catterick, the re-establishment of the Thornborough fort in the AD 160s, next to the *mansio* and its bath-house, was immediately accompanied by the development of several timber buildings along the link road running east to Dere Street.[80]

In contrast to the general pattern of expansion, however, the later second century onwards also witnessed a change of fortune at several of the industrial sites already discussed in the west Midlands–Cheshire plain area. The most clear-cut case is at Holditch, where the core of the industrial complex was in decline soon after *c.* AD 160, with only limited occupation being maintained henceforth into the early third century along the main road itself.[81] Likewise, at Wilderspool, it is clear that the industrial activity mainly flourished in the second century, followed by a general decline through to the mid third century to judge from the available pottery evidence.[82] This invites comparison with the recorded decline during the later second century at Heronbridge,[83] only 3 km (2 miles) south of the fortress at Chester, and also at Northwich in the post-military phase.[84] Moreover, at Whitchurch, the excavated areas show a change of use soon after AD 170, when at least one large stone building was constructed over the earlier industrial levels,[85] while at Droitwich there is evidence to suggest a change in the known character of the salt industry in or after the mid second century, though it clearly continued perhaps under different management or in a different location.[86] Only at Middlewich is third- and fourth-century activity better attested.[87] Clearly many of these sites flourished from the later first to early third centuries, with the emphasis on the mid second century; this decline and, in some cases, total demise of the manufacturing capacity with attendant de-urbanization, at a time when other small towns continued to experience relative prosperity, requires an explanation. It is all too tempting to link the industrial growth both here and at the comparable military *vici* noted earlier at Little Chester and Manchester to the government or army demands of the period and to explain their demise as a result of the settlement of the northern frontier and its subsequent reorganization under Severus and Caracalla.[88]

Such exceptions apart, however, by the end of the second century the familiar pattern of Romano-British small towns was well established, complementing and completing the urban network created by the chartered cities and self-governing civitas centres. How this was subsequently affected by the changing circumstances of the third century and beyond can be postponed until a later chapter.

THREE
INTERNAL
MORPHOLOGY

An understanding of the internal morphology and structural complexity of the small towns forms a vital framework upon which more detailed spatial, functional and developmental analyses can be built. It is unfortunate therefore that detailed research into such issues is still largely in its infancy. Generally speaking, the evidence from the major towns has attracted most attention in the literature, but recent syntheses of the material from the small towns have begun to redress the balance.[1] Such advances, however, are ultimately dependent upon the quality of the available evidence and their main conclusions, summarized here, may require some degree of modification as more material comes to light.

Three main sources of information can be used to shed light on the small towns, each one offering an important dimension to the overall picture but also suffering distinctive drawbacks. First and foremost, there is the evidence provided by aerial photography; when this is sufficiently extensive, as for example at Kenchester and Water Newton,[2] there is usually enough data to publish a composite plan of the internal morphology, though normally the picture is far more fragmentary. Such 'town plans' are eminently satisfying but also dangerously deceptive, because in the absence of excavation, they can only hint at the potential complexity involved. Second, there is the evidence derived from excavation itself, especially at those sites where the internal layout has been extensively sampled, as for example at Alcester,[3] Baldock[4] and Godmanchester.[5] This has the specific advantage of offering us a series of relatively detailed developmental sequences for individual areas within the plan, but unless such work has been sufficiently systematic, the resulting picture resembles at best an incomplete jigsaw. Third, and by far the most problematical, there is the spatial information derived from the distribution of occupation debris recorded during fieldwork or building activity. A considerable number of sites fall into this category, even when there has been some aerial photography and excavation, as for example at Braintree[6] and Horncastle.[7] The 'plans' so derived are the most difficult to interpret in terms of urban morphology, because their apparent size and shape may be deceptively inaccurate in the absence of structures and proper chronological information. Nevertheless, the evidence from all three sources can be integrated to paint a reasonably coherent picture of the small towns.

Discussions of internal morphology can be divided conveniently into three general sections:

(i) the range of individual building types recorded within the small towns;
(ii) the overall development of the settlement plan in relation to the internal roads and streets;
(iii) the internal organization of the buildings and land-use in relation to the roads and streets.

These aspects will be considered individually below.

Internal Buildings

Despite their importance as one of the basic features of internal morphology, the internal buildings have not always attracted the attention they deserve. In particular, the large romanized buildings have tended to dominate a disproportionate amount of past excavation at the expense of the more vernacular structures, even though recent evidence has begun to redress the

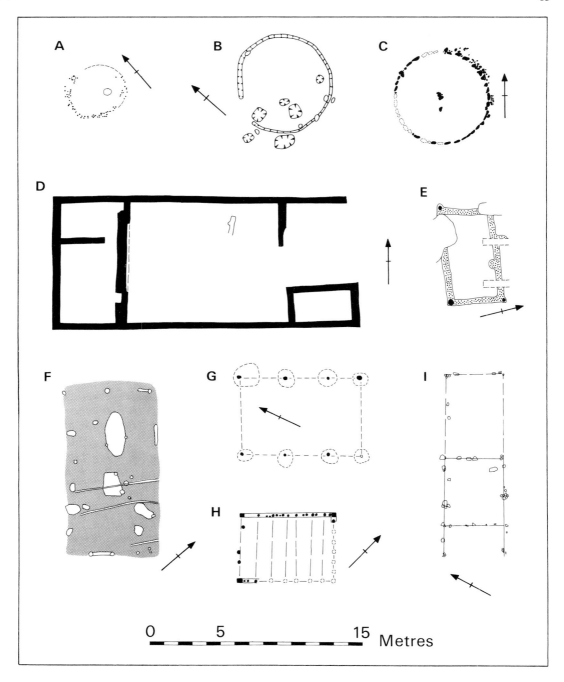

2 Plans of a selection of simple circular and rectilinear buildings: **A** Godmanchester (*after Green H. J. M.*); **B** Baldock (*after Stead and Rigby*); **C** Ashton (*after Hadman and Upex*); **D** Hibaldstow (*after Smith R. F.*); **E** Chelmsford (*after Drury*); **F** Scole (*after Rogerson*); **G** Brampton (*after Green C.*); **H** Godmanchester (*after Green H. J. M.*); **I** Wanborough (*after Wacher*)

balance. From what we know, however, the structural range found in the small towns is almost always far less diverse than in their larger urban counterparts. Buildings of essentially simple design, conforming to the different regional traditions, predominated and clearly provided the domestic and workshop accommodation for the bulk of the population. Alongside them, there is a marked scarcity of clearly Roman-inspired structures, especially those represented by the wealthy private houses, public and official buildings so common in the cities. The relative presence or absence of the latter is an important factor in distinguishing between different categories of small town.

Much of our knowledge about the domestic and workshop accommodation has been derived from aerial survey, supplemented in recent years by larger area excavations and improved recovery techniques. Particularly interesting is the continuity into the Roman period of the characteristic Iron-Age circular house, several examples of which are now known in the small towns (fig. 2 A–C). Fairly typical first-century examples are known at Godmanchester alongside a range of other structures.[8] They usually comprise a circle of stake-holes set into shallow trenches with stouter posts located at the doorways, suggesting a wickerwork construction with mud or clay daub walls and a thatched roof. These can be paralleled by three second-century structures at Baldock, represented by gullies and shallow post-holes.[9] Examples with stone foundations are also known at Bourton-on-the-Water[10] and Ashton, the latter with unusual upright limestone slabs.[11]

The retention of such traditional architectural patterns is hardly surprising, but, as yet, none has been found in third-century contexts. A few are known, however, in the fourth century, including a pair with turf walls in the extra-mural area at Towcester[12] and two late timber examples at Alcester.[13] Such circular buildings are not confined just to the domestic sphere, as those found in a religious context clearly demonstrate. Occasionally their exact function is uncertain, as in the case of the three structures in Normangate Field, Water Newton, one of which had a central post-hole and was originally floored with a red and white tessellated floor.[14]

The bulk of the domestic and workshop accommodation, however, falls into the category of simple rectilinear forms constructed in a variety of ways from timber and stone depending on the local availability of materials (cf. fig. 2 D–I). Most common, perhaps because they show up more easily, are the timber-framed buildings which rested upon stone foundations (D). These are known throughout the province, though regional variations are introduced by the use of flint, chalk, granite, limestone and sandstone among others. Elsewhere, buildings were entirely of timber-framed construction, either with their sills set into prepared trenches (E) or resting upon the ground surface (F) or based upon timber posts set into individual pits (G) or in linear trenches (H). A more interesting variant is introduced by those structures where the whole building appears to have been raised entirely above the ground, being represented only by lines of carefully levelled blocks used to support the timber joists (I).

Such diverse construction methods are not confined to particular types of building but rather reflect questions of cost and regional traditions which appear to have been relatively pronounced in Roman Britain. At some sites, where good building stone was scarce, timber-framed structures predominated throughout the Roman occupation, as for example at Great Chesterford,[15] where all the known buildings with the exception of the two late official structures were of timber construction with gravel or earth floors, plaster-covered wattle-and-daub walling and probably thatched roofs. Where stone foundations are normal, as at Catterick[16] and Hibaldstow,[17] regional variations reflect local sources: flint and chalk in areas dominated by the geological presence of chalk, limestones and sandstones in the area of the Jurassic ridge and granites and slates beyond.

It is interesting to note that rectilinear structures are frequently found in one of two distinctive locations, often accompanied by marked functional variations. First there are the buildings which are usually, though not exclusively, domestic in character, located in their own spacious plots of land or yards, often in association with a range of agricultural features. These are well represented at Godmanchester,[18] the first-century examples being generally rectangular cottages with a framework of vertical posts surrounding an earth floor. Second-century examples were somewhat larger, with a series of timber uprights defining two separate rooms. Both types were often set parallel with the road in an extensive plot of land. Similar buildings seem to predominate at Cambridge and Dragonby,[19] and, interestingly, at accepted 'village' sites like Catsgore,[20] a fact which must be important when trying to define the function and status of individual sites close to the town-village threshold.

The second distinctive group covers the well-known strip buildings which are set end-on to the road frontages, often in association with a range of specialized activities. Hence they are traditionally identified as the combined houses and workshops of resident craftsmen. Our evidence for them, derived from aerial photography and widespread excavation, is sufficiently well known to require little detailed comment here. Besides the numerous examples recorded at Corbridge along the main east-west and north-south streets,[21] and at Water Newton along Ermine Street and its side-streets,[22] comparable structures have been identified at many other small towns including Alchester, Camerton, Hibaldstow, Sapperton and Sea Mills.[23] Such buildings often have an associated yard to the rear. The presence of an open gable end, perhaps with some sort of arrangement to accommodate wooden shutters, indicates the commercial importance attached to such premises, as for example at Catterick.[24]

To judge by the size of individual examples, strip buildings tend to be larger than the domestic vernacular structures within their spacious plots. The second-century houses at Godmanchester measuring c. 5 by 11 m (16 by 36 ft) had an approximate floor area of less than 55 sq. m (576 sq. ft), assuming for the purpose a single-storey building; in contrast, the strip buildings at Hibaldstow and Sapperton, measuring c. 9.7 by 21.2 m (32 by 69 ft) and c. 11 by 20 m (36 by 66 ft)

3 Plans of a selection of winged-corridor houses:
A & B Camerton (*after Wedlake*); **C** Droitwich (*after Barfield*); **D** Droitwich (*after Gelling*);
E Great Chesterford (*after Brinson*);
F Margidunum (*after Todd*)

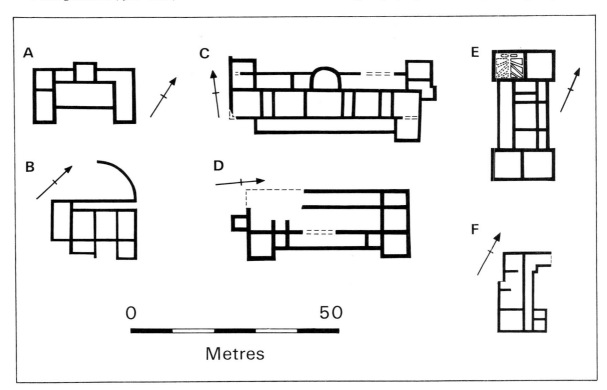

0   50

Metres

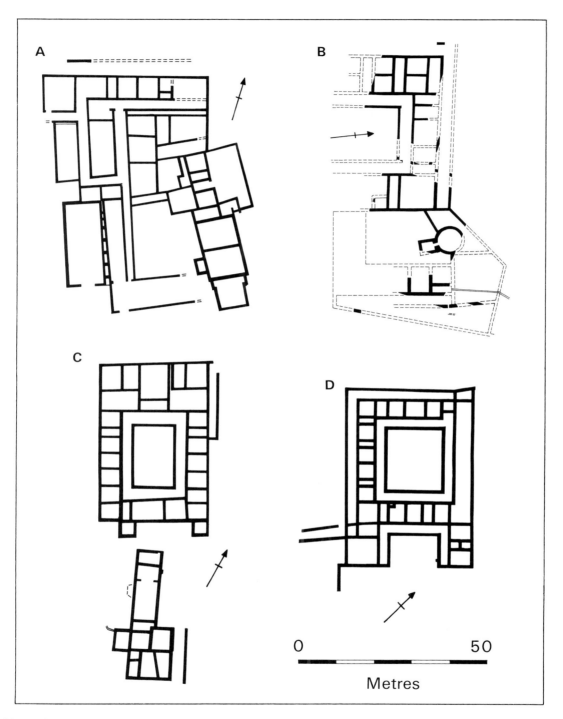

4 Plans of a selection of probable *mansiones*:
A Catterick (*after Wacher*); **B** Chelmsford (*after Drury*); **C** Godmanchester (*after Green H. J. M.*); **D** Wanborough (*after Phillips and Walters*)

0   50

Metres

respectively, offered somewhere in the region of 200 sq. m (2200 sq. ft) each. Such a variation in scale can often be matched by a corresponding degree of 'romanization', as in the timber examples at Great Chesterford with their tessellated floors and painted wall plaster.[25]

One further distinctive structure, the aisled building, might also be mentioned here. This was clearly a multi-purpose unit capable of functioning in agricultural, domestic, industrial or commercial capacities. Obvious agricultural examples existed at Ilchester and Neatham;[26] in an industrial context belongs the structure fronting Ermine Street in Normangate Field, Water Newton;[27] while the examples at Droitwich and Godmanchester appear in an official setting.[28] Such structures are generally therefore an integral part of the domestic and workshop accommodation available in all the small towns. Exceptions like the Godmanchester 'Basilica' clearly belong in another sphere.[29]

It has already been noted that buildings of more obviously romanized character play a less prominent role in the overall morphology of the small towns. Where they occur, they are often difficult to interpret in functional terms. A case in point is provided by the presence at various sites of more sophisticated houses, which can be compared with their better known counterparts in the major towns and the countryside (fig. 3). They were generally larger than the buildings described so far and were often more elaborate, with hypocausts, painted wall plaster or mosaic flooring. The late third- to early fourth-century winged-corridor house at Great Chesterford is fairly typical, offering a floor area of c. 400 sq. m (4350 sq. ft) and containing one room with a hypocaust and at least one tessellated floor.[30] Comparable houses have been recognized, individually or in pairs, elsewhere, as for example at Braughing, Camerton, Droitwich and Margidunum.[31] In contrast, a handful of small towns apparently contained several sophisticated houses, as the mosaic evidence from both Bath and Ilchester clearly demonstrates.[32] Aerial photography and excavation have also revealed at least three large houses at Kenchester.[33] The latter suggest the presence of several wealthy inhabitants, principally in the third and fourth centuries, but the individual examples could represent anything from rural establishments to official residences.

Larger, apparently official or public, structures have also been located within the small towns. Particularly characteristic are what appear to be large courtyard structures, often associated with a detached bath-house (fig. 4). A good example is the building at Chelmsford measuring 66 by 42.5 m (216 by 139 ft), with an internal corridor and an associated layout of rooms, and a less well-known bathing complex to the east;[34] the existing stone buildings were founded in c. AD 125–150, though the courtyard replaced an earlier timber predecessor and the baths incorporated an existing laconicum. A comparable building complex has also been examined at Godmanchester,[35] built c. AD 120, while a third is visible on the aerial photographs of Wanborough.[36] Their identification as mansiones, along with other similar buildings, is discussed below (p. 37).

Various other courtyard structures have been located, though in all cases their exact function is hard to define. These include two small examples (fig. 5 B and C), one at Cave's Inn[37] and the other, only partially excavated, at Whitchurch,[38] and two larger complexes visible on the aerial photographs at Water Newton.[39] To these might be added the enigmatic, though incomplete, courtyard building at Corbridge, which, at 65.5 by 67 m (214 by 219 ft), would have been one of the largest of all the structures in the small towns.[40]

Within the small towns, apparently independent bath-houses are more common than might have been expected given the general level of amenity provision (fig. 5 D–H). Among the known examples there is a marked variation in size, which ranges from the large many-roomed complex located close to the River Rib at Braughing,[41] down to the partly excavated building discovered at the rear of one of the frontage plots at Neatham.[42] These differences must relate to the function of the individual structures, though it is not clear how many were available to the local communities rather than serving otherwise unattested official uses.

The most marked contrast between the small towns and their larger counterparts is the relative paucity of large public buildings, especially those connected with amusement. Only a handful have been identified, frequently in very specific religious or industrial contexts. Pride of place must go to the bathing complexes at Bath, with their normal and curative facilities grouped

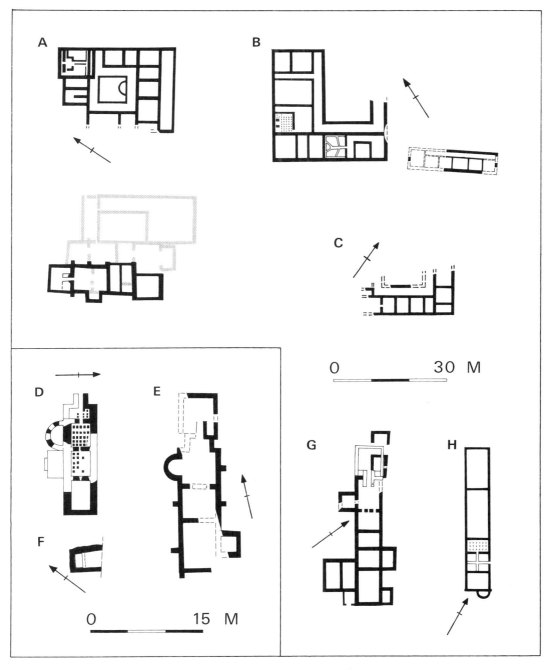

5 Plans of a selection of smaller courtyard buildings and bath-houses: **A** Wall (*after Lynam and Webster*); **B** Cave's Inn (*after Lucas*); **C** Whitchurch (*after Jones and Webster*); **D** Brampton (*after Knowles*); **E** Braughing (*after Partridge*); **F** Neatham (*after Millett and Graham*); **G** Cowbridge (*after Parkhouse*); **H** Margidunum (*after Oswald*)

around the hot springs and the Great Bath.[43] A smaller set of baths dependent upon mineral springs may also have existed at Buxton.[44] Theatres and amphitheatres are also rare, although two amphitheatres have been recognized: the well-known example at the mining settlement at Charterhouse, and the recently-discovered structure at the religious site of Frilford.[45] Recognized theatres appear to have been much less grandiose affairs, witness the enigmatic ovoid area at Wycomb and the possible theatre at Catterick.[46] These buildings reflect an important social or religious dimension about which more information is needed.

Religious structures are another category which have so far escaped attention, even though temples are well-established features at many small towns. Those of classical design and inspiration are infrequent, the most impressive being the tetrastyle prostyle temple set on a high podium and dedicated to Sulis Minerva at Bath.[47] At least some of the seven small buildings just outside the military compounds at Corbridge may also belong in this category.[48] By far the most common and distinctive type, however, are the Romano-Celtic temples of square, circular and octagonal plan. The numerous examples vary in importance and location. One important group lay within an enclosure at Springhead, apparently at the heart of the town itself.[49] At the height of its development, two main temples lay side by side amidst other structures and were approached through some form of monumental gateway to the east. Comparable enclosures with square temples are known at Water Newton and Irchester.[50] In contrast, other Romano-Celtic temples lay within larger enclosures set alongside or apart from the centre of the settlement, as for example at Harlow, where the temple and its associated precinct lay in the middle of a ditched enclosure 4.2 ha (10 acres) in extent.[51]

Besides the square form, octagonal examples have been excavated at both Chelmsford and Nettleton Shrub,[52] the latter being somewhat unusual having three concentric divisions. Circular temples are often difficult to identify unless they are clearly differentiated from their domestic counterparts. Examples include the circular building at Frilford and the structure in a precinct visible on photographs of Thorpe-by-Newark.[53]

The prominence of temples in the small towns is of some interest. In many cases, they are distinguished from the prevalent structural range by their degree of architectural pretension. With the exception of the private houses, and the public and official structures already described, such temples were often the most romanized element and were therefore visually as well as functionally important.

The final category in this section covers defences. Many of the small towns were supplied with fortifications during their lifetime. The earliest phase, in the last quarter of the second century, saw the construction of earthwork defences, many of which were subsequently modified by the insertion of a stone wall on the same alignment.[54] Apparent exceptions to this trend include sites like Chelmsford,[55] with no known stone defences, and Thorpe-by-Newark,[56] where they take a different alignment. While many sites were upgraded by the addition of walls to the existing earthworks during the third and fourth centuries, new stone defences, with or without a contemporary bank, were also provided elsewhere, reflecting an extension of this important protective function. The actual areas enclosed vary enormously, from the largest at Water Newton (18 ha/44 acres), down to sites like Mancetter with as little as 2.1 ha (5 acres). Outside there was usually at least one ditch and frequently more, often with evidence of recutting or later modifications.

Unfortunately very few gateways have been excavated, and at present no common trends can be discerned. Only the west gate at Kenchester provides a close parallel to the more monumental city gateways, with each side of its double carriageway flanked by an external semi-circular tower.[57] Other examples are generally far less elaborate, involving only a single carriageway. The north and south gates at Godmanchester fall into this category, with flanking guard chambers projecting equally to front and back, while at Chesterton-on-Fosse the guard towers were possibly added to the rear of the wall.[58] Complex changes are visible at the north gate at Great Chesterford.[59]

More obvious trends are visible among the external towers added during the last phase of defensive activity in the mid fourth century. Semi-octagonal towers are known at Kenchester and Mildenhall towards the west;[60] while in the east, three varieties can be distinguished, including rectangular (Great Casterton and Water Newton),[61] fan-shaped (Ancaster and Godmanchester)[62] and semi-circular (Caistor and Horncastle).[63] These trends are paralleled in the major centres, thereby reinforcing the suggestion that individual groups of sites may have been the responsibility of the same builders.

This section on internal buildings has necessarily covered a considerable amount of very detailed information and has inevitably had to be selective. Numerous miscellaneous and less easily classified structures have therefore been omitted from the discussions. It is possible nevertheless to draw several conclusions about the general range of structures and their relative importance in the small towns. Within the overall range, the overwhelming majority of the structures were of simple design and type, conforming to the traditions and materials of individual regions. In contrast, buildings of a more sophisticated, Roman character rarely form a significant element in the total structural make-up. Normally, excluding the relatively common temples or temple complexes, only one or two such complexes are found, usually taking the form of a more sophisticated house, a combined baths and courtyard building, or a detached bath-house. Only a handful of sites possessed a wider range of romanized buildings. Public buildings, whether administrative or cultural, are found only rarely within the range of structures, in contrast to defences which are relatively common at sites on the main communications network. Even if such buildings are the exception to the general norm, however, their architectural character, size and visual appearance would have served to distinguish them from their humbler domestic counterparts.

Settlement Layout and the Internal Street Network

Despite the inherent limitations of the evidence, a study of the internal road or street network can offer important insights into the sequence of development and its relative complexity. Most previous commentators on the small towns have distinguished them from their larger counter-parts on the basis of their usually haphazard and seemingly piecemeal development, though it has recently become clear that such a distinction, however useful, obscures recognizable variations among the surviving plans. They can be shown to range from sites entirely dependent upon the main road frontages, through those which developed a system of irregular internal streets and lanes, to the few with some form of organized street plan. From such a general classification, discussed in detail below, two very general conclusions can be shown to emerge: that several categories of small towns saw the provision of some form of internal street network to meet the needs of their inhabitants and that the existence of such a system, coupled with other morphological and functional indicators, might well reflect a higher degree of internal organization and urban complexity.

It is possible to identify five broad groups within the range of small-town plans. The first covers those sites where the main occupation is focused around the junction of two or more through routes. Such occupation is further characterized by the absence of any substantial developments beyond and away from the main frontages. Straightforward examples can be seen at Brampton in Norfolk,[64] where the extensive ribbon developments are confined to the junction itself and the main roads radiating east, south and west, and at Braintree,[65] where they occupy only the west and south-west approach roads at the expense of the staggered road junction itself (fig. 6 A and B). A less clear-cut example occurs at Frilford, where several distinct concentrations of debris are known in and around the *temenos* and the crossroads.[66] Some sites may have developed this type of location for reasons of overall convenience; others were clearly attracted by the economic potential of the crossroads. At Godmanchester, for instance, extensive ribbon developments spread outwards well beyond the line of the later defences, but with time, there was a more intense build-up in the area adjacent to the crossroads as the site became more economically specialized.[67] This centripetal tendency could eventually promote the construction of additional side-streets and lanes, as we shall see later.

These linear road junction sites clearly satisfied the basic land requirements of the resident population, and for many there were clearly no

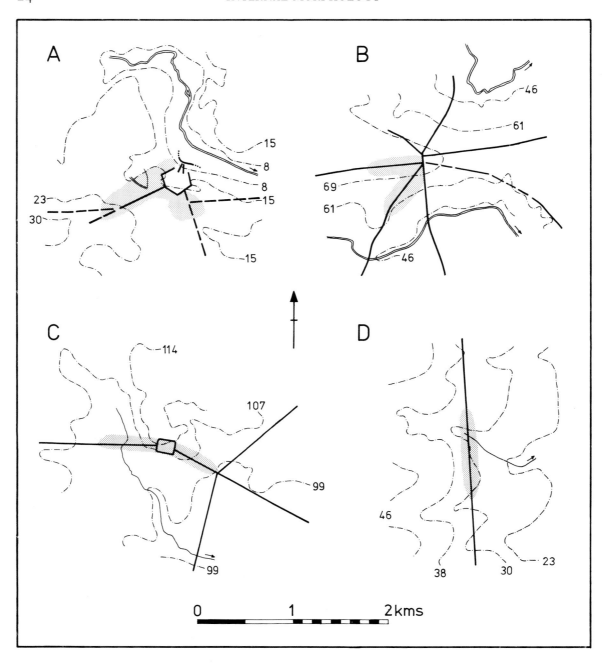

6 Examples of road junction and linear settlements:
   A Brampton (*after Green C. and Edwards*);
   B Braintree (*after Drury*); **C** Wall (*after Gould*);
   D Hibaldstow (*after Smith*)

social, economic or administrative pressures to encourage the creation of a more centralized and compact urban centre. This general conclusion applies whether the sites had Iron-Age antecedents or developed during the course of the Roman occupation.

The second category concerns one of the most characteristic classes of small towns, the so-called linear or ribbon developments, where the main occupation is confined to the frontages of a single main through route. Typical examples include Wall,[68] with debris known to extend up to 1.6 km (1 mile) along Watling Street, though in places it is clearly intermittent, and Hibaldstow,[69] where the known plots line Ermine Street for up to 800 m (2600 ft) (fig. 6 C and D). These sites, in their simplest form, betray little or no development away from the main frontages and there appears to have been no obvious urban focus within the plan.

Among students of small-town plans, linear settlements of this type have been seen as the commonest and the earliest form from which more complex plans evolved. This process usually involved the gradual and haphazard addition of side-streets and lanes so as to provide access to land beyond the immediate frontages. Examples of this outward expansion, combined with an increasing centralization, are confined not just to sites dependent on a single main road, as at Brough-on-Fosse,[70] but also to sites developing at road junctions as in the case of Great Chesterford.[71] Both can be seen to be intermediate in form between their humbler, undeveloped counterparts, and those sites characterized by a more complex irregular network of streets behind the frontages. Not all sites so developed, of course, and much more research is vital before we understand the full nuances of settlement expansion and contraction.

The third class of sites covers those developed linear and road-junction sites where increasingly centralized tendencies had been responsible for the growth of an irregular internal street system well beyond the initial main roads. A reasonably typical example is provided by Kenchester,[72] where the early ribbon development, extending over some 700 m (2300 ft), was apparently modified in the course of the second century by a much greater concentration of streets within the defended enclosure (see fig. 15). No attempt appears to have been made, however, to rationa-

lize the plan by linking up the side-streets and lanes by the provision of an *intervallum* road. The latter is one of the characteristic features at Water Newton, where the most complicated street system known in this category[73] lies within a walled area enclosing 18 ha (44 acres); it should not be forgotten, though, that extensive ribbon developments also existed to north and south along Ermine Street (see figs. 18 and 20). It is particularly unfortunate that in the absence of detailed excavations here, we can do little but hypothesize about the expansion of this small town.

This category of plan probably represents the outcome of a cumulative and spontaneous growth of internal streets, to meet a whole range of contributory factors including population growth, increasing functional complexity, the availability of resources and the intangible aspect of focal consciousness on the part of the resident community; hence its importance as an indicator of increased urban status. Two separate processes of expansion appear to be visible: an outward expansion along the roads, representing the primary use of convenient and ready-made frontages, and an outward expansion away from the roads into new land, reflecting a secondary process as and when the need for access to the centre became an overriding concern.

The fourth class of sites is also characterized by an irregular and haphazard network of internal streets and lanes, but one which apparently developed independently of major through routes. A characteristic example exists at Irchester,[74] where none of the three main roads thought to focus on the site has been conclusively located within the settlement (fig. 40). Almost all the surviving evidence for the streets is confined to the walled area which enclosed 8 ha (20 acres), even though occupation debris is known to be far more extensive. Here, the central north-south street, with a marked kink at its southern end, branches at its northern end to the north-west and north-east; along its course, further streets lead east and west with additional side-streets and lanes. Comparable irregularity also appears to be the rule at Ashton in the area west of the modern Oundle to Peterborough road,[75] though the excavated area is dominated by a single main road with several side-lanes, and in the evidence visible at the problematical sites of Dragonby and Kirmington.[76]

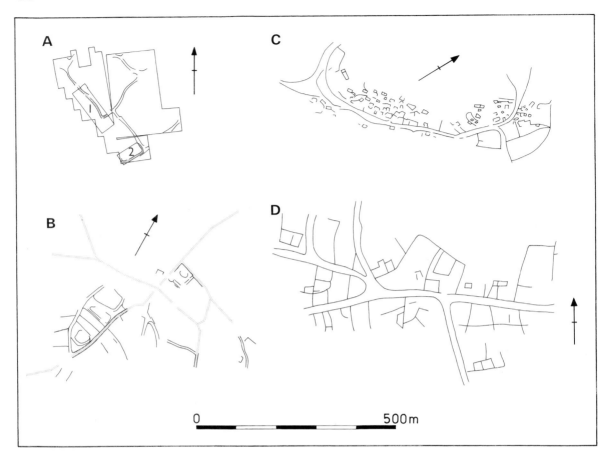

7 Comparative plans of some 'village' settlements:
A Dragonby (*after May*); **B** Kirmington (*after Riley*); **C** & **D** Chisenbury Warren and Hacconby Fen (*after Taylor*)

This particular category deserves closer attention, because the level of spontaneous internal development, independent of any main road(s), may well be the result of a native tradition flourishing in the Roman period. Interestingly all the examples quoted have some Iron-Age antecedents. Distinctive as the plans are, however, some of the less developed examples like Dragonby are difficult to differentiate from accepted 'villages' like Chisenbury Warren and Hacconby Fen,[77] thus reinforcing some of the problems of definition outlined in the introduction (fig. 7).

The final category of small towns covers those sites with an apparent element of planning or some form of recognizable street grid. Very few, however, appear to be planned in any way comparable with the cities of the province. Most are basically uncoordinated in that their planning probably represents the outcome of good fortune or minimal management. At Alchester, for instance, the defended area is quartered by the central crossroads (see fig. 24), while a further east-west street is indicated on aerial photographs.[78] Comparable arrangements are likely at Dorchester-on-Thames and Ilchester.[79] More organization may be visible at Corbridge, but the resulting *insulae* are still very irregular.[80]

Some sites possess a more co-ordinated layout, however, either as an original element or as a later addition. Among the former might well belong the apparently regular arrangement of internal streets of early Roman date on Wickham Hill at Braughing (see fig. 28).[81] If the fragmentary evidence from Baldock is comparable,[82] both might well represent a reshaping of an existing layout as part of a general Roman initiative or of native imitation of contemporary development in nearby cities. The street grid at Catterick, east of Dere Street and opposite the original settlement on the west (see fig. 30), appears to represent the best-known example of a later addition.[83] Traces of another such planned framework of uncertain date may also exist at Wanborough.[84] Such evidence confirms the general lack of real planning, however, so that most examples fall into line with the preceding categories where some sort of internal street network was developed as and when necessary to meet the needs of the resident community.

This discussion of the small towns, although descriptive, has helped to clarify our limited understanding of their settlement plans in relation to the organization and development of the internal roads and streets. While reiterating the apparent importance of a developed street network, we must be careful nevertheless to avoid oversimplifying the picture too far in the current state of the evidence. Most of our plans are little more than simplified abstractions derived from the overall spread of the known occupation debris, illuminated by infrequent excavation and aerial photography. Only rarely can we assess this spatial information in terms of settlement expansion and contraction through time. Such an historical perspective must be our long-term goal, even though for the present we can at best only hypothesize about the nature of the development processes at work.

Internal Land-use and Building Layout

Against the background of the known settlement plans, it is now possible to consider the internal arrangements of the building types and their associated patterns of land-use. Individual case-studies are presented below; here, the aim is to provide a more generalized picture by conflating information from all available sources. Several questions require specific treatment: what distinct zones existed within the sites and how were they used? Where were the individual building types and specialist facilities located? And how far can we determine development trends in the use of space?

Given the obvious importance of the main road and street frontages, it is hardly surprising that they provided the most attractive sites for occupation. Inevitably, therefore, almost every type of building can be found in just such a location, but here our interest lies in the recognition of broader trends of land-usage among the small towns. By far the most prominent pattern is represented by the regular development of narrow-fronted strip buildings along the main frontages in such a way as to accommodate the maximum number of properties in the space available. Their importance within the small towns has already been demonstrated (p. 18), and further detailed examples are unnecessary here. It is important, however, to consider their overall arrangement and that of their associated features.

At most sites, strip buildings appear to have been constructed as independent entities, separated from their neighbours by either alleys or narrow lanes. Sometimes, where occupation is particularly dense, there is little or no evidence for any associated property to the rear, suggesting that their occupants either worked land elsewhere or derived their livelihood from other specializations. This situation apparently applies at Water Newton.[85] Independence of this type was probably exceptional, however, and among the small towns strip buildings are usually known to lie at one end of a narrow plot or yard. This could be put to a variety of uses. At Chelmsford, the individual plots extend only 40–60 m (130–98 ft) and were sometimes occupied by lesser structures, pits and ovens.[86] Similar boundaries apparently lay 35 and 40 m (114 and 130 ft) respectively behind the buildings at Braughing and Neatham.[87] At Ashton and Holditch, the buildings lay in simple yards containing ovens and wells,[88] while at Middlewich, the land behind the frontages was used for related industrial activities.[89] In contrast, the plots at Penkridge, which were up to 30 m (100 ft) deep, may well have been employed as gardens or animal pens.[90] As might be expected, there is frequent evidence for the reconstruction of such strip building properties, the same property boundaries sometimes being retained over considerable periods, while at others a considerable level of property amalgamation and reorganization was involved.

A second prominent pattern of land-use along the frontages appears for the present to be confined to those sites with a marked agricultural bias. In them relatively spacious plots of varying dimensions were arranged along the frontages and housed a range of individual buildings and other related features. They are particularly prominent in the early stages of development at Godmanchester where, following the demise of the fort, a system of regular plots was apparently laid out, extending as a series of broad strips well into the territory surrounding the settlement.[91] These housed the characteristic domestic vernacular buildings already described (p. 17). Much the same picture emerges at Dragonby throughout the Roman period.[92] A further feature of this pattern can be distinguished at Braintree, where the plots have been shown to extend up to 105 m (343 ft) away from the frontages and appear therefore to represent smallholdings associated with the various buildings;[93] comparable dimensions have also been noted at Great Dunmow. Clearly the relative importance of such spacious plots within individual layouts, in contrast to the numbers of strip buildings, is of considerable interest to our understanding of their development and function, but precise details are difficult to obtain. At Dragonby, spacious plots appear to predominate in the excavated areas, but at Ilchester, they seem to be confined to the extramural frontages in the form of a double row of plots 20 by 50 m (66 by 165 ft) in size.[94] Such diversity is to be expected and may indicate different categories of settlement within the small-town range.

From what has been said, it is clear that the domestic and workshop accommodation, together with their associated properties and features, formed the predominant element along the frontages of the small towns. Of necessity, therefore, the larger, more sophisticated structures had to occupy whatever land was available, unless they were specifically imposed upon the plan by official action or were grouped together to form some sort of central focus within the layout. An examination of the location of particular groups of romanized structures allows us to determine general trends.

Mansiones usually occupy one of two specific locations, both probably reflecting the state of development at individual sites when the installations were added. One favoured location was directly alongside the main road frontages, as for example at Wall.[95] A similar location appears at Catterick and Great Casterton, and may also account for the courtyard structure parallel to Ermine Street at Water Newton.[96] The other favoured location was in the land immediately behind the frontage properties, served by either side-lanes or streets; examples are known at Chelmsford, Godmanchester and Wanborough.[97] These buildings are thus located wherever convenient land was available, though in the case of Godmanchester at least, properties were demolished in the process.

Much the same range of locations seems to prevail for the more romanized forms of housing. Where several wealthy houses are known to exist, they are usually later developments behind the main frontages and their buildings. This certainly seems to be the case with the larger structures located in the south-eastern part of the walled area at Water Newton,[98] and is more convincingly demonstrated at Kenchester, where at least three wealthy houses are known in similar locations, served by separate side-streets.[99] The buildings with mosaics at Bath, if domestic, may also come into this category.[100] In contrast, however, the two winged-corridor houses at Camerton may lie in a comparable location in relation to the Fosse Way but they clearly predate the well-known industrial expansion of the site along the frontages.[101]

Individual houses present more interesting contrasts. Examples are certainly known behind the main frontages in whatever land was available, as at both Margidunum and Mildenhall, just within their respective defences;[102] but they were frequently imposed on the main frontages, often overlying earlier occupation levels. The latter is true of the winged-corridor house at Great Chesterford and the building inside the defences at Thorpe,[103] suggesting that, on occasion, official action could override other concerns in matters of location.

Interesting trends also emerge for the location of temples. Some clearly occupied positions of convenience near to or alongside the main frontages, as for example at Chelmsford and probably Kenchester.[104] Yet others display associations with *mansiones*. The best attested case is the temple complex west of the *mansio* at Godmanchester,[105] though comparable examples may exist at Chelmsford and Water Newton.[106] But by far the most important are those small towns where a major temple complex provided a functional focus within the plan, as for example at Bath or Harlow.[107] This question of a more developed central core among the small towns is an important one which requires closer attention.

Urban growth is often reflected morphologically by the appearance of a distinctive central area. This is readily apparent among the cities of Roman Britain, where normally the *forum-basilica* lies at the centre, but among the small towns, the picture is much less strikingly developed. On current evidence, only a handful of sites seems to be involved. Such central foci generally take one of two forms, either the temple complex already mentioned, or one or more large and apparently important buildings. The first of these can be demonstrated at several sites where a religious element appears to predominate at the core; besides Harlow, with its ditched *temenos*, central precincts can also be seen at Irchester, Springhead and Wycomb,[108] while much the same level of importance may originally have attached to the enclosure at Frilford.[109] Such a religious focus perhaps indicates the primary function at these sites, in contrast to those where the temple occupies a somewhat subsidiary location in the known plan.

The second category is represented by several sites with some form of official or cultural focus. Particularly well known is the planned central core at Corbridge, developed in the later second and early third centuries on either side of the main east-west road.[110] To this might well be added the two large rectangular buildings and an associated temple compound at Water Newton, the combined temple and baths complex at Bath and the four major buildings in the heart of Braughing.[111] A different form of core appears to have existed from the third century at Godmanchester, after the creation of the open market-place and the construction of the official 'Basilica' building adjacent to the *mansio* compound.[112] Similar market-places are likely to have acted as a focus elsewhere.

Interestingly, only a small number of sites enjoyed such a distinctive central core, suggesting that in addition to a developed internal street network, this might be a further indicator of a higher level of urban development and complexity.

Behind the developed road and street frontages forming the settlement proper, what might be called the rural-urban fringe was reached. In its simplest form, this was often marked by the existence of field systems, as for example at Brampton,[113] where they are known immediately beyond the settled frontages and their associated manufacturing areas. But elsewhere the situation is far less clear, partly for lack of detailed evidence and partly because the boundary is not always precisely defined in archaeologically recognizable terms. At Water Newton, for instance, the fringes around the urban core appear to merge imperceptibly into the countryside; this is especially clear in the Normangate Field area, where the known kilns are interspersed with the urban workshops and shrines on the one hand and the droveways and rural estates of the villas on the other.[114] A comparable tendency has also been argued for Godmanchester, where the urban fields appear to merge into the enclosures associated with the villa at Rectory Farm.[115] At its extreme among the small towns, this blurring of the rural-urban boundary extends over the whole settlement, as at Dragonby,[116] and perhaps suggests some sort of link with the level of agricultural pre-occupation or functional specialization.

At one time the line of the defences used to be regarded as a significant rural-urban divide, but the repeated recognition of extensive extra-mural suburbs has necessarily shifted the emphasis of enquiry. It is now clear that the construction of the small-town defences provided an additional influence on their morphological development, depending upon the inclusion or exclusion of particular areas. These defences seldom attempted to enclose the total area of occupation, partly because of its pre-existing shape and extent, and partly because the defences were designed to perform a variety of different functions, many of which fell in the official sphere. Two broad groups seem to emerge from the known evidence (fig. 8), each with a different level of impact on the defended area itself and on the extra-mural suburbs.

The first category includes those small towns where the defences appear to rationalize an extensive urban scatter and to enclose a suitable urban core. Sites enclosing 8 ha (20 acres) or more

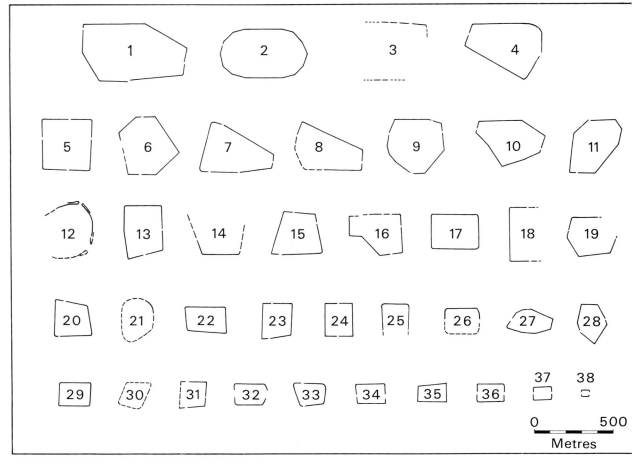

8 Comparative outline plans of small town fortifications: **1** Water Newton; **2** Great Chesterford; **3** Corbridge; **4** Towcester; **5** Alchester; **6** Godmanchester; **7** Ilchester; **8** Rochester; **9** Bath; **10** Kenchester; **11** Great Casterton; **12** Worcester; **13** Irchester; **14** Kelvedon; **15** Chelmsford; **16** Catterick; **17** Mildenhall; **18** Dorchester-on-Thames; **19** Brampton; **20** Whilton Lodge; **21** Alcester; **22** Dorn; **23** Ancaster; **24** Neatham; **25** Rocester; **26** Brough-on-Fosse; **27** Caistor (Lincs); **28** Margidunum; **29** Little Chester; **30** Droitwich; **31** Thorpe-by-Newark; **32** Mancetter; **33** Chesterton-on-Fosse; **34** Wall; **35** Horncastle; **36** Penkridge; **37** Cave's Inn; **38** Redhill

certainly belong here, though smaller examples like Catterick must also be considered on their individual merits. Construction of defences inevitably involved some small-scale demolition, seen, for example, at Chelmsford, Dorchester-on-Thames and Great Chesterford,[117] while some internal streets may have been blocked or altered as at Mildenhall and Irchester.[118] These disturbances must have been minimized, however, where the defences ran through the fringes of the main settlement, as they appear to have done at Kenchester. Once provided, two general trends are obvious: first, the intra-mural zone remained or soon became relatively well built-up, and second, there was no obvious contraction or shift in emphasis within the extra-mural zone prior to the mid fourth century at least. Both trends are well attested at Water Newton, especially in the Kate's Cabin suburb,[119] as well as at Ilchester and at Bath, where the appearance of mosaics might indicate some level of intra-mural concentration of wealth.[120]

Comparable trends are not found among the second category, which includes those sites where the defences are apparently arbitrarily imposed on a straggling ribbon development or urban scatter so as to provide a small defended strongpoint astride the road. Sites enclosing 4 ha (10 acres) or less are the norm, often including only a small fraction of the occupied area. Construction in these cases involved considerably more destruction to accommodate the defensive screen, as the evidence from Ancaster, Brough-on-Fosse and Mancetter clearly demonstrates.[121] Of particular importance, however, is the impact of such defensive provision upon the intra-mural zone; enclosures that are apparently almost empty have been noted at Caistor, Horncastle, Mancetter and Wall,[122] as well as at Margidunum with the exception of the late complex in the northern half.[123] The situation in the extra-mural areas is much less clear-cut, but the recovery of pottery appears to indicate some level of continued activity. Clearly the nature of the defences and their effect at individual sites may be yet another indicator of different levels of complexity and status.

It is worth recording also that urban contraction among the extra-mural areas does not appear to be a significant feature before the mid fourth century. Some sites were even able to expand as Catterick and Towcester attest.[124] But others show signs of change, especially those where fourth-century cemeteries developed in formerly built-up areas outside the defences; examples of this trend are well documented at Ancaster, Great Chesterford and Godmanchester.[125] Elsewhere, the nature of the fourth-century levels is difficult to interpret precisely. These trends will be considered in more detail below (p. 316).

Finally within the context of small-town morphology, we might briefly consider the question of the location of cemeteries. Despite their potential, however, as an indicator of relative size and development trends, little real systematic research has been undertaken. All too frequently, as well, cemeteries have been examined in isolation from other components of the plan. Large examples are known, however, more often than not on the fringes of the main occupied areas, as at Ashton, Baldock, Bath, Irchester and Water Newton.[126] To these can be added the fourth-century examples already mentioned, which clearly indicate some level of extra-mural contraction. This organized disposal of the dead in large communal cemeteries, set aside for the purpose, is a useful indicator of more complex communities, so that the appearance of isolated burial plots can be instructive; at Ilchester, the late burials within the extra-mural plots might well be indicative of the later Roman decline in standards within a contracting settlement.[127]

Discussion

From such a generalized synthesis of the morphology of the small towns, it is possible to begin to define several recurring features which can help to evaluate our understanding of the overall level of complexity at individual sites, although these will clearly need to be refined as more new evidence emerges from the ground. Particular attention has been drawn to the significance of a developing internal street network within the overall plan, in contrast to the ribbon developments which remained dependent upon the main roads. The nature of this development needs closer attention. Equally significant for the small towns is the existence of some form of central core within the plan, whether administrative, official, socio-economic or religious, around which the other elements are clearly structured. It has also been stressed that the overall range of individual building types can be a useful indicator of the level of settlement complexity; in particular, attention has been focused on the relative presence or absence of the larger, more obviously romanized, building complexes and their planned or *ad hoc* location within the layout. Just as important for the question of small-town function and status might be the relative proportions of strip buildings in contrast to the more spacious plots, since in general these are functionally distinct. Importance has also been attached to the nature of the defended area, whether 'urban-core' or 'strongpoint', and its relationship to the intra- and extra-mural zones so created. In addition, a close analysis of the organization and location of communal cemeteries should help to define higher orders of social organization and settlement complexity.

We must end this review by noting the relative simplicity of many of the small towns alongside modern notions of complex urban morphologies. Most would have appeared undistinguished and unsophisticated, especially those ribbon developments with a restricted range of internal structures. The exceptions, which have some form of developed street network, a more diverse range of buildings and perhaps even a central core, clearly stand out from the pack on current evidence, and they can thus be seen to compare most favourably with the urban patterns recognizable within the major towns and cities of the province.

FOUR
SPECIAL FUNCTIONS

As already indicated, there were sometimes special functions which at first aided the foundation, and later the survival, of certain small towns. But the existence of these functions does not mean that the towns depended on them exclusively and it did not prevent them from acquiring others from the normal expected range.

Chief among these special functions was a governmental or administrative duty at either local or provincial level or possibly both. Unfortunately there is all too little evidence from Britain to enable us to discern the precise nature of the relationship between the small towns and authority, although some tentative suggestions can be made. Consequently it is necessary to rely heavily on sources of information from across the Channel.

It is abundantly clear that when the time came to construct defences around many of these sites, the reason was not always primarily to protect the community. This is especially true of those, often identified as *burgi*, which protected only a very small part of the settlement (p. 35 below); but even where larger areas were enclosed, most included only a fraction of the total, as for example at Catterick,[1] Ilchester[2] and Water Newton,[3] where the inhabited extra-mural areas extended for considerable distances. This is not to say, though, that the interests of the local population were entirely ignored; for, if one of the primary purposes of fortifications was to guard the necessary physical organs of tax recording and collection and the necessary officials, then a secondary purpose may possibly be glimpsed in the simultaneous protection of some of the economic base from which many of the tax payments were derived; hence the inclusion of markets, shops, workshops and houses. An extreme and exceptional case is the small community outside the fort of Phasis in the province of Cappadocia, which was fortified by the governor solely to protect it from assault by invading Alans in the mid second century.[4] But this instance apart, there were presumably some official functions which the sites in this category possessed and which were physically concentrated within the defences and probably unrelated to local needs. Extrapolating from this, it is probably right to assume that these functions also (1) existed before the construction of the defences, but in a form which is not yet entirely visible to archaeology, and (2) can be connected with provincial rather than local administration.

Two types of evidence can give a clue to this particular function: inscriptions and structures. A handful of inscriptions from British sites and many more from other provinces refer to various provincial officials, usually soldiers seconded for duty to the governor's staff. It is probably no accident that they were to be found in most classes of urban or other settlements and in military *vici*. The commonest are those with the title *beneficiarius consularis*; where information is forthcoming from the inscriptions, almost all were legionaries. Most are found associated with forts or their *vici*, such as Lancaster,[5] Binchester,[6] Lanchester,[7] Housesteads,[8] Risingham,[9] Chesterholm[10] and Greta Bridge,[11] but they are also known from the civitas capitals of Wroxeter[12] and Winchester[13] and the small towns of Dorchester[14] and Catterick;[15] it is possible, though, that the latter were present when Catterick was still a military *vicus*, since one of the inscriptions is dated to AD 191.

The work of *beneficiarii* is by no means clear, but most authorities accept that they performed various police-type duties over the local populations, and supervised local tax collection. They have also been connected with the running of the *cursus publicus*, the empire-wide postal system created by Augustus for carrying official goods and despatches, and the intermediate stations – *mansiones* and *mutationes* – along its routes. It has also been claimed that they acted as Rome's representatives in areas devoid of large towns or cities, or military garrisons, but this hardly equates with the known distribution of most of the British-based officials in or near auxiliary forts. In sum, their duties probably varied from place to place and from time to time, although there was always likely to be a strong police element, especially in those areas on or near the frontiers where military government was paramount and where the natives enjoyed only limited autonomy. Even with auxiliary regiments present, there would still have been work for an official to oversee civilian activities. In Africa, for instance, standard-bearers of *Legio III Augusta* found themselves *agentes curam macelli*, or supervisors of markets;[16] a good equivalent here from more recent times might be the bazaar sergeant of British India. Indeed these officials are likely to have carried out the duties of assistant commissioner, resident magistrate, general arbitrator, tax-collector and market supervisor all rolled into one.

It is interesting that the number of *beneficiarii* greatly multiplied throughout the empire in the late second and third centuries, although they were not unknown before.[17] The principate of Severus probably saw the greatest expansion, and it is perhaps no coincidence that it may have been he who introduced the *annona militaris*, a tax paid in grain or other materials to meet the needs of the army. The *beneficiarii* might have been in charge of its annual assessment according to the quantity of the harvest, its collection and safe storage at some central point and its distribution to wherever it was needed. It must be remembered, though, that the Code of Justinian specifically states that 'no tax shall be exacted by the *stationarii*',[18] to which general category most officials probably belonged.

A *singularis consularis* is attested at Catterick on the altar which also records a *beneficiarius*, Q. Varius Vitalis.[19] Strictly *singulares* were members of governors' personal bodyguards, drawn from auxiliary regiments, but they may also have been employed for other duties. For instance, this altar

was dedicated by Titus Irdas to 'the god who devised roads and paths'. It is likely, therefore, that on a major route to the north he was on a duty connected with road-works or perhaps travel arrangements for the governor. Others are known from the military *vici* at Chesterholm,[20] Ribchester[21] and High Rochester.[22]

Rarer still are the officials entitled *stratores consularis*, known from the small town at Irchester[23] and the port at Dover.[24] Athough there is little agreement about their role, they seem to have had slightly more specialized duties. Strictly they were attached to the governor's staff as equerries or grooms, but as with *singulares* their duties may have taken them outside his immediate entourage. Anicius Saturninus at Irchester has been described as a remount officer securing new horses for the army, while O. Cordius Candidus at Dover may have been connected with the transport of horses across the Channel. Elsewhere, in the Danube province of Upper Moesia, *stratores* were to be found supervising road stations at both Niš (*Naissus*) and Čuprija (*Horreum Margi*),[25] and it is not impossible that they were doing the same in Britain.

Of more senior rank are the legionary centurions recorded as *centuriones regionarii*; they probably had wider responsibilities with oversight over whole districts and only four are known in Britain. One from Bath records the restoration of a vandalized religious shrine by G. Severius Emeritus;[26] he probably controlled a wide area including perhaps the nearby port at Sea Mills, although the situation may be more complicated, since Bath lay close to an imperial estate, the headquarters of which were at Combe Down just outside the town.[27] This would have come under the jurisdiction of the provincial *procurator*, one of whose assistants restored its headquarters building, and not that of the *regionarius*. The other two examples of *regionarii* come from the auxiliary fort at Ribchester,[28] where both Aelius Antonius and T. Floridius Natalis combined the post with that of *praepositus numeri* or fort commander. They were presumably responsible for supervising the civil settlement outside the fort and, in particular, the Sarmatian veterans who had been granted land in its vicinity.[29] These veterans had originally been recruited into the Roman army as heavy cavalry after the Sarmatian wars fought by Marcus Aurelius in the middle

Danube. One regiment was stationed at Ribchester from the late second century and its members were granted land as a gratuity upon retirement. This fact is recorded in the name of the *vicus, Bremetennaci Veteranorum*, which is contained in the Ravenna list.[30] This situation was not dissimilar to the frontier districts of eastern Syria, where villages were supervised by centurions seconded from the province's legions.[31]

Various other types of *stationarii*, to which general category most of these personnel probably belonged, are known in other provinces but none in Britain. *Frumentarii*, both cavalry decurions, for instance, are known to have served at Tiffen and Feldkirchen[32] in the mining district of Noricum, while an official bearing the title *immunis consularis curas agens vico Saloduro* is recorded from Solothurn near Augst;[33] as an *immunis* he had been relieved of all other military duties by the provincial governor in order to oversee the village community of the *Vicus Salodurus*.

The second category of evidence, that of structures, is more difficult to interpret successfully, although it is probably more plentiful in Britain. If we are to connect the small towns and other settlements which were provided with fortifications with the needs of provincial administration, then they should contain buildings identifiable as either the residences and offices of the local officials, or granaries and stores-buildings for the collection and security of taxes in kind. They may exist in conjunction with, or separately from, road-station buildings such as *mansiones* and *mutationes*, which may, or may not, have had their own officials. These buildings no doubt contrasted with the generally simple and unsophisticated structures found at most of the sites in question. A note of caution must be sounded, however. Although the existence of defences is being used here as the criterion for the presence of elements in the provincial administration, the reverse may not always be true. The same or similar elements could equally exist in unfortified sites, as indeed they probably did in the military *vici*.

The first structures to be considered must be the defences themselves, especially those which protected only an essential core, even though it may extend beyond the government installations. In Gallia Belgica there are a comparatively large number of small defended sites situated at intervals along main roads. They are most closely and evenly spaced along the road from Cologne to Bavai,[34] indicating the hand of the provincial administration; more may yet be found on other roads. These sites, usually called *burgi*, are small, that at Liberchies (Brunehaut) being only *c*. 2.5 ha (6 acres). This latter was situated beside the road and was not bisected by it, as was the larger fortified site at nearby Liberchies (Les Bons-Villers).[35] But these minor structures are not restricted to the west. They are found throughout the empire in the third and fourth centuries, although they were known elsewhere by different names: *castella, turres, centenaria* and by the Greek *pyrgoi*. They occur in the deserts of Africa, Syria and Arabia, and in the regions of the Rhine and Danube. They are found along *limites* and roads, at bridgeheads and crossroads. They were the late Roman Empire's answer to the weakness of linear barriers and provided a defence in depth which the latter could not. An attempt has been made to identify a similar system in Britain, comprising the sequence of five intermediate stations which lie along Watling Street between Towcester and Wroxeter, at Red Hill, Penkridge, Wall, Mancetter and Cave's Inn.[36] They were all fortified some time after the late third century and are characterized by their broadly rectangular shape and small size.

It need not stop here, however, because other sites in Britain might qualify for inclusion. These include the quartet of sites on the Fosse Way between Leicester and Lincoln, at Willoughby, Margidunum, Thorpe and Brough, and the trio between Leicester and Cirencester, at Chesterton, Dorn and Bourton. Unfortunately, very little is known about Brough, Dorn, Willoughby and Bourton, and defences have yet to be proven for the latter pair. Ancaster, Caistor and Horncastle might also be considered, the last two perhaps in connection with east coast defence; both are small, being 3 ha and 2.4 ha (7.5 and 5.9 acres) respectively. Ancaster lay on Ermine Street south of Lincoln.

It is still uncertain how these possible *burgi* operated. They may have contained either small units of the regular army or perhaps a locally-raised militia. Nor is it impossible that bands of *laeti* or *gentiles* were settled in some, if not all, during the late fourth century, but unfortunately the relevant chapter of the *Notitia Dignitatum*, which listed these barbarian recruits to the Roman army in Britain, is missing. It is doubly unfortunate that very few of the buckles and belt-plates, so often claimed as characteristic of late Roman military equipment,[37] have been found in these sites except for one at Cave's Inn. Elsewhere, isolated examples are recorded from Catterick, Wanborough and Wycomb, while among the small towns only Water Newton and Dorchester-on-Thames have produced significant numbers. An alternative explanation might see these fortified sites being used as bases for the storage of spare equipment and horses plus food and fodder for mobile cavalry units of the late Roman field army in Britain. This would account for the singular lack of internal buildings, even though a civilian element may have remained among the population as the sharp distinction between fort and town became increasingly blurred in the fourth century. Unfortunately little excavation has taken place in the interiors of these fortified sites and what has been is not very informative for, in many cases, the combination of stone-robbing and deep-ploughing has reduced even masonry buildings to amorphous scatters of stone.

Consideration of these sites, whether they were *burgi* or not, introduces another element into the discussion of fortified small towns. It has been pointed out that the insignia assigned to the *vicarius* of the British diocese, alone of such officers, consists of castellated enclosures instead of maidens, indicating that he commanded troops.[38] It is also generally accepted that during the fourth century not only were units of a field army serving in Britain but also regular troops were acting as urban garrisons.[39] These two sources of evidence together imply the presence of detachments of the field army stationed in both major and minor towns. This would explain the recovery of military equipment and weaponry from several sites, among them Cirencester with one of the largest collections. Apart from the small towns already mentioned at Dorchester-on-Thames and Water Newton, Catterick is perhaps the most interesting. Here, the characteristic buckles and belt-plates have been found, as well as a collection of weaponry, which included spears, lances and the barbed head from a *martio-barbulus*, a type of lead-weighted throwing dart used by the late Roman army. Three spurs have also come from late levels: they are uncommon finds on Romano-British sites and suggest the presence of a cavalry unit here in the late fourth century. In addition, excavations over a large area revealed considerable reconstruction and modification of existing buildings in the same period, as though the town was being forced to adapt to its new inhabitants. The buildings south of the main east-west street were chiefly affected, being united to form a major complex reminiscent of the *principia* and *praetorium* of a more normal fort.[40]

There are other structures, besides fortifications, which can indicate an official presence. These include *mansiones* and *mutationes*, the residences of officials such as *beneficiarii* if they are separate from the former, and warehouses and granaries for the collection of the *annona*. It must be stressed at the outset that correct identification is the chief problem.

Mansiones were normally large buildings with ranges of rooms grouped in suites around a central courtyard and a separate bath-house which would be additional to any urban bathing establishments. They provided overnight accommodation and food, as well as fresh horses, for members of the *cursus publicus*, and for some other official travellers. They are likely to be found in both large and small towns, provided they lie on the main roads, and therefore the Antonine Itinerary can be a useful indicator to their presence. Excellent examples are known at Heddernheim (*Nida*) and Kempten (*Cambodunum*) in Germany and Raetia respectively.[41] Perhaps the most characteristic British example is that in the civitas capital at Silchester, where it was the second largest building in the town after the forum and was situated close to the south gate.[42] In its final form, it contained some half dozen suites of rooms in two wings opposing each other across a central court. The third wing, which united the other two, possessed heated rooms which may have been in common use. All three wings had interior and exterior colonnades or arcades. The entrance divided the north wing into two unequal parts while the bath-house, placed beyond an outer court, was reached by a covered corridor. The excavations in the early part of this century have made this a difficult building to interpret, but it is clear from the published plan that alterations had been made to the original structure, which probably dates from the third century.

The best examples of *mansiones* yet excavated in the small towns are probably those at Chelmsford (p. 20), Godmanchester and Catterick (cf. fig. 4 A–C). That at Godmanchester is a nearly-symmetrical courtyard building, as at Silchester, but on a much reduced scale, with a separate bath-house close to the south wing.[43] It is thought to date to the Hadrianic period. Interestingly, spaces in the north wing flanking the entrance hall have been interpreted as stables and tack-rooms. Outside there appear to have been two aisled barns of second- and third-century date respectively, which were probably used for the safe storage of taxes collected in kind or goods in transit. This function is also reflected in two small square structures, projecting outwards from the south wall of the *mansio*, which have been interpreted as tower granaries. One of them remained in use after a disastrous fire in the late third century destroyed much of the town as well as the *mansio*, which was not rebuilt.

The *mansio* at Catterick was an altogether more asymmetrical building. As originally constructed by a ninth cohort, probably of *Legio VI*, it contained only two or three suites of rooms together with some which are best interpreted as having a communal function.[44] There was a small internal courtyard with an ornamental fountain and the old, first-century fort bath-house was rebuilt on a much larger scale. Both *mansio* and baths had their own water supply. Although the floors were at best concrete or *opus signinum*, most internal wall surfaces were covered in conventionally-ornamented painted plaster. The building was entered from the south through a porticoed doorway. It also enjoyed a pleasant situation on the south bank of the River Swale, close to a probable bridge carrying Dere Street. The *mansio* was constructed in the Hadrianic period, following the evacuation of the nearby fort, but it seems to have gone out of use and been demolished by the end of the second century. Why is not clear. The only part to survive was a later addition to the original building, a warehouse-like structure placed in front of and astride the main entrance. It was extremely well built, with buttresses along its eastern side and a very solid paved floor. As at Godmanchester, it was probably used as a collection and storage point.

Mansiones in other small towns are less well known. That at Wall is claimed on the evidence of the existence of a large and complex bath-house and an apparently contemporary adjoining court-yard house, both situated to the west of the later walled enclosure (fig. 5 A). Evidence indicates a destruction layer of *c.* AD 160 across the courtyard building, after which it was not rebuilt although the baths appear to have remained in use.[45] An aerial photograph also indicates a possible *mansio* at Wanborough (fig. 4 D), again apparently outside the defences.[46] Braughing seems to contain a courtyard structure about which nothing is known,[47] while a building at Cave's Inn is also difficult to interpret.[48] In the north, at Corbridge, a large building with a veranda and an ornamental fountain has been claimed as a *mansio*, although it started life as a winged-corridor house probably during the third century.[49] Some northern and Welsh *vici* also contained possible *mansiones*, such as Benwell,[50] Chesterholm,[51] Newstead[52] and Brecon[53]. As at Corbridge, they sometimes resemble rural dwellings, which should make us look again at some of the larger houses which occasionally occur in small towns further south. Buildings at Great Chesterford,[54] Margidunum[55] and Camerton[56] might have served as *mansiones*, although it should be stressed that separate bath-houses are absent, while it is difficult to identify the stables. One interesting factor, seemingly common to all buildings interpreted as *mansiones*, is the scarcity of broken pottery, coins and other trinkets. At Catterick, for instance, the only concentration of pottery was found in the ornamental fountain. In consequence, it has been claimed that the buildings were seldom used, but a more likely explanation is that they were kept scrupulously clean for official travellers. The size of most buildings would imply the simultaneous accommodation of several groups of messengers belonging to the *cursus publicus*. Moreover, despite the lack of artefacts, the bath-house at Catterick had been heavily used to judge by the state of the furnace cheeks, which had been rebuilt several times, and of the iron beams supporting the hot-water boilers, one of which had been completely burnt through.

Mutationes, which provided a change of horses but no accommodation, have proved much more difficult to identify, even though they should occur with greater frequency and at closer intervals than *mansiones*. Since their prime purpose was to stable horses, and perhaps to accommodate their grooms (though this could have been done in hay lofts at first-floor level), it is instructive to consider the space needs. Recent calculations suggest that a Roman cavalry horse required a space approximately 2.74 by 1.82 m (9 by 6 ft) if it was to have room to lie down and rise again and if other horses could pass to its rear.[57] This length could be reduced slightly if they were stabled *en echelon*. Consequently, it is necessary to seek buildings which conform to these figures or their multiples. One candidate is the building just inside the north gate at Thorpe-by-Newark, identifiable on the aerial photographs as a much bolder outline than any other structure in the town.[58] Excavation has revealed a long rectangular structure, constructed with substantial walls, but no more than mud floors, which was divided longitudinally into two very unequal parts by an internal wall (see figs. 91 and 92). The wider section measures *c*. 6 m (20 ft) in width which would accommodate two rows of stabled horses. The narrower part, *c*. 3 m (10 ft) wide, running the full length of the north side, could have been a service corridor or store for fodder; alternatively, this could have housed up to 15 or more horses, with the wider section accommodating carts, wagons, fodder or other stores. This building had succeeded another of equally substantial masonry but of different plan and probably different function, since quantities of painted plaster were recovered. Beyond this building at Thorpe, there is no other obvious candidate for a *mutatio* in Britain. Much of the difficulty of identification is caused by an almost complete ignorance of what we are looking for. Certainly if the building at Thorpe is a *mutatio*, then it is not visibly imitated elsewhere!

The last category of official building which ought to exist in many defended sites is the residence of the administrative officer, and there are a number of alternatives. The officers, whether *beneficiarii*, *stratores* or *regionarii*, might have been in charge of, and therefore accommodated in, the *mansio*, if one existed, though it has been argued that a *beneficiarius*, usually only a legionary, was too junior in status to have charge of such an important building. It is equally possible that these officials were billeted on local householders, a practice which became increasingly common among Roman army units in the late empire. The last alternative is that buildings were specifically constructed for them. As already noted above, small towns often contain one or two buildings of greater extent and more sophisticated plan than the general run. Examples are known at Great Chesterford, Camerton, Margidunum and Droitwich, among others.[59] But these structures on the whole resemble the familiar winged-corridor villas of the countryside, a building style which was restricted neither to Britain nor entirely to the countryside.[60] Care must therefore be observed in trying to identify them as the residences of minor provincial officials, for obviously they might be no more than the farmhouses of local landowners and in degree little different from a normal villa. Clearly archaeological evidence is insufficient in itself and absolute proof of official connections can come only from epigraphic sources.

There is one last function which small towns might have possessed at provincial level, that of acting as administrative centres for imperial estates. Again the evidence is sadly lacking, not only for the centres but also for the estates themselves. Nevertheless there are some indicators. In Britain, cases have been argued for the existence of estates in the Fens and around Salisbury Plain and Cranborne Chase,[61] while the inscription from the 'villa' at Combe Down near Bath provides irrefutable proof.[62] This records the restoration of a *principia* by Naevius, an assistant procurator, in the early third century. It cannot be the headquarters building of a normal fort and its association with a building which has all the appearances of a normal villa merely emphasizes the difficulties of interpretation; but for the inscription a villa it would be. Nothing is known about the location and extent of the associated estate; it could have been connected with stone-quarrying around Bath, which was being extracted and used for tombstones at Colchester before the Boudiccan revolt. A more certain case of an imperial estate is known in Gallia Belgica, in the Ardennes forest region, which was administered from the *curia Arduennae* (Amberloup).[63] What form of building this *curia* took is unknown, though it may not have been unlike a *principia*.

No small town in Britain can certainly qualify

as a centre for the administration of an imperial estate, although a case might be made for including Godmanchester and Water Newton. Both lie close to the Fen Edge, where there is some evidence to suggest that the land reclaimed under Hadrian between the Car Dyke and the Midfendic formed part of such an estate. Godmanchester contains an early third-century building, not unlike a *principia* in plan, which its excavator originally interpreted as a town hall.[64] It is difficult to accept this interpretation because there is no evidence to imply that the site was ever promoted to the rank of civitas capital, and it seems simplest to assume that it fulfilled some other official function. Using the Combe Down *principia* as a possible parallel, then an official link with an estate in the Fens is a serious possibility. Interestingly, the date of the building is roughly contemporary with the Combe Down inscription, coinciding with a considerable tightening of control over imperial estates under the emperor Severus, when the liberality which had been introduced first by Hadrian and later by Pertinax was largely cancelled. The repair of derelict, and the construction of new, buildings connected with these estates could be seen as part of the same policy. The case at Water Newton is rather less certain, but it has been argued that either one of the two large buildings visible at the centre of the defended area served as an administrative centre for the Fens, or that this function was performed by the remarkable complex identified at Castor to the north-east of the town's extramural suburbs.[65] Equally, these buildings may have been connected with the promotion of the town to the status of a civitas capital.

Many small towns probably played a part in the machinery of local government. It has been argued on a small amount of evidence from Britain and a greater quantity from Gaul, that most *civitates* were divided into constituent *pagi*, or rural areas, and that small towns acted as *pagus* centres.[66] This seems to have been the case among the Cantiaci and Durotriges, with secondary centres at Rochester and Ilchester respectively. It has also been suggested that several of these *pagus* centres were later promoted to the rank of civitas capitals in their own right; examples for which a case has been made on epigraphic grounds in Britain include Carlisle,[67] Ilchester[68] and Water Newton.[69]

Various local government officials were connected with both *pagi* and the *vici* which acted as their administrative centres. Again the evidence from southern Britain is scanty, and consequently reference must be made to the similarly organized settlements outside the northern forts. One class of administrator, the *magister*, is attested from the *vicus* outside the fort at Old Carlisle, on an altar dedicated by the *vikanorum magistri*.[70] Other communities of *vici* acting as corporate bodies are attested by inscriptions from Housesteads,[71] Chesterholm[72] and even as far north as Carriden[73] on the Antonine Wall. The famous inscription from Brough-on-Humber (*vicus Petuariensis*), attesting the presence of a theatre, shows that some *vici* possessed magistrates with the title of *aedile*, although we may be dealing here with a site which was also a civitas capital.[74] Several inscriptions from Gallia Belgica record officials with the title *curator*, such as the joint *curatores* attested at Bitburg (*Vicus Beda*) in the *civitas Treverorum*.[75] Alternatively, as at Old Carlisle, the simple title *magister* sufficed, as for example on the inscription dedicated to Mercury by Amilius, *magister vici Bodatii* (Vic-sur-Seille) in the territory of the Mediomatrices.[76] Another inscription from the same *civitas*, found at the capital of Metz, refers to *..nius Numidius magister pagi Io..* and demonstrates that *pagi* could also have their own officials.[77] There is at least one instance of an *aedile* of a *pagus*,[78] although we might suspect that the *praefectus pagi* of the Gallic Epotes lies outside the normal run of local government officials,[79] though it must be remembered that magistrates could appoint prefects to act for them in their absence. Whatever they were called, the duties of all these officials must have been much the same, acting as leaders of their communities, settling minor infractions and disputes, approving corporate actions of the inhabitants, especially in religious dedications, and acting generally as an essential link between government and people. It is, though, not entirely clear to what extent they were liable for tax collection and assessment. Ultimately, in most matters, they were probably subordinate to the authorities of the *civitas* in which they dwelt.

Not all small towns possessed governmental or administrative functions and even those which did more often than not combined them with others. Indeed, sites which were generally successful often attracted organs of government to them, as was the case with the cities and major towns, but in these and other instances it is always difficult to distinguish the primary function once it has been overlaid or mixed with others. Two other specialized functions, those of religion and industry, stand out from the mass and not surprisingly numerous settlements throughout the empire can be shown to have developed around important sanctuaries or centres of manufacturing and extraction.

One of the remarkable features of Gaul was the sometimes huge religious sites which developed often in out-of-the-way places. The example at Ribemont-sur-Ancre near Amiens[80] extended over 800 m (2600 ft) and contained, apart from the temple at the centre, a theatre, bath-house and numerous ancillary buildings. Others are known at Champlieu,[81] at the source of the River Seine,[82] and at Sanxay near Vienne,[83] while still others combined sanctuaries with *pagus* centres. In Britain, two major religious sites were connected with the spas at Bath and Buxton. Much is known about Bath,[84] where the hot springs were almost certainly venerated in the pre-Roman Iron Age. They attracted increased attention soon after the Roman conquest, so much so that by the end of the first century the great sanctuary and classical temple dedicated to Sulis Minerva, together with the bathing establishment, had been fully developed. The springs' curative properties were well enough known to attract visitors from other provinces[85] as well as several soldiers;[86] the latter raise the possibility that Bath was an official convalescent centre for the army as with some spas in Germany. Thanks to the fame of its springs, Bath became a prosperous community, providing services for visiting pilgrims and developing its own industries, one of which involved the production of pewter vessels.[87] As a successful town, it is not unlikely that it also became a *pagus* centre for part of the Dobunni and additionally the residence of the *regionarius* mentioned above (p. 34). It may also have acted as a service centre for the nearby imperial estate centred on Combe Down and for the numerous rich villas which grew up in the vicinity.[88] By contrast, very little is known about Buxton; but for its name, which includes the element *Aquae*, as with Bath, there would be little

to indicate the existence of a major Roman site.[89] Its name also implies that the mineral springs, which have continued in use until now, were once presided over by a patron deity called Arnemetia, goddess of the sacred grove. Somewhere, there must be the remains, of not only a Roman bathing establishment, but also a temple and sanctuary dedicated to this goddess.

Not all religious sites were so openly associated with water, however, despite its popularity in Celtic theology,[90] but caution is necessary when trying to identify religion as the primary function for a settlement's foundation and continued existence, as so many small towns possessed at least one temple. It is probably correct, nevertheless, to accept a dominant religious function for those sites where there is either a multiplicity of temples or a religious precinct with associated facilities. Such a site is Springhead between Rochester and London, where at least seven religious structures existed within a common *temenos*.[91] This group must have exerted a considerable attraction, enough to account for the growth of a small community containing shops, a bakery and blacksmiths. Another exists at Frilford, with a walled precinct containing at least one temple and now supplemented by the recently-discovered amphitheatre.[92] Similar types of settlement have also been identified at Harlow[93] and Wycomb[94] among others.

Some of these sanctuaries appear to lie on the boundaries between *civitates*, an indicator that they almost certainly date back to the Iron Age and marked tribal limits. Such is the case with Ribemont-sur-Ancre mentioned above, situated probably at the junction of three boundaries between the Ambiani, Viromandui and Gaulish Atrebates. In Britain, Frilford and Woodeaton may mark the boundary between the Catuvellauni and Dobunni, Harlow between the Trinovantes and Catuvellauni, and Brigstock between the Corieltavi and Catuvellauni. Since many of these religious sites supported markets and periodic fairs, it is not surprising that substantial settlements developed round them, often with Iron-Age antecedents. In the circumstances, it is therefore often difficult to be sure of the first arrival. Were the sites ancient inter-tribal meeting places, later sanctified by a religious presence, or did an existing sanctuary attract trades because of the volume of people attending? We shall probably never know; it is the classic chicken and egg situation!

The last class of small town to be considered in this chapter covers those which developed primarily around either extractive or manufacturing industries. Since the evidence for their existence is often of a less-perishable nature, it is easier to identify several in Britain. Elsewhere, settlements like the Magdalensburg and Feldkirchen in Noricum, which depended for their prosperity on the famous Norican iron, are good examples.[95] In Britain, several small towns grew up close to mining areas, though very little is known about them. The clearest example is Charterhouse which relied on the exploitation of lead and silver from the Mendips;[96] mining occurred over an extensive area, largely to the south-east of the town, which apparently possessed a complex street system and a small amphitheatre. A similar settlement seems likely at Weston-under-Penyard, where the widespread mass of slag and many furnaces has long pointed to the exploitation of iron from the Forest of Dean.[97] In these examples locations close to the sources of ore were of fundamental importance to their development, though distance did not always prevent sites further afield from profiting, as exemplified by pewter manufacture at Camerton and at Lansdown, near Bath, both within easy reach of the Mendips.[98] Mining settlements must also have existed at Dolaucothi[99] and in the vicinity of Pentre in Flintshire,[100] in association with the known reserves of gold and lead respectively, while a site at Carsington has recently been tentatively identified as *Lutudarum*, the headquarters of a mining company of that name, which operated the lead mines of the Peak District.[101]

The extraction of salt was also important to the economy, and at least two places in Britain bear the name *Salinae*. One can be confidently applied to Middlewich in Cheshire, where early exploitation of the inland brine springs is attested by the excavation of several brine pits and quantities of briquetage.[102] The other was placed by Ptolemy near the Wash in the territory of the Catuvellauni.[103] Certainly there is abundant evidence for the extraction of salt from sea water around the Wash, but so far no settlement has been found to match the name; on the distance from London alone, it ought to lie in the Sleaford or Heck-ington area. It is usually considered, though, that Ptolemy made a mistake with his co-ordinates, since the distance from London to his second *Salinae* also coincides conveniently with the distance to Droitwich, where inland salt production had been well established since prehistoric times. Although caution is necessary with this identification (p. 211), recent excavations have certainly demonstrated an expansion of the industry in the early Roman period, apparently focused on either side of the River Salwarpe.[104]

Most of these settlements were dependent upon the development of their respective extractive and processing activities. There are, however, several sites which apparently came to depend upon a range of processing and manufacturing activities, over and above the normal level of economic provision. A good example is Wilderspool, where excavation has revealed considerable metal-working activities, particularly in the second century, as well as the manufacture of glass, tile and pottery, including *mortaria*.[105] Much the same pattern emerges at Middlewich, where early salt production has already been mentioned; this was soon joined by iron-working and pottery production, as well as a range of service trades.[106] Their concentration with other sites in the west Midlands and Cheshire plain, has been mentioned above (p. 12), together with the probable importance of the early stimulus provided by the army.

Finally, the large-scale manufacture of ceramics, principally pottery and to a lesser extent brick and tile, was an important industry at several small towns. This was, of course, an extractive process partly dependent on the availability of suitable clay, together with supplies of wood for fuel and water; but there is no consistent link between towns and the known production centres, and many kiln sites are unrelated to settlements of any size, such as those at Farnham (Hants), the New Forest, Upchurch (Kent) and the extensive if dispersed area of kilns in the upper Nene valley between Duston and Irchester.[107] An exceptional case seems to be Brampton in Norfolk, where fieldwork and limited excavation have identified over 140 kilns in a well-defined and compact industrial quarter west of the defended area.[108] Usually, however, the production area is more widely scattered and the exact relationship with a given small town is harder to define. The best example is Water Newton, set beside the River Nene, in an area which until recently supplied numerous brickworks. Here, the largest of the towns considered in this volume grew at the centre of an extensive pottery industry which came to supply widespread military and civilian markets.[109] The town, known to have had the status of a *vicus*, is surrounded on all sides by numerous kiln sites and workshops which are everywhere interspersed with agricultural features and a number of substantial extra-mural houses or villas. In this case, at least, a close link can be discerned between the development of the pottery industry and the increasing size and prosperity of the town. Certainly the industry must have encouraged the growth of local villas and houses exploiting the potential of their agricultural resources to the full, while the town in its turn would have provided a workforce and essential access to the necessary marketing facilities. Even so, pottery production was only one of the factors at work. Elsewhere, the relationships are more difficult to define, usually because too little is known about the individual sites; examples include the extensive industries of Brockley Hill[110] and Mancetter-Hartshill,[111] while Dor-chester-on-Thames also lay on the fringes of the kiln area producing Oxford wares.[112]

One factor in the siting of many of these pottery industries and their associated centres was the ease of access to good transport systems, notably by water.[113] Water Newton was ideally placed on the River Nene running to the Wash, while Brampton enjoyed access to the coast along the River Bure. Mancetter was even better placed, being close to the head waters of three of the main river systems of Britain – the Avon and Severn, the Trent and Humber, and the Wash; the distribution of *mortaria* produced here reflects this geographical pattern.

It can be seen, therefore, that there were a number of small towns and settlements in Britain which clearly owed their origin and continued prosperity to certain specialized functions, while others acquired these functions with time, often as a result of direct imposition in accordance with central government policy. It should be stressed again, however, that although a specialized function might well exist, many small towns ultimately came to possess a range of functions, not least those which were most conveniently placed to exploit their full urban potential.

FIVE
ECONOMIC FUNCTIONS

Of all the functions which can be attributed to ancient urban settlements, the most universal was an economic one. No matter what the origin of a site was, at some stage during its development – and probably sooner rather than later – it will have acquired an economic role. It is not difficult to see why. People in even the simplest forms of developed economy required goods and services which they could not provide for themselves. When the same people were massed together, for whatever reason, they represented a lucrative market capable of attracting the providers of these goods and services. In time, this economic function may have grown strong enough to draw yet more people to it, so that it came to overshadow the original cause for the settlement's foundation.

Much has been written about the economy of the Roman Empire and its provinces, and the subject is something of a minefield for the unwary.[1] Summarized briefly, current opinions see the Roman economy as pre-eminently agricultural, occurring against a background of rising population, a growing proportion of which was not engaged in agricultural pursuits. Productivity also rose for a number of reasons of which taxation was probably the most important, although factors like technological improvements, peaceful conditions, access to wider markets and slavery must all have played a part. It has also been claimed that towns were centres of consumption rather than production and that even local trade was insignificant in volume because of poor transport facilities, while long-distance trade was with few exceptions restricted to luxuries because there was no mass-market. These views may well apply to the centre of the empire but require modification for the north-west provinces.

Good transport is vital to any trading activity. In the Roman world it was probably responsible for any expansions which occurred in trade and equally for any constraints that existed. Carriage by road was expensive but by water it was comparatively cheap. In this respect, the north-western provinces possessed a distinct advantage over the Mediterranean regions; here there was an abundance of navigable rivers, while Britain in particular had easy access to coastal transport. There is a good deal of evidence from these provinces to show that inland waterways were major thoroughfares; it ranges from the idiosyncratic distribution of pottery and other hardware to discoveries of the boats used, including the great flat-bottomed lighters which plied the Rhine and its tributaries. Using this evidence it can be shown that, in these regions, large quantities of certain products travelled considerable distances, and with some materials it is more than possible to detect the growth of a sizeable mass-market, despite the model of the Roman economy sketched above.

Roads, nevertheless, still played an important part and would have been used by all and sundry, even if they were originally built for military and political reasons. Indeed, some main roads represent corridors of distribution; objects like pottery are found along them and for a distance on either side, but the number of object-discoveries diminishes rapidly beyond a certain distance from the road. Yet so much has been written about the wonders of the Roman road system that probably not enough allowance is made for their often poor condition. Winter frosts would have annually disrupted the surfaces, as happened to the coach roads of the eighteenth and early nineteenth centuries before the invention of Mr Macadam; the end result would have been a series of monumental ruts and pot-holes. Repairs would have been difficult, if not pointless, in the depths of winter, so that almost a close season for carts and wagons might have been observed, with pedestrians and pack-animals being the only travellers.

Most small towns of any significance lay on the principal roads; some also enjoyed the advantages provided by a nearby river. Many were, therefore, in positions to take economic advantage of the transport system, which connected them not only with each other but also with major centres. The benefits of this system can be demonstrated by the example of the trader who carted a crate of whetstones from Craven Arms, or possibly from Stony Stratford, to Wroxeter for a market day, where he found himself in the company of other merchants selling *mortaria* as well as samian ware from Gaul.[2] It seems unlikely that they were the only merchants travelling considerable distances around Britain selling hardware; nor is it likely that they were unaccompanied by other traders in cloth, leather, wood, fruit and vegetables or other miscellaneous products.

Small towns, therefore, occupied a defined economic niche, even if it is but imperfectly understood. At one level, they would have supplied a range of services and facilities for a resident agricultural population and for travellers on the roads and rivers; at another, they would have provided periodic or permanent markets for the surrounding countryside in exchange for agricultural products. In most cases the development of these functions would have gone hand in hand with the growth of the settlement and would have been directly related to the increasing dependence of the surrounding hinterland on the goods and services which it could provide. The better and more diverse they were, then the greater the area of influence which could be 'captured', and correspondingly the more important a site in the economic and urban hierarchy.

Additionally it has been recognized that the largest concentrations of first-class villas often clustered around the small towns in preference to major towns or cities.[3] Thus in Kent, there are far more villas concentrated around Rochester than Canterbury, while elsewhere it is true of Bath, Ilchester and Water Newton, at the expense of Cirencester, Dorchester and Leicester respecti-

vely. Exceptions among the major towns are Chichester, Verulamium and Winchester. These distributions are difficult to explain, although they emphasize the importance of some small towns and imply an economic basis for the association. Villas were profit-making concerns which needed to dispose of their produce to remain viable; towns provided convenient markets, but why some small towns should have seemingly provided better markets than their larger counterparts remains unclear. The association could be related to the question of land-ownership and the availability of labour, and may have nothing whatever to do with markets.

The extent of these economic activities must have been constrained by the modes of transport available. For foot traffic, a distance of some 10–12 km (6–7 miles) would probably have been a more-than-adequate day's journey, especially if burdened with goods and needing to leave enough time for their disposal at the destination. Pack animals, with the driver also mounted, could probably have doubled the distance, as indeed could have most carts and wagons. A light chaise or unburdened pony could have extended this perhaps to 30 km (19 miles), but any distances above those quoted would have required an overnight stop and consequently an increase in the prices of the goods. While this might have proved acceptable for itinerant traders, to most local people it would have been unattractive and most would have preferred to be home by nightfall or soon after. It seems likely, therefore, that transport must always have been a limiting factor on trade. How often, for instance, did a normal inhabitant of Thorpe travel to Lincoln, his nearest major town, but some 30 km (19 miles) away? It is worth remembering that there are still people in Britain today who have never been to London.

Despite traffic and trade, all small towns maintained strong agricultural connections, because their inhabitants had to be fed, clothed and shod. Unfortunately, detailed evidence for the nature of these connections is limited, so it remains impossible to estimate how many of the inhabitants were involved in farming as opposed to other occupations. It is difficult to identify farms inside these settlements, while related field systems have been suggested at only a handful of sites, including the presumed Romano-British fields at Braintree[4] and the sequence of enclosures at Brampton.[5] Elsewhere, it is likely that the original boundaries between the fields will only be recognized through extensive survey and excavation.

Within many sites, however, there are ranges of buildings which often occupy enclosed strips of land not unlike medieval crofts, suggesting that some people, craftsmen included, were raising their own produce or keeping their own pigs and fowl. At Great Dunmow, for instance, it has been suggested that such strips were up to *c.* 100 m (327 ft) deep,[6] while the Fosse Way south-west of Ilchester was lined by two successive rows of enclosures some 50 by 20 m (165 by 66 ft) in size.[7] There is also evidence from Godmanchester to indicate an associated range of agricultural features, including two-post hay racks, hearths, corn-drying floors, threshing floors and a large number of wicker granaries.[8] Although we know very little about the tenurial and ownership patterns of these sites, it is likely that some of the inhabitants actually owned land outside the settlement and grew their own crops. It has also been suggested that they and other less-fortunately-placed inhabitants provided a reservoir of day-labourers for nearby landowners to help on the land at harvest time or on other labour-intensive occasions.

It is probably true to say, therefore, that most small towns, when taken with their immediate surroundings, were to some degree self-sufficient in basic agricultural produce. This would have included grain and a moderate supply of meat, from either stock or game. Limited supplies of fruit and vegetables must have been available, while an abundance of natural fruits and nuts could have been gathered in season, for either home consumption or for sale in the local market. Local resources were probably exploited to satisfy the demand for wool, leather and wood, while spinning, weaving, fulling and possibly dyeing were all essentially part of the normal domestic scene. It remains difficult, however, to measure this level of self-sufficiency on purely archaeological grounds. Some sites were clearly more dependent than others upon their own agricultural production, which encourages the belief that many small towns at the bottom end of the urban scale did not develop much in size or functional complexity beyond their large-village

counterparts. Higher up the scale, however, a greater reliance on produce from nearby rural estates might be expected, traded in exchange for a range of urban goods and services; however, it is precisely this aspect of economic co-operation which is difficult to establish on current evidence.

Beyond the agricultural connection, the main economic strength of a community resided in the number and variety of craftsmen which it could support. It is unfortunate, therefore, that the range of economic services carried out at individual small towns is never easy to define. In contrast to Gaul and Germany, where there are numerous inscriptions referring to craftsmen, as well as several sculptured reliefs,[9] hardly any relevant inscriptions, let alone sculptures, occur in Britain, and even they are usually divorced from the physical structures and workplaces. We must therefore depend almost exclusively on the archaeological record, even though the survival of crucial evidence for the range of shops and their resident craftsmen is frequently highly selective and difficult to interpret in the context of market-places and external economic contacts.

Archaeology has, however, revealed a growing number of very characteristic narrow rectangular structures stretching back from the available street frontages and often forming blocks or rows. These strip buildings are a common feature of urban sites throughout the empire and are usually identified as the shops and workshops of resident traders and craftsmen.[10] They are normally found to be divided into two very unequal parts. The larger part at the front often opens directly onto the street, but may have been protected by some form of veranda. The smaller portion to the rear is sometimes subdivided. The usual interpretation sees the front section as the shop or workshop and the rear as the accommodation for the shopkeeper. When the rear subdivision is absent, it is usually assumed, on very little evidence, that an upper storey acted as the domestic residence or, alternatively, as storage space.

A classic example was excavated at Catterick.[11] The front of the shop was open to the street, but large blocks of stone set at intervals across the threshold carried rebates for timber uprights, presumably to support the gable or perhaps an upper storey. A narrow slot ran in front of the rebates, which was clearly intended to take a series of wooden shutters to close the whole opening. The floors in the front, and larger, part of the premises were a confused mass of earthen layers, intermixed with ash and other deposits. Exactly what activity was being carried on remains uncertain, but it seems to have had commercial implications. At the rear of the shop were two rooms, set alongside a narrow passage leading to a back door. One room was heated by a hypocaust, fired from the shop; the other had a decent pink concrete floor, quarter-round moulding and plastered and painted walls. Clearly the shopkeeper lived in reasonably comfortable, if cramped quarters.

Comparable strip buildings are found in varying numbers in almost all small towns and they are, therefore, a useful indicator of a town's relative economic importance. Of course not all such structures can be certainly associated with commercial activities, which has led to the suggestion that many will have served as the homes of men working on the land.[12] Such caution has to be offset, however, by the rapidly growing body of evidence in favour of a commercial role, despite the fact that many important manufacturing and trading activities seldom left debris which survives except in the most favourable circumstances; the absence of recognizable evidence within individual buildings cannot be regarded, therefore, as proof of a non-specialist role. Moreover a shop would normally be emptied of its goods before abandonment, so that only a sudden catastrophe, like a fire, would catch it fully stocked. The relative importance of strip buildings in the urban plan has already been discussed (p. 27), and here it will suffice to mention only a few general examples.

At Corbridge, for instance, shops associated with various furnaces and ovens lined the main north-south and east-west roads from the early third century onwards.[13] An even more natural centre for economic growth was the junction of Ermine Street and Stane Street at Braughing, where, from the second century onwards, there were several possible strip buildings associated with bone-, iron- and copper-working.[14] Even more specialized in character would seem to be sites like Middlewich, where a number of strip buildings have already been noted in connection with iron- and copper-working, cobbling, weaving, glass and salt production (p. 41). This

evidence is echoed at a whole range of other small towns, and it is probably safe to suggest a similar interpretation for those sites where strip buildings are well attested but where either excavation or detailed evidence for trading activities is limited, as for example at Water Newton.[15]

Detailed evidence for the full range of craftsmen at individual small towns is inevitably lacking, but it is possible to assemble a general picture by using material from a wide variety of sources. Evidence is most abundant for specialists involved in ceramics and metal-working, because it survives better in the archaeological record. Individual workshops are relatively common, being identified by furnaces or industrial waste. Two examples can suffice. One is the second-century establishment at Godmanchester, manufacturing both iron and copper goods in a timber-framed workshop with an open front which contained four shaft furnaces and a bowl-shaped smithing furnace.[16] The other, at Ashton, is the second-century strip building with a wide entrance, which has been identified as a blacksmith's shop and contained five identifiable furnaces, a stone-lined quenching tank and numerous tools and completed metal objects.[17] Blacksmithing must have been a common occupation with one, or probably more, smith in each town and settlement, though it has to be remembered that some of the larger country estates, such as Chedworth, were virtually self-sufficient with their own resident smiths. Among the sites where characteristic evidence for iron extraction or smithing has been located might be included those at Ancaster, Braintree, Camerton, Holditch, Sapperton and Wilderspool.[18] The importance of the blacksmith is further attested by three ironwork hoards at Dorchester-on-Thames,[19] Great Chesterford[20] and Sandy.[21]

Copper-working was probably equally common, in view of the frequency of objects made from copper alloys. A practising coppersmith, who was also engaged in manufacturing fine champlevé enamel work, is certainly known from Catterick, where the bottom of a wooden waste tub was found intact, full of small filings and chippings and some tiny fragments of coloured enamels.[22] Several fine enamelled objects were found scattered on the floor, either representing part of his stock or else intended for scrap. Of particular interest was a pear-shaped enamelled perfume flask, since the nearest similar vessel has been found at Nijmegen, indicating some form of trade connection between Catterick and the Netherlands. Elsewhere, copper-working has been identified at several sites which include Brampton, Droitwich, Harlow, Neatham, Springhead and Wilderspool.[23] Additional insights into production are provided by the blanks for making brooches at Baldock,[24] while the counterfeiters' Severan coin-moulds at Ancaster[25] and the fourth-century examples at Duston[26] represent a less legal activity.

Other metal-workers are far less well represented in the small towns. Of particular interest is the goldsmith's establishment recorded in an inscription from Norton near Malton.[27] It was managed by a slave, who represents one of the classes of society present in the small towns. Archaeology can also demonstrate an interest in lead and its derivative alloy, pewter, from the evidence of workshops or stone moulds, as for example at Camerton,[28] Nettleton Shrub[29] and Towcester.[30]

Beyond the metal-workers, the only other regularly-attested craftsmen are the residential or semi-residential potters, working a single kiln and producing a range of wares largely for local consumption. It is important to remember, though, that the production need not have been a full-time or permanent occupation, nor necessarily an urban-based activity, as the much wider pattern of small- and large-scale production demonstrates. Several individual kilns are known in the small towns, sometimes in association with buildings. One example is the third-century kiln at Godmanchester, which can be related to a building in Pinfold Lane,[31] while a clay-floored structure at Hacheston was interestingly associated with both a third-century kiln producing grey wares and an iron-smithing furnace.[32] Elsewhere, kilns have been recorded at several sites, including Coddenham, Great Casterton, Ilchester, Sapperton and Springhead.[33] Larger-scale pottery production is considered elsewhere (p. 41).

Although the evidence for other craftsmen and traders is not nearly as well represented, being dependent in part upon the degree of archaeological survival, it can nevertheless reveal a surprisingly extensive range. Particular interest inevitably attaches to the limited number of inscriptions, including two from Bath, which mention Priscus, a *lapidarius* or stone-mason, and a *sculptor* Sulinus, who probably also worked at Cirencester.[34] Priscus was a native of the region around Chartres in Gaul and both may have been employed in the construction of the great bath and temple complex. Besides them epigraphy records a number of oculists' stamps from Bath,[35] Kenchester (two examples)[36] and Sandy,[37] each bearing the name of the individual concerned alongside his patent remedies for treating opthalmic disorders. They are likely to reflect an itinerant rather than a permanent presence.

Bath also had a resident gem-cutter, whose collection of 34 unmounted intaglios somehow ended up in the main drain carrying the overflow from the reservoir housing the hot spring.[38] Such craftsmen were considered more than mere artisans, and their products, especially set in seal rings, were highly esteemed. His presence at Bath indicates the town's prosperity and perhaps reflects the concentration of rich villas surrounding it. But he was by no means alone in Britain, for a combined silversmith and jeweller's stock is known at the extensive settlement of Snettisham in Norfolk.[39] This contained not only 110 unmounted intaglios, but also 17 more set in silver rings which formed part of a collection of 89 such rings; all of them, together with other items of silver jewellery, bars of silver, scraps of gold and two implements, were enclosed and hidden in a small pot.

Several sites provide evidence for leatherworking, though it is represented by only one identified tannery at Alcester,[40] which probably used the hides of cattle that grazed the water meadows of the River Avon. More usually, leather fragments and offcuts are the main indicators, as for example at Bath, Brampton, Carlisle, Middlewich and Water Newton.[41] The importance of shoe leather in some suggests a particular trade, confirmed by the cobbler's last from Sandy.[42] These activities were presumably far more common than the evidence so far suggests, given the widespread use of leather. It is likely that most small towns contained a tannery since the processes and equipment needed for the production of leather were not entirely suitable for domestic use, apart from the exceedingly unpleasant smell generated.

The corresponding evidence for textile manufacture and treatment on a commercial basis is everywhere lacking in Britain, except for the possible cloth-finisher's or dyer's shop at Chelmsford,[43] which contained several hearths and a large tile structure identified as a vat. But wool was available to all classes of society, and there are numerous references in classical art and literature to its collection from thickets and hedges where sheep grazed. Consequently a great deal of fulling, spinning, weaving and dyeing was carried out at domestic level, with plants probably being deliberately cultivated to provide dyes. Working in bone was also important; the debris normally survives and workshops have been recorded at Braughing, Catterick, Great Chesterford, Neatham and Springhead.[44]

Beyond the timber, brick and stone structures themselves and their tiled or slated roofs, there is virtually no direct evidence to confirm the presence of carpenters, masons, bricklayers, slaters, tilers and thatchers, and it is difficult to guess to what degree the local construction industry was a specialist concern. Tile-kilns have been located at Tiddington[45] and at Kelvedon,[46] south of the town, but as with pottery production they need not be urban-based and may also be seasonal. They probably served wider markets than the associated town, to judge from the tileries centred on Minety.[47] In contrast, the lime-kilns at Brampton[48] and Droitwich[49] were perhaps concerned with the construction of the defences. These two examples can hardly represent the total number which originally existed, although lime may have been produced in small, temporary clamps which have not survived later destruction. Production centres for window glass and glass vessels are, at present, few and far between, beyond the large glasshouse in the civitas capital at Caistor-by-Norwich.[50] Fairly extensive production can be envisaged at Wilderspool, where the good-quality local sand provided an essential ingredient.[51] Elsewhere among small towns, the evidence is restricted to Bath, Ilchester and Mancetter.[52] At the first, a building a short distance outside the town contained a furnace used for reworking coloured cullet. Evidence for more exotic trades is also rather limited, except for the suggested school of mosaicists and sculptors at Water Newton[53] and Carlisle[54] respectively; it is not surprising, therefore, that mosaics are generally rare in small towns, even though they often occur in nearby villas.

Evidence for traders associated with the food market and with the provision of accommodation for travellers is even more restricted. In the ancient world, the jobs of miller and baker were normally combined, but since much milling and baking was a domestic operation the presence of a professional must indicate the prosperity of the settlement. The evidence for grain-milling in small towns is limited but includes the third-century building with two millstones in the Kate's Cabin suburb at Water Newton,[55] the three millstones in the yard of building 16 at Springhead[56] and the very large millstone at Wanborough,[57] which implies the use of water or other mechanical power. Water-mills have been identified elsewhere,[58] notably on Hadrian's Wall and at Ickham in Kent,[59] where it probably lay on an estate near Canterbury. Bakeries have also been postulated at a handful of sites, including Holditch[60] and Springhead,[61] as well as the two second-century establishments at Chelmsford.[62] These examples at least seem clear; more often, buildings contain ovens or hearths which suggest bread-making but no other characteristic debris has been recognized. An example is one of the strip buildings at Sea Mills, which contained a number of ovens in the front room.[63] Alternatively it might have been a shop purveying cooked food, or it could have provided eating facilities for travellers along the road. An open-fronted building at Holditch, containing cooking vessels, a large quern and an oven might have provided a similar service,[64] while the evidence for a counter in the *vicus* at Greta Bridge points to another obvious gap in the evidence.[65]

Although the quantity and quality of all this information seems impressive at first glance, it is inevitably uneven in its coverage of different trades. This makes it difficult to define the precise level of services available in individual cases, but it does not prevent an attempt at drawing some general conclusions about the economic role of small towns. It has to be stressed at the outset that all sites provided some level of economic servicing, which will have originated in several ways. In some cases a pre-existing centre, which already possessed an economic role, will have been incorporated into the new system and perhaps attracted other functions as well. In others, the economic function will have followed in the wake of a variety of other causes, as when sites were founded as *vici* outside forts or posting stations or as administrative centres in the new local and provincial hierarchy. Once established, however, this function is likely to have assumed an over-riding importance at those towns which were most suitably placed to exploit its potential.

The evidence demonstrates that most small towns and even some villages provided a range of specialist goods and services. The range can be seen to be surprisingly restricted, however, with the emphasis on basic services (especially metal-working) at most sites; more specialized activities are less well represented. Almost all sites probably had one or more resident blacksmith and coppersmith, both repairing old items and manu-facturing new ones, whereas plumbers, pewterers and tinsmiths seem to have been rarer; only one goldsmith is known, while no silversmiths are attested. Less certain is the importance of car-penters, joiners, wheelwrights and coopers, even if all these occupations were distinct. Carpenters' tools turn up on several sites, together with a variety of nails, no doubt made by the local blacksmiths. More than enough work for at least one such practitioner must have existed in most towns, as there would have been for slaters, tilers and masons in those areas where building stone was in regular use. It is perhaps a mistake, though, to try to identify too many categories of independent craftsmen, even though the sources can attest a surprising level of specialization; in a small community, a jobbing builder could be his own mason, bricklayer, carpenter, tiler, thatcher, and slater, possibly even burning his own lime and making his own bricks. Other specialists might be expected, among them bone-workers, tanners, bakers and millers, and perhaps other food retailers, as well as a local potter and more rarely a glass-blower, where the necessary raw materials were available. Caution is necessary, however, because not all of these activities were certainly going on all the time. A single kiln, for instance, probably implies a potter's presence for only a short period in the life of a settlement; some may even have been itinerant or at best semi-residential, moving on once local demand had been satisfied. For luxury and exotic pro-ducts, such as mosaics, recourse would have to be made, save in exceptional circumstances, to the nearest major centre.

Most of these traders and craftsmen will have contributed directly to the self-sufficiency of the local community, much like the average nine-teenth-century village. Some will also have provided a range of facilities for those officials and private individuals travelling along the highways, which would have been an important element in those small towns which housed a *mansio* or, to a lesser extent, a *mutatio*, though there is surpris-ingly little evidence to demonstrate this. More importantly, many will have increasingly sup-plied goods and services to the nearby villas and rural settlements, as individual small towns came to act as centres for periodic or permanent local fairs or markets. These markets would have attracted a range of itinerant craftsmen and merchants, much like the trader in whetstones already mentioned (p. 44). But even now it is almost impossible to define the relative economic importance of each town from the available archaeological evidence; much of the interpre-tation depends on hypothesis.

Market buildings, in particular, have proved especially elusive in the small towns and there is little to compare with the forum or *macellum* of the cities. Various courtyard buildings have sometimes been interpreted as markets, but certainty of identification remains impossible on current evidence. They include the larger of the two central structures at Water Newton[66] and, more problematical, the unfinished Building XI at Corbridge.[67] Supposed market buildings at Alchester[68] and Braughing[69] have now more plausibly been reinterpreted as temples. In the apparent absence of identifiable buildings, market-places can only be inferred from the presence of large open areas near the centres of towns, which could have served for periodic markets and fairs. Sufficient examples are now known, sometimes in association with religious precincts or else with significant concentrations of third- and fourth-century coins, to suggest that they may have been more widespread. Examples include the area of metalling alongside the north-south road at Dorchester-on-Thames,[70] the open area south of the basilican building at Godmanchester,[71] the area south of the temple at Irchester[72] and the gravel areas flanking the temple at Wycomb, from which 1100 coins were recovered.[73] Not surprisingly the temporary structures erected in these areas have left few archaeological traces. More problemati-cally, open market areas need not be expected at all sites, because temporary stalls or even trestle tables could have been erected in side-streets, as in some modern towns today.

The uneven quality of the evidence also makes it difficult to establish the range of goods being traded and the area of influence of any particular market. One recent line of research has involved the investigation of pottery distributions as a possible indicator of a town's market area, partly because of its abundance and partly because it has been observed that pottery was not normally dispersed through permanent retail outlets. Promising results were certainly obtained from early studies, not least from the analysis of pottery produced in Savernake Forest near Mildenhall.[74] This seemed to indicate that its distribution corresponded to the town's market or service area, with more distant projections down the main roads. Doubts have been expressed, though, on this use of pottery distributions because the evidence can be interpreted in different ways,[75] and so care must be exercised in using these projections as indicators of market areas.

Even more difficult to establish is the relative economic importance of individual small towns in the regional and urban hierarchy; to what extent was a small town or village dependent on its major neighbours, and how much did the larger towns and cities rely on supplies from the former? Much would have depended on the distances involved and on the modes of transport available as already mentioned above (p. 44). The constraints imposed on the market area by travel, therefore, probably account for the limited range of goods and services being provided at many sites, while more specialized facilities and luxury items were only available in the larger population centres where demand was greater.

It remains to mention the evidence for harbours and quays in the small towns, as indicators of a possible role in the distribution of goods. Not surprisingly these features are principally confined to the cities of the province, though we might expect some form of provision at those sites where water transport clearly played a part in moving bulky products like building stone or pottery (p. 43). No certain civilian storehouses are known in the small towns, while quays are confined at present to those of the second century at Heronbridge near Chester,[76] probably for official use, the timber platform at Brampton[77] and the timber piles at Scole,[78] though the published evidence for the last is ambiguous. There is also the possibility of stone quays at Ilchester,[79] while harbour facilities might be predicted with reasonable certainty at Sea Mills, since its restored name should read *Portus Abonae*.[80]

It should be obvious from all that has been said that most small towns played a significant role in the economic life of the province, alongside the cities and major towns. What remains to be defined is the relative importance of these activities at individual sites, not least the degree of dependence upon crafts and the economic relationship between town and country. This is even a problem in better documented periods, and will only be resolved, if at all, by extensive research at the sites.

SIX
POTENTIAL CITIES

Carlisle (fig. 9)

'It is unfortunate that so little is known of Carlisle, *Luguvalium* (*Carvetiorum?*), although it seems to have grown to considerable size and may have exceeded 70 acres (28 ha).' So was written in 1973.[1] Fifteen years later the town of Carlisle is as much of an enigma as it was then, despite the expenditure of some very large sums of money and several large excavations. This is not the fault of the excavators, who have worked wonders with the early Roman military installations, but it simply demonstrates the fickleness of archaeological investigation, with the town continuing to prove elusive.

The town of Carlisle is correctly identified with the *Luguvalium* of the Antonine Itinerary[2] and the *Lagubalium* of the Ravenna Cosmography.[3] Comments on the Roman site have been made almost without a break since the Roman period. In AD 685 St Cuthbert perambulated '*illis murum civitatis*' and also saw a fountain working, implying that there was still a functioning aqueduct;[4] whether he was looking at the walls of a genuine town or of a fort is arguable. It has always been considered that he viewed the walls of the town, even though they have still to be located with absolute certainty. Later Bede,[5] William of Malmesbury,[6] Leland[7] and Camden[8] all either recorded or made comments on Roman remains at Carlisle. Excavations have been taking place almost continuously in Carlisle since the early 1950s, and a number of useful summaries have been published, beginning with Shaw's in 1923.[9]

The site lies on a low hill of red sandstone, which rises gently from the valley of the River Eden to the south but which terminates in two summits at present occupied by the cathedral and the castle. To north and west of the hill are steep slopes to the Rivers Eden and Calder respectively; on the east lies the River Petterill, while some kilometres further north the Solway forms the natural boundary to the Scottish lowlands. It is, therefore, a site of some strategic significance in any military context, a fact which has been recognized continuously since Roman times, when, at least under Agricola if not before, a fort was established here.

The most recent sequence of excavations has established that there was limited pre-Roman occupation of the site,[10] in the form of a round house, which may have been associated with areas of ploughed fields,[11] found below Roman levels in Annetwell Street, even though they had apparently reverted to pasture immediately before the arrival of the Romans. The date of their arrival is still disputed, although a temporary pre-Agricolan presence at least seems certain. Be that as it may, the first permanent construction was a fort of Agricolan date, whose south gate was situated just south of Annetwell Street, implying that the larger part of the fort lay towards the area of the castle.[12] Although its size is not yet known, suggestions have been made that it was larger than a normal auxiliary fort and may have accommodated either a vexillation, possibly of *Legio IX*, whose tile-works may have been situated some 8 km (5 miles) south of Carlisle at Scalesceugh,[13] (though the stamped tiles from there may belong to a slightly later period), or the *Ala Petriana* before its transfer to Stanwix over the river. The fort underwent several alterations before it seems to have been systematically demolished early in the second century.[14]

Excavations south of the fort have shown the existence of contemporary timber buildings as far south as Blackfriars Street. One, in the grounds of Tullie House Museum just outside the fort gate, was 12.2 m (40 ft) by at least 67 m (219 ft), with a

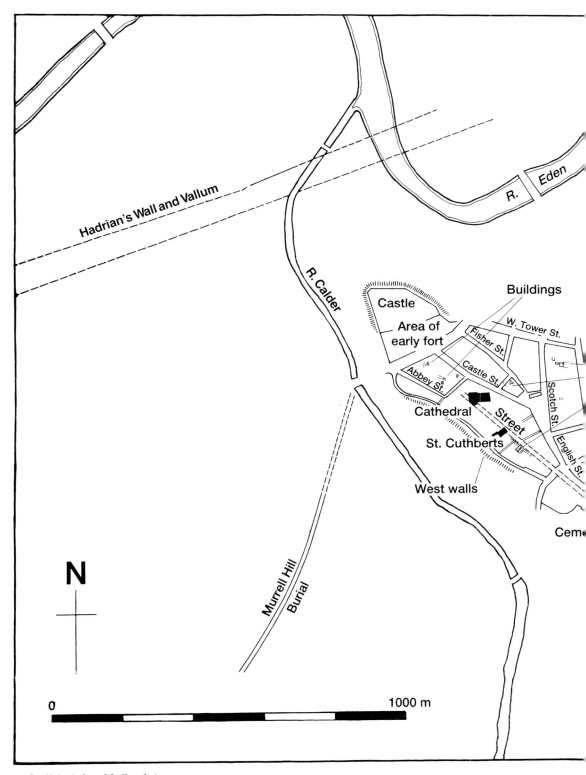

9 Carlisle (*after McCarthy*)

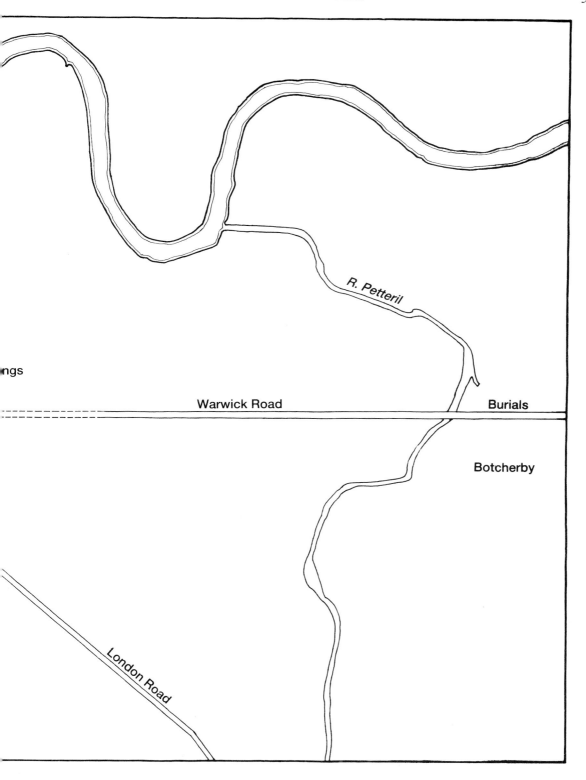

ngs

R. Petteril

Warwick Road   Burials

Botcherby

London Road

substantial plank floor over a solid foundation, and may have had a military function; attempts have also been made to interpret it as the base for a rampart surrounding an annexe to the fort. Two more structures fronting the main road, whose line is roughly perpetuated by Blackfriars Street leading south from the fort, were separated by side-streets and were planned more like domestic dwellings than military structures. It would seem, therefore, that a *vicus* grew in connection with the Agricolan fort; a writing tablet from Vindolanda records the presence of a *centurio regionarius*, who may have been connected with its administration.[15]

So much is certain. What is not clear, even now, is whether another fort was established in the vicinity before the construction of nearby Stanwix on Hadrian's Wall or whether the Carlisle position was left unguarded for a time. Higham and Jones[16] have argued, on the sole evidence of internal timber buildings, that another fort was constructed after a short interval early in the second century, and that it survived until it was demolished in the late second century; no contemporary fortifications for it have yet been recorded.

But the vital question still remains, no matter whether a second-century fort existed or not: at what point did the *vicus* become a genuine town? It would seem unlikely before the Hadrianic period at the earliest, if comparison is made with some other northern sites such as Aldborough; it might be thought to be more likely under Severus or Caracalla, when the whole northern frontier region was extensively reorganized. Much must also depend on the, as yet unknown, date of the constitution of the *civitas Carvetiorum*, for which it has been claimed that Carlisle acted as a capital. This assumption is based on the figure of 53 Roman miles, quoted on the Middleton milestone[17] as having been measured from Carlisle as the *caput viae*, and backed by the name of the *civitas* given on both the Brougham milestone[18] and the tombstone of Flavius Martius from Old Penrith (see below p. 58). The Brougham milestone dates to AD 258–68, so that the *civitas* must have been constituted by then. But the possibility that Kirkby Thore, also a walled town, and some 30 km (19 miles) south of Carlisle, was the capital cannot be entirely ruled out. One of the continuing difficulties about Carlisle is the

elusiveness of the town wall, and consequently the size of the town. In the past it has always been assumed that the wall followed the same line as its medieval successor. But a search in Annetwell Street and West Tower Street failed to find it.[19] Yet the first attempt in 1944 to find the Roman wall of Canterbury, which was also supposed to follow the line of the medieval wall, proved a failure,[20] so not too much should be read into the Carlisle evidence. Indeed reason would infer the existence of a wall, especially if the town became a civitas capital, and even more so if it became the capital of the late-formed province of *Valentia*. It is probably best, therefore, to reject McCarthy's view that the town was never completely enclosed.[21]

If virtually nothing is known of the town defences, only a little more can be said about the streets. The road leading out of the south gate of the Agricolan fort was adopted as the principal north-south street whose line, as mentioned above, is perpetuated most closely by Blackfriars Street; at one point near its north end there was a suggestion of a flanking portico. Another street at right angles to it was uncovered in Annetwell Street, where it was lined with timber buildings of second-century date, probably belonging to the fort. Other streets or lanes have been found at Tullie House, Castle Street and Keays Lane, but their alignments and positions do not fit a regular, rectangular grid. The main eastern axis of the system may, however, be represented by a major street on the line of Crown and Anchor Lane.

The second-century timber buildings in Annetwell Street mentioned above were replaced by masonry structures, possibly under Severus. Their plans are reminiscent of barrack blocks, with lanes separating them.[22] It has been tentatively suggested that they, together possibly with their timber predecessors, formed part of a military enclave within the civilian town, thus perhaps resembling Corbridge (see p. 60) with its two military arsenals. Other finds from the area which support this conclusion are 38 stamped tiles, representing *Legiones II Augusta*, *XX* and possibly *IX*; others were stamped IMP. Architectural and sculptural fragments, as well as parts of two inscriptions, one of which was a dedication by *Legio XX*, were also found.[23] If such an enclosure existed it would presumably, as at Corbridge, have been fortified by a masonry wall. It is not impossible that, if the enclosure was abandoned in the withdrawal of the Roman army from Britain, civilians might have moved in to take advantage of its protection. Were these the walls supposedly perambulated by St Cuthbert? Another possible official building, constructed of wood and dating to the late first or early second century, was discovered lying within its own ditched enclosure near Keays Lane. It has been tentatively interpreted as a *praetorium*, which could provide a residence for high-ranking officers or accommodation for them when travelling. It had been deliberately dismantled after a short life.[24]

Evidence for buildings that can most probably be associated with the civilian town is slight. Part of a massive structure with walls 2 m (6½ ft) thick was discovered at the junction of Castle and Fisher Streets; it was flanked on the west by a possible road running parallel to the main north-west to south-east axis. Lying as it does near the putative centre of the town, the building may have had some public function.[25] The wooden houses off Blackfriars Street, already referred to (p. 51), were ultimately rebuilt at least twice in masonry, and it is interesting to observe that there was little change in the original property boundaries through to post-Roman times, despite changes in use. Another masonry house, with a hypocaust, has been recorded at Keays Lane. Its life was extended, with alterations, into the third and fourth centuries. As an apparently domestic residence it seems strange that it replaced a timber structure which has been interpreted as a temple,[26] although time elapsed between the latter's destruction and the building of the house; it is unusual to find so deliberate a secularization of a religious site in the Roman world. But it must be admitted that the interpretation of the earlier building as a temple lacks conviction. It more closely resembles a market hall with one or more *tholoi* such as can be seen at *Lepcis Magna*. The stone-built house existed contemporaneously with a remarkably long-lived timber-framed building across a lane to the north, which was not dismantled until towards the end of the fourth century. The famous aqueduct seen working by St Cuthbert remains elusive, but a water tank inside the portico of a building uncovered at Tullie House was presumably fed by it. The most likely source of water was on the higher ground to the south.

Trade and industry are poorly represented in Carlisle, and what evidence there is, such as for copper-working and possibly tanning, may be military rather than civilian in character. Nevertheless, a dedication slab from nearby Bowness indicates that merchants were in the area,[27] and indeed, as a frontier town, Carlisle must have gained much of its wealth not only from the garrison on Hadrian's Wall but also from trade across the border. There is a direct comparison here, not only with neighbouring Corbridge, but also with Wroxeter on the Welsh frontier and with major towns and cities on other frontiers such as *Carnuntum*, where the main trade route from the south Baltic to north Italy crossed the Danube.

Despite the identification so far of only one temple, and that of a dubious nature, something of the religious interests of the inhabitants of Carlisle has survived in the form of inscriptions. A dedication to Cautes indicates the presence somewhere of a Mithraeum.[28] Variations on the theme of Mars also occur, such as Mars Barrex, Mars Belatucadrus and Mars Ocelus,[29] while a dedication probably to Mars Victor was observed by William of Malmesbury still in position on a vaulted building, which was presumably a temple;[30] these dedications are mainly by soldiers. Other deities recorded are the Mother Goddesses, the Fates, Mercury and Hercules,[31] while a small lead statuette of Diana came from the supposed temple site in Keays Lane. Christianity may be represented by a tombstone and a gold ring with an incised palm branch and the legend AMA ME, although this religion has more significance in post-Roman Carlisle. The largest cemetery with both inhumations and cremations extended southwards along the London Road, with more isolated burials at Murrell Hill and Botcherby.[32] The uninscribed tombstone from Murrell Hill is of some interest since it shows in relief a mother dressed in a tunic and seated in an upright chair, while holding an opened fan in her right hand. Beside her stands a child, who nurses a pet bird on her lap.[33] This tombstone probably also marks the line of a main road leading south-west from Carlisle to Old Carlisle and Papcastle and thence to the Cumberland coast. Other tombstones tell us a little about the inhabitants of the town, and include F. Antigonus Papias, a citizen of Greece and possibly a Christian, who

10 Corbridge (*after Salway and Bishop and Dore*)

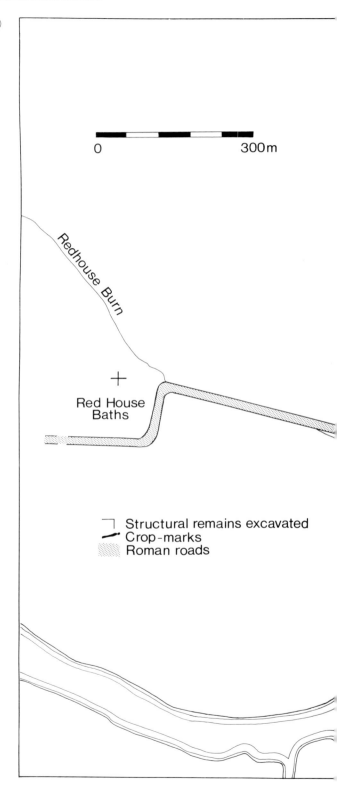

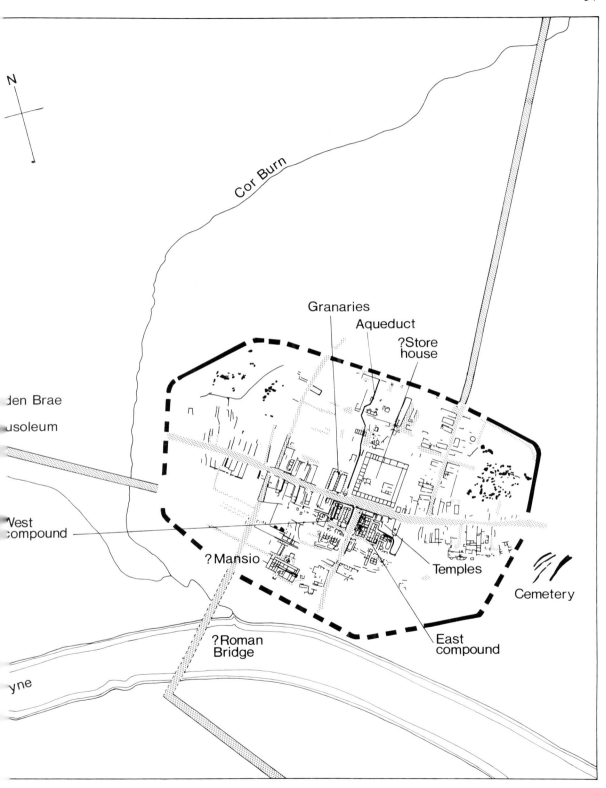

N

Cor Burn

Granaries

Aqueduct

?Store
house

den Brae

usoleum

West
compound

?Mansio

Temples

Cemetery

?Roman
Bridge

East
compound

yne

may also have been a merchant. More importantly, a tombstone from Old Penrith, some
distance south of Carlisle, refers to Flavius
Martius, who is described as a *senator* and
quaestor of the *civitas Carvetiorum*.[34] As a
member and officer of the council of the Carvetii,
he would have been well acquainted with
Carlisle.

The end of Roman Carlisle is inextricably
wedded to the account of St Cuthbert's visit, with
its implication that there was still a fortified urban
community in existence, headed by a *praepositus
civitatis* (an echo from Lincoln?) and with a still-
functioning aqueduct, towards the end of the
seventh century. But excavations have so far
failed to support this image and indeed have
indicated a town in decline. Certainly little
structural evidence has been found to support
this implication, although in the Blackfriars
Street excavations, timber buildings, possibly of
the fifth century, were replacing masonry structures on the same alignments. There came a time,
though, when even these were abandoned
and a large hall-like building was constructed on a
completely different alignment, which even
ignored the Roman street lines. But this evidence
still leaves a large gap to be filled between the
early fifth century and St Cuthbert's visit. Helping to fill it, though, is a recent argument that
Carlisle, as a civitas capital, was also a bishopric,
and one of the few in Britain which survived the
Romano-British to Anglo-Saxon transition;
indeed the *civitas* is seen as the homeland of St
Patrick.[35] In this way the Church, as in many
other parts of the western empire, would have
formed the bridge by which a moderately civi-
lized Romano-British community was maintained and eventually transformed into an English one.

Corbridge (figs. 10 and 11)

Corbridge, like Carlisle, lies just behind Hadrian's Wall on the Stanegate, and as with Carlisle
there is difficulty in disentangling the military
structures from the civilian.

Sometimes referred to as Corchester, the site is
to be identified with the *Corstopitum* of the
Antonine Itinerary,[36] and the *Corielopocarium* of
the Ravenna list.[37] It is generally considered that

the name *Corstopitum* is corrupt and Rivet and
Smith prefer *Coriosopitum*.[38] The site has been
known to many antiquaries from the eighteenth
century onwards; Gordon recorded that the
circuit of the walls was still conspicuous,[39] a
description which conflicts with the almost contemporary report of that other noted antiquarian
of Hadrian's Wall, John Horsley, who wrote that
the Roman site was almost entirely levelled and
under the plough. It is also worth noting that
Corbridge was the site of what must be one of the
earliest archaeological excavations ever to take
place in Britain, directed by King John in 1201
when he was seeking treasure. Apart from this
unfortunate monarch, a good deal of interest has
always been shown in the site, with a long
sequence of systematic excavation from 1906
down to the present day.[40] Unfortunately, as
some might say, the main objective of most of
these excavations has been the military sites, and
it is only in comparatively recent years that the
civil site has gained its just recognition.[41]

The earliest military site at Corbridge lies west
of the Roman town at Red House, where a large
Agricolan supply base and works depot was
discovered in excavations carried out before the
construction of the new bypass. The earliest fort
under the town dates to *c*. AD 90, and was followed
by a sequence of forts, with some chronological
gaps, down to *c*. AD 160, when part of the
conventional buildings were demolished and
replaced by workshops. This succession of forts
occupied an important position in the northern
military command. Not only did they guard the
bridge crossing the Tyne, but they also stood at
the junction of the Stanegate, running west
towards Carlisle, and Dere Street, one of the two
main arterial routes from York into central
southern Scotland. After Hadrian's Wall was
built, they would have helped to control traffic on
Dere Street passing through the Portgate, a
customs post on the Wall similar to that at Knag
Burn near Housesteads.

The military reconstructions *c*. AD 160 saw the
growth of buildings which were ultimately to
affect the planning of the civilian town. All the
barracks were demolished, leaving within the
defences only the granaries, now enclosed inside
their own compound, the headquarters building
and the commander's house. The structures
which replaced the barracks appear, from the

11 Corbridge looking east. The exposed buildings show to the left of centre (*Cambridge University Collection: copyright reserved*)

debris which they contained, to have been workshops, so anticipating the Severan arsenals. But this layout seemingly only lasted a comparatively short time, before it too was swept away, together with the buildings which had survived the previous changes and the fort defences. Work began on two new, larger, masonry granaries, although they were situated on the same site. Next to the eastern granary the aqueduct, which no doubt had served the successive forts, was provided with a new channel and distribution tanks; the source of water is unknown but presumably it lay on the higher ground to the north of Hadrian's Wall. The juxtaposition of a raised aqueduct close to the granary was not, one might think, a particularly sensible arrangement, as seepage from the aqueduct could well have made the granary, despite its raised floor, damper than was desirable. In the area previously occupied by the fort's headquarters and commander's house, a large masonry building was started; its plan encompassed an area 67 by 65.5 m (219 by 214 ft), with a central piazza or courtyard.

But work on these new buildings was suddenly interrupted, when some still-standing timber structures in the vicinity were also burnt. Unfortunately the date of this destruction, which may possibly be coupled with the similar fate of two nearby forts at Rudchester and Halton Chesters, is in dispute, and opinion is sharply divided over it; the date falls into one of the most vexed periods in the history of the northern British frontier. The modern view sees the destruction as occurring *c*. AD 180, to coincide with the account of an invasion of northern Britain by the historian Cassius Dio;[42] the wholesale acceptance of this view, though, causes some strains in interpretation which cannot be easily reconciled, chief among them being the implication that the damaged forts and other frontier works were left in a state of disrepair for the best part of 25 years, an unbelievable occurrence in Roman military affairs of the period. The alternative, and orthodox view, sees the damage as resulting from invasions from Scotland following the withdrawal of the garrisons by the governor of Britain and usurper emperor, Clodius Albinus, in AD 197.[43] A third but less acceptable possibility would place the invasion slightly later than this, in the governorship of Alfenus Senecio, *c*. AD 205–7.

Be that as it may, the work on the buildings, which it has been claimed were being constructed for a newly-constituted civitas capital, was at some time in the later second century violently interrupted and, with one exception, not resumed until the Severan period. The large courtyard building, mentioned above, was never completed. It has been variously interpreted as a military storehouse, a putative legionary *principia* and most recently as a forum for an embryonic *civitas*, to match Carlisle and the *civitas Carvetiorum* in the west (see p. 54). This would imply the promotion of another *pagus* of the Brigantes, and a possible candidate is that represented by the *curia Textoverdorum* mentioned on an altar from Chesterholm.[44] More likely, however, is the *pagus*, otherwise unattested, derived from the corrupted *curia* part of the name given to Cor-

bridge in the Ravenna list: *Corie Lopocarium*.[45] But if this *civitas* was constituted during the last half of the second century, the problem remains: why was the forum, if it was a forum, never completed? Only the south range seems to have found a later use as a row of shops fronting one of the main streets. It must be admitted, though, that it is not entirely convincing as a forum for a civitas capital; it lacks both *basilica* and civic offices. It makes better sense as a *macellum*, or market building, several of which are known in the larger towns of Britain, as well as in some Rhine and Danube frontier towns.

Although some building work had taken place in the pre-Severan period, notably two groups of temples on the south side of the east-west street, the main impetus to rebuild came under that emperor. Two new military compounds were constructed in the centre of the town and south of the same street; their enclosing walls respected the existing temples. The granaries were completed and provided with an imposing portico fronting the street; an imperial dedication jointly to Septimius Severus, Caracalla and Geta from one of them refers to the construction by an unknown legionary vexillation during the governorship of Alfenus Senecio.[46] A fragment of a badly damaged altar, found inside the south entrance of the west granary refers to a nameless officer in charge of the granaries. These two buildings were, therefore, clearly under military control, and it is most likely that they represented a collection centre for the *annona militaris*, a tax thought to have been introduced by Severus. The fountain-head and settling tank of the aqueduct were also rebuilt; two fragmentary inscriptions would suggest that the work was carried out by a detachment of *Legio XX*, possibly the same detachment that was responsible for the granaries.[47] Supply-lines were also laid from this *castellum aquae* to the two compounds.

The remaining buildings, defences and streets of the town are not well known, much of the information being derived from aerial photographs. The streets present considerable problems. What should be the main east-west street was inherited from the *via principalis* of the second-century forts and also represents the line of the Stanegate entering from the west. Although this road emerges on the eastern side of the town, attempts to trace it much further have failed. The main road north, Dere Street, must have described a dog-leg through the site, entering from the known site of the bridge over the Tyne to the south and emerging from the town on a more easterly line on its northward approach to the Portgate. It is interesting though that another internal street adheres closely to the line of the southward approach into the town, and may represent an earlier version of Dere Street before Hadrian's Wall was built. Short lengths of other internal streets have been identified but it is clear that, even though they intersect most often at right angles, there was no regular gridded system. One strange omission is the absence of a street running down the west side of the supposed forum, which would have linked a known street further north with that running between the two military compounds.

As far as can be seen from aerial photographs and minor excavations, most of the main streets seem to have been lined with strip buildings, which are usually interpreted as shops and workshops. They probably succeeded those of the second-century *vicus*, some evidence for which has been gained in excavations. Further military buildings, probably storehouses and also a bath-house, existed north of the supposed forum. A curiosity is the way in which the aqueduct channel by which, presumably, it was supplied with water, is diverted round the east end of the bath-house. The only other major building has been identified at the south end of the site, not far from the bridge crossing the Tyne.[48] It began life, probably in the Severan period, resembling a winged-corridor villa, which had been terraced into the slope which runs down to the river; it contained several heated rooms in the west wing and a water tank, possibly fed by local collection, in the front courtyard. Later additions and alterations greatly improved and enlarged the building; an ornamental fountain behind the house, from which came the famous Corbridge lion, was now linked to the aqueduct. The building was burnt to the ground in the disaster which overtook the town in AD 296, when the northern frontier was overrun by invaders, but it was soon rebuilt on an even more lavish scale, which possibly included a bath wing. The whole complex is usually interpreted as a *mansio*.

The fortifications of the town are no better

known than the streets. Traces of a rampart and a ditch have been identified by aerial photography and excavation in the north-eastern sector of the town, but doubt has been expressed as to their contemporaneity. The ditch, some 5 m (16 ft) wide by 2 m (6½ ft) deep, seems to have been deliberately filled with clay; the rampart, also of clay, some 4–5 m (13–16 ft) in width, was situated only about 1 m (3¼ ft) from the inner lip of the ditch. Foundations for a stone wall, 3–4 m (10–13 ft) wide, lay in front of the rampart and partly over the lip of the filled ditch.[49] Clearly more than one period of fortification is to be implied, with the likelihood that a masonry wall was added to the front of an existing bank, the contemporary ditch of which had to be solidly filled in order to carry its foundations; a date for the bank of not earlier than *c*. AD 130 has been provided by pottery, but no date can yet be given to the wall. Further excavation, though, may reveal a more complicated sequence.

The sites of two probable gates have been identified. At the point where Dere Street crosses the northern line of the curtain wall, two masonry foundations, 2.4 m (7¾ ft) square and 8.2 m (27 ft) apart were discovered in an excavation.[50] The distance between them would indicate a gate with at least two portals. On the south side of the town, just north of the bridge crossing the Tyne, a constriction in Dere Street has been noted, of the same width as between the foundations at the north gate; the length of the 'constriction' would have accommodated a wall and bank of nearly similar dimensions to that observed on the north side of the town.[51] Suggestive crop-marks at the point where the projected line of the defences meets the emerging east-west street have also been photographed from the air, but proof of another gate here will have to wait for excavation.

The religious observances of the inhabitants of Corbridge are well attested, not only through the structural remains of the six or so temples which lined the south side of the main east-west street near the military compounds but also through the number of dedications and items of religious sculpture which have been recovered from the site; quite a number, though, of the dedications were made by military personnel or army units.[52] Some of the cults mentioned are imports from the eastern provinces, presumably by soldiers or merchants, such as Jupiter Dolichenus,[53] Tyrian

Hercules and his consort Astarte, whose altars were inscribed in Greek,[54] and who were served by a priestess named Diodora and the Invincible Sun God, with its undertones of the Emperor Commodus.[55] The normal run of classical cults such as Mars,[56] Jupiter,[57] Juno,[58] Minerva,[59] Apollo[60] and Mercury[61] are represented, while there is a scattering of Celtic cults, sometimes coupled with their classical counterparts, as with the local patron deity, Brigantia, here linked with Jupiter Dolichenus,[62] and Maponus linked with Apollo;[63] also occurring is the 'Old God' Vitiris, or Veteris.[64]

Slight knowledge of other inhabitants comes from a small collection of material. A Greek presence is attested by the altars to Astarte and Hercules and by a gold betrothal ring inscribed in Greek to Aemilia.[65] Three tombstones are dedicated to children: 'Ertola properly called Vellibia',[66] Ahteha, whose name is probably a diminutive derived from the German,[67] and Julia Materna.[68] The most interesting example though is of a man whose name was probably Barathes;[69] he is described as a Palmyrene, from Syria, and also as a *vexillarius*, most likely a manufacturer or merchant of military standards, although the possibility that he was a standard-bearer cannot be entirely ruled out. It is not unlikely that he was the same man as Barates the Palmyrene whose wife Regina was buried at South Shields;[70] a Catuvellaunian by birth, she was at first his slave before he freed and married her. There was a considerable age difference at death, Barathes being 68 while his wife was only 30. Despite these few tombstones, the main cemeteries of Corbridge are not well attested. One seems to have been situated along the Stanegate, west of the town, where, in addition to single burials, a remarkable *mausoleum* has been investigated at Shorden Brae.[71] It consists of a massive foundation, 1.8 m (6 ft) deep and 9.7 by 10.3 m (32 by 34 ft), enclosing an irregular space about 4.3 by 4.9 m (14 by 16 ft), and clearly intended to support a superstructure of some weight. In the enclosed space there was an eccentrically-placed shaft, 1.2 m (4 ft) deep. This structure and shaft was surrounded by a walled enclosure approximately 41 m (134 ft) square; the wall was 1.7 m (5½ ft) thick. The corners of the enclosure were ornamented by sculptured funerary lions devouring stags. Despite the absence of any traces of body or coffin (apart from some nails in the fill) in the central pit, the whole monument would appear to be the probable grave – or cenotaph – of an important official which was erected sometime around the middle of the second century. Although other burials clustered around the enclosure, the internal area was respected, until the whole monument was dismantled at some time in the fourth century.

The later history of Corbridge is somewhat obscure. The date of the demise of the military arsenals is not known, although it could have been as early as the late third century. All the temples were totally demolished during the Roman period, probably by Christian iconoclasts, and the sites turned over to industrial use. The coin sequence for the site extends to the end of the fourth century, and there is enough evidence to show that a pagan Saxon cemetery exists somewhere in the area of the town. Beyond that it is not possible to go.

Ilchester (figs. 12 and 13)

Before this century, Roman Ilchester was poorly known, and even Haverfield, in 1906, thought it little more than a village.[72] The earliest excavations, however, in 1948–9 at Ivel House, supplemented by observation of local service trenches, revealed surprisingly complex occupation including buildings with *opus signinum* and mosaic floors,[73] at much the same time as Stevens argued for its status as a late civitas centre.[74] This pioneering work continued throughout the 1950s and early 1960s, but the results remain largely unpublished. Since then, larger-scale excavations have greatly extended our understanding of the town, focusing attention on the defensive sequence, on an area inside the northern defences in Kingshams Field, and on the suburbs along the Fosse Way and the Dorchester road, most of which are now fully published.[75] Recent work south of the town has revealed an apparently defended pre-Roman site,[76] while concerted watching briefs and limited excavations have added further information about the town's history and its cemeteries.[77] Such evidence provides useful insights into the site's morphological development, both inside and outside the central core.

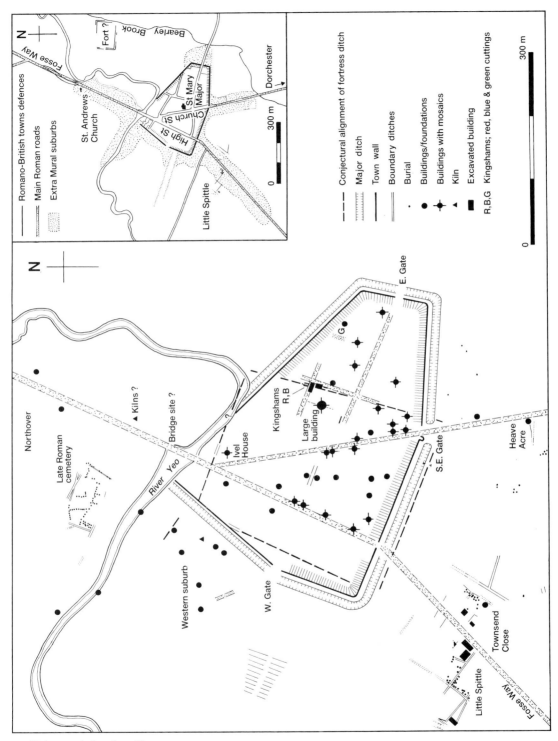

12 Ilchester (*after Leach*)

13 Ilchester, looking north-east along the line of the
Fosse Way through the centre of the modern
town (*Cambridge University Collection, Crown
Copyright*)

Ilchester lay on slightly raised ground above the floodplain of the River Yeo, where two roads joined the Fosse Way, one leading south-east from the centre towards Dorchester, the other branching north-westwards *c*. 600 m (2000 ft) north of the river. The Fosse Way was presumably important in the town's early development but its origins appear to be surprisingly complex. Although early and middle Iron-Age pottery has been located at various points, there is no evidence for any late Iron-Age settlement underlying the town, where the earliest levels are apparently military. The 1974 Kingshams excavation revealed two defensive phases in Blue Cutting,[78] commencing with a timber palisade and shallow ditch running north-south, fronting a rampart which probably lay to the west. A second ditch was cut in the berm west of the palisade, presumably necessitating its removal. This work enabled the turf-faced clay rampart located at Ivel House to be reinterpreted as the north side of a fort, while further excavations identified its probable southern and western sides, suggesting a vexillation fortress of *c*. 7 ha (17.3 acres).[79] Unfortunately little is known about its internal layout, while its date remains uncertain. More than likely it belongs in the decade AD 60–70, to judge from the presence of a coin of AD 67 in the truncated western rampart and the quantity of pre- and early-Flavian samian recovered in the Fosse Way suburb.[80] The late Flavian material in the upper fill of the inner Kingshams ditch probably represents early civilian rather than military activity (see below p. 66).

Aerial photographs have also suggested a second unexcavated fort to the north-east, between the Bearley Brook and the River Yeo, with a double-ditched enclosure *c*. 100 by 130 m (327 by 425 ft) enclosing *c*. 1.3 ha (3.2 acres), while a third site is suggested by numerous military finds within the Iron-Age hillfort of Ham Hill *c*. 8 km (5 miles) to the south-west.[81] Details are limited, but the evidence may indicate early use of the hillfort, followed by two successive installations in the valley related to the communications network. The actual status of Ham Hill is uncertain, but as one of the largest hillforts in the region it was probably occupied on the eve of the conquest, much like its counterpart at South Cadbury to the east.[82]

This sequence has been complicated, however, by the recent discovery south of the town near the Bearley Brook of a man-made earthwork enclosing *c*. 16 ha (40 acres).[83] Excavation revealed a flat-bottomed ditch 10 m (33 ft) wide, in front of a clay rampart, revetted in front by a low drystone wall to prevent slumping. Inside the enclosure, occupation horizons included the remains of at least one circular house, quantities of animal bone and metal-working slag, and characteristic late Iron-Age coarse pottery, matching material from Ham Hill and local Durotrigian wares; there was nothing definitely Roman in the sample. How this site fits into the overall picture remains uncertain, but it must surely indicate a significant shift in the local settlement pattern on the eve of the conquest.

Occupation outside the main fort at Ilchester clearly began at an early date and probably included native elements. Two apparently contemporary circular houses were identified at Ivel House,[84] while the 1975 excavation in Little Spittle alongside the Fosse Way recognized two early timber-framed buildings within a ditched compound west of the road.[85] The better preserved of the pair had apparently been dismantled, the pottery in the overlying silt horizon suggesting a later first-century date. Further rectilinear structures associated with Flavian material were also located in 1985 closer to the town.[86] This occupation was clearly contemporary with the fort, but it is uncertain whether it belongs to a *vicus* or a military depot. The complex sequence of sites in the Ilchester area raises several possibilities for early urban development, all involving a complicated interplay between military and civilian populations; much more work is vital to elucidate this.

The military withdrawal paved the way for the civilian development of the site, though details of the early occupation in the town centre have proved difficult to define. The most interesting aspect of the civil development is the recognition of several elements of a possible internal street grid, apparently laid out in line with or at right angles to the Fosse Way. Three internal streets were examined in the 1974 Red and Blue Cuttings at the west end of Kingshams Field, two being main thoroughfares throughout the history of the site, while the third was probably a service alley.[87] One main street (No. 1) lay parallel to the earlier military ditches, while the other (No.2) joined it at right angles, suggesting that the military plan influenced the layout. This new layout could not be dated precisely within the later first or early second century, though it may well have followed directly upon the final levelling of the military ditches, dated on pottery evidence to the late Flavian period.[88] If this was a civilian rather than a military operation, it must indicate a short hiatus between the military and civilian sequences in Kingshams Field, perhaps suggesting a post-military phase of settlement contraction. It would be dangerous to overstress its extent, however, because the site is well away from the central Fosse frontages, close to the north-eastern limits of the known second-century occupation; in Green Cutting to the east, the first and second centuries were represented only by buried soils interpreted as domestic refuse and possible cultivation.[89] Using the Kingshams evidence and other observations, Leach has postulated an early street grid within the later defences, making Ilchester unique at present among the small towns.[90] This hint of planning poses as yet unanswerable questions about the early impetus towards urban development.

Outside the central area, occupation spread along the road frontages south-west to Exeter, south-east to Dorchester and north-east across the river into the Northover suburb. Roads must also have led eastwards and westwards, the latter at least with offshoots serving an extensive suburb south of the river. Though such ribbon developments are a common small-town feature, at Ilchester their layout was partly constrained by the availability of higher ground above the river floodplain; to the south-west, for instance, the Fosse Way and its associated suburbs took advantage of a rise in the natural gravel which ensured a dry and attractive area for settlement. Within these suburbs, interesting variations are known in the date of the earliest civilian occupation.

Along the Fosse, there was apparently a lull in the sequence between the first-century activity of uncertain military or civilian origins already discussed and the earliest civilian horizons of the second.[91] West of the road in Little Spittle, the early levels were sealed by a grey-green sandy silt with charcoal flecks, probably deposited by floodwater silting. A comparable soil and silt horizon with charcoal flecks was tentatively identified east of the road in Townsend Close. Subsequent civilian activity is clearest west of the Fosse, represented by a series of ditched enclosures, the essential outlines of which were retained throughout the Roman period. A similar pattern is probably observable to the east. Recent excavations in the western suburb have also identified a lull in the sequence, between the earliest pits of the Flavian period and the more extensive second-century civilian activity.[92] An even more marked hiatus in the occupation sequence was recorded in the limited excavations in Heave Acre, alongside the Dorchester road, where traces of Flavian activity were overlain by a silt accumulation spanning the second century at least.[93] Thus the earliest civilian activity belongs to the third century with the main stone buildings dated to the fourth. Across the river in the northern suburb detailed information is lacking, though the known finds would suggest a second-century date for the earliest occupation.[94]

All this evidence demonstrates the complex character of the early occupation at Ilchester. After an initial post-military phase of contraction, development was apparently confined to the central area in the later first or early second century, followed by settlement in the roadside suburbs during the second and third; not until the third to fourth century did occupation reach its maximum extent of c. 20 ha (50 acres), extending north at least to St Andrew's Church and west along the river, south-east to the Bearley Brook and south-west for up to 600 m (2000 ft).

Within this broad framework, excavation has documented interesting morphological trends both in the central area and the suburbs. At Kingshams, the early streets were accompanied by contemporary timber buildings represented by two clay-filled gullies and several irregularly-placed stake-holes.[95] These survived throughout the second century, before being sealed by a thick deposit of silt and occupation debris suggesting a temporary break in occupation perhaps caused by flooding. The streets were quickly restored, however, accompanied by new buildings. One lay in the junction between streets 1 and 2, fronting onto the former, and originally comprised two rooms built of lias limestone, Hamstone and Pennant Sandstone with flint gravel floors. To the south lay several layers representing the floors and make-up of a timber building alongside streets 1 and 3. This was replaced by a stone structure, only partly examined in the excavated area. It comprised two rooms each c. 4 m (13 ft) square, laid out on either side of the alley (3), which presumably served further rooms and a yard to the rear. Contemporary with this, its northern counterpart was enlarged to c. 7 by 20 m (23 by 66 ft) by the addition of a third room in timber on the west, on a slightly different alignment, and the rebuilding of its east wall closer to the road, while its eastern room was subdivided lengthwise.

Elsewhere in the central area, enough structures are known to confirm the Kingshams picture, which indicates a dense arrangement of properties alongside the streets. There is, however, evidence for some 30 tessellated mosaic pavements within the later defences, mostly along the major frontages, suggesting a surprising level of affluence in the town.[96] Some clearly belonged to relatively small domestic and workshop premises, but others must have adorned larger private houses and official or religious complexes. At least one large building is known beneath the church and its graveyard, incorporating a range of rooms along its eastern side floored by tessellated pavements, but its precise function remains uncertain. Possible town houses are suggested by the mosaics found in the vicinity of Ivel House and in the area north of Limington Road close to Green Cutting in Kingshams Field.[97]

In the suburbs equally interesting trends are known. West of the Fosse in Little Spittle lay several rectangular enclosures defined by ditches.[98] The most northerly was apparently undivided, though only its southern ditch lay within the excavated area. At its eastern end two second-century buildings were identified, that to the south (Building 2a) lying at right angles to the frontage and apparently comprising a suite of rooms c. 7.5 by 3.5 m (24½ by 11½ ft), on Hamstone foundations. Its northern counterpart (Building 2b), though only partly excavated, had begun life as a timber structure with a gravel floor parallel to the frontage, before being widened to c. 7 m (23 ft) upon Hamstone foundations. Both ranges might have been independent structures, though excavations between them suggest a more complex L-shaped building with a courtyard to the rear and a timber colonnade along the frontage. Widespread evidence indicated that it had burnt down in the later second century. The frontage was subsequently occupied by a building (3a) on lias and Hamstone footings, measuring 18 by 6.5 m (59 by 21 ft), which originally comprised two rooms to which a third was added on the north. At the same time, the timber structure (2a) might have been partially (or totally?) rebuilt, though the details are unclear. It was certainly suppressed by the late third or fourth century when the stone building was provided with a corridor 4 m (13 ft) wide along its western side, comprising two and ultimately three rooms. This gave access to the old courtyard area. Such a complex timber to stone sequence is found elsewhere in Ilchester. Behind these buildings, the northern enclosure contains groups of post-holes, gullies and occasional pits.

The central enclosure, in contrast, was originally divided by a cross-ditch into two plots each measuring c. 50 by 28 m (165 by 92 ft). The eastern one was only partly examined, revealing towards the rear a series of pits probably dug for gravel, though no buildings were identified. Its western counterpart apparently remained open, being used at one stage for spelt cultivation. The most southerly of the three enclosures had also been subdivided, although little of its eastern half lay within the trench. Its western half remained open, except for a timber structure represented by two rows of six post-holes. Subsequent phases saw the amalgamation and redivision of these enclosures, presumably as ownership or tenurial arrangements changed, but the framework, once established, remained remarkably consistent over time, as the layout of the late inhumations attests.

Excavation east of the Fosse Way in Townsend Close was less extensive, though at least one length of boundary ditch suggests a comparable arrangement.[99] Occupation along the frontages was represented by several rather ill-defined second- and third-century timber and stone structures, succeeded by two fourth-century stone buildings, both badly damaged by a later ditch. Enough remained to show that the northern one was at least 9 by 7.5 m (29½ by 24½ ft), with two rooms of unequal size at the back, while its southern counterpart, of which only the rear 2.5

m (8 ft) was recovered, had apparently lain in a walled compound measuring 13 by 6 m (42½ by 19½ ft). Small-scale excavations in Heave Acre alongside the Dorchester road revealed a comparable timber to stone sequence, commencing in the third century.[100] This evidence from the southern suburbs clearly indicates an arrangement of elongated properties end-on to the frontages housing a variety of activities, but apart from a more generous allocation of space, little differentiates the associated buildings from their counterparts in the central area. In the western suburb likewise, limited work has suggested the development of a semi-industrial area in the second century, followed in the third and fourth by the erection of several stone-founded buildings, some with evidence for a degree of sophistication.[101]

The construction of the defences, enclosing *c.* 10 ha (25 acres) at the centre of the settlement, inevitably excluded the northern and western suburbs and the ribbon developments to the south-east and south-west. This apparently had little impact on the extent of these intra- and extra-mural zones, though it may have encouraged the enhanced development of the central area in the third and fourth centuries. The defences have been sampled at various points, revealing an interesting sequence.[102] The earliest phase comprised a clay dump rampart and a contemporary ditch, post-dating a range of Trajanic and Hadrianic material at several points. This would not be inconsistent with a late second- to early third-century date, in line with other sites, but more precise dating is essential. Excavations at the south-east gate astride the Dorchester road have suggested that its stone semi-circular tower was an integral part of these early defences. This recalls the sequence at several civitas capitals, including Cirencester and Exeter, but it remains unique to date at the small towns.[103]

In Kingshams Field, the bank was apparently partly levelled or cut away by the mid third century at least, prior to the construction of a stone building with a courtyard to the south.[104] This was only partially examined, but seemed to form part of an east-west range of rooms with at least two floor sequences. Comparable terracing has been noted elsewhere, at the south-east corner and along the south side, but the overall

effect on the efficiency of the defences remains uncertain.[105] The rampart front itself was subsequently cut away to accommodate a massive stone wall set on a foundation of limestone, clay and rubble lenses, which presumably incorporated the existing tower at the south-east gate. Dating evidence from the south-eastern part of the circuit includes a coin of AD 342–3 from the foundations. No evidence has yet been forthcoming for any external towers, the mortared stone foundation in Kingshams Field now being assigned to the medieval defences.[106]

From the excavated evidence, various aspects of the town's economic character can be defined. Few buildings provide any clue to their function, but a room in Building 2 in Kingshams Field contained a clay-lined hearth, a stone trough and a low platform, probably indicating a manufacturing or commercial role.[107] Elsewhere, we depend upon characteristic industrial debris, which includes iron-working in the courtyard south of Building 3 in Kingshams Field and two pottery kilns in the western suburb; bone-working is also attested by artefactual evidence, while the building trade is well represented.[108] The most interesting evidence, however, comes from the ditched enclosures in the Little Spittle suburb. The front row clearly housed small-scale industrial activities, indicated by metal-working debris and a glass-working hearth, while the rear plots were evidently agricultural, one at least being used for growing spelt, and a second probably containing a timber barn.[109] This combination of light industry and agriculture is probably typical of the suburbs where pressure on land was less acute than in the centre. Such plots are unlikely to have provided all the necessary food for their inhabitants, so not surprisingly traces of fields have been identified which predate the late cemetery in the Northover suburb.[110] There is also a possibility that the River Yeo had been artificially straightened in places in Roman times, suggesting that river transportation played a part in the life of the settlement.[111]

Surprisingly little is known about the settlement's religious life. No temples have been located and only two possible ritual pits have been identified, both in Little Spittle.[112] One second-century rectangular pit contained several pottery vessels, a dedicatory inscription and three republican coins, while a re-used fourth-century well had large quantities of animal bone including some complete carcasses and well-preserved plant, wood and leather remains. Neither is particularly distinctive, but comparable patterns have been noted elsewhere. A possible Christian presence has been suggested by several fourth-century burials in the Northover cemetery, because of their east-west orientation and similarities with Poundbury, but this evidence is insufficiently conclusive.[113]

Ilchester's status has been much discussed. In 1952, Stevens argued that two inscriptions from Hadrian's Wall, recording building operations by a levy from the *Civitas Durotrigum Lendinienses*, indicated a subdivision of the tribal territory, and that Ilchester was the obvious candidate for its administrative centre, given its identification with the *Lindinis* of the Ravenna Cosmography.[114] Although challenged, this remains the most convincing explanation. There is moreover archaeological evidence to suggest that Ilchester was more influential than most small towns, not least the developed central area and urban core defences. If the known mosaics belonged to private rather than official or religious buildings, this might indicate the presence of wealthier individuals who could have formed a town council, as might the marked concentration of late villas in the area, including that at Ilchester Mead, just outside the south-western suburbs.

Most information about the later phases of the town has come from several late Roman inhumation cemeteries. Finds of Hamstone and lead coffins at Northover House had long suggested an inhumation cemetery north of the river,[115] where excavation in 1982 revealed a ditched enclosure measuring *c.* 90 by 50 m (294 by 165 ft), which surrounded an estimated 1500 burials, apparently laid in rows east-west, some in coffins of lead, Hamstone or wood, others in lias limestone cists.[116] Excavation also revealed two contemporary buildings, while the burials extended eastwards beyond the enclosure towards the main road. All the associated grave goods belonged to the fourth century, the cemetery itself overlying earlier field boundaries and enclosures. Burials were also found in the south-western and south-eastern suburbs, the clearest pattern occurring in Little Spittle west of the Fosse.[117] Here Period V of late Roman date saw the imposition of an

inhumation cemetery upon the earlier pattern of ditched enclosures. Before this, much of Building 3 and its associated courtyard apparently went out of use, judging from an extensive stony layer deposited across their remains. The burials took their alignment, however, from the older boundaries, all but one lying in the plots nearest to the frontages. Forty-two extended inhumations, several with wooden coffins, were examined, 14 in the northern and 28 in the southern plot. The associated grave goods included everyday items like boots, knives and bracelets, though at least one burial contained a pot with chicken bones, and another a dog. The excavators assigned Period V to the late fourth and fifth centuries, though how long the tradition continued remains uncertain.

East of the Fosse in Townsend Close, the buildings apparently also went out of use, with their associated plots given over to burials, which again followed the earlier layouts and rarely contained any grave goods; observation of roadworks between Townsend Close and Heave Acre revealed yet more similar burials.[118] These southern burials are clearly very different from the co-ordinated northern cemetery, obviously occurring once the suburbs themselves were virtually derelict. This suggests important late fourth-century changes in the nature of Ilchester, probably involving a contraction of occupation to within the defences due to growing insecurity. Even so, the retention of the existing framework in the burial alignment suggests continuity within an essentially Roman context.

The recovery of later fourth-century coins and pottery in the town centre itself certainly also attests continued activity, but it is hard to determine how long this survived into the fifth century, given the cessation of both coinage and pottery supplies and the consequent problem of dating post-Roman levels.[119] In the western trenches in Kingshams Field, Buildings 1 and 2 certainly lasted into the fifth century, ultimately collapsing, to judge from an extensive rubble spread across the site, but no dating evidence was recovered. A similar undated sequence was recorded in Green Cutting to the east, where the courtyard had obviously been used for industrial activities prior to the demise of the associated building. A small quantity of excavated shell-tempered pottery and a few sherds of imported wares also suggest some fifth- to sixth-century survival, but these are not conclusive in the absence of *in situ* structures. Three sixth-century Anglo-Saxon brooches are probably stray finds. At present, there is little to suggest continued occupation at Ilchester by the time of full Saxon penetration in the seventh century.

Kenchester (figs. 14 and 15)

Kenchester's importance was first acknowledged by Leland in the sixteenth century[120], since when it has continued to attract attention. Antiquarian observers built up a picture of an important urban complex enclosed by a stone wall, within which traces of an irregular street system and numerous buildings were visible, some with evidence for tessellated pavements and painted wall plaster.[121] Modern research has expanded on this foundation, drawing upon the results of aerial reconnaissance and, to a lesser extent, excavation. Aerial survey in particular has revealed some of the intricacies of the site's internal morphology.[122] Excavation has, unfortunately, been limited in its extent and scope, with only the 1912–13 and 1924–5 sites sampling the interior;[123] more recent work has been confined to the defences and the west gate and to a settlement complex in the rural-urban fringe east of the town.[124] Inevitably, therefore, our understanding of the site's morphology is considerably clearer than its progressive stages of development.[125]

Kenchester is strategically located in the valley of the River Wye, close to the Iron-Age hillfort of Credenhill, and on an important east-west route heading towards the early military bases at Clifford and Clyro. Further roads probably led north-east, past Credenhill, towards Leintwardine and Wroxeter, and south across the Wye to Abergavenny. This must surely indicate that the site played a part in the Roman advance into the Welsh marches, and that the town owed its origins to an early military presence.[126] Such a fort would also have supervised the native population centre on Credenhill, which is one of the largest sites in the area, with univallate defences enclosing *c*. 20 ha (50 acres). Excavations in its interior demonstrated extensive occupation, which had apparently begun to decline in the AD 70s, perhaps in the wake of increasing migration

towards a more convenient centre on the road network.[127]

This attractive model of urban development has proved remarkably elusive on the ground. No trace of a fort has been located at or near the later town, and only three isolated pieces of military equipment are known.[128] Within the town, the earliest occupation is probably represented by Flavian pottery recovered from the limited excavations, but neither its extent nor its character can be defined.[129] Recent work in the eastern suburbs on the later winged-corridor building has added a further complexity, revealing an important sequence of later Iron-Age ditched enclosures alongside a stream, in one of which lay a two-phase timber round house associated with pottery, slag, bone and worked flints.[130] How extensive such activity was on the eve of any military operations remains uncertain, while its implications for the early stages of urban growth at Kenchester must await further research.

Our understanding of the civilian occupation at Kenchester is inevitably dominated by the aerial photographs, which reveal a 9 ha (22 acre) irregular defended enclosure set roughly astride an east-west road immediately to the west of its junction with two other roads. That to the north-east has not been examined, but its southern counterpart was sectioned south of the junction and shown to be 6.7 m (22 ft) wide with alternating bands of gravel, sand and cobbling.[131] Surprisingly little occupation is visible alongside this latter pair of roads, despite the normal potential of a crossroads, and is concentrated instead along the main east-west route, principally, but not exclusively, west of the junction. Within the defended area, the main road is well defined, with a prominent central channel or drain. It has been excavated at several points, both during the early excavations and in connection with the west gate, revealing informative sequences of relevance to our understanding of the site's development (see p. 73 below). This road forms the focus for an irregular network of side-streets and lanes which lead off at diverse angles and provide access to land and buildings behind the frontages. Many are quite short, some extend as far as the defences, and two at least apparently form a prominent central crossroads. Unlike Water Newton, no attempt was made to link these streets and lanes along the inner edge of

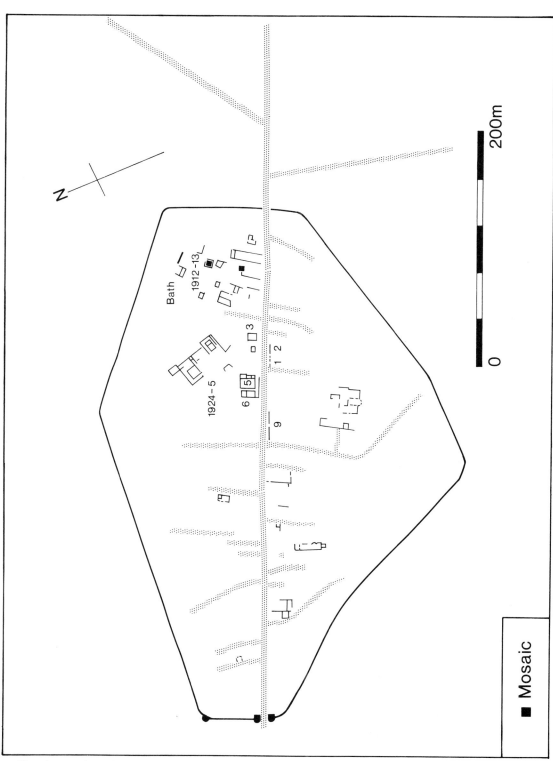

14 Kenchester, based on the aerial photographs with
additions from *Jack and Hayter*

the defences. Few have been sectioned, though
the central pair are known to be contemporary
with the main phase of the east-west road.[132]
Extra-mural ribbon development, accompanied
by several short side-streets and lanes, is also
visible, probably extending as far east as the
winged-corridor complex noted earlier. Numerous buildings are recognizable within this developed street system, though detailed plans can
rarely be drawn. The main frontages were
nevertheless crammed with closely packed buildings, while the land behind was evidently more
open and occasionally occupied by larger
structures.

The detailed phasing of this morphological
information presents major problems in the
absence of large-scale, modern excavations, but a
recent reassessment of the early excavation
reports has suggested that a major remodelling of
the town centre occurred apparently in the mid to
late second century.[133] This clearly involved the
construction of a new east-west road and at least
one contemporary north-south cross-street, the
provision of side drains within the defended area
and the erection of at least one probable public
building. This remodelling might also be contemporary with the decision to provide earthwork defences, though it could have preceded it
by several years on current dating evidence;
either way, such changes mark a significant
watershed in the town's development and pose
important questions about its status and
function.

Jack and Hayter sampled the main east-west
road at several points inside the defences, revealing a twofold sequence involving an earlier
roadway 9 m (29½ ft) wide, with sandstone-lined
drains on one or both sides, overlain by an often
narrower road with a central open channel.[134] In
the 1912–13 sections, the early road clearly
overlay a burnt horizon containing Flavian and
Antonine material, while the more informative
1924–5 sections demonstrated that the southern
drain overlay Antonine pottery at one point. This
makes it absolutely clear that the early road and
the drains belong in a mid to late second-century

context. None of these sections was apparently
bottomed if the drawings are to be believed, so we
do not know what underlay the burnt layer. One
of the 1924–5 sections also examined the central
north-south cross-street, demonstrating that its
construction matched that of the early road, with
which it was therefore contemporary.[135] The
east-west road has only been examined once since
the 1920s, during excavations on the west gate,
where it evidently comprised three separate
surfaces; the latest (road III) can probably be
identified with Jack and Hayter's later roadway;
the middle one (II) was contemporary with the
mid fourth-century gate and may be a localized
resurfacing; while the lowest (I) must represent
the east-west route in the preceding centuries.[136]
This latter remains undated, though it was not
the earliest feature on site, overlying at least one
slot-like channel. It had also been cut by a culvert
originally containing a wooden box drain, which
might be connected with the provision of the
sandstone-lined drains further east.[137] This
would suggest that the east-west road at this point
had not been substantially modified and that the
mid to late second-century redevelopment was
confined to the intra-mural zone.

Contemporary with the alterations to the main
east-west road, at least one or perhaps two
possible public buildings were constructed
immediately to the south on Sites 1 and 2, each
with a frontage carried on four columns and set so
close to the road that the new roadside drains had
to be diverted.[138] More importantly, however,
the remains overlay burnt material, while the
make-up levels on Site 2 contained Antonine
pottery, thus demonstrating that the building(s)
were part of an overall design reshaping the town
centre, which might also have included the first
phase of the defences. Excavations have been
largely confined to the western side, revealing an
earth rampart made up of material from at least
one contemporary ditch to the west.[139] A stone
wall had subsequently been inserted, obscuring
its original width. The best dating evidence came
in 1956, not only from the rampart itself and its
silted ditch, but also from the occupation layer
that it sealed. This included much mid second-
century pottery and one piece of samian of AD
140–80, in line with the normal sequence of late
second-century earthworks.

These impressive alterations probably represent an important event in the development of the site, even if we cannot define precisely what preceded it, how widespread it was and why it happened. It does, however, pose some interesting questions as to the nature and extent of earlier occupation on the site and whether the burnt level beneath the main road and the public building(s) represents simply site clearance or a more extensive fire. These can only be answered tentatively on present evidence. *In situ* occupation debris pre-dating the established mid to late second-century horizon has been located on several widely scattered sites, beyond that already noted beneath the east-west road and its side drains and the presumed public building(s). This includes the occupation sealed by the construction of the western defences, such as the material noted in the 1956 section and the pebbled surface preceding the ditches at the north-west corner.[140] South of the west gate, the wall had also cut through a hearth and a layer of charcoal and burnt clay deriving from a structure apparently levelled prior to the construction of the first defences.[141] Few other buildings can be assigned to this early occupation with any confidence. This evidence is surprisingly extensive, especially at the western end of the site, though more excavation is essential to clarify its distribution.

A recent reassessment of the site has suggested that elements of this earlier activity are also recognizable in the variations of the internal street alignments.[142] These are said to indicate two broad phases, one apparently following the line of the mid to late second-century north-south cross-street, which is especially prominent towards the western end of the defended enclosure, the other seemingly having its own distinctive alignment more akin to the line of the road running north from the main crossroads; this is more obvious at the eastern end, and might therefore be earlier in origin. This hypothesis cannot be convincingly proven on current evidence, but if accepted, it would suggest an early ribbon development with short side-streets and lanes, perhaps extending *c.* 700 m (2300 ft) either side of the main north-south road junction, followed by a mid to late second-century remodelling of the region to the west, perhaps contemporary with the new defences.

Within the developed street network, the evidence indicates a surprisingly wide range of buildings and a marked level of architectural pretension, though most of it clearly belongs in a third- or fourth-century context. The main east-west road was lined with strip buildings, very few of which have been excavated. Some, like the building on Site 3, were little more than flag floors, presumably supporting a timber superstructure, while others had stone foundations and concrete flooring; good examples of this type include the two buildings on Sites 5 and 6, fronted by a common veranda.[143] One was a simple two-roomed strip building, the other comprised a single large room with three smaller rooms along the east. More imposing structures also lined the frontages, including the public building, or pair of structures, represented by the columned façades on Sites 1 and 2; another is clearly known on Site 9, where an arrangement of four pillar bases suggests an identical function.[144] Lewis has interpreted these as classical temples, but not enough has survived to prove this suggestion.[145]

Much more interesting are the larger complexes which occupy the vacant land immediately behind the main frontages. At least three are known, each served by a short side-street or lane. One large example lay just inside the east gate, although its plan could not be reconstructed from the rather fragmentary remains which certainly included four hypocausts and two mosaics.[146] To the rear of the plot, excavation sampled part of a bath-house and an associated drain, close to where Stukeley recorded a monument with a niche. Whether this was all part of a single private house remains uncertain, because its location just inside one of the town's principal entrances might suggest an official function. North-west of this, another large building examined in 1924–5 extended over at least 52 m (170 ft) at an oblique angle to the prevailing internal morphology.[147] Its plan is also incomplete but seems to resemble a porticoed house with projecting wings. Pottery beneath its wall suggests a later second- or third-century date. A third complex can be identified on the aerial photographs in the south-east quarter, served by a lane from the north-south cross-street.[148] It has never been excavated but was clearly extensive. The location of these buildings and the limited dating evidence strongly suggests that all three are relatively late in the morphological sequence. Their recognition attests the presence of several wealthy individuals disposed to live in the town itself, while yet others occupied nearby villas, including the winged-corridor complex in the rural-urban fringe to the east, and the villa to the west at Bishopstone. Such evidence has an important bearing on the site's function.

Judging from the surviving architectural fragments, some of Kenchester's buildings were clearly imposing structures. Five Doric capitals and bases were recorded in the nineteenth century,[149] while several re-used blocks were found in 1957 in the foundations of the northwest tower; these blocks displayed cramp holes unrelated to the adjacent stones, and one at least was an elaborately moulded part of a plinth.[150] Obviously by the mid fourth century at the latest, some elaborate buildings had become redundant and could be demolished for re-use in the defences. Also of interest is the evidence for a stone and timber portico in the town's central area, apparently flanking the east-west road. This was partly formed by the stone façades located on Sites 1, 2 and 9, but elsewhere a series of morticed stones formed the foundation of a timber veranda.[151] It is arguable, however, that these stones belong stratigraphically with the later road surface, with its central channel, by which time the earlier drains had probably ceased to function; this would explain certain anomalies in their relative positions and have important implications for the site's later appearance.

Not surprisingly, our understanding of the town's everyday life is somewhat sketchy. Few buildings have revealed distinctive evidence for specialized activities, though several of the roadside examples contained furnaces and hearths which probably served an industrial role, while iron and lead slag indicates metal-working.[152] The latter is also known from the winged-corridor complex to the east.[153] Two otherwise unexpected specialists, T. Vindac[ius] Ariovistus and Aurelius Polychrinides, are recorded on oculists' stamps.[154] Religious activities are just as poorly represented, leaving aside the possible temples already described. Several altars have been recovered, mostly re-used in secondary contexts, as well as two busts of Minerva, a pipe-clay Venus and various miniature votive or ritual finds, including several bronze animals and an axe.[155] Equally little is known about the urban cemeteries which must exist, except for two inhumations found in 1920 near the main road leading south from the crossroads.[156]

Kenchester's status has been the subject of considerable discussion, not least because of the 1795 discovery of an inscribed milestone, apparently re-used in the northern defences.[157] This was originally erected in the reign of Numerian in AD 283–4 and apparently includes the reference to a R(es) P(ublica) C(ivitatis), most probably D(obunnorum) (of the Dobunni), though the latter reading and attribution have produced several fertile alternatives.[158] This raises the possibility of an administrative role for Kenchester, perhaps initially as a *pagus* centre, and then later as a full *civitas* centre. This promotional process cannot be proven, though it would not conflict with known Roman policy. Some support for this might come from the archaeological evidence, which attests Kenchester's increasing importance through time. This includes the upgrading of the central area, its architectural and civic (?) pretensions, the presence of possible public buildings, the provision of urban-core defences and the existence of several intra-mural houses and local villas whose owners could form the core of the local council. Such features are obviously not conclusive in themselves, but taken together they differentiate Kenchester from the majority of minor towns described in this volume.

Our detailed knowledge of the site's later history is largely dependent upon the excavations across the defences and at the west gate.[159] It is now clear that the earthen bank had been cut back to make way for a stone wall, resting on cobbled foundations up to 3 m (10 ft) wide, but unfortunately no precise dating evidence for its construction was recovered. Nor could its relationship to the external tower at the north-west corner or to the west gate be determined. At the former, stone-robbing had effectively removed the crucial junction on the steeply sloping ground; at the gate, it remained unclear whether the wall was already in existence or whether it had been constructed at the same time. Only further excavation can resolve this problem. Though only its rough foundations survived, the west gate turned out to be an impressive and imposing structure, comprising two towers with semi-circular fronts, flanking a dual carriageway. Its somewhat irregular shape and measurements were presumably counteracted as the building rose above ground level. It can be securely dated because its foundations sealed mid fourth-century pottery inside a carefully filled and levelled culvert. Interestingly, the two semi-circular towers had been built out over the filled ditch of the earlier rampart, as had the semi-octagonal external tower at the north-west corner. This was presumably one of several added in the fourth century, perhaps contemporary with a new wide ditch outside its predecessor. The tower's foundations were solidly built and included several fragments of re-used architectural masonry. Such impressive fortifications clearly attest Kenchester's continued importance well into the fourth century, though the sequence did not end here.

Sometime in the later fourth or early fifth century, major modifications occurred at the west gate, involving its remodelling as a single portal.[160] The original north passage was retained, with a new spina, while its southern counterpart was blocked and probably used as a guard chamber. A new road (III) was also laid, much narrower than its predecessor, which might tentatively be associated with the later road in the town centre with its central channel or drain. Such an identification has important implications for the morticed stones and the timber portico already mentioned, suggesting that the central area preserved some level of architectural pretension; this can only mean that early excavations failed to locate the contemporary timber buildings continuing Kenchester's urban tradition into the fifth century. Beyond this it is difficult to go; something was worth defending in this late period, but the archaeological evidence fails us. How long it lasted must also remain a mystery, as must the rise of its probable successor at Hereford, where Anglian settlers known as the Magonsaete were well established by AD 691.[161] It has been argued that they derived their name from that of Kenchester, which is identified as the *Magnis* of both the Antonine Itinerary and the Ravenna list, suggesting some tradition of local continuity, but there remain serious problems with this suggested derivation.[162]

Rochester (figs. 16 and 17)

The Roman site at Rochester lies on Watling Street, just east of its crossing of the River Medway. The town's generally accepted name is *Durobrivae*,[163] although variations occur in both the Antonine Itinerary[164] and Ravenna list.[165] The first systematic survey of Roman Rochester was carried out by George Payne towards the end of the last century; this account was slightly amplified in the Victoria County History.[166] Since then most archaeological work has been concentrated on the fortifications,[167] with all too little excavation being carried out in the interior,[168] mainly because of the presence of modern buildings.

Substantial traces of late Iron-Age settlement preceded the Roman foundation. Excavations in the High Street in 1961–2 revealed a metalled track and a large timber building; fragments of coin moulds, some 20 'tin' coins and slag would imply that there was a mint here.[169] It was clearly a site of some importance and it is not impossible that Rochester was the centre of one of the four Kentish kingdoms mentioned by Caesar,[170] although by the time of Claudius' invasion these kingdoms appear to have been united under one ruler. The River Medway narrows slightly to *c.* 150 m (490 ft) wide at Rochester, which is usually considered to be the lowest convenient crossing place. It is unlikely, though, that a bridge existed here in pre-Roman times, since it is usually argued that the first Roman crossing at the famous battle of the Medway took place further upstream towards Maidstone.[171] But after that victorious crossing, no time would have been wasted in building a bridge, possibly at first of boats, in the narrower Rochester section of the river. A fort was probably constructed to guard the bridgehead either at Rochester or at Strood on the opposite bank, although no traces have yet been found.

The excavations on the south side of the High Street in 1961–2 also revealed the earliest version of Watling Street, probably dating to the time of the conquest, with associated timber-framed buildings; the road was originally 2.7 m (9 ft) wide, although it was soon widened to 6.7 m (22 ft), and a central stone-built drain effectively divided it into two carriageways. The new carriageway was, however, short-lived, and a masonry

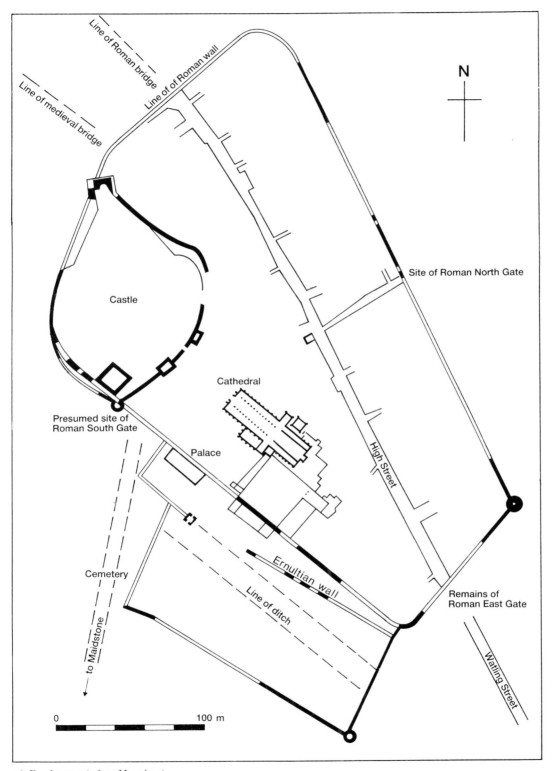

Line of Roman bridge

Line of of Roman wall

Line of Roman wall

Line of medieval bridge

N

Castle

Site of Roman North Gate

Cathedral

Presumed site of
Roman South Gate

Palace

High Street

Ernulfian wall

Cemetery

Line of ditch

Remains of
Roman East Gate

to Maidstone

Watling Street

0   100 m

16 Rochester *(after Harrison)*

17 Rochester, looking north-east. The castle and cathedral lie within the Roman town (*Cambridge University Collection: copyright reserved*)

building, probably a bath-house, was constructed across it at this point; the surviving carriageway appears to have been resurfaced seven times.

As indicated above, most of the information which has been gathered on Roman Rochester concerns the defences, which have now been identified more or less round the whole circuit, and which enclose an area of some 9.5 ha (23 acres). In 1968 it became clear that the stone wall had been preceded, as in many towns in Britain, by an earthwork, with a date of construction in the late second or early third century. So it would seem, but closer examination shows that the earthwork incorporated a good deal of turfwork, which in at least two places was laid on top of a layer of flints.[172]

Some time ago it was suggested that three east coast sites, at Brough-on-Humber, Caister-by-Yarmouth and Rochester, possessed late second-or early third-century fortifications which were different from the general run of urban defences of this date.[173] In all three cases the method of construction was changed, with turf on a stone, or part-stone, platform at Brough[174] and Rochester and with only a palisade at Caister.[175] Only very few other circuits are known to contain turf, and in one case at least, at Cirencester,[176] it was probably inserted as a repair. Moreover Brough had contemporary timber gates,[177] again a feature unrecognized at any other town, except for Silchester;[178] masonry gates were the norm elsewhere. These methods of construction, notably turf on a stone platform, employed at two of the three sites, timber gates at one at least and a palisade at the third, possess a martial appearance which remains unmatched at any other towns in Britain, where earthwork fortifications were normally of unrevetted dump construction, using material either scraped up from the surface or derived from digging ditches. Consequently it is worth reasserting that these three coastal sites may have functioned as secondary naval bases, supplementing the main bases at Dover, Lympne and Boulogne.[179]

The stone wall which was inserted in front of the existing rampart was just over 2 m (6¼ ft) in width and was constructed of Kentish ragstone faced with dressed blocks; bonding courses of tile have been recorded in places. The core of the wall is known to be still standing to a height of nearly 9 m (29½ ft) at its maximum. Outside the wall, except on the north side, where the river came to its foot, there appears to have been only a single ditch, some 6.5 m (21 ft) wide and 2.5 m (8 ft) deep, which had been truncated by the medieval ditch; it is most likely to have been contemporary with the early rampart. The date of construction of the wall, which has not been established with

any precision, would seem to lie in the third century. But there is little difference at present between the dates provided for both the early rampart and the wall.[180]

Very little has been discovered of the gates, although their sites can be predicted with tolerable certainty. Best known is the east gate which is thought to coincide with the site of the medieval East Gate. Here, when the Mathematical School was being rebuilt in 1894, part of a semi-circular tower of supposed Roman build was encountered beneath the medieval tower.[181] But excavations in 1969 in the East Gate area failed to add much to what was already known of the gate structure.[182] The only interesting point to emerge was that the Roman ditch continued an almost certainly unbroken course northwards past the medieval gate and its street to terminate 5.5 m (18 ft) beyond them, while both the early rampart and the Roman wall continued for an unknown distance beyond this end of the ditch. If this ditch is contemporary with the rampart then the gap for the gate between the rampart ends must have been much narrower than that left between the ditch ends. Whether the same applied to the wall cannot yet be established. But a further complicating factor is that Watling Street, in its latest phases, points directly to the medieval East Gate, strongly suggesting that here also lay the later Roman gate, most probably on a different site to that belonging to the early defences; if this is so, then the ditch must have been bridged at the gate. The north gate is presumed to lie at the point where modern Northgate Street cuts the line of the wall; a Roman street underlying the modern one here would seem to confirm the correctness of this assumption. Excavations nearby in 1961 failed to locate any structures.[183] This gate presumably led to a quay, or docks, and there are references to it in some Saxon charters. Similarly the south gate is usually assumed to be at the end of Southgate Street where an internal street points in the direction of Boley Hill; the existence of a cemetery in this region outside the walls would support this assumption. Two massive walls were recorded in 1891 lying at right angles to the line of the town wall under the modern street, but no proof of their Roman origin was obtained.[184]

There is greater doubt over the site of the west gate, since the exact line of the wall in this area

near the river has never been adequately established. Its position will also depend on the
whereabouts of the bridge across the river, which
is another unknown factor. Various opinions
have been expressed on the site of the latter.[185]
The medieval bridge, built in 1392 and demolished *c*. 1856, was a little distance south-west of
the modern road bridge and is recorded as having
been preceded by an earlier bridge on the same
line; it had ten waterways set between stone piers
and a timber superstructure, a method of construction commonly used by Roman engineers.
Yet the alignment of Watling Street as revealed
under the Guildhall would point to a crossing
slightly further north, and nearer the modern
line, along which a large number of Roman coins
have been found in the river bed. Massive
masonry was also encountered when the railway
bridge was constructed further north still of the
modern road bridge. But masonry of this nature
might equally be part of a dock or quay, so the
correct position of the Roman bridge still remains
in considerable doubt.

Little extra information about the streets of the
town, other than those already mentioned, has
been recovered in the course of excavations, but it
would seem that from present knowledge there
was no regular grid. Nevertheless, most of the
streets which have been sectioned were of substantial construction, in some of the wetter places
being provided with a substructure of timber
piles or a corduroy; otherwise local material such
as Kentish rag, crushed flints or chalk or gravel
were used. An attempt has been made by Nightingale to show that Rochester was the centre from
which an area of land to the north had been
centuriated on the regular basis of 20 by 20 *actus*
squares.[186] The main axes of the centuriation
were somewhat improbably and completely artificially taken as the eastward continuation of the
line of Watling Street, from before its deviation
slightly southwards at Salters Cross on its
approach to the suburb at Strood and to the
Medway bridge, and the extension northwards of
the alignment of the road from Maidstone to
Rochester. The area of suggested centuriation
lies well to the north of the town on Cliffe
Marshes, and Nightingale even claimed that a
plot measuring 2 by 1 *actus* (= 1 *iugerum*), which
features on the 1840 tithe map and is still in the
possession of a single owner, was a survivor of the
Roman survey. It must be admitted that the area
of Cliffe Marshes contains boundaries which
now, and on the map, correspond to centuriated
measurements, but there is no proof that they
date to the Roman period. Their extension
southwards to the imaginary axes situated near
Rochester is stretching the case beyond belief;
nevertheless Nightingale's arguments are
unequivocally supported by Dilke.[187]

Excavations have revealed fragmentary
remains of substantial masonry buildings within
the town walls, but no complete plans have been
recovered. The walls were normally constructed
of Kentish ragstone, with or without tile bonding
courses, or more rarely of brick; some, though,
were constructed with clay, a not uncommon
feature in the south-east of Britain. One building
beneath the Cathedral apparently contained an
apse with a floor of *opus signinum*, suggesting
perhaps the site of a bath-house hypocaust since
the floor was covered by a thick deposit of ash.[188]
Another possible bath-house has already been
mentioned, having been discovered in the excavation in the High Street in 1961–2. Elsewhere,
near the King's Head, the discovery of flue-tiles
carries a similar interpretation. Other major
buildings have been identified in the Northgate
area, where much painted plaster and fragments
of quarter-round mouldings have been recovered.[189] The buildings identified so far within
the town would imply a fairly dense distribution.

Although there are few indications of local
industries at Rochester itself, the town may well
have acted as the service centre for the potteries in
the Cliffe area to the north and those situated
downstream on both sides of the Medway estu-
ary. Best known, perhaps, are those at Upchurch,
on the right bank of the river below Rochester.[190]
The manufacture of pottery seems to have begun
there as early as AD 40 and continued at least until
the end of the second century. Another important
industrial activity carried on in the neighbourhood was the extraction of salt from sea water. A
band stretching along the south bank of the
Thames from Chalk to the Hoo peninsula, then
along the Medway marshes, and across the river
to the Isle of Sheppey seems to have been devoted
to this process. Large deposits of ash, burnt clay
and associated briquetage have been found in
numerous places along this coastal strip.[191] Salt
was an important item in the Roman economy,

over which some imperial control was probably exercised. It was not only used as a condiment, but was also the chief preservative of a large range of foodstuffs such as meat and fish, and in the preparation of skins and leather. If, indeed, production was under imperial control, then Rochester would have been the ideal centre for the administration.

Apart from cemeteries, little of religious significance has been found at Rochester. One large cemetery lay at Boley Hill outside the south gate, consisting chiefly of cremations, although a fragment of a decorated lead coffin has also been found there. A second cemetery has been identified at Borstal, about a mile south-west of the town near the river bank; it appears to have contained mainly inhumations, and the coins so far recovered would indicate a third- and fourth-century use.[192] Two other cemeteries, almost certainly connected with the town, existed across the river at Strood.[193] There is some evidence of ribbon development along Watling Street on the Strood side of the Medway, but this suburb was probably not large enough to account for the size of the cemeteries, which date from the middle of the first century until at least the third. Perhaps the oddest feature connected with the cemeteries is that no evidence has ever been found for one outside the East Gate. The ground outside this principal gate rises along Watling Street and it would seem a most suitable site for a large cemetery. A similar situation outside any other town would almost certainly have been used for such a purpose; it would seem, therefore, that there was some special reason, at present unknown, why this land was not so used at Rochester.

Lastly it is probable that Rochester acted as a service centre for the comparatively large number of villas situated in the surrounding countryside. The Darent valley, a short distance west of the town, contains several well-known examples such as Darent, Lullingstone and Farningham; others existed up the Medway valley in the Maidstone area. The contrast between the number of villas in the western half of the *civitas* of the Cantii and the comparative few in the east has long caused comment.[194] It is a phenomenon which is repeated at a number of other small towns such as Ilchester and Bath, but it cannot as yet be explained.

Water Newton (figs. 18 to 21)

Although Water Newton's remains attracted the attention of leading antiquarians from Camden to Stukeley, their full potential was not really appreciated until 1828, when Artis published copious illustrations of his 1820–7 excavations.[195] These revealed the industrial potential of the neighbourhood and a remarkable series of buildings ranging from simple workshops to elaborate private houses. By the early twentieth century, an impressive picture had been composed,[196] to which was soon added an important survey of the local road system and the fort near the Billing Brook.[197] Since then the most significant contribution has been made by aerial photography, such that we now possess a remarkably coherent record of the town's overall morphology.[198] These advances have not been accompanied, however, by any excavations within the defended enclosure, most work being confined to small areas in the extra-mural zones. This included rescue work south-east of the walled area[199] and the longer-term operations in Normangate Field north of the River Nene, most of which remain only in interim published form.[200] Just how little we know about the site's status and function is reinforced by recent spectacular discoveries, including the hoard of gold coins and the cache of Christian silverware.[201] Paradoxically, therefore, Water Newton is our clearest 'town plan', yet surprisingly little is known about its development through time.

The site has no obvious Iron-Age antecedents; more probably it originated as a civilian *vicus* outside the fort, which aerial photographs show as a multiple-ditched installation enclosing *c.* 2 ha (5 acres) on a gravel terrace north-west of the later defended nucleus and the Billing Brook.[202] It remains unexcavated, and therefore difficult to date, but it would logically belong in the pre-Flavian phase of consolidation, protecting an important river crossing on the main north-south line of communication, like the forts at Godmanchester and Great Casterton. At present there is no clear evidence for a pre-Flavian settlement associated with this site either north or south of the Billing Brook, though some of the later streets immediately outside the fort might perpetuate elements of an original *vicus*. This raises interesting questions, both about the layout of any early

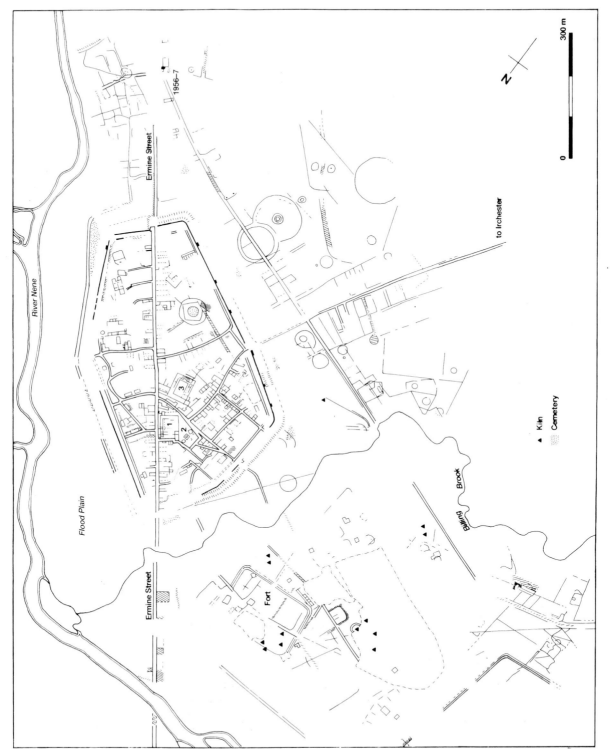

18 Water Newton, defended area south of the River
Nene (*after Mackreth*)

vicus and about its relationship with the later town where the morphology is apparently dependent upon the main road frontages and the associated side-streets. This was not the only military site in the vicinity, however; some 3.2 km (2 miles) down the river lay the vexillation fortress at Longthorpe, which, with its associated works depot and practice camps, is assigned to the period AD 47–62.[203] This was clearly a campaign base concerned with both east-west and north-south operations, but it does not seem to have been the focus for any civilian development.

The town's morphology can for convenience be considered in two sections, first the defended enclosure and the extra-mural suburbs south of the river (fig. 18), and second the extra-mural areas to the north and west (fig. 20). In its developed form, Water Newton is a classic case of increasing centralization leading to the creation of an irregular network of streets and lanes beyond the frontages of a main through-road. Its main axis was formed by Ermine Street, along which occupation stretched for *c.* 3 km (2 miles) on either side of the River Nene. Two sections across its line in Normangate Field, in 1961 and 1969,[204] showed it to be 7–8 m (23–26 ft) wide and up to 1.5 m (5 ft) high, reflecting the repeated resurfacings and repairs made necessary by heavy wear.

South of the river, above the flood plain, numerous side-streets and lanes run both obliquely and at right angles to the frontages, serving further densely occupied zones within the defended area which enclosed 18 ha (44 acres).[205] Unfortunately their relative chronology remains uncertain, but many are linked by cross-streets which perhaps suggest three or possibly four broad stages of growth: (1) The initial ribbon development along the Ermine Street frontages with only a few irregular side-lanes and possibly one large building (No. 1). This pattern occurs in second- and third-century contexts both at Kate's Cabin and in Normangate Field at the site's extremities,[206] and so probably began earlier within the defended area. (2) The extension of side-streets and lanes to serve land behind the frontages, and the provision of an 'inner ring road' linking some of them. This is most obvious east of Ermine Street, though there are traces to the west. (3) The construction of two more

regularly-shaped (planned?) *insulae* in the western part of the town, which might represent a separate stage if, as some photographs suggest, their principal axes originally extended beyond the defences. (4) The construction of the defences and the creation of an *intervallum* road connecting up an extended street layout. The two *insulae* may actually be contemporary with this, since they follow the line of the defences at this point. This would suggest that by the date of the walls, the interior was already well built-up; indeed excavations near the south-west gate showed the *intervallum* road to have been re-metalled six times indicating prolonged usage.[207]

Beyond the defended area, there are far fewer side-streets and lanes and occupation was concentrated along the main road frontages. Besides Ermine Street itself, a second road led south-westwards towards Irchester from a gap in the western defences, crossing in the process a further route which runs north-westwards from Ermine Street, roughly parallel with the enclosure, and heads off across the Billing Brook. Around the east side of the defences, a possible flood bank may also have doubled as a bypass road, though this is probably relatively late.

South of the River Nene, the pattern of intra- and extra-mural land-use and structural build-up is surprisingly clear, though there is little evidence upon which to base a discussion of its development. There are, however, considerable gaps in the visible building density, due to variable photographic conditions and the presence of unrecognized timber structures. At the centre of the defended enclosure lay two court-yard structures of uncertain function and a precinct housing several temple-like buildings.[208] One of the courtyard structures lay alongside Ermine Street (No. 1), with its other long side adjoining the precinct (No. 2) with which it may have been associated. Its larger counterpart (No. 3) lay at an oblique angle behind the buildings flanking the nearby frontages. Their locations might suggest that the former developed before the frontages were completely built up (though structures may have been cleared for it) while the latter had to use land behind them.

The intra-mural zone also contains other buildings, most of them relatively small and simple. Strip buildings of varying sizes are particularly prominent along the main frontages, some with additions to the rear, others with internal partitions, presumably providing the domestic and workshop accommodation for local craftsmen to judge from excavation in the suburbs. Few apparently have plots behind, perhaps indicating that their occupants were dependent upon specialized activities or farmed land elsewhere. Interspersed among these are at least three aisled buildings and several other rectangular structures running parallel to the frontages, some undivided, others with well-defined internal partitions; they usually lie along side-streets where pressure on land was probably less acute, and may represent a different class of structure socially or functionally.

Several apparently larger and more developed buildings lie at the ends of short side-lanes behind the main frontages. These are most evident at the south-eastern end of the enclosure and may be the wealthier houses noted by Artis, at least one of which had Alwalton marble slabs on its walls.[209] Such buildings suggest that some of the region's wealthier inhabitants resided within the town, which may have a bearing on the site's wider significance.

Outside the defences, interesting contrasts emerge in the extra-mural zones south of the river. Excavations during 1956–7 revealed extensive ribbon development along the road skirting the south-west side of the defences, close to its junction with Ermine Street.[210] Occupation began in the second century, being represented by pebbled spreads associated with several poorly recorded timber buildings, one of which contained ovens and hearths. By the third and fourth centuries at least eleven buildings lined the road, often separated by narrow side-streets or lanes. Five of these were fairly typical strip buildings, at least three with a room or cellar to the rear; two others were open walled enclosures; while there was also a possible shrine and a stone barn replacing a timber predecessor. They were associated with pits, ditches, ovens and hearths. Excavation in 1973 1 km (0.6 miles) to the south revealed further stone buildings fronting Ermine Street, though whether occupation was continuous between the two areas remains uncertain.[211]

Comparable buildings are also visible from the air north of the defences as far as the River Nene,

apart from the low-lying Billing Brook area. West of the walled area, the photographs reveal a complex of fenced or ditched compounds arranged end-on to the main road frontages and sometimes separated by short side-lanes. On the Irchester road, these are c. 25 m (81 ft) wide and extend over 100 m (327 ft) from the frontages; comparable plots line the cross-route parallel to the defences. No structures are traceable, so that their exact function is uncertain. North of the Billing Brook, further occupation including several side-streets flanked by buildings and numerous pottery kilns clearly overlies the redundant fort.[212] This material is largely undated, although it is clear that occupation along Ermine Street pre-dated the defences and continued with little or no change well into the fourth century.

North of the River Nene, aerial photographs and excavations have confirmed and extended Artis' work, demonstrating the presence of extensive extra-mural suburbs in Normangate Field (fig. 20). Ermine Street still formed the principal axis, lined by numerous strip buildings and associated kilns and pits, but various roads and streets branched eastwards from it, serving further densely occupied land.[213] Just north of the river, a main road branched north-north-east for c. 300 m (990 ft), with at least one prominent side-street, before swinging eastwards towards the Fen Road downstream. Its original alignment was roughly continued towards Castor, however, by a ditched trackway flanked by various enclosure boundaries. Further north along Ermine Street, another road branched northwards to follow the proposed alignment of King Street skirting the fen edge.

Within Normangate Field, additional side-streets and droveways can be seen following sinuous courses amid the crop-marks. One of the most obvious droveways, running roughly parallel with Ermine Street before turning eastwards at its northern end, was excavated between 1968 and 1973.[214] It was c. 5.5 m (18 ft) wide with traces of rough metalling surviving only in patches, with two side ditches 3 m (10 ft) wide and 1.8 m (5¾ ft) deep. Some 250 m (820 ft) to the north, another droveway running roughly north-south was examined in 1975;[215] this had originally consisted of fine gravel metalling set between shallow side ditches c. 1.3 m (4¼ ft) wide. These

19 Water Newton, the defended area south of the
River Nene looking north-west (*Cambridge
University Collection: copyright reserved*)

ditches were subsequently replaced by fences and
the road resurfaced with a spread of limestone
and river pebbles 7 m (23 ft) wide, later heavily
worn. These droveways formed the focus for a
wide range of agricultural and industrial
activities.

The development of this northern suburb is
better understood than its southern counterpart,
because enough small-scale excavation has taken
place to elaborate the information from the aerial
photographs.[216] Particularly interesting is the
system of ditched sub-rectangular land allotments visible alongside Ermine Street and the
associated streets and droveways and also located
by geophysical survey. These resemble the examples alongside the Irchester road, but here exca-

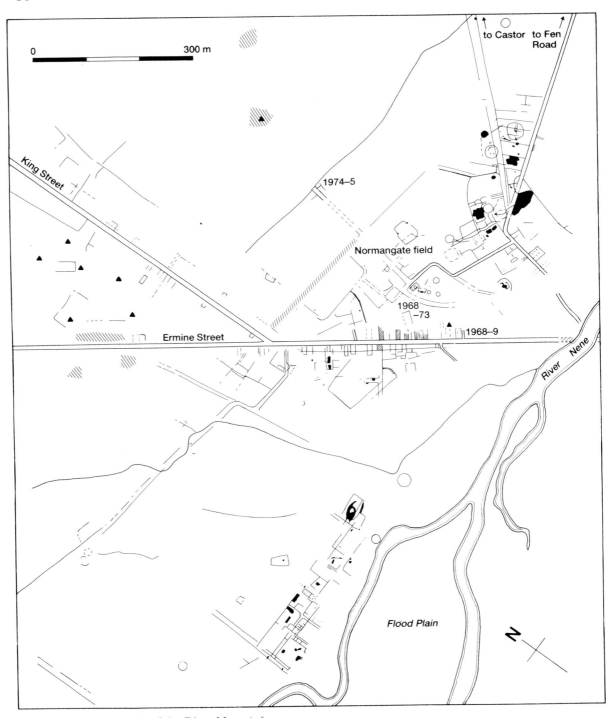

20 Water Newton, north of the River Nene (*after Mackreth*)

vations have clarified aspects of their chronology and function. Work at the north end of Normangate Field in 1974–5 dated the allotments here to the earlier second century at least,[217] thereby suggesting that land closer to the town centre must have been surveyed and allotted at this time or even earlier. This would argue for considerable community organization and official control of the division and leasing of land on the urban periphery.

The subsequent history of these properties varied somewhat. Those at the north end of Normangate Field remained essentially agricultural in character throughout the second century, after which they apparently went out of use.[218] A single plot of land c. 42 m (137½ ft) north-south by at least 18 m (59 ft) east-west containing a timber-built aisled barn, occupied the eastern side of the droveway, while on the west lay various shallow plots defined by post- and trench-built fence lines. Two of these, measuring 10 by at least 20 m (33 by 66 ft), and 6 by at least 16 m (20 by 52 ft) respectively, each contained a water hole, suggesting, in the absence of any recognizable buildings, their use as animal pens.

In contrast, the more commercially-attractive plots alongside Ermine Street soon attracted pottery production and then became built-up with strip buildings and workshops associated with various specialist activities, as Artis' excavations made clear. This sequence was confirmed by the 1968–9 excavation of an aisled workshop set end-on to Ermine Street and served by a metalled side-street 4.6 m (15 ft) wide along its southern side.[219] It had been erected in the second half of the second century to house a number of specialist kilns and furnaces, but clearly overlay the remains of earlier bonfire kilns and spreads of potters' clay. Initially many of the associated yards remained relatively open, but they gradually filled with furnaces, kilns and clay dumps, clearly reflecting increasing pressure on land. Most of the buildings lasted into the fourth century.

Excavations in 1969–73 along the eastern side of the droveway behind Ermine Street revealed a more complex picture, with a mid to late second-century encroachment onto hitherto open agricultural land by industrial concerns, represented by large areas of burnt sand covered by friable clay and wood ash.[220] These are interpreted as the remains of bonfire or clamp-type kilns, together with a few more substantial updraught examples. Then, surprisingly, this activity was superseded by buildings of very different, non-industrial, functions, including, from north to south, a circular structure replaced in the late third or early fourth century by an aisled barn, a rectangular shed later embellished with a portico and an internal apse, and two further circular buildings; opposite the latter to the west was a fourth-century *mausoleum*.[221] This marked change of land-use and the contrast with the Ermine Street frontages both indicate the level of potential complexity masked elsewhere by the absence of large-scale excavations.

Beyond these main extra-mural suburbs, it is difficult in some sectors to define a clear-cut dividing line between the town and the country-side. This is particularly true of the extensive areas involved with pottery production and iron-working, which merge into the estates of the surrounding villas. Many of these features were examined by Artis, though some have also benefited from recent fieldwork and excavation.[222] It has been demonstrated that the colour-coated pottery industries extended both upstream into the Sibson/Stibbington areas and downstream towards Stanground, in addition to the Billing Brook and Normangate Field sectors already mentioned. Iron-smelting was also carried out extensively to the west and north-west of the town, especially in the area of Bedford Purlieus. These areas are not strictly part of the town, though they were clearly important to its lifestyle and economy. Equally problematical are those villas within walking distance of the town at the rural-urban fringe. These include two large buildings in Water Newton parish to the west, the villa at Ailsworth north of the river and the courtyard house at Mill Hill to the east.[223] Even more imposing is the exceptionally large complex at Castor to the north-east, which has been variously identified as an official residence, a large villa and a rural sanctuary.[224]

Given the limited excavations at Water Newton, only a few buildings can be discussed in any detail. Of particular interest for the site's status and function are the two large buildings at the heart of the defended area.[225] The larger of the pair (No. 3) apparently comprised a courtyard measuring 36 by 22 m (117½ by 72 ft), surrounded

21 Normangate Field, Water Newton, looking
south-west. Elements of the street system and a
droveway, flanked by ditched enclosures, are
visible (*Cambridge University Collection:
copyright reserved*)

by rooms, though there are irregularities on the north. It must have been entered via a passage between other buildings. Its smaller counterpart (No. 1) is less distinct, but apparently involved a series of rooms arranged around one or two courtyards. Identifying their functions is difficult without excavation, suggestions including a *mansio* complex and a centre for the administration of the Fens respectively. The relationship between No. 1 and the temple precinct, however, is reminiscent of Godmanchester, suggesting that this is the *mansio*, while the larger structure might be tentatively identified as a market building or small forum complex, given the potential administrative status of the town; this would be unique among the small towns.

Of the remaining buildings, the circular and aisled varieties deserve closer attention. The 1969–73 Normangate Field excavations revealed three circular structures, the central one heavily robbed.[226] The northern example was 7.9 m (26 ft) in diameter with an unusual arrangement of limestone blocks ending in two post emplacements around its northern part and pitched stonework throughout the rest. At least three pitched stone supports along the inside may have supported engaged pilasters or a bench. Its southern counterpart, 9.1 m (29¾ ft) in diameter, had pitched limestone walls 0.8 m (2½ ft) wide and a central stone-packed post-hole supporting a timber superstructure and tiled roof. Inside was a red and white tessellated floor. All three dated to the third century, and were tentatively identified as shrines, as was the second phase of a nearby rectangular structure. This building, originally 13.4 by 6.1 m (44 by 20 ft), had a portico added on the west 1.4 m (4½ ft) wide incorporating an internal apse, a tessellated floor and painted walls.[227]

Three aisled buildings also came from Normangate Field.[228] The 1975 example was a simple post-built construction measuring *c.* 13 by 8 m (43 by 26 ft), though only its southern wall and aisles had survived later disturbance. The other two had pitched stone foundations, more normal for the area. The 1973 example replaced the northern of the three circular buildings already described, and measured *c.* 15.2 by 9.1 m (49 by 29¾ ft), with two rows of stone-packed post-holes. Its counterpart on Ermine Street was a two-phase structure, beginning life as a building measuring 25.9 by 13.1 m (84½ by 43 ft), with a shingled roof carried on two rows of massive posts 5.8 m (19 ft) apart. In the early third century it had been rebuilt with a new wall inside its robbed-out predecessor. It had functioned as a workshop throughout, in contrast with the other two which remained entirely agricultural.

Excavations at Water Newton have yielded little evidence about the settlement's everyday life apart from the industrial aspects already discussed, but there can be little doubt that it enjoyed a close relationship with the imperial estate in the Fens, by acting as a processing and marketing centre conveniently placed both for road and river transport. Unfortunately, little is known about the function of the numerous strip buildings within the defences, though examples examined in the suburbs may well be comparable. From south of the walled area comes evidence for metal-working, leather-working, and agricultural processing, represented by two millstones and a cache of cattle and horse bones, while from Normangate Field a single crucible with bronze droplets provides evidence for bronze-working.[229] In addition to these everyday activities, the suggestion of a fourth-century mosaic school based at Water Newton, coupled with the discovery of weights from a goldsmith's balance, hints at the presence of luxury trades.[230] More unusual activities are indicated by several moulds for forging coins of the Severan dynasty.[231]

The great bulk of the evidence from the town, however, concerns pottery production and iron-working. The earliest traces of pottery manufacture are found north of Billing Brook, where at least one late Flavian/early Trajanic kiln was producing calcite gritted wares, and in Normangate Field, represented by several second-century bonfire or clamp-type kilns.[232] These were superseded by more substantial updraught kilns which have been found right across the northern suburbs.[233] Evidence suggests that after an initial second-century surge of activity in Normangate Field, the number of kilns declined in the third and fourth, as manufacture gave way to other activities and moved further afield to more convenient locations. Iron-working is also attested in Normangate Field, principally by several probable furnaces in the aisled building alongside Ermine Street.[234]

Religious activities are not very well represented. The central temple complex (No. 2) has already been mentioned, but we know nothing of its chronology or its dedication. The aerial photographs suggest at least one Romano-Celtic temple alongside other circular or rectangular structures.[235] Numerous finds of statuettes include examples of Hercules, Ceres and Minerva, while a fragmentary inscription apparently dedicated to Mars was found west of the defences.[236] Less certain is the religious attribution of the three circular buildings in Normangate Field, despite their superficial resemblance to the circular tradition recognized at Brigstock and Collyweston. The apparent absence of conclusive religious finds might indeed suggest a purely secular domestic role.

Most interesting is the Water Newton treasure discovered in 1975 in the south-east of the defended enclosure.[237] It included 28 objects, many with obvious Christian implications. Besides cups and bowls with *chi-rho* symbols and apparently Christian inscriptions, several leaf-shaped plaques recall native Celtic votive objects, clearly transformed and Christianized by the incorporation of a *chi-rho* emblem. Such interaction between traditions is of special interest and it is most unfortunate that so little is known about the hoard's original findspot. Its exact interpretation remains debatable, but it can plausibly be seen as the more valuable possessions, perhaps the church plate, of a fourth-century Christian community focused on the town.[238]

Water Newton's defences enclose *c.* 18 ha (44 acres); this is comparable with Caerwent and larger than Caistor-by-Norwich and Carmarthen, all civitas capitals. They have been well known since the eighteenth century, when Stukeley recorded a stone wall fronted by a ditch 15 m (49 ft) wide.[239] This has been sectioned only once, on the south-west, revealing an apparently single-phase wall on a drystone foundation, backed by a clay bank, itself overlain by the *intervallum* road.[240] Doubts have been cast on this interpretation, but insufficient evidence is available to reassess it in terms of the more typical two-phase sequence. The second-century pottery sealed by the bank suggests a later second- or early third-century construction date, though this clearly requires confirmation elsewhere.

Three gates are visible, all unexcavated, two related to Ermine Street and the third to the Irchester road on the south-west.[241] The south-western and south-eastern examples were apparently staggered slightly, accounting for the odd diversion of Ermine Street on the south-east. Rectangular towers, also unexcavated, appear fairly evenly spaced along the exterior of the wall on at least two sides, but their relationship to the wall remains unknown. Such defences are clearly of urban-core type, designed to enclose a large part of the occupied area south of the river, including the official buildings. The very size of the defences emphasizes the local wealth available when compared with other large and small towns in the province.

Not surprisingly, given its apparent importance, Water Newton's status has been much discussed. The site has long been identified with the *Durobrivae* of the Antonine Itinerary and the Ravenna Cosmography, and its name is further recorded on several *mortarium* stamps.[242] One of these carries the legend *Cunoarus Fecit/Vico Durobrivis*, recording its manufacture at the *vicus* at *Durobrivae*, which is one of the rare instances in Roman Britain where epigraphy attests a site's status. It remains unclear, however, whether this relates to the whole community at *Durobrivae* or merely one ward within the town. The exact meaning of the word in relation to the status of the early civitas capitals is also still unresolved, but it is at least clear that we are dealing with a unit which enjoyed some measure of self-government.[243] Further evidence comes from a milestone found in 1785 in the ditch near the north-west gate, though it had probably been moved from its original location.[244] It had originally been erected in AD 276 in the reign of Florian, and records that it stood *M(ille) P(assuum) I* (i.e. one Roman mile) from its official point of measurement. It is usually accepted that such milestones were measured from civitas capitals or cities, suggesting that by the AD 270s Water Newton had achieved this rank and was responsible for the local government of its hinterland. Such an upgrading process is not unknown in the late Roman West,[245] and there are good archaeological grounds to support its occurrence at Water Newton, not least its increasing size and importance. This is reflected in the presence of possible public and official buildings forming an obvious urban focus, the recognition of several wealthy suburban villas and possible intra-mural houses, whose owners could have formed the core of the local council, and the provision of an extensive internal street network and of urban-core defences, all coupled with the obvious agricultural and industrial potential of its hinterland. Taken cumulatively, this archaeological evidence sets Water Newton apart from all the other minor towns studied in this volume.

There is little recent information about the town's cemeteries.[246] One clearly lay south of the road near the north-west gate, where Stukeley recorded urn burials and Artis noted stone coffins. Another lay outside the south-east corner, where Artis excavated several inhumations. The principal cemetery area, however, appears to have been that discovered during turnpike road construction in 1739 to the south and south-west. The finds included several urns and glass vessels as well as stone and lead coffins; some graves had even cut through the counterscarp bank of the town's ditch, suggesting prolonged usage. In 1754, further burials were discovered during the rebuilding of Kate's Cabin at the southern edge of the extra-mural area. Another large inhumation cemetery has also been recorded from scattered finds on the fringes of Normangate Field.[247] Several possible rectangular and circular *mausolea* have been noted alongside the Irchester road, but remain unexcavated.[248] They probably resemble the fourth-century example excavated alongside the droveway in Normangate Field, with rough stone footings enclosing four burials, one containing a pair of gold earrings, a silver brooch and bronze bracelets.[249] Lastly in the southern suburb several infant burials were found alongside the timber predecessor of the stone barn (p. 84).[250] Clearly Water Newton had a range of burial traditions which would benefit from modern excavation and research.

The fourth-century history of the town is somewhat unclear on current evidence, especially inside the defences, but some clues are available for the extra-mural zones. Within the southern suburb, many of the 1956–7 structures were apparently disused by the second half of the century, their footings being robbed out or cut by a new ditch alongside Ermine Street.[251] All this suggests contraction in this sector, although coins from the house of Theodosius attest casual occupation until the end of the century at least. The concentration of inhumation cemeteries close to the defences also suggests contraction, though several presumably earlier cremation urns from the same areas might counsel caution.

Occupation in Normangate Field also continued well into the fourth century. The droveways and drainage ditches were clearly well maintained throughout and began to silt up only during the currency of late colour-coated wares and coins of the house of Valentinian.[252] Buildings clearly fell gradually into disrepair, while the fourth-century *mausoleum* points to a shift in emphasis in at least one area. More importantly, few coins of the house of Theodosius have been recorded, indicating a fairly rapid end to the occupation. Further north, alongside the droveway excavated in 1975, the plots were actually vacant during the entire fourth century, suggesting changes here from an even earlier date.[253] Cumulatively this evidence points to later fourth-century decline in the extra-mural zones, but this is unlikely to be true of the defended area. The 1974 discovery of the Water Newton hoard,[254] a cache of 30 gold coins of the period AD 330–50, taken alongside the important fourth-century school of mosaicists,[255] clearly indicate continued wealth at the site, about which all too little is known.

The site's fifth-century history remains poorly known, though presumably neither its postulated administrative status nor its manufacturing capacity could have survived long once Roman authority lapsed and the roads became insecure. There can be no doubt that the countryside remained relatively productive, but we know little about how this influenced the fate of the town, principally because the relevant archaeological levels lie inside the defences where extensive plough damage in the past and the lack of systematic excavation combine to present a rather bleak picture.

SEVEN
MINOR TOWNS I

Alcester (figs. 22 and 23)

The extensive settlement at Alcester lies close to the confluence of the Rivers Alne and Arrow at a point where Ryknild Street, running between Wall and Bourton-on-the-Water, crosses the road from Droitwich to Tiddington. It has been identified as the *Alauna* of the Ravenna list[1] by Rivet and Smith,[2] although Richmond and Crawford earlier assigned this name to Alchester,[3] which in some ways makes better sense, since its neighbours quoted in the list would indicate that it lies on the road from Silchester to the south Midlands; nevertheless the derivation of the name of the River Alne from *Alauna*, and hence the name of the town on or near that river, is an attractive argument in favour of Rivet and Smith.

A fort has been identified by aerial photography on higher ground a little distance southeast of the later town.[4] It could be as early as the Claudian period, and it has the typical widely-spaced ditches of that period. At a later date, however, the fort was probably moved to lower ground and so closer to the site of the future town; two pieces of cavalry equipment from the Bleachfield Road area plus a few Claudian coins and some slight remains of early timber-framed buildings, might be thought to support this view. Apart from these fragments, though, the site of the town and its immediate suburbs have scarcely produced sufficient evidence to support the idea of a fort here before the Flavian period,[5] which, in view of the general military situation in the west Midlands at that time, would be unlikely.

Although a good deal of excavation has taken place at Alcester, especially in the south-western suburb around Birch Abbey, very little has received full publication.[6] Excavations in the fortified area of the town have always been difficult owing to the presence of modern buildings, but with new developments taking place, they have at last become feasible; even now, though, the line of the defences is still imperfectly known. A point worthy of comment is that the settlement grew up mostly in the north-east quadrant of the main road junction; the western boundary seems to have been along Ryknild Street, since a large cemetery was situated immediately across it. An area of marsh northwest of the fortified area, with peat formation taking place in Roman times, probably inhibited the construction of a through road to the town from that direction. Alcester therefore resembles a minority of other small towns which lie beside rather than athwart main roads, such as Dorn (p. 253). A complicated and often-changing irregular system of streets grew up around these main roads in the settlement area; most is known about those in the southern suburbs, for which the main road from Tiddington formed an axis, parallel to and south of the modern Stratford Road. Nevertheless changes must have occurred even in this route, for, during the fourth century, it was partly built over. One main street, set roughly at right angles, ran north and south from it; its northern arm, possibly Flavian in date, aimed at the southern end of the modern High Street where the south gate of the fortified centre was probably later established; a slight shift towards the west in its alignment in the late second century may have coincided with the construction of the first defences. The southern arm aimed towards the floodplain of the River Arrow, and was constructed in the middle of the second century.[7] Another street, also running approximately north-south, lay between it and Ryknild Street; the branch north of the Tiddington road

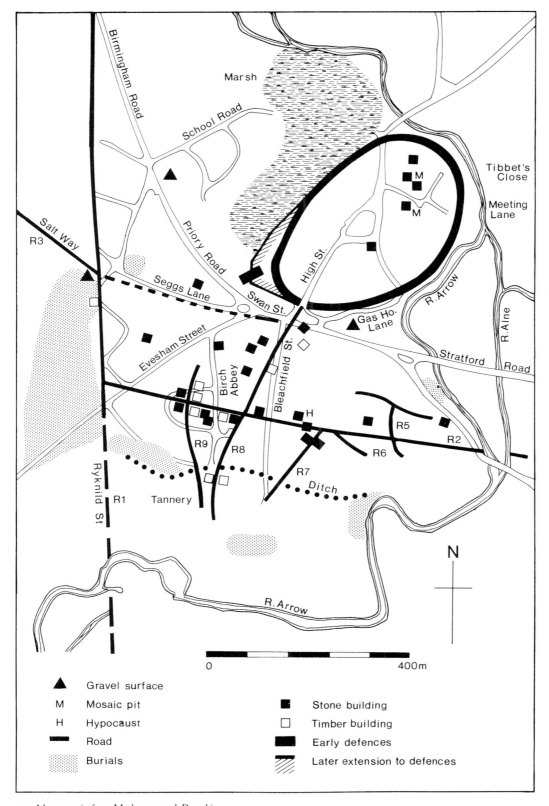

Legend:

▲ Gravel surface
M Mosaic pit
H Hypocaust
▬ Road
Burials

■ Stone building
□ Timber building
◼ Early defences
▨ Later extension to defences

22 Alcester (*after Mahany and Booth*)

23 Alcester, looking east at the Birch Abbey area (*Cambridge University Collection, Crown Copyright*)

was laid out late in the first century, but its continuation southwards was not constructed until the mid third century. At its southern end it turned sharply eastwards to cross the street described above, and possibly to link with yet another running south-west from the Tiddington road; it has been suggested that the latter was constructed as a short cut to Ryknild Street and skirted the southern suburb. Several other minor, and apparently random, streets were also found in this area when flood prevention works were carried out in 1970.[8] The somewhat cavalier way in which many of the internal streets were treated is illustrated by one which was found east of Bleachfield Street.[9] Dating to the later first century, it later provided a foundation for at least one substantial masonry building.

The defences of the enclosed area of the town have been identified on the north, east and south-west sides only. It would seem that on the north-west side, where they are still sought, the marshy area of ground formed a natural limit to their position. A section across the north-eastern side of the town near Gunnings Bridge revealed a clay bank, dated to the late second century, which was earlier than the masonry wall constructed in front of it.[10] The wall was 2.7 m (9 ft) wide and rested on a piled foundation. No ditch was observed here, presumably because the steep slope down to the River Alne rendered it unnecessary. A similar sequence is reported from the eastern side, in Malt Mill Lane, although no published information is available. On the south-western part of the circuit though, the line of the later wall departs from that of the early bank, here made of clay and gravel, and assumes an outer course. A ditch fronted the early bank at this point, while the piled foundation for the wall was here 3.8 m ($12\frac{1}{2}$ ft) wide. An early fourth-century building had been demolished to make way for the wall, thus providing an approximate date for its construction.[11] Alcester must be, therefore, almost the only town in Roman Britain where the later circuit of fortifications enclosed a greater area than that of its predecessor. The reason is probably not hard to seek. This quarter of the town appears to have contained buildings of quality which ran right up to and even over the defences of the late second century. Even then, despite the more generous line adopted by the wall in the fourth century, at least one major building had to be destroyed. Presumably an even more westerly line was ruled out by the presence of the marsh. In these same excavations a square external tower was also examined; it was thought to have been added to the wall at a later date. But with a date of construction for the wall extending well into the fourth century, and a date now being assigned for the general run of external towers somewhat earlier than that previously postulated in the Theodosian reconstruction of British towns and cities, it is difficult to avoid the conclusion that both may be contemporary. The wall at this point was recorded as robbed, and it is not easy to distinguish building phases when this has happened. Nothing is yet known of the gates of the town, although the position of the south gate can be inferred from the lines of the streets.

Alcester appears to have contained a number of buildings of quality, both inside and outside the fortifications. The structure which was destroyed by the construction of the town wall contained a row of some ten rooms; the walls were about 1 m ($3\frac{1}{4}$ ft) thick, and the structure had been roofed with limestone slates.[12] The surviving floors, though, were of clay, which might imply that there had once been plank floors above them. Also inside the defences in Tibbet's Close was a sequence of timber-framed buildings, with another masonry building nearby.[13] At least two mosaics have been recorded in the same area; mosaics are generally rare in small towns, and consequently these have considerable significance. Outside the walled area, a house built on a disused road (p. 94) began as an aisled structure but later had a corridor and two wings added to it. Two rooms had concrete floors, while a third, with a pebble floor, contained piles of charred grain; quantities of painted wall plaster were also recovered.[14] Another building, not far from the postulated south gate, had floors and walls of clay, except for the north end where the floor edge was marked by sandstone blocks. This may have been an open-ended shop with timber uprights based on the blocks, so providing both support for the gable end and a frame into which wooden shutters could be fitted when the shop was closed (see Catterick, p. 114).[15] One of the most interesting extra-mural buildings was uncovered in the Birch Abbey excavations. It was founded on horizontal timber beams and divided into at least four bays with a length in excess of 21 m (69 ft); the floor was of timber laid on shallow joists. It was associated with large waterlogged pits which contained leather offcuts, dung and other organic residues. Dated to the second half of the second century, it seems to have been a tannery and leather workshop, and is not only one of the few reliable instances yet found for this industry, but is also one of the few industries attested at Alcester.[16] Another masonry building was partly uncovered near the junction of the Tiddington road with the 'bypass' road (p. 94); one room contained a hypocaust, and a stamped tile was also found,[17] indicating perhaps a tilery in the neighbourhood. Numerous other fragments of buildings, many of barn-like or shop-like forms, have been discovered in the suburbs, representing almost the entire Roman period from the late first century onwards. There are also some ditched enclosures which obviously represent property boundaries; of most interest in this respect is a slightly meandering ditch, which appears to have acted as a southern limit for the suburb in the middle of the third century.[18] Some of the buildings were connected with small-scale metal-working,[19] including smithing, and one at least was decorated with painted plaster which included architectural motifs. A large pit containing over 50 unbroken mid-Antonine samian vessels might well be taken to indicate a pottery shop nearby.[20] Another trade is attested by the discovery of an *amphora* on which a black dipinto reads SCO FLOS SCOM[BRI], or 'prime extract of mackerel'.[21]

Almost every excavation which has been conducted in the area bounded by the River Alne on the east and north-east, the marsh on the north and north-west, Ryknild Street on the west and the boundary ditch on the south has produced evidence, however slight, for structures of one sort or another, and it is clear that the whole town was several times the size of the walled area. As observed above, the quality of some of the buildings is also better than that to be observed in many small towns, in which mosaics in particular are rare. This would seem to mark Alcester as something apart from the general category, and it is worth noting that the site lies almost equidistant, as the crow flies, from the major cities of Wroxeter, Leicester, Gloucester and Cirencester. It must therefore be situated not far from the junction of the three *civitates* of Cornovii, Corieltavi and Dobunni. Topographically it also enjoys a favoured position on a spur of ground which divides the Severn from the Avon valleys, and close to the fertile land in the Vale of Evesham. Yet this area is almost entirely devoid of villas. That being so, it might be argued that Alcester enjoyed an importance, above that of most small towns, for the rural area around it, providing not only its goods and services, but also the accommodation and ancillary buildings for the farmers of the neighbourhood. Thus it may have become the physical centre as well as the service centre for a considerable area of prime agricultural land near the junction of three units of local administration. It cannot therefore have failed to become an important centre in its own right after the administrative changes introduced in the

fourth century and it may have been promoted to the rank of civitas capital, although there is no evidence for the *civitas* over which it would have ruled. A Constantinian milestone, found re-used in a late fourth-century foundation, indicates road-works in the area at that time.[22]

The only area which seems to have been devoid of buildings almost throughout the Roman period lay near the main centre of occupation in Birch Abbey and Evesham Street. Up to 12 superimposed cobble and gravel surfaces were encountered,[23] and it was suggested by the excavators that the area was an open market. It thus resembles the open gravelled spaces in the centres of several small towns, among them Catterick (p. 114) and Godmanchester (p. 126), which, as well as Alcester, most likely functioned as markets for both local and itinerant traders.

Unfortunately, despite the widespread excavations at Alcester, little has been found which can be related to religious practices. Indeed the only recorded deity is Epona, the Celtic horse goddess, whose name had been scratched on the shoulder of a jar found in a pit in the Birch Abbey area.[24] This presumably implies that the contents had been consigned as an offering to the goddess, whose shrine or temple may have been nearby. 'Horsey' attributes associated with a small temple at Wroxeter might suggest that the goddess had a following in the Cornovian region.[25]

The sites of several cemeteries are known. The largest so far identified lies west of Ryknild Street, emphasizing the fact that the road may once have acted as a settlement boundary. Over 100 burials have been recorded here; one appears to have had a stone coffin, while other graves were lined with stones.[26] The cemetery as a whole would seem to be late Roman. A second-century cremation cemetery has been uncovered south of the defended area in Swan Street; it was claimed to have been receiving additional burials as late as the third and fourth centuries, when it must have lain within the built-up area.[27] Another, presumably later, inhumation cemetery lay in and around the southern boundary ditch at its Ryknild Street end.[28] Possibly even later, two burials have been recorded from Coulter's Garage just outside the south side of the defences;[29] these may be contemporary with the interment of a young girl who had been beheaded and ten infant burials in the garden of Lloyds Bank.[30]

There is very little evidence for the end of Roman Alcester. Some of the later structures, especially some timber buildings which had replaced masonry, may belong to the early fifth century, as indeed may some of the burials mentioned above, but there is no positive evidence in favour of such a date.

Alchester (figs. 24 to 26)

Alchester was first described in detail in 1724, when Stukeley noted its defences, the line of the north-south road and an artificial mound known as Castle Hill.[31] Surface irregularities in the meadows north and east of the defences were also interpreted as extra-mural buildings. Since then much has been lost, not least with the levelling of the presumed extra-mural suburbs and the robbing of the Castle Hill area for stone c. 1800, despite the recognition of its potential by Penrose in 1766.[32] The defended enclosure, which now lies within two fields, has also been extensively damaged, the northern field having been ploughed over many years, while its southern counterpart still retains traces of pronounced ridge and furrow. Against such a background of destruction, archaeological research has been restricted to limited investigations in the defended area in the nineteenth century[33] and to various small-scale excavations in the twentieth century. Investigations of the 1920s examined several internal buildings and the defences;[34] the 1974 sections clarified the defensive sequence[35] and the 1937 and 1983 campaigns sampled the supposed northern suburbs.[36] Inevitably therefore, our understanding of the site's urban morphology and history is somewhat sketchy, though aerial photography has added some valuable details.[37]

The site apparently lay c. 300 m (990 ft) south of the junction of two main Roman roads, one running north-south between Dorchester and Towcester, the other, Akeman Street, east-west between Cirencester and Verulamium. The former served as the town's central axis. A section in 1926,[38] immediately north of the centre, showed it to be c. 4.6 m (15 ft) wide with four or five re-metallings and a clay-lined ditch to its east, apparently belonging to the earliest phase of activity on the site. North of the town, it probably swung eastwards, along the line of the modern lane up to its junction with Akeman Street. This latter was sectioned west of the junction in 1937,[39] near Chesterton Lane, and shown to be c. 5.8 m (19 ft) wide with a ditch at least on the south. No dating evidence was recovered. East of the junction it probably followed the double line of trees straight to the river crossing. No satisfactory explanation has been advanced to account for the siting of the town away from this junction.

The morphology of the town is dominated by a central crossroads, formed by the Towcester-Dorchester road and an east-west street, which may have extended east as a link road to Akeman Street along Langford Lane up to Graven Hill. No corresponding extension west of the defences has been traced towards Castle Hill. To the south, a further east-west street is suggested by a parch mark across the southern of the two fields, though this requires confirmation by excavation.[40] Together these streets form a rudimentary street grid, comprising up to six regularly-shaped *insulae* around which the defences were constructed. Such apparently co-ordinated planning is rare among the small towns.

Not only is the site oddly located in relation to the major road crossing but it is also generally low-lying and liable to flooding. This is of interest for the origins and early development of the town, because there is no clear evidence for any pre-Roman activity. Excavations in the lowest levels (except for a gravel knoll at the town centre) have consistently hit the water table, and demonstrated that drainage of the site was a high priority in the early Roman period. Along the line of the eastern defences, in the 1920s, various ditches with associated gravel dumping were interpreted as an early defensive sequence;[41] their real function was identified in 1974 with the excavation of two drainage ditches of varying dimensions apparently traceable over c. 230 m (752 ft) from the north-eastern angle, parallel to the later defences.[42] These ditches had accumulated a black waterlogged silt, clearly indicating wet conditions and standing water. To their west, a sterile gravel layer indicated tipping to raise the ground level. Material from these ditch silts and associated levels indicated a mid first-century origin, with a later first-century infilling, and further levelling up in the early second century. A series of ditches was also excavated in 1937, north

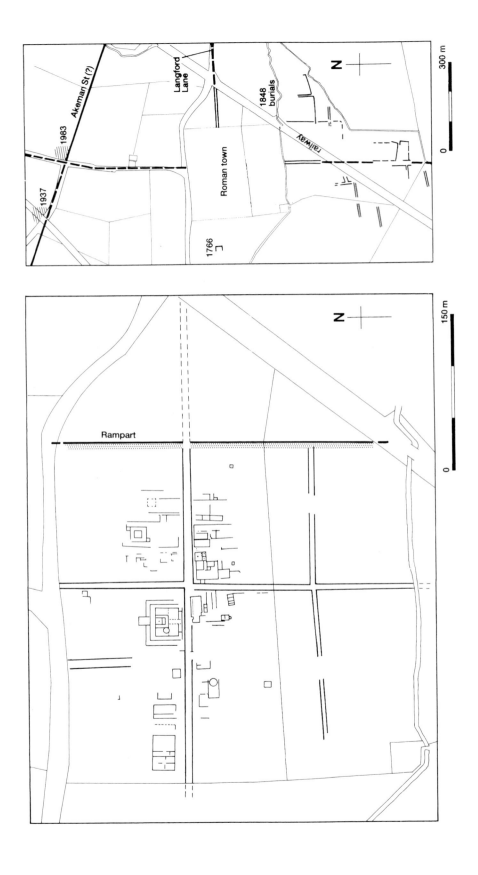

Akeman St (?)

1983

1937

Langford
Lane

1848
burials

railway

Roman town

1766

N

0   300 m

Rampart

N

0   150 m

24 (left) Alchester (*after Rowley and Mudd*)

25 (above) Alchester, looking east. The principal crossroads lie at the centre (*Cambridge University Collection: copyright reserved*)

of the line of Akeman Street;[43] some were probably property boundaries, though others closely parallel the 1984 sequence of frequently re-cut east-west ditches on the Faccenda Chicken Farm site.[44] Many had a consistent sequence of fills over a sticky grey clay, indicative of wet conditions. These ditches dated to the first and

second centuries, followed by a series of court-yards or cobbled spreads on the Chesterton Lane site and a layer of grey silt sand on the Faccenda site, perhaps indicating seasonal inundations. Iron-Age material from the 1937 excavations might indicate pre-Roman occupation, but more than likely it was the Roman period which saw a

26 Alchester, looking north along the main north-
south road. Both the crossroads and the internal
buildings are plainly visible (*C. Stanley*)

concerted attempt to intensify exploitation of the landscape surrounding the developing town. If so, the third-century decline on the north clearly requires further consideration.[45]

The levelling up of the drainage ditches on the east also involved a turfy deposit mixed with much charcoal and gravel.[46] From this came Flavian finds, which are clearly residual because they overlie layers containing later first-century material. This turfy deposit may have come from the levelling of a nearby military rampart, which might account for the quantities of mid first-century native and samian pottery, found alongside the probable remains of wattle-and-daub buildings in the earliest levels of the 1920s excavations.[47] Unfortunately too few convincing military finds came from these levels to postulate a military origin for the town,[48] though this might explain its location to the south of the obvious crossroads and the early interest in drainage.

The town's subsequent development is much more difficult to reconstruct, given the limitations of previous excavations. Indeed few buildings have been examined, and none to modern standards. The first recorded was the 'excavation' in 1766 of the Castle Hill building west of the main town centre, where a mosaic and hypocaust suggested a bath-house or private residence.[49] A second structure was examined in both 1850 and 1892 in the north-west corner of the central crossroads,[50] and shown to comprise a gravel quadrangle with a corridor to north, east and west and outer walls supported by shallow pilaster buttresses. An *opus signinum* floor and a room incorporating a stone-lined well on its northern side have suggested a religious function for this building, though it might also be a market-place.

Several buildings were also examined in the 1920s. One of second-century date was partly excavated just inside the north-east defences, and shown to comprise two rooms with mortar floors and a probable stone-paved corridor on the south.[51] It had apparently been destroyed by fire, perhaps as a prelude to the construction of the defences. Other stone buildings were also excavated in the north-east angle of the crossroads, though again only partial plans were recovered.[52] That to the west was a three-roomed structure with successive mortar and earth floors, built over the remains of its timber predecessors. It

originated in the second century and apparently survived into the fourth. Its eastern counterpart comprised at least two rooms, later replaced by a rectangular building in use in the fourth century. For the remainder of the site we have to depend upon aerial photography, which reveals numerous buildings regularly laid out along the main east-west street.[53] These include fairly typical strip buildings and several possible metalled yards, but occasionally somewhat larger buildings are visible, including what appears to be a large Romano-Celtic temple in a courtyard north-east of the crossroads. Air photographs taken in 1926[54] also indicate a rectangular building south-east of the railway, but no trace is now visible. Little can thus be said about the site's structural history, though it is interesting to note the replacement of timber by stone from the second century onwards.[55]

Alchester's defences, which probably enclose a roughly square area c. 10.5 ha (26 acres) in extent, were first investigated in 1892,[56] revealing a bank fronted by a rubble wall. Further work was undertaken in the 1920s, and again in 1974, when the sequence across the eastern defences was clarified.[57] Here they comprised a single-phase bank and ditch roughly following the line of the earlier drainage ditches. The wall was c. 2.5 m (8 ft) wide with pitched limestone slabs surviving three courses high, fronting a 6 m (20 ft) wide rampart of dumped sand and gravel, at the back of which there may have been a timber revetment. In front lay a shallow ditch 7 m (23 ft) wide, which was recut once, as fourth-century material in the fill clearly demonstrated. From the evidence of the samian and coarse wares included in the bank, these defences cannot be earlier than the late second century. Such a contemporary bank and wall is unusual alongside the more normal sequence known for Romano-British towns. Reconciling this evidence with that found in the 1920s has not always proved easy.[58] The 1927 work was clearly undertaken near the east gate, revealing at a surprising depth the pitched slab foundations of a wall 5.8 m (19 ft) wide; at its southern end, and immediately to the rear, a mass of solid rubble concrete on a stone foundation rested against the inner face. Although the superimposed stratigraphy is somewhat unclear, it is likely that the superstructure had been extensively robbed. Such substantial foundations may simply reflect the character of the surrounding ill-drained subsoil, close to the presumed site of the main east gate, while the internal rubble structure might be part of one of its towers. The 1928 examination of the north-east angle apparently located an angle tower comprising a massive stone footing, but the details are very unclear. If correctly identified, it would support the tradition, recorded by Stukeley, of four towers defending the town.

In the absence of large-scale excavations, our knowledge of Alchester's economic role is minimal. Many buildings along the streets no doubt functioned as workshops, but little has survived to identify the trades involved. One interesting find in 1926 from the three-roomed building near the centre was a bronze weight inscribed with a I on top and with CAES.AUG on one side,[59] apparently conforming to the Roman standard and perhaps indicating the maintenance of official weights and measures. Religious activity is also poorly known, with the possible exception of the building excavated north-west of the crossroads and the apparent Romano-Celtic temple already mentioned. Small finds from the site include a fragment of a white clay statuette found in the nineteenth century.[60]

Little attention has been directed at the extra-mural suburbs, despite antiquarian references which suggest they were extensive.[61] No structures were recovered in the 1937 or 1984 excavations north of Akeman Street, though most of the foundations visible in 1841 were actually south of this point. Cemetery evidence, of potential relevance to the extent of occupation, is also badly represented at Alchester, except for one unprovenanced glass cremation urn and the 28 skeletons discovered south-east of the town in 1848.[62] Though orientated east-west, their Roman date remains unproven in the absence of associated grave goods.

The end of the Roman town is difficult to reconstruct given the disturbed nature of the latest archaeological levels. In contrast with Dorchester-on-Thames (p. 121), however, there is a distinct shortage of any characteristic Saxon material from the site despite the fact that the coin list and the pottery suggest continued occupation into the early fifth century at least.[63] Decline, once it came, apparently set in relatively quickly before the Saxon presence made itself felt.

Braughing (figs. 27–9)

Braughing's potential was not fully appreciated until this century, despite the nineteenth-century discovery of finds in the vicinity of the railway station. Instead early antiquarians had focused on a site on Larks Hill, north of the River Rib, where Roman remains had reputedly been found.[64] Such uncertainty was finally dispelled in 1949 by the recognition of a street system on Wickham Hill and the partial excavation of a large stone building.[65] Subsequent investigations also clarified the local road network.[66] Our detailed understanding of the town's morphology and development depend, however, upon a series of excavations undertaken in advance of road-works and other redevelopment schemes from the late 1960s onwards.[67] Unfortunately, with one exception, none of these sampled the crucial settlement nucleus at the north end of the Hill; instead they were directed at areas peripheral to the main occupation, identifying extensive Iron-Age occupation, as well as several cemeteries, an isolated bath-house and various buildings fronting Ermine Street north of its junction with Stane Street. Thus we are better informed about the crucial late Iron-Age/early post-conquest period than we are about the development of the urban core, its street systems and its major buildings, all of which hint at an important urban complex, but one which, as yet, has produced no evidence for any defensive provision.[68]

Virtually all the main sections have produced evidence for late Iron-Age occupation, attesting not just its extent but also its importance. The earliest occupation was apparently focused east of the River Rib in the Gatesbury Wood area, where abundant finds were collected between 1935 and the late 1950s.[69] These included mid to late Iron-Age pottery, various imported wares and numerous moulds apparently used for making flans for silver coinage. This activity might have been centred originally on the 3 ha (7.5 acre) univallate enclosure on Gatesbury itself, although the site has never been systematically excavated. The pottery from other sites makes it clear, however, that occupation soon expanded westwards down into the valley and onto the narrow ridge of Wickham Hill, though not all the areas were necessarily occupied simultaneously or continuously. While it remains difficult to define the

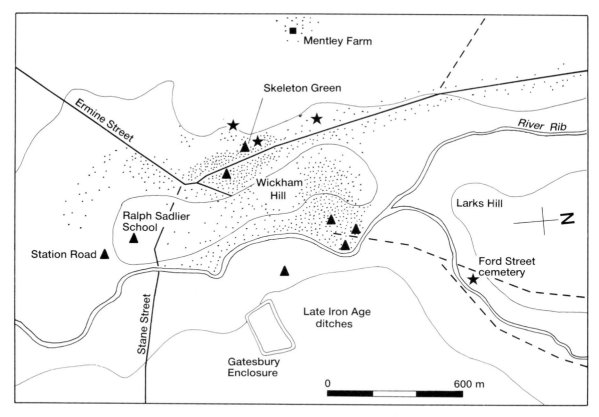

27 Braughing, late Iron-Age findspots and the Roman road network (*after Partridge*)

Key

——————— Roman Roads Known

– – – – –   „   „   Assumed

★   Roman cemeteries

▓   Finds of Roman Pottery

■   Villa

▲   Finds of pre-conquest material

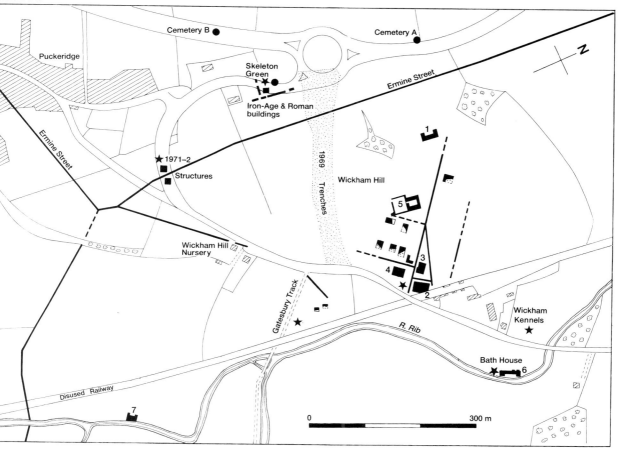

28 Braughing (*after Partridge*)

Key

— Roman roads known

- - - „ „ assumed

Roman buildings

Modern „

● Roman cemeteries

★ Late Iron Age Finds

29 Braughing, looking north. Both the line of
Ermine Street and the link road to Wickham Hill
are plainly visible in the centre foreground
(*Cambridge University Collection, Crown
Copyright*)

settlement's extent at any one point in time, the
recovery of large quantities of imported wares,
including   Gallo-Belgic   pottery,   flagons,
amphorae, *mortaria* and samian, has been vital to
the establishment of a detailed chronology.

Particularly important finds were made in the
1971–2 excavations at Skeleton Green, associated
with several successive rectangular timber buildings, some of which had been burnt down.[70]
Occupation had clearly begun *c*. 15 BC and
continued through to the Roman conquest with a

short hiatus during the AD 20s and early 30s. Another timber structure was identified in the earliest levels on Wickham Hill in 1949,[71] suggesting the possibility that occupation originally extended right across the later town site. That it extended north-east and south-east has been demonstrated on three separate sites. During the 1969–73 bath-house excavation, several pits and two dwellings were located, dating to c. AD 25–45.[72] Much the same date range was recorded at the nearby Wickham Kennels site in 1982 where various ditches and pits were associated with industrial waste, largely from metal-working.[73] To the south-east, however, the 1979 finds from near the Gatesbury Track revealed earlier occupation, apparently from c. 30–25 BC to the early first century AD.[74] Both the latter sites produced several coin moulds connected with the manufacture of gold, silver and bronze issues. Occupation also extended south-west to the later Roman road junction and even as far as the south end of Wickham Hill, where excavations in 1973 (Ralph Sadlier School)[75] and 1975–6 (Station Road)[76] revealed early activity – the former down to c. 10 BC with few or no imported Gallo-Belgic wares, the latter from the early first century AD into the Roman period. Less easily datable material has been found at several other points, while aerial photography has recorded a series of ditches and enclosures of probable Iron-Age date.[77] All this evidence attests the apparent extent of the site and its relatively rapid expansion, while the quantity and quality of the imports and the range of Iron-Age coins (several of continental origin) demonstrate its trading contacts. The coin moulds and metal-working debris also suggest a broader specialist role. Much remains uncertain, however, about the site's political status, but such a centre could hardly have been ignored when the Romans arrived.

Iron-Age Braughing must have been the focus for several trackways, linking it to neighbouring settlements. Not surprisingly, these were soon improved after the conquest, contemporary with the construction of Ermine Street as a new north-south route. These upgraded roads form the backbone of the new site, alongside the developments at the north-east end of Wickham Hill.[78] Ermine Street and Stane Street are of primary importance, creating a road junction west of the Hill and south of the main nucleus. Ermine Street approached this junction from the south-west, at which point it turned sharply northwards to follow a dry valley along the western side of Wickham Hill. Excavations, most notably in 1971–2,[79] revealed a primary cobbled surface 5.9 m (19 ft) wide, overlain by a road 10.1 m (33 ft) wide following a phase of mid first-century flooding. Two phases were also identified in 1970 at Pumps Mead,[80] though both were somewhat wider; they pre-dated a sand layer on the eastern frontage, itself cut by a pit containing late first-century material. Stane Street's course over its last 2 km (1.2 miles) has only recently been clarified, following an east-west line along existing field boundaries as far as the River Rib, where it swung slightly north-westwards towards the junction. Various sections along its course have revealed a hard-packed gravel surface which is curiously insubstantial in places. This might suggest that east-west traffic between Colchester and St Alban's followed a bypass road on a more southerly line, avoiding the town itself.

North of the junction, a side-street branched north-eastwards, though its line remains uncertain after the first 150 m (490 ft). A section in 1960–1[81] revealed a gravel surface 6.1 m (20 ft) wide with considerable signs of wear; further excavation by the Wickham Hill Nursery, near where the road is lost, sectioned two surfaces apparently on slightly different lines.[82] One was dated to the mid first century, the other was laid in the later first or early second century, apparently following a period of disuse. This side-street might have served the Wickham Hill nucleus, but could equally have linked up with the proposed routes heading north-eastwards towards Cambridge and Great Chesterford. These are poorly known, but are thought to converge upon the River Quin, south of Larks Hill, close to the Fordstreet cemetery; beyond here a single road headed for the River Rib close to the crossing of the modern B1368. Its side ditch was probably located in 1982[83] just west of the modern road on the Wickham Kennels site, whence it is a short distance to the side-street and the Ermine Street/Stane Street junction. How this proposed alignment related to the internal street network on Wickham Hill remains unknown. One further road approached from the north-west from Baldock, though its exact route has not proved easy to trace. It has been thought to align on Wickham Hill, but it could equally have joined Ermine Street further north. None of these roads can be securely dated, though the ditch on the Wickham Kennels site produced first- to third-century material.

Air photographs and limited excavations have revealed traces of an apparently planned internal street network at the north end of Wickham Hill, closely associated with several substantial stone buildings.[84] At no point can this be related, however, to the main roads discussed above. Excavation in 1949[85] sectioned the main east-west street, revealing a substantial build-up of road levels 0.9 m (3 ft) thick, the earliest of which was of flint and mortar construction, with a side-street at right angles. Claudio-Neronian finds from the associated roadside ditch suggest an early origin for both, though the side-street soon went out of use, being overlain by a pre-Flavian timber building. In the Flavian period, the main street was relaid, contemporary with the erection of a major stone building along its northern frontage and the demolition of the timber structure. This evidence, if repeated elsewhere on the Hill, might indicate an early Roman layout, replaced and modified in the Flavian era when the first large buildings were constructed. Possible traces of planning were also recorded at Skeleton Green,[86] where a road ran parallel to Ermine Street, with at least one secondary side-street at right angles. All this implies a very rapidly established and coherent urban plan, presumably rationalizing the existing Iron-Age occupation; this pattern of continuity and change clearly requires closer attention.

These internal developments were also accompanied by early Roman buildings, as for example at Skeleton Green, where the new streets served a series of timber buildings, which began life soon after AD 43 and apparently continued in use into the early AD 60s.[87] It has been suggested that the latter served official functions because of their early date, but the associated evidence is inconclusive. Early buildings are also attested on Wickham Hill, with both the L-shaped building near the railway station and the bath-house in the bend of the River Rib apparently originating in the Flavian period.[88] Surprisingly, however, few traces of early buildings were located north of the Ermine Street/Stane Street junction, alongside the new Ermine Street frontages.[89] The extent of this early Roman occupation and its subsequent development cannot be defined precisely, but the broad outlines at least can be established. On the north, the marshy ground on either side of the River Rib restricted occupation, while the river itself formed a natural boundary on the east, contrasting with the site's Iron-Age predecessor; to the west, occupation petered out beyond the Ermine Street frontages, where several first- to third-century cemeteries have been located; on the south, Stane Street probably provided a convenient boundary because no Roman occupation was located overlying the Iron-Age levels in 1973 or 1975–6 on the south side of Wickham Hill. Within these broad limits, occupation clearly varied in its intensity and character throughout the Roman period, but insufficient evidence is available to define more than localized trends.

One interesting sequence is provided by the 1971–2 excavations alongside Ermine Street.[90] Here the limited first-century occupation was succeeded, on both sides of the road, by much more intensive activity in the second century. This included several timber buildings which were clearly associated with commercial activities. These were replaced in their turn in the third century by further structures which encroached onto the road metalling. Behind them, at a distance of 35 m (114 ft), ran a fence defining their associated yards. Occupation here continued into the fourth century. Further north on Skeleton Green, in contrast, the short-lived, post-conquest occupation was succeeded, after a short interval, by a cremation cemetery[91] extending from the late first into the early third century; several later inhumations were also buried here. Elsewhere the story is less well defined. Limited work in the central area on Wickham Hill indicates prolonged usage from the late Iron Age onwards, with intense fourth-century occupation in the area of the main nucleus.[92] Trenches in 1969, however, across the ridge south of this, revealed a continuous spread of second-century material.[93] Such trends need clarification to define the nature and extent of the occupation at different stages in the life of the town.

A surprising amount is known about the range of buildings at Braughing, which includes a variety of domestic and workshop structures as well as several large masonry buildings. Considerable importance attaches to the late Iron-Age structures excavated at Skeleton Green.[94] They were all basically rectangular, with timber superstructures set into short beam slots or large post-holes surrounding floors of flint cobbles, rammed chalk or beaten earth. The latest and most substantial (No. VII) is fairly typical, and had been divided into two not quite equal parts, that on the west apparently being open on its south side where it was approached by a cobbled path. Equally interesting at Skeleton Green are the post-conquest structures alongside the two streets.[95] They were of sill-beam construction, with their main timbers resting directly on levelled flint and gravel platforms; apparently they had planked floors and thatched roofs. Their doorways were indicated either by areas of worn gravel, or by interconnected pathways leading in from the side-street. These structures have left little evidence for their function. Not so the buildings already mentioned alongside Ermine Street, which are distinguished by their commercial associations. No doubt such buildings were originally more extensive.

The presence of several large masonry buildings clearly distinguishes Braughing from most small towns, though only the bath-house (No.6) and the central L-shaped building of uncertain function (No.2) have been examined in any detail. The bath-house (see fig.5E) was apparently constructed c. AD 70–90,[96] because it incorporated *tegulae mammatae* rather than box-tiles, which became the norm in the later first century. It had flint and mortar foundations laid on a levelled platform cut into the natural chalk. These supported flint walls with tile bonding courses, faced internally with tufa blocks, presumably for insulation. It measured c. 22 by 4.5 m (72 by 15 ft) and comprised originally a range of three rooms with a furnace and stoke-hole on the north and a small rectangular room to the east. Later the wooden lean-to around the stoke-hole was replaced by a walled enclosure. Internally it had plastered and painted walls and *opus signinum* floors, those in the heated rooms supported by tile *pilae*. The baths lay apart from the settlement nucleus on Wickham Hill, immediately adjacent to the river, which may have encroached since Roman times. Fragmentary evidence suggests that it went out of use in the early to mid second century, after which it was robbed, first for the

roof tiles and later for the walling and hypocaust systems. Such an early demise is difficult to explain, as is the building's status because it seems too small for a public baths and is unattached to any official or private structure.

The central building, which is visible from the air, was first excavated in 1949 and re-examined in 1970.[97] It was L-shaped, measuring c. 35.4 m (114 ft) long by 18–21 m (59–69 ft) wide, built of limestone blocks set on a flint and mortar foundation, with a well-worn entrance and a veranda fronting the main east-west street. Pottery indicates that it too was constructed c. AD 75–85. Despite minor second- and third-century modifications, it retained its basic design well into the fourth century, hinting at an official function which is otherwise unknown. It has been variously interpreted as a temple complex and a market-place. Regardless of this problem, considerable significance attaches to the demonstrable Flavian date of these two large and imposing buildings, recalling the contemporary urban expansion at Verulamium and the parallel development of the temple compound at Harlow (p. 186).

Other substantial stone buildings are visible on aerial photographs, but their date and function remain uncertain.[98] At the west end of the Wickham Hill nucleus lay a winged-corridor house (No.1) apparently facing Ermine Street and suggesting at least one wealthy resident. To the south-east, roughly on the same alignment, there was a large double courtyard structure measuring c. 65 by 35 m (212½ by 114 ft) (No.5). This might have been a market building or a *mansio*, either of which would add significantly to our understanding of the site's development and status. Further large buildings are recognizable at the heart of the street nucleus (Nos. 3–4), but their plans remain ill-defined, while south-east of Wickham Hill, at least one more building is known next to the river (No. 7); its construction parallels that of the bath-house, but this is insufficient to presume a similar function without excavation.

These public buildings/large stone structures clearly attest a level of urban pretension alongside the apparent evidence for early planning and obviously indicate a site where defences might have been expected. Somewhat surprisingly, therefore, Braughing has failed to produce any convincing evidence for a defended circuit, thus making it a significant exception to recognizable trends. The reasons for this can only be guessed at, but if the evidence from the bath-house were repeated elsewhere it might hint at second-century stagnation in the face of competition from the better established site at Verulamium. Several wealthy Antonine burials in the Skeleton Green cemetery should warn against too much speculation, however.[99]

Despite Braughing's relative importance as an urban centre, little evidence has been forthcoming about its economic potential because of the rather limited and peripheral nature of most excavations. The site was certainly important in the Iron Age, judging from the metal-working evidence discovered on the Wickham Kennels site, and from the coin moulds also recorded here and elsewhere.[100] For the Roman period, nothing is known from the Wickham Hill nucleus, but there is evidence for iron-, bronze- and bone-working from the second- to third-century buildings alongside Ermine Street.[101] Such a commercial focus is hardly surprising and perhaps suggests that the earlier timber buildings were performing similar economic roles, even if characteristic debris is lacking. The town's inhabitants may also have been involved in the manufacture of pottery and tiles at Bromley Hall Farm, c. 3 km (2 miles) to the south-east, which flourished in the third and fourth centuries.[102] Equally little is known about the site's religious life, since the central L-shaped building cannot be conclusively identified as a temple complex. Elsewhere, evidence is confined to several small portable objects including two pipe-clay figures, one from a burial, and a probable lead curse, though its four lines of text have not proved to be decipherable.[103]

One feature of special interest at Braughing has been the examination of several cremation cemeteries in varying levels of detail. Most lie west of Ermine Street, except for the Fordstreet cemetery north of the River Quin at the possible junction of the Cambridge and Great Chesterford roads; this latter is poorly known and has not been subject to recent excavations.[104] The smallest cemetery (A) lay c. 200 m (650 ft) north of Skeleton Green and comprised only five burials, three of first-century and two of the mid to late second-century date, all with a range of grave

goods; a ditch on the south probably represents its original boundary marker.[105] A second cemetery (B) lay c. 100 m (327 ft) south-west of Skeleton Green, where despite the damage done during redevelopment, some 104 burials were recovered, apparently poorer than their northern counterparts and generally later in date; interestingly the second-century burials were generally located at the southern end of the excavated area, whereas the third- and early fourth-century examples were grouped at the north. The most interesting cemetery, however, was that excavated at Skeleton Green,[106] comprising 54 cremations and 5 late inhumations. In the late first to early second century the cemetery comprised a horseshoe-shaped enclosure apparently open on the south; this was subsequently enlarged in the early to mid second century, with a new bank and ditch enclosing extra land to the north. In its latest phase in the mid to late second century, the northern and eastern ditches were enlarged and an entrance provided on the north; part of the north-western corner was also separated off by a short ditch segment to accommodate an exclusive, richer, Antonine group of cremations. Most of the burials comprised a large urn containing the ashes and at least three or more associated vessels, but a distinctive group contained a wooden casket with elaborate hinges and locks. Several late inhumations were subsequently inserted into this cemetery, disturbing the earlier cremations. They were probably part of a more extensive late cemetery to the south, judging from the worn cobbled tracks which led in that direction.

Evidence for late Roman occupation at the site and its fifth-century survival is currently limited. Fourth-century occupation was certainly intense, not just along the Ermine Street frontages north of the Stane Street junction but also on the Wickham Hill nucleus, although excavation has shown that the L-shaped building had fallen into decay in the mid to late fourth century, and that a spread of earth and fourth-century material had accumulated across the uppermost surface of the main east-west street.[107] Likewise the fourth-century building debris from outside the main building suggests demolition in or near the settlement's core, but without excavation neither the extent nor character of these changes can be defined. Fourth-century coins are nevertheless abundant and include issues of Honorius and Arcadius, suggesting that activity continued into the fifth century in some guise, but as with so many sites, the archaeological evidence now fails us. We have no idea how long occupation was maintained and there is no certain Anglo-Saxon material from the site finds, let alone the cemeteries. There is at least the suspicion that a gradual contraction and decline was already underway in the fourth century, but what happened after this clearly requires urgent attention.

Catterick (figs. 30 and 31)

The small town and its extensive suburbs at Catterick are situated on Dere Street, the road which runs from York to Corbridge and beyond, where it crosses the River Swale. It is to be identified with the *Cataractonium* of Ptolemy,[108] the Antonine Itinerary[109] and the Ravenna Cosmography,[110] and lies within the *civitas* of the Brigantes. It has also been tentatively identified as the site of the battle of Catraeth, supposedly the last battle between the Britons and the Anglo-Saxons towards the end of the sixth century.[111]

The nearest major Iron-Age site lies at Stanwick some 12 km (7 miles) further north, where, it has been claimed, the Brigantian ruler Venutius made his last stand against Petillius Cerialis in AD 70 or 71.[112] More recent excavations, though, have cast doubt on some of Wheeler's interpretations.[113] But in 1969 an Iron-Age farmstead was excavated only a short distance south of the walled town near the racecourse.[114]

The walled site at Catterick has been known since at least the late eighteenth century and is recorded by Camden.[115] Before that, though, Cade had made some observations on the site,[116] while MacLaughlan surveyed the surviving walls and south gate in the middle of the nineteenth century.[117] Then also Sir William Lawson uncovered and restored part of the eastern wall on the racecourse. In 1939, prompted by plans for a proposed bypass for Catterick Village and Bridge, Hildyard and Wade initiated a series of excavations,[118] which were suspended by the advent of the Second World War. After the war, a number of excellent aerial photographs taken by St Joseph in 1949 showed outlines of walls,

streets and buildings, from which it became clear that the site was an unusually-shaped walled town and not a fort as had hitherto been supposed.[119] These photographs enabled Hildyard to undertake further excavations in 1952, when he identified a small building near the centre.[120] Since then three major campaigns of excavation have taken place, both inside and outside the town walls, in 1958–9,[121] 1972,[122] and 1981–2,[123] while a considerable number of smaller investigations have occurred spasmodically, mainly outside the walls.[124] The bypass, when it was finally constructed in 1958–60, cut a great swathe from north to south through the entire Roman site, which was observed to stretch from the southern end of Catterick Village almost continuously to the northern roundabout, where the bypass rejoins the old line of the Great North Road, a distance of some 4 km (3 miles), with the walled town forming only a small nucleus on the south bank of the River Swale.

The town owed its inception to the auxiliary fort which was constructed on the high ground at Thornborough Farm, looking north across the river, probably under Agricola. The outline of this fort, or a later version of it, was retained when the town was walled; it shows as a rectangular projection, of approximately the correct area for such a fort, on the west side of the town. Despite the supposed campaigns of Cerialis in the area, no trace of them has ever been found on the ground, and two small camps nearby are far too small to have accommodated his army.[125] The Agricolan fort seems to have possessed an annexe on its east side, in which a bath-house was situated, and where, in the following two or three decades, large quantities of organic waste, probably from a tannery, were dumped. In 1989, a writing tablet from Vindolanda was found by Dr Bowman to contain a reference to a delivery of hides from Catterick in the late second century. This must surely indicate the continuance of this activity beyond this date. There were also signs of metal-working, but whether of a civilian or military nature cannot be shown.

This first fort seems to have been abandoned *c.* AD 120, in line with many garrisons in Yorkshire, although a new military base was established north of the river *c.* AD 130; it would appear to have been a bridgehead defence constructed during a possible Brigantian rebellion.[126] Also

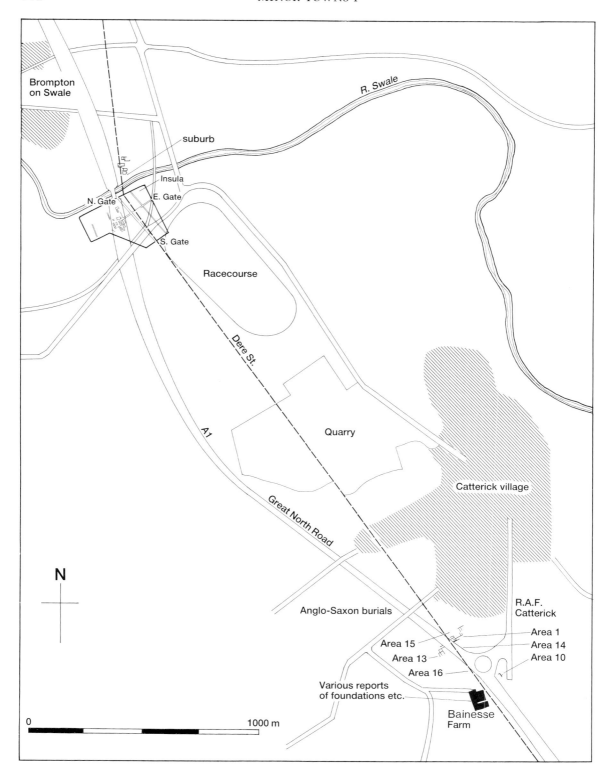

30 (left) Catterick (*after Wacher and Wilson*)

31 (above) Catterick, looking north before the construction of the bypass; the racecourse lies at bottom right (*Cambridge University Collection, Crown Copyright*)

during this period, a *mansio* was built south of the river close to the west edge of Dere Street; the fort bath-house was re-used and it was enlarged and rebuilt. Apart from the *mansio* there was little indication of other activity south of the river, where Hadrianic-Antonine material is generally scarce. But by the AD 160s, the fort to the north had been evacuated, and full-scale reoccupation of the south bank had been resumed. It was then that the first signs of a *vicus*, east of the fort and south of the *mansio*, began to appear. Its earliest buildings seem to have been flimsy wooden shops constructed over the midden, which had been sealed with a thick layer of clay, on the south side

of the street which led from Dere Street to the presumed east gate of the fort. An enclosure, surrounded by a stone wall, was also constructed in the south-western angle of these two streets. Its purpose is uncertain but it may have been a *temenos*. A temple somewhere in the vicinity is implied by the four altars which have come from the general area; one was found within the enclosure.

The *mansio* covered nearly 0.5 ha (1.2 acres) of ground, and consisted of two main groups of rooms set behind a veranda which faced across the river. A small internal courtyard contained an ornamental fountain,[127] while each group of rooms was provided with its own water supply, as was the reconstructed bath-house. The main entrance, contained within a small columned portico, faced south across an open gravelled area, to the street leading to the fort. A Jupiter column with ornate figured capital appears to have stood near the centre of this area.[128] The bath-house was set slightly askew to the layout of the *mansio*, since it followed the outlines of its predecessor, which had been terraced into the hillside; it contained three heated rooms, a hot bath, a cold room and a large plunge bath, a changing room and a small, square sweating room. Of considerable interest was the recovery during the excavations of one complete and one fragmentary iron beam, which had originally supported the hot water boiler over the stoke-hole.[129]

An extension to the *mansio* was built across the gravelled area at a slightly later date, and enclosed the original entrance portico which was in part destroyed. It was very well constructed, with a masonry drain running outside the eastern wall; buttresses were set across this drain, to give the wall added strength. The floor, which had been replaced several times, was made of stout flag-stones. When, towards the end of the second or early in the third century, the *mansio* was demolished, the only part to survive was this later addition, which was adapted to stand on its own. The *mansio* had been originally constructed by a COH VIIII, almost certainly of *Legio VI* from York.[130] Hence an official function is in no doubt and it must surely have been transferred to the only part of the whole building which survived the demolition. The wide front door and the care and solidity with which it had been constructed might suggest that it was a warehouse, perhaps even a granary, for the storage of taxes collected in kind. The site of the levelled *mansio* remained vacant and was not built on until almost the end of the Roman occupation, although at one stage a water pipe crossed it. This suggests strongly that the land remained in imperial ownership for most, if not all, this time and had not been sold.

The third and fourth centuries saw not only the development of a prosperous *vicus* but also the expansion of suburbs some distance from the fort. It is not yet known precisely when the latter was finally evacuated, although it would be reasonable to assume that it occurred before the fort area was enclosed within the town defences. These fortifications were probably built in the early fourth century, since they were constructed in the late Roman manner, with only a single wide ditch and no rampart behind the masonry wall. There are reasons, though, to suppose that a much more substantial wall had been planned, since the massive cobble foundations were nearly 4 m (13 ft) wide as compared with the 2.3 m ($7\frac{1}{2}$ ft) thickness of the superstructure. Neither internal nor external towers have yet been discovered, and the positions of north, south and east gates can only be inferred from the aerial photographs, while the existence of a west gate is still in doubt. These same photographs show a fairly regular street grid, which, in its subsidiary members, probably dates to the same period as the defences. Dere Street changes direction at the crossing of the Swale, where excavations on the north bank attempted, but failed, to find a bridge abutment. Nevertheless, the crossing of the river, whose fickle behaviour can raise its level by several metres in as many minutes, would almost certainly have required a bridge. North of the river, the road remained narrow for a time at the site of the north gate of the bridgehead fort, while in the fourth century buildings encroached on its east side.

The town was fortunate in inheriting the aqueduct which had at first supplied the fort and later the *mansio* and its baths. The source of the aqueduct probably lay to the west, most likely on Colburn Beck, a tributary of the Swale, where by means of a dam a sufficient head of water could have been impounded to provide a gravity flow to the fort. A distribution point somewhere on the high ground under Thornborough Farm is indicated by the direction of flow of all the subsidiary channels in the *mansio* and town. One channel, cut in contiguous blocks of stone, was inserted to run beside the main east-west street, crossing over from the north side to the south. It was intended to serve the civilian population since it fed a square, stone-built tank, situated outside a shop on the south side of the street, with the overflow escaping down the street.

As is to be expected, most of the buildings, first in the *vicus* and then in the town, were open-fronted shops and workshops. One such building had four large rectangular blocks of stone set in a line across the front. Rebates in the upper surfaces of the blocks showed where vertical posts had stood, presumably to support the front gable of the premises; slots cut in the blocks behind these rebates would indicate the positions of wooden shutters used to close the open front. This same shop also had a back door at the end of a short passage, which passed by two living rooms, one heated by a hypocaust, the other with a decent concrete floor and painted plaster on the walls. Another shop, of a slightly earlier period, had belonged to a coppersmith who had been engaged in the manufacture and sale of fine enamelled bronzes. Similar buildings occurred in the northern suburb over the river and as far south as Catterick Village; ordinary domestic houses were scarcer. The small building excavated by Hildyard just north of the main east-west street may be an example. Another, slightly more elaborate in plan (Building VII, 3), with a complicated history of reconstruction, was built around a small inner courtyard and possessed at least one heated room.

The early fourth century also saw an attempt to rebuild the derelict *mansio* baths, but on a less ambitious scale, presumably for use by the townspeople. The heated end, except for the outside wall of the furnace room, had been demolished to lower floor level and was now replaced by three small hot rooms only half the width of their predecessors. A new cold room was constructed to the west of the retained changing room; the plunge bath of the *mansio* period was also retained. But these efforts came to nought. No attempt was made to insert either wall-jackets or suspended floors; it was not roofed, and for a time the shell ended up as a convenient rubbish tip.

Some interesting developments took place probably *c*. AD 370, when a number of existing shops and domestic buildings seem to have been converted to other uses. All the open ends of the shops were blocked and Building VII, 3 was united with VII, 10; two small hypocausts were inserted into VII, 5, so small that they may have been intended for drying corn. Buildings VII, 5 and VII, 6 were united at the front and at the rear with VII, 3 to form a small L-shaped courtyard, which was entered through a grand, arched main gate, with a small wicket beside it. Other buildings, some with deep cobble foundations, some with only rows of stone blocks, were also con-

structed, mainly in the long-vacant area of the *mansio*. The shell of the unfinished bath-house was provided with massive stone floors, placed on top of the accumulated rubbish. The open front of a shop (Building VI, 8) down a side-street was closed by an apse. A marked change in materials of construction from pink sandstone to hard white limestone was observed; the standards of masonry also fell.

The alterations were associated with a collection of military equipment: three spearheads, a lance head, two barbed javelins and three spurs; the latter are rare finds in Britain.[131] Catterick has also produced zoomorphic buckles[132] of a type which has been ascribed to the equipment of soldiers in the late Roman army, or more improbably to *laeti* or *gentiles*. All would seem to point to the stationing of an army unit, probably cavalry, at Catterick during the Theodosian reorganization of Britain's defences. Buildings VII, 5 and 6 could be said roughly to resemble a *principia*, while Buildings VII, 3 and 10 are not unlike a *praetorium*; others take on the guise of barracks. The most likely explanation is that a unit of the comitatensian field army was billeted at Catterick in the late fourth century. Civilians may have been expelled in the process, which may have led in turn to considerable activity in the suburb over the river in the last half of the fourth century.

Despite the extent of the excavations little evidence has been accumulated for industrial activity. Only one workshop can be positively identified; this was the property of the coppersmith mentioned above. His shop contained a timber-lined wastebin into which all turnings, filings and chips of metal were swept so that metal could be separated from dross and recovered. A unique find was a pear-shaped, enamelled perfume flask, very similar to one from Nijmegen (the Netherlands). Traces of other metal-working have, though, been found as far south as Bainesse Farm. Another interesting find suggests that Catterick was a centre for the manufacture of querns. Several flat sandstone rough-outs had the positions for the circumference and central hole marked on them but they had never been completed because the stones broke, presumably during preparation. Apart from the bath-house, very little brick or tile was used anywhere on the site; abundant nearby stone supplied almost all building needs. Similarly, with main centres for the manufacture of pottery not far distant, no need was felt for local production. As already mentioned (p. 111), tanning may have been an important activity connected with the Agricolan-Trajanic fort; there is some slight evidence, in the form of very large, deep pits dating to the mid second century and situated beyond the later town wall to the south, that tanning was still being carried on at a later date. This would match the information from the Vindolanda tablet.

At least one temple has been identified in the northern suburb, while a suggestion for another, within a large *temenos* inside the walls, has been mentioned above (p. 113). The temple north of the river was set well back from the eastern edge of Dere Street and may have been associated with a small D-shaped building immediately to its south. The latter could be interpreted as a small theatre in which religious performances could take place. The temple itself was trapezoid in shape with two walls projecting outward from the front, probably enclosing a porticoed entrance. A great deal of late fourth-century pottery, mostly complete but crushed vessels, was recovered from this area; it included lamp-chimneys, ornamented with red-painted figures, *tazze*, a small oil lamp in the form of a duck, a vessel with a moulded figure of Mercury, and half of a life-size face mask in colour-coated ware. Although provided with loops and holes, possibly for attachment to the face, it is not unlike an *oscillum*, a ritual mask hung from a sacred tree or building to spin in the wind, probably to scare away evil spirits.

Four altars have been found at Catterick, but, apart from the information which two provide on the presence of Roman officials (see Chapter 4), they add little to the religious knowledge of the site. One, now lost,[133] invokes a nameless deity 'who devised roads and paths' and must surely refer to road-works in the vicinity in AD 191. A second[134] mentions a goddess Suria, while a third,[135] also lost, refers to Vheteris, usually considered to be the same deity as Veteris, Vitris or Huitris, and found only in northern Britain; a German origin is sometimes considered probable, and the name might be interpreted as 'the old gods'. A fourth altar,[136] dedicated to the Mother Goddesses of the Home, was found in the excavations of 1959, within the *temenos* and only a

short distance inside the south wall of the town. The only other inscribed stone of religious importance was found built into the outer wall of the fourth-century bath-house. It was a block on which a roughly carved *chi-rho* monogram[137] had been inscribed; it must almost certainly have come from another context, since its meaning and significance had been lost on the mason, who placed the stone on its side. Of a grimmer character altogether was the finding of the body of a new-born baby set in the foundations of Building VI, 8. A necklet of six phallic charms, once strung on a leather strap, accompanied it. Foundation offerings of this kind are not unknown in Roman Britain, although they are more normally found associated with temples.[138]

Small cemeteries have been found to the north-east and south of the walled town. A cremation in a glass bottle found by a mechanical excavator within the town area probably belongs to the period of the fort. Two tombstones had been re-used in inverted positions as door-sills in the early fourth-century bath-house; one commemorated Similinia Vera,[139] the other[140] had been too badly mutilated for names to survive, but would seem to have come from a large and splendidly-sculptured memorial.

One of the most interesting aspects of the site at Catterick is its survival as a Roman town and settlement, which must have lasted well into the fifth century. The best example to take to illustrate this survival is Building VI, 8, which had been altered in the last decades of the fourth century, along with other buildings in Insula VII, when an apse was added to the open west end. This apsidal building remained in use long enough for occupation material to collect on its floors, after which it fell into decay, with soil accumulating round its walls and over its floor until little or no visible remains can have shown above the ground. Then, and only then, a new building was constructed on the same site, but with its walls aligned differently and now built entirely of timber with individual posts set in the ground or on flat blocks of stone. The time which elapsed between the construction of the apsidal building and this timber-framed house would seem to be long enough for the latter to be safely attributed to the fifth century, even though no direct dating evidence was found. But this was not the only house to show these easily-distinguished structural features; several were found in Insula III, with fragments of others elsewhere. It would appear that a substantial Romano-British settlement still existed at Catterick, sheltered by its massive walls, at least in the first part of the fifth century; only five sherds of Anglo-Saxon pottery were found in the area excavated within the walls.

This contrasts strongly with evidence from north of the river, where an Anglo-Saxon *gruben-haus* had been dug through the paving of the possible theatre; it contained much domestic pottery and also a large fragment of a *buckelurn* of Sancton type,[141] which dates the dwelling to the fifth century. But that was not all. Anglian burials have been uncovered around Catterick Village, on the RAF base, where burials of this period were found inserted into the ruins of a Roman building[142] and at Bainesse Farm.[143] Further burials, with swords, spears and shield bosses were found immediately outside the south wall of the town, which gives some credence to the claim that Catterick was the site of the battle of Catraeth.[144] But it is clear that Anglo-Saxon immigrants had reached the site long before the battle and had settled in the vicinity of the town, whereas the later settlement (post-battle?) seems to have migrated to Catterick Village.

Dorchester-on-Thames (fig. 32)

The small town of Dorchester lay beside the west bank of the River Thame close to its junction with the River Thames and on the main road which ran north from Silchester and on to Alchester and Towcester. Bede[145] refers to the town as Dorcic, from which the name Dorocina was manufactured by the sham Richard of Cirencester. The correct name is not known for certain, although the *Tamese* of the Ravenna list[146] was applied by Richmond and Crawford to the town, or, more probably, to the site of the nearby Thames ferry.[147] The site has been recognized as Roman at least since Horsley's time.[148] A certain amount of limited excavation has taken place, mainly within the walled area. The western defences were explored in 1935–6[149] and further examined, together with the south side and some of the interior, in 1962–4.[150] An unsuccessful attempt was made to locate the eastern fortifications in

1972,[151] and the north-west corner of the town was explored in the same year.[152]

There is clear evidence at Dorchester of Iron-Age precursors. The promontory fort on Dyke Hills is a short distance south-west of the town,[153] and the hillfort on Castle Hill, Wittenham Clumps, lies across the River Thames, about 1 km (0.6 miles) to the south-west. The Dyke Hills fort has sometimes been interpreted as a Belgic *oppidum*.[154] Excavations in the town have also produced slight structural evidence as well as native Belgic pottery and coins which point to the settlement having once extended north of Dyke Hills. But most of this pottery was associated with Gallo-Belgic imports, which are normally considered to belong either to the very late pre-Roman Iron Age or even overlapping with the Roman conquest. It is not impossible, therefore, that in addition to being a native settlement the town of Dorchester grew partly as a *vicus* attached to a fort, the existence of which, although expected, has yet to be certainly determined. Aerial photographs revealed ditches some 200 m (650 ft) south of the town, but they are thought to be of agricultural origin.[155] Additionally the very large gravel-pit found to underlie the southern town defences[156] may represent the line of a military ditch, subsequently quarried for gravel, as at Cirencester.[157] Other features associated with a probable fort have included simple timber-framed buildings with clay floors beneath the southern part of the walled town;[158] their demolition post-dated a coin of AD 78. There is also an as yet unexplained ditch, which was located in the north-west part of the town running north to south; it contained first-century pottery and may belong if not to the fort then to an annexe.[159]

The earliest buildings of the town date to the middle of the second century. Not surprisingly they were constructed with timber frames and clay or gravel floors, a building tradition which continued into the third century. Unfortunately no complete plans have yet been recovered, but buildings seem to have been widely distributed over the site and fronted a number of streets. A later building of greater substance was partly excavated in the north-west corner of the walled town; it dated to the middle of the third century and appeared to have a range of rooms flanked on each side by corridors or verandas.[160] Painted and decorated wall plaster was recovered from it, but

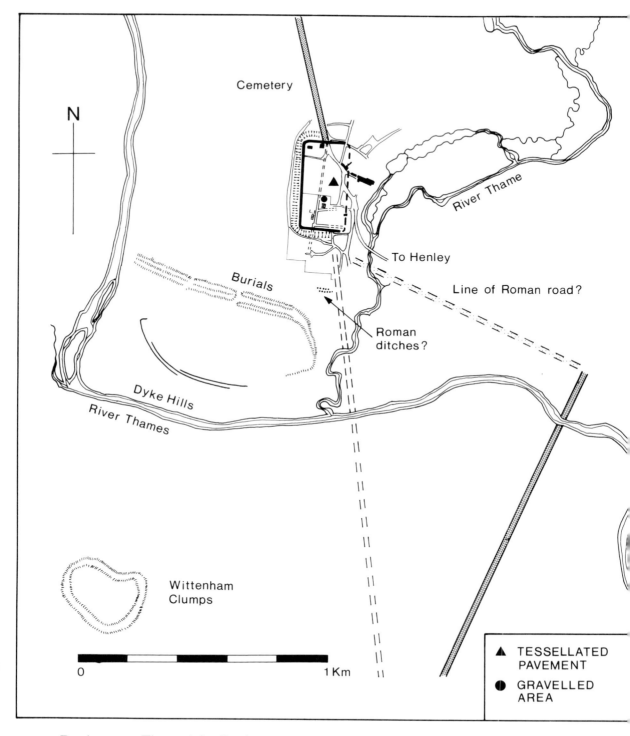

32 Dorchester-on-Thames (*after Frere*)

its life seems to have been comparatively short as, by the late third or fourth century, it had been converted to industrial use with the insertion of a number of kilns or ovens, which may have been for burning lime. By the later fourth century, the roof had collapsed, leaving an empty shell. Another building of merit was recorded near the centre of the eastern side of the town, opposite the churchyard, and is said to have had a tessellated pavement.[161] A tessellated pavement has also been recorded from the south-west quarter, while two others were found in buildings excavated in 1963.[162] No definite public or administrative buildings have yet been excavated, apart perhaps from that near the open gravelled space.

A number of internal streets have been identified, although some unsolved problems about the layout still exist. The road from Alchester and the north aims at a crossing of the River Thame a little to the south-east of the walled town. This line ought somehow to relate to the presumed axial north-south street, which has been shown to run slightly obliquely through most of the centre of the town. But at the southern end the course was found to have shifted slightly west before reaching the fortifications, which had stopped access; the street was sealed beneath at least the second rampart (below) and it is likely to have originally served houses which probably existed in the second century south of the later walled area. The causeway which appears on the line of the ditch outside the wall near this point has been shown to be false. Moreover, the road approaching from Silchester and the south diverges from its main alignment to aim at a crossing of the Thames some little distance downstream from its confluence with the Thame, where it perhaps joined a road approaching from Henley to the east. From there, to reach the southern side of Dorchester it would have had to veer north-west to cross the Thame near the town's south-east corner. A viable alternative involving an approach to the eastern rather than to the southern side of the town, would have required two or possibly three crossings of the Thame. Another alternative might envisage a second north-south street crossing the town towards a gate situated near the south-eastern corner; indeed a second-century street on this alignment was encountered in the unsuccessful attempt to locate the eastern defences in the grounds of the

Old Castle Inn, but it may lie too far east. It is odd, though, that an altogether more direct line was not adopted, which would have involved only one river crossing instead of two or more, by using a line running on the low ground between the eastern end of Dyke Hills and the Thame, but it may be that this area was too marshy in Roman times.

Two other internal streets existed at the southern end of the town; both ran approximately east-west. That nearest to the defences crossed the north-south street referred to above where it changed alignment, but the other, a little less than 100 m (327 ft) further north, formed a T-junction with it and aimed to the east.

The line of the fortifications is adequately known on the north, west and south sides, where it used to be marked by the hollow of a wide ditch; minor excavations have confirmed the position at the north-west corner and on the north side near the High Street. The west and south sides have been the subject of several later excavations. The east side is thought to have returned on a line parallel to the western fortifications, running between the High Street and Dorchester Abbey to complete a narrow rectangular enclosure; but despite excavations close to this line,[163] it has yet to be located. It is possible that this side assumed a more irregular layout, following more closely the west bank of the River Thame.

Excavations on the south and west sides have shown that the town was first defended by an earthwork, which in some places, unusually for civil ramparts, incorporated a good deal of turf.[164] On the south side, where it passed over a deep excavation, or quarry pit, it had been partly reinforced with horizontal timber strapping. A V-shaped ditch encountered in 1935–6 on the west side[165] is probably contemporary with this rampart, which has been dated to the late second century.[166] In the second half of the third century a masonry wall was inserted into the front of this rampart, which was itself widened and probably heightened. The wall had been extensively robbed leaving a trench about 3 m (10 ft) in width. It seems likely also that the V-shaped ditch of the early rampart was replaced when the wall was built, by the ditch, c. 30 m (98 ft) wide, whose hollow partly survives today; *mollusca* from its filling would imply the presence of permanent deep water.[167] It has been argued that this ditch was later than the curtain wall and would have been accompanied by the construction of external towers, as was the case in a number of other towns such as Great Casterton (p. 135) and Ancaster (p. 237). But since no trace of towers has ever been found, it might be better to assign the ditch to the same period as the wall; Catterick, where the wall was built in the early fourth century (p. 114), also had a wide ditch but no external towers. Similarly, no gates have yet been identified at Dorchester and, as indicated above, it is difficult even to suggest numbers, let alone positions.

As in the case of several other small towns, Dorchester appears to have had a nearly-central open gravelled space, 35 m (114 ft) wide, which was identified in 1963 as projecting 33 m (108 ft) to the east from the most westerly north-south street.[168] On the south side it was bounded by a major second- or third-century building containing a range of rooms flanked by verandas. As with other towns, this space probably served for a market-place; whether the building to the south, which is not unlike the range of a *macellum*, can be linked to it is not certain.

Dorchester is also one of the handful of small towns where the presence of an imperial official is attested by an inscription;[169] it was found in 1731 near the Red Lion Inn, but is now lost. It is a joint dedication to Jupiter Optimus Maximus and the deities of the emperors by M. Varius Severus, a *beneficiarius consularis*, and probably dates to the third century. The duties of these officers have never been precisely identified (see p. 33) but were probably multifarious. They may have been in charge of supplies for the army in one form or another, perhaps under the tax system. Certainly Dorchester was ideally placed, with both road and river communications, for tax collection and trans-shipment. It also lay in good agricultural territory along the Thames valley, with first-class grazing on the chalk downlands both above and to either side of it. Moreover this area also produced large quantities of distinctive pottery, some of which travelled as far afield as east Yorkshire.

In a region just noted for its pottery production, it would be surprising if Dorchester did not have some kilns in the vicinity. In fact it seems to have been very much on the southern edge of the production area, which was concentrated more around Oxford. Nevertheless two possible kilns have been identified close to the town, with a third definite example about 1.5 km (0.9 miles) north along the Alchester road.[170] The kilns produced both coarse and fine wares, and quantities of both were in use in the town itself from a comparatively early date. Yet it is worth recording also in this context that in the first and early second centuries *mortaria* in use at Dorchester came almost entirely from the Verulamium region; only later did local products supersede them. Dorchester also received considerable quantities of second-century black-burnished wares,[171] which were certainly not made in the neighbourhood. Apart, though, from pottery manufacture, there is little evidence for other industries. The kilns, ovens and hearths which were inserted into the ruined house in the north-west corner of the town have not been associated with the production of any specific goods.[172] The presence of a blacksmith, though, is perhaps attested by a small hoard of ironwork found lying on the latest street surface behind the southern rampart. It includes a coulter, a bar ploughshare and other items,[173] and also reflects on the agricultural needs of the area.

There is a marked lack of evidence associated with religious activities. The altar of M. Varius Severus, which also mentions the dedication of accompanying screens, might be taken to imply the presence somewhere in or around the town of a temple or small shrine, the site of which has yet to be discovered. A strange ceramic vessel, with a perforated interior flange and decorated with figures in creamy slip, might possibly have had a ritual use;[174] it came from the pre-rampart deposits at the southern end of the town. The town's close proximity to two rivers should have provided sufficient reason for the existence of temples or shrines to the relevant aquatic deities.

Unlike many small towns, the suburbs of Dorchester appear to have been slight. There is some evidence for occupation between the southern defences and the Dyke Hills, and a corresponding roadside scatter along the Alchester road to the north might be expected. There is evidence though that field systems ran up to the town boundaries in places, while a late farmstead was situated a short distance away to the north-west, on the left bank of the Thames.[175] It contained traces of a possible timber-framed building of late or post-Roman date.

A little more is known about the town's cemeteries, especially those belonging to the late Roman period; only one earlier burial, a third-century cremation, has been found south-west of the town.[176] One of the largest inhumation cemeteries lay at Queensford Mill, some 700 m (2300 ft) north-east of the fortified town. Here it was estimated that about 700 graves occupied a rectangular ditched enclosure, *c.* 1.3 ha (3.25 acres) in area,[177] of which some 200 were positively identified. Burials were orientated east-west in neat rows, not unlike the fourth-century cemetery at Ashton (p. 281). A radio-carbon date for a sample of bones indicates that the cemetery was being actively used in the late fourth to early fifth centuries; no grave goods were found. It could be argued that it was Christian in origin, although not all east-west burials without grave goods were necessarily Christian; but where a large number of burials all follow the same rite and where the cemetery is enclosed within a boundary, there must be a stronger presumption in favour of it having served a Christian community. Another major cemetery is known over 1 km (0.6 miles) away from the town in a west-north-west direction at Church Place, Warborough.[178] Again there seems to have been a ditched enclosure and again the burials were arranged in rows, but the orientation this time was west-north-west to east-south-east; one burial was in a lead coffin. A small rectangular building shows in aerial photographs of the enclosure at the south-east corner. Burials near the postulated crossing of the River Thame and on Dyke Hills indicate two other late cemeteries.

The distance of these two cemeteries from the town centre is worth comment, since it may reflect on the use of land in the area immediately around the town, where many field ditches imply heavy cultivation. This suggests perhaps that it was privately owned and that the owner was not prepared to sacrifice valuable farmland when the time came in the late fourth century for extra burial grounds to be found.

One of the most interesting aspects of the town at Dorchester is the information that has been gained for the period of transition from Roman Britain to Anglo-Saxon England. Dorchester is one of only a few sites in Britain where Theodosian coinage increases as a percentage of the total instead of declining, implying the continuing arrival of new batches of coins for official payments of one sort or another right up to the end of the fourth and possibly into the fifth century.[179] Frere's excavations in the southern part of the town were the first to uncover an interesting sequence of structures,[180] which may help to explain this coin pattern. The sequence began with a small building, probably half-timbered with masonry foundations (Building I.i), lying parallel and immediately adjacent to the westerly north-south street; it was divided into three roughly equal-sized rooms. The walls overlay a worn coin of Honorius (AD 394–5) and were in turn cut by the foundation trench of a Saxon timber-framed building. The date of construction, therefore, is likely to lie in the early to mid fifth century, although the life of the building cannot be determined. A scatter of sherds around the town, dating to the middle and later fifth century, carries the occupation beyond that of the building, although no structures contemporary with the sherds have so far been found. But a short distance to the north of Building I.i, a sixth-century *grubenhaus* was excavated; two phases of construction were apparent, both of which contained small hearths or ovens. The entrance in both phases projected to the north-east of the main sunken area down a short flight of steps possibly revetted with timber. As with the masonry building described above, the *grubenhaus* was set close to the west edge of the north-south street, onto which the entrance faced. It is tempting, therefore, to suggest that the street was still visible and in use in the sixth century. Later, after the *grubenhaus* had been destroyed, a much larger rectangular timber-framed building was constructed over its site, dating probably to about the ninth century. The foundation trenches for similar buildings were also encountered running obliquely down the street and over the site of Building I.i, but it cannot yet be said whether all were of the same date. Since these excavations in 1962, other *grubenhaüser* have been discovered in the north-west corner of the town and also near the eastern boundary,[181] and it seems clear that these few examples represent a widely-spread late Roman to Anglo-Saxon occupation within the walls, which began in the early fifth century and extended to at least the sixth century without a break; only after that were the streets disused, then becoming obliterated. This conclusion is backed by the presence of a number of burials from outside the walls. Two from the Dyke Hills cemetery were of a man and a woman. The man was buried with the accoutrements of a soldier in the late Roman army; while the woman, sometimes, but probably wrongly, reckoned to be his wife, was also wearing objects of similar style. North of the town, probably also from a late Roman cemetery, another woman was found to have been buried with comparable brooches.[182] Later still, probably in the seventh century, a small Saxon cemetery took over the site of the extra-mural farmstead mentioned above (p. 120).

These burials, together with the structural and coin evidence cited above, would seem to show the presence at Dorchester in the very late Roman period of a detachment of regular troops, probably recruited from north Germany, who either stayed after the final evacuation in the early fifth century or had been replaced or reinforced by *foederati* or *laeti* derived from the same area. That the latter arrived as family groups, which in turn attracted more settlers, would not seem to be in question. It is known that Dorchester became the seat of the first bishop of the West Saxons, Birinus, towards the middle of the seventh century and later the centre of the Mercian church. It seems unlikely that Birinus would have chosen the site for his evangelizing if there was not already in existence a substantial, protected settlement with good communications. It can be argued, therefore, that there is a good probability that the town was occupied continuously from the Roman to the English period, with the cultural and institutional changes between them occurring gradually over a span of time which might have extended for 200 years or more. Certainly it has been argued that the Silchester dykes, which face towards Dorchester and flank the main road running between the two towns, acted as a boundary between a surviving Romano-British enclave at Silchester, where there is little sign of early Saxon settlement, and an increasingly Anglicized community at Dorchester.[183] It is also interesting that this road, although it can still be followed with reasonable certainty at both ends, has a large gap in the middle where all traces have entirely disappeared, as though it became lost before the new land boundaries of the Saxon period were conso-

lidated.[184] This would imply a breakdown of communications between the two communities, which would help to account for the existence of the dykes. No date can yet be given to this episode, but it carries perhaps an echo of the revolt of the *foederati* mentioned by Gildas.

Godmanchester (figs. 33 and 34)

Few significant archaeological discoveries were made at Godmanchester prior to the current century,[185] principally because the central area of the Roman town still retained its late medieval layout of gardens, paddocks and closes, which offered few chances for detailed observation and recording. Its potential was first realized in the 1920s and 1930s during trenching for the water supply and sewers,[186] and was subsequently reinforced by the recognition in 1939 of a large building north of Pinfold Lane, represented by a hypocaust, *tesserae* and painted plaster.[187] During the past 30 years or so, infill development within the modern town has enabled several excavations to be undertaken, although most have been confined to garden areas and small derelict plots of land.[188] Even so, much of value has been recovered concerning the site's successive military and civilian phases, not least about its roads, defences and cemeteries, but also about its internal buildings, which include the *mansio* and its associated bath-house, two temples and various cottages, workshops and farm buildings. Several general publications have distilled the main conclusions from this work,[189] and this allows us to generalize about the town's morphology and development, though caution is necessary because many of the specific conclusions await detailed publication with all the supporting stratigraphic and dating evidence.

Like many sites on Ermine Street, the earliest activity at Godmanchester is military, reflecting the importance of the river crossing. On the dry approaches above the floodplain, the defences and internal buildings of what appear to be two successive forts have been identified.[190] The earlier, whose southern defences were traced over 170 m (556 ft) below the *mansio* and market-place, had a timber-revetted rampart 4 m (13 ft) wide, which was aligned east-west, and a double ditch system, the outer one of which was unfi-

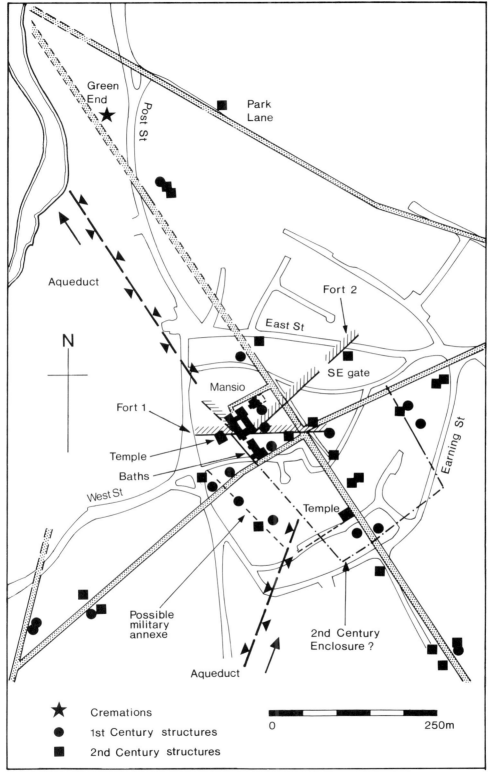

Green
End

Park
Lane

Post St

Aqueduct

N

Fort 2

East St

SE gate

Mansio

Fort 1

Temple

Baths

West St

Earning St

Temple

Possible
military
annexe

2nd Century
Enclosure ?

Aqueduct

★   Cremations

●   1st Century structures

■   2nd Century structures

0   250m

33 Godmanchester, first- and second-century
features (*after Green H. J. M.*)

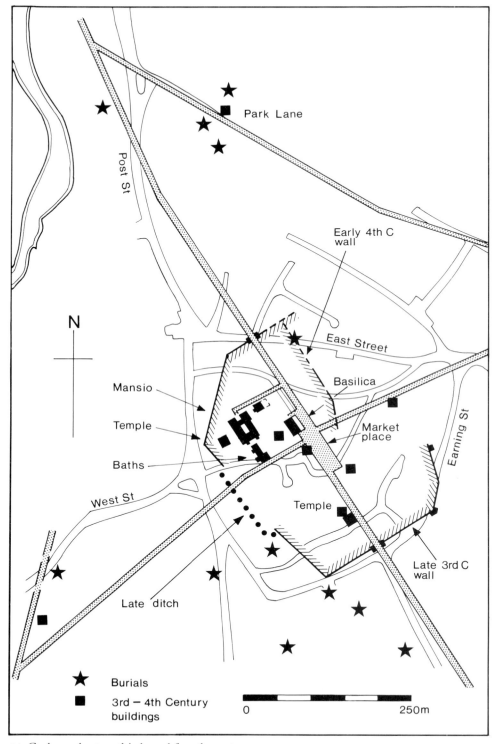

34 Godmanchester, third- and fourth-century
features (*after Green H. J. M.*)

nished.[191] A four-post interval tower was also located under the *mansio*. The size of this fort remains uncertain, because neither end of the southern defences has been identified. At one point in the vicinity of the basilican building, military buildings were sealed by the earliest gravel surface of Ermine Street, suggesting a Claudian date for the fort's construction. One mid first-century hut foundation, also pre-dating Ermine Street, has been located near the presumed northern defences and may well be part of an associated *vicus*.

The second fort was laid out on a different alignment running north-east/south-west across the earlier layout.[192] Again, only its south-eastern defences have been examined, but these included the position of the fort's southern corner and one of its principal gates in St Ann's Lane. This latter had a double carriageway flanked by timber towers, set between the timber-revetted ends of a box rampart 2.75 m (9 ft) wide, fronted by a single ditch. Behind lay a heavily worn *intervallum* road and a wattle-and-daub barrack. The position of these various features suggests a large military establishment, possibly of half-legionary size. Its date remains uncertain, but it may belong in a post-Boudiccan context alongside Great Chesterford because its ditch was not finally filled in and its timberwork not fully dismantled until the early second century. Perhaps associated with this fort was a large enclosure or annexe with military-type ditches lying west of Ermine Street.[193] It can be assigned to the Neronian era on the basis of the primary pottery groups found in its ditches. The road south-west towards Sandy and its original north-eastward extension have also been dated to the military phase because the latter seems to pre-date field boundaries assigned to the late first century, but this requires further corroboration.[194]

The site's later morphology was dominated by the main roads, in particular Ermine Street running south-eastwards from a ford over the river. Excavations demonstrate that it began as a cambered gravel surface varying in width from *c.* 6.1 m (20 ft) in the northern suburb near Post Street to 8.2–8.8 m (27–29 ft) closer to the centre.[195] It lay between flanking ditches, alongside which were a series of gravel-pits yielding finds suggesting a date in or after the mid first century. Several distinct resurfacings reflect both its importance and prolonged usage. Near the town centre it was joined by two roads roughly perpetuating the early military route already mentioned. That to the south-west towards Sandy has been sectioned at several points, including near Pinfold Lane, where there were two pre second-century surfaces and three successive northern ditches.[196] It was also located in 1987 beneath the early third-century basilican building, where it was flanked by side ditches and still retained its metalled surface. With the construction of the building, this section of the road was apparently diverted to the south into the market-place.[197]

Its north-eastern counterpart probably served as a link to the Cambridge road before continuing along the gravel terrace as a droveway. It was excavated at its junction with Ermine Street in 1986, revealing a steeply-cambered gravel road 3 m (10 ft) wide with at least four resurfacings; it was flanked by deep roadside ditches, the primary fill of which contained mid first-century pottery.[198] The Cambridge road remains unexcavated, but it has been traced bypassing the town on the north-east *en route* for the river crossing. In Park Lane, south-east of the latter, it was apparently flanked by occupation commencing in the mid first century, suggesting an early date for its establishment.[199] This early activity alongside the Cambridge road does not stand in isolation. Excavations in 1973 alongside Post Street north of the town centre identified a burnt deposit in the early fills of the gravel-pits and across the margins of Ermine Street, interpreted as the remains of timber structures dated by the associated pottery to the decade prior to AD 60.[200] This activity is probably best interpreted as part of an official *vicus* lying in the area to the north of the military establishments.

According to the excavator, the Flavian era saw a significant reorganization of the town centre, involving the laying out of a series of broad strips delineated by ditches extending outwards from Ermine Street onto the gravel terraces on either side.[201] The width of the plots, judging from the excavated setting-out posts, was 96.1 m (314 ft), which is presumed to represent a multiple of a traditional Celtic unit of measurement similar to the Roman *Pes Drusianus*. A system of infield and outfield agriculture, similar to later Scottish and Irish systems, has also been proposed on the basis of the pottery scatters around the town. Doubts have been cast upon these interpretations, however, even though elements of the land division are visible on aerial photographs amidst a palimpsest of Roman agricultural features to the north-east of the town, in the vicinity of the Rectory Farm villa complex.[202] Trenching here in 1975 revealed that the strips apparently ended on the line of a major cross-dyke marking the limits of the allocated land in this sector.

More detailed evidence is available for the late first-century expansion of the settlement along the main frontages, where ditched enclosures housed several types of structure, often set parallel to the road rather than end-on as with more normal strip buildings. These were accompanied by agricultural features including threshing floors, two-post hay racks, drying ovens and wicker granaries.[203] In addition to these, excavation has identified the premises of a resident baker and a metal-worker. The focus of this occupation apparently lay at the crossroads and along Ermine Street.

In the early second century several enclosures north-west of the crossroads were cleared to accommodate a courtyard building and associated bath-house.[204] A contemporary gravel lane served the north end of the courtyard complex, skirting the north side of a large aisled barn in the process, while to the west lay the first of three successive temples. Occupation, characterized by timber-framed buildings lying end-on to the roadside, also intensified along the frontages for some distance beyond the line of the later defences. Second-century buildings have been excavated just outside the later south gate and up to 180 m (589 ft) to the south, as well as on the Post Street and Park Lane sites alongside Ermine Street and the Cambridge road respectively.[205] At regular intervals, c. AD 150 and 200, Ermine Street was resurfaced after considerable wear; it was at its maximum c. 12 m (39 ft) wide with associated road ditches.

A few cremation burials, presumably denoting the rough limits of the occupied area, help to define the extent of this activity. To the north, eight second- to third-century cremations were found in 1955 at Green End, while to the south, one second-century cremation is known from Porch Farm.[206] Occupation on the branch roads certainly continued for some distance west of the

bath-house and east at least to Earning Street; beyond this, the three groups of cremation pots from 52 Cambridge Villas might represent an eastern cemetery.[207] One km (0.6 miles) east along the Cambridge road the Emmanuel Knoll barrow contained a primary second- to third-century cremation, though this probably belongs in a rural rather than an urban context.[208]

In the early third century, several late second-century timber buildings were apparently demolished at the central crossroads to accommodate a masonry basilican building with a forecourt to the east which encroached onto Ermine Street, necessitating its re-alignment slightly to the east.[209] Further south, this change apparently led to the creation of an open space between the two alignments of Ermine Street, best interpreted as a market-place at the town centre. This was substantiated in 1986 by the discovery of a two-period timber arcade with a gravelled paving along three sides of the square.[210]

The range of buildings in this undefended settlement has excited much interest, though few have been published in detail.[211] In first- and second-century contexts, examples of the traditional circular house are known on at least ten sites; generally they were stake-wall constructions set in a shallow trench, with substantial timbers only at the entrances.[212] That from St Ann's Lane in 1972 was 10 m (33 ft) in diameter, with a wicker-and-daub infill and a thatched roof, while two examples from Earning Street measured 6.1 m (20 ft). Until recently, it was thought that the type did not outlast the first century, but a second-century example is now known from elsewhere in St Ann's Lane. Alongside these, several other distinctive building types formed the bulk of the domestic and workshop accommodation throughout the settlement's life. Particularly common in the first century were square or rectangular cottages, with a framework of widely-spaced posts interspersed with vertical stakes infilled with clay and straw and set in a foundation trench, with an earth floor, a sunken hearth or fire-pit and a thatched roof. Numerous examples flanked the Sandy road in Pinfold Lane, associated with agricultural features, while others came from Earning Street to the east.[213]

New types in the second century include cob or *pisé* buildings constructed around a framework of posts supporting a thatched roof. Examples from the Stiles were mainly two-roomed structures with central or end-wall hearths. A good fourth-century example came from New Street, which was identified by the excavator as an early type of cruck structure.[214] Also new are timber-framed strip buildings with substantial corner posts and principals at intervals of 1 m (3¼ ft) infilled with wattle and daub. They had clay and gravel floors and thatched roofs. A typical example is the open-fronted metal-worker's shop measuring 7 by 5 m (23 by 16 ft) excavated in 1972 in St Ann's Lane.[215] It originated in the later first century, being rebuilt twice during the second century before being burnt down. Such buildings generally lie end-on to the frontages. Occasionally, more complex and sophisticated domestic accommodation has been excavated, such as the building 5.8 m (19 ft) wide in New Street with several rooms and a corridor on the north.[216]

Although some of these buildings were later rebuilt with stone sleeper walls, there were few major stone-built structures, the exceptions being either official or administrative. The most obvious lay north-west of the crossroads, including the courtyard building, the bath-house and the basilican structure. The courtyard building has not been definitively published, though its plan is reasonably clear (see fig. 4C).[217] It was apparently established early in Hadrian's reign, with its principal entrance on the north, giving access to rooms identified as stables and tack-rooms. Beyond these was a courtyard surrounded by a portico and by rooms to its east, south and west. Those to the east and west are interpreted as bedrooms, while the southern range probably included reception rooms, a dining room and a kitchen. Two projecting rooms on the south are probably tower granaries. South-east of the postulated kitchen lay rubbish pits spanning the early second to late third centuries, the effective life of the building.

Immediately south of this building lay the bath-house, which has been published in some detail.[218] The excavator argues that it was planned as a single suite of rooms but that during its construction there was a change of plan to incorporate two suites, one comprising Rooms 1–6 at the northern end close to the courtyard building, the other consisting of Rooms a–e at the southern end. These alterations raise the interesting possibility that the southern suite was

made available to the local community. The building itself was substantially built of flint rubble with tile bonding courses and a facing of sandstone blocks, supporting a roof of Colley-weston slates. It had *opus signinum* floors and plastered and painted internal walls. Other structures near the courtyard building and the bath-house probably performed related functions. East of the former lay the corner of a second- to third-century masonry building interpreted as an aisled barn, while to the west lay a small temple precinct, possibly part of the complex.

The plan of the basilican building has been reconstructed from small-scale excavations but is not yet fully published.[219] It was probably a single-aisled structure of six bays, measuring 24 by 12.9 m (78½ by 42 ft), with a forecourt to the east. It was substantially built of flint and ragstone walling with gravel floors and a Colleyweston slate roof. Its function has been much disputed, the excavator having proposed that it was an early third-century town hall, but more probably its closeness to the *mansio* complex indicates a related official function.

Although Godmanchester's stone defences were not begun until the later third century, it has been argued that an earlier second-century circuit ran on a different line.[220] This has been reconstructed from a V-shaped ditch, *c.* 3 m (10 ft) wide and 2 m (6½ ft) deep and running along the west of the baths and the courtyard building, and other possible sightings at points along the west and south. None of these is fully published and the reconstructed circuit is fraught with problems, not least the apparent absence of a rampart. On the west, the ditch doubled as a leat supplying the bath-house from the south, so that its defensive role must remain uncertain.

A surprising amount is known about the settlement's everyday life, indicating essentially agricultural roots combined with increasing economic activity and specialization. The overwhelming importance of agriculture is well attested in the roadside properties, where even the buildings set lengthwise to the frontages emphasize the early lack of pressure on land. Even so, some specialists served this agrarian community; witness the bakery at a prime site next to the central crossroads and the metal-worker's premises in St Ann's Lane.[221] The bakery began life in the Flavian period and comprised a two-roomed timber structure with an open shop fronting onto Ermine Street. The actual ovens lay in a compound at the rear of the building. The shop was rebuilt at least twice during the second century, the ovens being replaced by a large central hearth in the back-room, associated with bone pastry stamps. The various phases of the metal-worker's shop were associated with four shaft furnaces, a bowl-shaped smithing furnace and several crucibles, indicating copper- and iron-working. Metal-working was also indicated by iron slag covering the floors of various buildings elsewhere in the town.

The growing number of second-century strip buildings, and the creation of the market-place in the early third century, attest increasing econ-omic importance. Few crafts can be identified, although metal-working clearly continued; the iron-working furnace near a strip building in New Street suggests another blacksmith, while copper-working slag and crucibles came from the courtyard building's middens.[222] Other crafts included pottery production and bone casket manufacture, the former represented by an updraught kiln from Park Lane dated to AD 250, the latter by bone plates in the rubbish-filled ditch east of the temple precinct.[223] The third century apparently saw more workshops in and around the frontages near the market-place. Godmanchester thus shows an increasing depen-dence on specialized activities and trade, accom-panied by imposed official functions. This pro-gression presumably reflects the transition from village to small town, but even with this much evidence it is difficult to define the dividing line.

The settlement's religious life is also fairly well represented.[224] The most interesting complex, west of the courtyard building, is usually identi-fied as the shrine of Abandinus, recorded on a bronze votive feather from the late third-century deposit filling the old leat. It originated in the early second century as a simple 7 by 5 m (23 by 16 ft) timber structure with a 4 m (13 ft) diameter hut to its east; this was replaced later in the century by a larger temple of typical Romano-Celtic design comprising a central shrine sur-rounded by a 17 by 15 m (55½ by 49 ft) wooden veranda. It lasted through the third century before being destroyed along with the *mansio* complex. It may well have formed part of the

official complex because the latter's fence appar-ently enclosed it on the south at least. In the fourth century, it was replaced by a polygonal structure with a central masonry tank.

A second religious complex in the southern quarter of the town west of Ermine Street is indicated by a length of masonry wall and an imposing gateway astride an early third-century side-street, giving access to a structure which was only partly explored. Beneath the street lay a first-century entrance with a pipe-clay figure of Venus nearby, paralleling two examples from the *mansio* rubbish pits. These latter all had two dogs buried in the bottom, perhaps suggesting ritual overtones,[225] not unlike the comparable burials at Cambridge (p. 248).

Godmanchester's stone defences have now been examined at several points, revealing a somewhat unusual sequence.[226] When first exca-vated on the north-west in 1957 they were shown to comprise a 3 m (10 ft) wide wall and contem-porary rampart, fronted by a 10 m (33 ft) wide ditch.[227] A radio-carbon date from charcoal beneath the wall gave a date of AD 275 ± 45, which seemed to correspond well with a coin of Tetricus found in the rampart at the south gate. A second phase of defences seemed to be indicated by excavations at the south-eastern corner, which revealed a wide ditch and an apparently second-ary fan-shaped external tower which overlay an infilled earlier ditch.[228] In line with parallel evidence elsewhere, these changes were assigned to the mid to late fourth century. The town's two gates on Ermine Street are also known, though that on the north was only partially explored. It was probably similar, however, to its southern counterpart excavated in 1959–61.[229] This was 9.15 m (30 ft) wide, between two flanking towers which may have been built into a gap left in the walled circuit.

Unexpected complexities arose in 1978, how-ever, on the south-western side, where the 2.8 m (9 ft) wide foundations were shown to terminate in a butt end and to have been robbed apparently early in the fourth century.[230] No defences were then recognized over a distance of *c.* 100 m (327 ft), beyond which their line resumed again under Pinfold Lane *en route* for the north gate. Excava-tions in 1986 in Earning Street revealed a similar situation in the south-eastern sector, where the wall foundations and ditch ended abruptly at the site of a rectangular external tower.[231] Extensive trenching beyond this as far as St Ann's Lane failed to identify any further trace of the defensive line.

Clearly work on the defences had been interrupted during their construction. This can only be associated with the late third-century fire, which devastated the courtyard building, temple and bath-house.[232] Although the western tower granary and the north end of the baths were soon recommissioned, the coin evidence suggests that the *mansio* area remained open until the mid fourth century, when two new timber structures were built and the aisled building on the north re-roofed and used for industrial purposes. Contemporary with this, the *mansio* area was also apparently enclosed in a ditched compound, the ditches of which had been recut at least once.

Work meanwhile had recommenced on the defences. Excavation in 1981 in St Ann's Lane located a free-standing wall set in a 1.5 m (5 ft) wide trench fronted by a V-shaped ditch.[233] It contained re-used flue tiles and *tesserae* presumably derived from the demolition of the *mansio* complex after the fire. A continuation of this wall on a slightly different alignment was identified in 1986 on the south side of St Ann's Lane.[234] This defensive system, which is clearly secondary to the unfinished late third-century circuit, would appear to close off the north-west sector of the town where the main concentration of official buildings had always lain. Its southern end has yet to be traced.

The late history of the town remains poorly known, not least the fate of the official zone.[235] There are some clues, however, from elsewhere in the town. Ermine Street was last resurfaced in the early fourth century, after which a thick layer of rubbish accumulated containing late fourth-century finds. This has been noted at both the north gate and in the town centre, suggesting traffic had declined considerably. Fourth-century building activity is poorly recorded but was apparently commonest near the centre, suggesting contraction to within the defences or their immediate hinterland. No fourth-century occupation is published from Post Street north of the defences, while the northern half of the Park Lane site contained an inhumation cemetery. South of the unfinished defences, occupation had apparently ceased even earlier.[236]

Less certain evidence for contraction comes from the relatively extensive fourth-century cemeteries. The principal cemeteries lay in two areas, firstly in a wide arc around the south-west of the town, and secondly extending along the Cambridge road.[237] Most burials were in wooden coffins with few grave goods. How long these cemeteries continued in use remains uncertain. At the town centre, the reduced bath-house lasted into the late fourth century, when it was again modified, but it is unlikely that it lasted long into the fifth. Coins extend down to the House of Theodosius, indicating continued activity into the fifth century. More interestingly, early Saxon pottery has been identified from the *mansio* area, the town centre and the Cambridge road cemetery, but the only occupation site has been located on a housing estate to the north-east of the town.[238] How long activity continued into the fifth century remains unknown, though the pattern of Saxon occupation might indicate that, by the mid fifth century, the Roman town had reverted to the earlier Iron-Age distribution of farmsteads spaced along the gravel terrace.

EIGHT
MINOR TOWNS II

Great Casterton (figs. 35–37)

Although Stukeley and Gale had ridden around its defences in 1737, surprisingly little was known about Great Casterton prior to the excavations of the 1950s.[1] These were focused principally on the defences and external towers, and on a villa complex to the north-east,[2] while work in 1960 and 1962 investigated the fort visible on aerial photographs.[3] The interior was barely examined, however, except for several narrow trenches, which served to highlight both the extent of stone-robbing and plough-damage and the need for larger-scale excavations. Our understanding of the site's broader morphological and chronological aspects is thus somewhat sketchy, despite its being chosen for defensive protection on an impressive scale.

The site lay within a loop of the River Gwash, north of the Ermine Street crossing, having begun life as a *vicus* outside a military base, located just north-east of the later civilian defences c. 230 m (752 ft) from Ermine Street. Limited excavations revealed two successive forts facing south-east, where a single ditch apparently defines an annexe adjacent to the river.[4] The first fort enclosed c. 2.4 ha (5.9 acres) across its defences, with a rampart of limestone rubble 4.6 m (15 ft) wide supported by turf cheeks, fronted by a double-ditch system reminiscent of Hod Hill; a third ditch was also supplied between these on the weak south-eastern flank. It only had three gates, the south-eastern one at least of simple design, with four timber posts set between the rampart ends. Occupation began in the AD 40s and probably lasted on the pottery evidence until c. AD 70, when the fort was reduced to c. 2.1 ha (5 acres) by the construction of a new south-eastern rampart and

ditch inside the line of its demolished predecessor. Its gates were now much more complex, comprising two towers of six posts flanking a dual carriageway with a central two-post spina. This smaller installation probably lasted into the late AD 70s, when military operations would have necessitated its evacuation.

Not surprisingly, such a lengthy military occupation encouraged civilian settlement outside its defences, represented at various points by material of Claudian to early Flavian date. In 1950, two pits and a transverse gully were examined,[5] beneath the northern defences of the civilian site, all containing material of Iron-Age origin alongside south Gaulish samian of Claudian date, while an early Flavian timber building was located inside the defences in 1956,[6] represented by a much truncated sleeper beam beneath the later building sequence. This evidence, though limited, suggests a *vicus* outside the south-western defences of the forts, perhaps focused in part along the frontages of a road linking the fort gateway to Ermine Street, now perpetuated by Ryhall Road. Little else is known about its extent, or its morphology, nor can we define its relationship with the later civilian occupation primarily focused on Ermine Street.

This later occupation, prior to the construction of the defences, remains poorly known, though several basic morphological features can be recognized. With the growing importance of the communications network and the decline of the fort, there was probably a gradual shift in the settlement's focus towards the Ermine Street frontages, no doubt accelerated by the establishment of an official *mansio* in the later first century, the baths of which were located close to the modern church.[7] No trace of Ermine Street was recorded, however, during trenching, and so

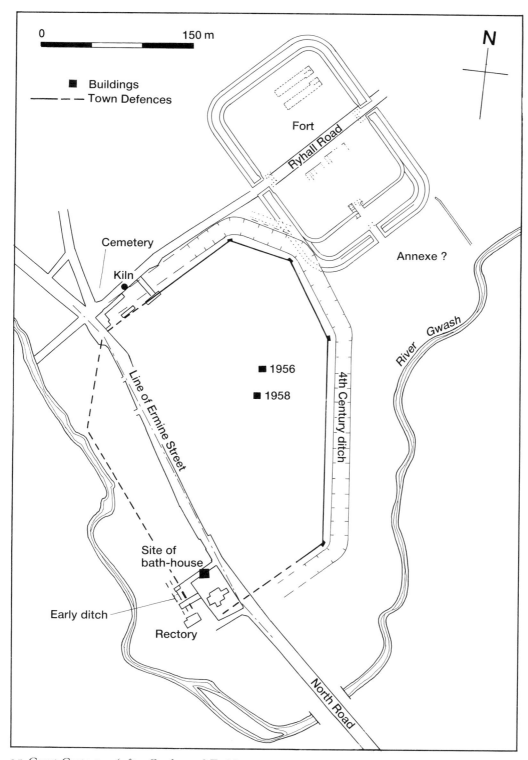

35 Great Casterton (*after Corder and Todd*)

36 Great Casterton, looking south; the late ditch
shows clearly along the north-eastern part of the
circuit (*Cambridge University Collection, Crown
Copyright*)

presumably its course is perpetuated by the line of the modern Great North Road. It would thus make two slight changes of alignment within the town, coinciding with the proposed line of the later defences, probably to avoid more than one bridging point across the Gwash. Nor did trenching recover any internal streets or lanes, though the rammed and trampled limestone apparently forming the Roman ground surface may have made an elaborate metalling unnecessary.[8] Some sort of network must originally have existed to provide access to the land east of Ermine Street which was subsequently enclosed by the defences. Fragmentary evidence from the 1950s trenching certainly suggests that occupation extended across this area, including a complex first- to fourth-century sequence located in 1956, midway between Ermine Street and the later defences.[9] Occupation lasting down to the late second century was also found in several defence sections cut between 1950 and 1956.[10] Much remains to be learnt about this early occupation, not least its extra-mural extent, which only large-scale excavation can resolve.

The defences form a significant morphological element enclosing c. 7.3 ha (18 acres), most of it east and north-east of Ermine Street, compensating for the constraints imposed by the River Gwash to the west and south. Several informative sections have been dug, all but one east of Ermine Street, revealing a single-phase wall and bank, apparently built in a series of straight stretches.[11] The wall had been heavily robbed, but had clearly been c. 2.1 m (6¾ ft) wide on a foundation of pitched limestone footings 2.4 m (7¾ ft) across. Behind lay an earthen bank up to 6.9 m (22½ ft) wide, made of interleaved lenses of stone, clay and occupation debris presumably derived in part from the ditches. This had apparently risen in stages as the wall itself was constructed because no obvious construction trench could be identified, while on the south, a layer of chippings under the rampart probably relates to the initial stages of the wall's construction. A considerable amount of dating evidence was recovered suggesting that the defences were built in or after the late second century; on the north, the rampart sealed a hearth and associated pottery no later than c. AD 190,[12] while on the east and south-east it sealed pottery no later than c. AD 175.[13] This uniformly early date for a contemporary stone wall and bank would make Great Casterton somewhat exceptional, whereas an early to mid third-century date might be more compatible with the sequence at sites like Ancaster (p. 237) and Alchester (p. 102). It is possible, however, that severe stone-robbing and the subsequent slumping of the rampart has disguised the original construction trench for a secondary stone wall, a suggestion which would bring Great Casterton into line with the two-stage sequence known elsewhere. Outside these early defences lay at least one V-shaped ditch, some 6.4 m (21 ft) wide and up to 3.7 m (12 ft) deep, which contained several second-century sherds in its primary silts.[14] On the weak north-eastern flank, however, three ditches were apparently supplied.[15] These defences clearly overlay earlier occupation, but given the nature of the excavations, it is difficult to define their impact on the newly created intra- and extra-mural zones.

Beyond the defences, our knowledge of the internal buildings is rather sketchy. Particular interest attaches to the bath-house, discovered in 1958, in a narrow trench along the lane north of the churchyard, which is undoubtedly related to the extensive building with hypocausts recorded during the nineteenth-century extension of the graveyard.[16] It lay c. 10 m (33 ft) west of Ermine Street and included a small semi-circular cold bath with evidence of painted plaster fragments and *tesserae* as well as two other rooms, both with *opus signinum* floors. Pottery in the relevant levels suggested a late first-century construction date, probably as part of a *mansio* complex directly alongside Ermine Street. This is the only known stone building pre-dating the defences; the rest were of timber construction, although only fragmentary details were recovered. Typical second-century examples include the post-built structures located in 1956, pre-dating the early third-century stone building with foundations of pitched limestone slabs set into a shallow construction trench.[17] This measured c. 11.6 by 6.1 m (38 by 20 ft), with at least one aisle parallel with its south wall, represented by three post-holes. A secondary hearth near the structure's south-east corner sealed mid fourth-century pottery, suggesting that it enjoyed a long life. Little else is known about the overall structural range within the town.

Excavation has not proved very informative

37 Great Casterton, looking north-west. The crop-
marks indicating the early fort can be seen
impinging on the northern corner of the later
town ditch (*Cambridge University Collection:
copyright reserved*)

about the town's everyday economic or religious aspects. Two pottery kilns have been located north of the defensive ditches near Ryhall Road, one in a pipe trench in 1958, the other in 1966.[18] Both were producing colour-coated wares amongst their repertoire, apparently successively from the mid second through to the early third centuries. Inside the defences, a typical late first-century bowl-shaped smelting hearth was found in the vicinity of the 1956 timber and stone buildings, presumably belonging to the post-military settlement. It measured 1.4 m (4½ ft) in diameter and 0.5 m (1½ ft) deep and contained iron-ore, slag and charcoal.[19] Iron-working debris was also located in 1958 in a small trench *c*. 18 m (59 ft) to the south, while the 1956 area produced a late second- or early third-century oven or kiln, though its precise function could not be ascertained.[20]

Knowledge of the site's later occupation revolves principally around the fourth-century defensive reorganization, supplemented by the villa excavations to the north-east. Like a growing number of small towns, Great Casterton was provided with external towers, four being known at the corners of the wall on its eastern side.[21] Prior to their construction, the original inner ditch had been infilled with material from a new wide ditch, comprising both freshly quarried rock and much looser sand and stones. The former provided an ideal foundation for the towers, but where the latter predominated, as at Bastion 3, it had proved necessary to re-excavate the material in order to provide the necessary foundations. All four towers were rectangular at their base, mostly made of freshly quarried slabs filled in with a thick mortar spread; in the case of Bastion 2, however, the lowest foundation comprised 12 large masonry blocks, some with redundant cramp-holes, indicating re-use from an earlier building. The new ditch, up to 18.3 m (60 ft) wide, has only been sectioned once, though surface traces suggest that it was originally supplied around the northern and eastern parts of the circuit.[22] The situation on the west near the river remains uncertain; west of the church, excavations located the first phase ditch, but this had not been infilled like its eastern counterpart, suggesting that the defensive alterations did not extend to this side.[23]

These changes are reasonably well dated on numismatic and pottery evidence.[24] Bastion 2 clearly sealed a coin of the mid AD 340s in the masons' chippings associated with its construction, while a coin of AD 354–8 came from in or under the contemporary turf-line on its northern side. Likewise, Bastion 3 post-dates another coin of AD 354–6. Clearly both towers belong after the mid AD 350s, a date paralleled by the mid fourth-century pottery from the primary silt of the wide ditch. This period also saw major changes commencing on the villa site to the north-east, where a new house was erected, replacing an earlier barn and drying floor.[25] Subsequently, *c*. AD 370–80 a separate south wing and self-contained bath-house were added. Unfortunately such evidence for relative prosperity cannot be compared with contemporary activity inside the defences, or in any potential extra-mural suburbs, because excavation has been too limited to define the relevant fourth-century horizons.

The town's fifth-century fate also presents problems. The only evidence comes from an extensive cemetery first recorded in 1959, *c*. 35–45 m (114–47 ft) beyond the site of the presumed north gate.[26] The burials were laid in rows with their feet to the east, some in fairly simple graves, others in stone-lined cists with flat covers. No grave goods were found, but pottery indicated a later third- to mid fourth-century date. Then in 1966, further inhumations were located near Ryhall Road, apparently cut into the counter-scarp bank of the wide ditch and clearly therefore of later fourth-century date.[27] These were also accompanied by several Anglo-Saxon cremations, suggesting a possible early presence in or near to the settlement. No Anglo-Saxon pottery has been reported, however, from the excavations inside the settlement, leaving us little upon which to build a plausible hypothesis for the fifth century. If the evidence from the villa is admissible as a guide, occupation clearly continued into the last decade of the fourth century if not beyond, because worn coins of AD 388–96 were found in its extensive destruction layer.[28] Even then, agricultural activity continued on the site, and presumably those who tilled the fields continued to inhabit the defended site astride Ermine Street; but for how long is pure speculation.

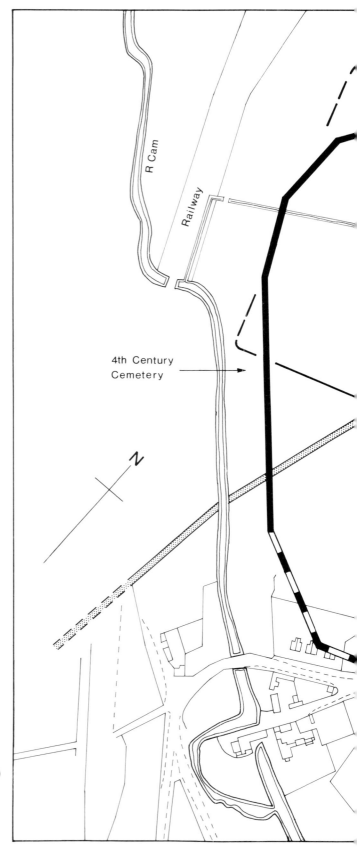

38 Great Chesterford (*after Rodwell and Going*)

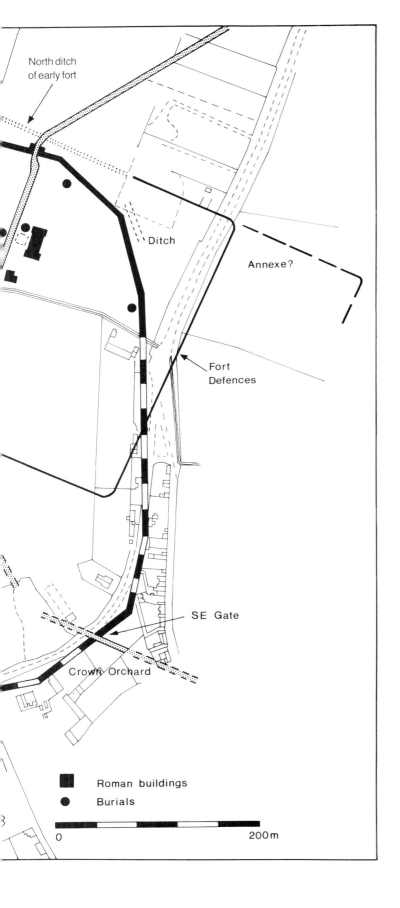

North ditch
of early fort

Ditch

Annexe?

Fort
Defences

SE Gate

Crown Orchard

■ Roman buildings

● Burials

0   200m

Great Chesterford (figs. 38 and 39)

Considerable vestiges of this Roman site were still visible in the eighteenth century, as Stukeley was able to record,[29] but since then it has been progressively ravaged, first by the systematic robbing of its defences for road-metalling, recorded in the 1770s, and second by extensive nineteenth- and twentieth-century gravel quarrying. Much of what we know has thus had to be salvaged in advance of these operations. Between 1845 and 1860, in particular, the site was investigated by R. C. Neville, who published detailed accounts of the cemeteries, the shafts and pits and the ironwork hoard.[30] Unfortunately, comparable finds later in the century were far less well recorded and illustrated. Twentieth-century gravel extraction reached a peak in the 1940s, prompting rescue excavations in the northern part of the defended area in 1948–9. These produced vital information about the site's Iron-Age and military phases and the broader structural development, but unfortunately the results are only available in interim form.[31] Later research has been limited, except for Rodwell's work on the military site and several small excavations, most notably along the eastern defences and on the temple 1.6 km (1 mile) east of the town.[32] Our understanding of the site's overall development is thus somewhat variable, though aerial photography has contributed some useful insights.[33]

There can be no doubt that the site had a military phase, but its pre-Roman status remains more problematical. The 1948–9 excavations beneath the Roman levels produced a quantity of late Iron-Age material, often filling typical rubbish pits, but unfortunately no *in situ* structures were recorded.[34] One of the occupation horizons below the late two-roomed building was even attributed to this phase, though no dating evidence was presented.[35] Sadly, little of the relevant material has been published, and the available descriptions are insufficiently precise to allow a detailed assessment of the site's date, importance and extent. More recently, the 1980 excavations in the Crown Orchard east of the defences located traces of a late Iron-Age house gully overlain by a first-century ditched enclosure.[36] This lends support to the case for an Iron-Age origin and suggests that occupation extended beyond the

1948–9 areas, but considerable clarification is essential, given the site's subsequent military role.

Prior to the 1940s, several authors had noted the site's strategic location on the River Cam, controlling the Icknield Way and several valley routes, but the only military find was what seemed to be a bronze mouthpiece from a trumpet.[37] Then in 1948–9, just outside the north gate, a ditch 4 m (13 ft) wide and 1.8 m (6ft) deep was located, with a slot at the bottom, running roughly east-west for *c.* 140 m (458 ft).[38] Beyond this, both ends had been truncated by quarrying. It had been deliberately backfilled, the associated finds suggesting a Neronian date. Later research on aerial photographs identified an apparent north-eastern corner and part of the southern defences, cutting across the centre of the later defended enclosure, close to where the town's principal road meets the routes running south-east and south-west respectively.[39] This suggested that the main road perpetuated the line of the fort's *via principalis*, and that the external roads were focused on its north and south gates. Although the western defences were not precisely located, the site's size was estimated as 14–15 ha (34.5–37 acres), large enough for a vexillation fortress of Longthorpe type. More recently, however, auger survey and trenching along the fort's eastern side have not confirmed the predicted line, revealing instead, some way inside it, a pair of ditches fronting a gravel base 6 m (20 ft) wide, which supported a timber-revetted rampart; this would enclose *c.* 9.9 ha (24.5 acres).[40] To date, no internal buildings have been located. This installation would have caused considerable disturbance for any pre-existing native site, but its nature and extent remain uncertain. It has been suggested that civilian settlement developed outside the south gate, subsequently spreading north across the abandoned fort, but the archaeological evidence for this is very fragmentary.[41]

The morphology of the later town was dominated by the main roads already mentioned, which were apparently established at an early stage. The principal roadway, following the old *via principalis*, was sectioned at several points in 1948–9.[42] Close to the centre it was 8.5 m (27½ ft) wide, with typical side ditches and evidence for several later resurfacings; further north, these

39 Great Chesterford, looking north-west
(*Cambridge University Collection: copyright reserved*)

resurfacings declined in number, first to three and then to two near the defences. This roadway clearly originated in the first century. Outside the later north gate it swung eastwards towards the Cambridge road, but this section has never been excavated. Of the two southern roads, that south-westwards towards Braughing is principally known from aerial photographs, but that heading south-eastwards was sectioned just outside the later defences in 1980.[43] It originated in the late first century, when it was 4.8 m (15½ ft) wide with side ditches, but was subsequently widened to 6.5 m (21 ft) in the late second century. Clearly the civilian town had developed around a framework determined not by its Iron-Age predecessor but by the main roads in conjunction with the known fort.

Early civilian occupation alongside these roads has proved difficult to identify, partly because of the rescue nature of much of the nineteenth- and twentieth-century excavations. Some of the latrine shafts probably belong in the first century but their distribution is too poorly known to help define the associated settlement. The earliest buildings apparently belong to the later first or early second century, being found alongside the main road frontages.[44] Most were rectangular with timber-framed superstructures and floors of gravel or beaten earth, though one had sandstone *tesserae*. Their wattle-and-daub walling had been impressed internally with a roller, forming a key for a coat of lime plaster, while the absence of tiles suggests a thatched roof. Such structures are well attested, especially beneath the two-roomed masonry building, where excavation revealed a complex first- to third-century sequence; the first structure was undated, the second had a gravel floor associated with several second- and third-century pits, and the third had a beaten clay floor.[45] As elsewhere on the site, these inherently flammable structures had obviously burnt down. It has been suggested, however, that a more extensive second-century fire might correspond with events reported elsewhere in Essex at this date.[46] Comparable second- to third-century buildings were also found in 1980 flanking the south-eastern road outside the later defences.[47] They had cobbled and tessellated floors and painted wall plaster, and were clearly associated with several yards, wells, ovens and hearths. One even had a latrine shaft in a post-built hut.

Although neither the settlement's extent nor its rate of expansion can be established in detail, some general trends emerge from the date and distribution of the various shafts excavated in the nineteenth and twentieth centuries. Unfortunately only 27 of the 68 recorded examples can be tentatively dated, but these are concentrated in the second and third centuries, 5 belonging to the second century, 3 to the second/third and 12 to the third.[48] They are distributed extensively both inside and outside the later defences, suggesting considerable expansion beyond the main road frontages. Neville certainly recorded shafts south of the walled area in the Rectory Gardens and to the west of the churchyard, as well as over 100 m (327 ft) outside the northern defences.[49] Like latrine pits elsewhere, they were often found in discrete clusters and thus remain our best guide to the original presence of timber buildings, though the original records are insufficiently precise to allow the identification of actual properties or allotments.

Another rough indicator of the site's extent is the cemetery evidence recorded in the nineteenth century, particularly the concentrations of cremation burials.[50] One was examined in 1847, apparently in the main northern cemetery c. 180 m (590 ft) outside the walls, the other in 1823–4 south-west of the River Cam close to the railway station. This extensive occupation beyond the road frontages, estimated in excess of c. 20–24 ha (50–60 acres), suggests the existence of an internal street system, but the only evidence for this visible on the aerial photographs includes two metalled side-streets close to the town centre and several unmetalled lanes running between the presumed building plots.[51]

Virtually all the excavated buildings were timber-framed, except for two masonry structures alongside the principal road. The first, originally excavated in 1848, was relocated in 1948 when something of its complex chronology was defined.[52] The earliest building consisted of several narrow walls sealed below the floors of its better preserved successor of winged-corridor type. This latter initially comprised a long central range incorporating a possible staircase well, with a single corridor on the west and pairs of wing rooms to north and south (see fig. 3E). The northern pair contained a hypocaust and tessellated floor respectively. Subsequent alterations included the subdivision of the central range into three, the addition of a corridor on the east and a new frontal wall along the west. Finds from the associated yards dated the earliest structure to the second and third centuries, and its winged successor to the later third or early fourth, roughly contemporary with the defences and the second masonry building to the south.

This second structure overlay several timber predecessors and a rubbish layer containing early fourth-century material.[53] It comprised two rooms, 9.1 by 6.1 m (29¾ by 20 ft) and 5.2 by 4.3 m (17 by 14 ft) respectively, with a yard or pull-in to the south leading into the larger room through a doorway 1.8 m (6 ft) wide. One of its walls had collapsed *in situ* with its carved clunch cornice, suggesting a building of some pretensions. Its outer face was plastered and painted with white above a red dado. Both buildings are clearly exceptional but their function remains uncertain. They could both belong in a rural setting but their date and apparent contemporaneity with the defences have long suggested an official role, the two-roomed structure being identified as a tax-collection centre.

Although the town's defences have been extensively robbed, excavations in 1948–9 and 1980 have helped to clarify their plan, extent and chronology.[54] The site was enclosed by a free-standing wall resting on a ragstone and cement foundation 3.7 m (12 ft) wide cut down into the gravel subsoil. Where it overlay earlier features, these had been diligently emptied and refilled with successive layers of rammed chalk and flint to prevent subsidence. Occasionally the builders missed one, as for example the 3.4 m (11 ft) deep shaft located in 1948–9 containing early fourth-century pottery. This suggested an early-mid fourth-century date for the defences, explaining the apparent absence of external towers. At the south-east gate, a prominent ditch 6 m (20 ft) wide by 3 m (10 ft) deep was excavated, fronted by two further ditches, though elsewhere only one ditch has been recorded.

Two of the three main gates have been examined, that on the north revealing a complex structural history.[55] It began as a gap through the wall 5.5 m (18 ft) wide, which was subsequently blocked by a substantial chalk foundation projecting internally and externally, presumably to support a tower. A new passage, 3.5 m (11½ ft) wide, was then cut through to the west and its new western terminal thickened on both sides as if to carry a tower across the top. This change of plan necessitated a re-alignment of the main road. Only the outer edge of the south-east gate was located and shown to be 11.5 m (38 ft) wide; outside it, the inner ditch terminated in two butt ends, which were linked by a small gully or culvert cut across the road.[56] Such free-standing defences are relatively rare, but they nevertheless enclosed something like 14.2 ha (35 acres) at the heart of the town, including the main crossroads, suggesting an attempt to protect both the settlement core and the official installations, perhaps represented by the two masonry buildings already described.

Knowledge of the site's economic basis is somewhat sketchy because none of the 1948–9 structures could be shown to have served specialist functions. Bone-working debris was recorded in 1980, alongside the buildings flanking the south-eastern road, suggesting that they combined domestic and workshop accommodation.[57] Elsewhere, commercial activity is attested by two steelyards, while the ironwork hoard and traces of metal-working remind us of the importance of the smith.[58]

The religious life of the town is better represented, not least by a stone fragment found before 1732 which apparently came from a substantial monument of octagonal plan, perhaps the base for a Jupiter column.[59] The four remaining faces were decorated with the head and torso of a deity in low relief set in a rounded niche. At least two or three more stones would be needed to complete the figures, identifiable as Venus, Mercury, Jupiter and probably Mars. More problematical are the numerous shafts which clearly originated as wells.[60] Their fills, however, which included a miniature axe and a range of animal and bird bones, suggested a religious connection to their excavator Neville, a suggestion perhaps reinforced by the interpretation of the ironwork hoard as a votive deposit.[61] Such evidence is inconclusive by itself, though unusually arranged fills have been noted elsewhere, suggesting that votive or ritual objects were included when the shafts ceased to perform their original functions.

Equally interesting, though difficult to relate to the town, is the Romano-Celtic temple located 1.6 km (1 mile) to the east inside a walled *temenos*.[62] Originally excavated in 1847, it was re-examined in 1978, when a silver mask with Celtic-type lentoid eyes and a moustache was discovered alongside other votive objects. The temple was 12.2 m (40 ft) square overall, built apparently in the second century and subsequently modified at least once during its long life. A link road may have connected it to the town.

The fourth century at Great Chesterford is well documented, not just by its defences and the contemporary masonry buildings, but also by its late cemeteries identified in the nineteenth century.[63] Two lay alongside the roads north and south-west respectively and a third on the west in the narrow corridor between the defences and the River Cam. Both the former began as cremation cemeteries, that on the south-west extending onto the west bank of the river. Most of the information recovered related to their later use for inhumations. The northern cemetery, examined in 1847 and 1859, revealed at least 100 burials accompanied by simple grave goods including pottery, late coins and bone pins. Its south-western counterpart, partly explored in 1823–4 and 1856, was very similar, though 25 child burials were discovered in one restricted area; a lead coffin was also reported from here in 1847.

The western cemetery is potentially the most interesting, because most of its active life post-dates the construction of the defences. Some 18 adult burials were discovered in 1856, accompanied by coins chiefly of the Constantines and Valentinian, while in the adjacent field lay a group of 15 infant burials, orientated east-west, with their heads to the west. The construction of the defences presumably made this a convenient area for burial, but both clearly overlay earlier occupation debris, suggesting some level of fourth-century contraction, at least on this western side. A possible tomb-base was also recorded west of the defences, though no actual burials were recovered.[64] Only its subterranean chamber, measuring 4.6 × 3 m (15 by 9¾ ft), had survived ploughing, but its rubble walls were plastered and painted, and there was a small doorway in one corner.

This evidence clearly indicates continued occupation throughout the fourth century and suggests survival into the fifth, though its extent and general level of prosperity remain uncertain.

Sadly, crucial evidence for the later history of the town has probably been destroyed by quarrying or ploughing, though there are hints of an Anglo-Saxon presence in the form of pottery and a large pagan cemetery.[65] The sherds were noted in 1948–9 at the north end of the town, but not in sufficient quantity to prove occupation on the site. The cemetery, of mid/late fifth- to early seventh-century date, was recorded outside the north gate of the town in the area of the known Roman cemetery, strengthening the case for continuity, though the relationship may be fortuitous. Rodwell has also suggested that the parish church in the cemetery area may have originated as an Anglo-Saxon minster, while parish boundaries may hint at an early post-Roman territorial definition of a still-significant town.[66] Clearly *in situ* structural evidence is now vital to elucidate this post-Roman sequence.

Irchester (figs. 40 and 41)

The small town of Irchester lies in the *civitas Catuvellaunorum* close to the River Nene at a junction of possibly three Roman roads: one coming south from Water Newton, another from the south-west, perhaps from Duston and Whilton Lodge, and a third pointing due south in the direction of Dropshort. It is surprising that there seems to be no direct line of communication with Towcester, its nearest major urban neighbour. It is probable that another road ran northwards to the large settlement at Kettering, and a massive agger can still be seen crossing the floodplain in that direction from the east gate. There does not seem to have been a north gate or a bridge over the Nene, and so no road left the town from that quarter. Despite these conjectural lines, though, there are still considerable difficulties to be overcome in elucidating the local road system because, apart from the agger mentioned above, no trace of roads entering the respective gates has ever been found or even seen on an aerial photograph; indeed, no through roads appear to cross the walled area. Any junctions that there might have been probably lay south of the town in an area now badly damaged by iron-stone mining.

Although no Roman name has survived and the town is not mentioned in any of the itineraries or

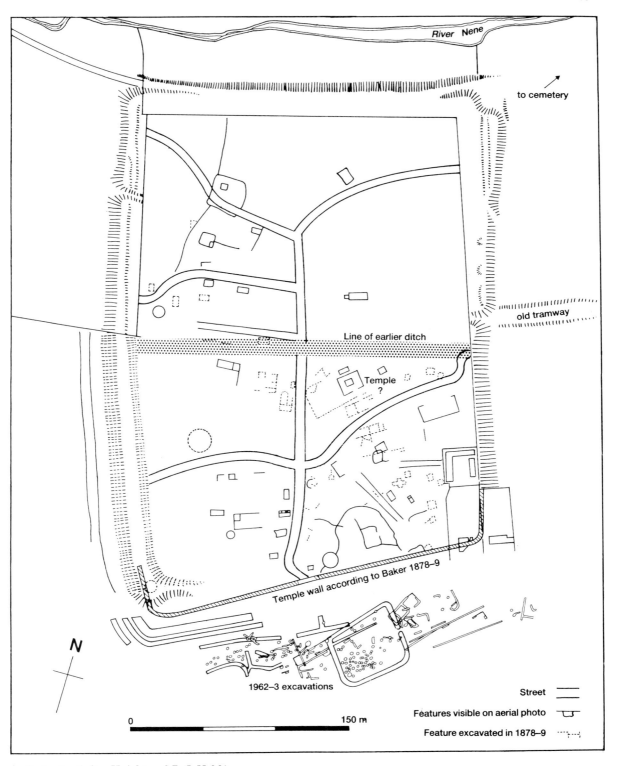

40 Irchester (*after Knight and R.C.H.M.*)

41 Irchester, looking north (*Cambridge University Collection: copyright reserved*)

other geographical sources, it has long been recognized as Roman. It was first referred to by Morton, who described the walls as still standing in the early eighteenth century,[67] while brief descriptions appeared in the updated editions of Camden's *Britannia*.[68] Iron-stone mining, especially in the eastern extra-mural area in the late nineteenth century, revealed an extensive cemetery, while the Revd R. S. Baker carried out excavations in the interior at about the same time.[69] The defences were explored in 1926,[70] while road-works south of the town and along the line of the south wall have resulted in two main series of excavations, in 1962–3 and 1981–4, and have been coupled with watching briefs.[71] The site has also been comprehensively photographed from the air with valuable results,[72] which has enabled a reasonable plan of the walled area and some of the suburbs to be constructed.[73]

The site seems to have had an extensive pre-Roman history, which included Iron-Age occupation south of the town walls; Hall and Nickerson refer to defensive ditches in this area, which they attributed to the Belgic Iron Age. Unfortunately, owing to an omission on one of their published plans, it is not possible to relate them, with conviction, to the site as a whole.[74] This occupation continued into the first century AD, and may have formed the *vicus* round an early fort, the existence of which is suspected but not yet proven. A dark linear crop-mark in the aerial photographs bisects the later town roughly from west to east and its ends coincide with slight changes in direction of the east and west defences of the town.[75] The dark band is earlier than the internal street system and may represent the ditch or multiple ditches of a fort of considerable size (10 ha/25 acres). A few minor items of military equipment have been found, but are not very significant.

Early fort or no, the settlement seems to have been flourishing by the late first century, with occupation extending over a far wider area than was later walled. On the south side of the town this occupation included masonry buildings of this date which seem to have replaced, though not necessarily immediately, quite substantial Iron-Age farmsteads. Little is known about the early occupation inside the walled enclosure, since only Baker's ill-recorded excavations have taken place; it should be noted that first-century coins are few.

This diffused early settlement is not properly recognizable as a town until the first phase of fortifications in earthwork were built, as in many towns elsewhere in the second half of the second century. Knight drew attention to the presence of pottery in the bank[76] similar to the dating levels of the Jewry Wall baths in Leicester, dated by Kenyon to AD 150–60 but now recognized as more likely to be slightly later.[77] Due, though, to the lack of excavations in the interior, almost all our knowledge of the buildings and streets has been derived from the aerial photographs, which show a good deal, but it must be remembered that these photographs probably show only the latest structures in the town; the earlier remain concealed beneath them.

One of the most significant features to appear in the photographs is the street layout.[78] This displays a haphazard irregularity that can only indicate an almost total lack of co-ordinated planning. Moreover, none of the streets appears to run beyond the line of the fortifications; consequently it might be assumed that none was laid out before the latter's construction. If that is not so, then the defences were constructed around an area sufficiently ample to include all streets, a hypothesis which is not perhaps so impossible since the south, the middle of the western trio and the most southerly of the two streets in the eastern half of the site, all approach the defences in a dog-legged fashion, as though they had to be extended to reach the new gates. If the defences had been there first, then surely the streets would have aimed straight for the gates. Of the streets which can be identified from the photographs, one runs northwards almost straight from the south gate (see below, p. 146) before dividing in the northern sector of the town to send sinuous offshoots approximately north-east and north-west towards the corners of the enclosure; no street approaches the north defences, and it is usually assumed therefore that there is no north gate. Two other streets branch roughly westwards and another north-eastwards from the central axis, while a lightly-metalled track was recorded just inside the southern rampart. For the future it would be interesting to excavate the junctions of the streets to see if all are contemporary or whether they developed successively as the need arose.

The town's fortifications, as indicated above, were first constructed of earthwork.[79] A massive bank, which on the south side was about 12 m (39 ft) wide, was thrown up, largely consisting of sterile iron-stone clay, probably derived from digging the ditches. There is, though, some confusion over the ditches. Hall and Nickerson record at the south-west corner a triple ditch system of apparently conventional Roman profile;[80] the inner ditch was about 6 m (20 ft) wide and 3 m (10 ft) deep and its inside lip was some 6 m (20 ft) from the front of the town wall. Knight, on the other hand, records in a trench across the southern defences not far east of the same corner only a single, wide and nearly flat-bottomed ditch; its width was c. 15 m (49 ft) and it was c. 1.7 m (5½ ft) deep, while its inner lip was also some 6 m (20 ft) in front of the wall.[81] How these two totally different systems are to be reconciled is very problematical. If the defences at Irchester followed the pattern of many towns elsewhere in Britain, then an early multiple-ditch system, as uncovered by Hall and Nickerson, would have been replaced by a single wide-ditch system in the fourth century, as found by Knight. But had that been the case, Knight should have recognized the truncated base at least of Hall and Nickerson's deepest ditch beneath his wide ditch; he did not. Resolution of the problem must await further excavation.

The earth rampart was cut back at the front for the insertion of a masonry wall, which has been recorded as being c. 2.7 m (9 ft) wide, although much of the external face seems to have been robbed, making a correct estimate difficult; the foundations though were up to 3 m (10 ft) wide.[82] No reliable dating evidence has yet been obtained for it, although Knight hazarded the guess, on the basis of his single wide ditch, that it should be assigned to the fourth century. He also recorded a heavily metalled strip on the inside of the berm, about 3 m (10 ft) wide, which he suggested was there to prevent erosion around the base of a nearby, hypothetical bastion.[83] Evidence for two, and possibly three gates came to light during Baker's excavation in 1878–9.[84] The south gate, roughly in the centre of the south wall, is correctly placed for the known internal street. He placed the west gate, though, at the point in the western defences where they make a slight change in direction. Here he recorded what he claimed was a massive stone gateway which had been dismantled and ruined at some period and

blocked with re-used stone. Unfortunately this position for a gate does not correspond to the line of any of the four westward-pointing streets. On the eastern side some heavy foundations were recorded as unexplored, but unlike those at the west gate, they are approximately in the correct position for the emergence of the most southerly of the two eastward-pointing internal streets. Excavations in 1962–3 in the south-west angle of the wall revealed a solid, trapezoid-shaped structure, contemporary with, or perhaps earlier than, the curtain wall, the inner facing of which rested on its rubble core.[85] It is not impossible that this corner tower, for so it seems to be, was contemporary with the earth rampart, in which case Irchester is the only small town where this is so, matching a similar sequence at Cirencester.[86]

The aerial photographs show that the main north-south street, at least on its west side, was lined with strip-like buildings, which are presumably shops and workshops; among them, though, are what appear to be more sophisticated structures, including a building resembling a winged-corridor house and another L-shaped building with one wing terminating in an apse. Stone spreads in the north-east sector of the town indicate other masonry buildings. There is evidence of painted wall plaster and tessellated floors, but no mosaics have yet been found. The most interesting building appearing on the photographs lies east of the main north-south street, in the angle made with it by the street leading to the east gate. It has the clear outlines of a Romano-Celtic temple set within its own *temenos*.[87] This was partly excavated in 1878–9, when a number of interesting discoveries was made in the courtyard.[88] Among them was a fragment of a composite figured capital, probably from a Jupiter column and similar to those found elsewhere in the north-western provinces, notably at Mainz,[89] Catterick[90] and Cirencester,[91] and a fragment of a much-weathered torso. It is interesting that Baker records that the fragment of capital was found not far from a column base which was surrounded by a worn pavement. More important perhaps were two other pieces of sculpture, which, it has been suggested, came from an octagonal monument or shrine.[92] It has been claimed that there is an octagonal building in the *insula* occupying the south-west corner of the town. There are also some circular structures visible in the aerial photographs which may or may not be shrines, but it should be remembered that round-houses with both timber and masonry foundations are a characteristic feature of this area in the first and second centuries.

A number of sizeable cemeteries have been located, mainly on the east side, but also to the south and west. One of the largest was in the Cherry Orchard area, where Baker found several hundred inhumations, mostly of late date.[93] Some were interred in stone coffins, one with a lead lining. Grave goods seem to have been scarce and there was no specific orientation. Other burials have been disturbed by quarrying south and west of the town. One memorial of interest was an inscribed tombstone, which had been re-used as a capping for a very late cist burial inside the walls just south of the east gate.[94] It comme-morates Anicius Saturninus, who was described as *strator consularis*, a soldier seconded from the army to care for the horses in the provincial governor's stables and to perform other eques-trian tasks for his master. Presumably he was on a tour of duty recruiting horses in the Midlands when he met his death; there is no reason to believe, as some would have it, that he would have been stationed permanently at Irchester.

Irchester is very similar to a large number of small walled towns, where the defended enclave only enclosed a small part of the total settlement. Here suburbs seem to extend in all directions except across the river to the north. As with the cemeteries, most of the western and southern suburbs have disappeared in iron-stone mining, with the exception of a small area immediately outside the southern defences, where a variety of buildings dating from the second to the fourth century were found in excavations which took place before the main road was widened.[95] The buildings seem to have been distributed hapha-zardly around the area, and most were simple rectangular structures; one possessed an apse. Another lay in the direct path of the most obvious line of approach of a road to the south gate; as indicated above (p. 145), the problems of the approach roads at Irchester still need to be resolved. One remarkable find in the area was a hoard estimated to contain about 42,000 third-century coins and weighing 125 kg (275 lb), which had been buried in a storage jar.[96]

Despite its position in an area containing several important minerals such as clay and iron-stone, there is virtually no evidence for industrial working in either the town or the suburbs. An isolated pottery kiln, probably of second-century date, was uncovered in the road-works south of the town,[97] but it was badly damaged before proper excavation could take place. Nevertheless there may have been a more developed pottery industry in the vicinity since Hall and Nickerson claimed that the indigenous black, shell-gritted wares were made from a local bed of fossiliferous Jurassic clay.[98] However, at nearby Rushden, large-scale manufacture of unusual vessels was taking place in the mid first century.[99] The kilns were not of normal Romano-British type but were constructed totally above ground with prefabricated fire-bars placed round a central pedestal. Production on a smaller scale seems to have continued here until at least the end of the second century. Hardwick Park, Wellingbor-ough, about the same distance away on the other side of Irchester, has also produced early kilns, which would seem to support the hypothesis that a fort at or near Irchester preceded the town.[100] At a later date a thriving industry grew up in the Northampton area, so possibly making the pro-duction of any quantities of pottery at Irchester unnecessary.[101]

The Nene valley and its hinterland around Irchester must have been a source of fertile agricultural land in the Roman period. At least five villas are known within a distance of 8 km (5 miles) or so of the town, together with several other farms and small settlements. It seems likely, therefore, that the primary function of Irchester was to provide a market and service centre for these outlying estates. The largest villa seems to have been at Stanwick, some 8 km (5 miles) downstream. Here recent excavations by David Neal have revealed a remarkable complex with a combination of residential and farm buildings, yards and compounds, spread over an area of some 30 ha (74 acres).[102] There is a hint of similarity with some of the huge north-Gaulish villas and estates, such as those in the Somme valley.[103] With prosperity of this nature within a short distance of Irchester, the town's economic position must have been assured.

Little is known about the end of Irchester. The possible blocking of the west gate, if gate it is, might indicate a rising feeling of insecurity in the late Roman period. The Royal Commission on Historical Monuments for England, repeating Knight, claims that 'the defences were remodelled in the fourth century, perhaps for artillery'.[104] This indeed is surprising when there is not the slightest evidence for the existence of external towers and where the only known internal tower was built before, or at the same time as, the masonry curtain wall. The latest building so far recorded in the town lay just to the rear of the metalled trackway which ran behind the southern rampart.[105] It was a timber structure of undetermined size with a roughly paved floor of limestone slabs, and it had been built over a rubbish tip containing late fourth-century coins and pottery. Also representative of the town's final days must be the hoard of bronze bowls and strainers which were found in 1873 buried in the eastern cemetery; they have been dated to the final years of the fourth, or to the opening years of the fifth, century.[106] Attempts by Knight to introduce a factor involving Irish raiders in the area, by virtue of the claim that Whilton Lodge (*Bannaventa*), some 40 km (25 miles) west of Irchester, was the birthplace of St Patrick and consequently the place from which he was captured, are no longer acceptable in view of Charles Thomas' careful reconsideration of all the evidence.[107] Nevertheless, there was early Saxon settlement associated with a late Roman occupation at Orton Hall Farm, just east of the neighbouring town of Water Newton,[108] and infiltration up the Nene would have been a simple matter.

Mildenhall (figs. 42 and 43)

Various discoveries in the aptly named Black Field south of the River Kennet, from the mid nineteenth century at least, have lent confirmation to the site's identification as the *Cunetio* of the Antonine Itinerary.[109] In 1880, the local vicar even noted the main roads and streets as cropmarks.[110] Little else of significance was recorded until the 1950s, when repeated aerial reconnaissance confirmed the existence of an internal street network and a two-phase defensive system.[111] Subsequently, several small-scale excavations partially clarified the line of the defences and sampled one of the internal buildings, but unfor-

tunately little has been published in detail.[112] Beyond the defences, however, our understanding of broader morphological and functional aspects is very sketchy. More worryingly, Black Field has been badly plough damaged, with serious implications for the latest archaeological levels.

Mildenhall lay at the junction of two roads, one running east-west between Silchester and Bath, the other roughly north-south between Wanborough and Winchester. This probably influenced the site's origin and early development, though the details remain poorly known. Current evidence suggests an early military presence in the vicinity. A few pieces of undoubted military equipment have been found, including a bronze apron mount, as well as several early coins including Republican issues and examples ranging from Augustus to Nero.[113] A well, excavated in 1963 beneath the stone wall south of the west gate, also produced samian of the period c. AD 50–60, together with Gallo-Belgic and other early Roman wares, alongside the locally produced Savernake ware, all within a relatively homogeneous fill.[114] This suggests a single backfilling operation, arguably in connection with the abandonment of a fort during the early AD 60s, but clearly *in situ* structural evidence is now required. This early material might also indicate a small civilian settlement, perhaps attracted from the supposed univallate hillfort of Forest Hill to the south-west, though few details have been recorded. This site later became the focus for a villa and, incidentally perhaps, also produced a fragment of military metalwork.[115]

The subsequent development of the town is much less clear given the limited nature of modern excavations. The 'plan' reconstructed from aerial photography is dominated by the two phases of defence, though traces of an internal street system and several stone buildings are also visible. The street system seems to be fairly regular, formed by two roughly parallel east-west streets and a single north-south street, all apparently pre-dating the defences to judge from the way both east-west streets were truncated at some point during their lifetime.[116] The original relationship between these streets and the main through-routes, known to be focused on the site, remains uncertain and may even have been complicated by the construction of the late

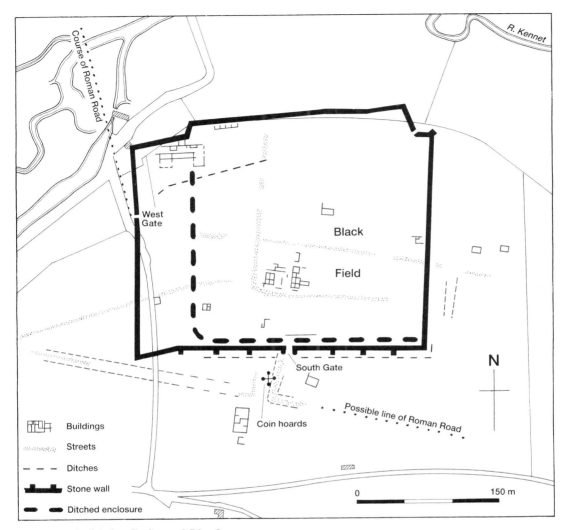

42 Mildenhall (*after Besley and Bland*)

defences. The east-west road may originally have coincided with the more northerly of the two east-west streets, although its course outside the defences remains poorly known for several kilometres. Margary, however, notes a prominent agger on a rough north-west to south-east alignment at Hill Barn south-east of Black Field, which, if projected, would apparently carry it past the southern end of the defences where traces of a street are visible from the air.[117] This might be the original alignment of the main road, though it could equally represent a bypass which replaced its northern predecessor once the stone wall cut across its line.

The north-south route presents more problems. Its northern arm is well known on a reasonably straight alignment north of its crossing of the River Kennet, which if projected would carry it down Cock-a-Troop Lane to a point near the west gate of the stone defences. Beyond this its original course is obscured by the wall, though it probably continued its known alignment, linking up with the next recognizable stretch of agger c. 1 km (0.6 miles) south of Black Field.[118] Most commentators, however, have suggested a more easterly alignment for this southern branch, corresponding with the original south gate and the main north-south street, though how this would relate to the river crossing and its northern arm remains unclear.[119] These unresolved issues can only be clarified by further excavation.

Most excavation has inevitably been directed at the defences, revealing two phases on slightly different alignments.[120] The earlier is represented by a double-ditched enclosure with prominent rounded corners enclosing c. 6 ha (15 acres). Its line is well attested on the south and west, but has not been conclusively proven on the north and east, although excavations have tentatively identified its ditches at two points beneath the later stone wall.[121] No trace has been found of an associated rampart, but this must have been levelled or removed at a later stage. On the south, the V-shaped outer ditch measured 3.7 m (12 ft) wide by 2.3 m (7½ ft) deep, while its inner counterpart, separated by a 1.8 m (6 ft) berm, was recorded as 4 m (14½ ft) deep. Sadly no reliable dating evidence was recovered. Only the south gate is known, represented by a causeway across the ditches. On the west, where a gate might have been expected, the ditches surprisingly cut

through one of the east-west streets.

This undated circuit was replaced by an apparently free-standing stone wall enclosing c. 7.5 ha (18.5 acres) on a slightly different and somewhat irregular alignment. On the north and east it probably coincided closely with the earlier ditches; on the south, where there is a suggestion of deliberate backfilling, it ran immediately outside them; while on the west it included a hitherto undefended area c. 80 m (264 ft) wide. Excavation has revealed a foundation of flint rubble 4.9 to 5.6 m (16 to 18 ft) wide, set in mortar with a front facing of oolitic limestone, which was probably reduced by offsets at the rear to c. 3.7 m (12 ft) above ground.

A series of external towers is also visible from the air, those on either side of the south gate being evenly spaced at c. 36 m (117½ ft) intervals. That nearest to the south-eastern corner, examined in 1958,[122] comprised a flint platform supporting a 7.3 by 5.1 m (24 by 16½ ft) projection represented by two courses of masonry, the lower of chalk blocks being semi-octagonal in plan, the upper of limestone being semi-circular. These were clearly bonded with the wall and therefore contemporary. Associated dating evidence included a coin from the primary silt of a ditch sealed beneath the wall at the west gate which was issued in AD 354–8, making this one of the latest defensive circuits in Roman Britain.[123]

Two gates are known. That on the south was of monumental design, with semi-circular external towers, but surprisingly it lay 35 m (114 ft) east of its predecessor represented by the causeway already mentioned.[124] The west gate, excavated in 1960, was a single-arched structure apparently designed to take wheeled traffic but apparently never used as such, as the absence of wheel ruts demonstrates; instead two sets of four shallow sockets were located at the western end, presumably housing iron grilles alongside a narrow wicket gate.[125] Surprisingly, no gate is known on the east, where the wall cuts across the main east-west side-street. This evidence clearly indicates that the late defences, in general contrast to their predecessors, paid little attention to pre-existing arrangements, which must seriously question their function in a purely civilian context.

Little attention has been directed at the buildings visible on the aerial photographs, and only one has been partly excavated, just inside the

43 Mildenhall, looking east. Besides the roads and defences, a large building complex is clearly visible at the centre (*Cambridge University Collection: copyright reserved*)

north-west corner of the stone defences.[126] This apparently comprised a range of rooms over 40 m (132 ft) long, fronted by a corridor with possible projecting rooms on the wings. Excavation also revealed an apsed room with painted walls in the main range projecting towards the defences. Its exact date could not be established, though it was certainly contemporary with or later than the wall. The excavators argued for an official function, but there was little to corroborate this. Equally impressive ranges of rooms are visible at the heart of the internal street system, the clearest aerial photographs suggesting a single large complex perhaps surrounding a courtyard.[127] Other smaller buildings can also be identified both inside and outside the defences, especially on the south alongside the postulated bypass road.

Next to nothing is known about the site's everyday life to match its self-evident defensive potential. Particularly tantalising is the discovery in 1978 of a hoard of 54,951 third-century *Antoniniani* from a site immediately outside the south gate of the early defences.[128] In reality, there were two separate hoards, a smaller one contained in a lead box and a much larger one buried in a storage jar let into a hole in the ground and covered with a limestone slab. Whether these were official in character, or whether they represent the private accumulation of a successful banker or businessman remains uncertain on current evidence. Little is known about the religious life of the settlement, while only one burial has been located, *c.* 120 m (390 ft) south of the defences.[129] It comprised a two-piece lead coffin encased within an outer wooden container.

It is somewhat ironic that the best dated sequences at Mildenhall concern the fourth-century stone wall and the building in the north-west corner, both providing a tantalising picture of a site of some importance to the central government at a time when other sites were showing signs of decline. Sadly we know little else about this late phase beyond the fourth-century well excavated in 1912, *c.* 60 m (198 ft) south of the south-east angle.[130] Nor can we begin to define its relationship to its presumed urban predecessor or its fifth-century fate, for which the relevant evidence may already be too plough damaged.

Towcester (figs. 44 and 45)

The Roman town of *Lactodurum* lies on Watling Street about 90 km (56 miles) north of London, at a point where it crosses the River Tove, and where the river forms a loop in conjunction with the Silverstone Brook. A minor road from Alchester joins the main road here, and another road might be expected to leave in the direction of Irchester or at least Duston, but no evidence for it has yet been found leading direct from the town. It has been suggested that it branched off Watling Street north of the town and beyond the river, where excavation has produced evidence for a gravelled surface. A third road is thought to head west-south-west towards Kings Sutton, roughly along the line of Brackley Road, while yet another was found branching in a generally southerly direction from the Alchester road, some 800 m (2600 ft) outside the town, possibly aiming towards Fleet Marston;[131] the latter had been added to the system.

Towcester probably lay in the *civitas Catuvellaunorum*; it is mentioned in the Antonine Itinerary and is called *Iaciodulma* in the Ravenna list.[132] The name of *Lactodurum* causes problems, but seems to imply the presence of an early fort in a region noted for its dairy-farmers.[133] Certainly this area around the central and east Midlands, which includes Leicestershire and Northamptonshire, is famed for the excellence of its pastures; in the northern and eastern parts, two famous cheeses are produced, and beasts are still transhumed from Wales in the winter.

The site has been recognized as Roman since Camden recorded coins, although he wrongly attributed the name of *Tripontium*.[134] Since then almost every early antiquary has made comments, the local antiquary Bridges being the first to draw attention to a circuit of probable defences;[135] not much of the latter can therefore have survived even in the eighteenth century. In contrast to Irchester, the Roman town at Towcester is almost entirely covered by the present modest market town. Consequently little excavation has been carried out inside the town. In the middle of the last century G. Baker plotted what he considered to be the line of the defences and also compiled a list of coins from the site.[136] Somewhat later, Haverfield summarized Baker's and other more recent discoveries, but repro-

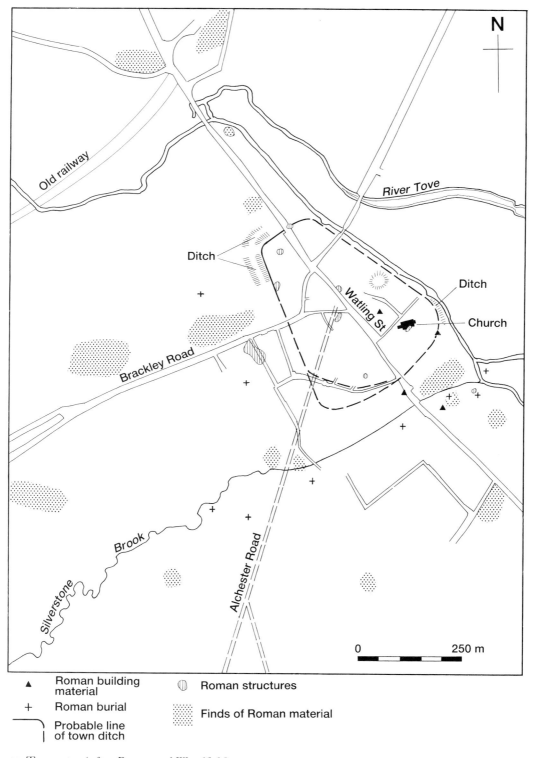

44 Towcester (*after Brown and Woodfield*)

45 Towcester, looking north (*Cambridge University Collection: copyright reserved*)

duced the former's probably erroneous map.[137] Since 1954 however, excavations, even then sometimes of a variable standard, have explored the fortifications, mainly in the northern part of the town and have uncovered parts of several substantial internal masonry buildings. The largest excavations, though, have been carried out in the suburbs, which extended for considerable distances, especially on the south and west sides.[138]

As indicated above, the name given to the site ought to imply the presence of an early fort in the district, probably not far removed from Watling Street. No evidence has yet been produced, but if the town developed from a *vicus* outside a fort, then the latter might perhaps be expected to lie outside its area, possibly on the rising ground to the south, or on the level but slightly higher ground across the River Tove. It should be emphasized that there is no indication of an immediately pre-Roman Iron-Age occupation under the town or in the immediate area surrounding it, so that this is unlikely to be the cause of Towcester's origin and foundation. Nevertheless, slight traces of early timber-framed buildings were found in excavations in the Park Street area.[139] Associated with the structures was an ornamental mount from the scabbard of a legionary's sword.[140] The only other items of possible military equipment are a leaf-shaped bronze pendant of a type often used by cavalry regiments and a bronze strap-end from the western side of the town.[141]

The slight traces of timber buildings referred to above, if not military, could represent either an early settlement forming round the new road junction or perhaps a *vicus*. Notwithstanding that so little is known of the town's earliest origins, a fair amount of activity is attested by finds of coins and pottery dated to the late first century. Somewhat surprisingly, also, one of the few identified buildings of this period was constructed in masonry, but then there is no shortage of good stone in the neighbourhood. The building was discovered on the south side of Park Street, set askew to the Alchester road and not far from its junction with Watling Street; it was substantial, with buttresses supporting at least one wall. The early date, allied with the materials of construction, might suggest an official use; its position close to an important road junction

would be ideal for a *mansio*. In the second century, following enlargement, it was replaced by two new masonry buildings, one of which encroached on the road.[142]

Casual finds would suggest that, by the middle of the second century, the main road frontages inside the town were mostly occupied by buildings, after the manner of many small towns; presumably the majority would have been shops and workshops. During the second century also, buildings began to appear in the areas away from the main roads and a bath-house may have existed beneath the church of St Lawrence, where floors of *opus signinum* and herringbone tiles, a reported hypocaust and box-flue tiles have all been found, overlying an earlier timber-framed structure;[143] a position in the lower end of the town would have facilitated drainage. Part of a late third-century timber-framed house was excavated a short distance south of the northwest corner of the town; it was replaced in the fourth century by a building with masonry foundations which had contained tessellated floors and painted wall plaster.[144]

Little is known about the internal streets, apart from the two main roads which join almost in the centre of the town. Traces of two others, linked to the Alchester road, have been found in Allens Yard in the south-west quarter. These same excavations also uncovered what was described as a concrete water channel or drain, 1.4 m ($4\frac{1}{2}$ ft) deep and 0.7 m ($2\frac{1}{4}$ ft) wide, associated with a cistern and a drainage system.[145] Considered in the broadest sense, this might imply that Towcester, unusually for a small town, possessed an aqueduct and a fairly sophisticated distribution system. The most likely sources would be the River Tove, the Silverstone Brook, tapped some distance upstream from the town, or any other of the known small streams in the area.

The line taken by the fortifications at Towcester is still in some doubt except in the north-west, where a single broad ditch can still be seen turning the corner. There is a less well-defined corresponding turn at the north-east corner, although doubt has been cast on the eastern line, which is now thought to lie further west of the mill leat originally considered to represent the ditch.[146] This is also despite the possible appearance of its inner lip in the north-eastern corner of the churchyard. On the south side, burials found during excavations in the T.M.T. yard, north of the Silverstone Brook, would indicate that the defences lay even further north.[147] Most controversy seems to surround the south-west angle, where two alternative lines have been proposed.[148] One, the inner course, closely follows the curving line of Richmond Road; the other makes a more pronounced angle to the south of it, and doubt must remain until excavation has established which is correct. There is also conflict over the nature of the defences, which, when first sectioned on the west side near the north-west angle, were found to comprise a single shallow ditch 9 m (29½ ft) wide, fronting a wall, mostly robbed but with foundations 3 m (10 ft) wide, backed by an apparently contemporary bank.[149] But a more recent drainage trench cut through the ditch, bank and robber trench of the wall, west of the north-east corner,[150] recorded a bank, perhaps of two periods. In 1954, when the first section was cut, early banks round Romano-British towns had not been generally recognized nor their existence accepted by many archaeologists. It is probably best, therefore, to assume that the first section was misinterpreted, and that Towcester, as at nearby Irchester, was provided with earthwork defences before the wall was built. It is interesting that the drawn and published section appears to have a vertical cut in the body of the robbing trench not far from its designated eastern edge. Generally where a wall has been robbed, it can be extremely difficult to distinguish between the cut made in a rampart for its insertion and the edge of the robbing trench.[151] Material from the core of the bank at Towcester dates to the later second century, comparable with other towns which were similarly fortified; no satisfactory date has yet been given to the wall. There ought to be at least three gates leading into the town. Massive masonry containing Roman brick has been recorded on the eastern side of Watling Street at a point roughly corresponding to the north gate, while foundations of what could be the south gate have also been noted. The position of the south-west gate carrying the Alchester road is as yet unknown. A fourth gate might exist on the Brackley Road line, since a cemetery and suburb exists beyond it.

One of the largest excavations to take place at Towcester has been a series carried out between 1967 and 1978 in a suburb south-west of the town, on both sides of the Alchester road; about 5.7 ha (14 acres) was examined in some detail with interesting results.[152] The metalled road was not, apparently, laid out until the late first century, although it might be suspected that an unmetalled track, following the same line, had been prepared somewhat earlier, especially if a fort was placed at Towcester. A series of fields, demarcated by ditches, lay west of the road and may have been connected with the nearby villa at Wood Burcote, which appears to be of the same date; equally they may represent the fields of farmers resident in the new town. Small circular structures, clearly forerunners of the more sophisticated round houses of this neighbourhood (see Irchester, p. 147), were found in some of these fields, and may indicate some sort of tenancy arrangement, or perhaps the allocation of land to native small-holders. These boundaries seem to have survived for about a century, when drastic replanning took place which, for the first time, affected both sides of the road. New plots were laid out, again bounded by ditches, and a standard measurement seems to have been employed, although differences between the opposite sides of the road might suggest that it was the boundary between two landowners and their respective estates. Buildings, mainly of timber or of timber and cob with unmortared stone foundations, appear at this stage, but were, unusually, set with their long axes parallel to the road and not, as is more normal with such structures, at right angles to it. There is slight evidence for industry in this period, notably smithing and pottery manufacture. Although general activity was intense here in the late second and early third centuries, it seems to have waned by the middle of the third century with buildings and farms even becoming derelict. The fact that this activity coincided with the construction of the first town defences may have a significance that cannot yet be appreciated.

A revival of interest in the area took place in the late third and early fourth centuries, when a new road 6 m (20 ft) wide was constructed branching from the main road in the direction of Fleet Marston, near Aylesbury. What new need caused this road to be built is not as yet identifiable, even if it was aiming at some intermediate but unknown site and not at Fleet Marston. At the same time as the road system around Towcester was being developed, the ditches flanking the Alchester road were cleaned out in such a way as to cut through many of the building sites which flanked it, a clear indication of the run down nature of the area. Towards the middle of the fourth century, though, there was renewed building activity. Some resemblances to the earlier plots, but with variations, were introduced giving a much more informal appearance. It would seem, therefore, that a semblance of the old property boundaries had survived either in records or on the ground. Distinctive buildings were erected in many of these new plots: the shapes were basically circular, ranging from 6 to 12 m (20 to 39 ft) in diameter, but it would seem that only half of the circumference was walled, probably in cob or possibly in turf; drainage ditches were dug round the walled sections of the circuits, and the open sides invariably faced the road. The structures, therefore, resemble shelters rather than proper dwellings, and appear to belong to the same tradition of vernacular building in this area of Roman Britain which gave rise to the circular houses noted above at Irchester, Stanwick and other places. West of the Alchester road, but not to the east, these structures were replaced after a shortish interval by rectangular timber buildings, possibly of aisled form, in which the internal uprights were based on stones or masonry pads; good-quality architectural pieces were re-used in some of them. It is worth remembering though that the area is low-lying, now producing water-logged deposits; probably in Roman times it was liable to flooding, conditions which, at Wanborough (p. 163), produced exceptional building methods to meet them. Unfortunately no levels were recorded from the tops of the masonry pads. Had they been made it might now be possible to argue the existence at Towcester of buildings similar to those at Wanborough, where the entire timber structure was raised above ground level on pads and stones of this nature. Both in these rectangular buildings and in the circular ones which preceded them, a good deal of evidence was found for smithing, iron-smelting, lead and possibly pewter and bronze manufacture; a pewter dish was among the objects recovered from the plumber's workshop. Alongside these industrial processes, there was also evidence for agricultural activity. Sheep and cattle were stalled, perhaps, since these plots appeared to be individual small-holdings, in the form of the house-cow and the fattened sheep for the family; also draught oxen may have been kept. In the fields behind the plots grazing would have been available, while the occurrence of insect pests associated with stored grain would suggest a degree of arable farming as well.

Reference was made in the last paragraph to re-used architectural masonry. Towcester has produced quite a number of such pieces as well as sculptured objects from both inside and outside the walls. These fragments include parts of column drums, capitals and cornice and frieze.[153] Many pieces were found where the Alchester road crossed the Silverstone Brook. This same area has also produced massive mortared foundations just south of the crossing and west of the road; two small silver votive axes, a silver ring, spoon and disc brooch, together with an unusual first-century bronze brooch, have also been found, while a large number of supposedly Roman horse skulls were observed on the site. Also recovered from the topsoil was an enamelled copper-alloy object described in the report as a 'miniature stool'. These interesting objects are not uncommonly associated with religious centres. A group of three from a coppersmith's workshop at Catterick had been made in diminishing sizes, so that the smallest sat above the middle which in turn sat on the largest. With their large central apertures it seems most likely that, set one on top of another, they formed some type of lamp or candle-holder; they are certainly not stools! Although it is likely that the architectural fragments came from more than one building, there is a strong presumption from the other evidence in favour of a religious establishment.[154] It is known that a petrifying stream runs into the Silverstone Brook, a phenomenon which was no doubt treated with some awe and wonder by the local inhabitants from earliest times onwards, and a suitable subject for propitiation; turning people and animals to stone has for long been deemed one of the great powers of witchcraft.

Some burials, mostly inhumations, were found in the Alchester road area. Other cemeteries are indicated by finds of skeletons, while an 'urnfield' near the Silverstone Brook was reported towards the end of the last century, when the course of the brook was being straightened; it would appear to have been a cremation cemetery. There certainly

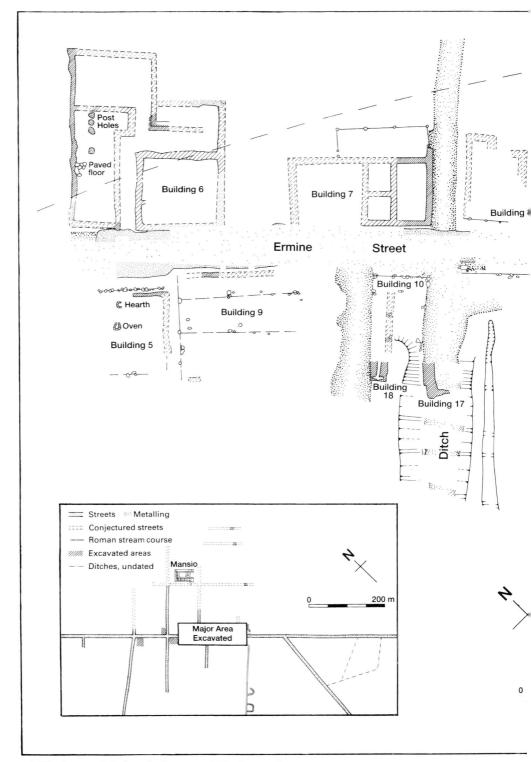

46 Wanborough (*after Anderson and Wacher, and Phillips and Walters*)

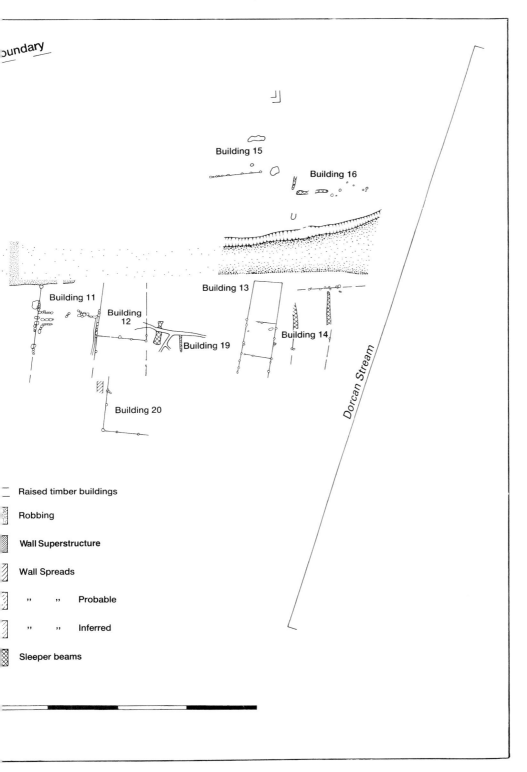

Boundary

Building 15

Building 16

U

Building 11

Building 12

Building 13

Building 19

Building 14

Dorcan Stream

Building 20

— Raised timber buildings

Robbing

Wall Superstructure

Wall Spreads

" " Probable

" " Inferred

Sleeper beams

were inhumation cemeteries outside the north gate. Another, which produced at least one cremation, existed along the present Brackley Road, indicating perhaps another gate and a road leading out of the town in this direction. The cemetery outside the south gate seems to have extended as far as the south-east corner. Generally, though, burials were fairly widely scattered and the cemeteries do not appear to have been intensively used.[155] A remarkable female stone head, apparently from within the town, has been identified as an underworld deity and may have come from a funerary monument.[156]

As at neighbouring Irchester there are a number of villas and other small settlements in the Towcester neighbourhood. The nearest is that at Wood Burcote, where a villa was built on a site which had been occupied from the middle of the first century AD. Pottery with late Iron-Age affinities was being manufactured there, probably in surface kilns of the type first identified at Rushden.[157] The villa replaced early timber-framed buildings in the late first century; an isolated stone building containing corn-driers some little distance away and beside a stream, has been interpreted as a water-mill, but there is no positive evidence.[158] It seems likely that Towcester acted as one of the service centres for part of the rich area of farmland which encompassed the whole of the Jurassic zone from the Cotswolds through modern Northamptonshire to Lincolnshire.

Although the demise of the villa at Wood Burcote seems to have taken place in the third century despite coins of the fourth century being found in the area, Towcester, in contrast, seems to have remained as a viable centre until the end of the Roman period. The masonry building uncovered near the north-west corner of the town apparently survived in use until the end of the fourth or even into the fifth century. Human skull fragments associated with the collapsed debris could indicate a violent end. Evidence, though, for the early Anglo-Saxon period is entirely lacking, despite the fact that by AD 917 the town had become a *burh*. In that year, following a siege, the site was refortified by Edward the Elder,[159] who made use of the Roman defences.

Wanborough (figs. 46 and 47)

The small town at Wanborough is usually identified with the *Durocornovium* of the Antonine Itinerary,[160] lying some 20 km (12 miles) south-east of Cirencester on Ermin Street, at a point where a branch road diverges to Mildenhall and just before the main road ascends the northern scarp of the Berkshire Downs on its way to Silchester. No evidence for Iron-Age occupation has ever been uncovered, and the nearest known major settlement of that period is Liddington Castle, on the scarp of the Downs some 5 km (3 miles) due south. The town probably lay within the *civitas* of the Dobunni, although it must have been close to the border with the Atrebates.

The site has been known since the seventeenth century.[161] Before its destruction in 1977, the central section was dominated by a visible linear depression which ran approximately north to south and terminated at the Dorcan Stream. This depression marked the line of Ermin Street, which although surviving in places had been largely robbed of its metalling. However, at one point close to the stream where metalling had survived, a long-cross penny of Henry III, embedded in the top surface, showed that the road was still in use in the middle ages. The site lies mainly on Kimmeridge clay and is therefore not particularly susceptible to aerial photography, although in the very dry summer of 1975 a series of photographs showed parch marks in grass of an extensive street grid to the north-east of the main road junction, as well as a major courtyard building set well back from Ermin Street.[162]

Three extensive campaigns of excavation took place in advance of the construction of a major road improvement scheme and flood prevention works in the area of the settlement known as Nine-Acre Field; between them they embraced much of the central area north of the stream, and took place in 1966 and 1968,[163] 1969–70[164] and 1976.[165] The first two campaigns were aimed mainly at identifying the area and density of settlement, especially adjacent to the main road, and consequently concentrated mostly on the later structures. The last campaign was designed to investigate the earlier occupation in much the same area. There has also been spasmodic excavation and rescue work carried out by Swindon

47 Wanborough, with the probable *mansio* showing
as a crop-mark in pasture (*Cambridge University
Collection: copyright reserved*)

Museum and other local bodies in the course of road construction. An attempt in 1970 to excavate in the field immediately south of the Dorcan Stream, where there are some interesting earthworks, had to be abandoned owing to the hostility of the landowner. Similar earthworks can also be seen in the field south of the junction of the two Roman roads; although one roughly resembles a wide but shallow ditch, the remainder of these surface features are so irregular as to be incapable of certain interpretation.

The site, even now, is low-lying and liable to flood, hence the construction of the present flood-water lagoon. In Roman times the same difficulty must have been experienced, which is accordingly reflected in the building techniques employed.

The earliest feature to be uncovered in the excavations was Ermin Street with its accompanying side ditches. The latter were set 23 m (75 ft) apart, a considerable distance for road ditches but not unparalleled elsewhere; they were not always continuous. Pottery from the west ditch suggested a construction date for the road in the Neronian period. These ditches also appeared to be part of a larger drainage system, again reflecting the low-lying nature of the ground. Buildings in this early period were sparse and constructed wholly of timber.[166]

No fort has yet been found at Wanborough, but the situation on a main road some 20 km (12 miles) south-east of the fort at Cirencester, makes it a likely candidate, a supposition borne out by finds of military metalwork, coins and good-quality pottery.[167] The most probable position for a fort is on the slightly higher ground rising towards Stratton St Margaret; if correct, then the lower-lying ground between it and the stream could have developed as a *vicus* or possibly as a workshop area. This early occupation terminated *c.* AD 80, which probably means that the fort was then evacuated, in line with that at nearby Cirencester.[168] The deposition of large quantities of industrial waste, notably iron and glass slag, together with numerous pottery vessels – some still unbroken – in the roadside ditches is reminiscent of the clearing of a fort during an evacuation.

It is not certain, though, that the settlement which developed here in the late first and early second century was a direct descendant of the *vicus*, since a break occurred in the occupation in the areas which have been examined. Much must depend on the date of the *mansio* which has been revealed in an aerial photograph as being situated some 150 m (490 ft) to the north-east.[169] If the *vicus* did not survive the fort's evacuation, then the construction of a *mansio*, perhaps afterwards, could have provided the impetus for the growth of a new civilian settlement.

The *mansio* was a large courtyard building, measuring *c.* 48 by 34 m (157 by 111 ft) (see fig. 4D). Ranges of rooms and some cross-corridors were placed along an ambulatory which surrounds three sides of the central court; the fourth side appears to contain only one long room, but internal partitions may have been robbed or may have been of wood. This side, though, was treated differently since it lacks the external ambulatory which encloses two of the other sides and part of the third; this fourth side, facing south-east, also has two projecting wings, suggesting perhaps that it contained the main entrance. It is thought that a bath-house existed near the southern corner where, although the ground is less sensitive to aerial photography, box-flue tiles, *pila* tiles and wall plaster have been discovered.[170] The *mansio* is aligned on a regular grid of streets, suggesting a system which is either earlier or contemporary with it, and stretching for unequal distances on each side of Ermin Street.[171] Several short side-streets were added to the system in later centuries, presumably to provide access to the rears of new buildings.

One interesting feature is the later treatment of Ermin Street. Although the early, widely-spaced, side ditches were probably filled by the end of the first century, the area between them was, most likely in the second or third centuries, covered in a layer of carefully graded hard chalk or limestone aggregate some centimetres thick. It had been closely compacted and the surface showed considerable wear. It is difficult to be certain about its purpose, since the later running surfaces of the road occupied only a much lesser width in the middle. The most likely explanation would be that it was designed as an apron to prevent the underlying clay from being washed away from beneath the metalling in times of flood. The full width could never have been intended to act as the road, since buildings rapidly encroached upon it from both sides, and ultimately new ditches were dug through it immediately adjacent to the road. A further interesting feature was observed as the road approached the Dorcan Stream.[172] Not only did these new ditches diverge away from the central line of the road some distance short of the stream, but also at the same point the worn, compacted metalling of the surface gave way to looser, unworn rubble. This might suggest that the road rose on an embankment as it neared the stream, hence implying the presence of a bridge and not a ford at the crossing.

An attempt seems to have been made in the late second or early third century to fortify the core of the town. A large ditch, c. 9 m (29½ ft) wide, was found to the west of Ermin Street and some 70 m (230 ft) north-west of the stream crossing, although no corresponding ditch could be found east of the street. The ditch was associated with a clay rampart on its north-west flank, which may have been fronted by a stone wall, c. 1.2 m (4 ft) wide; only a somewhat indeterminate robbing trench survived, so that the relationship between rampart and wall could not be established.[173] During the third century, a cobbled surface, delimited by a fence of wooden posts along its north edge, ran down into the ditch. The excavation was much confused and difficult to interpret, but there also appeared to be slight traces of a gate structure adjacent to Ermin Street. On present evidence it would seem that, although normal fortifications were started, perhaps at first in earthwork, they were never completed. Certainly if the line of the ditch was continued eastwards it would have either encroached upon the *mansio* or turned before reaching it, so excluding it from the fortified area. Moreover, the projected line of the ditch east of Ermin Street was blocked by a substantial side-street running in the same direction and by a well-constructed masonry building situated in the angle of the two streets. Obviously much more investigation is required before the whereabouts and history of the defences can be satisfactorily explained.

The main area of the settlement, along both sides of Ermin Street as it approached the stream, saw much building activity in the later Roman period, when both frontages were occupied almost continuously for some distance north. Most of the buildings were constructed with masonry foundations, often of large sarsen blocks, but were probably half-timbered. Burnt daub indicated the presence of timber-framed

structures based on sleeper-beams, some of which were placed directly on the ground and not in trenches, in recognition, perhaps, of its wetness. Further recognition of this disadvantage led to the use of a building method which was, at the time of discovery, unique in Roman Britain.[174] Noted in one building at first, but subsequently exposed in others, single stones were observed to form straight lines with distances of up to 1 m (3¼ ft) or more between them. The stones were often quite small and the upper surfaces were seldom flat, so they would not have made suitable bases for upright posts; yet the highest points of all the stones in a given group were on virtually the same level, with only small variations of a few centimetres between them. It was concluded, therefore, that these stones acted as levellers for the ends of wooden floor joists, so that the entire building was raised above the ground, in the manner of modern prefabricated garden sheds. It was also noted that only small sherds of pottery were found within the area of a building, although the number of small finds, such as coins and other metal objects, was greater than might be expected. Presumably the latter could fall easily between the floorboards or through knot holes and could not then be recovered. Unfortunately, although the outline of a building constructed in this way could be traced without much difficulty – providing individual stones had not been too disturbed – the lines of internal partitions cannot be established.

There is some evidence for industrial activities at Wanborough. Although the site lay sufficiently close to the major pottery factories at Savernake[175] and in the Thames valley[176] for these wares to be strongly represented, more local manufacture took place at Whitehill Farm and Purton, just north and west of Swindon, and possibly at Wanborough itself; no kilns have yet been found, but some types of fabrics, including fine wares, some glazed wares and some unusual relief-decorated beakers are peculiar to the area.[177] Bricks stamped with a maker's or a factory's name or initials are not uncommon, and can be paralleled at Cirencester and some other Gloucestershire sites;[178] they may have been manufactured at the large, but mainly-unexplored, factory at Minety only some few kilometres north-west of Wanborough.[179] TPF and IVC DIGNI occur most commonly. All excavators at Wanborough have recorded large quantities of bun-shaped lumps of iron slag. Iron ore, as nodules and as pan, occurs naturally in the Kimmeridge Clay, which underlies most of the site, and they were no doubt exploited, although smelting furnaces have yet to be found. Ovens, possibly for baking bread, were found in a number of buildings, while the discovery of a very large quern, of Midlands millstone grit, in a courtyard building on the north-east side of Ermin Street may have come from a mechanically-driven mill, implying the production of flour on a commercial rather than a domestic level; the stone was fractured and an attempt had been made to mend it with iron cramps sealed with lead.[180] There was no shortage of building materials in the neighbourhood, shelly limestone outcropping at Swindon and chalk and flint available not far distant on the Berkshire Downs.

It is likely that a temple once existed, although the site has yet to be positively identified. Heavy stone foundations have been reputedly recorded in a field south of Lotmead Farm, while unconfirmed reports of fragments of white marble being found close to the Dorcan Stream not far from the *mansio* site are, if true, evidence for a building of some merit. But the firmest evidence for the existence of a religious establishment was the finding of a lead *defixio* or curse.[181] They were normally fixed to some outside part of a temple, and usually invoked dire consequences on a malefactor. Unfortunately this curse is not complete, and neither the name of the deity, whose help was being requested nor the name or names of the person or people being cursed have survived. Religion on a more domestic level is probably represented by a fragment of the head of a female pipe-clay figurine, possibly of a mother goddess.[182] So far the only indications of a cemetery lie some 30 m (98 ft) to the west of Ermin Street, where both cremations and inhumations have been found.[183] The nearness of this cemetery to the main road must be taken to indicate that the main bulk of the town lies to the east and that only a narrow strip of settlement bounded the west of the road. One street, though, which branched off Ermin Street to the west, seems to extend well beyond the limits of the settlement and appears to be aiming at Swindon Old Town where, on the hilltop, Roman buildings have been identified, as well as a later Anglo-Saxon settlement.[184] It seems too far away to be a suburb, and the buildings may have been connected with either a nearby villa, of which a number exist round Wanborough, or with stone quarrying or pottery manufacture.

The end of the Roman period at Wanborough saw the use of much late pottery, while the coin series contains pieces representing the later emperors. What caused the final dissolution of the settlement can only be a matter for conjecture, but it may be that a wetter climate, coupled with a rising water table in the late fourth or early fifth centuries rendered the site uninhabitable. Hence the ultimate migration to the better-drained hilltop of Swindon by the earliest Anglo-Saxon immigrants.

NINE
SPECIALIZED SITES I: RELIGIOUS

Bath (figs. 48–52)

Of all the small towns, Bath is perhaps the best known, with a long tradition of antiquarian discoveries stretching back as far as Leland and Camden. The site was also fortunate in attracting the attention of various individuals during the eighteenth and nineteenth centuries, among them Englefield, Lysons, Irvine and Davis, at a time when redevelopment first exposed the principal Roman remains to view.[1] The various elements of the temple precinct were recorded in 1790 and 1867–89; the great bathing establishment was pieced together from discoveries most notably in 1755 and 1878–96; and the main reservoir was examined in 1878–9. Nor were these the only significant finds, as Haverfield's masterly summary in 1906 clearly demonstrated.[2] Thereafter Bath slept for almost half a century, with the exception of work at the east end of the bathing establishment in 1923.[3] Then in 1954, prompted by the increasing pace of redevelopment, a programme of excavations and research was begun which was to last, on and off, through to the mid 1980s under the successive direction of Sir Ian Richmond and Prof. Barry Cunliffe. Work concentrated on elucidating the developmental sequence of the principal religious and curative facilities at the heart of the defended area,[4] coupled with rescue operations at several other sites.[5] To this can be added the considerable corpus of epigraphic and sculptural material from the town, so vital to our understanding of the resident population.[6] The big building complexes apart, however, surprisingly little is known about the rest of the settlement and its morphological development, which makes it difficult to define its broader role in relation to a wider hinterland.[7]

Bath's origins remain obscure, but must be related in part to the presence of three mineral springs rising to the surface north of the Avon, and in part to its strategic location on the Fosse Way. The springs, which include the main King's Bath spring and the subsidiary Hetlin and Cross Bath springs, clearly gave rise to its Roman name, *Aquae Sulis*, which itself strongly suggests a pre-Roman religious origin for the site.[8] Little trace of any Iron-Age activity has survived the extensive Roman building operations, however, though it has been suggested that a gravel ridge approaching the main spring from the south might represent a pre-Roman causeway from which votive offerings could be thrown; this could well account for the 17 Celtic coins of Dobunnic and Durotrigian derivation, though these were actually found alongside Roman material in the sand fill of the later reservoir.[9] Bath's military potential at a strategic river crossing has also attracted attention.[10] Several finds of Claudio-Neronian pottery and coins have long suggested an early military presence, as have a number of apparently early military tombstones, but no actual structural evidence has yet come to light. A recent reassessment of the road network has suggested that the principal routes converge on a river crossing near Bathwick, well to the north of the later curative focus around the springs.[11] Here, on the west bank, early finds indicate an extensive settlement nucleus on the slopes of Snow Hill extending southwards along the river, while on the east side, finds of Claudio-Neronian samian from a slightly elevated gravel terrace might well point to the site of an early fort. All this would make the springs and any existing religious focus peripheral to the early Roman nucleus astride the river crossing.

Attention was soon directed at the develop-

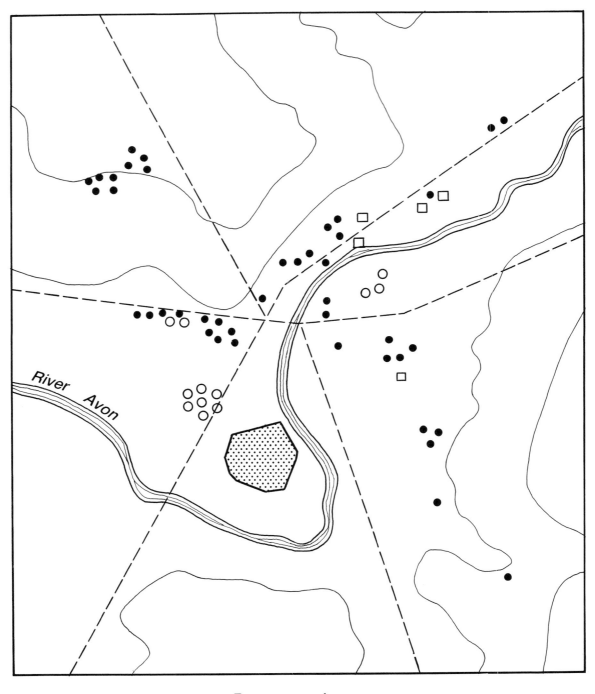

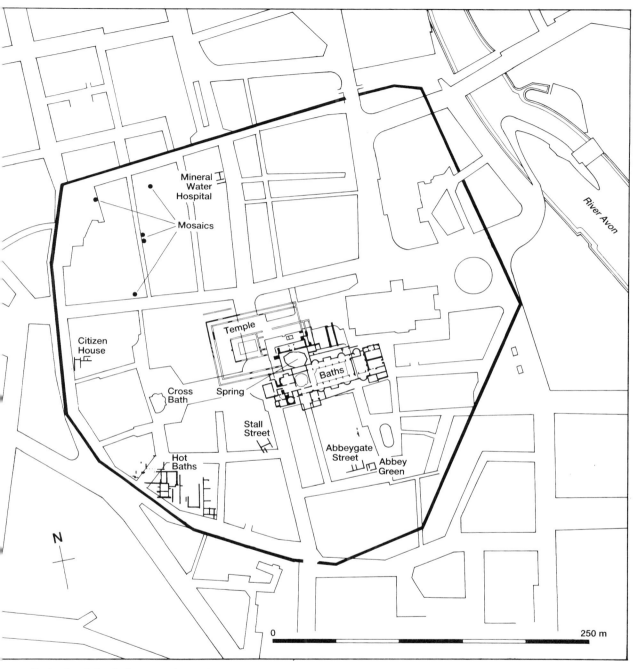

49 Bath, the defended area and associated building complexes (*after Cunliffe*)

ment of the King's Bath spring, however, which was to become the central focus of a large complex comprising the Temple of Sulis Minerva to the north and the principal bathing establishment to the south (fig. 50). Here the Roman engineers constructed a reservoir and settling tank to help contain the spring and its daily output of a 1,137,500 l (250,000 gallons).[12] First a working platform was constructed on oak piles, just inside the projected line of the reservoir wall, with a gap opposite a substantial drainage channel to remove the excess water. This lowered the water level sufficiently in the building area to allow the mud clogging the spring to be removed. Then a foundation trench was dug alongside the working platform into which was set the reservoir wall, probably on a series of oak piles. Contemporary with this the drainage channel was converted into a permanent stone-lined drain and the principal elements of the baths begun. Finally the reservoir was waterproofed with massive sheets of lead, the lower ends of which were sealed between a layer of blue lias clay and a thick concrete slab. With a sluice gate fitted across the drain, the water was allowed to fill the reservoir. In its original design, the spring was probably surrounded by a low balustrade and open to the air.

Immediately to the north of the reservoir lay a 28.8 by 17.9 m (94 by 58½ ft) paved area fronting the Temple of Sulis Minerva, which flanked its western side. The whole was enclosed within a colonnaded precinct 72 m (235 ft) east-west by 52 m (170 ft) north-south. In its first phase, the temple was approached by a flight of steps from the east and stood on a 9 by 14 m (29½ by 46 ft) podium of concrete rubble probably faced by freestone blocks.[13] Numerous elements of its superstructure have survived, allowing it to be reconstructed as a tetra-style Corinthian façade with a roughly square *cella* behind.[14] The columns supported a normal architrave and frieze, of which little is known, surmounted by the well-known Sulis pediment with its central oak-wreathed shield incorporating a male 'Gorgon's' head, held aloft by two winged Victories who perch on globes; in the corners probably reclined sea-creatures or Tritons, while other spaces were occupied by at least one Corinthian helmet and an owl perched on another, both appropriate to Minerva.[15] East of the temple in the paved area

lay the altar, constructed at the point where the east-west axis of the temple complex crosses the north-south axis of the reservoir and the entrance hall of the baths beyond.[16] It seems to have been 2.2 m (7 ft) square originally, resting on a platform of raised limestone blocks, though only three of its corner blocks and a single capping slab have survived. The former carry representations of various Roman deities including Bacchus, Hercules and Apollo. To the east of the paved area, lay the main wall of the precinct incorporating a centrally-placed doorway.

The chronology of these developments depends primarily on a stylistic assessment of the surviving architectural fragments, which can be assigned with reasonable confidence to the period *c*. AD 65–75.[17] This is very much in line with the limited dating evidence from the baths, which must in any case have formed an integral development with the reservoir. In its earliest phase, the establishment comprised three elements, with a spacious entrance hall flanked by a series of rooms to the south and west and a sequence of thermal baths to the east.[18] The main entrance hall with its north and south arcades lay immediately south of the spring, and three windows in its north wall were clearly designed to offer a view over the reservoir into the precinct beyond. The rooms to the south and west underwent numerous later modifications, but originally comprised a simple suite of baths including both a *tepidarium* and a *caldarium* with two recesses. Immediately east of the hall lay the Great Bath, set within a 33.2 by 20.4 m (108½ by 67 ft) aisled hall, with arcades along its north and south sides housing a series of rectangular or semi-circular niches. The bath itself, which measured 22 by 8.8 m (72 by 29 ft), had four steep steps and was entirely lead-lined. It was filled from the reservoir by a lead box-pipe at its north-western corner. From the arcades of the Great Bath, doors led east into the so-called Lucas Bath, measuring 13.1 by 6.1 m (43 by 20 ft), beyond which lay yet another smaller swimming pool. Both were supplied in sequence from the Great Bath, suggesting a series of thermal baths declining in size, grandeur and temperature. The evidence indicates that all three originally possessed a timber roof, while the heated rooms to the west probably had concrete vaults.

This massive redevelopment of the spring and

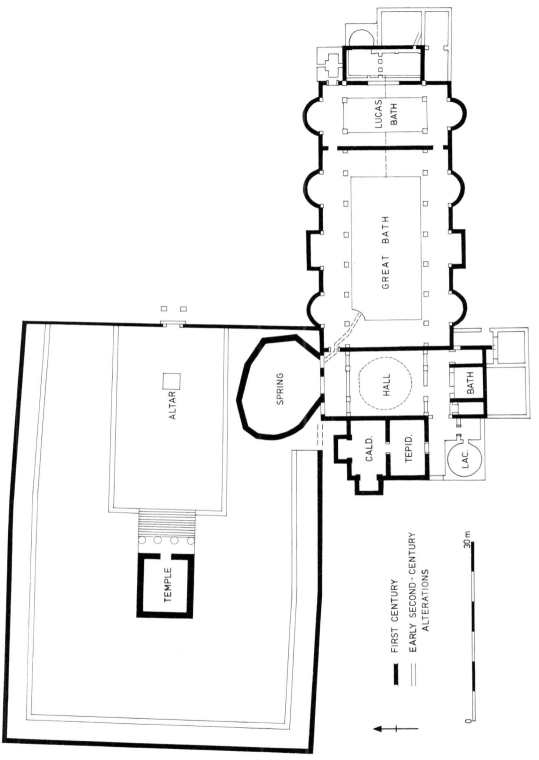

50 Bath, the Temple of Sulis Minerva and the Baths
in the first and early second centuries (*after
Cunliffe*)

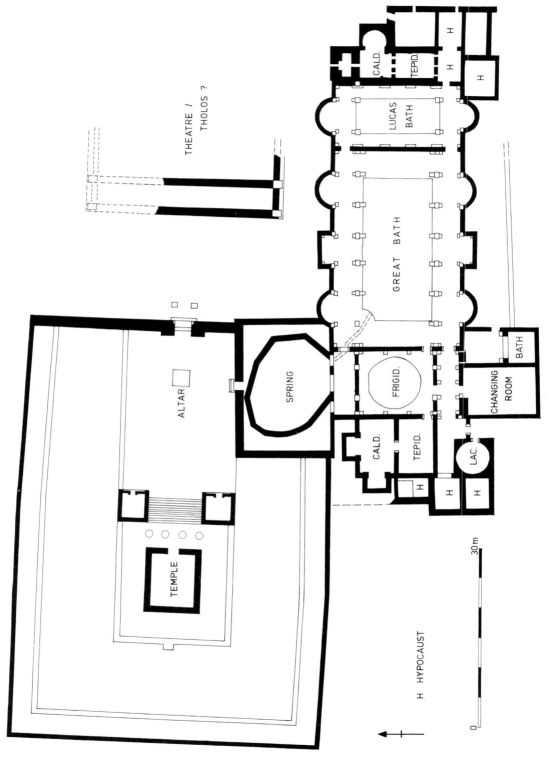

51 Bath, the Temple of Sulis Minerva and the Baths
in the later second and early third centuries (*after
Cunliffe*)

its immediate environs, apparently in the later Neronian or early Flavian period, is in marked contrast with the situation not only at all other small towns but also at many of the province's main administrative centres. This all presupposes a considerable investment of capital and the presence of large numbers of skilled foreign craftsmen, all working to a very specific classical design.[19] As suggested above, this new expansion seems to have occurred on the periphery of the original early settlement astride the river crossing. Occupation here certainly continued, judging by the later first- and second-century finds, though none of these has actually come from controlled modern excavations. Within the bathing establishment itself, the second century witnessed major changes which affected the facilities at both the east and west ends.[20] On the east, the smallest of the thermal pools was dismantled and replaced by a new suite of heated rooms and an associated changing room, all entered via a door in the south-eastern corner of the Lucas Bath. Equally complex changes occurred at the west end, apparently involving an extension of the facilities to include a *laconicum* alongside the existing moist heat baths. The original entrance hall was now converted to house a circular plunge bath and its arcades were walled up to form independent corridors. The new bath served both the original warm rooms to the west and the new *laconicum*, which lay at the west end of the extended southern corridor. Existing rooms along the south side of the old entrance hall were also replaced at this stage. These changes are generally assigned on somewhat limited dating evidence to the Hadrianic period, though their contemporaneity remains in doubt. Even so, they reflect the need for an increased range of facilities consequent upon the success of the spa both locally and in the wider context.

More far-reaching changes, affecting not just the baths but also the reservoir and the temple precinct, seem to have occurred in the late second or early third century, though the available dating evidence is exceptionally meagre (fig. 51). The principal modification to the baths was the decision to replace the original timber roofing by a series of barrel vaults, which necessitated considerable alterations to counter the problems of lateral thrust.[21] These are best seen in the Great Bath, where the existing arcade piers were

cut back and thickened and where new piers were added along the external north and south walls alongside the niches. These supported a central barrel vault and two lower tunnel vaults. Similar modifications were made to the Lucas Bath to the east and the circular bath to the west. Presumably as part of these changes, new heated rooms were added to the facilities at both ends, though the overall design clearly remained much the same.[22] These alterations must have caused considerable disruption to the functioning of the baths, but, once completed, must have had the effect of making the whole complex even more impressive. Contemporary with all this, the reservoir was enclosed within a 23.4 by 15.3 m (76 by 50 ft) chamber with a central doorway set into its north wall opposite the altar.[23] This chamber supported a new tile and concrete vault, which integrated the reservoir into the overall design of the baths. The reservoir area was also heightened, necessitating the provision of three steps by the door to compensate for the change in levels. These changes meant that access to the spring was now significantly restricted to either the door in the north wall or the three windows in the south.

Equally important changes occurred in the temple precinct, most notably to the temple itself.[24] The original podium structure remained intact but it was now surrounded on the north, west and south by a raised ambulatory which effectively doubled its size. The exact arrangement of this new structure remains uncertain, since it might have been either a raised walkway or the foundation for a colonnade and a lean-to roof. Across the east flank, a new monumental façade was created, incorporating a flight of steps flanked by two small rooms, possibly shrines; both had a central doorway and their engaged pilasters probably supported a pediment. The implications of these changes in religious and ritual terms is hard to define, though the overall effect was to convert an existing classical building into one closer in form to the Romano-British norm. Elsewhere in the precinct, the altar platform was extended and the eastern enclosure wall was partly rebuilt to include a much more ornamental entrance.

The nineteenth- and twentieth-century preoccupation with these religious and curative facilities has inevitably given us only limited

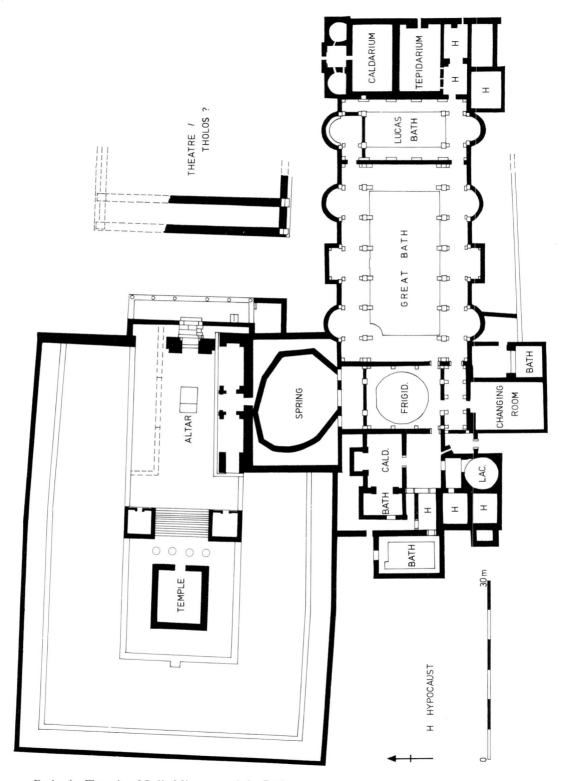

52 Bath, the Temple of Sulis Minerva and the Baths
in the later third century (*after Cunliffe*)

insights into the rest of the settlement morphology and its development, but enough has been recorded from the later defended core to reinforce the picture of relative prosperity. Particular interest attaches to the existence of several other romanized building complexes. East of the main Sulis-Minerva temple precinct and north of the baths lay a structure with massive foundations which has never been properly explored.[25] It has sometimes been identified as a possible *forum-basilica* or more plausibly as a theatre, but recently it has been interpreted as yet another religious precinct of the Hadrianic period, probably housing a richly ornamented *tholos*. Besides the King's Bath spring, Bath's other two springs also attracted the attentions of the Roman engineers and architects. During the nineteenth century, work on the Hetlin or Hot Baths spring defined a sequence of building periods, the latest of which comprised an elaborate suite of baths replacing an earlier demolished structure of uncertain date and function; this suggests a second public bathing establishment, perhaps also related to a religious area attested by three altars from the vicinity.[26] The Cross Bath spring has so far produced no evidence for elaborate buildings but was instead simply enclosed as a large oval pool. Its religious and medicinal associations seem secured, however, by a single dedication and at least one carved block depicting the Aesculapius legend.[27] An even more monumental building is represented by four fragments of a decorated cornice found in 1869, but nothing else is known about its character or its original location.[28]

At some point in the third century, the north wall of the King's Bath spring reservoir began to show signs of collapse under the weight of the barrel vault, and major improvements became necessary (fig. 52).[29] The new schema involved the addition of a raised portico along the north side of the enclosure wall, extending nearly 5 m (16 ft) into the original paved precinct. This formed the foundation for three substantial buttresses which were built against the affected structure. Little survives of the western structure, which had to be totally rebuilt at a later date, but its eastern counterpart was built of massive stone blocks fastened together with iron cramps. The central buttress flanking the existing door to the spring was constructed as a monumental

doorway in the form of a quadrifrons. Its four piers probably supported an arched attic surmounted by a pediment, the centrepiece of which was a roundel containing the head of the sun god held aloft by two nymphs on either side of a rock. Contemporary with these changes, the eastern enclosure wall of the temple precinct was partly demolished and rebuilt 2.3 m (7½ ft) to the east, though its original monumental gateway was retained as a free-standing structure. Little is known about any corresponding changes in the northern part of the paved precinct, though it has been argued that some sort of structure would have been necessary to balance the south portico and retain the symmetry of the temple approaches. The discovery of numerous fragments from a monument known as the Façade of the Four Seasons, incorporating a pediment with a central head of the moon goddess in the relevant area, is thus highly suggestive.[30] The baths to the south of the reservoir may not have been immune from change during this period either, though the exact chronology remains uncertain.[31] The east end certainly underwent massive alterations, involving the replacement of the old *tepidarium* and *caldarium* by two much larger heated rooms, one with two apsidal baths flanking the main flue. Corresponding changes are also indicated by the surviving evidence at the west end, but the entire plan has not yet been recovered. No doubt the general aim was to extend yet further the available facilities.

Interestingly, it was the area occupied by the three springs and their related religious and bathing facilities which was selected for defensive provision rather than the alternative focus by the road junction further north. The details are not yet beyond dispute, but it seems to have enclosed *c.* 10 ha (25 acres) and to have protected only the principal buildings.[32] Excavations in 1963 along the north side suggested an initial clay and gravel rampart *c.* 9.1 m (29¾ ft) wide, containing pottery down to the later years of the second century, in line with the programme of defensive provision elsewhere. These details were confirmed in 1980, when it was also demonstrated that the bank had been cut back to receive a stone wall resting on a 2.9 m (9½ ft) wide footing of rubble and clay. Beyond the associated berm lay a wide flat-bottomed ditch. No such relationship had been recognized in 1963, though there was a suggestion that the bank had been raised, sealing a mass of fresh stone chippings probably derived from the wall's construction. Dating evidence for the insertion of the stone defences is very limited, but it is generally assigned to the later third or early fourth century. Pottery of that date had certainly accumulated across the back of the rampart tail. No gates or external towers have been recorded.

The construction of the defences led to a gradual change in the character of the intra-mural areas around the principal buildings. Much of this area had apparently remained under-developed in the first and second centuries, but now there is evidence to suggest an increase in the number of buildings, including several with mosaics indicative of wealthy private housing or additional facilities.[33] Examples are known west of the Hot Bath spring, where Irvine recorded a large town house with at least seven rooms (one at least with a hypocaust and mosaic), and at the Mineral Water Hospital, which possessed at least three mosaics. In total it is now clear that the defended area contained at least 11 major buildings of some size and pretensions, a fact which separates Bath in the late period from all other small towns.

Outside the walls, our understanding of the second- to fourth-century settlement is very limited, because so little controlled excavation has been possible.[34] Occupation certainly seems to have spread northwards along the level strip of land skirting the River Avon, presumably forming a ribbon development as far as the original nucleus by the river crossing. Not enough is known, however, to say whether the intensification of intra-mural activity already noted was a consequence of contraction in the suburbs as the population migrated into the walled area.

Beyond all this lay the cemeteries, though the evidence, largely from nineteenth- and early twentieth-century rescue observations, has not been well recorded or published.[35] The principal cemetery extended north-east of the settlement along the line of the Fosse Way, now represented by the London Road. Here several funerary inscriptions, including those of the soldier Iulius Vitalis and of Vibia Iucunda,[36] suggest a degree of wealth and sophistication, though the majority of burials were either simple urned cremations or inhumations in stone coffins with covers. A second cemetery is also indicated by cremation and inhumation burials alongside and to the south of the supposed Roman road running west of the settlement through Julian Road and Victoria Park. Yet another extensive cemetery seems to have lain in the Bathwick area on the opposite side of the River Avon, where at least one priest of Sulis Minerva was buried.[37] These would seem to be the main urban cemeteries, though large numbers of burials have been recorded across a wide hinterland, suggesting the fragmentary nature of our knowledge.

Inevitably our understanding of Bath's everyday life is dominated by its religious and curative establishments, supplemented by the wealth of lead curses and votive objects recovered from the main spring. This makes it difficult to assess the site's broader significance in relation to a wider economic hinterland. Epigraphy attests various professionals directly or indirectly associated with the temple, amongst them a priest, Caius Calpurnius Receptus, and a specialist *haruspex*, Lucius Marcius Memor, as well as the 'doctor' Tiberius Julianus, represented by his oculist's stamp.[38] It also records the cosmopolitan attraction of the facilities, which were no doubt catered for by a range of otherwise unattested officials, innkeepers, shopkeepers and medical practitioners, skilled or otherwise. Numerous soldiers certainly came to Bath, and at least one lost his discharge diploma,[39] while citizens are recorded from as far away as the regions of modern Chartres and Metz.[40] The religious attraction of the site is also well attested by the finds from the spring, which included a huge number of coins, numerous metal vessels, some 130 lead curses and a range of other ritual objects.[41] The curses especially tell us much about the ordinary people and their everyday aspirations and worries, while also suggesting the presence of scribes skilled in the requisite official language. Yet more detail is provided by the inscribed altars and monuments, in particular the public beneficence of Claudius Ligur and Gaius Protacius who paid for the restoration and repainting of one of the religious buildings.[42]

This evidence provides us with a picture of a flourishing and prosperous religious settlement, but Bath clearly also lay at the centre of an extensive economic hinterland, noted for the marked concentration of some 30 villas within a 25 km (16 mile) radius.[43] Unfortunately little is

known about the relevant service trades, and
direct evidence for marketing facilities is entirely
absent. Archaeology attests the presence of iron-
working in the form of two small furnaces in a late
third- or fourth-century workshop on the Citizen
House site,[44] as well as leather-working represented by a cache of shoes and offcuts from a
second-century pit in Walcot Street.[45] Lead-
working has also been recorded in Abbey Green,
pre-dating a second-century masonry building,
but this is likely to be related to the plumbing and
roofing of the baths.[46] The buildings themselves,
of course, attest the importance of stone quarrying and all the related construction trades, while
the reference to the sculptor Sulinus points to
complementary trades.[47] Beyond such evidence,
it has been suggested that Bath served in an
administrative capacity, given the distances
between it and the nearest other urban centres at
Cirencester, Mildenhall and Ilchester, but there
is little direct information to support this. There
is a reference to a *centurio regionarius* who
restored 'a holy place wrecked by insolent hands'
in the fourth century, but there is nothing to
connect him specifically with the town itself.[48]

The later history of Bath presents an interesting story, though much of the evidence has to be
drawn from the principal complexes already
described. The north wall of the reservoir continued to give problems despite the third-century
modifications and, as a consequence, further
changes became necessary in the early fourth
century.[49] The north-western buttress was
clearly dismantled and rebuilt as a solid masonry
block, while a new buttress was added along the
western wall. Probably contemporary with this,
the podium and the precinct around the altar
were restored. This may well be the context for
the rebuilding of the ambulatory wall and its
reflooring, though the details remain uncertain.[50]
These changes represent the last serious attempt
to maintain the temple precinct as a monumental
religious complex. In the baths, further alterations are recorded at the west end, involving
among other features the insertion of a swimming
bath into the old *caldarium* and the addition of a
new heat source to the *tepidarium*. At the east end,
drastic modifications were necessitated by periods of flooding which affected the underfloor
heating arrangements; this involved the removal
of the hypocaust floors and their replacement at a

higher level.[51] The effect would have been to
reduce the facilities available for considerable
periods, a problem which progressively wor-
sened with time. All this has to be set against the
background of relative fourth-century prosperity
reflected in the intra-mural mosaics and the local
villas.

From *c*. AD 350 onwards, the character of the
temple precinct began to change, perhaps as a
result of the rise of Christianity. Much of the
colonnade and stylobate of the outer precinct
were demolished and new, probably secular,
buildings are recorded along the north side and in
the south-west corner.[52] Within the inner paved
precinct, a complex sequence has been defined,
comprising a prolonged accumulation of rubbish
and soil interspersed by six phases of cobbling
and repaving, most of which contained variable
quantities of re-used building materials and
sculptural blocks.[53] These indicate that the
monuments in and about the precinct (including
the temple itself) were being progressively dismantled and that its function had largely lapsed.
The successive cobble spreads had seen considerable wear, however, reflecting continued usage of
the area which still provided access to the
functional reservoir. The absolute chronology of
this activity remains uncertain, but even on
conservative estimates it must have continued
well into the fifth century if not beyond. Then
came a period of deliberate demolition affecting
the entablature of the reservoir and its two
buttresses, as well as what remained of the
quadrifrons and other monuments, apparently in
search of the iron cramps and their lead seal-
ings.[54] Thus weakened, this would be the logical
point at which the reservoir vault collapsed,
marking a significant break in the development
and the function of the site. It has been argued
that this occurred in the sixth or seventh century,
after which the site remained derelict.

No such impressive sequences were established for the baths by the early excavators, so
that we know little about their ultimate demise.
No doubt the problem of periodic flooding
continued until eventually the will to repair the
damage and the money ran out. This process may
have been hastened by Britain's separation from
the Roman world in the fifth century, but how
quickly it all occurred is impossible to define. The
final stage in the drama would have seen the

collapse of the vaulting to leave 'The Ruin', so vividly described in an Anglo-Saxon poem.[55] Beyond these central complexes, archaeology provides only limited clues to the end of Roman Bath. Particularly interesting evidence for survival has come from the Abbeygate Street site, where the latest Roman building collapsed late in the fourth century.[56] After an interval, a new structure was erected on a different alignment, the associated stratigraphy arguing for survival well beyond the traditional end of Roman Britain. Clearly the story varies from site to site, but such a varied picture of continuity and decline must have given the town a somewhat unusual air after its period of prosperity. Enough must have survived into the sixth century, however, for the Saxons to inherit in the aftermath of the Battle of Dyrham in AD 577, when Bath is listed in the Anglo-Saxon Chronicle as one of the three towns to have been captured.[57]

Buxton (fig. 53)

Almost our entire knowledge of this important site in the Pennines, near the Peak District, is derived from its name: *Aquae Arnemetiae*. In the Ravenna list it is called *Aquis Arnemeza*.[58] As at Bath (*Aquae Sulis*, p. 165) the name clearly refers to a spa with springs of a health-giving character, which still run today. The temperature of the water, at 28°C, is only a little more than half that at Bath (50°C), while the flow per day at 846,000 litres (186,100 gallons) is somewhat less (1,137,500 litres/250,000 gallons). Also as at Bath, the name associates the springs with a goddess, here Arnemetia, which is derived from the Celtic *nemeton*, a sacred grove.[59]

The Roman town lies below its modern counterpart, much of which contains buildings listed for their architectural merit. The chances to excavate, therefore, have been few and far between, and virtually no recent explorations have taken place. Camden conjectured that the site was Roman, from the behaviour in its vicinity of a recognized Roman road, Bathamgate, but he recorded no Roman remains at Buxton. The eighteenth century saw the first discoveries being made during the development of the present spa town, and these continued from time to time until

the early part of this century but little has come to light since.[60]

The town lies in a valley at the crossing of two main roads: that from Little Chester to Manchester, and that from Brough-on-Noe across the moors to Buxton and on then towards the Stoke-on-Trent district; the first section is called Bathamgate. A milestone[61] was found at the south-east corner of Hardwick Square in Silverlands; it gives a distance of 10 Roman miles to Brough, whereas the correct distance is nearly 11 Roman miles. It cannot, therefore, have been found in its original position. Unfortunately also, the upper half of the stone, containing the main part of the dedication, has broken away; consequently it cannot be dated. Flavian pottery has been recovered from the Silverlands area and consequently a fort has been postulated.[62] But apart from the pottery and the road junction, and the fact that there was almost certainly a pre-Roman shrine to Arnemetia, probably with an accompanying settlement, there is little tactical, and even less strategic, significance for siting a fort here. Nevertheless, once into the area, the Roman army may well have expanded the spring's facilities for their own use, as they clearly did at Bath and at other spa towns on the continent.

Fort or no, there were reasons enough for Buxton to develop as a small town in the Roman period. The existence of both hot and cold chalybeate springs, and of an important religious sanctuary, would have been a considerable attraction first to the army, and secondly to civilians following in its wake. The medicinal properties might have been sought by many; if Bath is a guide, they could have come from far afield, even from other provinces. Obviously, though, it never became as popular, or as large a town as Bath, being situated 300 m (990 ft) above sea level in a generally inhospitable landscape and winter climate.

Fragments of the bathing establishment have occasionally been observed in the area around St Ann's Crescent, and close to the site of the springs or St Ann's Well.[63] The latter, according to records made in 1709, rose into a stone basin surrounded by walls of Roman brick. Nearby was found a massive lead-covered structure, which must have been a lined bath; with the Peak District only a short distance away, there would

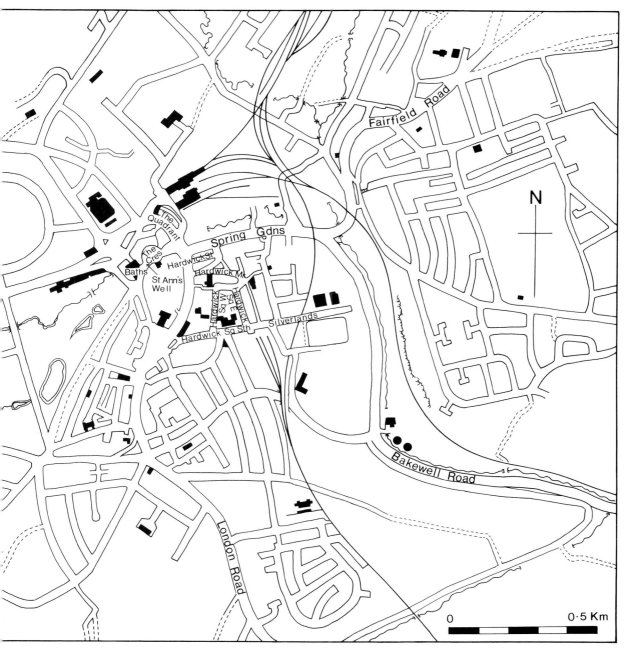

53 Buxton

have been no shortage of lead. During the development of St Ann's Crescent, yet another bath, some 7 by 4.5 m (23 by 15 ft), was revealed, into which the water flowed from one of the several outlets of the hot spring through a lead pipe with a diameter of about 200 mm (8 in). The waste water departed through what was described as a 'floodgate', which was presumably some form of sluice which could be raised or lowered as the need arose, but whether of stone or timber was not stated. This bath was floored, if the description is reinterpreted, with a layer of *opus signinum* 150 mm (6 in) thick. One curious feature was the 'strong oak beams' laid along the tops of the walls, which were about 1 m (3¼ ft) high. This account sounds as though they were only sleeper-walls and that the superstructure had been half-timbered.

In 1787, excavations in the area of what is now the Terrace revealed a massive base, composed of stiff blue clay surrounded by a substantial dry-stone wall with four offsets; the superstructure was said to have been of large, well-dressed stones, and the whole was *c.* 14 by 8 m (46 by 26 ft) and stood 1.2 m (4 ft) high.[64] The excavator, H. Rooke, suggested that this was the foundation for a temple, although Haverfield dismissed the idea without paying much attention to it. Yet it was clearly a massive foundation for a major building, which to some extent matches the podium of the Temple of Claudius at Colchester, where earth-filled masonry vaults provided the foundation. Moreover, the dimensions, although overall slightly smaller, are not far from being of the same proportions as the podium at Bath. The unmortared large but well-dressed masonry blocks also resemble the lower podia of some of the smaller temples at Corbridge (p. 60). The position on a low hill immediately facing the baths around St Ann's Well, as described above, would have been ideal for the temple of Arnemetia, and the hilltop itself may once have been crowned with the sacred grove. As far as can be determined, a considerable area of rough limestone paving was discovered a little distance east, when Holker Road was being developed. This could be the foundation for a better quality surface of slabs, acting perhaps as a yard for a house nearby or even as part of a *temenos*; three large hearths, though, had been built on it at about equal distances apart, so that if a proper

pavement once existed, the top paving-stones must have been removed before the hearths were built.

There is no indication that the small spa town of Buxton, and its associated bathing establishment, survived beyond the end of the Roman period, if as long as that; late coins are not common. The solution to this problem is perhaps related to a number of caves near Buxton, which remained inhabited for part at least of the Roman period. The spa and the small town which grew alongside it perhaps had no great attraction for the local residents of the neighbourhood, and was left largely to the variable whims of visitors.

Frilford (figs. 54 and 55)

Prior to the 1970s, Frilford was regarded as little more than a small rural shrine, with a probable Iron-Age predecessor, around which had developed a small native settlement. Knowledge was confined to a late Roman/early Saxon cemetery, originally discovered during nineteenth-century quarrying,[65] and to the supposed Iron-Age and Roman religious buildings first excavated in 1937–8[66] and re-examined in 1964.[67] Then between 1978 and 1984 a programme of field-work, aerial reconnaissance and small-scale excavations transformed our perception of the site,[68] revealing an extensive religious complex with a surprising level of associated settlement of probable urban character. This included a 30 ha (74 acre) spread of occupation debris in and around the temple area, a *temenos* compound and an amphitheatre. Even so, much remains uncertain about its morphology and development, beyond the known debris scatter and the limited windows afforded by excavation.

During 1937–8, excavations on three sites sampled an area of apparently extensive Iron-Age and Roman occupation, revealing in the process two fairly typical Romano-British shrines, which seemingly replaced two middle Iron-Age structures. This suggested an Iron-Age origin for the site and the significant possibility of religious continuity. This was clearest on Site C,[69] where a circular Roman building succeeded a *c.* 12 m (39 ft) diameter penannular ditched enclosure with an entrance on the west and two rows of three post-holes in the interior; one of

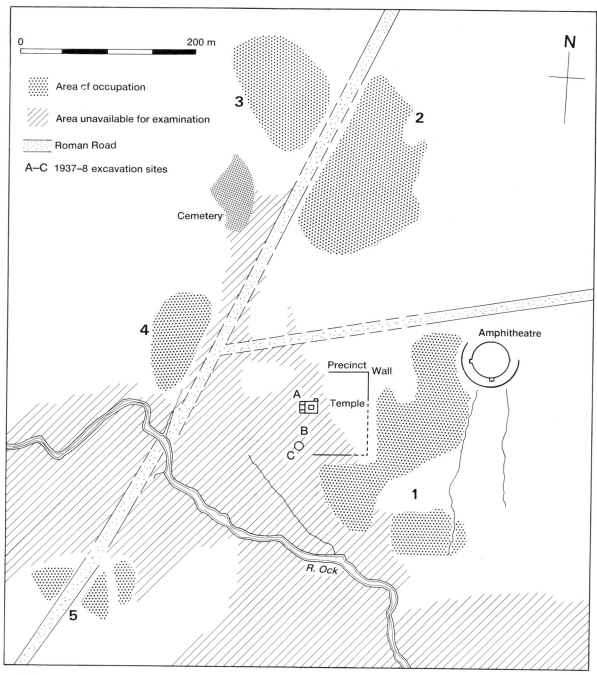

54 Frilford (*after Hingley*)

55 Frilford, looking south; the amphitheatre is
clearly visible left of centre (*Cambridge
University Collection: copyright reserved*)

these contained an iron ploughshare, and the posts themselves had probably been replaced several times. The ditch itself cut through earlier pits and gullies, indicating that it was not a primary feature. The excavators argued that both the ditch and the post-holes had been sealed by a thick clay deposit, apparently laid down prior to the commencement of Roman building operations. This seemed to support a case for continuity between the Roman building and its Iron-Age predecessor, though the pottery associated with the latter clearly belonged to the early to middle Iron Age, while the absence of later Iron-Age and early Roman pottery from the clay infilling suggests that it had been levelled by the first century BC.[70] Most commentators have accepted the religious association of the ditched enclosure, drawing attention to its dubious henge-like affinities and to the ritual character of the ploughshare deposit, but a domestic attribution seems equally plausible.[71] This is clearly the case on Site B,[72] between here and the other potential religious area to the north, where several Iron-Age pits and at least one post-built structure belonged to the early and middle Iron Age.

Comparable stratigraphic continuity was originally proposed for Site A,[73] where a Romano-Celtic temple was seen to replace a rather fragmentary timber building, which had apparently burnt down, creating a 0.45 m (1½ ft) thick layer of debris across the site. This was subsequently shown to belong to an 8.5 m (27½ ft) diameter stake-wall structure with a four-post doorway on the south-east.[74] The 1930s excavators had linked its destruction to levelling up operations prior to the construction of the Romano-Celtic temple in the Flavian period, but the 1964 re-examination of the site questioned this attractive hypothesis, not least because it found no further trace of burnt debris, and proposed re-dating the temple to the later second century. There was equally little to suggest that the Iron-Age structure lasted into the first century AD, most features in the vicinity producing early to middle Iron-Age pottery, down to the end of the first century BC.[75] Its religious identification also presents problems, because there was little to differentiate it from a range of other domestic alternatives.

This uncertainty over the interpretation of the excavated evidence demonstrates that modern opinion is now less dogmatic about Frilford's supposed religious significance in the late Iron Age and about its pre-Roman origins. Certainly there was extensive early to middle Iron-Age occupation on the three sites, some perhaps ritual in character, but the scarcity of later Iron-Age material suggests either a phase of abandonment or a general decline in its extent and importance.[76] Further excavation is obviously essential to clarify both the chronology and the extent of any pre-Roman focus, not least because the site's re-emergence in the Roman era, and its self-evident religious importance, must surely indicate some thread of continuity (perhaps of a ritual nature?) capable of providing the necessary stimulus. Even with the rejection of the evidence for *in situ* Iron-Age ritual structures, Stevens' hypothesis that the site originated as a religious focus on a tribal boundary between the Dobunni and the Atrebates still remains plausible, paralleling several Gallic religious complexes.[77]

In contrast to its predecessor, the Romano-British settlement is better known from the scatter of occupation debris, even if its developmental details remain somewhat sketchy. The main features in the plan are the two presumed Roman roads north of the River Ock, the *temenos* precinct and the amphitheatre, around which lay at least five distinct areas of Romano-British occupation debris.[78] The principal road apparently ran north-east/south-west through the site, probably between Alchester and Mildenhall, though its exact course and date are poorly known. Four of the principal debris spreads are found along its frontages (Areas 2–5), as is the late Roman/early Saxon cemetery, presumably representing ribbon developments north and south of the river. Those west of the road (Areas 3–5) have produced only third- and fourth-century pottery, while only Area 4 revealed definite building evidence in the form of stone foundations and tiled roofs. In contrast, Area 2 east of the road produced pottery spanning the whole Roman period alongside comparable building debris. North of the river, and immediately opposite Area 4, a second Roman road probably branched eastwards, running to the north of the main religious complex and the remaining spread of occupation debris (Area 1). The temples lay in a substantial stone-walled enclosure, the north, east and south sides of which are clearly visible on aerial photographs; if the main temple was centrally located, as the plan suggests, then its overall dimensions must have been *c.* 130 by 100 m (425 by 327 ft). East of this, between the *temenos* and the amphitheatre, was a considerable spread of occupation debris (Area 1) characterized by pottery spanning the Roman period and by building debris in the form of stone foundations and tiled roofs; several red *tesserae* even hint at a structure of greater pretensions. Although difficult to interpret in detail, this evidence might suggest that the earliest occupation began in and between the temple complex and the amphitheatre, and to the north (Areas 1 and 2), with later occupation developing along the western frontages of the north-east/south-west road. More detailed work should clarify this basic model.

The recognition of the *temenos* confirms the focal importance of the Roman buildings on Sites A and C. The most imposing was the Romano-Celtic temple constructed along the precinct's east-west axis, probably at its centre.[79] Its walls had been heavily robbed, making dating difficult, but its plan and general development were reasonably clear. It originated as a simple *cella* 7.6 m (25 ft) square surrounded by a portico 16.8 m (55 ft) square, both with foundations 1.1 m (3½ ft) wide; there had clearly been painted wall plaster and a red brick tessellated floor. Along its northern side there was evidence for a contemporary gravel surround, while a 6.7 m (22 ft) wide pathway, with at least three separate surfacings, extended *c.* 9 m (29½ ft) to the east. Two separate annexes had subsequently been added to this building, that on the north-east comprising a single small room, *c.* 3.8 by 2.4 m (12½ by 7¾ ft) internally with foundations 0.75 m (2½ ft) wide, which had cut through the original gravel surround. The other annexe, comprising three rooms, extended across the western side of the building, resting on a foundation of stone, tile and occupation debris, to the west of which was a gravel layer overlying a coin of Trajan. Little dating evidence survived, though the 1930s excavators argued for a Flavian origin on the basis of a samian sherd of AD 60–70 in the make-up level. This seemed to fit in with the lowest of the gravel paths leading to the eastern door, while the more substantial second layer, containing second-century samian and a second- to third-century grey vessel, was connected with the construction of at least the western annexe. The 1964 excavations, however, demonstrated that the building could not have been erected before the later second century, presumably contemporary with the second gravel path, while the main annexe was attributed to the early fourth, along with the uppermost gravel surface.[80]

On Site C to the south, a second religious structure was located just inside the precinct's south wall.[81] It comprised a circular building, 11 m (36 ft) in diameter, with foundations 0.75 m (2½ ft) wide, inside which were the remains of a hearth; to it probably belonged the ritual pit containing a bronze votive sword and shield and a fragmentary iron spearhead. Excavation suggested that it had burnt down. Dating again proved difficult, the excavators arguing for a first-century origin contemporary with the main building, but this may now need revision.

The religious potential of the Frilford complex is clearly reinforced by the discovery of an amphitheatre,[82] closely paralleling the theatres, or hybrid theatre-amphitheatres, known at several other sites both in Britain and more especially in Gaul. Though badly levelled, aerial photography and excavation have defined its basic plan, which comprised an arena, *c.* 45 m (147 ft) in diameter, obviously cut down into the ground to provide raw material for the clay and rubble banks which were 11 to 12 m (36 to 39 ft) wide and supported the wooden seating. These were retained by a stone wall around the arena, which was served by two entrances on the east and west. A small alcove on the south may have been a shrine or beast-cage, or may have supported an above ground structure. No clear dating evidence was recovered from the excavations, which also suggested some sort of timber predecessor, much as has been found at Silchester, though this can hardly indicate a comparably early date.[83] Such a complex hints at the provision of other facilities, including a bath-house and visitor accommodation.

The range of smaller domestic buildings at Frilford is currently poorly known, though their existence is attested by building stone and roof tiles. Even less is known about the site's economic basis as a counterbalance to its obvious religious importance, which makes it difficult to define how far it developed a range of urban services over and above those related to the temple area. Only large-scale excavation can resolve such problems.

Our understanding of the site's later history depends upon the excavated evidence from the Romano-Celtic temple and from the cemetery area west of the north-east/south-west road. Unlike its circular counterpart on Site C, the temple apparently lasted throughout the fourth century;[84] the final resurfacing of the approach path was overlain by 78 fourth-century coins, including several whose usage must have continued into the succeeding century. Theodosian coins were not as abundant here, however, as in the cemetery area, where most were very worn, suggesting that activity was not as prolonged and perhaps began to decline at a somewhat earlier date, though when this occurred remains uncertain.[85] The cemetery itself has been examined on several occasions and some 359 graves have been recovered, spanning both the later Roman and Anglo-Saxon periods.[86] The late Roman burials are generally cut into the bedrock and aligned in rows roughly west-north-west by east-south-east. A few wore hobnail boots and had coins in their mouths, while five were buried in lead coffins.

The cemetery was also used for both early Saxon cremations and inhumations. The cremations, in patterned or plain urns, had very few grave goods, whereas the inhumations were accompanied by various objects, including spears, knives, ear- and tooth-picks; some were in stone-lined graves, apparently following the Roman alignment, while others were less deeply buried and variably aligned. The datable grave goods span the fifth and sixth centuries, apparently indicating some overlap between the various burial traditions. Unfortunately there are no detailed plans for the early excavations and the more recently located burials lie in discrete areas, the Roman to the north and the early Saxon to the east of the quarried area, where the vital area of overlap examined by Rolleston had clearly lain; hence their exact relationship and chronology cannot now be re-examined.[87] Early Saxon occupation is also suggested by hand-made pottery recovered during field survey south of the river in Area 5, and perhaps by several fragmentary sherds discovered in the amphitheatre, but only

large-scale excavation can hope to define the fifth-century sequence in further detail.[88]

Harlow (figs. 56 and 57)

Harlow has long been regarded as a site of religious significance, since the 1927 discovery of a Romano-Celtic temple on the summit of an elongated hill east of the River Stort.[89] Subsequent investigations of the complex, both in 1962–71 and again in 1985–8,[90] confirmed this general picture, revealing a complex sequence spanning the later Iron-Age and Romano-British periods. But this is only part of the story, because a tradition of discoveries north and east of the hill has emphasized that the temple did not stand in isolation but was actually accompanied by an extensive settlement.[91] Unfortunately this has never been systematically examined, beyond a series of small-scale rescue excavations in advance of redevelopment work in Old Harlow, most notably in the Holbrooks area[92] and in the vicinity of Stafford House.[93] This limited evidence inevitably makes it difficult to assess the site's morphological development and its wider role in relation to the temple complex, questions which only further excavation can resolve.

Particular interest attaches to the realization that the Romano-Celtic temple succeeded a pre-existing religious site, though the evidence for this has inevitably been disturbed by the construction of the later buildings. Suggestive features were first located during the 1960s excavations, alongside abundant late Iron-Age material in the old land surface.[94] The temple foundations had certainly cut two otherwise undated post-holes and a V-shaped gully, while several round patches, some containing carbonized wood, were interpreted as possible post-holes, though no definite pattern emerged in the excavated areas. From the old land surface came some 232 Iron-Age coins, numerous pre-Flavian bronze and iron brooches and a range of bracelets, pins, rings and other toilet articles, as well as a quantity of animal bones. Many of the brooches and other small finds had been bent or damaged prior to deposition, all highly suggestive of their being votive offerings at or near a religious site. Interesting, though difficult to interpret, is the

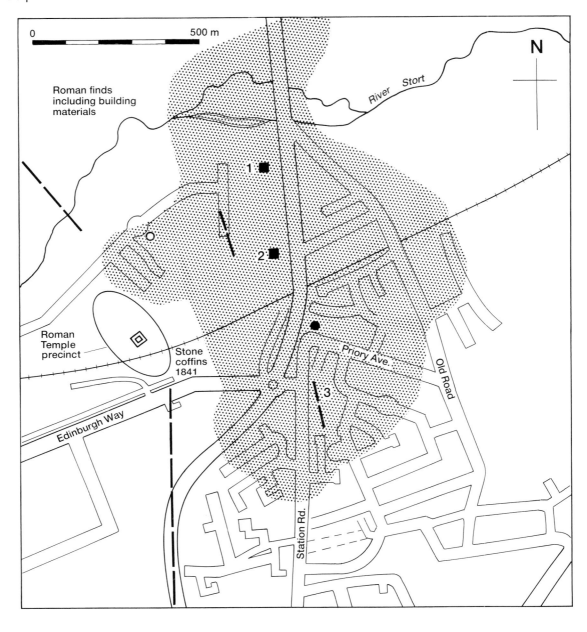

56 Harlow (*after Bartlett*)

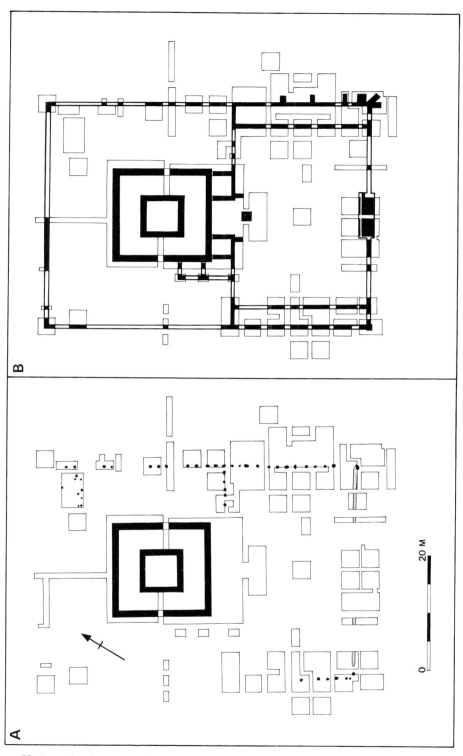

57 Harlow; development of Romano–Celtic temple
(*after France and Gobel*)

evidence that all the stratified gold coins found in 1962–71 were restricted to the area later enclosed by the ambulatory wall of the temple, whereas the large number of mint bronze issues from various rulers (including Tasciovanus and Cunobelinus) were distributed, often in discrete clusters, right across the southern part of the precinct.[95]

Further details about the site have come from renewed excavations between 1985 and 88. These revealed the ring ditch of a mid to late Iron-Age circular house, sealed beneath the temple courtyard, as well as numerous finds including a bronze scabbard mount, a bronze leaf and brooches and some 555 coins.[96] Such abundant material clearly emphasizes the Iron-Age ancestry of the site, though the practice of ritual deposition certainly extended into the early Roman period as is clearly demonstrated by the recovery of several coins, a small quantity of samian and a few pieces of military equipment from the old land surface.[97] Pre-Roman activity may not have been confined solely to the hilltop and the temple precinct, however, because comparable coins and pottery came from the Holbrook's area to the north-east.[98] This could represent either a separate settlement area or another religious site, to judge from the overlying Roman features, but neither its character nor its extent could be recorded in the time available.

The development of the religious precinct on the hill during the Roman period is now tolerably well known,[99] commencing with the construction of a typical Romano-Celtic temple 14.8 m (48½ ft) square; this had a *cella* 7.6 m (25 ft) square and an ambulatory 3.7 m (12 ft) wide, the foundations of which cut into the original land surface (fig. 57A). Its walls, though heavily robbed, had been of flint and mortar construction with tile bonding courses, resting on foundations *c.* 0.9 m (3 ft) wide; they had been plastered and painted. Little of the original flooring survived, but enough mosaic *tesserae* were recovered in the associated debris to suggest its former character. East of the temple, and obviously contemporary with it, lay an area of flint cobbling presumably laid as a new ground surface. Where this and the temple sealed the old ground surface, the latest datable finds belong to the period *c.* AD 60–80, suggesting that the remodelling of the sanctuary probably occurred in the Flavian era; in contrast, the latest

pottery finds from the old ground surface under the stone forebuildings belonged to the second century. This early transformation of a native site compares favourably with developments elsewhere, including Braughing (p. 109) and Verulamium,[100] and reflects the policy of romanization so often attributed to the Flavian governors.

Early in the second century, after 150–200 mm (6–8 in) of debris had accumulated across the earlier cobbling, a rectangular palisade was added, probably surrounding the temple on all four sides. It was clearly traceable on the northeast and south-west, where its 0.5 m (1¾ ft) posts lay *c.* 10 m (33 ft) from the ambulatory. Across the front of the temple, these individual posts were partly replaced by a palisade slot. A line of posts also ran at right angles to the main northeast side, heading for the east corner of the ambulatory; assuming a corresponding set on the opposite side, this would have created a rectangular enclosure in front of the temple much like its stone successor.

The next significant stage, soon after *c.* AD 200, saw the removal of the palisade and the levelling up of the whole area in front of the temple prior to its redevelopment (fig. 57B). Two small rooms were now added to the south-eastern side of the ambulatory, thereby creating a porch-like effect flanking the entrance. Their flint walls had been extensively robbed, and little of their floor levels survived, though a small portion of red *tesserae* and wall plaster gave a good clue to their original decoration. The front walls of these rooms coincided with the rear wall of a new rectangular courtyard 28.7 by 22.6 m (93 by 74 ft), which dominated the approach to the temple and housed the main altar. It was entered through a substantial gateway opposite the temple, set on a flint and clay raft, while its two shorter sides were flanked by a pair of galleries 3.7 m (12 ft) wide, both with tessellated floors and painted wall plaster. That on the north-east had required external buttressing, though little of its superstructure survived to explain why this was necessary. The external walls of these galleries also extended along both flanks of the temple and across the back, recalling the design of the earlier timber enclosure. Besides the new rooms flanking the temple entrance, two more small rooms were constructed along its south-western side, though their design and function could not be determined.

This comprehensive reconstruction emphasizes the continuing importance attached to the Roman precinct, which apparently stood on the summit of a low hill rising *c*. 6 m (7 yd) above the flood plain of the river. This was further defined by a ditch *c*. 4.6 m (15 ft) wide enclosing *c*. 4 ha (10 acres), with a single causeway entrance at its southern end, which is usually interpreted as a boundary marker for the whole precinct.[101] The prominent hollow at the northern end of the hill, often identified as a theatre or a pond, proved in 1962 to be a natural feature.[102] Although the temple's dedication remains uncertain, one fragmentary inscription found in 1962–71 mentions the *Numen* of the Emperors, while a recently discovered limestone head has been identified as Minerva.[103]

This religious importance is further reinforced by material recovered from the Holbrook's site.[104] Besides a range of essentially domestic items including bone and bronze pins, bracelets, rings, toilet items and numerous brooches, mainly of first-century date, not unlike the temple assemblage, there were other finds of votive or ritual character otherwise unattested at the temple. These included gilt bronze letters and bronze leaves, several miniature axes, a small pewter vessel and a silver sheet with leaf decoration, as well as over 200 fragments of bronze sheet, some decorated, some scored and cut, and some riveted and pierced. Much of this was not closely stratified or dated, though at least one axe, a bronze leaf and the silver sheet were found together in Pit 1 in a late second- to early third-century context. Equally interesting is the folded lead sheet with a dedication and request to Mercury from a third- to fourth-century context in Pit 2.[105]

Not surprisingly, such an important religious complex provided the focus for an extensive settlement in its immediate vicinity, estimated as covering over 12 ha (30 acres).[106] Its western side was partly delimited by the ditched precinct itself but beyond this it extended in a broad arc north and north-east towards the river and the Holbrooks site, east and south-east onto the Stafford House site and south towards Old Harlow. Little can be said about the internal road network, though three routes are thought to be focused on the site.[107] One apparently ran south from the temple towards Epping; another probably led north-east from the river crossing; and a third is known heading north-west to Braughing, its course perhaps represented by occupation debris found north of the river.[108] Sketchy traces of internal streets have been recorded during excavations, but the details remain unpublished.

To date, the most informative excavations have been directed at the Holbrook's and Stafford House sites. As early as 1935–6, work on the Holbrook's factory had revealed part of a tessellated floor indicating at least one building of some pretensions.[109] North of this in 1970–1, redevelopment work revealed more such evidence, though detailed excavation and recording was impossible in the time available.[110] One major structure was briefly examined, comprising at least three rooms, one with red *tesserae* flooring and painted plaster, another with a tessellated floor. Its construction date could not be established, but a nearby pit apparently containing building debris alongside late second- to early third-century finds, might suggest occupation in the second century. To the south-east lay various other cobbled areas and fragmentary walls, as well as several pits and hearths. Across the Holbrook's site, occupation clearly began in the first century BC and continued throughout the Roman period.

Of particular interest on this site is the evidence for manufacturing activity, which includes at least one hearth of first- or second-century date, over 200 fragments of bronze sheet as well as slag with a high copper and tin content and a quantity of iron slag and lead waste.[111] Its interpretation presents problems, however, though the favoured hypothesis is that votive objects were manufactured on the Holbrook's site for use in the ritual associated with the temple, hence the preponderance of apparently ritual and domestic finds. A bronze-worker's hearth discovered to the south in Priory Avenue might point in a similar direction.[112] The 37 lead weights and over 600 coins might also indicate a broader commercial role providing specialist services for a wider hinterland, as might the leather finds discovered in a well in 1980.[113] An alternative hypothesis, however, would interpret the finds of ritual character and the substantial romanized building as belonging to a second temple complex on the Holbrook's site itself, with the three fragments of an imported pipe-clay theatre mask perhaps hinting at other amenities nearby.[114] Such a grouping of religious precincts would not be unparalleled, but more evidence is vital to clarify the position. This uncertainty reflects the serious shortcomings of the settlement evidence, which only further research can resolve.

The predominantly agricultural features excavated on the Stafford House site contrast with the Holbrook's material, though several iron-working hearths were recorded.[115] Features recovered included a timber building measuring 5 by 4 m (16½ by 13 ft) sealed beneath an early fourth-century gravel-yard and a two-phase farmstead defined by a palisaded enclosure.[116] The latter originated as a barn-like structure measuring 9 by 4 m (29½ by 13 ft) subsequently replaced by an aisled building 15 m (49 ft) wide by at least 15 m (49 ft) long, associated with a gravel-yard, several ditches and a well. How far this farmstead was an integral feature of the settlement as opposed to a satellite of the main religious nucleus remains unclear, but its apparent integration highlights the importance of farmers in the population at many small towns.

Surprisingly little is known about the settlement's associated cemeteries beyond isolated burials; these include six coffins found in 1841 during construction work on the railway.[117]

Most of our evidence about Harlow's late Roman occupation comes from the temple excavations,[118] which demonstrate that the main precinct was destroyed by fire and systematically dismantled in the later fourth century; in the long room east of the courtyard, fallen wall plaster sealed two coins of AD 330–5, while in one of the small rooms flanking the temple entrance similar plaster overlay a pit with a contemporary imitation of an *Urbs Roma* coin. This room also contained a hearth and associated stake-holes as its latest internal features, for which a religious interpretation seems unlikely. This evidence may not be typical of the site as a whole, though any part of the associated settlement which depended upon the precinct for its livelihood must have suffered in the wake of its demise. Unfortunately any changes of this kind may not be easily distinguished from the broader pattern of late Roman contraction affecting other sites in the south and east.

Just as problematical is the fifth-century fate of the settlement in the absence of any detailed stratigraphic sequences. Little was found from either the temple or the other excavated sites to suggest prolonged usage, while the known coin evidence generally ends with issues of Valentinian.[119] Some pagan Saxon sherds have been found both at the Temple and the Holbrook's site, but as yet no early burials are recorded near the settlement.[120] With its primary religious function in decline, there may have been little to prolong its active life far into the fifth century and even less to attract new functions, but such a speculative conclusion needs archaeological confirmation.

Nettleton (fig. 58)

Nettleton, or Nettleton Scrub or Shrub as it is sometimes called, lies on the Fosse Way, some 17 km (10 miles) north-east of Bath. The settlement is surrounded on the north and west sides by steep banks or escarpments of limestone, which are transected by the Broadmead Brook running roughly from west to east. The excavations showed that the modern course of the brook had changed since Roman times. A sharp-sided dry coombe, the Wick Valley, runs down to the brook from the south; only on the east does the ground open out into a wider valley. Consequently the settlement was always somewhat constricted. The Fosse Way entered from the north-east and appears to bifurcate through the settlement before resuming a united course, which was considered by the excavator to run close to the modern road; this is not entirely clear from his published plan, especially since an exit is marked through the southern boundary bank which crossed the Wick Valley; it would seem to offer a more probable course.[121]

The Roman site has been recognized for some time. About 1911, a fragmentary statue of Diana and a hound was discovered during the construction of a lime kiln against the escarpment on the north side of the valley. From 1938 almost up until his death in 1956, excavations were carried out by W. C. Priestley on the north side of the river, where he located the site from which the sculpture came.[122] From 1956–71, the excavations, solely south of the brook, were continued by W. J. Wedlake.[123]

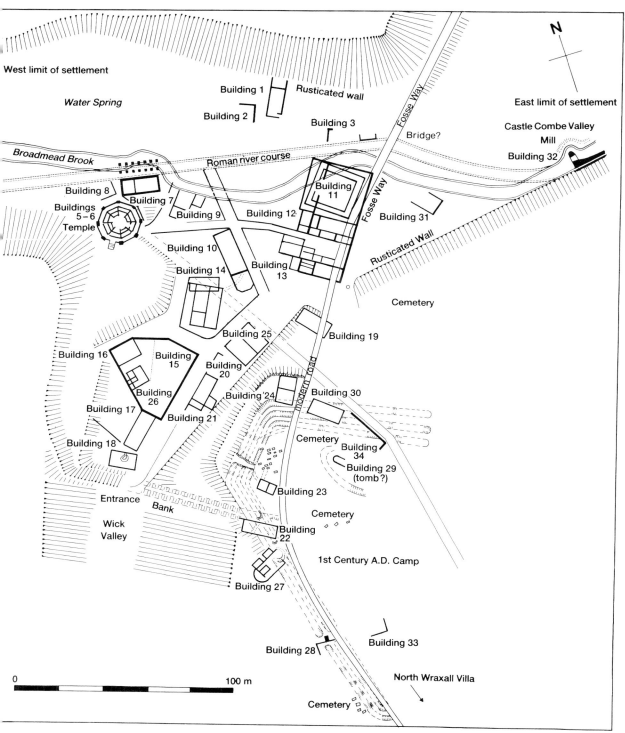

West limit of settlement

Water Spring

Building 1

Rusticated wall

Building 2

Building 3

Fosse Way

Bridge?

East limit of settlement

Castle Combe Valley

Mill

Building 32

Broadmead Brook

Roman river course

Building 8

Building 7

Buildings 5–6 Temple

Building 9

Building 12

Building 11

Fosse Way

Building 31

Rusticated Wall

Building 10

Building 14

Building 13

Cemetery

Building 25

Building 19

Building 16

Building 15

Building 20

Building 24

modern road

Building 30

Building 26

Building 17

Building 21

Building 18

Cemetery

Building 34

Building 29 (tomb?)

Entrance Bank

Building 23

Cemetery

Wick Valley

Building 22

1st Century A.D. Camp

Building 27

Building 33

0   100 m

Building 28

North Wraxall Villa

Cemetery

58 Nettleton (*after Wedlake*)

There are slight but definite remains of pre-Roman Iron-Age settlement in the form of a ditch, a quantity of pottery and two Dobunnic coins,[124] in which *civitas* it must lie. The earliest Roman activity in the area was probably connected with the construction of the Fosse Way, although the road itself has not been positively identified. An enclosure, possibly associated with this work, was situated on the higher ground south-east of the later settlement;[125] it was surrounded by three ditches of no great width or depth. These ditches contained material dating from Claudius to Trajan, on the strength of which Wedlake assigned them to the Claudian period, and suggested that they surrounded a work camp associated with the Fosse Way. Although the excavation report mentions finds of military equipment, presumably from inside the enclosure, nothing of certain Claudian date was published. Its north-west and south-west sides were established with some confidence, but doubt must remain over the suggested lines of the north and south-east sides, which give it an unusual triangular shape. As regards the interior, Wedlake records 'small clay-lined pits about 0.6–0.9 m (2–3 ft) in diameter, and about the same in depth. The pits contained much burnt material, including fragments of iron and bronze slag. There were also several large stones in each pit.' This description would fit that of post-pits dug by the Roman army, and might suggest that there had been timber-framed buildings inside the enclosure, which were deliberately demolished on evacuation, when any scrap wood was burnt. Unfortunately the positions of none of these pits are shown on the published plan.

The most important building within the settlement, from the beginning, was the shrine or temple dedicated to Apollo Cunomaglos, a hitherto unrecorded Celtic god conjoined with a classical deity;[126] it seems likely, therefore, that the site was of pre-Roman sanctity. In addition to the altar found in the temple, a bronze intaglio ring and a bronze plaque recovered from the same area both mention Apollo. But other deities including Silvanus, Diana, Mercury and Rosmerta, and some unnamed, are attested, two at least from the north side of the river where a spring rose almost immediately opposite the temple. The altar to Silvanus was jointly dedicated to the *numen Augusti*.

The first temple, dated by Wedlake to the first century AD, was a simple circular building with eight internal and external pilasters, erected on a slight prominence just south of the brook on the west side of the settlement; a street ran towards it from the Fosse Way.[127] But Wedlake's date might be questioned since he records ambiguously a hoard of coins found in a small pit 'below the floor level.' Unfortunately he does not specify whether the pit cut the floor level or was sealed by it. The hoard contained coins down to Marcus Aurelius, so that, if it was sealed below the floor, the temple could have been built as late as AD 180; unfortunately also, the detailed coin list is devoid of site provenances.[128] Once established, though, the temple enjoyed a long life and underwent several major alterations, the first of which, towards the mid third century, saw the construction, in rusticated masonry, of an octagonal podium round the circular shrine. Slightly later the circular shrine was destroyed by fire, which does not seem to have harmed the podium. Consequently when the central part was rebuilt after the fire it was not only enlarged but also made to mirror the octagonal shape of the podium; new internal radiating walls created eight trapezoidal-shaped compartments opening off a central space.[129] Further alteration took place in the first half of the fourth century, when four alternate side-chambers were closed off from the centre. It was suggested by the excavator that the cruciform plan so produced implied that the building had been converted to a Christian church.[130] Be that as it may, its life in this phase was short; it soon became derelict and a new rudimentary shrine was reconstructed in the ruins. Before long, however, the surviving parts of the building were incorporated in a farmhouse, which could date to the late fourth or even fifth century.

Another interesting building (Building 7) connected intimately with the temple was constructed along the river bank to the north-east; of simple rectangular form, it probably dated to the second or early third century. It was chiefly distinguished by the thickness of its walls and by fragments recovered in the excavations, which showed it to be a building of some architectural merit. The side which lay along the river bank appears to have consisted of an arcade, the piers of which were matched at a later date, according to Wedlake, by a corresponding series of piers in the river bed; Priestley is reputed to have found a similarly constructed wall on the opposite bank.[131] Since the main dedication of the temple was to Apollo, a recognized deity of healing, it is not impossible that taking the waters in the neighbouring stream was seen as part of a ritual cure. A covered arcade built out over the stream would have provided an ideally-regulated bathing place.

Other buildings seemingly connected with this religious centre were a house (Building 9), which it was suggested was the dwelling of a resident priest, a shop (Building 10) and, situated slightly further away and closer to the main road, an inn or hostelry (Buildings 11 and 12, with a possible extension to 13). The whole establishment, therefore, looks not too dissimilar to many small rural religious centres in the western provinces. This function, therefore, must have been the primary reason for the settlement's foundation and growth. It lacks a theatre, though, which suggests only a moderate popularity of the cults, despite its situation on a main road.

The topography of the site would have made the construction of adequate fortifications almost an impossibility, yet the limestone scarp on the north side and the steep slopes to the south-east, as well as those on the west side of the Wick Valley, were cut back to vertical faces and limestone walls with rusticated masonry were constructed along them.[132] These walls would hardly qualify as defences and they were most likely built to prevent weathering of the scarps and slopes and consequently the danger of falling rocks; they would have given the settlement a neat and tidy prospect. From the similarity between the masonry of these walls and the temple podium, they were assigned a mid third-century date. Traces of an earth bank and a slight ditch, which Wedlake dated tentatively to the early or mid fourth century, crossed the neck of the Wick Valley.[133] They might represent a southern boundary for the settlement, or even a lackadaisical attempt at fortification; whatever they were, they were clearly no longer operative by the late fourth century, for two buildings (22, 27) were constructed outside them.

Apart from the main temple of Apollo, Priestley claimed that he had excavated another temple on the north side of the brook (Building 1), near which the fragmentary statue of Diana was found. It had been constructed against the revetting wall of the limestone scarp; consequently it must be later in date than the mid third century. A partition wall divided the building into two unequal parts, the northernmost of which contained a spring that had been channelled southwards through the building. While a religious function is very possible, the lack of proof must be stressed.[134]

During the fourth century a number of buildings were either adapted or freshly built for industrial purposes, a change which may have been caused by the declining importance of the cult centre.[135] Building 21 was used for the manufacture of pewter tableware and a number of stone mould fragments were recovered, similar to those found at Camerton (see p. 295 below). Other fragments were found within the general area of the Wick Valley. Bronze-smelting seems to have been carried on during the late fourth century in Building 13, while at the same time slight evidence for iron founding and smithing occurred in Buildings 16 and 26. Quantities of slag and a bar of wrought iron were recovered from the vicinity.

Perhaps one of the most interesting buildings to be discovered accidentally in the settlement, since their occurrence is so rare in Roman Britain, was the water-mill situated a short distance downstream (Building 32).[136] It was revealed when the destructive storm of 1968 swept away parts of the river bank. A well-constructed mill-race, with its bed curving downwards to accommodate the curvature of the wheel was uncovered; the wheel was about 2.5 m (8 ft) in diameter and would probably have been of the undershot variety. The main stream had been diverted round the north side of the race where it was retained by a stone revetted bank. A sluice gate at this point, to raise the water in the race to the height of the wheel, must once have operated.

A number of cemeteries are known to be connected with the settlement, mainly in the area of the first-century enclosure.[137] One of them seems to have been Christian, with all the graves orientated east-west. Wedlake suggested that Building 23, close by, served as a mortuary chapel; it is though somewhat reminiscent of the masonry *mausolea* at Dorchester.[138] Not far from Building 23 lay another narrow building with an apsidal end, and possibly enclosed by a small ditch; it too may have been a *mausoleum*.

The settlement seems to have retained some of its vitality well into the fifth century, since a large number of late coins covering the period AD 330–402 have been recovered, although it must be realized that some of them could have come from dispersed hoards. The find of a lead-weighted javelin, a *plumbata*, would imply at least a visit of soldiers of the late Roman army. Several buildings had been burnt and Wedlake attributed the destruction to two consecutive raids in *c.* AD 370, although caution should be exercised in accepting such closely assigned dates and explanation. Moreover fires in buildings containing large furnaces for metallurgical use cannot have been uncommon. But the final end of the settlement seems to have come at a later date, possibly as late as the sixth century, when the remaining inhabitants were put to the sword; quantities of fragmentary human bones bearing evidence of extensive injuries during life were found in and around the farmhouse, which had been built on the temple ruins. Dated to *c.* AD 392 by Wedlake, this massacre could, of course, have occurred at any time after that date.[139] The nearby villa at North Wraxall seems to have suffered a similar fate, although here the coin sequence ends with Gratian.[140] It is not perhaps going too far beyond the bounds of possibility for a date as late as AD 577 to be postulated, for Nettleton lies within a short distance of Dyrham Park, the reputed site of the final battle in western England against the Saxons, after which the towns of Bath, Cirencester and Gloucester fell to the invader; any nearby settlements or farms could have suffered a violent end following the battle.

Springhead (figs. 59 and 60)

The small settlement at Springhead lies in a valley on Watling Street about two-thirds of the distance from London to Rochester. It is mentioned in the Antonine Itinerary[141] as *Vagniacis*, a name which is a combination of two British words probably meaning a 'marshy place'. The ending *-is* is normally taken to imply an estate,[142] so the name means 'the estate of, or by, or at, the marshy place'. A number of early ditch systems, and pits said to be of a votive character, are known to underlie the Romano-British settlement. It

seems likely, therefore, that the site was of ancient sanctity before the creation of the Romano-British religious centre.[143] It is well known that marshes, bogs, streams, rivers and springs – indeed, almost anything connected with water – were often venerated in the Iron Age, a practice which was frequently carried through into the later period. The springs which formed the marsh of the ancient name, as well as being the origin of the modern name, were still active until the late 1930s when they finally dried up, owing to the lowering of the water table by numerous nearby chalk-pits.

It has been argued that the creek, created by the springs, which was navigable until 1939, was also navigable in the Roman period when there might have been an even greater depth of water. The headwaters of the creek were, in the Roman period, revetted by flints and surrounded by a metalled area, so forming a 'dock' which penetrated virtually right into the settlement.[144] Equally these features could have formed the base and surrounds for a *nymphaeum* from which visitors could cast their offerings into the spring. Unfortunately it was emptied some time ago and the basin filled with concrete.

Apart from the pre-Roman material referred to above, there is also evidence of early Roman occupation; a substantial ditch, 3 m (10 ft) wide and 2.7 m (9 ft) deep, has been traced at the southern end of the site, forming two sides of a rectangular enclosure.[145] An early, short-lived fort is not impossible; alternatively the ditch may mark the boundary of a pre-Roman religious enclosure, of the type recognized at Gosbecks Farm, Colchester,[146] or it might even be, if Penn's first-century date is amended, the ditch belonging to some urban fortifications (p. 197 below).

Somewhat naturally, Watling Street forms the main axis for the site, although its course, as far as it is known, is somewhat sinuous, due perhaps to the need to avoid marshy ground round the head of the spring; in places the road had been raised up to 6 m (20 ft), presumably because of these conditions. On approaching from the south-east, it turns, for a short distance, almost due west, before resuming a north-westerly by north course on leaving the settlement. There is some conflict between Penn and Harker on the last part of the alignment. Penn considered that the road (numbered R1) continued on its westerly course and that Harker's Watling Street was only a secondary road (numbered R2 by Penn),[147] although Penn admittedly refers to R2 as both wide and substantial. Harker, though, has cast doubt on the actual existence of Penn's R1 alignment.[148] Clearly more work needs to be done to settle the matter, although for the moment Harker's assessment is probably nearer the truth. It should be noted, though, that the course of Watling Street cuts obliquely across the ditched enclosure referred to above (p. 192), apparently entering through the south-east corner.

There can be little doubt that the small town of Springhead grew round, and because of, a major religious sanctuary, which was most likely associated with the springs and marsh, and which was probably pre-Roman in origin. On the south side of Watling Street near the centre of the settlement, an area bounded by the main road and two side-streets contained at least seven structures which have been interpreted as temples, shrines or other religious buildings. It was enclosed by a wall round the north-eastern corner,[149] but not elsewhere. A line of large posts, some 2.4 m (7¾ ft) apart, was noted at another point on the perimeter but must have been more than a fence. A sizeable square building, situated near the middle of the eastern side, was interpreted as a gatehouse or, possibly, another temple.[150] It had been constructed against the *temenos* wall and dated to the late second or early third century. Steps descended from the inside floor down to the *temenos* and so indicated the position of a door. A small square base of tiles was situated in the centre of the floor, with what was probably a votive pit between it and the door. But the whole structure much more resembles a small temple, built against the *temenos* wall, than a gateway.

Within the remainder of the *temenos* there were two principal temples, situated adjacent to one another in a row facing east; each was flanked by a smaller temple. Temple 1, north of 2, was basically of conventional Romano-Celtic type, with some embellishments.[151] It dated originally to the late first or early second century, although its foundation had cut through deposits as early as the Claudian period; an earlier timber-framed temple might therefore be expected to have lain beneath. The temple appears to have been rebuilt during the second half of the second century when certain modifications were introduced,

notably the construction of a semi-circular *suggestus* in the *cella*, a rare feature in Roman Britain. Slightly later, but probably still in the second century, projecting wings were added flanking the main entrance to the portico, while a mosaic was inserted between them on the approach across the portico to the *cella*. The whole floor area of the *cella* and portico had been tessellated during the first rebuilding. A small, uninscribed but suitably decorated altar was found lying on the floor of the *cella* and was accompanied by a variety of other votive and religious objects. It has not, though, been possible to identify the principal dedication, but there may have been a connection with Venus.

Temple 2, almost identical in size to 1, was architecturally quite different, even though it still conformed to the basic Romano-Celtic plan.[152] The normal *cella* walls had been replaced by eight plinths; a ninth, and larger one, opposite the probable entrance, was interpreted as the base for a cult statue. The *cella*, therefore, would appear to have been an openwork structure, with the roof supported on pillars or columns, since there were no traces of connecting walls between the bases. The wings, however, were here part of the original building. A small plinth for an altar stood a short distance in front of the steps leading up to the portico; the base of the altar was found nearby. This temple was considerably later in date than Temple 1, belonging to the late second or early third century, and it was perhaps contemporary with the reconstruction of the latter. Temples '3' and 4, though situated to the north of Temple 1, were intermediate, dating probably to the mid second century. They were also of completely different form,[153] both being simple rectangular buildings. 'Temple 3' was distinguished by its extremely thick walls (1 m/3¼ ft) and an apparent absence of any entrances; the floor was clay and the inside surfaces of the walls had been lined with thick *opus signinum*. Penn's interpretation that it was a sacred pool may therefore be correct, and it would have had obvious associations with the aquatic deities of the springs and marsh of the area.

Temple 4, much smaller than the others, was situated close to the northern *temenos* wall and at an angle to it. The interior was divided by a cross-wall into two unequal halves. The larger half contained a base for a cult statue placed against

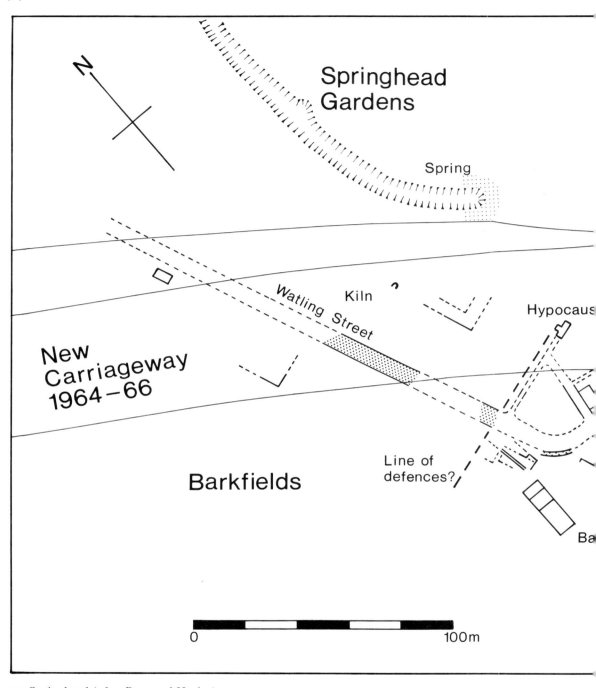

59 Springhead (*after Penn and Harker*)

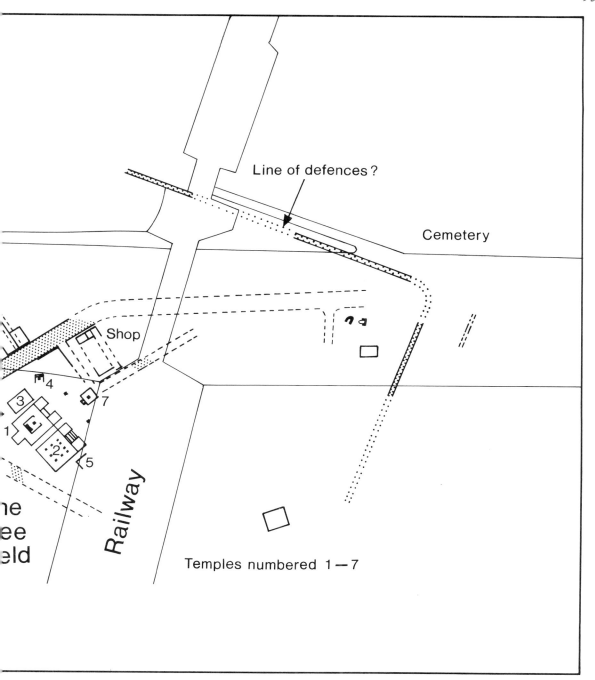

Line of defences?

Cemetery

Shop

Railway

Temples numbered 1 — 7

60 Springhead, looking south-east. The angle in
Watling Street and the possible bakery show
extremely clearly (*Cambridge University
Collection, Crown Copyright*)

the dividing wall. A grimmer note was struck by the finding of four burials of six-month-old infants, one to each corner of this room, which had been deposited in two separate ceremonies; two had been decapitated and they were undoubtedly foundation sacrifices, an unusual find in the Roman world with, here in Britain, possible atavistic links to Celtic religious practices.

Temple 5 could be only partly investigated since most of it lay under the railway embankment.[154] It was, as with Temple 4, much smaller than 1 and 2, and also much later, dating to the late third or early fourth century; the chief discovery of note was that the rear wall had collapsed in such a way as to carry the eaves of the roof with it in an unbroken line of *tegulae* and *imbrices*. The last temple to be discovered was 6, again of Romano-Celtic form and situated in the north-west corner of the *temenos*.[155] It appears to have had a very limited life, being dismantled in the early second century when Temple 1 was constructed.[156]

Another feature of interest was observed in the *temenos* in front of Temple 1. This was a well-founded base of concrete with a brick super-structure,[157] which was dated to the early second century but may be later. Beside it lay a pit containing several fragments of a large Corinthian capital; other fragments have come from within the *temenos*, together with pieces of column shaft bearing an imbricated leaf pattern. It seems most likely that these fragments came from a Jupiter column which had originally stood on this base.[158] Although distributed mainly in Germany and northern Gaul, a dozen or so of these columns are known from Britain, including three from other small towns: Catterick (p. 114), Irchester (p. 146) and Corbridge (p. 61).

There were several other interesting buildings in the settlement. One (B2) fronted Watling Street east of the *temenos* and was interpreted as a shop.[159] It was a rectangular timber building set at right angles to the street frontage with what appeared to be a corridor or veranda running down the east side; it was dated to the late second century. Two small rooms formed the frontage, but the remainder of the building was inaccessible under the railway embankment. It seems to have burnt down before being reconstructed in masonry. Another substantial tripartite building (B10) fronted onto Watling Street opposite the

temenos.[160] Dating to the early second century, it too was almost certainly at first a shop. It underwent various modifications in the late second or early third century, in one of which a corn-drier was inserted into the smaller of the rooms. Largely ruinous by the end of the third century, it became the workshop of a blacksmith who laboured under a crude shelter erected in the shell. By the end of the fourth century it was covered by a street. A much smaller building (B8) nearby, dating to the second quarter of the second century, possessed a hypocaust which appeared never to have been used.[161] A possible hardware shop is indicated at the southern end of the town, where a timber-framed building (B18) had been partly burnt down; it contained much samian ware.[162]

Perhaps, though, the most interesting building outside the *temenos* was the supposed bakery.[163] Constructed probably in the early second century, it was divided into three rooms of unequal size; the outside walls were buttressed, implying perhaps an upper storey. The front, and smallest, room resembled a portico, with a wide door giving access to the next room. This second room, and its much larger neighbour to the south, both contained sizeable ovens, one of which, at least, had originally had a domed ceiling. Part of a large quern was also found.

The tantalising fragments of a building with a corridor possibly surrounding it (B9) were discovered during construction of the new carriageway of the modern main road.[164] Its situation, coupled with its closeness to the hypocausted building mentioned above, might mean that it was a *mansio* or even a guest-house for pilgrims visiting the religious sanctuary, as at Lydney.[165] It is known to have contained at least one tessellated floor.

The town was served by a number of side-streets and lanes laid out in a haphazard manner, of which the most important were those bounding the *temenos*. Another street led off Watling Street, opposite the western *temenos* road, to join a small lane which appeared to lead to the hypocausted building. The fortification of the town is a question which has already been raised in connection with the large ditch at the south end. This needs to be considered in conjunction with another ditch of almost equal dimensions on the line of Penn's road R5, which Harker has now reinterpreted as the upcast from the ditch;[166] the latter, though, had caused a subsidence in the surfaces of Watling Street, which would not be expected if it was part of a circuit of urban fortifications.

Industrial activity on the site is not well represented, although there is a scatter of evidence showing small-scale working typical of any small town. A pottery kiln is claimed to have been discovered in 1922.[167] Iron slag, with furnace brick still adhering, has also been reported,[168] while hammer scale was associated with the blacksmith's shop in Building B10 as also in the derelict Temple 1.

Apart from numerous child burials in the settlement itself, not all of which were necessarily sacrificial (p. 197), some other burials were found in 1921–2 in an area well to the south-east of the town; both cremated and inhumed bodies were located.[169] One walled *mausoleum* was noted which contained the bodies of two infants in lead coffins, one of which was decked out in gold ornaments,[170] as well as a number of cremations. Of funerary interest also was the discovery of several fragments of sculptured lion, about 1.5 m (5 ft) long.[171] In a far-reaching article, Penn has attempted to link the child burials, 14 of which occurred along the north side of the *temenos* where they were all covered by a thick layer of clay, with the arrival in Britain of an epidemic known to have spread from the east under Marcus Aurelius in AD 166. His arguments are interesting and ingenious but lack sound evidence.[172]

There is a certain amount of evidence for the end of the Roman town, after which it reverted to open fields. Temple 1 ceased to be used about the middle of the fourth century when a blacksmith took up residence in the west portico.[173] Although safe evidence is lacking for the disuse of Temples 2 and 5, a similar date would not be out of place.[174] No dates have been given for the demise of Temples 3 and 4. Elsewhere in the town, activities, with alterations and falling standards, seem to have extended until the end of the fourth, or, more probably, early fifth century.

Springhead was a site obviously of some significance in the religious life of the Cantiaci, spanning both the Iron-Age and Roman periods, and presumably only declining with the enhanced rise of Christianity after the middle of the fourth century. It is perhaps surprising that there are no obvious signs of Christian iconoclasm, sometimes recognizable elsewhere. Once the main reason for its existence was removed, the town seems to have collapsed fairly rapidly from a place of some wealth and sophistication to something little more than an agricultural village. The religious function can, therefore, be seen as pre-eminent in its foundation, and, while it lasted, its continued prosperity.

Wycomb (figs. 61 and 62)

Wycomb lies in the upper reaches of the valley of the River Coln, also known locally as the Syreford stream, some 4 km (2.5 miles) east of the western scarp of the Cotswolds and only a short distance from Cheltenham. Its Roman name is unknown, although the modern name is obviously derived from the Latin '*vicus*'.[175] Neither does the site appear to have any connections with a major road, lying between the Salt Way, about 3 km (2 miles) to the east, and the White Way, about the same distance west; this may, though, have formed part of a direct link between Gloucester and Bourton.

The site has been recognized as Roman since at least the seventeenth century. A good deal of excavation has taken place, the earliest by the local landowner, W. L. Lawrence in 1863–4, after which the construction of two railway tracks and a junction not only bisected the site from north-east to south-west but also cut off the southern end.[176] In turn the railway was extinguished and the southern track was used for the construction of the Andoversford bypass along the line of the A40. Again, excavations preceded its construction, but they have not been adequately published, the reports being distributed between the county journal and some more ephemeral sources.[177] Fortunately some clear aerial photographs have been taken which show a main street bifurcating and running approximately north-north-east to south-south-west, off which a number of side-streets project.[178] There also appears to be a central area at the northern point of bifurcation, bounded by streets, which is thought to have contained a major temple; unfortunately most of this is now sealed by railway embankment. There is enough Iron-Age material scattered over a large part of the site to

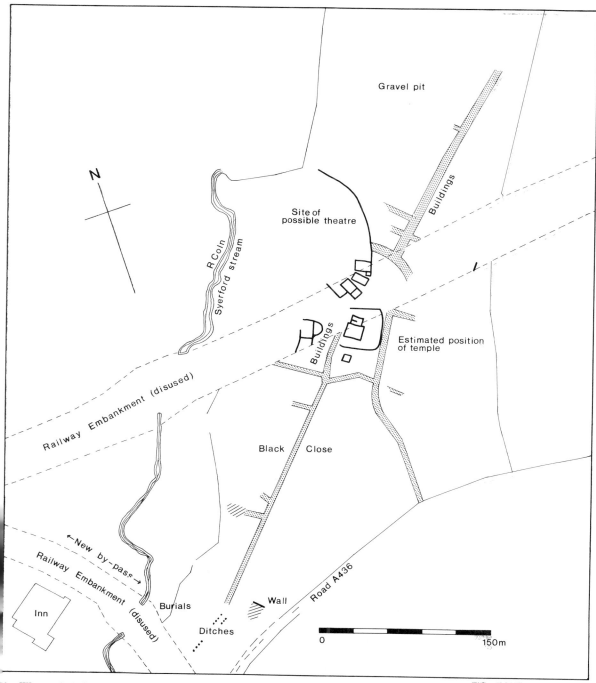

Gravel pit

Buildings

Site of possible theatre

R Coln

Syerford stream

Estimated position of temple

Buildings

Railway Embankment (disused)

Black Close

New by-pass

Railway Embankment (disused)

Inn

Burials

Ditches

Wall

Road A436

0 150m

61 Wycomb (*after Lawrence and Rawes*)

62 Wycomb, looking north-east (*Cambridge University Collection: copyright reserved*)

conclude that the Roman town grew from an existing settlement; three Dobunnic coins, brooches and contemporary pottery have been recovered. First-century timber-framed buildings and artefacts at the south end might suggest an early fort.

The central feature in the settlement is usually regarded as a temple set in a *temenos*. Two successive buildings, with one partly superimposed on the other, have been identified. The second has the outlines of a standard Romano-Celtic temple about 12 m (39 ft) square, although no *cella* is apparent. The first was a two-celled structure set slightly west of the second; architectural fragments were found nearby, but it is not possible either to say from which building they came or to ascribe a date.[179] The coin sequence, though, starts with Flavian issues, so they are unlikely to be much earlier. Their central position would make it highly probable that they were the centre of attraction for the settlement's foundation and continued existence, and it is probable that they were preceded by an Iron-Age shrine. The settlement's isolation, away from main roads, would debar it from the category of road stations.

As might be expected, a number of objects with religious associations have been recovered from the site. They include two stone panels incorporating *genii cucullati*, and Professor Toynbee has referred to the marked similarity between them.[180] These little hooded figures are, of course, common in the Cotswold region and clearly represent some form of popular local deity. A fragment of a third panel was recovered in the excavations in 1969–70 at the southern end of the settlement.[181] There are also two small, carved figures, one with grotesque head and arms,[182] and a small bronze statuette of Mars, 76 mm (3 in) high.[183] A miniature bronze votive axe has now been lost, but a piece of a temple lamp chimney was recovered at the south end of the town in 1969–70. The temple area has also produced over 500 coins dating from the Flavian period to the end of the Roman occupation.[184]

Another feature found by Lawrence lying just north of the *temenos* was a curving wall which he traced for 23 m (75 ft). It has sometimes been interpreted as the outer retaining wall of a theatre, which, given the nature of the settlement, is not impossible, although the wall is of comparatively slight build, less than 1 m (3¼ ft) thick. If the *cavea* was an earth bank and the rest of the structure had been of timber, Lawrence is unlikely to have observed the surviving traces.[185] But if the wall belonged to a reasonably conventional theatre, its approximate diameter would have been in the region of 130 m (425 ft), which might be considered as excessive for a small country shrine; the Gosbecks Farm theatre is only 80 m (264 ft). Lawrence also records at least four other masonry buildings, of shop-like proportions, on the line of this curving wall, which might imply that, if a theatre, it had a limited life, being later disused and built over; alternatively they might represent internal radiating walls.

One of Lawrence's principal buildings was No. 13.[186] This was recorded as having an apse projecting to the east; hypocausts, flue-tiles and *tesserae* were associated with it. It was claimed to have been destroyed by fire, but the burning was most probably derived from functioning hypocausts, and so Lawrence was misled; it was possibly a bath-house. Another substantial building was discovered near the boundary between Wycomb Close and Black Close.[187] The usual bric-a-brac expected from a small town is also present, with tools and agricultural implements being well represented.

One puzzling feature found in 1969–70 at the south end of the site was a large ditch, originally reckoned to be over 2 m (6½ ft) deep and 7.3 m (24 ft) wide, which ran on a sinuous course almost coinciding with the line of the main street.[188] It was reported as being flat-bottomed with a layer of uniformly-sized pebbles covering the undisturbed gravel. One interpretation suggested that it was a 'ceremonial way' leading towards the temple. Ceremonial or not, its line might well represent a hollow way for the main north-south street, no other evidence for which was found in this area. Alternatively it might represent an earlier natural or even artificial channel for the Coln Brook, which now runs a little further to the north-west. It certainly was not a defensive ditch for the town, since it not only ran in the wrong direction but also did not keep to a straight enough course. It is difficult, though, lacking a published section, to make a reasoned reassessment. The filling of the ditch apparently contained only late Roman material, including coins, calcite-gritted pottery and animal bones.

There are suggestions of cemeteries north of the settlement, where a cremation burial has been found in gravel working, while six inhumation burials have been discovered near the banks of the Coln Brook at the south end; no grave goods were recorded.[189]

The end of Wycomb seems to have been delayed until the fifth century. Late coins, down to Arcadius, are the commonest. A single chip-carved buckle of typical late fourth-century type came from the southern end of the site, together with a fragment of grass-tempered pottery, which in this part of Britain is normally given a fifth-century date. But the demise of Wycomb as a town may have come earlier, when Christianizing influences, present at Chedworth villa, only 7 km (4.5 miles) away, and at Cirencester a little further, may have removed the primary reason for its existence. Some residual functions, though, may have survived in a service centre for the six or so villas which existed within 8 km (5 miles) of the site.

TEN

SPECIALIZED SITES II: INDUSTRIAL

Brampton (figs. 63 and 64)

Beyond several cremation urns recorded in 1667 and a few finds made in the nineteenth century, there was little to indicate the existence of a large Roman site at or near Brampton before 1966, since when its character and overall extent have become apparent as a result of local fieldwork and excavation. Much is now known about an industrial zone to the west, the defended enclosure at the centre of the settlement with its small bath-house, and a range of buildings and related features alongside the main roads.[1] Aerial photography has also added details about the surrounding landscape, though the chronology of the visible crop-marks can only be defined by excavation.[2] Though much of the work remains only in interim form, we still know a surprising amount about the morphology and extent of an apparently important industrial complex south of the River Bure.[3]

The earliest origins of the town remain uncertain, despite the discovery of several Iron-Age finds and of various objects of possible military origin, including two bronze skillets. Few details have been published, however, and there are no *in situ* structures to indicate either a pre-Roman presence or the existence of an early fort.[4] Instead the site probably began life at the focus of several roads on the slightly rising ground above the crossing of the River Bure, eventually expanding to cover an area of *c.* 50 ha (124 acres) on either side of the river, though it is likely that only the immediate road frontages were ever intensely built-up.[5] One principal axis approached the centre of the later ditched enclosure from the south, following the line of the modern road, but its exact course beyond this remains uncertain. It probably continued its alignment north of the

ditched enclosure, with a branch road leading east across the river into the Oxnead suburb. Two side-streets also branched north-eastwards inside the defended area, apparently converging on a timber wharf alongside an old course of the river. The northern one has been sectioned at several points, revealing in 1979 a *c.* 3.5 m (11½ ft) wide layer of compacted gravel up to 200 mm (8 in) thick.[6] An earlier section in 1976 recorded its side ditches and noted that it sealed a pit containing late first-century pottery, perhaps suggesting an early second-century construction date.[7]

A second principal road approached from the east and made a T-junction with the north-south route *c.* 100 m (327 ft) south of the ditched enclosure. Excavation near the junction suggests a late first-century date for this,[8] thereby also providing a context for the main north-south road. A third main road led south-westwards through the industrial suburb, originating at a crossroads in the centre of the later ditched enclosure. It has been excavated at several points, revealing in 1973–4 a surface of sand and gravel 7.5 m (24½ ft) wide and up to 0.45 m (1½ ft) thick.[9] It had apparently been laid out early in the life of the settlement because it sealed a hollow containing a sherd of first-century pottery. Excavation at one point also identified evidence for a third-century remetalling, though elsewhere it had simply been patched as need arose. At the western end of the industrial zone there appears to have been a junction, the main road leading away in a more westerly direction. Besides these main roads, aerial photographs suggest several other possible tracks or droveways, the two most obvious converging just north of the main road to the west of the ditched enclosure.[10]

These roads formed the focus for typical ribbon developments, which have been recorded

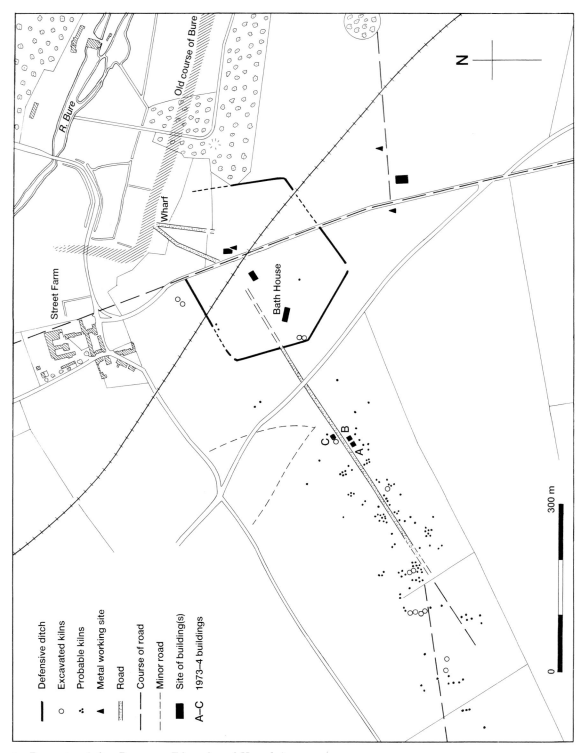

63 Brampton (*after Rogerson, Edwards and Knowles*)

in detail not just at the centre of the town but also alongside the principal approaches. Most information has come from the western suburb, where extensive industrial activity has been documented and where excavation in 1973–4 revealed an interesting sequence.[11] In the later first century, there was already evidence for pottery production north of the road, while to the south a ditch at right angles to the main roadside ditch clearly indicates the subdivision of the frontages into separate enclosures. This pattern was further reinforced in the late second to third century by the construction of two buildings within the plots and by the redefinition of their boundary line by a new ditch. Comparable enclosures, extending both north and south of the main road, appear on aerial photographs, though their chronology remains uncertain. This sequence might well parallel the evidence at Water Newton (p. 87), the area being initially divided up into plots given over to pottery production and then being subsequently occupied by buildings as the pressure on land increased. This trend might also have seen a westward shift in the pottery production.

Limited excavations in the southern suburbs, alongside the north-south road and its eastern counterpart, have identified a comparable pattern of building debris along the frontages with a system of enclosures behind; their overall chronology is not yet fully defined.[12] At the centre of the site, prolonged excavations have pieced together an equally complex sequence alongside the northern branch road to the wharf.[13] The principal elements include several successive timber buildings and workshops, numerous wells lined with oak planks, and a series of pits, gullies and post-holes. Occupation apparently began in the later first century, prior to the construction of the road, and certainly lasted well into the fourth.

Most of the excavated buildings have been of simple design except for the bath-house. Fairly typical examples were found in 1973–4.[14] Building A was represented by 17 post-holes of varying sizes set in two lines at right angles to the road, defining a structure c. 9 by 5.5 m (29½ by 18 ft) in size. Building B to the west was of roughly comparable dimensions, c. 8.7 by 5.7 m (28½ by 18½ ft), with a more regular series of eight post-holes set in two rows. Little of their super-structure survived, but it probably consisted of a wattle-and-daub infill perhaps with a thatched roof, though there is evidence of roof tiles from the central area. A different design is probably represented by Building C north of the road, though only two of its walls lay within the excavated area. Two bands of flint were set into the natural, upon which must have rested sill beams for the wooden superstructure. Comparable buildings with flint wall footings and bases have been recorded elsewhere in the central area and the southern suburbs.[15]

Of particular interest is the detached bath-house excavated in 1971–2 (fig. 5D).[16] It originally measured 12.8 by 4.6 m (42 by 15 ft) and incorporated, from east to west, the normal sequence of cold, warm and hot rooms. To the south projected a series of semi-circular or rectangular foundations, tentatively identified as the remains of an entrance lobby and additional plunge facilities. At a secondary stage, the hot plunge was dismantled and the baths extended westwards by 1.8 m (6 ft) to include an extra hot room. The walls of the structure were of flint and mortar construction, with tile bonding courses, while inside there is evidence for *opus signinum* floors and plastered and painted walls. Unfortunately, the building has been extensively robbed and its dating is uncertain, though finds in the vicinity attest occupation throughout the Roman period from c. AD 80–350. Excavations north of the baths in 1976 revealed a robbed structure 4.3 by 3.7 m (14 by 12 ft), originally attached to the north wall of the hot and warm rooms.[17] This has been identified as a latrine. There was also evidence for an earlier building on the site. Why such a bath-house was supplied at Brampton remains uncertain, given the absence of such amenities from all but a handful of small towns, but it is perhaps best regarded as an adjunct to the site's other specialized functions represented by the ditched enclosure and the level of industrial activity.

The ditched enclosure was first recognized on aerial photographs in 1974, enclosing c. 6 ha (15 acres) at the heart of the settlement, though its north-eastern side remains unclear.[18] It thus includes the central crossroads, the bath-house and the access to the wharf. Excavation at two points on the south and west revealed a ditch c. 2 m (6½ ft) deep and up to 7 m (23 ft) wide, but any associated rampart has probably been ploughed away. Its date can only be determined from the material included within the two distinct phases of infilling. The lowest sand and clay lenses included pottery of the late second to early third centuries, while the uppermost levels included late third- to early fourth-century finds within industrial and occupation debris.

This suggests a relatively short life for the enclosure, which apparently never received a secondary stone wall. This evidence probably accounts for the absence of any obvious impact on the character of the intra- and extra-mural zones. The function of such an enclosure presents problems, but it must be presumed that the site performed specialist activities of a type likely to attract officially-inspired defences, but whether this can be associated with the settlement's industrial character remains uncertain. Taken alongside the baths, however, the ditched enclosure reinforces the unexpected potential of the Brampton complex.

The most striking feature of the town's everyday life is the importance of pottery production and iron-working. The former is mainly concentrated along the road leading to the south-west, where some 132 kilns have been identified;[19] a further 13 are also known, scattered across the rest of the site. Only 14 kilns have been excavated, all of updraught type with a single flue; some were circular with a variety of different floor types, while others were rectangular or square. From the large and well-built nature of several examples, it is clear that some potters were involved in specialized *mortaria* and flagon production, probably on a large scale for export to a wider market. This is confirmed by the distribution of the stamped *mortaria* attributed to Aesuminus, which have been found as far north as Corbridge during the period *c*. AD 160–200, while one of the herring-bone stamps has even been recorded at Cramond.

Other kiln products include grey burnished vessels related to Black-Burnished 2 wares and rusticated vessels of late first- to early second-century date. It has been argued that the latter indicate a military origin for the industry because it was an early type introduced from the continent for the military market, but the single kiln so far identified is insufficiently conclusive.[20]

Pottery production clearly spanned the late first to the mid third centuries, with the emphasis falling in the second. The excavation of a probable wharf in 1973 reinforces the likelihood that long-distance water transport played a significant role in stimulating the location and expansion of the Brampton complex.[21] It comprised a platform of re-used timbers, retained by large horizontal wooden beams, set alongside a side channel at right angles to the main course of the river. This in turn was overlain by a layer of rammed sand, gravel and chalk. Some 30 m (100 ft) to the west, further vertical timbers are known, apparently indicating a structure originally built out into the river.

The evidence for iron-working is also surprisingly extensive, with many pits and gullies across the site containing large quantities of slag. The 1973–4 excavations noted a significant concentration of debris north of Building B, including 14 kg (31 lb) of smithing slag and 200 g (0.4 lb) of furnace lining, possibly associated with a furnace or hearth represented by a patch of burnt clay; likewise, east of Building A, Pit B contained 5 kg (11 lb) of smithing slag in its successive fills.[22] This activity probably belongs in the late second and third century, contemporary with the buildings. Comparable evidence has been found elsewhere,[23] both inside and outside the ditched enclosure, while the upper fill of the ditch itself contained a considerable amount of industrial debris. Alongside the northern branch road to the wharf, there was at least one third-century workshop involved in iron- and bronze-working, while in the southern suburb metal-working is attested close to the main junction and alongside the east-west road. Such a significant level of large-scale industrial activity is only rarely found among the small towns.

There were also other craft-specialists among the population, providing basic everyday services. Examples include the dump of leather offcuts from shoe manufacture found in the wharf area and the clay-lined oven associated with lime burning in the zone to the south.[24] These activities must be balanced, however, by the evidence for agricultural occupations, represented by the system of enclosures on the aerial photographs.

Evidence for the religious life of the settlement is scarce, being confined to several miniature votive objects (including an axe and a spear),[25] two pipe-clay Venuses, a statuette of Hercules and two figurines of Minerva and Jupiter.[26]

64 Brampton, looking east. Both the polygonal
defences and the main road leading south-west
into the pottery-making sector are plainly visible
(*Cambridge University Collection: copyright
reserved*)

Several possible ritual pits have also been excavated, one of which contained four dogs while another yielded an ox skull, a cat skull and a bronze bell.[27] Equally little is known about the site's cemeteries, beyond isolated burials. Southwest of the baths, for instance, a single cremation was located, while a nearby gully contained the body of a young woman;[28] elsewhere, in the workshop area near to the branch road, two late third-century cremations have been excavated, together with a pit containing the hastily buried body of another young woman.[29] These finds are clearly not indicative of normal cemetery areas but their full significance remains uncertain.

The town's later history is difficult to piece together on current evidence, not least because the archaeological deposits have been extensively plough damaged. Pottery production had certainly ceased by the fourth century, as perhaps had the metal-working concerns, though it is clear that occupation continued well into the century. In the 1973–4 area alongside the western road, later fourth-century activity was represented by Building C, a ditch and two pits on the northern side and a spread of occupation debris across the eastern half of the road to the south.[30] This might indicate a decline in the level of traffic passing along the road, though confirmation is needed from elsewhere along its course. No post-Roman material was recorded above these late levels. Much the same pattern emerges elsewhere in the site, the northern branch road to the wharf in particular being overlain at one point by a fourth-century post-built structure, and cut in another by a ditch.[31] This evidence argues for a gradual decline in the course of the fourth century, with little to suggest any significant level of continuity beyond this.

Charterhouse (figs. 65 and 66)

Despite being one of the most important Romano-British extractive centres, Charterhouse has never benefited from detailed research or excavation. Its ruins were first recorded by Skinner in 1819–20, while the principal discoveries were made between 1867 and 1876, when the vast mining tips were extensively re-exploited; most of the finds were made in the area of the modern Town Field and Upper and Lower Rains

Batch but, unfortunately, few records were maintained and little is known about any associated buildings.[32] Beyond this, our understanding of the site's development and morphology depends entirely upon small-scale excavations (principally on the amphitheatre) and limited fieldwork and aerial reconnaissance, together with the evidence of the lead pigs.[33] This is not much on which to base an assessment, not least because so little excavation has been done within the settlement. Equally problematical is the extent of ancient mining, because so much of the area has been extensively exploited and re-worked in more recent times, especially along Blackmoor and Velvet Bottom, though traces of possible early trenching have been recognized.

No *in situ* evidence exists for pre-Roman mining, though the objects from the Glastonbury 'lake village' clearly attest some activity.[34] This would account for the early Roman interest apparently represented by a 1.2 ha (3 acre) fort south of the known settlement, close to the main centre of mining.[35] Although unexcavated, flooding in 1968 exposed enough Claudio-Neronian pottery to indicate its main period of occupation. This early military presence is reinforced by two well-known lead pigs from Wookey Hole and Blagdon, both traditionally dated as early as AD 49, though this has recently been questioned;[36] a further pig from St Valéry sur Somme, dated to the reign of Nero, also carries the stamp of *Legio II*, indicating continued military control.[37] How long this was maintained cannot be determined, though it must have diminished in importance, if not lapsed altogether, once the first imperial agents or procuratorial officials were appointed.

Only one Roman road is known, heading towards Blackmoor from the south-east, but its course is lost east of the fort, as it approaches the lower-lying ground. Thus its relationship both to the fort and the civil site remains uncertain. Because the settlement has never been systematically examined, its chronology remains unknown. Aerial photographs and fieldwork suggest that occupation extended over at least 12.1 ha (30 acres), being focused around a system of irregular streets defining a row of roughly square plots running east-west with less regular blocks to north and south.[38] Finds from this area include numerous inscribed and uninscribed lead pigs, several lead weights, over 200 brooches and

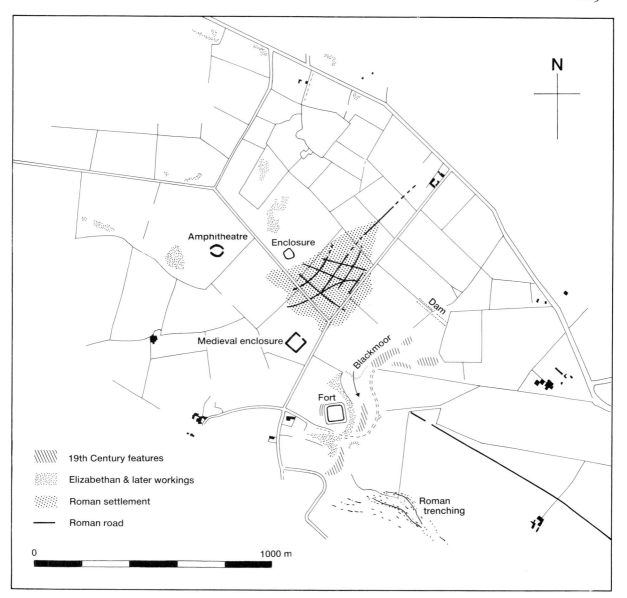

65 Charterhouse (*after Jones*)

various other domestic items, while nineteenth-century writers mention considerable amounts of charcoal, scoriae and probable smelting furnaces, as well as several clay crucibles, all attesting the site's industrial character. Limited confirmation of this was provided by small-scale trenching in the 1960s, but few new details were added.[39] An early reference to well-made drains 0.9–1.2 m (3–4 ft) deep might indicate a bath-house somewhere on the site.[40]

West of the settlement lay the amphitheatre, apparently detached from the main settlement area.[41] Excavated in 1908, it measured *c.* 70 by 61 m (230 by 200 ft) with an arena *c.* 32 by 24.4 m

66 Charterhouse, looking south-west; the details of the street system are well defined, as are two probably later enclosures (*Cambridge University Collection: copyright reserved*)

(105 by 79 ft), served by two entrances on the east and west respectively. Its bank had a sand core, overlain in places by a make-up of clay, sand, gravel and scoriae from lead-working. It had largely been built up by excavating the arena into the natural sand, though an external ditch was also sectioned along the northern side. The Roman date of this earthwork is apparently confirmed by the recovery of several pottery fragments (including some samian) from the bank, the east entrance and the ditch. The size and abraded nature of these sherds, however, coupled with the presence of numerous prehistoric flint flakes, has suggested to some writers that they are residual,[42] but since no post-Roman material has ever been located, its interpretation as a small amphitheatre still seems the most plausible. Two other finds of interest from the settlement include a bronze mask and fragments of a pipe-clay figurine.[43]

Given existing evidence, it is impossible to define the chronology of the mining site, or the precise details of its layout. The associated mining area was presumably extensive, but only one area of trenching south-east of the fort above the lower-lying ground has been tentatively assigned to the Roman period.[44] It consists of several vertical-sided, relatively narrow trenches, exploiting the lead outcrops to a depth of c. 5 m (16 ft) in places, clearly recalling Pliny's statement that British lead was easily accessible and close to the surface,[45] though we should be cautious about dating mining remains on purely surface evidence, as the much later Derbyshire lead rakes make abundantly clear. In the absence of clear dating evidence from the settlement and the mining areas, the history of exploitation must be pieced together from the surviving lead pigs.

These suggest that after the initial military activity, production passed into the hands of several individuals who might be imperial agents or procuratorial officials, or civilian prospectors in their own right. The earliest, C. Nipius Ascanius, is recorded on a pig from Stockbridge dated to AD 60, while two of his successors, G. Publius C[. . . and Tiberius Claudius Trifer[na], were operating in the Vespasianic period.[46] The former is also associated with the *Novaec. Societas*, the only mining company actually attested for the Mendips on a pig found at Syde. Such inscribed pigs are common under Vespasian,

attesting the industry's rapid expansion, and again in the second century through to the AD 160s, after which the inscribed series comes to an end.[47] After this, demand may well have declined, with mining operations falling increasingly into private hands, which no longer produced large inscribed ingots, though confirmation of this is hard to find. Occupation at the site certainly continued into the fourth century judging from the coinage, but later fourth-century issues appear to be absent.[48] Whether this reflects a gradual decline is difficult to prove on current evidence.

Droitwich (figs. 67 and 68)

There are at least two places in Britain with the name *Salinae*. Both are mentioned in the Ravenna list.[49] One, in addition, is mentioned by Ptolemy as lying within the tribal *civitas* of the Catuvellauni.[50] The identification of the first site causes little problem and the name is usually attributed to Middlewich (p. 227); the other lies on a road north of Gloucester. Rivet and Smith,[51] however, equate the latter with Ptolemy's *Salinae* and give the name to the modern town of Droitwich, noted, as with Middlewich, for its salt production since the Iron Age. They argue that Ptolemy made a cardinal error in his bearing, although his distance from London to *Salinae* (Droitwich) was nearly correct. They consider that a town near the Wash, where the bearing would place it, would not only lie outside Catuvellaunian territory but also be unlikely to have developed as a salt-producing centre by the late first century, to which date Ptolemy's information probably belongs. Yet Rivet earlier attributed Cambridge and Godmanchester, both towns lying on the Fen margin, to the Catuvellauni;[52] moreover salt was being produced in the Fens from the Iron Age onwards.[53] It is all too easy to say that Ptolemy was wrong when his figures do not fit modern hypotheses; it has happened before over the identification of *Isca* (Exeter) with the fortress of *Legio II Augusta*. If he is allowed to be right, then there may be three sites in Britain called *Salinae*, of which Droitwich was one but with the third still to be located.

The Roman site at Droitwich has been known since at least the late eighteenth century when the first canal was constructed. Further discoveries

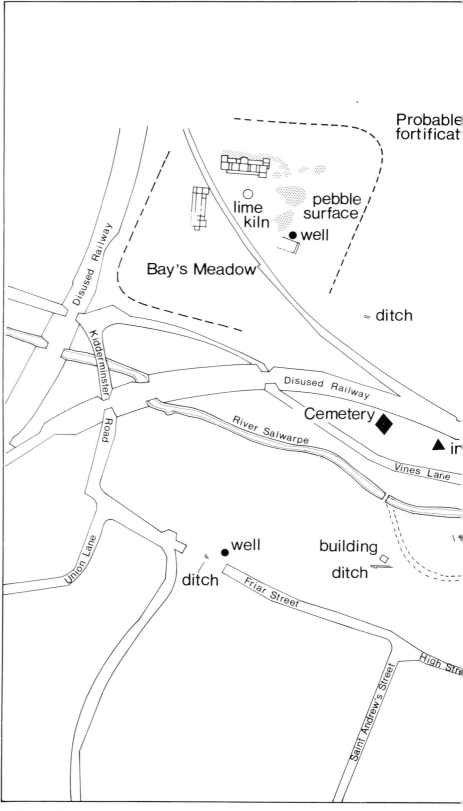

67 Droitwich (*after Hurst, D.*)

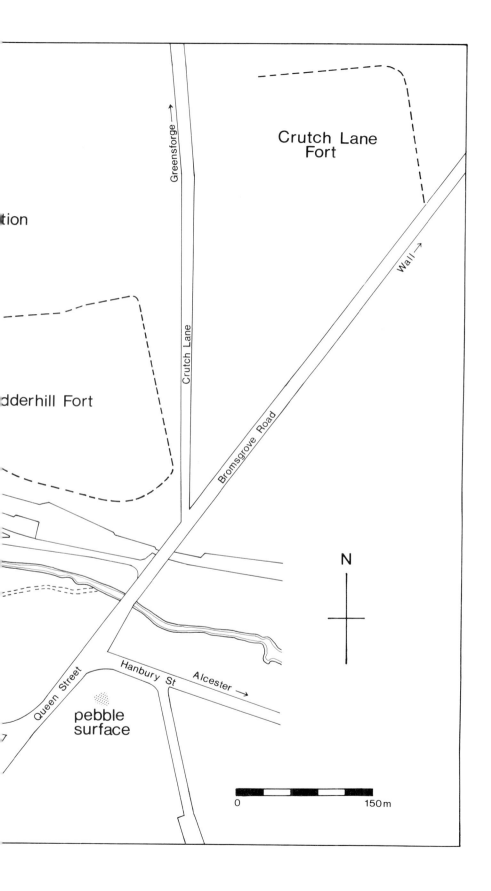

tion

dderhill Fort

Crutch Lane
Fort

Greensforge →

Crutch Lane

Wall →

Bromsgrove Road

N

Queen Street

Hanbury St

Alcester →

pebble
surface

0   150m

were made when it was extended and when the railways were built in the middle of the nineteenth century.[54] The installation of the main sewers slightly later produced yet more finds, but they were ill-recorded, as with all the earlier discoveries.

The Roman town of *Salinae* lay on the River Salwarpe not far from its junction with the Severn.[55] Roads from Gloucester, Metchley, Alcester and possibly Wroxeter met here. The brine springs were used in the Iron Age, and there is little doubt that this was the industrial base which caused the foundation and growth of the Roman town. Salt was a product of considerable economic value in the Roman Empire and its extraction was often carried out under imperial control. The recognition of this importance probably influenced the decision to place a fort here in the years immediately after the invasion. But whereas the Iron-Age settlement and subsequently the Roman town mainly occupied the valley site, the fort was situated on higher ground to the north at Dodderhill. Two parallel ditches were found there in 1937, enclosing an area which may have been as great as 4 ha (10 acres). Pottery and coins of the Claudio-Neronian period have been found,[56] while later investigations traced more of the outline, established two periods of internal timber building,[57] and also produced more contemporary coins, brooches and military equipment. The first military occupation ceased *c*. AD 70, but a second followed from *c*. AD 120–50 and may have represented a revived imperial interest in the production of salt. The site of the fort has recently been the subject of a successful prosecution by English Heritage under the Ancient Monuments Act; a large area was levelled for a playing field without permission or excavation and has consequently been lost for all time.

From this commanding position overlooking the river valley and close to the main road junction, the fort would have been in an ideal position to supervise the local labour producing this valuable commodity. Excavations in Friar Street on the site of the new fire station revealed wood-lined pits, probably used for the storage of brine.[58] On disuse, they had been filled with much ash and briquetage, containing pre-Roman Iron-Age pottery; this activity continued here until *c*. AD 100. Comparable early Roman activity was also located on the Old Bowling Green site.[59] A separate area of settlement seems to have developed as well to the north of the river valley, in the area now known as Bays Meadow, which is roughly bisected by a disused railway line.

North-east of the railway, surface features were believed to represent the wide ditch of a fortified circuit of the town. Excavations southwest of the railway line, where the ditch might be expected to continue, established that there was not only the wide ditch but also another smaller ditch on an inner alignment,[60] which caused the excavator some confusion. A re-examination of the published section, however, shows possibly a more complicated sequence than he described. There are no questionable points about the outer ditch, but the inner ditch could be interpreted as the robber trench for a shallow-founded masonry wall superimposed on a deliberately-filled ditch. Indeed the excavator raised the possibility that it marked the line of a robbed wall, *later* converted to a ditch. The same feature was followed for some distance south-westwards to Vines Lane, towards which it ran in a straight line. More recent excavations, in 1971–2 on the southeastern and north-eastern sides of the circuit, have now established beyond doubt that a masonry wall, probably contemporary with the wide ditch, succeeded what was seemingly an earthwork fortification, the ditch of which ran below the wall and its rampart. The latter contained a coin of Carausius, so it and the wall probably date to the very late third or fourth century.[61] The date of the earlier earthwork is still not known. No sign of gates, or of internal or external towers has yet been seen. The relationship, therefore, of the walled circuit to the road system cannot be established. But the main Worcester to Metchley road is thought to run along the line of the modern Bromsgrove road, well to the east of the fortifications, from which the Wroxeter road diverges along Crutch Lane on the eastern side of Dodderhill. The Hanbury road probably represents the line to Alcester. It seems likely, therefore, that Droitwich is yet another of those small towns, such as Dorn (p. 253) and Alcester (p. 92) where the main roads pass by, without entering the fortified circuit.

A number of major buildings have been identi-

68 Droitwich, looking south-west. The line of the
ditch in Bays Meadow can be seen to the right of
centre (*Cambridge University Collection: copyright
reserved*)

fied, including what would seem to be two conventional winged-corridor houses situated at right angles to one another in the northern part of the defended area. That to the west[62] was well built with its main walls nearly 1 m (3¼ ft) thick; there was at least one heated room in the south-west corner (see fig. 3D). The house dates to just after the middle of the third century, and there does not seem to have been a predecessor. A twin pair of T-shaped drying kilns, interpreted by the excavator as corn-driers, was found in front of the house. This may be so, although there was no evidence of burnt grain. It is not impossible, therefore, that they might have been used for brine evaporation.

The second house, close to the northern defences, was first discovered when the now-disused railway line was constructed; it was shown to contain two much-damaged tessellated pavements, one incorporating a simple geometric mosaic.[63] It was partly re-examined in 1924,[64] while later investigations showed that it had been built at about the same time and to much the same plan as the western house, although on a larger and more lavish scale (see fig. 3C); wall plaster painted with human figures, foliage and animals was recovered.[65] A well in the front courtyard provided water. The house appears, though, to have had a short life, being destroyed by the end of the third century, in contrast to the other, which may well have been occupied down to the early fifth century. In a rural context, both of these houses would be called villas, and there are clearly agricultural connections, with the poss-ible corn-driers, and burnt grain found on the floor of another building. So while the salt industry probably provided the principal reason for the town's foundation and continued exis-tence, its secondary function as an agricultural centre for internal or nearby farms cannot be dismissed.

Part of another building, also with an external corridor, was found in the area in front of these two houses; its date and function are obscure.[66] In the southern part of the site, a fourth-century building resembling an aisled barn or farmhouse was discovered. There was also an outhouse situated along most of its south side, the floor of which was covered with charred grain; the building may have been a granary.[67] Another possible granary was identified, together with

other fourth-century buildings, behind the ram-part in the north-eastern part of the site.[68] Little evidence has been obtained so far for buildings earlier than the third century within the area of the fortifications.

Most of the industrial evidence from the town has, somewhat naturally, been related to the extraction of salt, to which reference has already been made (p. 214). In the Roman period, briquetage, an oval oven and fragments of unusual conical vessels were found beneath the rampart of the eastern defences and were clearly related to the preparation of salt.[69] In the area of the Old Bowling Green, further large quantities of briquetage were recovered, together with six oval clay-lined pits, up to 2.3 m (7½ ft) across, which were located near brine springs and which were probably used as storage or settlement tanks for the liquid; they may once have been covered. Iron-Age pottery was present, although the pits dated to later in the first century. A second-century masonry building stood nearby. At a later date, probably around the late third century, four wooden barrels had been cut in half length-ways and the halves laid in pits, again presumably as part of the salt-extracting process,[70] which seems to have been carried out in the Roman period along a considerable length of the Sal-warpe valley, with evidence occurring as far east as the Hanbury Road. It has been claimed that special ceramic vessels were made in the Malvern potteries as containers for the salt produced at Droitwich. The only other evidence for an industrial activity associated with the town was a very large lime-kiln, 3 m (10 ft) in diameter, which was found buried beneath a later building in front of the northern corridor house in Bays Meadow. It had presumably supplied lime for the considerable building programme which took place in the second half of the third century.[71]

So far little evidence has been obtained for cemeteries, but in Vines Lane, just outside the southern fortifications, 14 inhumations have been discovered, orientated east-west; there were no grave goods, but one at least had been buried in a coffin.[72] The spacing of the burials would suggest a well-organized graveyard of a type which is becoming more familiar in late Roman small towns, such as those at Ashton (p. 281) and Alcester (p. 96). Whether these cemeteries are Christian or not, they obviously represent a departure from the old, haphazard inhumed style of burial, where quite often early interments were disturbed by the later. It would be reasonable to suppose that the graves were marked in some way, or even that a plan was kept to avoid this happening. If they were pagan, then it might be that the better-ordered way of Christian burial was being copied.

Considerable quantities of late Roman pottery and coins have been recovered from Droitwich, and one coin at least,[73] associated with the westerly of the corridor houses in Bays Meadow, dates to the first quarter of the fifth century. Salt presumably kept its value in the late Roman Empire, and there is no reason why production at Droitwich should have ceased until it became impossible to send it to market.

Holditch (fig. 69)

Until the late 1950s, the settlement at Holditch was entirely unsuspected. Small-scale excavations had instead concentrated upon Chesterton c. 1 km (0.6 miles) to the north-west, where antiquarian tradition suggested a Roman military establishment, but no significant structural remains were located, despite the presence of suggestive early samian.[74] Ironically, the fort was not discovered until 1969,[75] several years after redevelopment work at Holditch revealed a surprisingly extensive civilian site apparently performing specialized industrial functions.[76] Trial trenching initially sought to determine the extent of the settlement, but later more intensive investigation was directed at the buildings fronting its north-east/south-west street. These small-scale excavations inevitably restrict our understanding of the site's morphology, though they did prove informative about its developmental sequence and its wider functional role.

Holditch's origins and early status are somewhat obscure. Military activity in the region began with the Neronian fort at Trent Vale, c. 6 km (4 miles) to the south-east.[77] This was probably replaced by the early Flavian site on the higher ground at Chesterton, where small-scale excavation in 1969 revealed the south-eastern defences of an auxiliary fort, comprising two ditches and a 7.6 m (25 ft) wide rampart of sandstone fragments set between turf revetments.[78] The fort apparently faced north-east

because its south-eastern gate lies off-centre, while a Roman road has been traced approaching what, on topographical grounds, must be the centre of its south-western side. Excavations south-west of the fort along the boundary of Top Field located a further ditch, perhaps representing an external annexe or an earlier and larger temporary camp. At an uncertain date, the front turf revetment had been thrown down into the inner ditch.

There is as yet no evidence for a *vicus* outside the Chesterton site, though it was perhaps too short-lived to facilitate this. More problematical is the relationship between the latter and the civilian settlement at Holditch, which apparently also developed in the early Flavian period.[79] Given the distance between them, Holditch is unlikely to have originated as a *vicus* attached to the Chesterton fort, unless specific conditions about its location had been laid down by the military. An independent origin thus seems likely, taking advantage of the communications network and locally available raw materials to develop a specialist role in conjunction with a nearby garrison and the wider military market. A less likely alternative, given the close link elsewhere in the north-west between forts and specialized *vici*, is that an undiscovered successor to the Chesterton fort lies closer to Holditch itself.[80]

Whatever its origins, Holditch apparently expanded quickly in the later first century. Occupation debris is spread over at least 400 m (1300 ft) from south-west to north-east, from the Metanodic factory to beyond the A34 and up to 250 m (820 ft) across its other dimension.[81] Within this area, excavations had initially expected to locate the main road south-east from Chesterton, heading for Rocester and Little Chester, but revealed instead a 7.3 m (24 ft) wide street on a north-east to south-west alignment. The main road must therefore follow the A34/A52 London Road through the east side of the settlement. The internal street was substantially built, with an original surface of chippings and gravel resting upon a foundation of large sandstone blocks.[82] It had been resurfaced at least three times, once with a 50 mm (2 in) layer of molten iron slag, which had run together to form a solid mass. This street probably linked the main Roman road with a large building known to lie

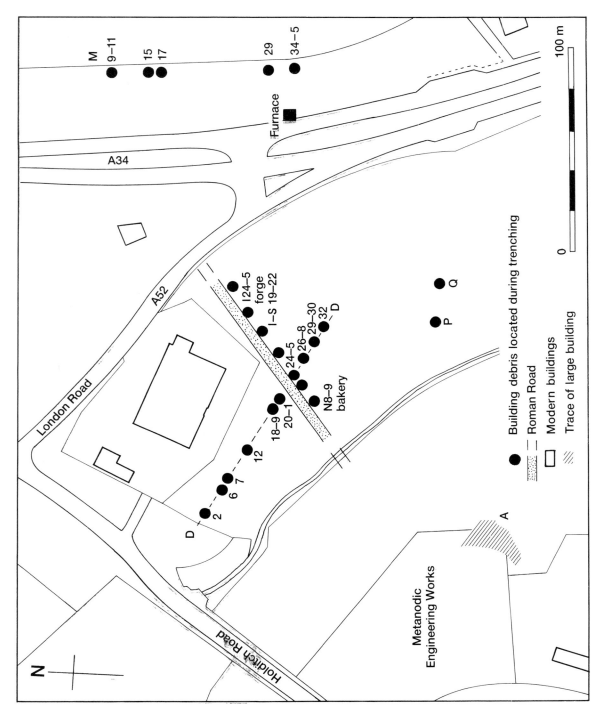

69 Holditch (*after Charlton*)

under the Metanodic factory, though its line south-west of the Ashfield Brook has been destroyed by later activities. No other internal streets are known, but such an extensive site would require further provision to accommodate the known buildings.

Trenching throughout the settlement identified numerous buildings which had been successively rebuilt and replaced over time, though few complete plans were recovered. Most consisted of floors of clay or well-laid sandstone blocks, supporting a timber superstructure infilled with clay, and a tiled roof. In 1958 for instance, the exploratory Trench D cut obliquely across the main street, thereby sampling a complex sequence of buildings on and behind its frontages.[83] Those to the south extended across boxes 24–32. Close to the frontages, the earliest activity consisted of a clay and pebble floor in 24 and a clay floor in 25, both overlain by a more substantial second-century floor of sandstone blocks; the surrounding foundation trench still contained fragments of its oak superstructure. Behind in 26–27 lay another sandstone floor, and beyond that a pebble and mortar floor in 27–28. Further clay floors were located in 29–30, and again in 32, some 30 m (100 ft) from the frontage; beyond this no further structures were found, though occupation debris was abundant. Comparable timber structures were located north of the street, those nearest to the frontages in boxes 20–21 and 18–19 resting on sandstone floors, while further north there were several clay floors in 12, 7, 6 and 2. This evidence suggests that activity was heaviest along the frontages, with lesser structures and yards to the rear, all apparently associated with specialized industrial activities. Occupation began in the later first century and apparently ended soon after the mid second.

More extensive excavations in 1960–1 examined the buildings along the southern frontage in Trenches I-S, 19–21, though work on the intricately superimposed structures was hampered by adverse weather.[84] Most were of simple design like their Trench D counterparts. The late first-century buildings, with their stone floors, were very fragmentary, but in I-S 21 they were replaced on a slightly different alignment by a second-century timber-framed strip building with several successive sandstone or pebble floors. Its plan during its separate phases was not

easy to reconstruct, but seems to have included an open veranda, two rooms and a yard containing an oven. Buildings of this general type were not confined to the frontages, however; Trenches P and Q to the south-east revealed sandstone block floors, timber and clay walls and tiled roofs, while east of the A34 further timber buildings were located at various points in Trench M.[85]

This extensive occupation is also accompanied by a marked emphasis on specialized industrial activities, represented by large amounts of charcoal, coal and cinder ash, and by lead waste, iron-ore and slag.[86] The importance of iron-working is well attested by the use of slag as a road metalling, already described, and by the regular recovery of iron slag in first- and second-century contexts across the site; south of the street in Trench D, for instance, charcoal and slag were frequently found on the earliest clay floors, while the early building in I 24–25 has been identified as a forge.[87] These activities probably spread east of the A34, where large quantities of iron slag were found near a furnace measuring 1.7 by 1.1 m (5½ by 3½ ft) on Site H.[88] This metal-working was accompanied by other service trades, best attested by the bakery in N 8–9.[89] Little of its structure survived, but a succession of four or possibly five ovens was recorded, the latest pair being built on a circular pebble floor set in clay with a hard-baked clay dome across the top. Commercial activity is also represented by several lead weights and possibly by the later building on Site I 19–22 identified as an open-fronted food shop or eating house.[90] These specialized activities recall several other industrial sites in this north-western area.

The settlement's chronology is also interesting. Significant late first-century expansion is well represented by the buildings already described along the street frontages, where occupation began c. AD 70–80, while its second-century extent is well attested by the distribution of structural debris and pottery across the site. After c. AD 160, however, there is cumulative evidence for the settlement's contraction and decline. The sandstone floors in D 24–25 and 26–27, for instance, and the clay floor in 29–30, were all overlain by debris including collapsed stone, roof tiles and nails, a pattern repeated in I 19–22.[91] The presence of charcoal in the upper levels might suggest that some structures were des-

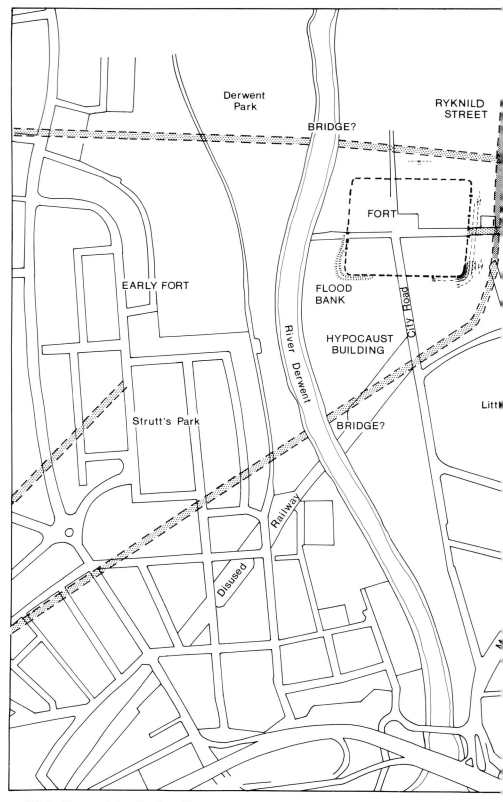

70 Little Chester (*after Dool et al.*)

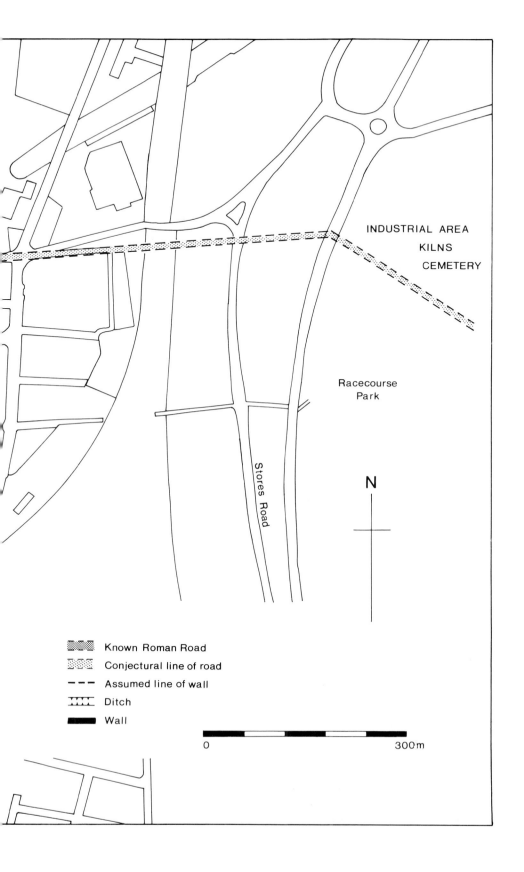

INDUSTRIAL AREA

KILNS

CEMETERY

Racecourse
Park

Stores Road

N

Known Roman Road
Conjectural line of road
Assumed line of wall
Ditch
Wall

0   300m

troyed by fire, but a major conflagration seems unlikely. Most had simply been abandoned and subsequently collapsed. Wherever this occurred, debris sealed material of mid second-century date. This evidence for abandonment is currently confined to the areas alongside the north-east/south-west street, suggesting that the problem initially affected the settlement's lower-lying areas. Occupation certainly continued east of the A34, though apparently on a reduced scale to judge from the quantity of third-century pottery.[92] But even this area succumbed eventually, because there is a complete absence of fourth-century finds. The reasons for such a decline remain unclear, though it is not without parallel at other sites with specialized industrial interests.

Though a military successor to the Chesterton fort nearer to Holditch remains hypothetical, the site may not have been entirely devoid of an official presence during its lifetime. The main street apparently led to a large building thought to underlie the Metanodic factory, though only a fragment of its wall has been located.[93] This was 0.8 m (2½ ft) wide and extended at least 9 m (29½ ft) without any obvious cross-walls. The associated finds included large quantities of tile and brick, fragments of window glass, a stone column drum cut for railings and a fragmentary centurial stone apparently reading *C(enturia)* GAL[... This latter might suggest a military or official interest not only in the building's construction, but also in its subsequent function within the settlement. Unfortunately this cannot be proved from the surviving remains, which were tentatively assigned to the Hadrianic period. Such an official building fits in well with what is known about the site's short chronology and its specialized industrial associations, thereby lending support to the view that such industrial functions were its primary *raison d'être* in the context of local and regional military requirements.

Little Chester (figs. 70 and 71)

Little Chester lies on the northern outskirts of the modern city of Derby. It is mentioned in the Ravenna list as *Derbentione*,[94] and is consequently a place where a river name *Derventio* (Derwent) has been attached first to a fort and then to the settlement.[95] It lay at the junction of a number of roads. Most important probably was Ryknild Street, running north from Wall and on to the fort at Templeborough; another road ran almost due west from Little Chester to Rocester and then on to Wilderspool and the Lancashire coast, while a third probably aimed at Buxton and the Peak District. A fourth road connected Little Chester with the Roman site at Sawley on the north bank of the River Trent, but whether it then crossed the river is not known.

The site has been recognized as Roman at least since 1721, when Stukeley surveyed the plan of a rectangular, walled enclosure bounded by a wide depression marking the position of a ditch.[96] Since then finds of Roman material have been made from time to time, followed by several small-scale investigations,[97] prior to the more protracted series of excavations which took place between 1968–83,[98] and again in 1987.[99]

The earliest Roman occupation of Little Chester, where there is no evidence for an Iron-Age settlement, was on the west bank of the Derwent. Excavations in Strutts Park have produced sufficient evidence to show that a Neronian fort was established there, probably under the governor A. Didius Gallus, which remained until the early Flavian period.[100] It was then probably superseded by another fort on the opposite bank of the Derwent, dating to *c.* AD 80–120, although no fortifications for this period have yet been found. But the internal buildings would suggest more irregular planning than is usual in a conventional fort of this time; moreover, these buildings passed under the Antonine rampart near the south-east corner, indicating a fort of greater size than its successor.[101] This fairly intense period of occupation was followed by a distinct decline under Hadrian, when the fort was probably evacuated, to be replaced in the Antonine period by another whose outlines were recorded by Stukeley.

By the end of the second century, the fort seems again to have outlived its usefulness. The

71 Little Chester, looking north. The line of Ryknild Street, north of the fort, can be seen most clearly in the allotments at the top left (*Cambridge University Collection: copyright reserved*)

defences were remodelled; the clay bank, revetted by timber, was retained, but a single ditch replaced the earlier pair. It may have been at this stage that a masonry gate, earlier than the later curtain wall, was inserted on the west side.[102] Internal buildings were demolished and the site was sealed with a thick layer of gravel. In the north-east corner there were signs of industrial activity, with hearths fed from a central stockpile of coal. It is difficult to escape the conclusion that the fort had become more of a civilian town, with the inhabitants of the *vicus* moving inside the defences. But not for long, as within 25 years the interior was at least partly covered with a thick layer of dark soil, which the excavators likened to cultivation soil. It is not known where it came from, but there must have been a great amount; neither can its use be explained, unless it was to create a large, walled market-garden. Thereafter, the interior of the fort remained virtually unoccupied until the late third century.[103]

When the second, Flavian, fort was founded, a *vicus* grew with it to the east, towards what is now the racecourse, and flanking the road to Sawley. Potteries were established by *c.* AD 100, containing a number of unusual kilns. Many were no more than 1 m (3¼ ft) across and some were much less; several were grouped around common stoking-pits. The wares they produced were uncompromisingly Roman in form and fabric and included quite large quantities of green-glazed vessels; presumably galena from the Peak District was used. Prototypes of later Derbyshire wares were also being made. But this activity lasted for only a comparatively short time, generally terminating *c.* AD 110–20, although a minority of kilns continued production until the middle of the century.[104] In the later second century the area seems to have blossomed into an industrial centre, with flimsy timber-framed buildings being constructed along the roadsides. A number of furnaces and hearths and the quantities of slag imply the working-up of impure iron blooms and the manufacture of ironwork. Small amounts of smelting slag and iron ore would indicate that iron was smelted but not on the sites explored. Some of the hearths may have been used for non-ferrous metals, although no other specific evidence was recovered.[105]

The behaviour of the main roads at Little Chester obviously affected the development of the *vicus* nearer to the fort. Stukeley was the first to show that Ryknild Street did not enter the fort but ran past it on the east side, before curving south-westwards near the south-east angle towards a crossing of the Derwent. He also mentioned a gravel road parallel to the northern defences, which formed a crossroads with Ryknild Street and aimed westwards at the river, where he recorded the piers of an early, and therefore probably Roman, bridge; presumably this is the road to Rocester. Both roads have since been confirmed by excavation.[106] Traces of timber and masonry buildings have been uncovered in and around the area of the crossroads, as has the crossing of Ryknild Street by the road leading out from the fort's east gate. One building of the third to fourth century was recorded as having a colonnade. South of the fort, near the bridge over the river, a hypocaust has been discovered, which was said to date to the early fourth century; it was associated with painted plaster.[107]

The late third or early fourth century saw some notable changes at Little Chester. The rampart of the Antonine fort was now supplemented by a wall 3 m (10 ft) thick, and a new wide ditch replaced that of the earlier periods. These fortifications have now been recorded on the west, south and east sides but not on the north;[108] an opportunity to determine the north line was recently let slip by English Heritage.[109] Some rebuilding also took place within the walled enclosure; its character would seem to be civilian rather than military, even given the vagaries of the late Roman army. This attempt to create what is probably a conventional walled town did not affect the *vicus*, which, at least around the south-east corner, continued in occupation while the industrial centre on the racecourse was still busy.

It is very difficult to suggest an acceptable reason for these developments. There are indications that Little Chester became an industrial centre, but no more than Wilderspool, which never received fortifications, although it had passed its peak before urban defences became common. Similarities exist between Little Chester and Catterick (p. 111), where an early fort was later walled with the town, although there the walls also surrounded part of the *vicus*, which at Little Chester was left wholly unenclosed. An answer can come only with more exploratory work inside the fortifications, which is becoming increasingly difficult to achieve as opportunities are lost.

In one respect, though, Little Chester exceeds many other small towns in the unusual quality of its burials, although the earliest probably belonged to the army. A row of five squarish masonry *mausolea* was situated along the north side of the Sawley road where it crosses the modern racecourse and after it had left the Roman industrial area; one *mausoleum* had been preceded by a timber-framed version.[110] Cremation burials were found in three, with a variety of grave goods and in each a cremated pig. The other two had completely solid foundations with no evidence of burials, which may have been placed in parts of the superstructure. All are dated to the early second century and they presumably represent the burials of officers from the fort. The *vicus* is unlikely to have contained so many wealthy residents by that date, unless it early became connected with the burgeoning lead industry of south Derbyshire, which was operating by *c.* AD 80. Perhaps here were the graves of some unknown Italians like Ti. Claudius Triferna whose name appears on a lead pig from the area.[111] Their presence might account for the high-grade pottery which was being produced. Some other solitary cremation burials had also been made around the area, dating to much the same period, before yet another unusual feature was constructed. This was a walled cemetery, set further back from the road and behind the row of *mausolea*; its external measurements were about 14 m (46 ft) square.[112] The earliest cremation burials were made in it in the mid to late second century, after which it seems to have been used continuously, if spasmodically, until the middle of the fourth century, mainly for inhumations, although cremation did not altogether cease. A total of 61 inhumations were recovered. One odd feature was the three burials which had cut through the enclosing wall, suggesting that it can never have been of great height. The social background to such a small cemetery is not easy to define. If a family is represented, then it had remarkable powers of survival averaging some six members per ten generations spread over the best part of 200 years. Alternatively, it may have been owned by a burial club, which must have had a very small and select membership and which

included men, women and children. Walled cemeteries of this type are unusual so far north, most belonging to south-eastern Britain and north-west Gaul and Germany. It may perhaps be taken as an indicator of the origins of at least a small part of the settlement's population.

The *vicus* and its suburbs at Little Chester do not seem to have outlived the fourth century, generally terminating well before its end. It may be that the later levels have all succumbed to post-Roman disturbance, but neither the coin list nor the pottery would support a later date. The next identifiable phase in the life of the settlement only came in the sixth century, when a number of Anglian burials were made inside the south-eastern defences.

Middlewich (fig. 72)

A Roman presence at Middlewich was first demonstrated in the nineteenth century by the recovery of numerous finds over a wide area, including several fired clay bricks resembling salt-working briquetage.[113] Such discoveries have continued in the twentieth century, most notably the discharge diploma of a retired auxiliary,[114] but the first excavations were only begun in 1960 (Site A), since when several important sites have been investigated, including a salt-working complex (Site C), various iron-working compounds (Site J) and several strip building complexes (Sites C and G).[115] Though the bulk of the evidence remains in interim form, this work has added enormously to our understanding of the settlement's morphology and development. It is clear, however, that fourth-century levels have been badly disturbed by later activity and that much has been lost through the construction of the Trent and Mersey Canal and the railway.

There is little to suggest an Iron-Age origin for Middlewich or its salt-working industry, unlike Droitwich. Activity characterized by several brine pits apparently commenced in the Flavian period.[116] One example on Site K, at the southern end of the site, contained pottery of *c.* AD 70–80 in its lowest fill, while a second on Site C close to the centre had been in use from the later first century, to judge from the associated finds. Buildings of comparable date have been identified at several

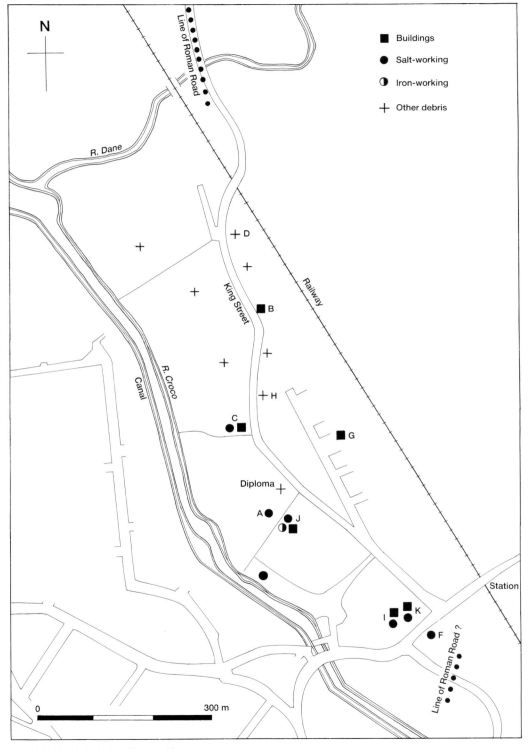

72 Middlewich (*after Bestwick*)

points, as for example on Sites B, C and I,[117] attesting to the rapid development of the site and its industrial activity, though whether this was a civilian concern independent of a military stimulus remains uncertain, because the site is eminently suitable for an early fort, standing on rising ground above the confluence of the Dane and Croco. As yet no distinctive military items have been found, but the numerous examples of early Flavian samian might perhaps indicate a military presence.[118] Somewhat more interesting is the presence of a retired auxiliary in the early second-century population, perhaps drawn back to the site as a consequence of the potential profits to be won from its principal product, salt.

The morphology of the town is known only from the distribution of occupation debris, which extends over an estimated area of c. 35 ha (86 acres), from the River Dane on the north to well beyond the railway station on the south, a distance of over 1.2 km (0.8 miles).[119] In places it spreads up to 300 m (990 ft), suggesting a fairly typical ribbon development along the road frontages, though unfortunately the internal road network remains poorly understood. Two principal roads are focused upon the site, presumably forming a junction somewhere at its southern end.[120] One ran north-west to south-east, though only its north-western branch beyond the River Dane is well known; south-east of the town, its course has probably been lost to industrial development and the canal. Within the settlement, the only possible sighting came in 1962, when excavations revealed a spread of pebbles to the east of the modern King Street, with two parallel north-south ditches, the smaller of which might be a roadside ditch.[121] A second main road apparently ran south-west to north-east, though only its south-western portion from Whitchurch can be clearly traced; Watkin recorded a possible line near the station, but its extension beyond this to the north-east remains unknown.[122] Within the settlement, no internal streets are known.

Excavations along the projected north-west to south-east road have identified various timber strip buildings, dating from the later first century onwards. They were apparently crowded end-on to the frontages to make use of all the available space, those on Sites I and K to the south lying at 70 degrees to the presumed road, unlike the examples on Sites C and G at the centre.[123]

Behind these frontages, the picture changes. On Site J, for instance, a system of ditches, 0.7 m (2¼ ft) wide, ran east-west and north-south, defining a series of ditched enclosures within which lay several iron-working furnaces; beyond lay yet more industrial debris, including heaps of slag and salt-working briquetage extending to the steep slope at the western fringe of the settlement.[124] This picture is admittedly rather sketchy but suggests that buildings stood along the frontages while the land behind was divided into plots devoted to various industrial uses; the intensity of occupation and industrial usage apparently declines with distance away from the roads.

Few detailed plans of the buildings are published, but clearly they were all of timber-framed construction and simple design, as the sequence of strip buildings and related structures on Site C clearly demonstrates.[125] Particularly interesting are two second-century buildings flanking the north and south sides of a central yard. The northern one, only partly explored, had a door in its south wall leading into the yard. Its southern counterpart was c. 5 m (16 ft) wide by at least 16 m (52 ft) long, comprising three rooms within the excavated area; it too had a door leading into the yard. Both buildings were recognized from their sill-beam trenches. The site was subsequently occupied by several later third- and fourth-century structures, including a house 13.1 m (43 ft) wide with a corridor 2.7 m (9 ft) wide on the north. Comparable buildings elsewhere include those on Sites I and K, the former rebuilt three times during the second century each time with different flooring, the latter measuring at least 27.7 m (90 ft) long by 6.1 m (20 ft) wide.[126] Surprisingly few fourth-century structures are known, but they include a partly excavated open-sided workshop on Site J represented by six large post-holes.[127] There is no evidence for more sophisticated buildings at Middlewich.

As with other sites in the area, Middlewich reveals a surprising level of specialized industrial activities, especially salt production, the importance of which is reinforced by its identification with one of the two *Salinae* place names recorded in documentary sources.[128] The earliest evidence comes from several late first-century brine pits on Sites C, I and K, while its early extent can be gauged from deposits of briquetage on Sites F and K, the latter extending over at least 100 by 150 m (327 by 490 ft) and up to 0.6 m (2 ft) thick in places.[129] On Site C, these early levels were overlain by a salt-working complex focused on an open yard, which was subsequently enclosed by a windbreak or rain shelter across its western end, between the two buildings already described.[130] Within this lay another brine pit, two types of brine-kiln or hearth and the remains of two *dolia* or large *amphorae* for brine storage; these latter were set fast in the ground with three others, of which only the impressions survived. One was inscribed with the graffito 'AMURCA', traditionally interpreted as 'waste from the brine'.[131] Finds indicate that the complex flourished in the second century.

The regularity with which briquetage has been found, particularly along the settlement's western side, confirms the large-scale nature of the later first- and second-century activities, though how long they lasted remains uncertain. Three different kiln types have been identified, including trough-kilns, rectangular open hearths and circular kilns, all presumably used for brine evaporation.[132] A good example of the first was excavated on Site A, revealing a clay-lined trough 3.05 by 0.61 m (10 by 2 ft) with a ledge along both sides 0.31 m (1 ft) above the floor. Its charcoal and clay fill contained the bulk of its kiln furniture, including a complete firebar, eight wedge-shaped bricks, nine cylindrical supports and five rectangular clay plates. A second example was found on Site C alongside a rectangular open hearth, the latter measuring little more than 0.6 by 0.9 m (2 by 3 ft). Five circular kilns were excavated on Site I, each one averaging *c.* 0.91 m (3 ft) in diameter and being laid out as one of a pair in a figure of eight arrangement. Their fills contained briquetage and firebars.

Salt was not the only important industry, however. Several ditched enclosures behind the frontages on Site J contained both circular and rectangular iron-working furnaces, apparently in use during the late second and early third centuries.[133] Associated slags derive mainly from forging and scaling, though the recognition of some smelting slag and attached furnace fragments also suggests smelting nearby. Further west, the enclosures contained no further furnaces but slag heaps were abundant.[134]

There is also evidence from Middlewich for other craftsmen serving basic economic needs, and many strip buildings clearly combined domestic and workshop accommodation, reflecting their role as shops. Trades identified on Site C include metal-working (iron, bronze and lead), window glass manufacture, weaving and cobbling, the latter represented by 18 kg (39 lb) of leather offcuts from the fill of the early brine pit.[135] Excavations here and elsewhere have also recovered large quantities of animal bones, principally the leg bones and skulls, suggesting a specialized interest in meat products. On Site G, four small kilns and a large quantity of wasters attest a short-lived phase of pottery production.[136] Clearly industrial activity and craft specialization played a significant role from the later first century onwards, though there is some evidence to suggest a relative decline during the third century. This would conform with the trends at other industrial sites in the region, but contraction was clearly not on anything like the scale witnessed at Holditch (p. 219) and Wilderspool (p. 231).

Nothing is known about the site's religious life or its burial areas. Likewise the nature and extent of its later occupation presents problems, given the levels of disturbance already mentioned. Fourth-century buildings are known, however, including the corridor house (Site C) and open-fronted workshop (Site J) described earlier, while there is a surprising scatter of coins and pottery across the site. These are insufficient to construct a detailed account, but seem to indicate an increased level of fourth-century activity following the uncertainties of the third.[137] How long it lasted remains uncertain, though the relative shortage of later fourth-century material must surely suggest an accelerating decline, helping to account for the absence of any recognizable post-Roman activity. Only the recovery of stratified material, however, coupled with publication of the existing information, can give more precision to this late sequence.

Wilderspool (fig. 73)

The Roman site at Wilderspool lies mainly on the south bank of the River Mersey and straddles the modern counties of Lancashire and Cheshire. It has always been something of an enigma, which the construction of the Manchester Ship Canal and other waterways and the expansion of the industrial town of Warrington have done little to solve. It has been known as a Roman site since the late eighteenth and early nineteenth centuries, when the Bridgewater and Old Quay canals were cut through it and the Greenall Whitley brewery was constructed on another part. Roman foundations were then reported, together with bases, shafts and capitals of columns, and ashlars large enough to be equipped with Lewis holes.[138] Subsequently excavations were carried out by Thomas May from 1895–1905[139] and, more recently, by Manchester University and the Department of the Environment (formerly the Ministry of Public Buildings and Works).[140]

In the Roman period, Wilderspool was situated at the point where the road from Little Chester, here called King Street, which skirted the base of the Pennines through Rocester and Middlewich, crossed the River Mersey at probably its lowest fordable point, thence continuing to Walton le Dale and Lancaster, on which stretch it ran almost parallel with the Manchester-Ribchester road. It is not known if the Mersey was crossed by a bridge, but it would be a reasonable assumption in view of the road's importance; the large ashlars with Lewis holes recorded from beneath the brewery could have come from an abutment. There are only slight indications of a direct route to Manchester, the traveller otherwise having to journey via Northwich, but a road pointing south-west from Wilderspool aims at Chester.

It has been argued that there was an Agricolan fort at Wilderspool ever since May not only recorded a 'rampart' and 'ditch' on the west side of the site but also claimed to have found them on the other three sides. Certainly an important river crossing might be thought to have warranted a fort in the Agricolan strategy for northern Britain.[141] Unfortunately, the evidence taken as a whole does not support May's claim. In the first place, more recent excavations have failed to confirm his military fortifications;[142]

secondly, the irregular outline of his proposed fort would be unlikely, even if not impossible in the Flavian period, while thirdly, the industrial development which May recorded as having succeeded the fort is now known to have begun much earlier, probably c. AD 85–90, but was not apparently under military control; this occupation lay over much of the site of his claimed fort.

If May's fort is discarded, but not forgetting that a fort on another site may yet be found (early coins have come from the centre of Warrington), all the other evidence points to a settlement being founded during the late first century for no very clear reason. It rapidly became an industrial centre of some magnitude with activity intensifying up to the middle, or slightly later, second century. Yet, apart from supplies of good-quality quartz sand for glass and clay for making pottery, there was no base for other industries relating to copper, iron and possibly lead. Not only has the question of ore supplies to be answered, but also the question of the markets for the finished products, since it seems unlikely that Wilderspool was ever large enough to have consumed entirely its own products. Some iron ores occur locally in association with surface coal seams; copper could have come from Alderley Edge, North Wales or Anglesey, better iron ore (haematite) from Cumbria and lead from Flintshire or the Pennines. Much could have been carried by river or coastwise by sea and then up the River Mersey. This leaves the question: why concentrate such industries here when the raw materials had to be brought from such scattered and comparatively distant . places? Inevitably this brings in the second question of where were the markets, if it is assumed that production was on a scale which exceeded local consumption? A clue here may be provided by the companion pottery industry. Ordinary Wilderspool wares seem to have been distributed throughout most of the forts and *vici* of the Lancashire-Cheshire plain. Special and more readily identifiable vessels, such as triple-vases and *mortaria*, seem to have had wider markets, with the former reaching across the Pennines and as far north as the west end of Hadrian's Wall, while the latter not only covered the same general area, but also penetrated even further north to Scotland and the Antonine Wall.[143] To what extent other goods followed the tracks of these pots must remain a

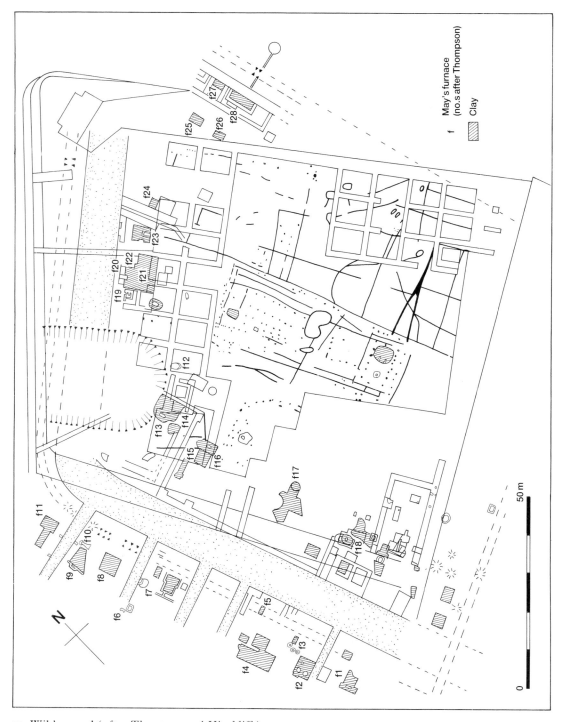

73 Wilderspool (*after Thompson and Hinchliffe*)

subject for conjecture; nevertheless the distribution provides a pattern for other possible markets.

There is another important factor to be considered for Wilderspool. As with Northwich and Middlewich, it enjoyed a period of intense activity, growing from the late first century to a peak in the Hadrianic-Antonine periods, then declining from c. AD 160 until, by the early third century, the settlement seems to have been but a shadow of its former self.[144] To some extent the decline may have been started by the forward movements of the army into Scotland, which caused the evacuation of many of the Brigantian forts, although significantly this advance did not affect those in the north-west so much; the apparent loss of military customers may not, therefore, be the full explanation. Moreover many Pennine and other northern forts were reoccupied, following the withdrawal from Scotland, at just about the same time as the start of the decline at Wilderspool can be detected, c. AD 160–70. Nor does it seem entirely likely, as the Victoria County History has argued, that it was the second advance into Scotland under Severus which caused the decline.[145] This advance was much more short-lived and did not lead, as before, to the wholesale evacuation of forts in Brigantia. Moreover the third century saw a general increase in prosperity, which frequently surpassed that of the second, in many of the northern *vici*. But the trend was reversed at Wilderspool. Some potters, in consequence, uprooted themselves and re-established their factories further north, presumably to follow their markets;[146] potters from elsewhere in the Midlands followed them. The decline would seem, therefore, to have been the result of a number of interrelated factors, most of which are still to seek. It is certainly true though that third-century coins and pottery are scarce, although there may have been a limited recovery in the fourth.

Apart from the recent excavations, it is very difficult to interpret the structures earlier revealed by May and other workers. The architectural fragments mentioned above (p. 229), would imply at least some buildings of substance, including perhaps a temple or a shrine, or a good-quality residence. Apart from these, masonry buildings are rare, and May recorded only a small

number north of the Ship Canal and one south of it at Stockton Heath. All except two were situated along King Street and were interspersed with slighter, presumably timber-framed buildings, of which May was sadly only able to record their clay floors;[147] the ovens, furnaces and hearths of various metal-workers were set on them. A number of lanes leading westwards off the main road provided access to these premises. Among the furnaces and hearths that May recorded were shaft and bowl furnaces for the smelting of iron and the subsequent working of the blooms, and smithing furnaces, usually identified by the presence of hammer-scale, for the manufacture of iron fittings and tools.[148] A furnace that had been equipped to contain seven small crucibles was used for melting copper alloys; a crucible with metal residue still adhering was found nearby. Other similar crucibles were found elsewhere. Samples of frit and other colouring matter were claimed by May as evidence that enamelling was carried on; a number of enamelled objects such as brooches were found on the site. The absence of moulds (but see p. 232 below) need not be a bar to this suggestion, since none was found in the coppersmith's workshop at Catterick (p. 115). The preparation of lead products, perhaps pipes and sheets, seems to have been carried on in another workshop; two glass-houses equipped with furnaces and containing waste and scrap glass together with raw materials were also discovered. Whether glass vessels, as well as the commoner window glass, were made is difficult to say, but one of the houses may have been manufacturing beads and counters. Three pottery kilns were located in Stockton Heath, south of the Ship Canal, and there was also a structure which, from the description, could be interpreted either as a hypocaust or possibly as a tile-kiln;[149] the Warrington Museum collections contain tile wasters.

The more recent excavations, largely in the area to the east of May's, and up to 1 km (0.6 miles) distant, also revealed a series of buildings, almost all of which were constructed of timber. In this area a trackway ran from north-east to south-west; it was defined by fences and ditches, which had been recut several times. The ground on both sides of the track had been partitioned into ditched enclosures, which contained circular, oval and rectangular buildings. Here also there was evidence of industrial activity in the form of hearths, a crucible which had been used for copper alloys and mould fragments, presumably for casting these alloys. In a later phase, a stone-lined tank, equipped with an overflow, had been inserted into the northern ditch of the track, presumably as a public water supply; it is reminiscent of similar tanks found at Corbridge (p. 59) and Catterick (p. 114) and may indicate the presence of a functioning aqueduct with a distribution network. The recovery of fragments of column drums as well as part of a Corinthian or composite capital would imply that better-class buildings existed somewhere in this area. Pottery recovered from these sites not only supports a late first-century start for the occupation but here also carries the likelihood of a continuation into the fourth century, in contrast to the areas further west.[150] It is not impossible, therefore, that the settlement gradually migrated eastwards along the track, which may represent the line of a road aiming in the Manchester direction; increasingly wet conditions near the Mersey in the late Roman period might have caused the movement.

Despite the size of the settlement, which may at its peak have covered 10 ha (25 acres) or more, virtually nothing is known of its cemeteries. Isolated burials have been found, including one in a lead-lined wooden coffin on the north bank of the Ship Canal, from near which was also recovered a cremation in an urn; another similar coffin and two infant cremations came from the brewery site. The main cemeteries, therefore, were probably located south and east of the settlement.[151]

Although Wilderspool seems to have declined from the late second century, the final end cannot be determined, even given a fourth-century resurgence, perhaps coupled with a geographical shift eastwards.

Worcester (fig. 74)

Less is known about the small town of Worcester than probably almost any other in Britain. Yet it has been recognized as a Roman site since Camden[152] confused it with the *Bravonium* of the Antonine Itinerary,[153] which is now generally accepted as applying to Leintwardine.[154] In the Ravenna list there is a place named *Vertis*,[155]

which Rivet and Smith consider corrupt,[156] but it is the second stage out on the route from Gloucester to Droitwich and could, therefore, represent Worcester. If this is so, there can be no connection between this name and the modern name Worcester apart from the -*ceaster* element, which would imply that the earliest Saxon immigrants probably found an abandoned settlement of which even the name had lapsed.

Worcester lies on the east bank of the River Severn on the road from Gloucester to Droitwich; this has been located at Sidbury, east of the cathedral, where it was 4 m (13 ft) wide,[157] and had been resurfaced several times. Barker has argued that a street, discovered in a northern suburb, was on a line aiming at Greensforge, to which a road also ran direct from Droitwich;[158] two almost parallel roads so close together would seem unlikely. As yet, the existence of a Roman bridge over the Severn has to be proved, although it seems a reasonable assumption; a road is thought to run from Worcester to Stretton Grandison and thence on to Kenchester, so some form of crossing would have been necessary.

But a river crossing, probably a ford, even in the pre-Roman Iron Age, is indicated by the presence of a promontory fort on the higher ground on the east bank overlooking the river. Iron-Age pottery and coins, four of them Dobunnic, the tribe to which the area belonged, have been found, as well as the ditch of the fort in the Lich Street area.[159] Although a Roman fort has long been suspected, in view of the tactical importance of the river crossing, no certain structural evidence has yet been discovered although there is a scatter of early coins including Augustan, Tiberian and quite a number of Claudian issues. Excavations south of the cathedral cut a ditch, which in one place had the characteristic Roman cleaning channel at the bottom; it had been recut twice, but no Roman pottery was found in the successive fillings. Later work nearby found a similar ditch containing medieval pottery, so its Roman origin must remain in doubt.[160] But another, first-century, ditch found in the Lich Street excavations may belong to a fort,[161] as also one east of the cathedral.[162]

In so far as the town is concerned, virtually nothing is known of it apart from the fortifica-

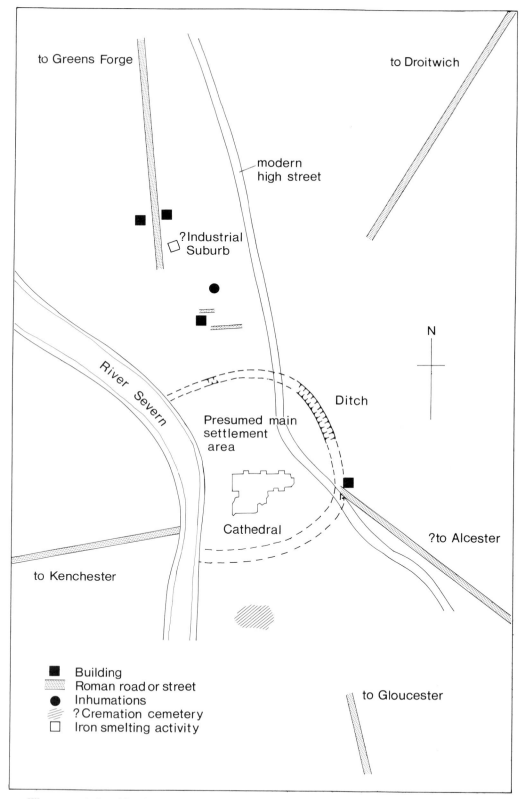

to Greens Forge

to Droitwich

modern
high street

?Industrial
Suburb

N

River Severn

Ditch

Presumed main
settlement
area

Cathedral

?to Alcester

to Kenchester

to Gloucester

■ Building
▨ Roman road or street
● Inhumations
▨ ?Cremation cemetery
□ Iron smelting activity

74 Worcester (*after Mundy*)

tions, and even here knowledge is limited to the north and east parts of the circuit. Excavations in Lich Street,[163] Little Fish Street[164] and the Technical College area,[165] have revealed the line of a very big, wet ditch, 27 m (88 ft) wide and 7.6 m (25 ft) deep; it has been claimed that part of it may have been a natural water-course, utilized by the builders of the fortifications. Late second-century pottery in the primary silt can give only an approximate date for its construction, although its size and shape belong more properly to the fourth century. All traces of a contemporary rampart, or for that matter, a wall, had there been one, were swept away when the site was levelled in the post-Roman periods. The southern limit of the town, though, may be indicated by the presence of a likely cemetery under the castle mound, which was demolished between 1826 and 1833. Unbroken glass vessels were recovered, but no inhumations were recorded which would suggest that the cemetery was mostly used for cremations.[166]

The only building of probable Roman date and of any substance found so far was a circular structure, 9 m (29½ ft) in diameter, situated in Britannia Square. A number of coins of the late third and fourth century were associated with it;[167] its shape and size would suggest a circular temple or shrine. Timber-framed buildings, though, have been excavated in Sidbury, east of the cathedral, where also was found a street, running south-east to north-west, made entirely of iron slag. But it is not known if these features lie inside or outside the town's defences.[168] An unusual discovery here was two wooden water-pipe lines, of which the iron junctions survived.[169] Clearly Worcester, unlike most small towns, possessed an aqueduct with a distribution system.

One area which has recently revealed information is that around Broad Street, north of the town.[170] Here developed, in the second century, a residential suburb of some class, where at least one house, probably timber-framed, possessed decorative wall-paintings. Access to this suburb was gained by the road, thought to run towards Greensforge (p. 232), which, with an ultimate width of 9 m (29½ ft) and an accumulated depth of successive surfaces of 1.8 m (6 ft), would seem excessive for a minor suburban street. At a later date, probably in the third century, an iron foundry with at least six smelting hearths was established in the area. Quantities of slag from the smelting carried out in this foundry, and possibly from elsewhere in the town, were used for surfacing roads. Indeed the regular use of slag as a surfacing and the frequency with which iron slag has been recorded strongly suggests that the processing of ore, brought in by boat, almost certainly from the Forest of Dean, and its subsequent redistribution, was a significant activity at the town.[171] The only articles claimed to be possibly manufactured here were a mass of nails.

In so far as the end of Roman Worcester is concerned, ephemeral timber buildings were built on the surface of the Gloucester road and were associated with many butchered cattle bones and fourth-century pottery,[172] implying a fairly rapid breakdown in communications with the south. Little more can be said about Worcester until the seventh century when it became a bishopric. In the interval it seems to have been abandoned.

ELEVEN
MINOR DEFENDED SETTLEMENTS

Ancaster (figs. 75 and 76)

Ancaster's Roman past was first described in 1870 by the Ven. Edward Trollope, who recorded not only its defences but also several other significant finds, including the late Roman and early Anglo-Saxon cemetery south of the town and the *Deae Matres* relief.[1] Our current understanding of the site's development and morphology derives principally from a series of excavations undertaken between 1962 and 1971, which focused on the fort ditches and the underlying Iron-Age settlement, the town defences, certain extra-mural complexes (as in the Castle Pits site) and the late Roman inhumation cemeteries.[2] Even so, the picture remains sketchy because many of the detailed conclusions (with the exception of the defences) remain unpublished, while little work has actually been done inside the defences.[3]

Ancaster is strategically located where the Ancaster Gap cuts the Jurassic limestone ridge, making it a focus for overland communications. Here an important north-south prehistoric trackway along the ridge was met by an east-west route linking the Trent river systems with the Fenland and the coast. This explains the late prehistoric settlements in and around Ancaster and the establishment of at least two military sites in the vicinity.[4] The late Iron-Age occupation beneath the Roman town has not been extensively sampled and its overall extent remains uncertain; finds suggest that it lay primarily on the western side of the area occupied in Roman times.[5] Its structural details are somewhat limited, but the surviving ditches and gullies yielded a rich assemblage including imported Gallo-Belgic wares and fineware pottery of Belgic type, as well as several Iron-Age brooches and a number of

Corieltavian silver coins. These indicate a site of some importance, benefiting from overland trade, and so an early Roman military presence is not surprising.

In 1974, aerial reconnaissance revealed a marching camp of 11.3 ha (28 acres) on the north side of the Ancaster Gap, probably reflecting early supervision of the prehistoric trackways. A more permanent establishment, at Ancaster itself, is represented by two ditches west of the later urban defences beneath the inhumation cemetery.[6] Both ran east to west, the northern one being V-shaped, while the southern one resembled a *fossa punica*; they terminated on the east in a butt end, where a gravelled causeway probably indicates a gateway. No rampart structure was located, so that it remains uncertain whether the fort originally lay to north or south; modern opinion favours the latter, but this cannot account for the timber building *c.* 18 m (59 ft) to the north, apparently on the same alignment as the ditches.

This juxtaposition between a pre-existing site and an early Roman fort raises interesting questions about the origins and early development of the later small town, but unfortunately not enough is known of the vital stratigraphic sequences to examine the problem of settlement continuity in detail. What disturbance, for instance, arose from the imposition of the fort upon a pre-existing settlement, and what happened to the natives? How quickly did a civilian *vicus* develop alongside the fort? And how did the post-military civilian occupation perpetuate the character and layout of its native and *vicus* predecessors, if at all? Answers to such vital questions are currently unavailable, and must await the outcome of future investigation.

The limited nature of past research affects our understanding of the site's morphology and the

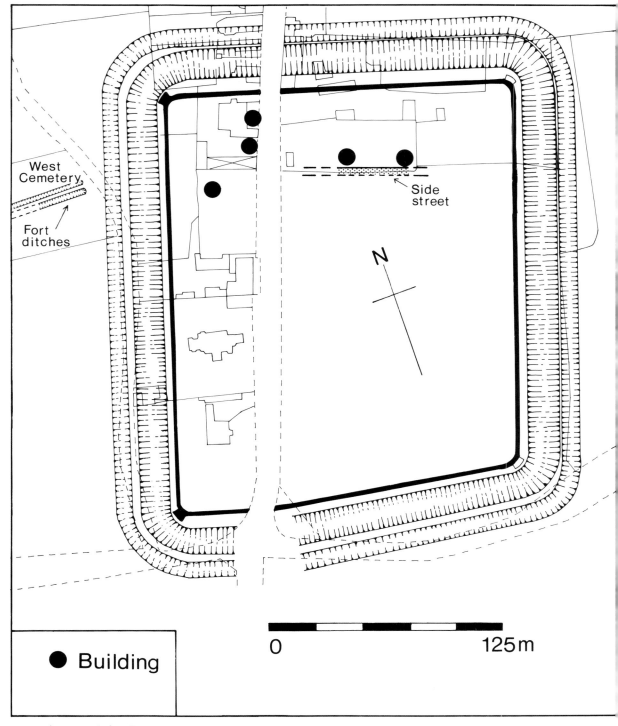

75 Ancaster (*after Todd*)

character of its development. The primary focus for settlement was probably the main north-south line of Ermine Street, but judging from the distribution of second-century material occupation soon extended well beyond its frontages, even into areas that were to become extra-mural suburbs. In most excavated sections, the defences overlay pre-existing first- and second-century occupation, as for example in Trenches 3 and 18 on the east and in Trench 4c on the south; on the north, in Trench 19, a building may even have been dismantled prior to their construction.[7] Beyond the defences, second-century buildings have also been located to the east in Field 109, and perhaps also on the Castle Pits site to the south-east.[8] This evidence suggests that Ancaster experienced an extensive and fairly rapid second-century expansion prior to the imposition of the defended circuit, enclosing a roughly rectangular core of c. 3.7 ha (9.1 acres) astride Ermine Street. Surprisingly, the latter did not occupy a central north-south location but ran much closer to the western defences.

This extensive occupation, estimated at c. 24–8 ha (59–69 acres), should indicate the existence of an internal street network providing access to buildings and land beyond the Ermine Street frontages. Unfortunately, only one side-street has been recorded, running east at the northern end of the defended enclosure; where partially sectioned in 1955 it was at least 3.4 m (11 ft) wide.[9] It has also been suggested that the irregularity in the alignment of the southern defences may have been caused by an existing east-west road beneath the modern A153, but this remains unproven.[10]

Although little is known about the internal layout, small-scale excavation within the defended enclosure in 1955 and 1960–1 revealed several structures flanking the side-streets already noted.[11] Sadly few complete plans could be recovered in the space available. On Site I, east of Ermine Street, three structures were partially explored, all aligned end-on to the frontage, though only the most easterly could be reconstructed in any detail, being 4.6 m (15 ft) wide with a central door opening onto the street. West of Ermine Street, on Site II, only one reasonably complete rectangular structure, with an earth floor and central hearth was recorded. Little evidence was found to date their earliest phases,

though occupation certainly continued into the fourth century. Further buildings were recovered incidentally during the 1962–71 sections across the defences, especially in Trenches 3 and 18, where a poorly constructed stone building with two north-south walls and a pair of crushed limestone floors provided useful dating evidence for the construction of the town wall.[12] Excavation has also examined the building sequence in the Castle Pits area, c. 180 m (590 ft) south of the defences, in what may have been an extra-mural suburb or a satellite agricultural settlement.[13] Earlier occupation here was succeeded by an aisled building measuring 15.2 by 8.5 m (49 by 27½ ft), constructed no earlier than the later third century then modified in the fourth by the insertion of a new corn-drier and the replacement of its predecessor by a circular oven. Later fourth-century rubbish across the western part of its floor may indicate its date of abandonment.

Considerable attention has been directed at Ancaster's defensive sequence, making it one of the best known among the small towns. Numerous sections have revealed a remarkably consistent picture, involving a contemporary stone wall and bank, later reinforced by external towers, most probably at all four corners.[14] Where the wall survived later robbing, it was 2.3–2.4 m (7½–7¾ ft) wide and made of trimmed blocks resting upon a wider foundation of pitched stones, themselves apparently set in a construction trench just wide enough for the footings. The contemporaneity of the associated bank was demonstrated most notably in Trench 1, where its deposits included interleaved lenses of white mortar presumably derived from the wall's construction. Likewise in Trench 19, the deposits ran up to the six surviving wall courses, though a turf line might indicate more than one stage in the bank's construction. The date of these defences is tolerably well known, though the lack of absolute precision is noteworthy given the number of excavated sections. Pottery in and under the bank extended down to the early third century and included none of the characteristic mid to late third-century wares that are so common elsewhere at Ancaster. Equally useful is the evidence from Trenches 3 and 18 where c. 150–250 mm (6–10 in) of wind-blown sand had accumulated over the rampart tail, prior to the construction of the stone building already discussed; between its two

76 Ancaster, looking south along the line of Ermine
Street. The defences, which enclose the church
to the right of the main road, can just be seen
parallel to the line of trees in the bottom lefthand
corner (*Cambridge University Collection:
copyright reserved*)

floors, five coins of AD 268–75 were found, suggesting that the bank was built some time before *c.* AD 280. On balance this suggests a date before AD 225, although a slightly later date remains possible.

Beyond the wall lay two ditches, the inner one being up to 16.8 m (55 ft) wide in places, though its depth varied between 2.4 and 4.9 m (7¾ ft and 16 ft); its outer counterpart was equally variable, being up to 9 m (29½ ft) wide and between 1.5 and 2.7 m (5 and 9 ft) deep. Limited evidence suggests a fourth-century date, but this seems doubtful in the apparent absence of any earlier ditches. Presumably they were well maintained, accounting for the paucity of satisfactorily stratified material relating to their original excavation. Research at the north-west and south-west angles has revealed characteristically fan-shaped external towers, added probably during the fourth century, though little well-stratified dating evidence has been recovered. That on the north-west, though badly robbed, stood upon a pitched cobble foundation set into a foundation trench with a 250–350 mm (10–14 in) gap between it and the wall footings; much the same was found at the heavily-robbed south-west angle. No gates have been located, though these must have existed to accommodate Ermine Street.

Several interesting sculptures from Ancaster relate to its religious life, probably derived from a shrine or religious precinct near the modern churchyard west of Ermine Street. In 1831, a relief of three *Deae Matres* was found apparently *in situ* on a foundation of two superimposed stones.[15] The foundation measured 0.48 by 0.41 m (19 by 16 in), with the figures seated on a long couch and draped in high-waisted dresses. In their hands, they clasp various items, including a basket filled with fruit and several *paterae*. In front of the relief and its support lay a small altar, set on a circular slab surmounting a column 0.69 m (27 in) high. Further sculptures were recovered in 1960, during work on the north-east buttress of the church, both probably derived from the same building or precinct as the 1831 finds.[16] One depicts a male head with a drooping moustache and thick curly hair, the other includes two female heads within a rectangular niche. Two more pieces were found re-used as late grave covers in the cemetery west of the defences,

though both probably came from the same source.[17] One was a male torso wearing a cloak, the other was a dedicatory inscription to an otherwise unknown god Viridius, recording the erection of an arch by a native called Trenico. Their re-use in a late Roman context might indicate either the demise of the precinct or a change in its role, perhaps under Christian influence.

Our understanding of the site's economic activities is somewhat sketchy, though the recovery of so much religious sculpture, as well as several stone coffins, all made from local oolite, seems to indicate the existence of a flourishing school of local sculptors. A link with local quarrying also seems likely. Other trades are sketchily represented by a pottery kiln discovered in 1865 north of the town and east of Ermine Street, and by a second-century iron-working area below the enclosure associated with the Castle Pits building.[18] No certain workshops have been identified, though the building with a hearth on Site II could have served other than domestic functions.[19] One interesting, if somewhat dubious, occupation is represented by several moulds used for coin forging during the Severan period.[20]

The construction of the defences must have had some impact on the settlement morphology, as for example in Trench 19, where the wall and bank overlay the remains of a building, which may have been specifically dismantled to make way for the defensive screen. Whether there were corresponding changes in the extra-mural suburbs at this date is unknown, though the fourth-century picture is now a little clearer as a result of excavations in the late inhumation cemetery west of the defences.[21] This revealed over 300 inhumations, mostly aligned east-west and apparently laid out in a reasonably organized manner. Some had been buried in local stone coffins, but most were in stone-lined graves or wooden coffins; some were apparently unmarked, others had stones at the head and foot. Few had associated grave goods, though occasionally personal items such as bracelets had been included. These suggest a late third- and fourth-century date, while one burial had coins down to the AD 360s. This cemetery so close to the defences might indicate extra-mural contraction, a suggestion perhaps reinforced by other known burials similarly located.

These include the inhumations on the site of the former Angel Inn, north of the town and west of Ermine Street, and the rather fragmentary evidence south-west of Ant House farm.[22] The latter may be an extension of the inhumation cemetery, recorded by Trollope, south of the defences and east of Ermine Street, which also included some 40 Anglo-Saxon cremation urns of the period prior to AD 450.[23] These early cremations in the southern cemetery are not yet paralleled by comparable evidence either from the northern area or from the well-excavated western cemetery, but they still hint at early settlement in the vicinity of Ancaster. Certainly, as Todd emphasizes, the region was popular with Germanic settlers, judging from comparable material in the Loveden cemetery only 4 km (2.5 miles) to the west.[24] Little diagnostic Anglo-Saxon material has been recorded within the settlement, and only one piece is apparently securely stratified alongside late Roman pottery, but the absence of concrete structural evidence cannot be taken as conclusive, given the small-scale nature of past excavations. More detailed information is needed to clarify the fifth-century fate of the town.

Caistor and Horncastle (figs. 77–80)

It is most convenient to consider these two sites together, as there are many similarities between them, not least the small amount known about them. Both occupy land near or at the base, and to the west, of the Lincolnshire Wolds: Caistor on the lower chalk, Horncastle on a gravel terrace of the River Bain. Neither site is specifically mentioned in the literary sources, although the Ravenna list includes a place called *Bannovalium*, which could be applied to either.[25] Neither seems to be closely connected to the Roman road network, but they are joined together by a prehistoric ridgeway known as the Caistor High Street, which originally ran between the Humber and the Wash. There is, however, a road running west from Caistor possibly intended to meet Ermine Street at Hibaldstow, but doubt has been cast on its Roman origin. The main road east from Lincoln aims between the two sites and

bifurcates before the Wolds, one branch turning south-east towards Burgh-le-Marsh, the other, if it continues, pointing at the Lincolnshire coast and at a place now probably destroyed by the sea. Horncastle may also in Roman times have stood at the head of a navigable inlet formed by the River Witham and its tributary the Bain. The defences of both towns were recorded by Stukeley and by other antiquaries since his day;[26] a summary of knowledge to date was published by Hawkes in 1946.[27] Since then limited excavations have been carried out at both places,[28] but an opportunity for further work at Caistor was missed in 1986, when the County Council carried out building operations within the scheduled area[29] without archaeological investigations taking place.

There was certainly an extensive Iron-Age settlement at Horncastle, but less is known about the origins of Caistor. The settlement at Horncastle continued, seemingly without interruption, into the Roman period, and it has been suggested that an early fort was founded here. It should be noted, though, that no military equipment has been recovered and that all the early pottery could be accounted for by the settlement. Chance discoveries and aerial photography have shown that this lies in the area contained by the Rivers Bain to the west and Waring to the north; the walled site is situated across the latter. Finds from the settlement date from the first to fourth centuries and include buildings with masonry walls, painted plaster and mortar floors.[30] Scatters of pottery have been found outside the walls of Caistor to the west and north, but structural evidence is lacking; two third- or fourth-century pottery kilns have also been recorded on the western side.[31]

The defences of both places have certain points of similarity as well as differences.[32] The wall at Caistor follows the contours of the ground to trace an irregular ovoid, while Horncastle presents a more regular, trapezoid, appearance. At both sites the walls have been subjected to robbing; the foundations at Caistor were 3.5 m (11½ ft) wide in contrast to the 5.5 m (18 ft) at Horncastle, where the superstructure was in excess of 3 m (10 ft). No trace of a rampart has yet been detected at Caistor, but there is ample evidence for one at Horncastle. A ditch (or ditches) at Caistor has still to be proved, but

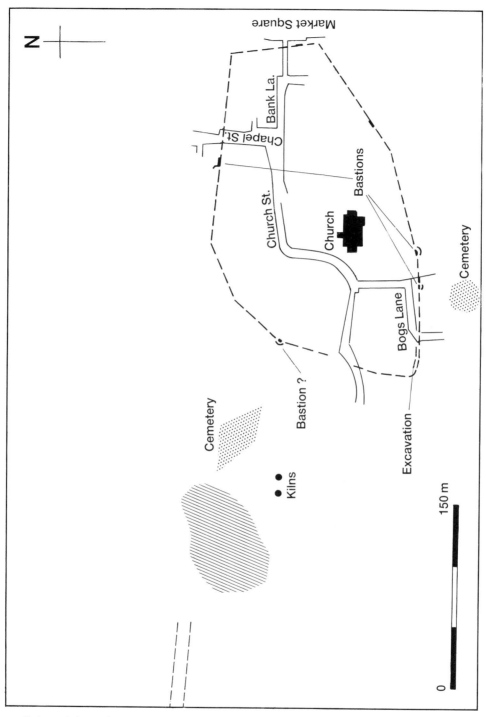

77 Caistor (*after Rahtz*)

78 Caistor, looking north-east (*Cambridge University Collection: copyright reserved*)

slight evidence for at least one, if not more, has emerged at Horncastle. Both sites, though, had external towers, which were considered to be contemporary with the curtain wall. Those at Caistor, despite being heavily robbed, appear to have been semi-circular in plan. The corner towers at Horncastle were an unusual shape, projecting squarely from the angles but with rounded outer faces. No gates have yet been located at either site, but changes in alignment of the curtain wall in the middle of both the east and the west sides at Horncastle suggest likely positions, in which case the gates would resemble the staggered east gate at Brough-on-Humber.[33] At Caistor a possible gate has been identified near the centre of the east side, where two massive parallel walls have been found only 5.5 m (18 ft) apart and at right angles to the line of the curtain wall; it has also been suggested that the external

79 Horncastle, looking north-east; the church left of
centre lies within the walled area (*Cambridge
University Collection: copyright reserved*)

80 Horncastle (*after Field and Turner*)

tower just west of Chapel Street on the north wall may possibly be a gate tower.

The dating of both circuits still requires greater precision although it is generally agreed that neither can be earlier than the late third century. Both, though, could be later, especially if the external towers are contemporary with the walls; this is common in the late third century in northern Gaul and Germany but is unusual for urban sites in Britain, where external towers were almost always added at a date put firmly in the middle of the fourth century, if not later; the exceptions are some of the forts of the Saxon Shore. As with Wall (p. 276) and Mancetter (p. 259) there is a marked absence of even casual finds inside the walls at both sites, although excavations in the High Street, Horncastle, revealed part of a timber-framed building and a metalled surface; wells have also been found.[34] This general lack of structures raises the possibility that Horncastle and Caistor were part of a defensive system which, perhaps in conjunction with coastal sites now lost to erosion, was intended to protect the hinterland, including Lincoln, when the need arose. Lincoln almost certainly became a provincial capital in the fourth century, and a place of considerable importance. The odd feature, though, if this is the explanation, is that there are no direct roads between Lincoln and Horncastle and Caistor, or between the latter pair and the coast. But if this assumption – that they were defensive strongpoints – is correct, and it is very difficult to accept them as normal fortified urban centres, then it would follow that the defenders who used them had no need for metalled roads, for instance cavalry, who could range at will over the Wolds and the lower ground to the east and west. The field armies of the fourth century were intended to be mobile, but even mobile forces need protected bases in which extra horses, fodder, food-stocks and spare equipment could be kept. Only comparatively flimsy wooden buildings, together with some grazing, would be required for stores, while a handful of men would be sufficient to care for them behind their strong fortifications. It is well known that early Saxons, and Picts for that matter, were largely incapable of storming a walled site. Given these secure bases, which also could always be used as refuges in emergency if the pressure of the enemy became too great, a mobile unit could function with great efficiency. Of course, such a limited use would leave few traces for archaeological recovery!

Cemeteries have not yet been located at Caistor but are indicated by inhumation burials to the west and south-west of the walled circuit. A single item of possible religious significance is an ornamental lead casket, four fragments from which were discovered inside the walled area just west of the churchyard. A cast inscription, repeated on each side, reads *Cunobarrus fecit vivas*, undoubtedly recording the Celtic name of the maker.[35] The casket almost certainly dates to the fourth century and the use of the word *vivas* has been taken to be a reference to Christianity, although in this instance the relationship can only be slight. Nevertheless it indicates the presence, for at least a short time, of one wealthy person at Caistor.

Burials at Horncastle are known only from south of the walled circuit, in the same general area as the civil settlement.[36] A concentration of inhumations around Croft Street and Bryant Close would seem to indicate a cemetery; three lead coffins were recovered, as well as infant and adult skeletal material; a little further south, two more lead coffins were found, and it has been claimed that they may have contained gypsum burials, which again carries a hint of Christianity.[37] What was once probably a large cremation cemetery was also encountered south of the Wong. The pottery and coins recovered from it would suggest an extended period of use terminating in the fourth century.

It is not known when Horncastle ceased to be of importance in the Roman world; the pottery and coins hardly carry the occupation beyond the middle of the fourth century. Caistor, in contrast, is represented by an interesting inhumation cemetery of the fifth-century Anglian period and by an unusual inscription found in 1770 at Castle Hill; it is now lost, but is thought to date to the ninth century.[38] These features, although exceedingly slight, show a tenuous connection between the Roman, or sub-Roman, period with that of the early Saxon.

Cambridge (fig. 81)

Despite a long tradition of discoveries at Cambridge, especially on Castle Hill, little was known about the character and extent of the Roman settlement prior to a series of excavations which began in 1956.[39] Most have been directed, however, at the morphology and development of the defended area, either side of Castle Street, while little is known about the character of the suburbs along the principal approach roads or the occupation south-east of the River Cam. Beyond various interim reports and a few general accounts, the detailed conclusions remain unpublished.[40]

Settlement clearly began on the hilltop beside the river in the late first century BC, with a succession of oval or circular ditched enclosures occupied into the early Roman period.[41] Examples are known on several sites including Ridgeons Gardens, the Shire Hall and Comet Place. A fairly typical sequence in Gloucester Terrace[42] commenced with two sides of a ditched and palisaded enclosure associated with several pits. This was replaced by a horseshoe-shaped enclosure within which lay a chalk marl floor, a clay fireplace and traces of wattle-and-daub walling. After the ditch had silted, it too was replaced by a larger enclosure making use of the existing entrance, which contained various post-holes and a hearth. Such enclosures extend over c. 2.8 ha (6.9 acres), most being relatively simple and apparently indicating a small agricultural settlement on the higher ground above the floodplain.

There is little to indicate specialized activities, except for the coins from four British tribes, which suggest an economic role, and the much larger Enclosure 9 in Ridgeons Gardens.[43] This latter comprised a series of recut ditches and gullies along its south-eastern and south-western sides, the dating of which points to a long-established boundary being maintained into the early Roman period. Few internal features were recognized, and so its function remains uncertain.

The early Roman period is difficult to interpret at present, though Cambridge is an obvious site for a fort, being strategically located where a gravel ridge provides a narrow crossing over the floodplain. In the 1930s, two ditches were recorded at right angles under the Shire Hall, both apparently yielding Claudian material which is no longer identifiable.[44] Both were confidently assigned to a fort but they have not been traced in later excavations and so their character and dating must remain uncertain. A further Claudian ditch was also recorded by the west corner of the Shire Hall in 1984, where the first-century ground surface was shown to be intact contrary to speculation in the 1930s.[45]

Several features in Ridgeons Gardens may also belong in a military context, though the supporting evidence is inconclusive.[46] Immediately outside the south-eastern boundary of the late Iron-Age Enclosure 9 ran a Claudian ditch itself replaced by a substantial timber palisade c. 2.5 m (8 ft) deep and 0.8 m (2½ ft) wide with a central causeway. Two short lengths of Claudian ditch were also recorded along the south-western flank. More importantly, on the north-eastern and north-western sides of Ridgeons Gardens lay the corner of a large rectangular enclosure defined by two successive V-shaped ditches up to 4 m (13 ft) wide and 2 m (6½ ft) deep, their fill including a military strap-end. This certainly extended over 60 m (198 ft) along both axes and its north-eastern side terminated in a butt end probably representing one side of a gateway. Related finds date the enclosure to the period c. AD 70–120, suggesting its identification as a small road station of military or official origin. Support for a military presence at Cambridge can also be drawn from other sectors of Castle Hill, where the late Iron-Age enclosures went out of use, perhaps in the wake of deliberate army clearances.[47]

Despite some uncertainty over the early Roman occupation, civilian activity becomes increasingly recognizable in the early second century, focused on a series of internal roads and streets. Traditionally the principal axis was thought to be the north-west/south-east road, running east of the modern Castle Street down to the river crossing, along with its junction with Akeman Street aligned north-north-east/south-south-west. Excavation has, however, revealed a more complex picture. The junction of the north-western and north-north-eastern routes was located in 1983, Akeman Street at least being 7 m (23 ft) wide with a well-cobbled surface.[48] Interestingly, it was aligned on the possible entrance to the road station, indicating its first-century origin. Its north-western counterpart was examined more fully in 1985 at the north-west gate, where it

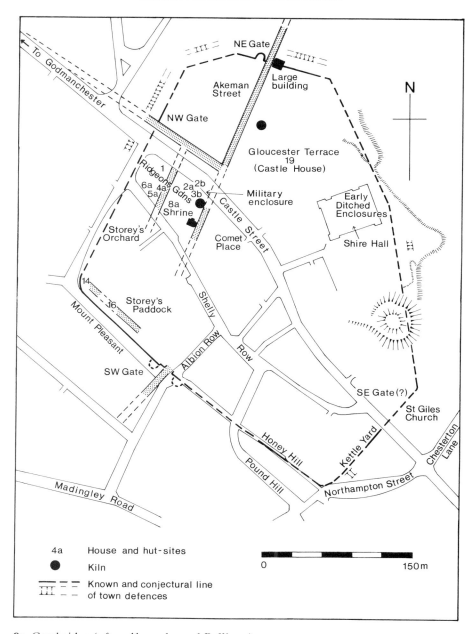

81 Cambridge (*after Alexander and Pullinger*)

was well-made with a cambered cobbled sur-face.[49] Surprisingly no road was traceable south-east of the junction, where a second-century structure was excavated, and so its precise align-ment down to the possible south-east gate under St Giles Church and thence to the river must remain uncertain.

In the early second century, two side-streets were constructed in Ridgeons Gardens, one being a continuation of Akeman Street south-south-west of the main junction.[50] Both were *c.* 4 m (13 ft) wide with up to four successive orange gravel surfaces, overlying, and thus perpetuating the alignment of the enclosures already dis-cussed. Whether such streets were restricted to this north-western sector is uncertain, though a more extensive system seems likely given that occupation was widespread not just on Castle Hill but also downslope to the river. Ribbon development also occurred south-east of the river, where scattered finds are known alongside Bridge Street.[51]

The associated civilian occupation is charac-terized by several ditched and fenced properties entered through substantial gates. Besides the domestic accommodation, their gravelled yards contained a range of ovens, hearths, rubbish pits, wells and latrines. Typical examples were found in Ridgeons Gardens, Storeys Paddock and Mount Pleasant.[52] One building in Ridgeons Gardens (3b) lay in a yard measuring 12 by 8 m (39 by 26 ft), which comprised a chalk and gravel spread supporting two ovens, while another (1) was a timber structure measuring 5.2 by 4.8 m (17 by 15½ ft), with wattle-and-daub walls, cement floor and tiled roof. Others had gravel and chalk flooring and thatched roofs, while occasionally the walls were lime plastered and painted. Once established, the majority enjoyed a long life, being rebuilt or modified on several occasions. In contrast, excavation has identified only one sub-stantial stone-walled building of second- to third-century date, sealed beneath the later defences close to the north gate.[53] Although much damaged, this had originally comprised at least one hypocausted room while there is also evi-dence for *opus signinum* flooring and painted wall plaster. None of the associated finds suggested a domestic function to the excavator. *Tesserae*, tiles and *opus signinum* have been located elsewhere, however, especially on the slope down towards

the river, perhaps indicating a larger structure in the vicinity.[54]

Cambridge apparently expanded quite rapidly in the second century, but there is some evidence to suggest a third-century contraction. Several of the structures already described went out of use, and in some, such as Building 5a/6a, the asso-ciated yard was actually dug into by several pits. Whether this was localized or more widespread remains uncertain, becuse other structures con-tinued in use throughout; Buildings 14 and 15 certainly lasted into the early fourth century at least, the latter with a substantial cement floor.[55] Even so, the settlement's overall character was maintained, the buildings and their associated features emphasizing the agricultural occupa-tions of the resident population. There is surpris-ingly little evidence for specialized activities, beyond the iron slag found in both Iron-Age and Roman contexts, the bone pin products from a well in Ridgeons Gardens and two kilns, one of them off Akeman Street producing large indented beakers.[56] Kiln debris and wasters are also known from Jesus Lane in the postulated southern suburb.[57]

The site's religious life is represented by a probable timber shrine found alongside the continuation of Akeman Street in Ridgeons Gardens.[58] Constructed in the late second century, it comprised a subterranean cellar 8 m (26 ft) long, 4 m (13 ft) wide and 3 m (10 ft) deep with an apsidal end and a niche; several post-holes at the edges measuring 0.4 by 0.6 m (1¼ by 2 ft) supported a substantial timber super-structure. Its religious associations are suggested by various finds in the immediate vicinity, including the burial of two dogs and a bull's head in the gravel flooring and an unusual sequence of animal burials in the ash layers derived from the building's early third-century destruction; these comprised a sacrificed horse surrounded by seven complete pottery vessels, a bull and a sheep, and three dogs arranged in triangular formation around a pot. Immediately above the ash layer a large quantity of pottery was found, including samian and colour-coated wares, at least 256 flagons and a quantity of glass vessels, all suggest-ing some specific event. This was all sealed with clay and subsequent rubbish dumping. North-west of the shrine, along the line of earlier features associated with Enclosure 9, lay some 13 later third- and fourth-century shafts.[59] Each contained a mature dog and one or two infant burials in a wicker-work basket or on a rush mat, together with a pair of child's shoes. This repeated assemblage suggests ritual activities.

The town's character probably changed with the construction of the fourth-century defences enclosing c. 10 ha (25 acres).[60] These comprised a contemporary wall and bank separated from a broad shallow ditch by a 12 m (39 ft) wide berm. Although heavily robbed, sections show that the wall comprised alternate layers of stone and mortar laid into a 3 m (10 ft) wide foundation trench; in Mount Pleasant, this overlay early fourth-century levels associated with the demolished remains of Buildings 14 and 15. Three of the site's four gates have been examined,[61] that on the north-west being little more than a simple gap with no evidence for an associated gatehouse. In contrast, the north-eastern and south-western gates were more elaborate, apparently comprising a single carriageway with semi-circular projecting towers and recessed guard-rooms. No other external towers have been identified, though these may have been removed by subsequent stone robbing. Unlike its north-eastern counterpart which lay astride Akeman Street, the south-western gate in Mount Pleasant lay several metres south-east of its projected line presumably necessitating some level of road realignment.

Contemporary with the defences, intra-mural occupation intensified, with the construction of new buildings alongside existing structures.[62] Building 4a, 4.9 m (16 ft) square, in Ridgeons Gardens is typical, with wattle-and-daub walls and painted lime plaster supporting a tiled roof. To the west lay a sand and gravel yard, 7.7 by 6 m (25 by 20 ft), and an associated well. Comparable new structures were located in Storeys Paddock, where Building 20 apparently survived into the fifth century. Sadly little is known about the fate of the contemporary suburbs. Equally poorly recorded are the town's cemeteries.[63] The most important lay to the south-west in the Madingley Road and Mount Pleasant areas but also extended onto the St John's College cricket fields, where there is confused evidence for both Roman inhumation and Anglo-Saxon cremation burials, raising an interesting question of continuity. Other burials may have existed to the north-north-east along Akeman Street, but it is unlikely

that they extended as far as the Arbury Road settlement, where a small rectangular stone *mausoleum* has been examined; this probably belongs in a rural rather than an urban context.

Unfortunately the fate of the Roman town is poorly known despite the cemetery evidence. Occupation certainly continued into the fifth century, while the coin series extends down to the reign of Honorius. There is evidence at several points in the town centre for a featureless build-up of loam above the latest Roman levels before the earliest post-Roman features, suggesting a significant decline in activity.[64] There are some possible exceptions, as for example the fifth- to sixth-century *grubenhaus* in Ridgeons Gardens and the sixth-century brooch from the Storeys area,[65] but even these cannot argue for any significant continuity in urban traditions through to the renewed activity on the hilltop in the eighth century.

Chesterton-on-Fosse (figs. 82 and 83)

The small, fortified road station at Chesterton lies on the Fosse Way about half-way between Dorn and High Cross and about 10 km (6 miles) north of the crossing made by the road from Alcester to Alchester and the Fosse. Very clear aerial photographs show two conjoined streets emerging from what appears to be a south-east gate, but neither line has ever been investigated further afield.[66] It is also unfortunate that this section of the Fosse Way is not included in either the Antonine Itinerary or the Ravenna list or in Ptolemy, so that its original name is not known.

The outline of the town's fortifications can still be seen as low, grass-covered mounds and depressions, enclosing a sub-rectangular area which is cut in two unequal parts by the Fosse Way. The larger half has been made the subject of a management agreement by English Heritage, which should save it from further ploughing, but the widening of the modern Fosse Way caused the destruction of both north and south gates, of which only the former could be excavated.

The earliest excavations took place in 1921–3 when long narrow trenches were driven across the eastern part of the enclosure. An area of tessellated pavement was uncovered, which had been the floor of a room with painted plaster

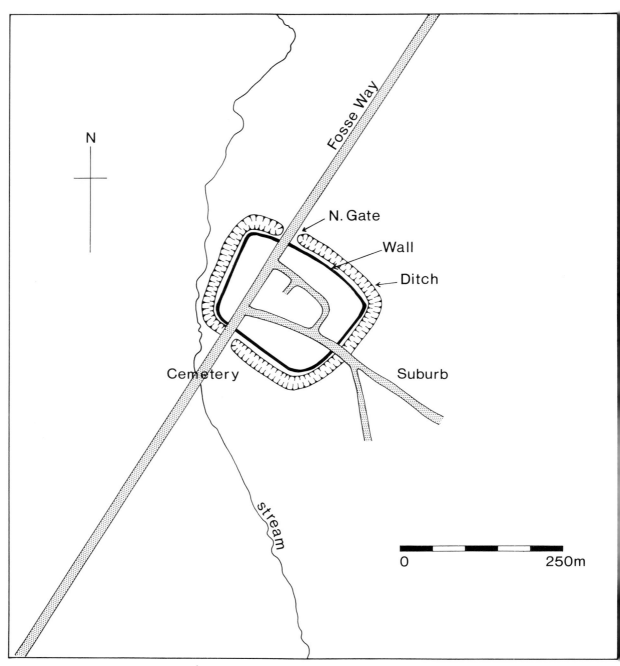

82 Chesterton-on-Fosse, based on the aerial
photographs

83 Chesterton-on-Fosse, looking north (*Cambridge University Collection: copyright reserved*)

walls; flue-tiles recovered probably from this same area would indicate a hypocaust.[67] A fragment of a lead *defixio* inscribed . . .]*sethaus*[. . . | . . .] *dalmaticum* [. . . | . . .]*nisiii*[. . . is referring to someone's cloak (a *dalmaticum*) being stolen;[68] it would imply also that there was a temple nearby, perhaps associated with the small brook which runs round part of the south and west sides of the site, but nothing is visible on the aerial photographs.

More recently, excavations took place in 1961, before the modern road was widened, and again in 1967 in the western part of the site to assess the degree of survival of the structures inside the town and to explore the fortifications near the north corner. The north gate was revealed as a single passageway, just over 3 m (10 ft) wide, which was flanked by internal rectangular towers. The entrance was slightly staggered, since the two ends of the town wall, here 2.75 m (9 ft) thick, were not on the same line. The masonry had been badly robbed, but the robbing had been carried out in such a way as to suggest that the towers were not built at the same time as the wall. A rampart, 9 m (29½ ft) wide and described as of clay, lay behind the wall, and at the time was thought to be contemporary with it; a single broad ditch had possibly replaced two of smaller dimensions. The earliest cambered surface of the Fosse Way had the remarkable width of 9 m (29½ ft).[69]

The section cut through the north-western defences in 1967 showed conclusively that the wall, here 3.4 m (11 ft) thick, had been inserted in front of an existing 'turf' (*sic*) rampart. Confirmation, though, was obtained that the wide ditch was later than the smaller inner ditch, which had been deliberately filled with clay; the outer ditch, however, was deemed to be contemporary with the new, wide inner ditch. There are clearly conflicts between these results and those of 1961; only further excavation will resolve them. No date has yet been given to the earthwork phase of fortifications, but early fourth-century coins at the bottom of the wide ditch provide a probable date for when it was dug and possibly also for the construction of the wall. The north angle was examined but was found to have been heavily damaged; no sign of internal or external towers was observed.[70]

The earliest buildings, with timber frames, to be excavated so far within the walls lie in the northern corner; they were dated to the Antonine period. Along the north-western road frontage several phases of timber buildings were ultimately replaced by a simple rectangular stone structure, all apparently within the third century; the latter had encroached upon the ditch of the Fosse Way, which had been about 1 m (3¼ ft) deep but was by then filled with silt. It was placed with its long axis at right angles to the road, in the traditional position for a shop, but it contained seven rooms, one of which at the rear was semicircular while another was floored with concrete and had been decorated with painted wall plaster; again the resemblance to the internal arrangements of a shop is very marked, and the finding of a bronze steelyard might be taken as additional evidence of trade. Slightly later, probably in the fourth century, another large timber building was erected further south.[71]

The aerial photographs clearly show some internal streets which, in conjunction with the Fosse Way, form a trapezoid area roughly in the centre of the town. From its south corner another street aims for the south-east gate. Light patches also appear in these photographs, which could be interpreted as stone spreads, probably indicating the sites of other masonry buildings.

The coin sequence from both early and late excavations is remarkably constant, beginning in the middle of the third century and terminating towards the end of the fourth. There is no Iron-Age material, virtually nothing datable to the first or early second century, and so nothing to show why the settlement was established where it was, and this probably not until well into the second century. Yet, if the site warranted the construction of earthwork fortifications, probably, as with most towns, in the fourth quarter of the second century, it must by then have reached some degree of importance, which it retained through the third and for most of the fourth centuries. Some local government function might be suspected, but until more excavation has been carried out in the interior it is not possible to be more precise.

Scatters of pottery in neighbouring fields may indicate extra-mural suburbs, while burials of an unspecified date are reported to have been found along the Fosse Way, south-west of the town.[72]

Dorn (figs. 84 and 85)

Though known since the seventeenth century, Dorn has unfortunately never been subject to detailed research. Thus our understanding of the site's morphology and development is somewhat sketchy, depending upon the surviving earthworks of its defences, the evidence derived from aerial reconnaissance and the limited excavations undertaken in 1937–9. Much else has also been noted incidentally during repeated ploughing, which has caused considerable disturbance to the latest archaeological deposits.[73]

The surviving remains are those of a roughly rectangular 4 ha (10 acre) defended enclosure lying immediately west of the Fosse Way c. 300 m (990 ft) north of its junction with another possible road running east-west. The shape and location of this enclosure alongside the main road have suggested that the settlement perpetuated an original fort site, but nothing has been found to substantiate this, since the limited first-century pottery, including butt-beaker and

84 Dorn (*after R.C.H.M.*)

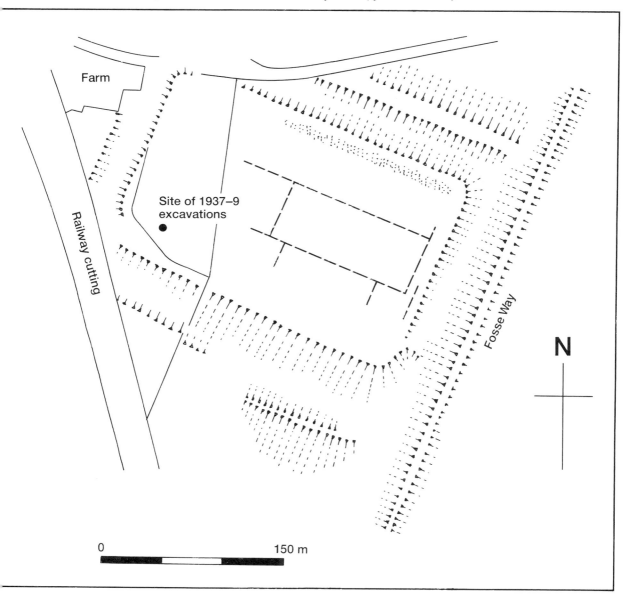

Farm

Site of 1937–9
excavations

Railway cutting

Fosse Way

N

0   150 m

85 Dorn, looking south-west (*Cambridge University Collection: copyright reserved*)

samian, is just as likely to belong in a civilian context as in a military one.[74] The defences are most prominent on the north and south sides, being defined by a low and well-spread rampart fronted by a ditch apparently 45–60 m (147–198 ft) wide; on the east the situation is complicated by the Fosse Way, while the western end has been obscured by the modern farm and the railway cutting. No excavations have been undertaken, and so neither the structural history nor the chronology of the defences is known, though analogy with comparable small, roughly rectangular enclosures elsewhere might suggest a later rather than an earlier date.[75]

Within the defences, aerial reconnaissance has revealed an apparent system of internal streets forming a compact grid; two streets can be seen to run parallel to the main axis of the bank, being crossed at right angles by two further lanes parallel to the Fosse.[76] This distinctive morphological feature needs detailed investigation to define its chronology and the character of the related occupation, but to date, excavation has only sampled a small area in the south-western corner. Besides the late building discussed below, this revealed second-century occupation well away from the Fosse frontage, comprising two wells and a clay and gravel floor, overlain by a deposit of pink ash apparently derived from the demolition of the building.[77] Several possible contemporary wells or rubbish pits were recorded last century during the cutting of the railway outside the south-western corner of the defences.[78] The 1937–9 excavations also recorded the fragmentary plan of a late Roman building, with at least four rooms and a courtyard or road along its north side. Its superstructure with plastered walls rested upon diagonal stone footings and clearly supported a tiled roof. Unfortunately, few other features of the settlement's morphology have been examined, and the extent of any extra-mural occupation remains unknown.

The most interesting nineteenth-century discoveries, apparently during ploughing east of the railway, were two sculptured stones probably derived from a shrine or a religious precinct.[79] Both were altar-shaped, with a sunken panel on the face housing a small figure in relief; one was badly worn but it probably resembled its better preserved counterpart, which depicted a *Genius* draped in a cloak wrapped around his waist and descending as far as his knees. He appeared to be holding a *patera* over a low altar and a cornucopia. Unfortunately both are now lost, as is a roughly-hewn altar recorded in 1902.[80]

Little is known about the economic basis of the settlement beyond two steelyards recovered from the floor of the second-century building excavated in 1937–9.[81] These probably indicate commercial activity at this date, but nothing is recorded for the later occupation. With the disturbance to the latest levels, the site's post-Roman fate remains unknown; coin evidence certainly continues to the end of the fourth century, but this is the limit of our knowledge.

Mancetter (figs. 86 and 87)

As with Wall (p. 276), the small town at Mancetter consists of a roughly rectangular enclosure sitting astride Watling Street between Wall and High Cross. Another known main road from the site strikes off in a north-easterly direction to Leicester, from a point a short distance south-east of the walled town, while yet another ran south-east towards Hartshill. The site lies south-east of the River Anker, half being in the parish of Witherley and half in the parish of Mancetter village, which is over the river. As with Wall, it has been claimed as one of five fourth-century *burgi* on Watling Street, similar to those found along some of the main roads in northern Gaul and Germany.[82] Mancetter is mentioned in the Antonine Itinerary as *Manduessedo*,[83] but is not included in the Ravenna list. The site is mentioned by Dugdale, Stukeley and other antiquaries.[84] It became part of a very large and important industrial area which extended for several kilometres southwards to Hartshill, near Nuneaton, and which distinguishes it from Wall. But the similarity with Wall reappears when origins are considered. Recent aerial photographs and excavations have shown that a two-phase vexillation fortress was established in the pre-Flavian period under the modern village of Mancetter.[85] It is not, though, the only military installation here, and traces of earlier and later forts or camps on different alignments have been discovered, together with very early Claudian samian and a hoard of coins, which suggests that there was an extended period of military occupation, in one

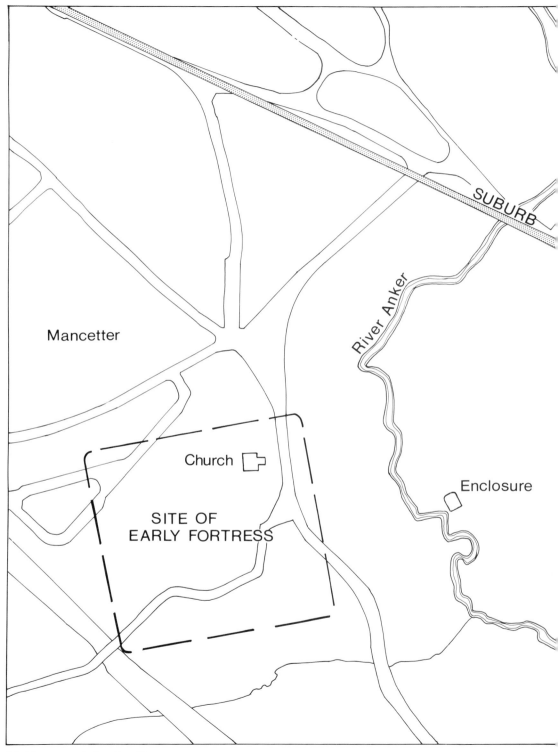

86 Mancetter (*after Booth*)

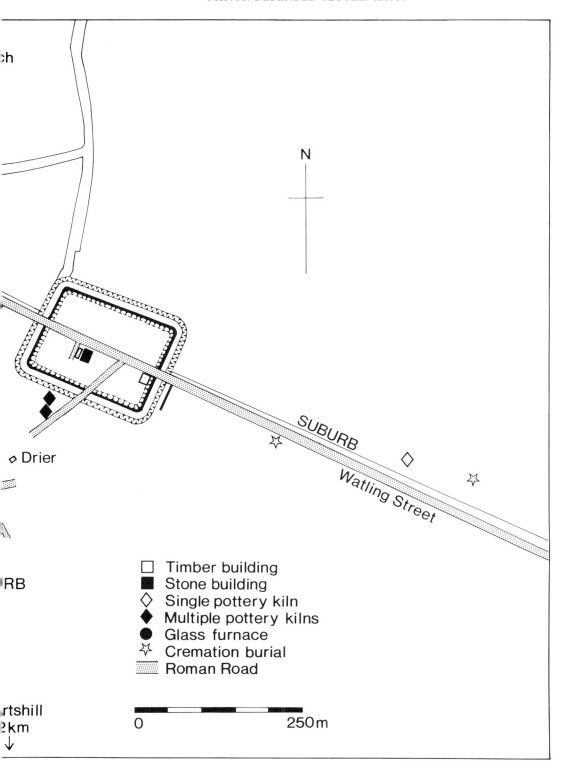

N

SUBURB

Watling Street

Drier

RB

rtshill
2km
↓

□ Timber building
■ Stone building
◇ Single pottery kiln
◆ Multiple pottery kilns
● Glass furnace
☆ Cremation burial
▒ Roman Road

0   250m

87 Mancetter, looking south. The line of the ditch
of the late fortifications can be most clearly seen
on the north side (*Cambridge University
Collection: copyright reserved*)

stage of which a vexillation was the garrison; Webster has even claimed that the escarpment south of Mancetter was the final battleground where Suetonius Paullinus defeated Boudicca.[86]

Not a great deal is known of the civil settlement, which at first was the usual jumble of buildings lining both sides of Watling Street stretching south-eastwards from the river. Pottery of the pre-Flavian period has been found, although the first buildings, of timber with a variety of clay, gravel and mortar floors, are thought to date to the Flavian period. Presumably these earliest inhabitants were primarily attracted by the presence of the garrison, which at one stage was larger and more prosperous than an auxiliary regiment.

Industrial production began with pottery in the early second century; chief among the products were *mortaria*, which were frequently stamped with makers' names or factories. At least a dozen potters are known by name from Mancetter and more from Hartshill, spanning the period until the fourth century; some potters, notably Iunius and Sarrus, worked in both places. The distribution of their products is interesting, since it covers the entire northern half of Britain up to and beyond the Antonine Wall, north Wales, and the south Midlands.[87] Apart from the presence of suitable clay, Mancetter enjoyed another benefit that was seldom found at other major potteries. It lay close to the sources of three of the largest river systems of Britain: those leading into the Wash, the Severn and the Humber. This may have lain behind the reason to construct the 'short-cut' road to Leicester to give immediate access to the Trent and thence the Humber. It is well known that water was the cheapest and most reliable form of transport for pottery in the Roman Empire, and it is significant that the distribution of Mancetter and Hartshill wares reflects the available water routes, up to the points where they entered into competition with vessels from other centres such as the Oxfordshire kilns. For a time though, the Mancetter and district potters saturated the midland and northern markets with their *mortaria*, and it is not unlikely that much of their success began with army contracts.

The kilns at Mancetter seem to have been located almost entirely on the south-western side of the town, which, if the prevailing wind was from that quarter, must have caused a considerable nuisance to those living alongside Watling Street.[88] Simple timber buildings have been found, some of which may have been drying-sheds or workshops. One such drying-shed seems to have doubled as a corn-drier during the harvest season.[89] The area was provided with adequate water from a number of wells, from one of which a channel had been cut to carry water to other parts of the site; it was eventually filled and sealed by a side-street.[90] Pottery, though, was not the only material manufactured here, since a glass-furnace was found in which cullet was being used.[91]

The fortifications of the Watling Street enclosure have been excavated in a number of places, the earliest on the north-east side in 1927.[92] Further investigations were carried out in 1954–5[93] and again in 1964.[94] A trench cut through the south-east side in 1964, probably near a gate, showed that timber buildings of the second or third centuries had been demolished to make way for the defences. They combined a masonry wall, which had been robbed to the foundations leaving a trench 5.5 m (18 ft) wide, and a contemporary clay rampart; unusually, posts revetted the back of the bank. Two ditches were encountered outside the wall; the inner was separated from the wall by a very wide berm. The defences were dated to the late third or early fourth century.[95] The only unexplained feature so far is a large ditch underlying these later fortifications, which was located in 1954–5 and which was dated to the first century; its excavators argued that it had enclosed an early settlement.[96] This is unlikely. It may have belonged to a military circuit, but the possibility that it represents a late second-century earthwork fortification for the town cannot yet be entirely dismissed. No external towers have so far been identified, but the wide berm of *c.* 20 m (66 ft) might be taken to show that they have still to be found.

Unlike Wall, Mancetter has produced slightly more evidence for occupation within the fortified enclosure during the fourth century, although even here remains are scarce. Buildings of both masonry and timber were found just inside the south-east gate, while a good deal of pottery dating to this period has also been recovered. The production and distribution of *mortaria* certainly continued until *c.* AD 360, so there is no reason why the settlement should not have survived until then. But, as at Wall, the crucial problem remains. What was the function of these fortified enclosures and why were they built? Is it possible that they were constructed as permanent campaign camps for the field army of the fourth century, which were used only when the need arose? The late Roman army, like its imperial predecessor, was presumably familiar with tents.

Margidunum[97] (figs. 88 and 89)

Although known since the eighteenth century,[98] Margidunum attracted little attention prior to a series of excavations which began initially in 1910.[99] By then, unfortunately, extensive stone-robbing and repeated ploughing had severely damaged the archaeological levels. Much of what we know about the site's morphology and general development is derived from F. Oswald's 1920–36 excavations,[100] which examined c. 0.6 ha (1.5 acres) west of the Fosse Way; to him we owe the plans of the buildings in the western part of the defended area and a tantalising glimpse of the site's early industrial history, though much was either misinterpreted as evidence for a fort or inadequately recorded, such that chronological precision is now impossible. Fortunately, less extensive excavations in 1966–8,[101] in advance of the construction of a new roundabout, clarified some of the phasing, adding significantly to our understanding of the southern defences, the buildings along the Fosse Way and the early industrial activity. Without these, the story would be very sketchy.

The most prominent surface feature, until its partial destruction in 1968, was an irregular defended enclosure on a slight rise astride the Fosse Way, c. 1.6 km (1 mile) south-east of the River Trent, which Oswald interpreted as part of his conquest period fort. Although we now know this to be erroneous, his excavations west of the Fosse clearly suggested a military origin for the site, revealing extensive first-century deposits with high quality Claudio-Neronian pottery and several metal objects with probable military associations.[102] These deposits make little sense as part of a fort, however, because they apparently include at least two ditched compounds enclosing various timber buildings and several

rectangular pits containing iron slag; that immediately inside the southern defences of the later civilian site, for instance, was defined by two ditches, and contained at least seven separate slag pits.[103] Unfortunately, detailed accounts of these early levels were never published, but comparable ditched enclosures, some containing quantities of iron slag, were located in the 1960s, both north and south of Oswald's trenches (Sites 2 and 3) and on a site bordering Newton Lane c. 300 m (990 ft) south-west of the defences.[104]

The combined dating evidence from these early levels clearly indicates intensive occupation between c. AD 50–75. Excavation and fieldwork demonstrate that it was also extensive, covering a narrow strip of ground close to the Fosse, as far south as the Newton Lane site and as far north as two ditches located on Site 4 just outside the civilian defences. This is far too extensive for an early vicus, and a more likely explanation, given the apparent importance of specialized iron-working in some of the compounds, is that the site housed a works depot or industrial annexe, perhaps related to an adjacent fort. This specialist function helps to explain the site's spectacular extent and expansion, and its apparent later first-century decline in the wake of the military withdrawal. The location of the fort remains unresolved, though the larger of the two ditches mentioned above, west of the Fosse, might be part of its defences.[105] This was V-shaped, 2.7 m (9 ft) wide by 1.7 m (5½ ft) deep with a cleaning channel at its base, and terminated in a rounded end; it had initially silted up prior to being deliberately levelled. Much remains uncertain about this important early episode and its impact on the local economy.

Little is known about the occupation between the end of the proposed military phase and the mid second century, when the earliest stone buildings appeared alongside the Fosse. No structures were identified in the 1966–8 excavations, while nothing in Oswald's accounts can be assigned to this period. What this means in settlement terms is unclear, though the site can hardly have been deserted in the interval. With the reappearance of archaeologically identifiable and datable structures, the essential features of the site's internal morphology become recognizable, though much remains to be resolved.[106] The main focus for occupation remained the Fosse

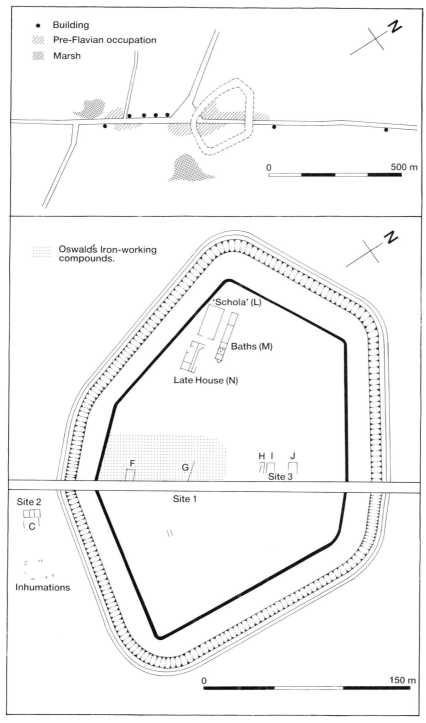

88 Margidunum (*after Todd*)

89 Margidunum, looking north-west before the roadworks. The defences straddle the road across the centre (*Cambridge University Collection: copyright reserved*)

Way frontages, forming a characteristic linear or ribbon development. The only known side-road probably branches west from the Fosse immediately south of the defended area, before following the line of its medieval and later successor down to the Trent crossing. Elsewhere, short lengths of metalling served individual buildings, as for example the gravel lane 3 m (10 ft) wide on Site 2. Building debris is known to extend over a distance of *c.* 800 m (2600 ft), but excavation has shown that it remained scattered and discontinuous throughout the settlement's history. East of the Fosse, for instance, opposite Site 3, trenching revealed hardly any buildings, despite this being the central part of the defended enclosure. This characteristic apparently became more pronounced with time.

The internal buildings present some interesting contrasts. The majority are of traditional strip-building type, best represented by the three complexes (H, I and J) on Site 3 on the western margins of the Fosse.[107] All were quite simple in design, with a beaten clay floor and foundations of local skerry blocks supporting a timber-framed superstructure and a thatched roof, judging from the absence of tiles or slates. Oswald excavated comparable buildings, including the small rectangular structure (F), identified as a 'stable', and the fragmentary remains ambitiously reconstructed as his 'Commandant's House' (G).[108] These structures have proved notoriously difficult to date precisely, but most apparently belong in the years after the mid second century, as does the slightly more elaborate three-roomed cottage (C) examined on Site 2 beneath the upcast of the defensive ditches.[109] It measured 14.3 by 5.8 m ($46\frac{1}{2}$ by 19 ft), with foundations of packed skerry blocks, set between facing stones of the same material, a technique at present unparalleled at Margidunum. It lay c. 14 m (46 ft) back from the east edge of the Fosse, being bounded on the east by a yard defined by two short walls, within which a rubbish deposit had accumulated spanning the period AD 150–250.

Particular interest in architectural and functional terms attaches to the structures excavated by Oswald towards the western end of the defended enclosure, though their structural history and dating remain uncertain. All three share the same alignment, suggesting that they originated as part of the same complex. The most distinctive is the so-called 'late house' (N),[110] apparently comprising a range of four rooms joined by a corridor with projecting wings, though the surviving plan clearly confuses several phases (see fig. 3F). Its floors were of opus signinum while the walls were embellished with painted plaster. Oswald noted that in one place its flooring overlay fourth-century pottery, indicating a late construction date at this point, though the building itself probably originated at an earlier stage. More importantly, from the point of

view of the late town, it clearly continued in use beyond AD 350.

North of the house lay an enigmatic rectangular building identified by Oswald as a 'schola'.[111] It measured c. 25.6 by 11.9 m ($83\frac{1}{2}$ by 39 ft) with no obvious internal subdivisions. It probably dates from the second century, judging from the pottery recorded beneath and on its floors, which apparently contained no third- or fourth-century material. East of this, across a narrow street or yard, lay a small three-roomed baths complex (M),[112] attached to a pair of larger rooms forming a structure 39.2 by 6.7 m (128 by 22 ft) (see fig. 5H). On the south lay an unheated room with a small semi-circular apse, followed in sequence to the north by two heated rooms, the first with a cruciform hypocaust, and the second with brick pilae supporting the floor; the main stoke-hole clearly fed the central room and thence the northern room. Sadly, this important building is not securely dated, though a scatter of second-century material recalls the evidence from the 'schola'. It would logically belong with the winged-corridor house, but there is insufficient evidence to demonstrate its survival into the fourth century. Oswald's rather sketchy sections[113] certainly suggest that both the 'schola' and the baths went out of use sufficiently early for a marshy deposit (?) to develop, prior to the area being covered by builders' debris and associated third- and fourth-century pottery; this latter might derive from the rebuilding of the 'late house' suggested by its plan.

This complex of buildings contrasts sharply with the overall structural range, posing interesting questions about their function. The same problem surrounds the construction of an irregular defended circuit at the core of the roadside settlement, enclosing c. 2.8 ha (6.9 acres). Knowledge of its constructional history largely depends on the 1960s excavations across the southern side,[114] though Oswald had earlier noted its principal features without appreciating their correct function. Two main stages are recognizable, commencing with a rampart 7.8 m ($25\frac{1}{2}$ ft) wide, fronted by at least one ditch which had been subsequently infilled and replaced by a new ditch further out on a slightly different alignment. Now or slightly later the rampart was considerably enlarged and fronted by a stone wall of which only the robber trench c. 3 m (10 ft) wide remains.

Subsequently two entirely new ditches were dug outside.

Given the limited nature of the excavations, these successive phases are difficult to date, not least the stone wall, which had been so extensively robbed that little stratified material was recovered. The original rampart sealed samian of c. AD 140 beneath it and so probably belongs to the well-known phase of later second-century earthworks. Both the early ditches contained residual material, though the excavators thought that they had been filled by the early third century; the otherwise undated wall must post-date this, because it sealed the inner ditch at one point. The later ditches are uncertainly dated, though they were still in use in the fourth century, judging from the large quantities of rubbish of that date in their fill. Neither of the presumed gates astride the Fosse Way has been examined, while there is nothing to indicate the existence of external towers.

The construction and subsequent modification of these defences must have affected the central part of the site, not least any buildings which stood in the way. Indeed, the three-roomed cottage already described (p. 263) may have been demolished when its northern part was buried by the upcast from the late defensive ditches. The provision of defences might also have influenced the development of the intra- and extra-mural zones, though too little excavation has been done to confirm this.[115] Occupation clearly remained scattered and discontinuous, but this apparently became even more pronounced with time. None of the buildings excavated in the 1960s revealed evidence for fourth-century occupation, while inside the walled enclosure, only Oswald's 'late house' apparently continued in use after AD 300. This would suggest that the intra-mural area was rather empty and that there was no obvious late trend to pack buildings inside for protection. Corresponding evidence for the late extra-mural suburbs is sadly lacking, but there is little about the site as a whole to indicate a lively fourth-century township; quite the reverse in fact! Caution is necessary, however, because there is no shortage of third- and fourth-century coins and pottery, suggesting that subsequent ploughing has seriously disturbed the associated structural evidence.

Little is known about the site's everyday functional aspects. None of the buildings has revealed any characteristic internal features or diagnostic debris, and so they may have housed a largely agricultural population. One blacksmith at least is attested by a workshop deposit located on Site 1, including six or seven worn hones and a range of iron objects.[116] Religious activities are only attested by two *deae nutrices* from the rubbish deposit associated with the three-roomed cottage, though an unprovenanced stone relief depicting a mounted warrior might have come from a religious structure.[117]

As elsewhere, the latest Roman evidence is represented by an inhumation cemetery cut into and extending beyond the upcast bank of the southern defensive ditches.[118] It may originally have been more extensive, perhaps linking up with the cemetery mentioned in 1857 outside the south-east angle.[119] Of the 12 burials excavated in the 1960s, most were simple in character, laid irregularly in shallow graves without grave goods. Two were buried in rather crude lead coffins, while a third lay in a stone-lined grave; one had been decapitated, another had hobnail boots and yet another had an assortment of bronze grave goods. Their dating depends on the associated finds, which indicate a late fourth- to early fifth-century context. The cemetery area also produced one fragment of Anglo-Saxon pottery to add to the other unstratified finds made elsewhere, including at least one Anglo-Saxon brooch and pendant.[120] The full significance of this material is hard to assess in the absence of *in situ* settlement, but this is hardly surprising given the subsequent land-use history of the site, whereby even late Roman features have been difficult to find. More than likely little now remains to clarify the fifth-century fate of the site.

Neatham (fig. 90)

Despite the discovery in 1959 of occupation debris on the terrace north of the River Wey at Neatham,[121] little was known about the site prior to the excavations and watching briefs of 1969–76 and 1979.[122] Though these were limited in Areas E and F at the south end, the more northerly Areas A to D sampled reasonably extensive areas alongside or at right angles to the road frontages, giving useful cross-sections through the site's morphology and an outline of its chronological development, as well as revealing a range of fairly typical domestic buildings frequently lacking elsewhere. Neatham is thus a good example of a small town with ribbon developments along the main road frontages.

So far there is no evidence for any nearby military presence, the site apparently developing around the junction of two Roman roads.[123] One of these, the main Silchester to Chichester road, running north-west to south-east, formed the principal axis of the settlement. Sections at several points in Areas A, B and E revealed a patchy spread of large flints rammed into the natural gravel, though in Area C there was a made surface, perhaps connected with the later defended enclosure. It was accompanied by an early V-shaped ditch *c.* 1 m (3¼ ft) deep, located 20 m (66 ft) west of the frontage in both Areas A and B. This had been deliberately backfilled early in the second century, prior to the intensified development of the frontages and the construction of a second road in Area A, running at right angles to the Silchester-Chichester road, towards Farnham and Winchester. This was somewhat more substantial, consisting of cobbling laid directly onto the natural gravel, though it had been modified in the later third century by an extensive spread of gravel affecting the whole of the central crossroads. Besides these two roads, there was at least one other, apparently running east towards the Alice Holt potteries. This was located on Site E close to its junction with the Silchester-Chichester road, where it comprised a gravel strip bounded on the south by a ditch.

Besides these primary roads, at least two side-streets or lanes have been excavated. One short gravel lane, probably of third- to fourth-century date, led south-west from the Silchester-Chichester road to a bath-house (No. 27), close to the settlement boundary. The other, undated, street left the main road at an oblique angle further to the north in Area B and may well have joined the Alice Holt road near the cemetery in Area F. This too had a gravel surface bounded by a short length of gully along part of its northern side. The simple construction of most of these roads and streets, and the suitability as a surface of the natural gravel, suggests that side-streets and lanes were originally more common, though now somewhat difficult to identify.

These roads form the framework for a characteristic pattern of relatively shallow ribbon developments alongside the frontages. The earliest occupation, dated to *c.* AD 70–90, was apparently centred near the later crossroads, principally along the Silchester-Chichester road. In Area A,[124] three late first- to early second-century timber buildings (Nos. 1–3) have been recovered along its eastern side, while a scatter of post-holes and a gully lay to the west. Elsewhere, in Area F,[125] the sequence of cremation burials apparently commences in the mid to late first century. Unfortunately these early levels are generally disturbed by later activities, and their extent remains uncertain when compared with the later expansion of the settlement.

The earliest stage in this expansion involved the creation of the central crossroads in Area A by the addition of the Winchester-Farnham road already mentioned. This reorganization inevitably encouraged a replanning of adjacent areas, with buildings being re-aligned along all the available frontages. Much of the evidence belongs to the third and fourth centuries, but the essential framework dates from the mid second. East of the Silchester-Chichester road, two new timber structures (Nos. 4 and 5) with an associated yard and well replaced their earlier counterparts; No. 4 at least belongs in a third-century context. West of this, at least four buildings (Nos. 6 to 9) lay alongside the new Winchester-Farnham road, though only the earliest phase of No. 7 was certainly contemporary with this road, sealing an unworn samian bowl of the period AD 100–125. In the small areas excavated, the evidence was somewhat difficult to interpret, but the buildings appeared to be separated by open yards with wells, ovens and pits.

In the mid second century also, an apparently organized layout straddles the Silchester-Chichester road in Area B.[126] To the west, two adjacent properties are indicated by clusters of second- to fourth-century wells, cisterns and pits (Nos. 8–13 and 14–20), bounded by a ditch (2) and possible fence line, running roughly parallel to the road and *c.* 40 m (130 ft) from it. This boundary clearly remained important until a very late date, as the paucity of later occupation debris beyond its line suggests. Within these individual properties, only one building (No. 13) could be reconstructed with any confidence. To the east, a

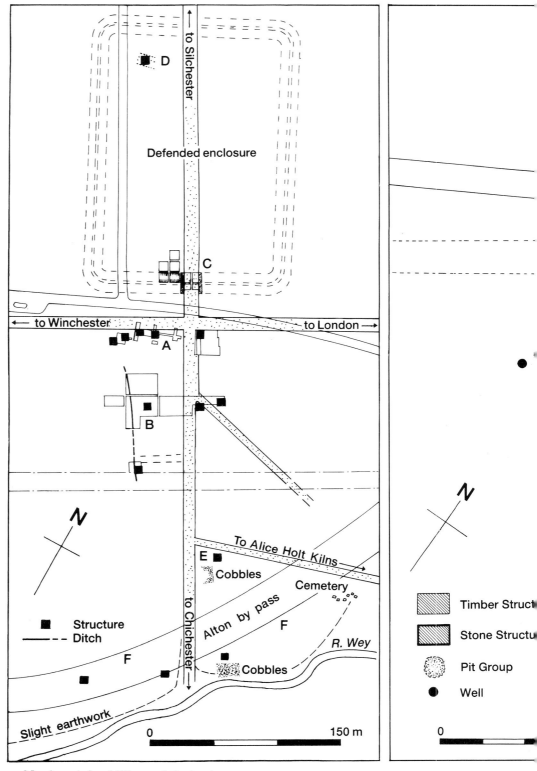

90 Neatham (*after Millett and Graham*)

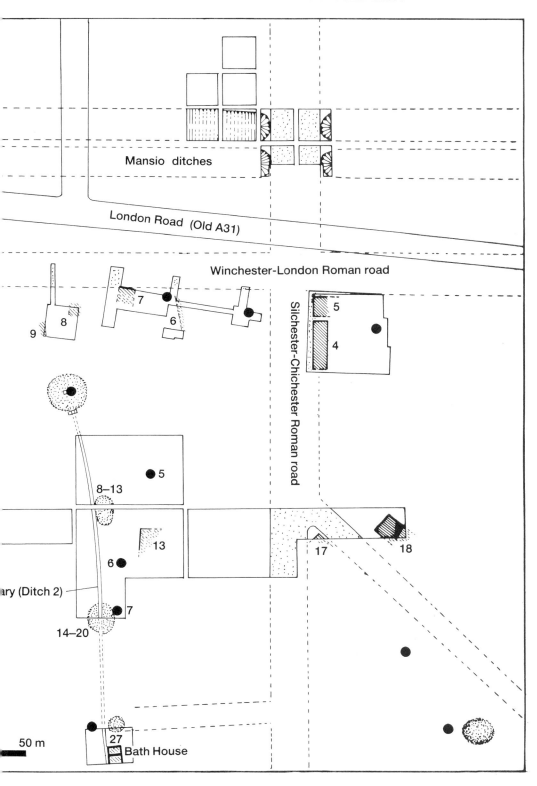

Mansio ditches

London Road (Old A31)

Winchester-London Roman road

Silchester-Chichester Roman road

9 8 7 6

5 4

8–13 5

13

6

ary (Ditch 2)

14–20 7

17 18

50 m

27

Bath House

side-street complicates the picture, which was otherwise broadly comparable to judge from the two excavated structures. A similar new layout may also have extended north of the crossroads onto Area D,[127] where the coin loss figures point to intensified activity in the mid to late second century, though the earliest levels were not fully excavated. The principal third-century feature was an aisled building (No. 19) associated with an oven and well. Development in this northern sector may have been influenced, however, by the construction of the defended enclosure, though the details remain unclear.

This evidence about the second- and third-century ribbon developments strongly suggests a series of properties of relatively standardized size, with a common boundary c. 40 m (130 ft) from the main frontages.[128] Moreover the pit clusters in Area B spaced at intervals of c. 25 m (81 ft) seem to indicate regular property divisions, though the structures in Area A were apparently more closely spaced. Each property must have contained one or more buildings, together with their water supplies, ovens and cess-pits, the latter being attested by a fragment from a wooden lavatory seat. These yards or plots were probably multi-functional, combining domestic accommodation with horticultural and other specialist activities. Though many of the excavated features are of post second-century date, the overall design clearly originated at this earlier date during the settlement's expansion. Whether this organization was imposed from above or was achieved by communal co-operation remains unclear.

Equally interesting is a second major reorganization in Area A in the later third century,[129] involving the laying of an extensive gravel spread across the central crossroads and the line of the Winchester-Farnham road. This had been regularly re-patched throughout the fourth century and had probably supported a range of timber buildings. This change in the layout indicates considerable overall organization, causing the suppression of existing property boundaries and structures. In contrast, the existing layout in Area B was unaffected and was apparently maintained throughout the fourth century and perhaps even beyond.

There is also evidence for significant third- and fourth-century expansion southwards towards the river, onto the hitherto peripheral Areas E and F,[130] where virtually all the buildings, yards and associated features and perhaps the Alice Holt road belonged in this context. Coin losses also increased markedly in the late third century onwards, suggesting that the expansion of the site might have involved a shift in the main centre of occupation southwards from the original centre; this hypothesis clearly needs further investigation.

Important evidence has also been produced about Neatham's internal buildings.[131] Admittedly all but two are of timber construction and most belong in a third- or fourth-century context, but they still provide a representative sample of basic structural types. Different construction techniques included straightforward post-hole and sill-beam structures and buildings set on stone post-bases. Building 4, for example, east of the main Silchester-Chichester road in Area A, is a typical post-hole construction set parallel to the frontage; it comprised two rows of posts c. 3.2 m (10½ ft) apart, forming a rectangular structure at least 13 m (43 ft) long. Comparable buildings in Area B included No. 13 set well back from the frontage and No. 17 in the angle between the main road and the side-street.

The early buildings in Area A were however of sill-beam construction, for example No. 3, which had beam slots to front and rear housing the main structural timbers, with a row of post-holes fronting the street suggesting an impressive timber-post veranda. Its predecessors on the same site (Nos. 1 and 2) had only one principal beam slot at the front, indicating that the remaining sill-beams rested on the ground. Disturbance or destruction by later activities often renders such buildings difficult to recognize archaeologically. No. 19 in Area D represents an equally vulnerable type, where the posts for the timber superstructure were set on stone post-bases, clearly forming an aisled building c. 9.5 m (31 ft) wide by at least 18 m (59 ft) long, set back from the road frontage. Where evidence survived, most structures had clay or gravel floors and were probably thatched, since few tiles are recorded. Most lay in their own yards, sometimes alongside the frontages, sometimes end-on and sometimes set well back.

The only obviously romanized building so far identified is the bath-house (No. 27) in Area

B(v).[132] This is served by a short side-lane, alongside and apparently respecting the course of the original boundary ditch. The limited portion examined included a *frigidarium* 2.1 m (6¾ ft) wide with a cold plunge to the north (see fig. 5F). Its massive flint and mortar walls stood in a substantial construction trench, with the sequence of rooms running north to south. It began life in the mid third century and lasted until the mid to late fourth. Its exact status is uncertain, its size and location towards the rear of a normal property suggest a private rather than an official role, but its immediate surroundings have been insufficiently explored. The presence of such a small bath-house reminds us, however, of the potential of these sites and of the wealth of some of their inhabitants. *Tesserae* and hypocaust tiles have also come from the defensive ditch in Area C, suggesting a larger building somewhere near the defended enclosure.[133]

Excavations have yielded a surprising amount about the everyday economic activities being performed.[134] The range of objects and querns demonstrates the importance of agriculture, but more specialized activities are also indicated, suggesting that the site provided services to a wider hinterland. Metal-working debris is particularly prominent, with most areas producing iron slag, but more significant are the traces of copper- and bronze-working particularly associated with the very fragmentary Building 23 in Area F. Successive floor levels contained quantities of ash together with slag, crucible fragments and metal droplets. In Area B also, a late Roman well (5) produced a pewter mould, while a possible industrial furnace was inserted into the sinkage above Pits 7–18 and 20. A marked concentration of bone pins from Area C and unfinished pieces from Pits 14 and 16 in Area B both suggest specialist bone-working, while numerous wasters from a late pit (3) in Area A indicate pottery production near the site. These surprisingly widespread activities, together with the discovery of two pieces of steelyard, clearly reflect a commercial role. The excavators have also argued that Neatham may have been involved in marketing and distributing Alice Holt/Farnham pottery during the third and fourth centuries, perhaps partially accounting for its increased size and importance during this period.[135]

The short-lived defended enclosure was an especially prominent feature of the settlement morphology. Evidence first appeared in Area C, where the butt ends of a pair of defensive ditches were recorded on either side of the Silchester-Chichester road.[136] Both were *c.* 7 m (23 ft) wide by 2.5 m (8 ft) deep, with primary silting including coarse pottery of late second- to early third-century date. They were subsequently recut, above which fairly rapid and deliberate backfilling contained mid third-century pottery and a few coins down to AD 270–3. Fieldwork and aerial photography indicate that these ditches formed part of a 2.5 ha (6 acre) enclosure bisected by the Silchester-Chichester road. Such a small strongpoint defence clearly does not protect the entire occupied area, so its function is probably official rather than urban. Insufficient of the enclosed area has been examined to define its exact role, but it may well have protected an official installation or *mansio*, to which the tiles and *tesserae* already mentioned might belong. A second bank, apparently with an inturned entrance, now under the line of the bypass, has been claimed as a later defended enclosure, but this interpretation requires confirmation by excavation.[137]

Religious activity at the site is sparsely documented, finds consisting of a single fragment of a pipe-clay Venus, together with some of the fills of pits and wells which may have had ritual overtones.[138] Pits 14 and 16 in Area B each had a Rhenish motto beaker and contained 11 and 19 complete coarseware vessels respectively; their animal bone assemblages are also peculiar, Pit 16 including a complete cock skeleton and Pit 14 a range of cock bones. All these may have been included as votive offerings when the function of the individual features changed.

Only one small cemetery has been located,[139] alongside the Alice Holt road in Area F. Excavations revealed two inhumations in a single grave pit and five cremations, one with a wooden casket, 11 vessels and a pair of hobnailed shoes, and the largest with 65 vessels. The dating of the cremations suggests usage by a single family with a common burial tradition between the mid first and mid second centuries. The only other burial, found and dispersed by workmen in 1979, lay somewhere to the west of the boundary ditch in

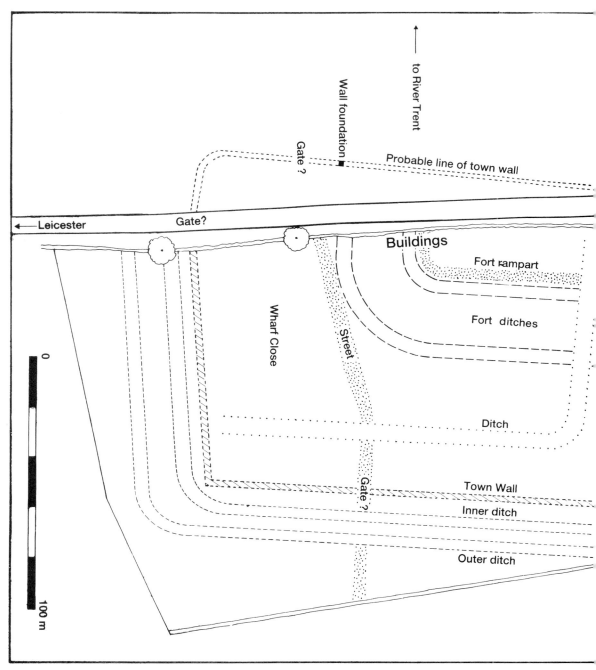

91 Thorpe (*after Wacher*)

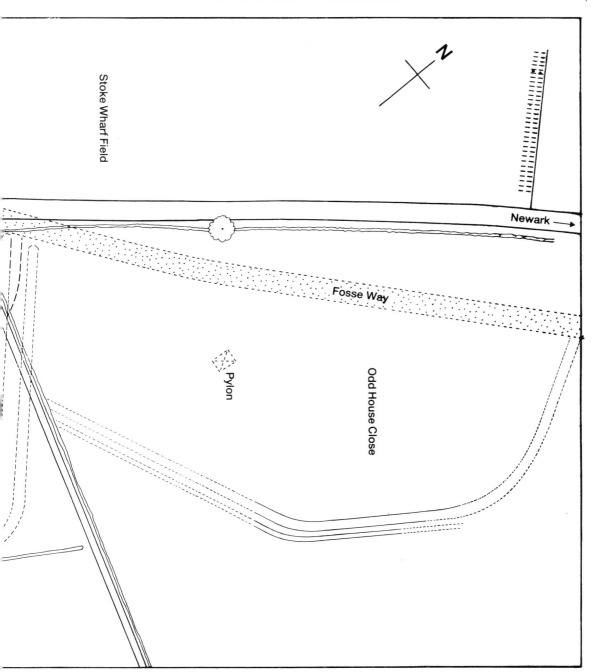

Stoke Wharf Field

Newark →

Fosse Way

Pylon

Odd House Close

Area B, suggesting that other cremations may lie on the edges of the settlement.

The end of Roman Neatham is also rather poorly known. The coinage certainly continues down to AD 388–402, presumably reflecting continued activity into the fifth century, but how long this was maintained in the wake of economic decline, especially in the pottery industry, is difficult to determine. Two *grubenhaüser*[140] provide the only evidence for Saxon occupation, one from Area B west of the main road, the other *c.* 40 m (130 ft) to the south-west. The former had been built into the sunken fill of Well 5, overlying coins of AD 388–402, but associated pottery suggested a sixth- to seventh-century date for the building. There is little to suggest continuity in the interval and it seems likely that the rationale for Neatham declined with the economy, and the settlement gradually became deserted.

Thorpe (figs. 91 and 92)

The site of Thorpe lies a short distance south of Newark on the Fosse Way and is one of at least four small towns situated on the road between Leicester and Lincoln. It therefore fell in the *civitas* of the Corieltavi and is to be identified with the site named *Ad Pontem* in the Antonine Itinerary. The name implies a crossing of the River Trent, which lies close to the west side of the town.[141]

Two sets of aerial photographs,[142] taken at different times, show a site of some complexity, which had been variously interpreted by several investigators[143] until the excavations carried out in 1963 and 1965[144] defined more accurately the different enclosures and their chronological relationships. Most of the features which show on the aerial photographs are enclosed within the two modern fields of Oddhouse Close to the north and Wharf Close to the south. Much of the metalling of the Fosse Way north of the town had been robbed in the middle ages, presumably to provide material for the present course of the A46; in this respect it resembles Ermin Street at Wanborough (p. 160). Hence the road shows as a dark, rather than a light, mark on the aerial photographs. The area west of the Fosse Way, although containing about a quarter of the town, which was subjected to limited excavation in 1952,[145] has been much confused by the flood actions of the River Trent, and it is only possible to identify tentatively the western side of the walled site.

Two phases of pre-Roman occupation have been found in Wharf Close, although it is possible that the second overlapped the Roman conquest.[146] The first was represented by a circular house, which was later replaced by a rectangular building. These buildings could be related to the numerous field boundaries which show on aerial photographs of Oddhouse Close; some have been identified as being earlier than the fort annexe, although no datable material was recovered from them. Both buildings were partly overlain by the rampart of the Roman fort which was constructed in the late Claudian/early Neronian period. A large polygonal annexe extended on the fort's north flank as far as the northern end of Oddhouse Close.[147] There are no signs of a contemporary *vicus*. Both fort and annexe were probably abandoned early in the Flavian period, when it would seem that the visible line of the Fosse Way across Oddhouse Close was laid out and consolidated; the earlier line has not been located.

Numerous quarry pits for gravel were revealed in both the aerial photographs and the excavations. Timber buildings, of which one at least was burnt, began to line the main road in the early second century, and during this century part of the site was enclosed within a single large ditch, which lies principally in Wharf Close but which could have extended further south. Timber buildings, especially along the frontages of the Fosse Way in this field, were gradually replaced by masonry, although continued ploughing and robbing has reduced them to disordered spreads of stone, with only small unconnected areas of paved floors surviving. The enclosing ditch was gradually filled with domestic rubbish during the third century, and in the late third or early fourth century a new defensive line was adopted. This consisted of a wall, with foundations 2.5 m (8 ft) thick, no visible sign of a rampart and, at first, two ditches, which were ultimately replaced by a single wide ditch. External towers, which were sometimes an adjunct to the alteration of urban ditch systems in Britain, do not seem to have been added; none is visible on the aerial photographs, although the wall had been so badly robbed that all traces of towers may likewise have been obliterated.

The only substantial building which can now be identified is situated just within the north gate. It shows clearly in the aerial photographs and was partly excavated in 1963. It lies over the filled ditch of the second-century fortifications and must therefore date to the third or fourth century. At least two periods of construction were revealed, with the plan of the second differing from that of the first. The walls were substantial and a good deal of painted plaster was recovered.

As already suggested (p. 38), the building was probably connected with some administrative function, perhaps as a *mutatio*.

Only one internal street shows on the aerial photographs, running approximately due east from the Fosse Way seemingly towards gates in the successive defences. There may have been an equivalent western projection towards the River Trent, where presumably the bridge which gave the town its name is to be sought. A rough stone

92 Thorpe, looking north-west towards the River Trent. The outline of the late walled enclosure shows most clearly, also the substantial building just inside the north gate (*Cambridge University Collection: copyright reserved*)

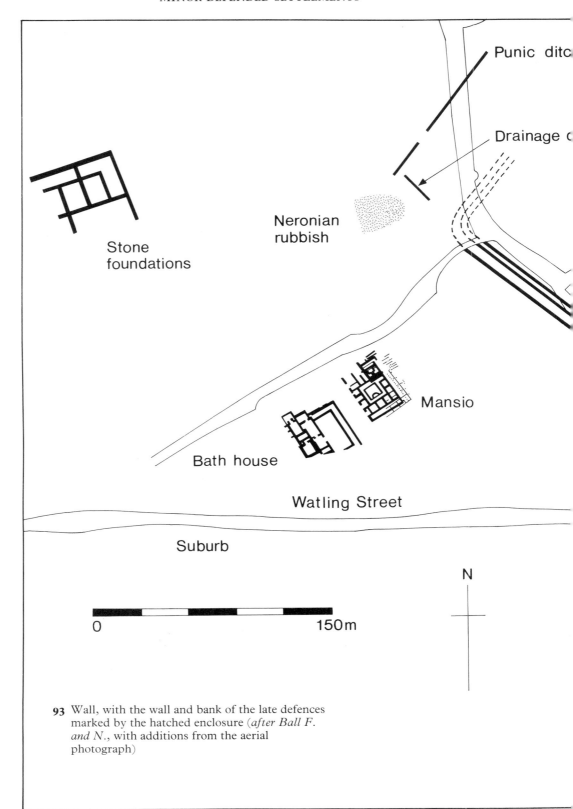

93 Wall, with the wall and bank of the late defences
marked by the hatched enclosure (*after Ball F.
and N.*, with additions from the aerial
photograph)

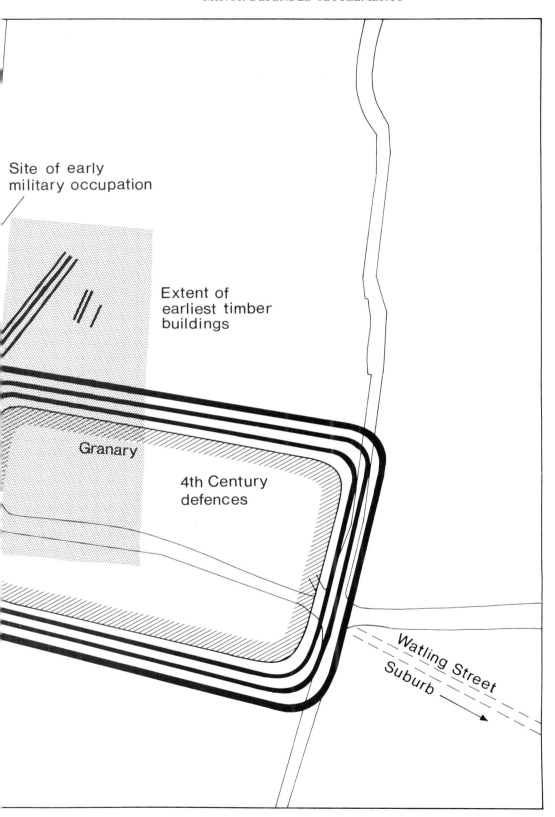

Site of early
military occupation

Extent of
earliest timber
buildings

Granary

4th Century
defences

Watling Street

Suburb

relief, probably representing the Celtic deities Sucellus and Nantosuelta, found nearby at East Stoke[148] would imply the presence somewhere of a shrine or temple, perhaps outside the town. Little is known of any cemeteries, although single burials have been recorded.

Wall (figs. 93 and 94)

The small fortified town at Wall, together with Mancetter (p. 255) is one of five situated on Watling Street north of Towcester which, it has been argued, formed a chain of *burgi*;[149] it also lies close to the junction of Watling Street and Ryknild Street. The site is mentioned in the Antonine Itinerary as *Etoceto*[150] and in the Ravenna list as *Letoceto*,[151] the latter being the preferred name. Stukeley noted Roman walls still standing in the early eighteenth century,[152] although he was by no means the first to do so.[153] Excavations, under the auspices of the North Staffordshire Field Club, began in the early 1900s, when the bath-house and its adjacent building were uncovered. Both are now exposed to view in the care of English Heritage, having first been re-excavated before consolidation of the masonry.[154] Aerial photography[155] has revealed the south-east corner of a fortified enclosure astride Watling Street, which has now been traced round a sub-rectangular circuit. Further excavations have also uncovered several periods of military occupation on the higher ground to the north, the earliest of which dates probably to the Claudian period. A vexillation fortress, possibly for part of *Legio XIV*, was established slightly later, followed by a series of reductions which ended with a small fort dated to the early second century.[156]

This succession of military bases, combined with the effects caused by a major crossroads, attracted a civil settlement which seems, in the second century, to have been spread along both sides of Watling Street for a distance of about 3 km (2 miles).[157] Late in the military phase an attempt was made to construct a bath-house on the south-west slope below the fort, but it was not apparently completed. Somewhat later, this was replaced by a new bath-house on different building lines which comprised a single range of rooms measuring some 17.4 by 7.9 m (57 by 26 ft) overall. This was subsequently enlarged with additional rooms, probably in the second half of the second century, while some time in the third century, an aqueduct may have been extended to it from the north-east.[158] This bath-house may from the beginning have been associated with another masonry building situated higher up the slope and separated from it by a gravel road or yard (see fig. 5A). It dated to the Hadrianic period and occupied the site of an earlier timber building, which may have been deliberately demolished prior to its construction. The new structure contained a peristyled courtyard surrounded by ranges of rooms, with a veranda running the full length of the south-east side. Its plan, taken together with the proximity of a bath-house, would suggest that it was a *mansio*, admittedly of small dimensions. It was destroyed by fire in the late second century and was not rebuilt, although the bath-house remained in independent operation, presumably being used by the town's inhabitants.[159]

One of the greatest puzzles at Wall is the fortified roadside enclosure. The defences, which had rounded corners, consisted of a wall, nearly 3 m (10 ft) thick and backed by a contemporary or later rampart, which was described as being of turf; there were three ditches in front of the wall, which is thought to date to the fourth century.[160] The ditches were refilled quite soon after they had been dug. Surprisingly this enclosure, and also the similar one at Mancetter, apparently contained no buildings of any substance. Admittedly not a great deal of excavation has taken place and it may be that contemporary masonry buildings have been destroyed by ploughing; but even then there ought to be spreads of stone, and it is also curious that very little pottery and only a few coins of the fourth century have been recovered, the latest being one of Valentinian I. The late Roman army on occasion reverted to timber buildings, sometimes, as at Porchester,[161] placing sill beams directly on the ground surface, which are almost impossible to detect in an excavation. But this would not explain the paucity of pottery and coins, unless the occupation was very short. It seems, though, to rule out the hypothesis that these Watling Street *burgi*, if *burgi* they were, can be dated to the reorganization of Count Theodosius in the years after AD 367.[162] However, the

94 Wall, looking west. The ditches on the south side
of the walled enclosure are clearly visible and
have been transferred to the preceding plan
(*Cambridge University Collection: copyright
reserved*)

explanation already proposed for Mancetter (p. 259) may equally apply here.

When the *mansio* was being excavated, seven carved stones were found to have been re-used in the walls; two more had been located in 1912. They displayed the outlines of crùdely-carved human heads and figures. One carries a club and two carry what appear to be shields; on another, the head is horned. They seem to have belonged to a stone screen, associated with a Flavian concrete floor, all of which formed part of a substantial timber building which pre-dated the *mansio* and which may have been destroyed during its erection.[163] It might have been part of a shrine, in which a strong Celtic element was allied to a classical theme, since the club-bearing figure could be a representation of Hercules, while the horned head was probably Cernunnos. The only other find of religious significance at Wall has been a bronze bowl bearing a *chi-rho* monogram; unfortunately its exact provenance is not known.[164]

There is little evidence of industry at Wall. Traces of copper-working have been reported in the military period, and fragments of iron slag are quite common. Cemeteries existed west of the modern village, where some burials had been overtaken by the westward extension of the settlement; both inhumations and cremations have been located, one of the former in a stone coffin.[165]

The end of Wall seems to have followed a genuine decline in occupation during the fourth century; there is no evidence to link it with the fifth century, by which time the settlement may have moved to Lichfield.

TWELVE
UNDEFENDED SETTLEMENTS

Ashton (fig. 95)

The settlement at Ashton occupies a situation, very similar to Sapperton (p. 304) and Hibaldstow (p. 300), on the road that followed the valley of the River Nene from Water Newton to Thrapston and then presumably on to Irchester. Aerial photography has revealed a maze of crop-marks in the general area of the settlement lying between the river and the road, but most of them were probably associated with agriculture.[1] The existence of a pre-Roman Iron-Age community has yet to be proved, though 'Belgic' pottery and two coins of Tasciovanus have been found.[2] These could equally have come from an early post-conquest native settlement, but the foundation of a brand new settlement here in the Claudian period is not easy to explain, unless there was a fort which has still to be discovered; this is not impossible but it is unlikely in view of the nearness of the fort at Water Newton. Otherwise, apart from the crossing of the River Nene, where there was probably a bridge, there are no very obvious reasons to explain a new foundation; a pre-existing Iron-Age settlement is far more likely.

The site at Ashton first attracted attention when the railway line from Peterborough to Oundle was constructed;[3] a cemetery was discovered in the station area. But it was the construction of the Oundle bypass in the early 1980s which prompted the series of investigations that have provided most knowledge of the site.[4]

The Roman settlement is a classic of its type, consisting largely of strip buildings strung out on both sides of the main road for some distance, with side-lanes giving access to the backs of these premises and to others situated somewhat haphazardly behind the main property frontages. At an early stage, probably dating to the mid first century, a number of enclosures were laid out, at least on the north-western side of the main road; some had tracks left between them which later became metalled streets. At the southern end of the site the backs of these plots were truncated by another street, which approached the main road at an acute angle from the north and which, with possible building plots on its western side, seems to have formed something of a western boundary to the main part of the settlement. About 100 m (327 ft) further north another street from the west made a crossroads, continuing in an easterly direction for an unknown distance. The plots were first defined by ditches but, as they silted, fences were constructed.

By the second half of the second century, masonry buildings were being erected in the northern part of the excavated area. They seem to have ignored the earlier land divisions, and a radical change must have taken place in the property boundaries. They were characteristically strip buildings, although they were not crowded together; each seems to have had a generous allotment of land both at the sides and also at the backs; a number of properties possessed their own wells. A more complex building occupied the south-west angle of the crossroads.[5] The actual corner was occupied by a simple, well-built, rectangular structure, but its street-side walls were extended beyond its limits to form part of a yard or enclosure, the boundaries of which were completed by a range of three rooms in the south-west corner and another, only partly excavated, building to the west. A well, over 8 m (26 ft) deep, was situated in the northern part of the courtyard, only the front part of which was metalled. The main building contained five furnaces, a stone-lined water tank and consider-

95 Ashton (*after Dix*)

able quantities of iron slag, numerous nails and other iron objects, as well as a smith's hammer and portable anvil; presumably this was the smithy of a reasonably prosperous blacksmith. Several other buildings in the settlement had similar functions. Indeed it is a surprising feature of many small towns that there was such a demand for the services of blacksmiths, which reinforces the importance both of this particular craft to urban and rural communities and of iron in the economy.

One important find of a religious nature has been made. The well mentioned above contained a complete lead tank which had been thrown into it together with fragments of another. The complete tank was marked with a *chi-rho* monogram denoting Christian ownership or use.[6] These tanks are not uncommon in Britain, most frequently occurring in eastern areas of the province and on rural sites. Sometimes the monogram is flanked with an alpha and omega; tanks without either are also known, such as those from Bourton-on-the-Water (p. 289). Their purpose has long been disputed. They have been called baptismal fonts, but as baptism in the early Church was by effusion and not immersion they seem over-large for the purpose. Another suggestion would associate them with cemeteries, as sources of water for diluting wine drunk at the feasts held at shrines in honour of the dead. Certainly they are often found near cemeteries and water,[7] as at Bourton and Ashton, but since lead-poisoning was recognized in the Roman world, this might be considered an unsafe, if not downright dangerous, practice.

The context of these tanks leads directly to a cemetery which was situated at the south-west end of the built-up area of the settlement.[8] It seems to have been deliberately planned within a boundary ditch on the east side and a possible hedge planted to the north. The burials themselves, of which 178 have been identified, were arranged in moderately neat rows and orientated east-west. As with Dorchester-on-Thames (p. 121), some form of marking of individual graves must have been employed, or a plan kept, to avoid disturbance of old graves by new. Grave goods were almost entirely absent, those which occurred being of fourth-century date. This is in contrast with other contemporary burials, which were mainly to the rear of the plots mentioned

above (p. 279) and in which orientations also varied. Several came close to the boundaries of the graveyard but none upset the ordered regularity within it. In the circumstances it would be hard to rebut a presumption that this was a cemetery used entirely by a Christian community living within the settlement in the fourth century. A very rough calculation might equate the rate of burial, over say a hundred years, with some ten or so family groups. It is worth remembering in this context the large collection of Church plate which was discovered within the walls of Water Newton (p. 90), only a little over 10 km (6 miles) away to the north-east.[9] Presumably somewhere at Ashton there is a church or chapel still to be found.

Coins of Arcadius and Honorius would indicate continuing activity at the site until the early fifth century, although little structural evidence of the fourth century has been recovered, except for pits, ditches and wells. This absence may be due to ploughing, or perhaps to a shift in the settlement, caused by a rising water-table and consequential flooding, to the higher ground in the neighbourhood of Oundle across the River Nene, where was later established a monastery in the early eighth century.

Baldock (fig. 96)

Baldock's potential was first realized in the 1920s, when an extensive cemetery was excavated towards the south-eastern end of Walls Field (Site P), a discovery which prompted several other small-scale excavations.[10] Here the matter rested until the discovery in 1967 of a rich La Tène III burial (Site F) and the subsequent programme of investigations undertaken in advance of redevelopment between 1968–72.[11] This initially involved trial trenching at various points and a watching brief near to where the burial had been found (Sites G-K), followed by area excavations in Upper Walls Common, in Walls Field and Brewery Field, and in advance of the construction of a telephone exchange (Sites A-C and L). Extensive geophysical surveys were also undertaken in 1970 and 1979, revealing details of the site's street system and a series of ditched enclosures right across Upper Walls Common and into Walls Field. Further development after 1980 prompted renewed excavations, focusing in particular on various sites along the western side of Upper Walls Common (principally Sites S, U and V).[12] As a result something like 4 ha (10 acres) has now been excavated, and yet more is tolerably well known from the associated surveys, especially along its north-eastern and eastern flanks. Baldock thus ranks as one of our better-known sites, despite problems of plough damage and the poor survival of buildings. Sadly much has now been lost to development.

Baldock is an obvious site for human settlement, being located where the chalk ridge is intersected by a gap and where several springs rise; here, too, overland communications met in both the later prehistoric and the Roman periods, most notably the Icknield Way along the ridge itself and the routes south-east to Braughing, south-west to Verulamium and north-west to Sandy. These provided the focus for an extensive late Iron-Age settlement, originating in the first century BC, traces of which were first located in 1967, when a rich burial was unearthed during bulldozing on the south-western side of Clothall Road (Site F).[13] Though much damaged, it had originally lain in a grave pit 1.6 m (5 ft) in diameter accompanied by a large bronze cauldron with an iron rim and ring handles, a Dressel 1A *amphora*, two iron firedogs, two bronze dishes and two wooden buckets with bronze bands and handle mounts.

Several contemporary and later burials have been found to the north-east in Upper Walls Common. Excavations on Site V in 1980–1 revealed another rich burial set inside a ditched enclosure 33 m (108 ft) square with an original south-eastern entrance, subsequently blocked by several shallow ditches.[14] The main burial lay in the centre, surrounded by satellite cremations, paralleling the evidence at King Harry Lane, Verulamium; the truncated grave contained a late Iron-Age pedestal urn, a wooden bucket with bronze and iron fittings, three partially complete pigs' skeletons and several fragments of chain mail. To the north-west lay a much smaller enclosure measuring 9 by 8 m (29½ by 26 ft), located in 1984 within the confines of a late Roman inhumation cemetery.[15] This too had a south-eastern entrance and contained at least three cremations. Comparable small enclosures were examined in 1970–1 towards the south-western end of Site A, measuring 7 by 7.5 m (23

by 24½ ft) and 10 by 12 m (33 by 39 ft) respectively, though only the former, which had escaped later Roman disturbance, revealed a central burial.[16] These burial enclosures probably lay close to the settlement fringes, especially along the north-eastern flank.

Associated occupation has been traced on several sites (B, D and U), though its full extent remains uncertain.[17] Early activity was suggested by several pits on Site D at the south end of Clothall Road, containing few or no Gallo-Belgic imports. With this may belong the 1967 burial with its Dressel 1A *amphora* and the prominent boundary on Site B, traceable on the geophysical survey running over *c.* 540 m (1780 ft) north-west to south-east, an orientation which apparently dictated the line of several contemporary features as well as many later Romano-British elements. No buildings were located, so these may be farm plots or small fields. By the early first century AD, the area south-west of this boundary on Site B had been redefined, the two newly-created plots apparently bordering a roadway and two possible side junctions, all later integrated into the early Roman street system. Beyond these lay the burial enclosures already described in Upper Walls Common. South-east of the latter, on Site U, a Belgic enclosure was excavated in 1981–2, containing two round houses and four cremations. This extensive Iron-Age occupation is also reinforced by some 130 pre-Roman coins and by the quantity of Gallo-Belgic imports, which rank it sixth in league behind such sites as Braughing and Verulamium.[18]

Despite its strategic location and established population, no early military presence has been identified, while Ermine Street bypassed the town some kilometres to the east. This inevitably left Baldock at a disadvantage in official terms, though it clearly continued to prosper as a local centre. Its importance as an Iron-Age road focus continued in the Roman era, though the detailed layout can only be partially reconstructed.[19] Clothall Road has long been recognized as the line of the Sandy to Braughing road, running north-west to south-east, though it has only been sectioned once inside the settlement, by the unpublished Brewery Field excavations in 1968 (Site L). At Baldock it met the Icknield Way, which is usually represented as skirting around the northern fringe of the settlement. This suggests that the junction was not a significant feature in the site's morphology. The course of the road south-west towards Verulamium is well attested by the London Road just outside the settlement, but instead of following this alignment direct to Clothall Road it is now known to have pursued a more northerly line to link up with the known internal streets.

Baldock's internal morphology was only partly determined by the frontages of these roads. Occupation debris covered at least 30 ha (74 acres), extending both east and west of the Clothall Road axis as well as southwards along the Verulamium road onto the Tesco site (R).[20] Its outer limits are probably indicated partly by the absence of debris, as on its north-western side, and partly by the location of several large cemeteries (especially Sites D, E, S, P and W). Within these boundaries, intensive occupation is attested, spanning most of the Roman period. Our understanding of the site's developmental history derives principally from the excavations in Walls Field and Upper Walls Common, though geophysical survey suggests that they are fairly representative of the broader picture along the eastern and north-eastern flank. The situation elsewhere is far less certain; west of Clothall Road at least three substantial buildings suggest a different story.

The most interesting feature to emerge is an extensive street system, confined at present mostly to the area east of Clothall Road.[21] The first segment, examined in 1970–2, ran north-east to south-west across Sites A and B. Its south-western end on Site B already existed in the late Iron Age, but early in the Roman period it was redefined by new ditches contemporary with its extension north-eastwards across Site A. Here it ran on a slightly different line and measured 6–6.5 m (20–21 ft) wide. Originally its entire length had been metalled, but this had become heavily worn such that by the fourth century on Site B it was represented by a hollow way 3–4 m (10–13 ft) wide. Two side-streets branched north-west and south-east on Site B, roughly perpetuating the earlier Iron-Age boundary alignments. These can be traced right across the site in the geophysical survey, which also revealed two further north-east to south-west streets running parallel to, and on either side of, the 1970–1 example. In the early 1980s, these were shown to be c. 6 m (20 ft) wide

between their respective side-ditches, with extensively worn metalled surfaces.[22] Elsewhere, patches of metalling hint at additional side-lanes.

This evidence indicates at least one main north-west/south-east street crossed by three roughly parallel north-east/south-west streets, all originally defined by ditches and maintained throughout the Roman period. Most were apparently established early in the post-conquest period, because on Site A the surviving metalling sealed early Roman features and its ditches contained Claudio-Neronian material. At first glance, this early planning seems to indicate an attempt to romanize the settlement, paralleling contemporary urban trends at neighbouring sites; but if this were the case, there is little to suggest the contemporary appearance of specialized buildings or amenities. An alternative hypothesis about the site's evolution is that the street system was an early Roman extension of an existing settlement layout defined by specifically native traditions. This is clearest on Site B, where the north-east/south-west street (and perhaps its side junctions) clearly perpetuated a pre-existing trackway. This would suggest a native site with its own inbuilt impetus spanning the late Iron-Age and early Roman periods. Clearly more evidence is vital to decide the issue, particularly because we seem to be just on the edge of the specifically Iron-Age component.

Alongside these streets lay a series of successive enclosures, with ditches up to 2 m (6½ ft) wide and 1 m (3¼ ft) deep, defining individual plots, presumably with a hedge or fence. It has proved difficult, however, to define and date individual phases, because of the residual and abraded nature of the pottery in their fills.[23] In the later first and early second centuries, few well-dated ditches have been recognized, despite considerable evidence for occupation on Sites A and B. By the mid second century, however, a large enclosure had been established in the north-eastern part of Site A, with a well-defined two-phase timber gateway on the south-east served by a lane, and an apparently contemporary circular hut at its centre. South-west of this on Sites A and B, further enclosures were established in the early third century, clearly perpetuating earlier first-century alignments despite the absence of recognizable markers in the intervening periods.

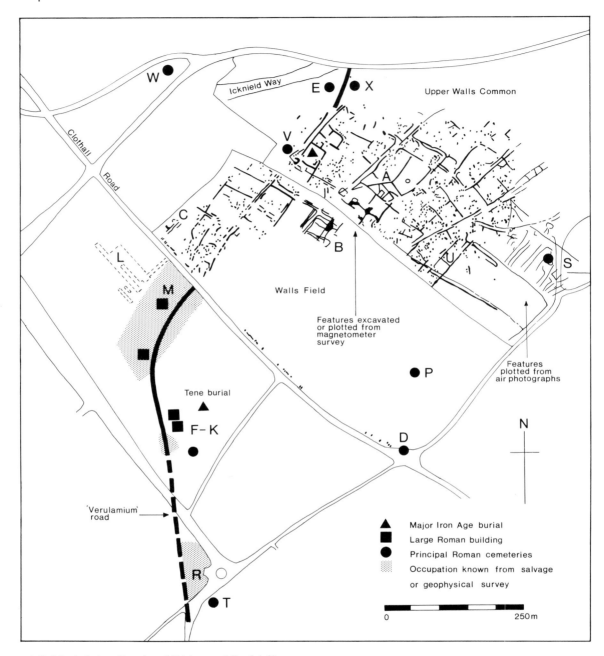

96 Baldock (*after Stead and Rigby, and Burleigh*)

These enclosures were associated with a range of ovens, wells, pits and quarries, though surprisingly few buildings were recovered.[24] Most of the wells were round, c. 0.8–0.9 m (2½–3 ft) in diameter, and up to 9–12 m (29½–39 ft) deep, all with foot-hole notches down their sides. One type of pit was very similar in construction and design, though the associated fills were characteristic of cess-pits.

The associated buildings have not survived well, partly because most were of wattle-and-daub, cob or adobe construction, and partly because of extensive plough damage.[25] East of Clothall Road, only two stone buildings are known, one set back from one of the roads on Site A, the other nearby in a fourth-century ditched enclosure. The walls of the former, measuring 13.5 by 7 m (44 by 23 ft), survived only where they had been built over and into earlier features, as on the south, where it cut into a ditch filled in the third century. Material of comparable date lay under its pounded chalk floor. Rectangular timber buildings are more normal, built either around a framework of timber posts, as in the case of Building 1 on Site A, or upon timber sill-beams as in the 6 by 2.5 m (20 by 8 ft) example excavated in 1981 on Site V,[26] although this may belong to the fifth century. Alongside these, the traditional circular house also continued in use. Besides the late Iron-Age examples already mentioned, three Roman examples have been excavated.[27] Building 6 comprised two short lengths of gully c. 9–9.5 m (29½–31 ft) in diameter with gaps to the north-west and south-east, inside which were several post-holes defining part of a concentric ring c. 7.5 m (24½ ft) in diameter. It was apparently built in the mid first century and its north-eastern gully was cut by a Hadrianic pit. The other two were of different construction, comprising a vertical-sided foundation trench apparently supporting a row of timber uprights. Building 7 was 6–6.8 m (20–22½ ft) in diameter and probably belongs to the early second century, judging from the pottery in the fill of its trench and at least one associated burial. Building 5 was probably contemporary with the mid second-century enclosure on Site A, its foundation trench 7 m (23 ft) in diameter being backfilled after c. AD 160 on the basis of the associated pottery. The survival of this circular tradition well into the Roman period indicates an element of native continuity, com-paring favourably with earlier suggestions about the street system.

In contrast to these relatively simple structures, few buildings of any real substance have been identified, except for the Romano-Celtic temple visible on aerial photographs west of the Clothall Road (Site M).[28] Two other stone buildings of some pretensions may also lie in this western sector, though only fragmentary traces were seen during watching briefs.[29] At various points on Site H, a wall of flint nodules set in mortar was noted, with an internal opus signinum floor, while on Site G, the corner of a chalk and flint structure with tile quoins was identified on a similar alignment. Neither their function nor their date could be determined, though the building at Site G post-dated a pit containing second-century pottery, suggesting a third- or fourth-century construction. The presence of three potentially substantial buildings west of the Clothall Road suggests a higher level of development than in the excavated and surveyed areas to the east, although this could be the result of less serious plough damage. Any future chance to sample these variations must be a high priority.

Knowledge of the settlement's everyday life depends upon the excavated areas, which indicate a predominantly agricultural basis coupled with some specialization. The ditched enclosures themselves find close parallels with predominantly rural sites, with each of the buildings probably lying in its own compound, associated with a range of ovens, wells and cess-pits. Further confirmation comes from several probable corn-drying or malting ovens located in Upper Walls Common.[30] More specialized activities are represented by one in situ iron-working furnace, while a specialist role might be suggested by metal slag on the floor of the building 6 by 2.5 m (20 by 8 ft) already noted.[31] Far more interesting is the metal scrap, three brooch blanks and several crucibles, found over a relatively restricted area on Site A, close to an oven of uncertain function, suggesting a bronze-worker in the vicinity.[32] Several other kilns and ovens appear to be domestic rather than specialized in function. This balance between agriculture and small-scale manufacturing accords well with the picture at other sites.

Religious activities are also attested, not least by the Romano-Celtic temple already mentioned, known only from aerial photographs and geophysical survey. A second religious area may be represented by a concentration of ritual finds at the north-eastern end of Site A, all from an early third-century context. They include three votive models (two axes and a spear), a 'ritual' iron rattle, a bronze fragment possibly from a statue and 44 iron spearheads, 33 found in the same feature.[33] Some of the excavated shafts and pits might also have contained ritual deposits, but this is far from certain. Elsewhere there is evidence for more individualized devotions, including a pipe-clay Venus figurine and the lead curse referring to a lady called Tacita which was found in a burial in the 1920s cemetery.[34] From Site B comes a larger than life-size face mask, probably of second-century date, which may also have had a religious connection with some form of theatrical performances.[35]

Excavations at Baldock have revealed a surprising number of cemeteries and isolated burials. The earliest to be excavated, on Site P, between 1925 and 1930, contained at least 320 cremations, which were placed in small chalk-cut pits and accompanied by a range of grave goods, mostly in the form of pottery.[36] In places, they were much disturbed by later inhumations. Trenching south-west of this in 1968, on Site D, located eight slightly earlier cremations of the later first century, the richest contained within a wooden casket surrounded by eight samian vessels, a flagon and several unburnt animal bones.[37] More recently, in 1982, a third cemetery was found on this south-eastern flank (Site S), including at least 160 cremations and 20 inhumations, some belonging to the first century.[38] At the settlement's north end, trenching in 1969 revealed part of another early cremation cemetery apparently in use by the early second century (Site E). This was extensively examined in 1986–8, adding c. 400 burials, mostly cremations, to the 13 already known; to the east lay a late inhumation cemetery partially excavated in 1987 (Site X).[39]

Two other late inhumation cemeteries are also known, both apparently inside the area previously occupied, suggesting some level of settlement contraction. That on the north, examined in 1982–5 (Site V), lay in a ditched enclosure 30 by 26 m (100 by 85 ft) alongside the most northerly of the north-east/south-west streets.[40] It contained some 60 graves, some re-used to give a total of c. 100 burials, all orientated with the enclosure ditches. Many were in coffins, associated with pottery vessels, hobnails and finger rings, and some had been decapitated. The second cemetery was recorded during a watching brief in 1968 near the Tene (Site J), where 21 inhumations were apparently aligned east-west with no associated grave goods, suggesting a relatively late Roman date; a further 50–100 similar burials were disturbed by building work in 1978.[41] These organized burial areas, along with others on Sites T and W, contrast sharply with a number of isolated burials found across the site. Some are relatively easy to explain, as for example the newly-born infants buried close to Buildings 3 and 7 on Site A, but the late inhumations in the top of various wells are more problematical.[42]

Later Roman activity is somewhat difficult to piece together from current evidence. Few of the enclosure ditches can be confidently assigned to the fourth century, with one exception, though occupation clearly continued well into the century, judging from the finds associated with the hollow way on Site B and with several wells.[43] The late cemetery evidence, however, together with the absence of Oxford red-slipped wares from Site A, might suggest fourth-century contraction to a more central location on either side of Clothall Road, though only detailed excavations in the relevant areas can confirm this.[44] Even more suggestive of changing circumstances is the late (fifth-century?) tendency to insert burials into the top of well shafts, as happened on Sites A, B and V, in marked contrast to the organized ritual of earlier cemeteries.[45] Attention has also been drawn to the animal remains, including two red deer, two hares and a fox, found down a well on Site B, apparently indicating a stage when animals were browsing amid the ruins and happened to fall in, though the date at which this occurred remains unknown. None of this helps to determine how long the Roman site continued in use after c. AD 400. Until the 1980s, no Saxon activity was known, and there appeared to be a break in the occupation from the fifth to the twelfth centuries, but recently a possible sub-Roman/Saxon(?) building measuring 10 by 5 m (33 by 16 ft) has been located, cut into the dark-earth sequence above the late Roman layers.[46] Its

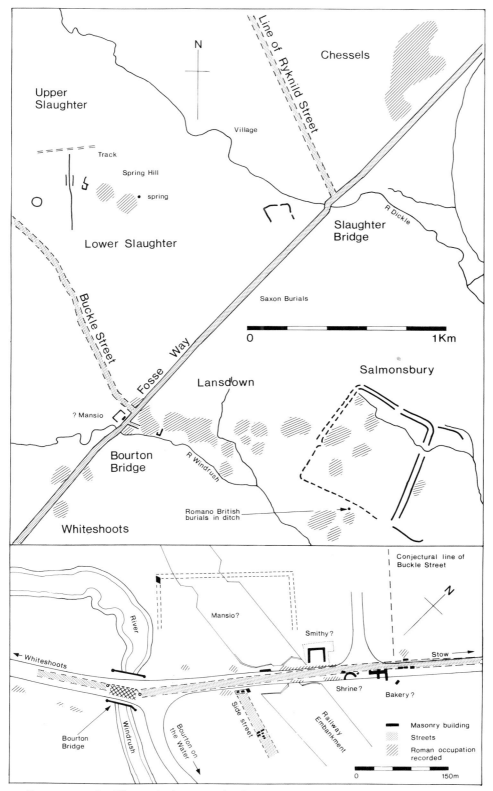

97 Bourton-on-the-Water; the larger-scale plan
shows the area just north of the bridge in greater
detail (*after O'Neil*)

exact date is uncertain, but it hardly argues for any high level of continuity; it would thus seem likely that a marked decline set in during the fifth century, not to be rekindled for some considerable time.

Bourton-on-the-Water (fig. 97)

This scattered, unfortified site lies on the Fosse Way, about half-way between Dorn and Cirencester, in the valley of the River Windrush. At the north-eastern end of the settlement Ryknild Street strikes off to Alcester, while Buckle Street, running almost parallel from a point just north of Bourton Bridge, is also possibly of Roman origin. The Roman settlement was first discovered in 1875 when gravel-digging took place in a field about 90 m (294 ft) from Bourton Bridge, while considerably more was recovered when, shortly after, the Cheltenham-Bourton railway was constructed.[47]

The origins of the Roman settlement belong in the large, bivallate Iron-Age fortification at nearby Salmonsbury,[48] but there may have been a secondary religious centre in the Chessels (p. 289). Salmonsbury, although built in the manner and to the scale of a hillfort, occupies a gravel plateau near the valley bottom between the Windrush and the River Dikler. All Iron-Age cultures are represented in the occupation down to the 'Belgic' immediately before the Roman conquest. There is no evidence for a Roman fort, so that the sprawling settlement along both sides of not only the Fosse Way but also the Windrush must have grown from the migration of the local people to the new roads, perhaps helped by the establishment of some kind of posting station. It is interesting that, although the defences of Salmonsbury were not maintained, occupation continued both inside and out throughout the Roman period, the coin series running from Claudius to the late fourth century.[49]

The main core of the settlement appears to have been situated close to Bourton Bridge.[50] In Roman times the Fosse Way crossed the Windrush by a substantial paved ford, which still exists under the modern bridge. Beside it was found a series of small stone piers, deemed to be part of a footbridge, but it is curious that this major road did not warrant a vehicular bridge. When the railway was constructed remains of a large masonry building, with walls reported to be standing 1.5 m (5 ft) high and occupying an area of some 73 by 43 m (239 by 140 ft), were revealed just north of the bridge on the north-west side of the Fosse Way; a column base indicated a building of some architectural merit. It has been reasonably suggested that it was a *mansio* or *mutatio*; material dating from the later second to the middle of the fourth centuries was recovered from it.[51] In 1967 an opportunity occurred to excavate along the line of the Fosse after the railway embankment, now disused, had been cut back in order to widen the modern road. Immediately north-east of the postulated *mansio*, a masonry building of some size was found, set at right angles to the Fosse; the heavy-duty floor was part cobbles and part flagstones. A furnace, interpreted as a forge, with an oven nearby, had been built against the inside of the south-west wall, outside which lay a cobbled yard. The building was interpreted as a stable, with accompanying smithy, belonging to the *mansio*. A number of coins on the floor dated from the late third to late fourth centuries.[52]

Three other buildings in this area, but on the opposite side of the Fosse Way, were partly excavated. One, interpreted as a bakery, had two large ovens built through a wall so that they could be stoked from outside the building. The building was active in the fourth century and the coins recovered from the destruction debris imply a possible continuation into the fifth. Attached to this bakery was another structure with a hearth and a considerable dump of household refuse; it was well built, with walls 0.7 m (2¼ ft) thick, and probably fronted onto the Fosse Way in the typical manner of a shop or workshop.[53] A short distance to the south-west another building with an unusual apsidal or circular form was constructed of compacted small stone rubble topped with gravel set between single lines of facing stones; an entrance through the head of the apse faced onto the Fosse. A timber superstructure was suggested, and the space between the curving walls was described as an ambulatory. Two short discrete lengths of wall flanked the entrance. This curious structure was interpreted as a wayside shrine, although no objects of religious significance were recovered; dating was difficult but the building is later than the late second century.[54]

The distribution of other buildings in the settlement is extensive, not only north and south along the Fosse Way, but also south-eastwards along the Windrush valley towards Salmonsbury and under the modern village. One building at Leadenwell was identified as a 'villa' dating from the second to the fourth century. It contained two lead tanks in addition to a well and an oven. A minor but well-constructed street ran south-eastwards from the Fosse, from a point a short distance north-east of the ford, and aimed towards this part of the settlement.[55] Elsewhere, south of the river, excavation has examined several circular structures with stone foundations and a slabbed floor.[56]

It is not easy to define the relationship of the settlement clustered around Bourton Bridge with that known at the Chessels, some 2 km (1.5 miles) north-east on the north-west side of the Fosse, or with that almost due north on Springhill. Chessels covers a considerable area and consists mostly of ditched enclosures, although three masonry and some timber structures have been located; wells, burials and coin hoards have also been found.[57] Of most interest, though, was a collection of sculptures from a well, which contained a small relief of Minerva, two uninscribed altars, votive plaques of Mars and of *genii cucullati*, two small statuettes and some architectural fragments.[58] The finds overall date from the second to the fourth centuries, with a concentration in the latter. It would seem that a religious building of some importance lay in this area, which could account for the growth of this part of the settlement round it, almost completely divorced from Bourton Bridge. It may indeed, as with so many of these rural shrines, particularly in this part of Britain, have origins in the Iron Age. Other finds, including an anvil, an iron pig and an assortment of tools and fittings, would imply the presence of a blacksmith. Other items of possible religious use are the two lead tanks from Leadenwell;[59] they were uninscribed, but elsewhere such tanks have been found adorned with the *chi-rho* monogram, as the one from Ashton (p. 281).

Apart from the scatter of burials at Chessels, only two have been recorded at Bourton Bridge. They were found in the south-west ditch of Salmonsbury camp; one was contained in a stone sarcophagus.[60]

It is clear that the Roman settlement at Bourton-on-the-Water was a large and thriving, if sprawling, community. Although structural evidence remains scarce, the quantity of other finds has been considerable. It is interesting that two, if not three, main centres can be identified, which appear to relate to (1) what was probably a native religious site, and to (2) a *mansio* of the Roman administration. Why they were not combined is now impossible to say; but if the *mansio* was equipped with its own bath-house, as many were, a situation close to the Windrush may have provided better water supply and drainage. Coins as late as those of Honorius suggest survival until at least the early fifth century.

Braintree (fig. 98)

Despite chance discoveries in the nineteenth and twentieth centuries, little was known about Braintree prior to several small-scale excavations in the 1970s, which focused on the Stane Street frontages west of the town and on the Coggeshall Road earthworks.[61] Most information, however, comes from the gazetteer of previous finds compiled by Drury, which helps to establish the site's overall extent and its relationship to the road network.[62] Despite this, our understanding of broader morphological and chronological issues is somewhat sketchy, not least for the early phase of development and its immediate Iron-Age predecessor.

The site's morphology is dominated by several major and minor roads apparently forming a staggered road junction at the modern town centre. Three roads (3, 5 and 7) aim for a point at the north end of Bank Street, while the remaining four (1, 2, 4 and 6) converge at its southern end, a development which is difficult to explain on current evidence so long as their relative chronology can only be tentatively established. The most recent assessment has been based on a detailed landscape survey of the roads, the Coggeshall Road earthwork and the local field systems, combined with the limited excavation evidence.[63]

The principal axes during the Roman period seem to have been Stane Street running east-west (roads 4 and 5) and the north-east/south-west road from Ixworth to Chelmsford (6 and 7). Neither follows a straight course through the

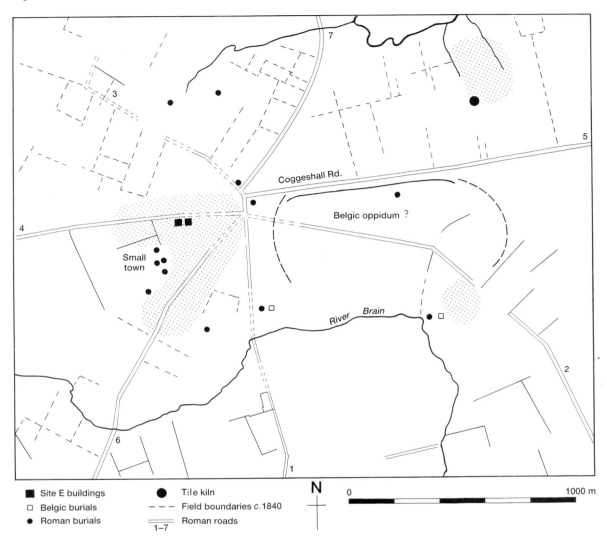

98 Braintree (*after Drury*)

settlement, suggesting that they were not original features. Stane Street may have originated as a late Iron-Age trackway, though its current line was presumably formalized in the mid first century AD judging from the pottery recovered on Site E.[64] While its western branch (4) was focused on the south end of Bank Street, its eastern arm (5) was apparently deflected northwards to skirt around a pre-existing earthwork south of the modern Coggeshall Road, thereby joining the staggered junction at its northern end. This

earthwork will be considered below, but its relationship with the early east-west road at this point suggests a late Iron-Age date. The Chelmsford-Ixworth road has not been examined at Braintree, but near Little Waltham it was dated to the mid first century, perhaps in the immediate post-Boudiccan era, making it the later of the two Roman roads.[65] Hence the alignment of its two branches would have been conditioned by existing arrangements. Three other roads also featured in the developmental sequence of the junction, one leading north-west from the northern junction (3), a second running south-west from the southern junction (2), while a third, perpetuating the line of Bank Street, runs due south (1). Though poorly known, their early date seems reasonably certain; Drury has noted that the Chelmsford road (6), south-west of the town, apparently overlies several boundaries whose general alignment conforms to two of the minor roads (1 and 2), suggesting that they are contemporary with a system of early Roman, or more probably, late Iron-Age land divisions. Road 1 also forms the spine of the Bank Street stagger at the centre, which tends to confirm its primary status.

This late Iron-Age origin for part of the road framework suggests the existence of a pre-Roman settlement, for which present evidence is somewhat scattered. Discussion has centred on the Coggeshall Road earthwork, already mentioned, a bank and ditch running east-west for c. 800 m (2600 ft), parallel to the eastern branch of Stane Street (5), which it apparently predates.[66] It was first described in 1833, since when much has been levelled and landscaped. At its north-west corner lies the prominent earthwork in Mount House, beyond which its extension southwards is lost; on the east, its line presumably followed the curve of Cressing Road, whence it probably turned south-west towards the river. It has been interpreted as part of an *oppidum* complex, enclosing c. 50–60 ha (120–150 acres), though such estimates seem unconvincing on present evidence. Excavations in 1976 and 1979 examined the earthwork at three points, though the results proved disappointing because of post-Roman disturbances.[67] Only the Cressing Road trenches at the north-eastern corner produced convincing evidence for a truncated bank, which presumably predates the second-century pottery found in the lowest levels of its eroded tail. More disturbing results were obtained, however, in 1984, when the Mount House earthwork was shown to be more recent in date, suggesting that a reassessment of the whole is necessary.[68] Iron-Age occupation is known, however, from the vicinity of the '*oppidum* site', though not as yet from the hypothetical interior or from beneath the small town. The 1983 excavations at the Fountain, near the modern town centre, revealed a late Iron-Age circular house with stake-holes, while Drury's gazetteer

lists two Belgic cremation cemeteries south-east and south-west of the projected *oppidum* circuit.[69] This evidence is highly suggestive of an Iron-Age origin but is insufficiently conclusive about its character, extent or status.

By contrast, its Romano-British successor is better known, the occupation debris forming distinctive ribbon developments not at the junction itself, surprisingly, but along the frontages of the main roads leading west and south-west (4 and 6).[70] The reasons for this lopsided development remain uncertain. Though dating evidence is limited, the south-western branch developed remarkably quickly, first-century material being known from several points along its frontages. This was followed by a second-century extension along the western arm, well illustrated on Site E, where the earliest buildings alongside Stane Street were only constructed towards the end of the second century, indicating that even by that date, significant parts of the frontages were not built up.[71] A small group of early samian on this site has suggested the presence of a post-Boudiccan fort in the vicinity, but this seems unlikely given the current absence of any characteristic military finds from the small town.[72]

Braintree is thus typical of those sites where the occupation remained tied to the main roads, debris rarely extending more than 100 m (327 ft) from the frontages. No side-streets or lanes have been recorded, though provision must have been made to serve the cemetery areas. Most of the occupied area was probably taken up by long plots of land given over to agricultural or horticultural functions, the rear boundary of which may be represented by a possible ditch located c. 105 m (343 ft) from the western frontage of road 6.[73] The excavated plots on Site E were at least 16 m (52 ft) wide, apparently defined by fences or ditches which were frequently replaced, reflecting the maintenance of fixed property boundaries.[74] Within these, the buildings were mostly set lengthwise and not end-on to the frontages. The pair on Site E are probably typical of the structural range, though both have suffered from post-Roman disturbances. In the eastern plot, Building A was a timber-framed structure measuring c. 13 by 6 m (43 by 20 ft), with ground-laid timbers resting on a prepared ground surface. It was constructed in the later second century and lasted for about a hundred years. Its neighbour in the western plot, Building B, apparently combined ground-laid timbers with posts set into the ground, though its dimensions and plan proved difficult to define. It began life in the later third century and lasted into the mid fourth. Not all the buildings were entirely timber-framed, however, as the structures with stone foundations excavated at the Fountain in 1983 demonstrate.[75] No substantial public or official buildings have been recognized.

Given the limited amount of excavation, it is hardly surprising that the site's everyday aspects remain poorly known. The nature of the plots astride the frontages suggests an agricultural emphasis, but this must be set against the involvement of their inhabitants in limited manufacturing. Iron-working was clearly being undertaken close to Site E during the lifetime of Building A, while Building B was obviously a focus for later operations, judging from the quantity of fired-clay fragments, iron objects and smithing slag; several of the excavated features in the western plot may even represent the stunted remains of its hearths.[76] The presence of a blacksmith at Braintree is not surprising, but there is also evidence for bone- and antler-working from a third-century pit in the western compound.[77] Less certainly related to the town is a probable tilery recorded north-east of the centre on Bradford's Farm Estate; the kiln itself was located in 1966, while its products have been found at various points in the vicinity.[78]

Evidence for religious activity at Braintree is even more scanty, being confined to a single pipe-clay *dea nutrix* from the excavations on Site E.[79] Several cremations have been located, however, concentrated in the angle between the two principal axes of settlement. They probably represent the main first- and second-century cemetery, though the details are poorly recorded.[80] Other cemeteries apparently lay at the periphery of the settled areas, examples being known near the road junction and south-east of the Chelmsford road (6). No certain inhumation cemeteries are known, the single east-west burial in a stone coffin, from south of the Coggeshall Road earthwork, being somewhat isolated and probably relating to a nearby villa or farm complex.[81]

The later history of the small town is also somewhat difficult to elucidate on current evidence. The quantity of burnt Antonine samian might suggest that Braintree suffered some level of late second-century disturbance, as has been noted elsewhere in Essex, but the material is insufficiently well dated and stratified to allow a definitive assessment.[82] Occupation on both main roads continued into the fourth century, though its intensity and extent are difficult to estimate; Site E, for instance, was certainly abandoned in the AD 360s, suggesting some level of contraction on the western road.[83] No decline seems likely on its south-western counterpart, judging from the known finds, but only excavation can clarify the issue. The fifth-century fate of the town remains uncertain in the absence of any stratified sequences or closely datable finds. No Saxon occupation has been recognized, beyond a few pottery sherds and the references to one 'Saxon Urn' and several burials in the area of the early Roman cemetery.[84] These are too poorly recorded to be regarded as reliable evidence, and, in any case, the burials are probably of seventh- or eighth-century date. Whatever happened in the interval at Braintree is currently unknown.

Camerton (figs. 99 and 100)

The small Roman town at Camerton in Somerset lies on the Fosse Way about 12 km (7 miles) south-west of Bath. The first records were made by Collinson in 1791, who mentioned foundations and a tessellated pavement.[85] Slightly later, the Revd Skinner, rector of Camerton 1800–37, made many detailed records, preserved in his 99-volume diary, now in the British Museum.[86] His results have been summarized by the Revd Scarth[87] and also by the Victoria County History.[88] In 1926 Abbot Horne of Downside Abbey excavated an Anglo-Saxon cemetery north of the Roman settlement[89] and then began excavations on the latter until 1946, when direction was taken over by William Wedlake;[90] the excavations continued until the late 1950s.

The site lies on a limestone ridge between the Rivers Cam and Wellow. There are extensive traces of prehistoric use of the ridge from Neolithic times onwards, with a considerable Iron-Age occupation; huts of the later Iron Age were located beneath the Roman town, and the site has produced six Dobunnic coins.[91] Despite

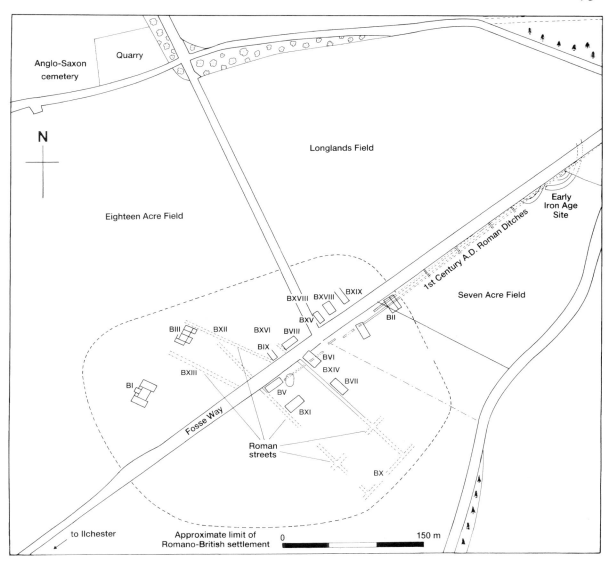

99 Camerton (*after Wedlake*)

Ptolemy's attribution of Bath and hence Camerton to the *civitas Belgarum*, it is far more likely that both lay in the territory of the Dobunni.[92]

Wedlake postulated the existence of a small fort or camp north-east of the later settlement, which he thought may have provided accommodation for workers building the Fosse Way; so far no evidence has been found in support of this.[93] The Fosse Way here seems to have been constructed *c*. AD 50. It was flanked on both sides by ditches set some little distance apart; their layout, however, was not regular. At one point, on the south-east side, there were two ditches, one of which consisted of discontinuous lengths, not all on the same line. Indeed, the whole road layout here is not dissimilar to that of Ermin Street at Wanborough (p. 162). In both places the gaps left in the side ditches may have been to allow access, not only to buildings but also possibly to agricul-

100 Camerton, looking north-east (*Cambridge University Collection: copyright reserved*)

tural land. Although no first-century building
plans were recovered in the excavations, quantities of burnt daub were found in first-century pits
north-west of the Fosse Way and imply the
presence of timber-framed houses, although destruction deposits of this type could have come
from Iron-Age houses demolished when the road
was laid out. But if they were Iron-Age buildings,
then it would create a remarkably long gap in the
history of the occupation, since Wedlake was
unable to find any masonry buildings earlier than
the mid to late second century.

Two of the earliest masonry structures to be
discovered were situated on the western perimeter of the settlement. Streets were constructed
to give access from the Fosse Way, but they were
not laid out either at right angles or aligned to it.
Building I strongly resembles a winged-corridor
villa in plan, as to a lesser extent does Building III
(see fig. 3A and B).[94] Indeed, if both existed in
isolation, there would be no difficulty in calling
them villas. The other contemporary buildings
had been constructed on the same side of the
Fosse Way, as though the road acted as a property
boundary. This may be important in considering
the origins of this so-called town. The unproven
first-century buildings apart, the earliest substantial development did not take place until the
middle of the second century or later, round these
two villa-like buildings. Was this, therefore, a
straightforward rural estate, with perhaps a small
vicus growing on it? Even in later periods in the
third and fourth centuries, when building took
place on both sides of the Fosse Way, all the
structures were very similar, most being, with
one exception, of a simple rectangular shape. But
unlike shops and workshops of a genuine town
they did not cluster along the main road frontages; instead several were placed some distance
from them, with their main axes parallel with,
rather than at right angles to, the road. Some
distance was always maintained between one
building and another, and several possessed their
own metalled yards. Side-streets were constructed to serve the buildings south-east of the
Fosse Way. If the removal of the enclosing
curtain wall at Gatcombe,[95] a major villa some
kilometres north of Bath, is envisaged hypotheti-
cally, the surviving layout would not be dissimilar to Camerton. Recent excavations have also
shown that the villa at Catsgore, not far from

Ilchester, was also surrounded by what appears
to be a village-like community.[96]

Soon after the middle of the third century, the
settlement not only expanded but it also appears
to have changed its character. Masonry buildings
were then constructed for the first time on the
south-east side of the Fosse Way and were
matched by others across the road; all were of a
simple rectangular pattern, although Building II
later had a narrow room or veranda added to its
eastern side.[97] This building also had exceptionally thick walls, just under 1 m ($3\frac{1}{4}$ ft) wide. The
slate roof had collapsed into the interior, which
had originally been floored with slabs of old red
sandstone laid on a thick layer of small chippings.

A common feature in almost all the buildings of
this date was the provision of a variety of hearths
and furnaces, which the excavator suggested was
caused by a change from an agricultural to an
industrial function. He claimed that iron-smelting took place on the site, since quantities of slag
were found, especially towards the eastern end.
One large pit, over 9 m ($29\frac{1}{2}$ ft) across and about 1
m ($3\frac{1}{4}$ ft) deep may have been used for smelting
as early as the late first century, which would
imply that Wedlake's contention that industry
only appeared in the third century was somewhat
misguided. But despite the large amounts of slag
in the pit and the presence of a well-made hearth,
no proof was obtained that it was definitely used
for smelting.[98] Nevertheless there was better
evidence for this process in and round Building
XVII, where there was also evidence for pewter-
working. The lower stone from a mould for
casting shallow, oval pewter dishes was discovered close to a sunken furnace; two other moulds
were found in the same building.[99] Wedlake
suggested that a pile of coal outside it was used for
smelting iron; this is unlikely since coal, containing a high proportion of sulphur, is not suitable
for this purpose, unless it has been changed to
coke beforehand by pre-heating. Evidence for
smithing came from Buildings VI and XIV,
although the furnace associated with the latter is
not dissimilar to some types of corn-drier.[100]

At no time was the settlement fortified, but
another general phase of building seems to have
taken place early in the fourth century, this time
only on the north-western side of the Fosse
Way.[101] This is interesting, as it again contrasts
with the expansion to the other side of the road in

the third century. If this settlement is a *vicus* attached to a villa it might point to changing property boundaries which involved the main road.

The only objects of religious significance to be found at Camerton were discovered by Skinner in Building XVI and post-dated the late fourth-century rebuild.[102] Two column drums and a base indicate a structure of some architectural distinction. One of the drums, though, may have been used to support a crudely-carved stone statuette of a seated figure, some 200 mm (8 in) high. Nearby was also found a 'grotesque' head, some 100 mm (4 in) high. Other finds in the area were a stone spearhead and a fragmentary inscription dating to AD 235. The latter appears to be part of a formal dedication and mentions the consuls Severus and Quintianus.[103] Apart from the fact that there was clearly a religious shrine in the area of Building XVI, the inscription sheds a little more light on the nature of the settlement. Dedications of this nature are rare in rural establishments. The suggestion has already been made that Camerton represents the *vicus* attached to an estate based on the villa-like Building I. Yet for a villa this building is very modestly proportioned and lacks much in the way of refinements. We could, therefore, possibly be dealing with an estate run by a manager, or, if it was an imperial estate, which is not impossible, by an assistant *procurator*, as at Combe Down just outside Bath.[104]

One other structure at Camerton deserves a brief mention. It is the so-called 'amphitheatre' situated a short distance south of the church in Camerton village, which is 0.8 km (0.5 miles) from the Roman settlement. A limited excavation carried out by Wedlake showed a series of stepped levels arranged around three sides of a square; there was a ditch under each step. There appeared to be an entrance in the centre of the north side, with a well-made trackway leading to it. A good deal of Roman pottery was found in association with the earthwork, but a definite Roman date for its construction must remain in doubt.[105] It was suggested by Hawkes, in correspondence with Wedlake, that it was a gathering place for a nearby religious centre, perhaps situated underneath the church. This is not impossible, but the terraces could equally have been for cultivation, with, since it lies at the head

of a small combe, provision for irrigation; it could be of Roman or medieval date.

The end of the settlement is shrouded in uncertainty. The coin sequence declines rapidly after the Constantian period,[106] although Wedlake considered that most of the buildings still in existence in the early fourth century survived into the early fifth; certainly Buildings VIII, IX and XV seem to have done so, and he also points to 'squatters' occupying other near-derelict houses. But the Anglo-Saxon cemetery nearby was dated to the sixth and seventh centuries[107] and presumably represents the transfer of the settlement to the site of the modern village.

Cowbridge (fig. 101)

Despite a range of finds and a long tradition identifying Cowbridge with the *Bomium* of the Antonine Itinerary, the site's potential was not fully appreciated before the 1970s.[108] Since then the pace of development in the modern town has necessitated several excavations alongside and to the north of the High Street frontages, supplemented by extensive geophysical surveys in the Bear Field.[109] Much of this work is yet to be published in detail, but the interim statements have revealed a hitherto unexpected 'small town' with at least one short-lived substantial building and a preoccupation with metal-working.[110] Given the limited nature of the excavations, details of the site's overall morphology and development remain uncertain.

The settlement is thought to have originated outside an early military establishment on the east-west route between Cardiff and Neath. Support for this comes from several roof tiles stamped LEG II AUG on the Arthur John car park site, together with a *ballista* bolt and several pieces of military equipment, though none has been found in characteristically military contexts.[111] Excavation on the Midland Bank site also revealed a short length of ditch aligned north-east to south-west, which had apparently been back-filled towards the end of the second century.[112] Although its depth could not be determined because of the high water-table, surviving tip lines suggested a width of *c.* 7–8 m (23–26 ft). This was tentatively identified as one side of a hypothetical 2 ha (5 acre) fort, but this interpretation now seems unconvincing for several reasons, not least the absence of any associated rampart. It would also lie diagonally across the line of the early Roman road located just to the west in 75 High Street. Much therefore remains uncertain about any military presence at Cowbridge, which only further excavation can clarify.

The situation is further complicated by the nearby multivallate hillfort of Caer Dynnaf on Llanblethian Hill, enclosing c. 4.9 ha (12.1 acres).[113] Within the interior, aerial photographs have indicated characteristic traces of terracing and several hollows, but the excavations of 1965–7 revealed only first- to fourth-century pottery and quernstones, suggesting usage throughout the Roman period contemporary with Cowbridge; only one pit apparently contained purely Iron-Age pottery. Normally a process of migration from an existing Iron-Age site to a newly-established roadside centre might have been expected, but this was seemingly not what happened to any obvious extent. Clearly further work is necessary to clarify the relative contribution of both sites to the landscape.

The morphology of the civilian settlement has to be reconstructed from a few small-scale excavations and the recorded distribution of occupation debris. Its principal axis was the main Roman road running east-west along the line of the modern High Street. Although unexcavated, its northern ditch was located at 75 High Street, where it was 1.5 m (5 ft) wide, 0.8 m (2½ ft) deep, and at least 6 m (20 ft) from the presumed edge of the road.[114] It had been filled relatively quickly with rubbish and then overlain by buildings. The associated evidence suggests a late first-century date for its construction, probably contemporary with any early military presence. Subsequent civilian activity apparently extended at least 350 m (1100 ft) west of the river crossing but it may originally have extended even further if the material in Hopyard Meadow was part of the settlement rather than a separate rural establishment.[115] Within the former area, excavation has principally taken place north of High Street, revealing occupation extending some way back from the frontages into the Bear Field and the Arthur John car park; whether the same pattern pertains south of the road remains uncertain. This work inside the settlement has allowed the definition of several interesting variations in the pattern of internal land-use.

Alongside High Street a range of buildings occupied the road frontages, examples being recorded at Nos 75, 77 and 83.[116] The pair at No. 75 were of timber, resting on either sleeper beams or stone wall footings, with clay and gravel floors. They were set at a slight angle to each other, the intervening space being paved with limestone slabs. Of the two, the eastern one was more fully excavated, being at least 18 m (59 ft) long with an internal row of four timber uprights, perhaps suggesting an aisled construction. Both buildings overlay the early roadside ditch and lasted into the third century, when they were burnt down. Further west at No. 83, part of another building of late third- or early fourth-century date was uncovered c. 40 m (130 ft) from the frontage. A timber superstructure rested on rubble-filled foundation trenches with an internal clay floor or make-up. If this pattern is characteristic of the High Street frontages, Cowbridge would be a typical ribbon development.

North of the High Street frontages, geophysical survey and trenching during 1979 revealed a surprising archaeological potential.[117] This was subsequently corroborated by work on the Bear Barn site, where a clay and stone layer containing Romano-British material sealed several gullies and post-holes, the former being 0.8–1.7 m (2½–5½ ft) wide with V-shaped or rounded bottoms.[118] These clearly formed part of an extensive system of enclosures of varying sizes on a markedly different alignment to the High Street frontages. Further details were recorded in 1983 during the extensive geophysical surveys of the Bear Field,[119] while excavations here in 1983–4 identified a series of rectangular enclosures whose boundaries were defined by sequences of ditches and gullies.[120] At least three phases of activity were recognized, the earliest gullies belonging to the mid second century with subsequent modifications extending into the fourth. Few earlier features were recorded. Within the enclosures, activity had clearly been intense, but no traces of flooring had survived, suggesting that any buildings originally stood on horizontal timbers laid directly on the ground. Not enough is yet known about these enclosures to define their full extent, but they clearly form a significant element along

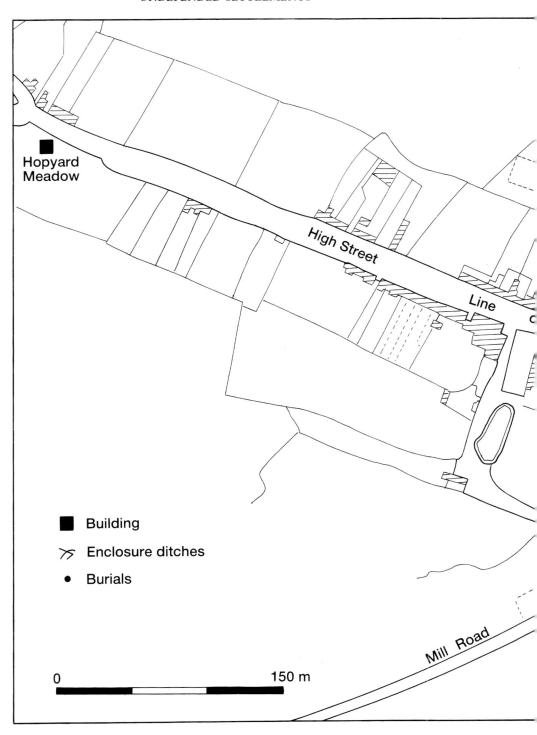

101 Cowbridge (*after Parkhouse*)

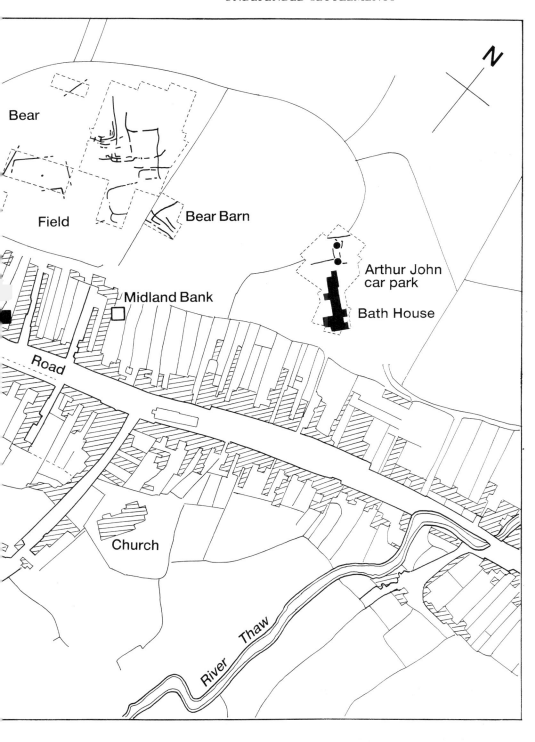

Bear
Field
Bear Barn
Midland Bank
Arthur John car park
Bath House
Road
Church
River Thaw

the northern fringe of the settlement west of the bath-house, whose alignment they share.

One further element in this northern area is the substantial bath-house located in the Arthur John car park (see fig. 5G), beyond the postulated line of the fort's north-eastern defences.[121] It was apparently in use for only some 20 years, being abandoned *c.* AD 120 because of drainage problems. Originally it comprised a row of five rooms with a sixth projecting on its eastern side, but during construction or slightly later a two-roomed furnace was added on the north and a second projecting room on the west. Later an enlarged furnace area replaced its two-roomed predecessor, while four more rooms were added on the south. This building has obvious military or official parallels in terms of both its plan and its date. It also incorporated roof tiles made under the auspices of the second legion based at Caerleon, thereby strengthening the case for a fort or a specialist concern for which a bath-house was a necessary adjunct.

Our understanding of the site's everyday life is still rather sketchy despite assertions that it was an important local centre. None of the excavated buildings has revealed distinctive debris and the most interesting evidence concerns the metal-working activities recorded in the Bear Barn and Bear Field areas. Large quantities of iron slag were first noted under the Bear Barn, both in the underlying clay and stone layer and in the fills of the underlying gullies.[122] Comparable evidence also came from the Bear Field, the topsoil alone containing 61 kg (134 lb) of slag in one 10 m (33 ft) square.[123] None of the material was found *in situ* and no furnaces or hearths have been identified, such that the exact nature and extent of the metal-working still remain to be defined. Most of the slag probably derives from smithing, but some haematite and probable tap slag might also suggest smelting. Judging from the context of the slag and related finds, activity apparently began in the mid second century and lasted through to the fourth. Much remains to be clarified about this aspect of the settlement.

Nothing is known about the site's religious life, while only a handful of isolated burials have been located.[124] The discovery of a probable funerary lion must, however, indicate at least one tomb of some pretension nearby.[125] Equally little is known of the settlement's later occupation

despite the recovery of fourth-century pottery and coins. Current evidence suggests a more obviously agriculturally-based site, especially the probable corn-driers close to the robbed-out baths and in the latest enclosures in the Bear Field.[126] Occupation certainly continued well into the late fourth century in the latter, which is in marked contrast to the High Street frontages where late buildings have proved difficult to identify. Only one possible structure has been excavated to the west in Hopyard Meadow, but this may lie in a rural context and have little bearing on the fate of Cowbridge.[127] It was represented by several cobble-filled trenches post-dating a number of late third- to mid fourth-century ditches, but was otherwise undated. Not surprisingly, there is little evidence to indicate how long occupation lasted into the fifth century.

Hibaldstow (figs. 102 and 103)

The Roman settlement at Hibaldstow lies on both sides of Ermine Street, a little over 30 km (19 miles) north of Lincoln, where the road crosses a stream at the bottom of a valley. A road eastwards may exist to link the settlement with North Kelsey and Caistor. The site does not appear to have been much known before the 1930s,[128] except for a passing reference in the early eighteenth century to the foundations of many buildings in the fields alongside the road. But the burying of a gas pipeline and the widening of the modern road, which is here on the same alignment as Ermine Street, led to excavations in the 1970s on both its east and its west sides respectively.[129] The settlement appears to extend for some 800 m (2600 ft) along the road, but only selected areas on its western length could be properly sampled.

Hibaldstow has been described as the site of a possible early fort, on the strength of some mid first-century finds, although none is specifically military in character. There is no evidence for an Iron-Age settlement, and the earliest pottery from the area is late first century in date. Again, therefore, as at Ashton (p. 279), no sound reason can yet be put forward to explain the foundation of a settlement here at that precise time.

Even though occupation began in the late first

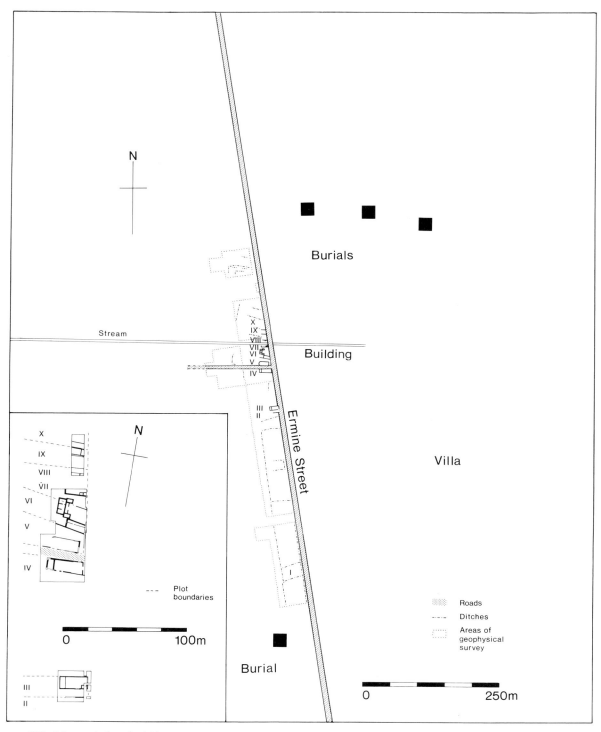

102 Hibaldstow (*after Smith*)

century little is known of the early settlement. One of the first effects of the construction of Ermine Street was to dam the stream, which formed a pond against the agger; surprisingly no drain was inserted. Vegetable matter preserved in the waterlogged levels, which were ultimately built upon, shows that the landscape around the settlement was open grassland, carrying perhaps a hint of Iron-Age clearances. Traces of timber buildings belonging to the early settlement have been discovered but no building plans have been obtained.

Of most significance though in the early period is the setting out of what a modern estate agent would call 'building plots'.[130] The entire length of the settlement west of Ermine Street seems to have been so treated, although not all the plots were of the same size or orientation; the angle which some made to the road may have been dictated by either the lie of the ground or the fact that not all plots were laid out simultaneously. The plots were bounded by ditches, and in one or two places gaps were left between adjacent plots to allow access to the rear; some were later metalled as side-streets or lanes. These plots say much about the way in which the settlement could have started. If all were contemporary, some form of over-riding authority can be postulated, or at least some form of owners', or perhaps tenants', co-operative, which could make decisions on the size and position of each parcel of land; much would depend on who, if anyone, owned the land beforehand, which it is now impossible to say. Three villas are known to the east and north-east of the site; there is also the 'winged-corridor building' which eventually emerged in the late third century, set well back from the west side of Ermine Street and in a most desirable position just south of the stream. Any of them, more especially the first three, could have been the residence of a large landowner. If, in contrast, the land was not previously owned by anyone, then presumably a prospective settler could stake out his own claim. But if this had been the means of allocation, a greater degree of irregularity might be expected. Consequently it is probably best to postulate the existence of at least a measure of authority or prior ownership. Once established, though, economic forces came into being and plots could have been bought or sold. Indeed, the winged-corridor house men-

tioned above, though modest, must reflect the development of personal wealth on the part of the owner; it lay astride two plots which must have been amalgamated by either purchase or inheritance. The house had been preceded by an aisled barn or farmhouse of conventional form, and the progression from this to a winged-corridor house can likewise be seen as part of the success achieved by the owner.[131]

Apart from this single more sophisticated house, most of the others follow the accepted pattern and were ordinary strip buildings, placed in their plots, and with the earliest dating to the late second century. Several phases of rebuilding or reconditioning were observed, which prolonged the life of most into the fourth century. At least two then became derelict, only to be reoccupied or rebuilt in timber. A zoomorphic buckle and a silver spoon,[132] dated to the late fourth century, came from one building.

There was little to indicate the specific functions of these structures, although their plans would indicate shops or workshops. Two contained ovens, one of which was suggested by the excavator to be a corn-drier. Burnt seed grains recovered from them show that spelt was being cultivated, as well as rye, oats, hulled six-row barley and the Celtic bean. Other seeds recovered represent the normal flora of the neighbourhood, such as elder, sunspurge, corn cockle, speedwell and birdsfoot trefoil, all species which can be found in north Lincolnshire today.[133] Surprisingly, no evidence of metallurgical activity was found, despite its frequency on other sites. It is a reminder that, in the Roman world, the workshops of artificers of the same kind were often grouped together in the same quarter of a town or village, which may not yet have been located at Hibaldstow.

One building in this group (V,2) was exceptional in that its west end was formed by a flattened apse; its frontage also lay further back from Ermine Street, and was at first built of timber. In a second phase the eastern end was rebuilt in masonry, nearer to the road, and most of the building was divided longitudinally. Several stone-built ovens were also found, as well as a small copper-alloy statue of Jupiter in a layer of rubble outside the building to the north.[134]

The building material for the masonry structures seems to have come from a quarry, which is

103 Hibaldstow, looking north with part of the
roadside excavations visible north of centre
(*Cambridge University Collection: copyright
reserved*)

still marked by a depression in a field surface south-west of the settlement. Exceptionally, though, roofing slates of coal-measures sandstone are more likely to have come from Yorkshire, together with coal found in one of the houses; coal was also identified as coming from the Durham fields.

A number of burials were encountered at the southern end of the settlement, at the back end of the building plot described above, and may be part of a larger cemetery.[135] Their position might either indicate a change of land-use, or else, as at Ashton (p. 281), the non-observance of the law which forbade burial within the boundaries of a town or fort. It might also reflect on the status of these roadside settlements which, perhaps, were not deemed to be in the urban hierarchy. If, though, they were classed as *vici*, there must have been an essential difference between the *vici* which were civitas capitals, where the burial laws were normally applied, and those which were not, such as Hibaldstow. Other inhumation and cremation burials have been reported from fields north-east of the settlement and presumably mark the site of another cemetery.[136]

Late pottery and coins of the House of Theodosius indicate the survival of the settlement to the late fourth or possibly early fifth century, although by then there is some evidence of a decline in housing standards. Beyond that it is not possible to go.

Sapperton (fig. 104)

The small unfortified town at Sapperton is situated beside the main road which runs north from Bourne to join Ermine Street at Ancaster. Building debris and a scatter of other finds cover an area of about 4 ha (10 acres). The site has been recognized as Roman for at least 150 years, and observations made in the 1930s recorded a possible hypocaust of brick. The Roman road is said to be marked by the line of the modern lane, known locally as Long Hollow, though the settlement seemingly lies along a parallel road about 100 m (327 ft) to its west. An open mind should be kept on the matter, however, since Long Hollow could have been formed as a post-Roman diversion round ruinous buildings and collapsed debris on the original main road

through Sapperton. Another road is thought to run east-west to join up salt-making sites in the Fens with Leicestershire. A little distance east of the centre of the settlement is a villa, now ploughed out, which once had mosaics and hypocausts; another villa may lie to the west.

Excavations and fieldwork have now been carried out at Sapperton annually since the early 1970s.[137] In consequence, a large area west of the main street has been cleared to show the plans of a number of late Roman strip buildings set with their long axes at right angles to the street, in the manner common to shops and workshops. A somewhat smaller area has been examined in depth to find out as much as possible about the origins of the settlement. All the structures appear to lie within a western boundary ditch.

The earliest activity on the site was the digging of a number of large quarry pits for gravel, presumably to supply the aggregate for the first road, which, unusually, was constructed of concrete; no accurate date can yet be given to it, although it is almost certainly first century. The pits had been filled by *c*. AD 100 with material which included Iron-Age pottery and two Corieltavian coins.[138] It seems reasonable to suppose, therefore, that the origins of the Roman settlement lay in a local Iron-Age community, although no structures of this period have yet been located. Iron-working was introduced to the area soon after the filling of the pits, with quantities of iron slag being deposited on the west side of the street. The sites of these smithies are not yet known; nor is it known from where the iron-ore came, although it is distributed fairly widely throughout the Jurassic zone and occurs locally as limonite. Both smelting and forging slags have been identified. The first buildings in this area followed in Hadrian's principate, after a period of agricultural use; they seem to have been constructed of masonry as there was an abundance of local building stone, although half-timbering cannot be discounted.

The early to middle third century saw successive redevelopment of the buildings right across the area excavated. One, built of good quality masonry, was probably a smithy. Apart from several hearths, a scatter of iron slag and coal was found in the main workshop at the front of the building, while the room to the rear, with painted plaster walls and a plaster floor, served as the

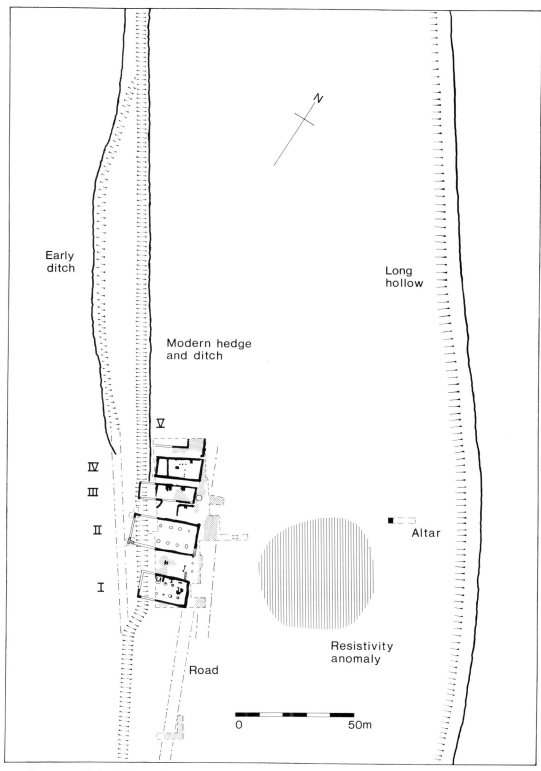

Early
ditch

Long
hollow

Modern hedge
and ditch

V

IV

III

II

Altar

I

Resistivity
anomaly

Road

0   50m

104 Sapperton (*after Simmons*)

living quarters.[139] These structures lasted until the early fourth century, when a more radical redevelopment took place. At the start a new street of cobbles was first laid, slightly east of its predecessor; the fronts of the new buildings encroached a little upon the line of the old street. Two of them were constructed as aisled buildings, and the positions and quantities of structural ironwork and window glass would imply half-timbered superstructures with, in two cases, glazed clerestories.[140] All were once more associated with hearths and ovens, which were situated in the fronts of the premises with the rear rooms again being used as living quarters; more painted plaster, some with architectural and geometric designs, was recovered from a shallow pit later dug through the floor of the living room in Building IV.[141]

Building V was more unusual, being separated from the street by a wide metalled courtyard or corridor, which also ran round its south side; towards the rear of the building the metalling was composed of iron slag and furnace waste, showing that smithing was still a profitable industry.[142] A curious feature was connected with Building III. This was a curving length of wall projecting south of the building to form part of an apse, in the north-eastern corner of which the burials of three very young infants had been interred; it is possible that this part of the building served as a shrine, though infant burials are not uncommon in Romano-British settlements, and four more came from the neighbouring building to the north.[143] Other objects of religious significance have been found, including an uninscribed and broken altar and a very rudely-carved stone figurine some 120 mm (4½ in) high. Another shrine or temple may have been situated near where the altar was found, to the east of the street; a large circular anomaly, nearly 50 m (165 ft) across, has been located here by a resistivity survey.[144]

Sapperton, therefore, has the characteristic plan, origins and chronology of many similar roadside settlements in Britain. Usually fairly compact in the vicinity of the main thoroughfares, these settlements tended to sprawl outwards to a greater or lesser extent, depending on the individual circumstances of each settlement; the degree of expansion, or lack of it, can probably be taken as a measure of its economic strength or weakness. But what is not yet known at Sapperton is the relationship of the two villas to each other and, together or individually, to the settlement lying between them. There is nothing to prevent the settlement from having been a *vicus* on one or other's private estate, as may be the case at Hibaldstow, or even Camerton.

There is a little evidence, in the form of a possible *grubenhaus* dug in the ruins of Building IV, for the decline of Sapperton.[145] Measuring 4 m (13 ft) long, 2.5 m (8 ft) wide and 0.3 m (1 ft) deep, it contained shells and animal bones and had a central hearth. A large corn-drier inserted into Building I in the late fourth century would indicate a continuing interest in food production.[146] A curious burial was also found inserted into the robber trench of one of the walls of Building V and so presumably post-Roman in date. Fragments of skull, pelvis and long-bones had been interred in a small stone-lined pit, with most other bones missing; it was thought to be a re-interment, but of what date is not known.[147]

Staines (fig. 105)

Tradition has long associated Staines with the site of Roman *Pontibus* mentioned in the Antonine Itinerary, but not until the nineteenth century did chance finds lend credence to this identification.[148] These even included a reference in 1880 to a bath-house and tessellated pavement. Here the matter rested until the pace of new development in the modern town necessitated salvage excavations in 1969 on the Barclays Bank site alongside High Street,[149] since when several sites have been examined. Those at Elmsleigh House and the Friends' Burial Ground have been published, but the rest remain only in interim form.[150] Even so, the results have added considerably to our understanding of the site's overall morphology and its development, though crucial questions still remain.

Occupation is focused principally on a gravel island east of the confluence of the Rivers Thames and Colne, along the line of the London to Silchester road roughly perpetuated by the modern High Street. It apparently stretches eastwards from the site of the presumed Roman bridge, at least as far as the Sweeps Ditch, where debris is known on the Mumford and Lobb site, if

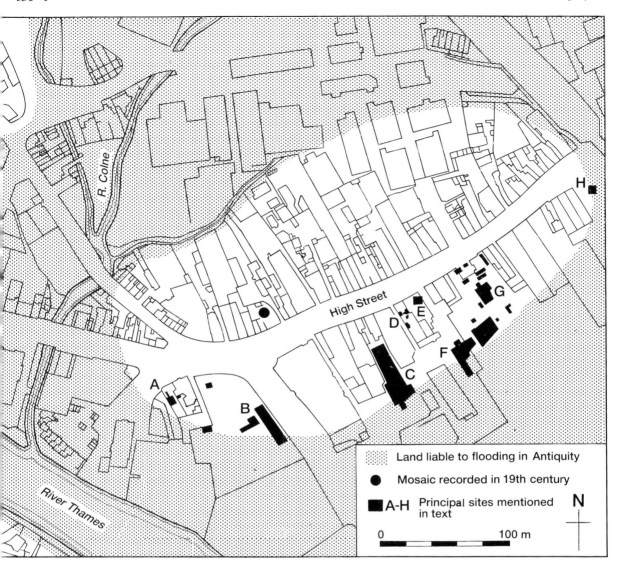

105 Staines (*after Bird and Jones*). Sites mentioned in text: **A** Market Square; **B** Johnson and Clark; **C** Friends' Burial Ground; **D** National Westminster Bank; **E** Barclays Bank; **F** Elmsleigh House; **G** Central Area Development; **H** Mumford and Lobb

not further.[151] This island was surrounded in antiquity by either flowing water or marshland, which was always liable to flooding. Further gravel islands lay to the north-west across the Colne and to the west across the Thames, on both of which traces of Roman occupation have been located, despite the extremely limited nature of recent archaeological research.[152]

Nothing suggests Iron-Age settlement at Staines, despite its strategic potential as a crossing point over the Thames, nor is there any good evidence for early Roman activity, let alone a fort, in the wake of the military operations in the area. The earliest activity on the Barclays Bank site seems to have been associated with pottery of early Flavian (or at the earliest late Neronian) date and the only certain military find was an unstratified cheek-piece from a cavalry helmet of the later first or early second century.[153] A spread of burnt material on this site was also located on the nearby National Westminster Bank site in 1976, but the number of buildings involved and the date of their destruction was not determined.[154] Further pre-Flavian activity was recorded in 1978 in the Central Area Development in the form of a series of large quarry pits which were subsequently infilled during the course of the late first century.[155] Early activity has also been claimed on the Friends' Burial Ground, behind the High Street frontages, characterized by several pits and ditches associated with a gravel spread, but the dating seems to be too early given the published pottery evidence.[156]

This evidence is clearly not very extensive and is not diagnostically military, thus archaeology cannot sustain a fort origin for Staines despite the site's obvious potential. Whatever the status of these early levels, civilian settlement seems to have expanded markedly in the early to mid Flavian period and to have lasted through to the end of the second century when significant changes occurred. This is recognizable on several sites alongside the High Street frontages. A typical sequence was recorded in the Central Area Development, where the infilled quarry pits were replaced by a series of late first-/early second-century timber buildings thought to be shop-houses, some of which were replaced in their turn by further structures on flint and ragstone foundations in the mid second.[157] A somewhat similar sequence emerged on the National Westminster Bank site.[158] Excavation in the Friends' Burial Ground, towards the rear of the frontage plots, also clipped two phases of building activity, one dating to the later first century, the other to the mid second. Behind these lay various features suggesting specialized activities in an associated yard.[159] Further west in Market Square, towards the west end of the High Street island, the later first century was represented by two successive round houses and associated rubbish deposits, replaced in the second by a series of ovens and subsequently by a well.[160]

Cumulatively, this evidence indicates the growth of a fairly typical ribbon development with no side-streets or lanes being recorded in the excavated areas. A variety of buildings seem to have occupied the roadside frontages, some of them quite sophisticated, with associated properties to the rear. In the Central Area Development, the late first-century structures were timber-framed constructions with clay walls. Their second-century successors were more elaborate, however, one having plastered and painted walls with *opus signinum* and clay floors, the other a possible tessellated floor represented by *tesserae* fragments.[161] The 1985–6 excavations on the Johnson and Clark site, though primarily in the land behind the frontages, also recovered much painted plaster as well as *opus signinum* and *tesserae* cubes presumably from buildings alongside High Street.[162] Comparable evidence came from the Barclays Bank site, where the finds indicate a timber-framed structure with a tiled roof and wattle-and-daub walls surrounding floors of clay, chalk and gravel.[163] The associated wall plaster had been painted with a floral motif. This evidence suggests a surprising level of second-century prosperity.

The site's fortunes appear to have changed dramatically in the later second and third centuries. Buildings were evidently demolished or destroyed early in this period at various points along High Street, while intensified flooding affected the shoreline of the settlement. Certainly, no third-century occupation was located in the Central Area Development following the deliberate demolition of the second-century structures, while the building on the Barclays Bank site may have suffered a similar fate, though the evidence is admittedly fragmentary.[164] Further west, the Market Square site was also abandoned from the early third century onwards.[165] On the Friends' Burial Ground, a small ditched enclosure was apparently infilled in the third century, while a complicated flood sequence sealed earlier levels at the south end of the site, thus rendering it uninhabitable for the rest of the century at least.[166]

No convincing explanations have been advanced to account for these changes, which apparently involved considerable settlement contraction and the abandonment of occupied frontage plots. This phenomenon has been noted elsewhere in the south-east.[167] It is extremely unlikely that the whole site was abandoned, even though third-century contexts have proved difficult to identify. Even when occupation was resumed in the later third and fourth centuries, its nature and extent seem to have been very different. The evidence would suggest that it was much more dispersed and perhaps extended further than the core of the first- to second-century town. Fourth-century buildings have been identified in the Central Area Development and at Elmsleigh House.[168] The latter lay alongside a late gravel spread and were generally simple clay and timber structures surrounding clay floors with little evidence for romanization. This might reflect the changing fortunes of the settlement, though it has to be remembered that they were probably outbuildings in the backlands and that we know all too little about the late road frontages. Much, therefore, remains uncertain about the character of the third- and fourth-century occupation at Staines, which only detailed excavation can resolve.

Information about the site's everyday life is somewhat limited, though its economy in the later first and second centuries was reasonably healthy, judging from the range of imported continental material. Iron slag has been recorded in all the excavated areas, as for example in the Flavian to Hadrianic pit on the Friends' Burial Ground, but so far has not been found in association with any *in situ* hearths or furnaces.[169] Another specialized interest concerned with animal products may be represented by a cache of cow skulls in a second pit on the same site.[170] The situation in the later period is less clear, given the site's changed fortunes, though metal-working is still suggested by iron slag in a fourth-century pit on the Friends' Burial Ground.[171] The site's religious life is represented by various small finds, including a *Dea Nutrix* figurine, and probably also by the well on the Market Square site, which contained 17 complete dog skeletons suggestive of a ritual function.[172] Our understanding of the site's cemeteries is extremely limited, depending on a record of several groups of vessels on a site east of the town.[173]

The site's later history remains poorly known, though recent work has contributed in particular

to our understanding of the area behind the frontages. At Elmsleigh House, for instance, the latest building had probably been dismantled in the mid fourth century judging from the pottery in its beam slots; this evidence perhaps hints at further contraction or a change of land-use along the site's southern fringes.[174] During the later fourth/early fifth century, the whole area along the western and southern shores of the High Street island was progressively affected by episodes of major flooding, which must have hastened those changes already underway.[175] Elsewhere little is known about the late Roman levels. On several sites, including Market Square, the Central Area Development and the Friends' Burial Ground, a characteristic 'black soil' has been found paralleling that recorded at London and elsewhere.[176] This is never directly associated with any other features and so its exact interpretation and date present problems. On the Johnson and Clark site, at least, it had clearly accumulated over the latest Roman levels.[177]

The latest flood horizons across the southern fringes of the site progressively cut into an iron-panned clay layer which had accumulated along the shoreline.[178] The earliest deposits above this floodline contained a few sherds of late Roman pottery, but their rolled condition does not indicate occupation nearby. At a yet later date, the iron-panned clay was cut by a series of interrupted and intersecting gullies, interpreted as a flood defence, which have been traced over 120 m (390 ft) from the Johnson and Clark site on the west to the Central Area Development on the east. These gullies contained several rolled late Roman sherds as well as a quantity of Saxon grass/chaff-tempered wares, though unfortunately none can be closely dated within the early to mid Saxon phase. Such pottery has been found right across the southern end of the town and in small quantities near the central High Street frontages but does not apparently spread westwards for any great distance. Some early Saxon occupation seems to be indicated by an early spearhead and several sherds of decorated pottery, but little is known about its character or extent.

The interpretation of this evidence depends ultimately on the elucidation of the late Roman activity at the site and the precise dating of the Saxon grass/chaff-tempered wares currently assigned to the fifth to ninth centuries. One line of reasoning argues for sub-Roman continuity alongside a growing Saxon presence; another argues for a marked decline followed by a Saxon reoccupation in or after the fifth century. Only extensive excavation can clarify the issue, though the answer may lie somewhere in between.[179] Staines' survival and importance inevitably depended upon several factors not least the level of political stability on either side of the Thames and the importance of the river crossing: in times of relative peace the site could flourish, in times of stress it would decline. Episodes of flooding would no doubt contribute to the problems. This model could account for the vagaries of the archaeological record throughout the fifth to eleventh centuries, though at present it remains essentially speculative.

Tiddington (figs. 106 and 107)

Serious excavations began at Tiddington in the 1920s, revealing a large cemetery in 1923–4, a smaller burial area in 1925 and an apparent 'industrial' zone in 1926–7. Only the last of these was published in detail,[180] while further unpublished discoveries were made in the 1930s.[181] Little else was recorded until the late 1970s, when redevelopment threatened several areas including the 4 ha (10 acre) field close to the 1925–7 sites. This necessitated large-scale excavations between 1980 and 1983, preceded in one case by extensive geophysical survey.[182] Though only a relatively small area has been examined, a coherent picture has emerged of an extensive settlement with a mixed agricultural and light industrial base typical of many sites in the grey area between small towns and villages.

The site apparently developed alongside a trackway running north-east to south-west along the south bank of the River Avon, close to an early ford. The 1980–1 excavation revealed middle Iron-Age occupation, probably from scattered farmsteads, followed much later by a first-century AD round house with associated rubbish pits and drainage or boundary gullies at the north end of the site.[183] First-century ditched enclosures and round houses were also recorded in 1982.[184] These enclosures had seen long usage, being re-cut several times, and were associated

with at least one Iron-Age coin and with pottery of native 'Belgic type' belonging to the early to mid or late first century. The chronology of this early occupation needs clarification, because it could represent either a pre-conquest settlement or an early *vicus* outside a fort. The former seems more likely, given the apparent lifespan of the enclosures, the associated pottery assemblage and the absence of any obvious military features or finds. A pre-conquest origin would explain the short-lived military site at Orchard Hill Farm, 3 km (2 miles) south of Tiddington, the early army presence being designed to supervise an existing centre and one of several convenient fords.[185]

Whatever its origin, the site expanded in the later first and early second centuries, despite being bypassed by the main road from Alcester to the Fosse Way, which crossed the river *c.* 2.4 km (1.5 miles) downstream. Excavations have revealed several internal streets and lanes running irregularly to the north and south of the presumed trackway along the river, thought to follow the line of the modern Tiddington Road. A roadway defined by ditches and extensive rubbish pits ran eastwards across the 1980–1 site,[186] being traced again further east in 1983,[187] where a gap 10 m (33 ft) wide between the adjacent features marked its course. A more complicated arrangement of streets defined by ditches was located in 1982,[188] including a prominent north-south street which apparently joined an east-west roadway across the north end of the site; a third street ran north-west to south-east in a natural hollow across the centre. This had been widened in the mid second century with a gravel surface, which became heavily rutted. Alongside these streets lay several ditched enclosures containing relatively simple domestic and agricultural buildings, rubbish pits, corn-driers and wells, demonstrating clearly that the excavated areas were never intensively built-up during the life of the settlement. This occupation has been thought to extend over *c.* 22 ha (54 acres), being defined on the north by the river floodplain, on the west by the 1923–4 cemetery and on the south-east by further burials and the fourth-century ditch, but this may be an over-estimate.[189]

The third century onwards saw some interesting contrasts in the character of the occupied areas.[190] At the south-east corner, occupation expanded southwards across the 1980–1 site as

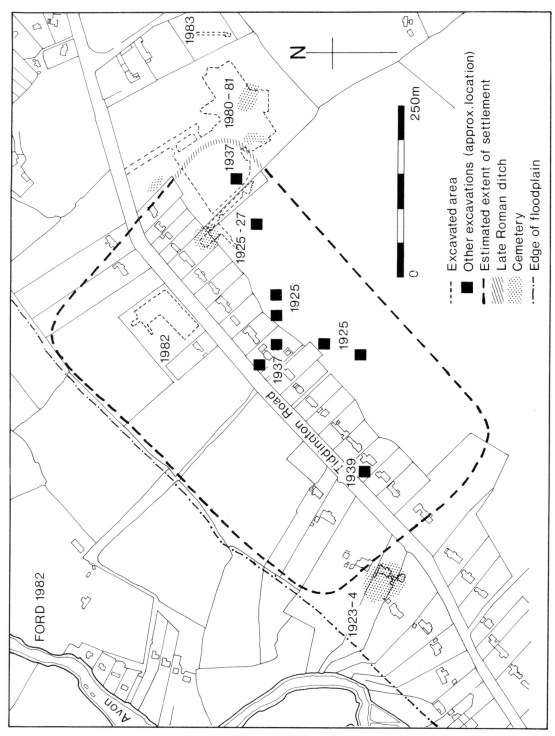

106 Tiddington (*after Palmer*)

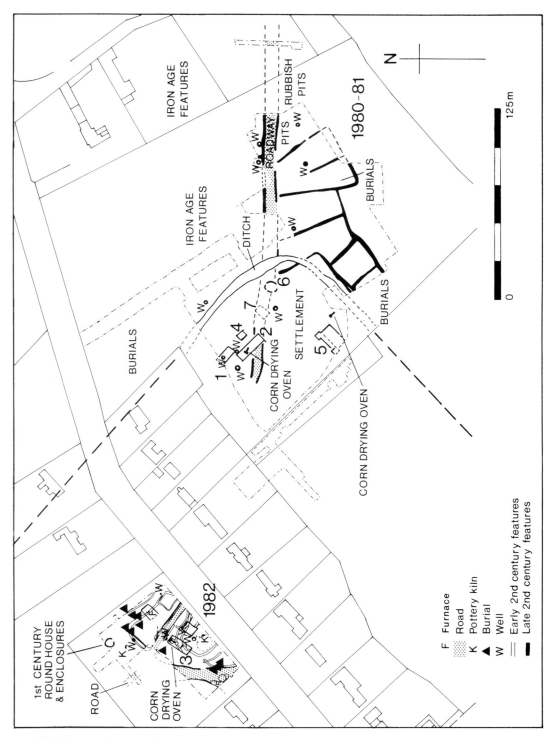

107 Tiddington, the area of the 1980–3 excavations
(*after Palmer*)

new buildings, pits and wells demonstrate. In contrast, while some of the streets were maintained on the 1982 site, the latest buildings belonged to the early third century, while the fourth century was represented only by scattered burials. The mid to late fourth century also saw significant changes on the 1980–1 site, where a large ditch up to 7 m (23 ft) wide and 2 m (6½ ft) deep was dug along and through the southern and eastern sides of the occupied area, actually cutting the line of the earlier roadway.[191] It was probably defensive in character, presumably with an internal bank, though its irregular width and depth make it difficult to include in the known sequences of provincial defence.

Excavated buildings are all of simple type and design, the majority of timber and thatch construction within individual plots.[192] Examples include, on the 1980–1 site, the structure set in beam trenches and the building on post-bases, measuring 11 by 5.5 m (36 by 18 ft) and 21 by 7 m (69 by 23 ft) respectively, and in the 1982 area, the post-built structure 15 m (49 ft) long by 6 m (20 ft) wide. Stone-built structures are rare but include, on the 1980–1 site, a granary 5 m (16 ft) square on rough stone footings and an aisled building measuring 15 by 11 m (49 by 36 ft) with square projecting rooms along its north-western side, resembling a humble winged-corridor house.

everyday life. Its agricultural basis is represented by at least five corn-drying ovens and by the remains of a field system south-east of the site, including several small paddocks containing wells alongside the 1980–1 roadway.[193] Several buildings also belong in this sphere: one complex on the 1980–1 site included a possible stockade and a rubble raft incorporating a stone-lined drain, both presumably for animals, while one of the 1982 structures contained a small bread oven and a corn-drying oven.[194] There is also evidence

for limited specialization, including an iron-smithing hearth excavated in 1927, to which can be added an abundance of smithing slag, traces of bronze-working, small-scale bone- and antler-working and two late first- to early second-century pottery kilns producing coarse-ware jars on the 1982 site.[195] Contrary to the interpretation of the 1925–7 excavations, there is little to indicate large-scale industrial activities; indeed the so-called tile-kiln has been reinterpreted as a corn-drier, while the lead-working evidence has been rejected as unconvincing.[196] Such small-scale specialization alongside a predominantly agricultural population is fairly typical of sites at the small town/village threshold.

Other everyday aspects are poorly known. One large cemetery of some 220 graves, including several cremations, was examined in 1923–4 at the site's western end, but the details remain unpublished,[197] while scattered burials have been noted elsewhere. Ten burials were located in 1925 near the 'industrial' sector; 35 burials, including 6 cremations, were found in the 1980–1 excavations; and some 12 burials were noted in 1982 singly or in clusters by the internal streets.[198] This apparent lack of organization in certain areas contrasts markedly with the late cemeteries at other small towns and may be another indicator of the site's less well developed character.

Recent excavations have done little to clarify how long occupation was maintained into the fifth century and beyond. An early Saxon presence in the vicinity is attested by cemeteries at Bidford and Bridgetown, but their relationship, if any, to the Tiddington settlement remains uncertain.[199] By the sixth century, the focus of activity had probably moved downstream to Bridgetown and thence to Stratford itself, by which time little will have remained at the original Romano-British nucleus.

THIRTEEN
CHANGE AND CONTINUITY

In most small towns, the second century had been one of expansion, though there had been exceptions to this trend late in the century, most notably in the specialized industrial sites of the north-west. What followed in the third and fourth centuries presents some interesting contrasts, as some towns experienced a period of change, if not decline, while others continued to grow.

Evidence for contraction or decline in the level of third-century occupation has been noted in several small towns, despite the well-known difficulty of dating third-century deposits. At Staines, for instance, flooding certainly led to the abandonment of previously-occupied land along the southern fringes of the site in the half century or so after AD 220, though a marked decline in the settlement's prosperity has also been noted in several areas much closer to the High Street axis.[1] At Kelvedon too, recent if limited excavations have suggested that there was a significant decline in activity in the later third century, especially along the southern edges previously occupied by the defences; at the same time, the original road through the centre of the site had clearly fallen into disuse, though all could be explained by a shift in occupation northwards to the line of the modern High Street, where so far excavation has been limited.[2] The demise of the earthwork defences at Kelvedon, however, and also of those at Chelmsford, where neither were apparently replaced by a stone wall, might be seen to indicate a change in their respective official roles, which must have had repercussions in other functional spheres.[3]

Late third-century changes have also been suggested at Worcester, on the basis of third- and fourth-century pottery and coin evidence, but most of this has come from sites away from the core of the town and may thus not be representative.[4] There can be no doubt, however, that occupation had ceased in at least one part of the central area of Tiddington in the third century, even though some of the internal streets were still being maintained.[5] These examples of small towns are generally too scattered to identify specific patterns, but they reinforce the need for much more detailed research so as to develop a better understanding of expansion and contraction through time both at individual sites and at the regional level.

Change is to be expected, of course, in the third century, reflecting the wider upheavals which affected the Roman west as well as more localized provincial trends, but not all Romano-British small towns present such a gloomy picture. The evidence tends to be somewhat limited and difficult to interpret for individual sites, but taken altogether it indicates that the sites located most advantageously benefited from an expansion of their economic role, so that they came to play a progressively more important part in servicing their immediate hinterlands; some may even have become civitas capitals.

Public and religious buildings continued to be maintained at a number of sites and in several cases they were improved and enlarged. Without doubt the best examples are the late second- and third-century additions to the temple and bathing complex at Bath,[6] but they do not stand in isolation. Significant modifications were now made as well to the temple and its precinct at Harlow[7] and perhaps also to two temples at Springhead (Nos. 1 and 2), though the chronology at this latter site needs considerable clarification.[8] Likewise, the temple at Frilford was enlarged in the late third or early fourth century by the addition of at least a western annexe.[9] The third century also saw the construction of new official buildings, though their impact on the civilian occupation and on the status of the sites involved is hard to define. These include the large stone 'basilica' at Godmanchester, constructed in the early third century south-east of the existing *mansio* complex,[10] the two villas in the Bays Meadow area at Droitwich[11] and the long stone 'storehouse' excavated at Alcester, which apparently replaced a timber predecessor in the later third century.[12]

These activities in the public, religious or official spheres can, more importantly, be paralleled by continued third-century economic prosperity as well as expansion, making it clear that urban life in many small towns was far from moribund. At Godmanchester, for instance, the number of known workshops apparently increased in the third century and these may have been associated with the proposed market-place.[13] A comparable expansion can be seen late in the century at Camerton,[14] reflecting the economic growth of the Bath region, and at several other sites including Great Chesterford[15] and Hibaldstow,[16] all of which enjoyed some degree of economic success. Considerable extra-mural occupation is well attested at Water Newton, both at Kate's Cabin south of the walled area and in Normangate Field north of the river,[17] reflecting the expansion of the pottery industry and the prosperity of the site and its immediate hinterland. The third century also witnessed the replacement of existing timber structures by masonry buildings or by timber-frames set on stone foundations at many sites including Alcester, Catterick and Ilchester.[18]

Cumulatively this evidence suggests that the third-century changes among the small towns caused the differentiation of the more important economic centres from their lesser counterparts, which may not have fared so well. This culminated, during the later third and fourth centuries, in a period of considerable prosperity in these small towns, reflecting their enhanced importance in the marketing hierarchy alongside the major centres. It must be remembered that this was also an era of significant developments in the countryside, which saw the emergence of numerous wealthy villas and the widespread appearance of mosaics.[19] The marked concentrations around Bath, Ilchester and Water Newton are examples.

In the north, a relatively peaceful time was enjoyed in the wake of the Severan campaigns and the subsequent military reforms. Not only did many of the northern military *vici* flourish outside their respective forts, but so too did the larger urban settlements at Corbridge and Carlisle, the latter perhaps as the civitas capital of the Carvetii.[20] At Catterick too, evidence for expansion is visible on the aerial photographs in the form of a new street layout to the east of Dere Street, while buildings are also known to have stretched along the road north of the river and as far south as Catterick village.[21]

During the third century, there was also an increasing concern about the provision of defences at the small towns. This was often no more than a simple strengthening of existing earthwork fortifications, but it was also now directed at a much wider range of hitherto undefended sites.[22] Comparable trends are evident among the provincial cities and, from the later third century, among the urban centres of Gaul and Germany in the aftermath of the barbarian invasions. Early stone defences were apparently provided at new sites like Alchester,[23] Ancaster[24] and Water Newton,[25] where earthworks are currently unknown, but the most significant burst of activity seems to have come in the later part of the third and the early part of the fourth centuries, though absolute precision is impossible on current evidence.

Large areas continued to be enclosed at a handful of sites such as Great Chesterford,[26] but the most distinctive trend saw the provision at several towns of small strongpoint defences; these were usually constructed at the hearts of long straggling roadside developments and, where evidence is available, often seem to be characteristically devoid of internal structural evidence. Examples include the well-known sites in the west Midlands, as for example at Mancetter and Wall,[27] but other roadside sites were probably involved, such as Brough-on-Fosse and Dorn (p. 35). Their location at almost standard intervals along the main roads would seem to indicate an official rather than a civilian function and suggests that the late third century was a significant period of change in the role of many roadside sites. It remains difficult, however, to define the impact of these changes on other aspects of the civilian occupation, given the poor quality of most of the excavated evidence.

Although the later history of the cities has been the subject of much debate,[28] that of the small towns has received considerably less attention. This is hardly surprising, considering the character of much of our late evidence. The fourth century is generally easier to handle, information being both relatively more abundant and usually more readily datable, whereas the fifth century onwards is much less simple, with convincing trends absent at all but a handful of sites.

The process of fortification already mentioned continued well into the fourth century, when more towns were fortified for the first time. They include the contemporary walls and external towers at Caistor[29] and Horncastle[30] on the Lincolnshire Wolds, the latter somewhat to the north of the actual settlement. Both were small, conforming to the strongpoint type of defence, and both were presumably concerned with official matters. A new circuit with a contemporary wall and external towers was also built at Mildenhall on a slightly different alignment to its earthwork predecessor.[31] Stone walls may also have been added at this time to existing earthworks at other sites, although they remain undated.

The addition of external towers to urban walls in the fourth century is a well-attested phenomenon, but so far only a select number of small towns are known to have been involved. They include a string of sites along the eastern side of the province running from Ancaster southwards to Godmanchester via Great Casterton and Water Newton.[32] Their location at important river crossings on the main north road from London must surely hint at official thinking behind their selection. Any comparable system in the west is far less clear but certainly includes the towers at Kenchester.[33] The general pattern is further reinforced by comparable developments at the provincial cities. They are usually assigned to a date in or after the mid fourth century, though there is a considerable amount of debate over their precise context.[34] Their presence might indicate a garrison of some form, though concrete evidence for this has proved very elusive (p. 36).

By their nature these defences belong in an official context. They do not, therefore, tell us much about the equally important civilian dimension at individual small towns. Whatever their individual fates, the fourth century is normally represented as a period of relative prosperity in town and country, despite the upheavals caused by the events of the AD 360s and their aftermath. Although this might be true for those small towns providing a range of official and socio-economic services, evidence from several others suggests that the winds of change may have been appearing at variable dates throughout the century and generally gathering pace in the later years.

Several defended sites apparently contracted in the fourth century, since inhumation cemeteries developed in previously occupied areas outside the walls. This has already been established at Ancaster,[35] Godmanchester[36] and Great Chesterford,[37] though we remain uncertain as to whether it was accompanied by increased internal activity. At Ilchester, likewise, former properties in the suburbs alongside the main roads were used for burials,[38] while at Water Newton a fourth-century *mausoleum* in Normangate Field indicates a corresponding change of land-use.[39] Several of the smaller strongpoint defences also appear surprisingly empty, even allowing for later disturbances to the uppermost archaeological deposits. This was certainly the case at Margidunum, and seems also to be true of sites like Caistor, Horncastle, Mancetter and Wall (p. 31).

At yet other sites, previously built-up areas both official and civilian ceased to be occupied during the fourth century. In the former context, much of the *mansio* complex at Godmanchester was destroyed by fire *c.* AD 300, after which it was not rebuilt, and the site remained vacant.[40] This fire also seems to have interrupted work on the defences. In a civilian context, various examples have been recognized. At Chelmsford, for instance, Site S became part of an open enclosure in the fourth century, following the demolition of earlier structures,[41] while at Braintree occupation ceased in the excavated site alongside the Braughing road *c.* AD 360–70.[42] Likewise the excavated area at Scole was abandoned in the fourth century.[43] At Braughing, too, late occupation debris is fairly restricted, though intensive where it has been recorded.[44] It is difficult to assess the full significance of such open areas without more extensive excavation, but a declining population seems to have led to a process of intermittent contraction.

At several small towns, excavation has revealed the demise of probable focal structures, not infrequently temples, perhaps reflecting not only a change in religious attitudes but also a decline in upkeep and importance. The clearest example is at Bath, where the temple of Sulis Minerva and its precinct were certainly in decline by the mid fourth century,[45] while a comparable trend has also been recognized at Braughing.[46] Here the possible double temple on Wickham Hill fell into ruin in the later part of the century, though even before that, the associated road had apparently ceased to be used, while the surrounding land was covered with debris from nearby buildings. Similarly the temple at Harlow was systematically dismantled in the later fourth century,[47] while at Springhead, a thick layer of slag and iron fragments over part of the floor of Temple 1 must surely indicate its use by a blacksmith some time after AD 341.[48]

Some small towns apparently experienced a change of emphasis, with an increasing military presence after the AD 360s. This is clearest at Catterick, where part of the central area was seemingly converted for military use.[49] In the northern extra-mural suburb, this is reflected by increased civilian activity presumably linked to the expulsion of people from their houses inside the town. The recognition of other sites housing late garrisons has proved difficult but one possibility is Dorchester-on-Thames, where military metalwork and the high level of Theodosian coinage may be indicative.[50] Such a military presence will inevitably have been disruptive for the resident population, who might have been dispossessed in the process, but it must also have provided an important economic stimulus for those in a position to benefit. All these trends could be multiplied to demonstrate the changing fortunes within fourth-century small towns, but it would be dangerous to overemphasize decline before the end of this century as most sites apparently survived in some form into the fifth century.

The question of subsequent continuity and decline, following the traditional 'end' of Roman Britain in AD 410, is difficult to reconstruct in detail: large numbers of sites have produced no information of value for these latest periods (usually because of limited excavations, plough damage or later building disturbance), and only a handful of individual case-studies is available from which to generalize. The situation is further complicated by the regional and chronological variations in the speed and character of Germanic expansion and settlement and by the recurring argument over the possible continuity between Roman towns and their successors on the same sites. There has also been a tendency to seek simple monocausal explanations to cover all the available evidence, but not surprisingly they have not gained widespread acceptance. In reality, several different trends are recognizable among small towns, suggesting that the situation varied from region to region and site to site.

In the south and east, where Germanic settlement generally occurred at a relatively early date, several sites provide evidence for a foreign presence, perhaps indicating some integration with the resident population. This can occasionally be recognized by distinctive house types within the settlement itself or, less conclusively, by Germanic burials within or closely associated with late Roman cemeteries which apparently continued in use. Heybridge falls into the former category.[51] Excavation has revealed several *grubenhaüser* of early fifth-century date within a well-defined area of the small town, though interestingly occupation seems to have ceased around AD 450. Elsewhere these buildings tend to be somewhat later in date, as for example at Cambridge[52] and Neatham,[53] and so the case for continuity is much more difficult to argue.

Germanic burials have been located at several small towns, but they are rarely accompanied by any distinctive evidence for internal settlement. At Kelvedon, for instance, the late Roman cemetery north-east of the town contained several well-furnished fifth-century Anglo-Saxon burials, while the south cemetery clearly also continued in use.[54] A similar pattern may exist at Great Chesterford, where large fifth- and sixth-century cemeteries have been identified and where the late Roman cemetery between the town and the river probably overlapped with the Saxon cemetery to the north.[55] Early fifth-century cremations have been excavated at Ancaster close to a late Roman cemetery,[56] while later Roman and Germanic burials have been found together at Cambridge,[57] Frilford[58] and

Great Casterton.[59] Most of these sites have also produced pagan Saxon pottery, thereby strengthening the case for a continuing occupation, even if its extent and duration remain uncertain.

These examples seem reasonably well established, but elsewhere the evidence for an overlap between Roman and Saxon is far from conclusive. At Staines, for instance, a surprising amount of Saxon activity has been recorded, including a series of floodwater ditches along the southern end of the site, but the associated pottery cannot be accurately dated within the fifth to ninth centuries;[60] thus a direct overlap between the late Roman and Saxon sequences cannot as yet be conclusively demonstrated. Much the same problem arises at Dorchester-on-Thames, despite the site's self-evident importance in the late Roman period and in the mid seventh century.[61]

In contrast, at other small towns in the south and east, there is as yet little or no evidence for a Germanic presence during the fifth and sixth centuries. This is often matched by a relative scarcity of well stratified and dated archaeological sequences, thereby making it difficult to detect either the existence or the duration of any continuity. At Water Newton, for instance, while there is evidence to suggest a decline in the later fourth century in the northern and southern suburbs, we know next to nothing about the crucial intra-mural area where continuity is most likely.[62] This problem is further complicated by the fact that late Roman coinage probably continued to circulate into the mid fifth century, following the disruption of the regular supply of new coins from the imperial mints, which has made it difficult to define and date the latest pottery sequences with any absolute precision. Usually the only evidence is in the form of 'late Roman pottery' and 'coins of the House of Theodosius', which are little use as pointers to the length of fifth-century survival.

When stratified sequences have been identified, there is usually enough to suggest that activity continued into the fifth century, though it rarely seems to have been extensive. At Chelmsford, the octagonal temple lasted at least until AD 402, after which its portico was used as a dwelling and later still it was totally robbed.[63] Subsequent occupation was represented by a single structure containing an oven and several pits. Likewise at Godmanchester, excavation has revealed several rubbish pits and ditches of post-Roman date, but these can tell us little about how long occupation lasted.[64] Numerous other sites in the south and east clearly fall into this category, but few can provide any extra insights. Only the recovery of well stratified and closely datable sequences to match the oft-quoted example at Verulamium will help to resolve such issues.[65]

Further north and west, Germanic expansion was delayed until the sixth century, convenient markers being the battles of Dyrham (AD 577), in which Gloucester, Cirencester and Bath were reportedly taken, and Catraeth of c. AD 590. In these areas, small towns had a greater chance of survival for which the relevant evidence might be expected. As in the south and east, however, it is often difficult to interpret and to date, for reasons which have already been outlined. Some exceptions emerge nevertheless. At Carlisle, a particularly remarkable level of continuity seems to be indicated by the tradition that, in AD 685, St Cuthbert perambulated the walls and saw a still-running fountain.[66] Unfortunately this historical evidence has not yet been substantiated by excavation, which makes it difficult to assess.

Far better evidence has been forthcoming from the excavations at Bath, in particular those in the inner precinct to the east of the Temple of Sulis. The bathing establishment does not seem to have survived long into the fifth century because of increased flooding, but the reservoir and the precinct to the north clearly continued in use for some time.[67] This is represented by a deep accumulation of silts and cobbled surfaces probably spanning the fifth and sixth centuries. On top lay the tumbled remnants of the southern façade, which had collapsed along with the reservoir vault following a period of renewed demolition. This evidence hints at what might be expected elsewhere given adequate survival of the relevant deposits. An equally interesting sequence also emerged from the excavation of the west gate at Kenchester. Here there was evidence for a late phase of defensive reorganization, in which the original southern entrance was blocked to create a single-passage gateway.[68] Clearly there was still something worth defending into the fifth century, though little was recorded in the early excavation.

It would be dangerous, however, to try to

extrapolate from these few examples to the majority of northern and western sites. The excavations at Ilchester have revealed only very small quantities of fifth- and sixth-century material, suggesting a relatively sharp decline and ultimate desertion.[69] Likewise, at Catterick, occupation inside the defences continued into the fifth century after the evacuation of the late garrison, while a *grubenhaus* was found in the suburb north of the river dating to this period. Otherwise its extent and duration seem limited, and no clear link has been established with the Anglian burials around Catterick village.[70]

This post-Roman picture is clearly very complicated both for individual small towns and at a regional level; the dangers of seeking simple explanations for the pattern of continuity and decline are clearly emphasized. Part of the problem stems from the nature and limitations of our evidence; but it is also derived from a confusion in some archaeologists' minds over the different meanings of continuity. It can apply simply to the continued occupation of a small town site, without any reference to either its character or its intensity. Alternatively, it can refer to the continued existence of traditional socio-economic and institutional patterns along Roman or quasi-Roman lines. The former is easy to demonstrate, and all too often the evidence is evaluated solely in these terms. The latter is much more difficult to determine, not least because it is possible to question the character of several sites even as early as the fourth century.

At a general level, the fifth century saw the evacuation of the remaining military units of the Roman army and the removal of the official representation, which had been important at numerous sites and especially those involved in local administration. This effectively ended the system that had maintained a particular pattern of small town growth in Roman Britain and also had repercussions, alongside other factors, on their capacity to service both the local and the wider hinterland, except where the local inhabitants were capable of maintaining it for themselves. In such a situation, urban contraction was inevitable as sites became agriculturally more self-supporting and progressively less dependent on providing services for an external market. The character and speed of this decline still needs considerable clarification in both the fourth and the fifth centuries because it clearly varied markedly from site to site according to a range of conditions. It is perhaps arguable, however, that for most small towns at least, this process extinguished the last vestiges of urban continuity in its second sense; those which subsequently re-emerged at a later date probably did so because they were suitably placed to form part of an entirely new political and socio-economic framework.

FOURTEEN
THE FUTURE

This survey of some 54 out of 80 or more so-called 'small towns' in Roman Britain has, if anything, served to show just how lamentably ignorant we are about them. Of the walled sites, it can be claimed that we have a tolerable knowledge of some half-dozen, such as Corbridge and Catterick, and the same can probably be said of the unfortified variety, such as Wilderspool and Springhead. At the other end of the scale are places like Buxton and Caistor where almost total ignorance reigns. In between lie most of the sites where information is at best patchy and merely serves to heighten anticipation for the future.

As a class, the small towns remain one of the least well known of Romano-British sites. That it should be so is due to two reasons. Firstly, almost all our information, as with monuments of all periods, has been, since the war, and is still being, gained through rescue excavations. Selection of sites for investigation is therefore totally capricious and haphazard and is brought about not through the designs of archaeologists but by the intentions of property developers, quarry-owners, farmers and the like, to which an entirely unnecessary additional unknown factor is added through the whims of the state and allied archaeological services as to whether money will be available for any one threatened site. The second main reason arises from the condition of the sites. Most excavators who have worked on them will testify to the generally poor rate of structural survival, often caused by the ephemeral nature of many of the buildings and by the lack of deep, well-stratified deposits. Usually, but by no means always, only the most substantial masonry buildings have survived the attentions of both stone-robbers and the plough. As an example, a small town in the Midlands, excavated by one of the present writers, produced some depth of strati-fied deposits, but they formed unconnected 'islands' of superimposed floors surrounded by totally irregular, deep disturbances filled with modern cultivation soil; it was impossible either to relate the floors to any kind of structure or to identify clear robber trenches. A visit one day by the farmer and his wife solved all. 'Oh yes,' said the wife, addressing her husband, 'isn't this where you pulled out all those cart-loads of stone which we used to remake the yard?'

Probably, therefore, the first priority for the future is to protect as many remaining small towns as possible from any further depredations of agriculture and development. Chesterton-on-Fosse is an example where this has been attempted and where English Heritage has entered into a management agreement with the owner not to plough the area within or over the walls. Unfortunately the area covered by the agreement is not large enough and barely covers the ditches, let alone possible suburbs and cemeteries. That, it may be claimed, is one of the main points which this study has emphasized: it is essential to remember that these sites, whether walled or not, and almost without exception, frequently cover many hectares of land. Often there is a central core, which in some cases becomes fortified and which is usually surrounded by sprawling and low density suburbs interspersed with tracks, fields, enclosures and cemeteries. The sites will never be properly understood if these areas are ignored.

Once protected, if more is to be found out about small towns, a proper research strategy should be implemented,[1] not only to originate new investigations but also, where necessary, to clarify or increase the results of rescue excavations, which frequently leave more questions unanswered than there were at the start. The programme would probably be too large for an individual, or even a university department or museum, to undertake. But there is no good reason why a learned society, such as the Roman Society, or a body like the Urban History Centre at Leicester University, with its own small towns programme of research, should not sponsor a scheme similar to the Royal Archaeological Institute's research programme for castles. Failing that, why should not a number of like-minded archaeologists, interested in the problems of small towns, form an independent organization, possibly on the lines of the Medieval Village Research Group, which has now functioned with conspicuous success for several decades. Once established, the new organization could set about collecting an archive of information, propose a research strategy and sponsor detailed surveys. It might also instigate the long-term excavation of a single site, on the lines of the MVRG's researches at Wharram Percy. The site would need to be selected so as to be as representative as possible: a microcosm of all the problems associated with small towns. It would also need to have a good survival rate for structures and artifacts. Catterick (p. 111) would not be a bad choice. The survival of both masonry and timber buildings is good, as is that of metal, ceramic and other artifacts. A broad chronological knowledge has already been obtained for the site, although it is capable of refinement; there are also Iron-Age settlements nearby. It represents the transition from an early multi-period military to a civilian occupation and back again to military in the late fourth century; it has evidence for the sub-Roman and early Anglo-Saxon periods; and it has extensive suburbs stretching for a kilometre or more north and south of the walled area. It had a *mansio*, and inscriptions show governmental connections. Unusually for small towns, it also possessed a sophisticated water distribution system, which needs to be further examined and the aqueduct sought. It has produced evidence for domestic, industrial and religious buildings. Of additional interest is the possibility that more waterlogged areas may be found, with important implications for determining the local environment, as well as for detecting the evidence for industrial and economic activity involving organic materials. Other suitable sites with equal potential, but where less is already known, might

be Alchester (p. 97), Mildenhall (p. 148), or Sapperton (p. 304) where, indeed, the type of research excavation here being recommended has now been continuing for over a decade. As an extension to the 'one site' aim, a far more ambitious programme might be mounted to investigate a site in each of the categories represented in this book by Chapters 6–12. It might be objected that such a programme of research would be far too expensive to undertake in the present conditions of financial restraint. But there is no good reason why, if properly structured, it would not attract grants, which, on the lowest level of activity, might need to be no more than a few thousand pounds a year.

What then would be the basis for this programme of research? It can probably now be claimed that a good deal is known about origins. Most sites have been sufficiently examined to show the origin to be either an existing Iron-Age settlement or religious site or the establishment of a Roman military base, or both. Of more interest, therefore, is the handful of sites, such as Hibaldstow, where neither factor seems to be involved. Equally of interest is the investigation of early plot or property boundaries, as with those at Hibaldstow (p. 302) and Ashton (p. 279); all too few examples can be quoted. Now also moderately well recorded are the extents of many small towns, although chronologies still have to be established in most for the expansions or contractions which took place. Broad dates have been provided for the construction of fortifications, where they exist, although all are capable of refinement, which will only come with much more excavation, preferably not as sections cut across the lines, but as linear clearances along them. This method will also help to reveal subsidiary features such as repairs, junctions between building gangs, internal and external towers and gates and the sequence of ditch systems, about which all too little is known at most sites; in some places, such as Towcester (p. 156) the relationship of the wall to the rampart still needs clarification. Other ancillary features such as drains passing through defences would also repay study.

Careful attention should be paid to street junctions. It is abundantly clear that minor streets in many of the small towns were only constructed as and when they were required. The relationship of one street to another will be encapsulated in the junction; if chronologies can also be established, then these investigations would be one of the quickest ways to show the growth of a settlement. Streets in themselves are also worthy of study, not by a quick section across them, but by stripping lengths, which will show the use of different types of aggregate, the way in which it has been laid down, the amount of wear on any given surface and the frequency and extent of repair or patching. Apart from these factors, streets were also the most commonly used routes for drains and fresh-water pipelines or channels. Variations in the type of aggregate used can also reflect on other matters. Sometimes a change from gravel to stone rubble occurs at the same time as the construction of masonry walls; presumably masons' waste was being put to good use, and a chronological link between the construction of masonry defences and internal buildings, can, therefore, sometimes be established through the streets.

More excavation is required of 'official' buildings, which are notoriously difficult to identify. Only when sufficient have been examined and comparisons made between their plans will identification become increasingly certain. This stage is already being approached with *mansiones*, where there is usually a strong element of similarity between one plan and another, with certain features common to all. But conviction is still totally lacking over the interpretation of any building as a *mutatio*; ignorance still reigns here, as it does with other possible buildings with an 'official' function such as granaries, stores buildings and the like. Taxes in kind must have been stored somewhere, before distribution. Moreover, some small towns had officials such as *beneficiarii*, *stratores* and *regionarii*, yet their residences still have to be identified, if indeed they existed. Were they billeted on the townspeople; or did they use the local *mansio*?

This survey of small towns has shown up two other facts. In almost every place the earliest buildings were timber-framed, but there was an almost uniform transition to masonry in the second half of the second or early third century, with only a few exceptions. This not only must represent an architectural revolution but also hints at considerable social and economic changes. Yet no explanation for the transition and

its results has ever been attempted, despite it happening all over the province. The other fact is that by far the commonest plan of any structure to be found in all these sites is the shop or workshop strip building, whether of timber or masonry, aisled or not; internal arrangements may vary, possibly according to the use to which the building was put, and an internal analysis might be revealing. Following on, it becomes important to pay more attention to those buildings which do not conform to this plan and which may represent a whole range of functions varying from the growth of purely residential accommodation to religious uses. Another factor which can be seen in most small towns is the lower density of buildings when compared with the civitas capitals. In the latter the shops usually form continuous blocks of property with, at the most, only narrow alleys between them. In small towns, where it might be argued that land prices were not so high nor competition for the best sites so great, more generous allocations of space normally surrounded each building. Particular attention should, therefore, be paid to those examples where this does not happen, as it may be evidence for different economic circumstances.

Another surprising feature to emerge from this study is the large amount of metallurgical processing, especially iron-working, which was carried out on these sites. A careful assessment of, for example, the number of smithies in existence at any one town at any given time would probably show considerable spare capacity over and above satisfying the demands of the immediate local community. This would reflect on the connection between a small town and its surrounding rural areas, and the services which it could provide.

Those sites which have been identified as *burgi*, such as Wall and Mancetter and possibly Caistor and Horncastle, should also be investigated. As already outlined in the section dealing with this group (p. 235), their interiors are very different from the normal run of small towns; a tentative explanation has already been put forward (p. 245). It seems likely that most contemporary buildings inside these defences were timber-framed and probably of a very ephemeral character; additionally there might be fenced or hedged enclosures for horses or stock. In many cases the surviving remains of these structures will have been subjected to plough damage, if not to more drastic forms of destruction; earthworms will also have been active near the surface. The damage that the latter can cause is well-recorded,[2] but possibly not in so dramatic a form as in a late fourth-century building at Catterick. After this building had been demolished it was replaced by a timber-framed structure on a slightly different alignment; the timber uprights were supported on large blocks of stone placed directly on the superimposed sandy floors of the preceding building. Earthworms cannot, of course, work through solid stone, so that the only surviving patches of these floors were preserved under the stone blocks; elsewhere they had been reduced to a uniform black humic soil to a depth of 0.5 m ($1\frac{3}{4}$ ft) or more. A considerable reward must therefore await someone who can devise a method for distinguishing the original layers, post-holes, pits and beam slots from this apparently uniform mass of garden soil. In the meantime there would be much to be said in favour of stripping a good-sized area inside one of these *burgi* by the methods so successfully employed by Barker at Hen Domen and Wroxeter.[3]

Most excavations in small towns have tended to concentrate particularly on the fortified centres. More attention should be paid to the outlying buildings in the suburbs, where the best chance will be obtained of recording fluctuations in the prosperity of the whole settlement, since they represent the barometer areas, most likely to be occupied when the town thrives but abandoned when in decline. So far, also, few cemeteries have been identified or properly excavated. There are indications that the normal laws covering burial in the Roman world were not always being observed in some small towns; this may be significant in attempts to distinguish between the status of one settlement and another.

Lastly, more time and effort should be put into recreating the whole urban topography and environment. It is just not good enough now to make imagined reconstruction drawings of buildings, no matter how life-like they may look. Apparently it is theoretically possible to calculate the distributed weight of a building by examining the depths of the depressions made by the foundations in certain types of soil.[4] This should make estimates of a building's height much more accurate. It is also the present custom for reconstruction drawings to be clothed with fuzzy, look-alike vegetation, even in the best examples of the art; in reality all vegetation varies considerably in colour, size, form and texture. What is most urgently needed here is a series of representative waterlogged deposits, which may yield evidence for the local vegetational cover; no opportunity should be missed. So often we read in excavation reports that such-and-such a well could not be fully emptied because of the lack of time, money, suitable labour, proper pumps, safety equipment, or any number of other excuses. There is really no need for such lapses any longer; given adequate laboratory facilities, deposits of this nature contain the information for re-creating much of the original visual appearance of a site. The avowed aim of every excavator should be the total restoration of the visual appearance, the function, the people and their environment in every small town. At present much of this can only be wishful thinking, but goals never set are never achieved.

NOTES

All referencing in this volume conforms to the Harvard convention, with the following exceptions:

1. *J. Roman Studs.* and *Britannia* references throughout refer to the yearly 'Roman Britain in . . .' summaries published in the *Journal of Roman Studies* and *Britannia* respectively;
2. D.O.E. *Arch. Excavations* also relates to the yearly summaries published by the Department of the Environment (H.M.S.O.);
3. All ancient sources (e.g. Tacitus, Bede), which have been quoted in full at the relevant place.

Chapter 1 (pp. 1–6)

1. Todd 1970.
2. Rodwell and Rowley 1975.
3. Rivet 1975.
4. Crickmore 1984b.
5. Smith 1987.
6. Ordnance Survey 1956 and 1979.
7. For these sites, see Wacher 1975a.
8. *Ibid.*, 405–10; Rivet 1975, 113.
9. Leech 1982; Ellis 1984; Branigan 1985, 138 and fig. 34.
10. Specific references to individual sites have not been included in this introductory chapter because the detailed evidence is presented elsewhere.
11. The Latin name *Margidunum* is retained throughout the text because no acceptable English alternative has found favour.
12. Crickmore 1984b provides the best summary.
13. Initially by Rodwell 1975.
14. Useful summaries appear in St Joseph 1966; Wilson 1975; Frere and St Joseph 1983, 166–81.

15. Rivet 1975, 114.
16. Fulford 1982, 407–8.

Chapter 2 (pp. 7–14)

1. Cunliffe 1984.
2. See for example Hodder and Hassall 1971; Hodder 1972; 1975.
3. Webster 1966; Frere 1975.
4. Cunliffe 1976b; 1978, 285–6; 1985; Burnham 1979.
5. Cf. R.I.B. 899 (Old Carlisle) and 1616 (Housesteads).
6. Frere and St Joseph 1983, pls. 57 and 60; Sommer 1984, 70 and 98–9.
7. Sommer 1984, 76, 83 and 92; Higham and Jones 1985, fig. 29.
8. Sommer 1984, 77.
9. Salway 1965, 46–7.
10. McCarthy 1984, 65 and 68.
11. Webster 1966.
12. Frere 1975 on small towns; Rivet 1977 extended the argument to the civitas capitals.
13. Crickmore 1984b, 37.
14. Green H. J. M. 1975, 185 and 190.
15. Webster 1981, 65–71 and 82.
16. Cf. Webster 1981, 65 (Alcester); 76–8 and fig. 32 (Penkridge); Mackreth 1979, fig. 11 (Water Newton).
17. Cf. Burnham 1986.
18. See especially Partridge 1981.
19. Chaplin 1963, l; *J. Roman Studs.* 53, (1963), 158.
20. Cunliffe 1988, 1.
21. Bartlett 1988b.
22. Harker 1980, 288.
23. May 1976, 166–8; Todd 1981, 4.
24. Wacher 1975a, 315–16.
25. R.C.H.M. 1975, 60–3; Shortt 1976, 6–8.
26. Stanford 1970; Wilmott 1980, 119–21.

27. Lambrick *et al.* 1980, 39–40 and 113–14.
28. Crickmore 1984b, 38–40.
29. Freezer 1979.
30. Charlton 1961; 1962.
31. Burnham 1986, 194–6.
32. Cf. May 1976, figs. 7 and 8.
33. Wedlake 1958, 47ff.
34. Drury 1988, 125–35 (Chelmsford); Lynam 1913, 140–2; Webster 1958b; Crickmore 1984b and references (Wall).
35. Elkington 1976, 183ff.
36. Cunliffe and Davenport 1985, 178–9.
37. Green H. J. M. 1975; 1977.
38. For the walled area, cf. Mackreth 1979, fig. 11 and *J. Roman Studs.* 48, (1958), 139; for Normangate Field, see Dannell and Wild 1971; 1974; 1976; Dannell 1974.
39. Breeze 1982; Frere 1987, chs. 4–7.
40. Wacher 1975a.
41. Tacitus *Agricola* 21.
42. Cunliffe 1969, 129; Blagg 1979.
43. Wacher 1975a, 294–8 (Cirencester); Frere 1983, 55–72 (Verulamium).
44. Hebditch and Mellor 1973, 40–1 (Leicester); R.I.B. 288 (Wroxeter).
45. France and Gobel 1985, 23–35.
46. Harker 1972; 1974.
47. Holmes 1955, 102–5; Wilson 1975, 13, pl. IXA.
48. Stead and Rigby 1986, 84–5.
49. Wilkes and Elrington 1978, 41.
50. May 1970, 228–9 and 234.
51. *Britannia* 12, (1971), 278, fig. 12; Elkington 1976, nos. 1, 5 and 7 (lead pigs); the dating of the earliest lead pigs has been questioned by Clement Whittick 1982.
52. Walters 1908, 187; Bridgewater 1967.
53. Charlton 1961, 31–2; 1962, 62 and 64.
54. Bestwick 1975b; *J. Roman Studs.* 59, (1969), 210–11; Petch 1987, 202–8.
55. Thompson 1965, 73–80; Petch 1987, 194–8.
56. Freezer 1979, 4.
57. Jones and Webster 1968, 203 and 210.
58. D.O.E. *Arch. Excavations* 1972, 42–3; Jones 1972; Jones and Reynolds 1983; Petch 1987, 198–202.
59. Dool 1986b (Little Chester); Jones and Reynolds 1978 (Manchester).
60. Oswald 1952, 3–6; Todd 1969, 22–7.
61. Green H. J. M. 1975, 191; 1977, 9.

62. Drury 1972, 10.
63. Drury 1976, 124–5.
64. Greenfield and Webster 1965, 3 (High Cross); St Joseph 1958b, 3–4; Barton 1958, 6–9 (Penkridge).
65. Todd 1969, 40 and note 2.
66. Partridge 1975, 148.
67. Drury 1988, 130–5.
68. Green H. J. M. 1975, 196–8.
69. Wacher 1971a, 170–71.
70. Lynam 1913, 140–2; Round 1974b.
71. Booth 1980, 7.
72. R.C.H.M. 1979, 91.
73. Green H. J. M. 1975, 201–2.
74. Hadman and Upex 1977; *Britannia* 14, (1983), 305–6.
75. Mackreth 1979, fig. 11.
76. Wilmott 1980, 123–5.
77. For a general discussion, see Crickmore 1984a.
78. Salway 1965, 47–9; Daniels 1978, 93–7.
79. McCarthy 1984, 70–2.
80. Wacher 1971a, 170.
81. Charlton 1961, 31.
82. Thompson 1965, 80; Webster 1975.
83. Hartley and Kaine 1954, 19.
84. Petch 1987, 202.
85. Jones and Webster 1968, 205–7.
86. Hunt 1975, 49; Sawle 1978, 79.
87. *J. Roman Studs.* 59, (1969), 210–11; Bestwick 1974, 30; 1975b, 70.
88. Breeze and Dobson 1987, 127–44.

Chapter 3 (pp. 15–32)
1. See for example Burnham 1988 and 1989.
2. Frere and St Joseph 1983, 169–70 and 172–6.
3. Booth 1980; *Britannia* 17, (1986), 394–5.
4. Burleigh 1982; Stead and Rigby 1986.
5. Interim accounts in Green H. J. M. 1975 and 1977, now in need of revision.
6. Drury 1976.
7. Field and Hurst 1983.
8. Green H. J. M. 1975, 196.
9. Stead and Rigby 1986, 36–8.
10. *Britannia* 10, (1979), 318; 12, (1981), 354.
11. Hadman and Upex 1979, 29.
12. Brown *et al.* 1983, 134.
13. Taylor 1969; Booth 1977.
14. Dannell and Wild 1971, 11–12; 1974, 87–8; Dannell 1974, 7–9.
15. Brinson 1963, 78.

16. Wacher 1971a, 171.
17. Smith 1987, 189–94.
18. Green H. J. M. 1975, 196 and 201.
19. Wilkes and Elrington 1978, 41–2 (Cambridge); May 1970, 228–9 and 234 (Dragonby).
20. Leech 1982.
21. Cf. Bishop and Dore 1988, fig. 5.
22. Cf. Mackreth 1979, fig. 11.
23. Stanley 1979 (Alchester); Wedlake 1958 (Camerton); Smith 1987, 189–94; *Britannia* 8, (1977), 389; 9, (1978), 433 (Hibaldstow); Simmons 1985; Oetgen 1987 (Sapperton); Ellis 1987, 18–34 (Sea Mills).
24. Wacher 1978, 88.
25. *Britannia* 12, (1981), 350.
26. Leach 1982, 71 (Ilchester); Millett and Graham 1986, 46–7 (Neatham).
27. *Britannia* 1, (1970), 286–7.
28. Barfield and Tomlinson 1971 (Droitwich); D.O.E. *Arch. Excavations* 1975, 36–7.
29. Green H. J. M. 1975, 202.
30. Brinson 1963, 79.
31. Partridge 1975, 148 (Braughing); Wedlake 1958, 48–52 (Camerton); Gelling 1959a, 3–7; Tomlinson 1967, 7; Barfield and Tomlinson 1971 (Droitwich); Oswald 1941, 44–5; Todd 1969, 57 (Margidunum).
32. Cunliffe 1984, 169–72 (Bath); inf. on Ilchester from Mr P.J. Leach.
33. Jack 1916, pl. 12; Jack and Hayter 1926, pl. 1; Frere and St Joseph 1983, 169.
34. Drury 1988, 130–5.
35. Green H. J. M. 1975, 196–8.
36. Phillips and Walters 1977.
37. Lucas 1981, 27–31.
38. Jones and Webster 1968, 205–9.
39. Wilson 1975, 9; Mackreth 1979.
40. Daniels 1978, 93–4.
41. Partridge 1975, 148.
42. Millett and Graham 1986, 33–6.
43. For baths, see Cunliffe 1969, 89–131 and 1976a; for the possible theatre see 1969, 148–9 and reservations noted in this volume (p. 173).
44. Haverfield 1905, 223.
45. Gray 1910 (Charterhouse); Hingley 1982, 306–9 (Frilford).
46. Lawrence 1864a, 304; Lewis 1966, 130 (Wycomb); *Britannia* 4 (1973), 280 (Catterick).
47. Cunliffe and Davenport 1985.
48. Lewis 1966, 64–5 and 71.
49. For the two main temples, see Penn 1959; 1963.
50. Wilson 1975, 9 (Water Newton); Haverfield 1902, 180–1 (Irchester).
51. France and Gobel 1985, 23–48.
52. Drury 1972, 13–24 (Chelmsford); Wedlake 1982 (Nettleton).
53. Bradford and Goodchild 1939, 36 (Frilford); Wilson 1975, 12 (Thorpe).
54. For earthworks and defences in general, see Wacher 1966a; 1975b; Frere 1984; Crickmore 1984a.
55. Drury 1975, 170–1.
56. *J. Roman Studs.* 54, (1964), 159.
57. Heys and Thomas 1963.
58. Green H. J. M. 1975, 204 (Godmanchester); *J. Roman Studs.* 52, (1962), 171–2 (Chesterton).
59. Brinson 1963, 76.
60. Heys and Thomas 1959, 100 and 102 (Kenchester); Annable 1960, 235 (Mildenhall).
61. Corder 1961, 20–8 (Gt. Casterton); St Joseph 1966, 25 (Water Newton).
62. Todd 1975, 217 (Ancaster); Green H. J. M. 1975, 206 (Godmanchester).
63. Corder 1955, 38–9. Technically, those at Horncastle have rounded outer faces and straight sides; Field and Hurst 1983, 54–6.
64. Green C. 1977; Knowles 1977.
65. Drury 1976.
66. Hingley 1982.
67. Green H. J. M. 1975; 1977.
68. Gould 1964; Oswald 1968.
69. Smith 1987, 189.
70. St Joseph 1965, 87.
71. Rodwell 1972; Wilson 1975, 10.
72. Wilmott 1980; Frere and St Joseph 1983, 169.
73. St Joseph 1966, 25–6; Wilson 1975, 9–10.
74. R.C.H.M. 1979, 91–5.
75. Hadman and Upex 1975, 15.
76. May 1970 (Dragonby); Riley 1977 (Kirmington).
77. Cf. Taylor 1983, figs. 29–30.
78. Rowley 1975; Stanley 1979.
79. Frere 1962, 121; *Britannia* 4, (1973), 297 (Dorchester); inf. on Ilchester from Mr P.J. Leach; the grid proposed in Leach

1982, fig. 3 must be treated with caution.

80. Bishop and Dore 1988, fig. 5.
81. Partridge 1975, fig. 4.
82. Stead and Rigby 1986, fig. 3.
83. Wacher 1971a, fig. 24.
84. Phillips and Walters 1977; *Britannia* 16, (1985), 310.
85. Cf. Mackreth 1979, fig. 11.
86. Drury 1972, 10.
87. D.O.E. *Arch. Excavations* 1972, 54 (Braughing); Millett and Graham 1986, 27 (Neatham).
88. Hadman and Upex 1977, 8 (Ashton); Charlton 1962, 62 (Holditch).
89. *Britannia* 6, (1975), 242; 7, (1976), 321.
90. St Joseph 1958b, 4.
91. Green H. J. M. 1975, 185.
92. May 1970.
93. Drury 1976, 124.
94. Leach 1982, 65–82.
95. Lynam 1913 with corrections in Gould 1968 and Round 1972.
96. Wacher 1971a, 170 (Catterick); Corder 1961, 49–50 (Gt. Casterton); Mackreth 1979 (Water Newton).
97. Drury 1988, 130–5 (Chelmsford); Green H. J. M. 1975, 196 and 198 (Godmanchester); Phillips and Walters 1977 (Wanborough).
98. Mackreth 1979, fig. 11.
99. Frere and St Joseph 1983, 169–70.
100. Cunliffe 1984, 169–72.
101. Wedlake 1958, 48–52.
102. Todd 1969, 57 (Margidunum); St Joseph 1953, 90–1 (Mildenhall).
103. Brinson 1963, 79 (Gt. Chesterford); *J. Roman Studs.* 54, (1964), 159 (Thorpe).
104. Drury 1972, 21–5 (Chelmsford); Jack and Hayter 1926, 21 and 26 (Kenchester).
105. Green H. J. M. 1975, 201.
106. Drury and Rodwell 1980, 65–7 (Chelmsford); Wilson 1975, 9 (Water Newton).
107. Cunliffe 1984 (Bath); France and Gobel 1985 (Harlow).
108. R.C.H.M. 1979, 94 (Irchester); Harker 1980 (Springhead); R.C.H.M. 1976, 125 (Wycomb).
109. Hingley 1982.
110. Daniels 1978, 95–7; Bishop and Dore 1988, fig. 5.
111. Mackreth 1979, fig. 11 (Water Newton); Cunliffe 1984 (Bath); Partridge 1975, 148 (Braughing).
112. Green H. J. M. 1975, 204.
113. Edwards 1977, fig. 100.
114. Cf. Dannell 1974.
115. Green 1978.
116. May 1970.
117. *Britannia* 4, (1973), 302 (Chelmsford); Frere 1962, 118 (Dorchester); Alexander 1975, 108 (Gt. Chesterford).
118. Wilson 1975, 12 (Mildenhall); R.C.H.M. 1979, fig. 89 (Irchester).
119. *J. Roman Studs.* 48, (1958), 140.
120. Leach 1982 and unpub. inf. (Ilchester); Cunliffe 1984, 169–72.
121. Todd 1981, 21 (Ancaster); St Joseph 1953, 91 (Brough); Mahany 1971, 24 (Mancetter).
122. Rahtz 1960, 178 (Caistor); Field and Hurst 1983 (Horncastle); O'Neil 1931, 177 (Mancetter); Gould 1964, 16 (Wall).
123. Todd 1969, 70.
124. *Britannia* 4, (1973), 250 (Catterick); Brown *et al.* 1983, 134 (Towcester).
125. Todd 1975, 221 (Ancaster); Brinson 1963, 86–8 (Gt. Chesterford); Green H. J. M. 1977, 18 (Godmanchester).
126. *Britannia* 15, (1984), 300 (Ashton); Stead and Rigby 1986, 61–75; *Britannia* 15, (1984), 304; 17, (1986), 401; 18, (1987), 327 and unpub. inf. from Mr G. Burliegh (Baldock); Haverfield 1906, 264–7; Norton in Cunliffe 1969, 212–18 (Bath); Baker 1875 (Irchester); Haverfield 1902, 170; Taylor 1926, 233–4 (Water Newton).
127. Leach 1982, 84–8.

Chapter 4 (pp. 33–42)
1. Wacher 1971a; Wilson 1984.
2. Leach 1982.
3. Frere *et al.* 1987, plan V.
4. Arrian, *Periplus*, 9.
5. R.I.B. 602
6. R.I.B. 1030–1.
7. R.I.B. 1085.
8. R.I.B. 1599.
9. R.I.B. 1225.
10. R.I.B. 1696.
11. R.I.B. 745.
12. R.I.B. 293.
13. R.I.B. 88.

14. R.I.B. 235.
15. R.I.B. 725–6.
16. C.I.L. VIII 18224.
17. MacMullen 1963, 157.
18. *Codex Justinianus* 4, 61, 5.
19. R.I.B. 725.
20. R.I.B. 1713.
21. R.I.B. 594.
22. R.I.B. 1266.
23. R.I.B. 233.
24. *Britannia* 8, (1977), 426.
25. C.I.L. III 1674–6, 8244, 8249, 12672 = 14561;
26. R.I.B. 152.
27. R.I.B. 179.
28. R.I.B. 583 and 587.
29. R.I.B. 583, 594–5.
30. Ravenna Cosmography, 107.7.
31. Harper 1928.
32. C.I.L. III, 4806 = I.L.S. 4863; Alföldy 1974, 258, 334 n.36.
33. C.I.L. XIII, 5170.
34. Wightman 1985, 208–9.
35. Mertens and Brulet 1974.
36. Webster 1971.
37. Hawkes and Dunning 1961.
38. *Notitia Dignitatum Occ.* XXIII.
39. Frere 1987, 346.
40. Wacher 1971a, 171–2.
41. Mylius 1936, 299; Kleiss 1962.
42. Boon 1974, 138–47.
43. Green H. J. M. 1975, 196–201.
44. Wacher 1971a, 170.
45. Lynam 1913; Webster 1958b; Round 1974b.
46. Phillips and Walters 1977.
47. Partridge 1975, 148.
48. Lucas 1981, 27–31.
49. Salway 1965, 50–5.
50. Petch 1928.
51. Birley 1977, 44–6.
52. Curle 1911, 92–103.
53. Wheeler 1926, 60–8.
54. Brinson 1963, 79.
55. Todd 1969, 57.
56. Wedlake 1958, 47–52.
57. Frere and St Joseph 1974, 24.
58. *J. Roman Studs.* 54, (1964), 159.
59. C.f. Todd 1970, 120.
60. Wacher 1974.
61. Hawkes 1947, 27; Wacher 1978, 129–32.
62. R.I.B. 179.
63. C.I.L. XIII 3631; Meyers 1964, 126.
64. Green H. J. M. 1975, 202–3.
65. Wild 1978.
66. E.g. C.I.L. XIII, 4636, from Naix.
67. R.I.B. 2283.
68. R.I.B. 1672–3.
69. R.I.B. 2235.
70. R.I.B. 899.
71. R.I.B. 1616.
72. R.I.B. 1700.
73. *J. Roman Studs.* 47, (1957), 230.
74. R.I.B. 707.
75. C.I.L. XIII 4131.
76. C.I.L. XIII 4310.
77. C.I.L. XIII 4316.
78. C.I.L. I 1279.
79. *Bulletin Épigraphique de la Gaule* 5, (1885), 179.
80. Cadoux 1971; Agache 1978, 404–10.
81. Espérandieu 1913, 94–5; Grenier 1958, 407–15.
82. Vaillat 1932, 53–4; Grenier 1960, 608–39.
83. Formigé 1944; Grenier 1960, 553–67.
84. Cunliffe 1984.
85. R.I.B. 140 and 163.
86. R.I.B. 139, 143–4, 146–7 and 156–60.
87. For the stone moulds from Lansdown, see Bush 1908.
88. Rivet 1955, 31.
89. Haverfield 1905, 222–7.
90. Alcock 1966.
91. Harker 1980.
92. Bradford and Goodchild 1939; Hingley 1982.
93. France and Gobel 1985.
94. R.C.H.M. 1976, 125–6.
95. Alföldy 1974, 113–14.
96. Jones and Lewis 1974; Elkington 1976, 183ff.
97. Walters 1908, 187; Bridgewater 1967; Shoesmith 1969.
98. Wedlake 1958, 82–4 (Camerton); Bush 1908 (Lansdown, near Bath).
99. Lewis and Jones 1969; Lewis 1977.
100. O'Leary and Davey 1977; *Britannia* 18, (1987), 302–3 and refs.; 19, (1988), 416–17.
101. Selkirk 1981, 125–6; *Britannia* 15, (1984), 290; 16, (1985), 282.
102. Bestwick 1975b.
103. Ptolemy, *Geography* II, 3, 11.
104. Hunt 1975; Sawle 1978; Freezer 1979.

105. Thompson 1965, 73–80; Hartley and Webster 1973.
106. *J. Roman Studs.* 59, (1969), 210–11.
107. Lyne and Jefferies 1979; Fulford 1975; Monaghan 1987; Woods 1974.
108. Knowles 1977.
109. Hartley 1972.
110. Swan 1984, 97–8 and refs.
111. Hartley 1973b; Swan 1984, 98–101.
112. Young 1977.
113. Fulford 1977.

Chapter 5 (pp. 43–50)
1. See for instance Finley 1973; Duncan-Jones 1974; Garnsey, Hopkins and Whittaker 1983; Greene 1986.
2. Atkinson 1942, 125–46.
3. Rivet 1955, 31–2; 1969a.
4. Drury 1976, fig. 49.
5. Edwards 1977, fig. 100.
6. Drury 1976, 124.
7. Leach 1982, 65–82.
8. Green H. J. M. 1975, 191; 1977, 9.
9. Cf. Elbe 1977 and La Baume (not dated).
10. Richmond 1966; Wacher 1975a, 63–5.
11. Inf. from excavator (J.S.W.).
12. Todd 1970, 121.
13. Birley 1954, 17–18.
14. Potter and Trow 1988, 9–12.
15. Mackreth 1979.
16. *Britannia* 4, (1973), 288–90.
17. Hadman and Upex 1975, 12.
18. *Britannia* 2, (1971), 257 (Ancaster); Tylecote, Bayley and Biek, in Drury 1976, 94–6 (Braintree); Wedlake 1958, 59, 66–7 (Camerton); Charlton 1962, 64 (Holditch); Simmons 1985, 18 (Sapperton); Bestwick and Cleland 1974, 146–7; Thompson 1965, 73ff. (Wilderspool).
19. Frere 1962, 119; Manning, in Frere 1985, 139–52.
20. Neville 1856.
21. Johnston 1974, 45.
22. Inf. from excavator (J. S. W.).
23. Knowles 1977, 213 (Brampton); Barfield 1975, 48 (Droitwich); *J. Roman Studs.* 53, (1963), 138 (Harlow); Harker 1971, 190 (Springhead); Millett and Graham 1986, 52–3 (Neatham); *Britannia* 8, (1977), 385 (Wilderspool).
24. Foster, in Stead and Rigby 1986, 143.
25. Hawkes 1946, 20.
26. Haverfield 1902, 197.
27. R.I.B. 712.
28. Wedlake 1958, 82–4.
29. Wedlake 1982, 68–74.
30. *Britannia* 6, (1975), 255.
31. Green H. J. M. 1977, 19.
32. *Britannia* 5, (1974), 439.
33. D.O.E. *Arch. Excavations* 1973, 58 (Coddenham); Corder 1961, 50; Whitwell and Dean 1966, 46 (Gt. Casterton); Leach 1982, 10 (Ilchester); D.O.E. *Arch. Excavations* 1974, 52 (Sapperton); Jessup 1928, 339 (Springhead).
34. R.I.B. 149 and 151.
35. Cunliffe 1984, 190.
36. Walters 1908, 180; *J. Roman Studs.* 54, (1964), 181, no. 20.
37. Johnston 1974, 46.
38. Cunliffe 1984, 188–9.
39. *Britannia* 17, (1986), 403.
40. *J. Roman Studs.* 56, (1966), 206.
41. Ambrose, in Cunliffe 1979, 115–22 (Bath); *Britannia* 5, (1974), 438 (Brampton); *Britannia* 9, (1978), 423 (Carlisle); *J. Roman Studs.* 59, (1969), 211 (Middlewich); Wild 1974, 167 (Water Newton).
42. Johnston 1974, 45.
43. *Britannia* 7, (1976), 343.
44. Potter and Trow 1988, 10 (Braughing); Inf. from excavator (J. S. W.) (Catterick); *Britannia* 12, (1981), 350 (Gt. Chesterford); Millett and Graham 1986, 157 (Neatham); Penn 1958, 74 (Springhead).
45. Fieldhouse, May and Wellstood 1931, 5–6.
46. Rodwell 1975, 96.
47. McWhirr 1979, 181–2.
48. *Britannia* 5, (1974), 438.
49. *Britannia* 3, (1972), 317.
50. Atkinson 1931, pl. XII.
51. Thompson 1965, 177–8.
52. *Britannia* 17, (1986), 415 (Bath); Leach 1982, 78 (Ilchester); D.O.E. *Arch. Excavations* 1969, 23 (Mancetter).
53. Smith 1969, 107–9.
54. Phillips 1976.
55. *J. Roman Studs.* 48, (1958), 139.
56. *J. Roman Studs.* 58, (1968), 205.
57. Anderson and Wacher 1980, 119.

58. Spain 1984.
59. Simpson 1976, 26–49; Young 1981, 32–9.
60. Charlton 1961, 31.
61. Penn 1958, 55–61.
62. *Britannia* 7, (1976), 342; 13, (1982), 371.
63. Ellis 1987, 21–5.
64. Charlton 1962, 64.
65. *Britannia* 6, (1975), 235.
66. Mackreth 1979.
67. Daniels 1978, 94.
68. Myres 1892; St Joseph 1953, 92.
69. Holmes 1955, 94ff.; Todd 1970, 123.
70. *J. Roman Studs.* 55, (1965), 210–11.
71. Green H. J. M. 1975, 204.
72. Knight 1968, 102.
73. Lawrence 1864a, 422 and 425.
74. Hodder 1974a, b and c.
75. Cf. Hodder 1979, 193–4.
76. Hartley and Kaine 1954, 19–21.
77. Knowles 1977, 211.
78. *J. Roman Studs.* 27, (1937), 239.
79. Leach 1982, 11.
80. Rivet and Smith 1979, 240.

Chapter 6 (pp. 51–91)
1. Wacher 1975a, 406. If anything the degree of certainty then expressed as to the area of the town was much too optimistic.
2. Antonine Itinerary 467.2 (Iter II); 476.6 (Iter V).
3. Richmond and Crawford 1949, 129.
4. Bede, *Vita Sancti Cuthberti*, 4.
5. *Ibid.*, 4, 27.
6. William of Malmesbury, *Gesta Pontificum Anglorum*, 3.
7. Leland 1744, 7, 54.
8. Camden 1695, 833.
9. Shaw 1924; Hogg 1956; 1964; Salway 1965, 41–5; Daniels 1978, 239–43; Charlesworth 1979; McCarthy 1979; 1980; 1984; McCarthy *et al.* 1982; McCarthy and Dacre 1983; Caruana 1983; Higham and Jones 1985, 52–9 (the plan, fig. 28, is wrongly labelled); Cleary 1987, 28–30. See also annual summaries in *J. Roman Studs.* 45, (1955), 124; 46, (1956), 124; 47, (1957), 202; *Britannia* 5, (1974), 410–11; 7, (1976), 310–11; 8, (1977), 376; 9, (1978), 421–3; 10, (1979), 281; 11, (1980), 359–60; 12, (1981), 325; 13, (1982), 343–4; 14, (1983), 290–2; 15, (1984), 280; 16, (1985), 274–6.

10. McCarthy *et al.* 1982, 82.
11. *Britannia* 9, (1978), 422–3; 16, (1985), 274; McCarthy 1979, 270.
12. Charlesworth 1980.
13. Haverfield 1916, 282.
14. *Britannia* 16, (1985), 276.
15. Bowman and Thomas 1983, 110.
16. Higham and Jones 1985, 55.
17. R.I.B. 2283.
18. *J. Roman Studs.* 55, (1965), 224.
19. *Britannia* 5, (1974), 411; Cleary (1987, 28), though, is of the opinion that the lower courses of masonry found in West Tower Street, below the medieval work, were of Roman origin, and that a ditch containing second-century pottery uncovered in Lowther Street, represents the defences on the east side.
20. Williams 1947, 7–9.
21. McCarthy 1984, 73. This suggestion that the Roman settlement – apart from the forts – was undefended has recently been restated (*Current Archaeology* 116, 1989, 300), but it is always dangerous in archaeology to claim an absence of something because it is impossible to prove; it may be due solely to excavators looking in the wrong places, or to other circumstances totally beyond our control! Not so long ago it used to be claimed that Leicester had no west wall, and Grimes in 1968 even went so far as to state for London: 'that there was no continuous defence along the river in Roman times'. It might be best, therefore, for the time being, to suspend judgement on Carlisle.
22. *Britannia* 13, (1982), 344.
23. *Ibid.* and 410.
24. McCarthy *et al.* 1982, 81; McCarthy 1984, 68; Caruana 1983, 77–8.
25. *Britannia* 9, (1978), 423.
26. McCarthy *et al.* 1982, 81; McCarthy 1984, 68; Caruana 1983, 78–80.
27. R.I.B. 2059.
28. R.I.B. 943.
29. R.I.B. 947–9.
30. R.I.B. 950.
31. R.I.B. 951–3.
32. Patten 1974.
33. Toynbee 1962, no. 89.
34. R.I.B. 933.
35. Thomas 1981, ch. 13.

36. Antonine Itinerary 464.3 (Iter I).
37. Ravenna Cosmography, 107.18.
38. Rivet and Smith 1979, 322.
39. Gordon 1726–7, 176.
40. A convenient bibliography covering these excavations down to 1978 can be found in Daniels 1978, 331. For more recent excavations see *Britannia* 8, (1977), 372; 12, (1981), 322; Bishop and Dore 1988.
41. Viz. Salway 1965, 45–60; Daniels 1978, 93–100.
42. Dio Cassius, *History of Rome*, 73, 8. For a recent view, see Daniels 1978, 6, and put more forcibly, Breeze 1982, 126–9.
43. Frere 1987, 147–57.
44. R.I.B. 1695.
45. See Rivet and Smith 1979, 323, who canvass the possibility of *Curia Lopocarium*.
46. R.I.B. 1151.
47. R.I.B. 1164–5.
48. Woolley 1907, 174–7; Forster 1908, 215–18.
49. Forster 1915, 235–7.
50. Forster and Knowles 1914, 288 and plate VIII.
51. Forster 1908, 211.
52. Richmond 1943.
53. R.I.B. 1131.
54. R.I.B. 1124 and 1129.
55. R.I.B. 1137.
56. R.I.B. 1132.
57. R.I.B. 1130.
58. Richmond 1943, 156–8.
59. R.I.B. 1134.
60. R.I.B. 1120–2.
61. R.I.B. 1123 and 1133.
62. R.I.B. 1131.
63. R.I.B. 1120–2.
64. R.I.B. 1139–41.
65. Cowen 1936, 312; Thomas 1981, 130.
66. R.I.B. 1181. For an alternative reading, see Salway 1965, 229.
67. R.I.B. 1180.
68. R.I.B. 1182.
69. R.I.B. 1171.
70. R.I.B. 1065.
71. Gillam and Daniels 1961.
72. Haverfield 1906, 294–9.
73. Cox 1952; 1982.
74. Stevens 1952.
75. Leach 1982.

76. Leach and Thew 1985.
77. Most of these will be published in the Ilchester Volume 2, access to which in typescript was generously provided by Mr P. J. Leach. Short interims appear in Burrow 1981; 1984; Leach and Ellis 1985 and Leach 1987, as well as *Britannia* 13, (1982), 381; 14, (1983), 319–20.
78. Leach 1982, 21.
79. Leach and Ellis 1985, 2; inf. from Mr P. J. Leach.
80. Rodwell, in Leach 1982, 129–30; inf. from Mr P. J. Leach.
81. Leach 1982, 5; Webster 1958a, 80–3.
82. Alcock 1973b, chs. 6–7.
83. Leach and Thew 1985.
84. Cox 1952.
85. Leach 1982, 61–5.
86. Inf. from Mr P. J. Leach.
87. Leach 1982, 24.
88. *Ibid.*, 21.
89. *Ibid.*, 41.
90. The original reconstruction published in Leach 1982, fig. 3, should now be treated with extreme caution.
91. Leach 1982, 65 and 93–5.
92. Leach 1987, 6–7; inf. from Mr P. J. Leach.
93. Leach 1982, 109.
94. *Ibid.*, 8.
95. *Ibid.*, 24–30.
96. Inf. from Mr P. J. Leach, based on the work of J. S. Cox.
97. Cox 1952; Burrow 1981; 1984.
98. Leach 1982, 65–82 and fig. 34.
99. *Ibid.*, 95–100 and fig. 51.
100. *Ibid.*, 109.
101. Leach 1987, 6–7.
102. For details of the defences, see Leach 1982, 9 and 41–52 and *Britannia* 13, (1982), 381. Inf. on south gate and further sections on the west and south-east from Mr P. J. Leach.
103. Wacher 1975a, 75.
104. Leach 1982, 41.
105. *Britannia* 13, (1982), 381; inf. from Mr P. J. Leach.
106. Leach 1982, 50–2; inf. from Mr P. J. Leach.
107. Leach 1982, 26–8.
108. *Ibid.*, 9–10, 43 and 52; inf. from Mr P. J. Leach.

109. *Ibid.*, 68, 71 and 78.
110. Burrow 1984, 22.
111. Inf. from Mr P. J. Leach.
112. Leach 1982, 71–4 and 82.
113. Inf. from Mr P. J. Leach.
114. Ravenna Cosmography 106.11; Stevens 1952.
115. For summary, see Gray 1934.
116. Burrow 1984; *Britannia* 14, (1983), 319–20.
117. Leach 1982, 82–8.
118. *Ibid.*, 100–3 and 108.
119. For the latest levels and the evidence from Kingshams, see Leach 1982, 12, 31 and 52.
120. Leland 1744, V, 66; VII, 152.
121. For a summary of the antiquarian literature, see Walters 1908, 176–80.
122. St Joseph 1953, 92 and pl. XIV, 1; 1958a, 98; 1966, 25–6; Baker 1966; Wilson 1975, 10 and pl. IV; Frere and St Joseph 1983, 170 and pl. 103.
123. Jack 1916; Jack and Hayter 1926.
124. Webster 1957; Heys and Thomas 1959; 1963; Rahtz 1977; Wilmott 1978; Wilmott and Rahtz 1985.
125. For a reassessment of the evidence, see Wilmott 1980.
126. As has been argued by Davies 1980, 260.
127. Stanford 1970.
128. Webster 1958a, 83.
129. Jack 1916, 176; Jack and Hayter 1926, 13–15.
130. Wilmott 1978, 70.
131. Jack and Hayter 1926, 9.
132. *Ibid.*, 15.
133. Wilmott 1980, 123–5.
134. Jack 1916, 178–9 and pls. 2–3; Jack and Hayter 1926, 13–15 and pls. 11–13.
135. Jack and Hayter 1926, 15.
136. Heys and Thomas 1963, 155–8.
137. *Ibid.*, 154.
138. Jack and Hayter 1926, 9.
139. Webster 1957, 141–2.
140. Heys and Thomas 1959, 108.
141. Heys and Thomas 1963, 161–2.
142. Wilmott 1980, 121–3 and figs. 3–4.
143. Jack and Hayter 1926, 23–5.
144. *Ibid.*, 25.
145. Lewis 1966, 71.
146. Jack 1916, 24–7.
147. Jack and Hayter 1926, 25.
148. Wilson 1975, 10.
149. Walters 1908, 180.
150. Heys and Thomas 1959, 102–3.
151. Jack and Hayter 1926, 21, 23–4 and 26.
152. Jack 1916, 179; Jack and Hayter 1926, 23.
153. Rahtz 1977, 35.
154. Walters 1908, 181–2; *J. Roman Studs.* 54, (1964), 181, no. 20.
155. For the miniature objects, see Walters 1908, 182–3; for the pipe-clay figure, Jack and Hayter 1926, pl. 35. See also Green 1976, 169.
156. Jack and Hayter 1926, 9.
157. Lysons 1806, 391–2 and pl. 27; R.I.B. 2250.
158. E.g. Stanford 1980, 120–1 and 158–9.
159. Webster 1957; Heys and Thomas 1959; 1963.
160. Heys and Thomas 1963, 156–8 and 165–6.
161. Stenton 1971, 47.
162. For discussion and references, see Wilmott 1980, 129–30; for identification, see Rivet and Smith 1979, 407; Antonine Itinerary 484.7 (Iter XII); Ravenna Cosmography 106.27.
163. Rivet and Smith 1979, 346.
164. Antonine Itinerary 472.3 (Iter II); 473.3 (Iter III); 473.8 (Iter IV).
165. Ravenna Cosmography, 106.37; 106.39.
166. Payne 1895; Wheeler *et al.* 1932, 80–8.
167. Harrison and Flight 1969; Harrison 1971; 1973; Flight and Harrison 1979; Harrison and Williams 1980; Harrison 1982; 1986; Flight and Harrison 1987.
168. Chaplin 1963; *J. Roman Studs.* 53, (1963), 158; Harrison 1971.
169. Chaplin 1963, l; full publication is still awaited.
170. Caesar, *De Bello Gallico* V, 22.
171. For an alternative view see Thornhill 1977.
172. One of the writers (J. S. W) saw both these sections: Harrison and Flight 1969, 58 (fig. 4) and facing p.61 (fig. 6). In his opinion the layers described as the early rampart in Cutting A were clearly derived from turf, while in Cutting C the rampart appeared to have a front cheek of turf revetting sandy and gravelly material.
173. Wacher 1975a, 395; 1978, 52.
174. Wacher 1969, 29–34.
175. *J. Roman Studs.* 42, (1952), 96; Ellison 1962.

176. Wacher 1961, fig. 2.
177. Wacher 1969, 32.
178. Fulford 1984, 51–8.
179. Two recent writers have rejected this view, but neither has attempted to explain the differences outlined here: Ramm 1978, 60; Cleary 1987, 17 and 128. The latter claims 'that the nature and sequence of the defences [at Rochester] can be more easily paralleled at towns.' This is clearly not so at Rochester and even less so at Brough and Caistor.
180. Harrison and Flight 1969, 77; Frere 1984, 71.
181. Payne 1895, 52 is now discredited in Harrison 1973, 130.
182. Harrison 1973, 129–30.
183. Harrison and Flight 1969, 70.
184. Payne 1895, 6.
185. Arnold 1921; Robson 1921; for the position of Strood causeway see Thornhill 1979.
186. Nightingale 1952.
187. Dilke 1971, 191–3.
188. Hope 1898, 214.
189. Harrison 1982, 95.
190. Monaghan 1987.
191. Miles 1975, 26–31.
192. Wheeler et al. 1932, 87–8.
193. Ibid., 88 and 169.
194. Rivet 1955, 29–34.
195. Artis 1828. Unfortunately there is no accompanying text to the illustrations, though some of the gaps are filled by Trollope 1873.
196. See the summaries in Haverfield 1902, 166–78; R.C.H.M. 1926, 52; Taylor 1926, 228–47.
197. Margary 1935; 1939; Hawkes 1939.
198. St Joseph 1953, 91; 1958a, 98 and pl. XIV; 1961a, 132 and pl. XI; 1965, 87; 1966, 25–6 and pl. IV; 1969, 127; Wilson 1975, 9–10 and pls. 1–3; Frere and St Joseph 1983, 173–6 and pls. 105–7. For a compilation of the evidence inside the defences, see Mackreth 1979.
199. J. Roman Studs. 48, (1958), 139–40; 49, (1959), 117–18; Britannia 5, (1974), 433.
200. The principal accounts are Dannell and Wild 1969; 1971; 1974; 1976; Dannell 1974; Wild 1976. Cf. also R.C.H.M. 1969. Short summaries appear in J. Roman

Studs. 52, (1962), 169; 53, (1963), 135; 54, (1964), 164; 59, (1969), 219; Britannia 1, (1970), 286–7; 2, (1971), 264; 5, (1974), 431–3; 6, (1975), 250; 7, (1976), 332–3.
201. Johns and Carson 1975; Painter 1977.
202. Hawkes 1939; Margary 1939; St Joseph 1953, 82–3 and pl. IX.
203. Frere and St Joseph 1974; Dannell and Wild 1987.
204. J. Roman Studs. 52, (1962), 169; Dannell and Wild 1971, 12.
205. For the morphology and buildings in the area south of the River Nene, see Mackreth 1979, fig. 11, based on the available aerial photographs.
206. J. Roman Studs. 48, (1958), 140; Dannell 1974, 7.
207. J. Roman Studs. 48, (1958), 139.
208. Mackreth 1979, 19–21.
209. Artis 1828, pl. XXVI (1) and (2).
210. J. Roman Studs. 48, (1958), 140; 49, (1959), 117–18.
211. Britannia 5, (1974), 433.
212. Wilson 1975, 10.
213. R.C.H.M. 1969, 22–4; Margary 1935. Margary's Road III is now known not to be a road; Inf. from Dr J. P. Wild.
214. Dannell and Wild 1969, 7; 1971, 11.
215. Dannell and Wild 1976, 187; Wild 1976.
216. See especially Dannell and Wild 1969; 1971; 1974; 1976; Dannell 1974; Wild 1976.
217. Dannell and Wild 1976, 190–1.
218. Ibid., 188–9.
219. Dannell and Wild 1971, 7–11.
220. Dannell 1974, 7.
221. Dannell and Wild 1969, 7; 1971, 11–14; 1974, 87–8.
222. For brief details, see Wild 1974, 160–7; the pottery industry is also discussed by Hartley 1972.
223. Wild 1974, 151, quoting Artis 1828.
224. Wild 1978.
225. Wilson 1975, 9; Mackreth 1979, 19–21.
226. Dannell and Wild 1971, 11–12; 1974, 87.
227. Dannell and Wild 1971, 13–14.
228. For the aisled buildings, see Dannell and Wild 1971, 8–9; 1974, 88; 1976, 189.
229. J. Roman Studs. 48, (1958), 140; Dannell and Wild 1976, 186.
230. For the mosaic school, Smith 1969, 107–9; for the weights, Dannell 1974, 7.

231. Trollope 1873, 138–9.
232. Wild 1974, 161; Dannell and Wild 1974, 87.
233. *J. Roman Studs*. 49, (1959), 117–18; Dannell and Wild 1969, 8–11; Hartley 1972, 12–13.
234. *J. Roman Studs*. 53, (1963), 135; Dannell 1974, 7; Wild 1974, 165.
235. Mackreth 1979, 21.
236. Green 1976, 207–8; the inscription was recorded by Trollope 1873, 133.
237. Painter 1977.
238. Thomas 1981, 113.
239. Haverfield 1902, 169.
240. *J. Roman Studs*. 48, (1958), 139.
241. For the gates and external towers, see Frere and St Joseph 1983, 173.
242. For the identification, see Wild 1974, 147 and Rivet and Smith 1979, 348.
243. Cf. Johnson 1975; Frere 1987, 197.
244. R.I.B. 2235.
245. Jones 1964, 715.
246. For details, see Haverfield 1902, 170; R.C.H.M. 1926, 52; Taylor 1926, 233–4.
247. Inf. from Mr D. F. Mackreth.
248. Wilson 1975, 10.
249. Dannell and Wild 1969, 7.
250. *J. Roman Studs*. 48, (1958), 140.
251. *Ibid.*
252. Dannell 1974, 8.
253. Dannell and Wild 1976, 190.
254. Johns and Carson 1975.
255. Smith 1969, 107–9.

Chapter 7 (pp. 92–129)
1. Ravenna Cosmography, 106.39.
2. Rivet and Smith 1979, 224.
3. Richmond and Crawford 1949, 7, 18.
4. Webster 1981, 65, pl. 11.
5. Booth 1980, 6–7.
6. Brief notes appear in *J. Roman Studs*. 51, (1961), 172–3; 53, (1963), 134; 55, (1965), 208–9; 56, (1966), 206; 57, (1967), 185; and in *Britannia* 2, (1971), 262; 4, (1973), 288; 5, (1974), 430; 7, (1976), 331; 8, (1977), 397; 9, (1978), 439–40; 10, (1979), 299; 11, (1980), 368–9; 12, (1981), 339; 13, (1982), 361; 15, (1984), 295; 17, (1986), 393–5 and gazetteer; 19, (1988), 449–50. Comparable notes appear in the *West Midlands Archaeological News Sheet*, as do several longer interims including

Booth 1976; 1977; 1979. A useful short synthesis of material appears in Booth 1980.
7. D.O.E. *Arch. Excavations* 1970, 22; Mahany (forthcoming).
8. *Britannia* 7, (1976), 331; D.O.E. *Arch. Excavations* 1970, 22.
9. *J. Roman Studs*. 51, (1961), 172–3.
10. *J. Roman Studs*. 56, (1966), 206; 57, (1967), 185.
11. *Britannia* 17, (1986), 393.
12. Booth 1979; *Britannia* 11, (1980), 368–9.
13. *Britannia* 15, (1984), 295.
14. *J. Roman Studs*. 51, (1961), 173; 55, (1965), 209; Hughes 1960, 15–16.
15. *Britannia* 9, (1978), 439.
16. *J. Roman Studs*. 55, (1965), 209; 56, (1966), 206.
17. Davis 1930. The stamp TCD recorded in *J. Roman Studs*. 53, (1963), 165, can be compared with the commoner TCM, distributed solely in the north Cotswolds and Severn Valley areas north of Gloucester and Cirencester (McWhirr and Viner 1978, 369). Two other similar stamps are known; none occurs outside Alcester. Another tile stamped . . . RNI was found in a pit; *J. Roman Studs*. 56, (1966), 223. This stamp has not been recorded elsewhere.
18. *J. Roman Studs*. 55, (1965), 209.
19. Booth 1980, 16.
20. *Ibid.*, 18.
21. *J. Roman Studs*. 56, (1966), 224.
22. *Ibid.*, 220.
23. *Britannia* 4, (1973), 288; 15, (1984), 295.
24. *J. Roman Studs*. 56, (1966), 224.
25. Wacher 1978, 260.
26. *J. Roman Studs*. 53, (1963), 134.
27. Hughes 1960.
28. *J. Roman Studs*. 55, (1965), 209.
29. *Britannia* 11, (1980), 369.
30. *Britannia* 7, (1976), 331.
31. Stukeley 1724, 39–40 (= 1776, 41–3).
32. Penrose's 'excavations' are recorded alongside other details in Marshall and Brown 1858.
33. *Ibid.*, 138–40 and Myres 1892. For a summary of such early work, see Harden 1939, 283–5.
34. Hawkes 1927; Iliffe 1929; 1932.
35. Young 1975.

36. Harden 1937; Foreman and Rahtz 1984.
37. St Joseph 1953, 92; Wilson 1975, 11 and pl. VIb; Stanley 1979, pl. LXX.
38. Hawkes 1927, 160–1.
39. Harden 1937, 29–30.
40. Wilson 1975, 11. The street sometimes shown running north-south parallel to the eastern defences is probably a misinterpretation of a medieval plough-ridge; inf. from Mr T. Rowley.
41. Iliffe 1929, 114–16.
42. Young 1975, 139–40 and 151–2.
43. Harden 1937, 26–9.
44. Foreman and Rahtz 1984, 24–9.
45. *Ibid.*, 45–6.
46. Young 1975, 152.
47. Hawkes 1927, 158 and 162–3; Iliffe 1929, 116–17; 1932, 43–5.
48. For a bronze harness clip, see Webster 1958a, 69.
49. Marshall and Brown 1858, 125.
50. *Ibid.*, 139; Myres 1892.
51. Iliffe 1932, 41–3.
52. Hawkes 1927, 161–2 and 164–5.
53. See especially Stanley 1979. Mr T. Rowley kindly supplied an updated plan which reveals a much more extensive spread of buildings than hitherto realized, cf. Rowley 1975, fig. 4.
54. Harden 1939, 283.
55. Rowley 1975, 123.
56. Myres 1892.
57. Iliffe 1929, 114–19; 1932, 40–1; Young 1975, 138–41 and 150–1.
58. Young 1975, 152–4.
59. Hawkes 1927, 181–2.
60. Cuming 1856, 177.
61. See for example, Hussey 1841 and Marshall and Brown 1858.
62. Marshall and Brown 1858, 130.
63. Rowley 1975, 123.
64. For a summary of the nineteenth-century finds and the antiquarian accounts of Larks Hill, see Gerish 1900 and Page and Taylor 1912.
65. Holmes 1955.
66. Barr and Gillam 1964.
67. The principal excavation reports are those by Stead 1970; Partridge 1978; 1980; 1981; 1982; Potter and Trow 1988.
68. For a general account of the discoveries, see Partridge 1975.
69. Westell 1936, 362–3; Henderson 1938; Partridge 1981, 323–50.
70. Partridge 1981, 32–4 and relevant specialist reports therein.
71. Holmes 1955, 102.
72. Partridge 1978, 25.
73. Partridge 1982, 41–2.
74. Partridge 1980, 97–101 and 130.
75. Partridge 1978, 87–90.
76. Partridge 1980, 30–3.
77. Partridge 1981, 28 and fig. 3.
78. For a discussion of the roads, see Barr and Gillam 1964 and Partridge 1975, 145–6.
79. *Britannia* 4, (1973), 299–300.
80. *Britannia* 2, (1971), 270.
81. Barr and Gillam 1964, 115.
82. Partridge 1978, 91.
83. Partridge 1982, 42.
84. Wilson 1975, 13 and pl. IXA.
85. Holmes 1955, 102–5.
86. Partridge 1981, 50–1.
87. Partridge 1981, 34.
88. Holmes 1955, 104; Partridge 1978, 25.
89. Potter and Trow 1988, 9.
90. *Ibid.*, 9–13.
91. Partridge 1981, 34–5.
92. Holmes 1955; Partridge 1975, 150.
93. Stead 1970.
94. Partridge 1981, 37–40.
95. *Ibid.*, 49–50.
96. Partridge 1978, 25–32.
97. Holmes 1955, 94–6 and 104–6; Partridge 1978, 65–7.
98. For the other masonry buildings, see Partridge 1975, 148–9.
99. Partridge 1981, 248.
100. Partridge 1980, 128–9; 1981, 326; 1982, 40 and 57.
101. Tribbick 1974; Potter and Trow 1988, 9–12 and 160.
102. Partridge 1975, 153.
103. *Britannia* 17, (1986), 436.
104. Holmes 1955, 100; Partridge 1978, 98.
105. For cemeteries A and B, see Partridge 1978, 68–83.
106. Partridge 1981, 245–321.
107. Holmes 1955, 106.
108. Ptolemy, *Geography* II, 3, 16; I, 24, 1; VIII, 3, 8.
109. Antonine Itinerary 465.2 (Iter I); 468.2 (Iter II), 476.2 (Iter V).

110. Ravenna Cosmography, 107.14; Richmond and Crawford 1949, 18 (no. 136).

111. Williams 1938; Jackson 1939, 32–4. This identification of Catterick as Catraeth has now been seriously questioned by Alcock (1983).

112. Wheeler 1954.

113. *Britannia* 13, (1982), 348; 16, (1985), 278; 17, (1986), 384; Haselgrove 1984, 21–2.

114. D.O.E. *Arch. Excavations* 1969, 14.

115. Camden (Gough edn 1806), 3, 336.

116. Cade 1789; 1792.

117. MacLaughlan 1849, 215–16.

118. Hildyard and Wade 1951a.

119. St Joseph 1953, 90; Hildyard and Wade 1951b.

120. Hildyard 1957.

121. Excavations inside the walled area; *J. Roman Studs.* 50, (1960), 217. For a summary, see Wacher 1971a.

122. Excavations north of the River Swale; *Britannia* 4, (1973), 278–80.

123. Excavations at Bainesse Farm, Catterick Village; *Britannia* 7, (1976), 314; 13, (1982), 346–8; 14, (1983), 293; Wilson 1984, 77–81.

124. Excavations at Catterick Village; Hildyard 1953; *J. Roman Studs.* 57, (1967), 208. Excavations north of River Swale; *J. Roman Studs.* 59, (1969), 207; *Britannia* 2, (1971), 251; 3, (1972), 309; 5, (1974), 413; 6, (1975), 235; 7, (1976), 314; 11, (1980), 363; 15, (1984), 281. Excavations on the racecourse; *Britannia* 16, (1985), 278.

125. St Joseph 1955, 82.

126. *Pace* Jarrett 1976.

127. *J. Roman Studs.* 50, (1960), pl. XXII, 1.

128. *Ibid.*, pl. XXII, 2.

129. Wacher 1971b, pl. XXIIA.

130. *J. Roman Studs.* 50, (1960), 237. A stamped tile of this legion, of a die known at York, was found in excavations in the 1960s at RAF Catterick; *J. Roman Studs.* 57, (1967), 208. A complete hypocaust brick, stamped LEGVIV, was found in roadworks in 1981; *Britannia* 13, (1982), 420. It also appears to be from a known die (Wright 1976, 228, no. 44).

131. Wacher 1971a, figs. 26 and 27. See also Shortt 1959; 1964.

132. Hawkes and Dunning 1961, 43 (no. 2) and 62 (no. 1); another has been found at Stanwick; *ibid.*, 49 (no. 10).

133. R.I.B. 725.

134. R.I.B. 726.

135. R.I.B. 727.

136. *J. Roman Studs.* 50, (1960), 237.

137. *J. Roman Studs.* 51, (1961), 193.

138. As at Springhead, Temple 4, see p. 197; Penn 1961, 121.

139. *J. Roman Studs.* 57, (1967), 204; 58, (1968), pl. XIX, 1.

140. *Britannia* 7, (1976), 380, pl. XXXVIIA. Despite n.13 it should be recorded that *both* stones came from the bath-house where they had been used as door-sills.

141. Myres 1969, *passim*.

142. Hildyard 1953.

143. *Britannia* 13, (1982), 346; Whitaker 1822, 22.

144. *Pace* the objections by Alcock 1983.

145. Bede, *Historia Ecclesiastica Gentis Anglorum*, III, 7.

146. Ravenna Cosmography, 106.38.

147. Richmond and Crawford 1949, 46.

148. For a summary of finds, see Harden 1939, 288–96.

149. Hogg and Stevens 1937.

150. Frere 1962.

151. Bradley 1978.

152. Rowley and Brown 1981.

153. Allen 1938.

154. Cunliffe 1976b, 145.

155. Frere 1962, 115; 1985, 91.

156. Frere 1962, fig. 4 facing p.119.

157. Wacher and McWhirr 1982, 34.

158. Frere 1985, 95–8.

159. Rowley 1975, 118.

160. Rowley and Brown 1981, 6–8.

161. Harden 1939, 292.

162. *Ibid.*, 293; Frere 1985, 93.

163. Bradley 1978, 17. A wall 2.5 m (8 ft) wide has been observed, however, beneath the High Street.

164. See p. 79 for comments on the use of turf in urban ramparts.

165. Hogg and Stevens 1937.

166. Frere 1962, 129; amplified in Frere 1984, 71.

167. Hogg and Stevens 1937, 70.

168. Frere 1985, 93 and 98–100.

169. R.I.B. 235.

170. Young 1977, *passim*.
171. Frere 1962, 129.
172. Rowley and Brown 1981, 8–9.
173. Frere 1962, 119; Manning, in Frere 1985, 139–52.
174. Frere 1962, 139, pl. VIIb, fig. 17.
175. May 1977.
176. Harman *et al.* 1978, 3.
177. Durham and Rowley 1972; Harman *et al.* 1978, 3–6.
178. Harman *et al.* 1978, 6–16.
179. Reece, in Frere 1985, 135.
180. Frere 1962, 121–8.
181. Bradley 1978, 23; Rowley and Brown 1981, 10–12.
182. Kirk and Leeds 1953; Hawkes and Dunning 1961, 1–10.
183. O'Neil 1944.
184. Margary 1973, 165–6.
185. For brief details, see Taylor 1926, 252–4.
186. E.g. Garrood 1927 and 1937.
187. Hunnybun 1952.
188. Interim summaries appear in *J. Roman Studs.* 47, (1957), 214; 48, (1958), 138; 49, (1959), 118; 52, (1962), 174; 54, (1964), 164; 55, (1965), 209; 57, (1967), 186; 59, (1969), 219; and in *Britannia* 1, (1970), 287; 2, (1971), 264; 3, (1972), 320; 4, (1973), 288–90; 5, (1974), 433; 6, (1975), 250–1; 7, (1976), 333; 8, (1977), 398; 10, (1979), 300–1; 12, (1981), 340; 13, (1982), 363. Compare also D.O.E. *Arch. Excavations* 1970, 18–19; 1971, 19–20; 1972, 55; 1973, 45–6; 1974, 36–7; 1975, 50.
189. Green H. J. M. 1959; 1960a and b; 1961a and b; 1969; 1975; 1977; 1978; 1986. Considerable advice and unpublished information was also generously supplied by Mr H. J. M. Green.
190. Details on the sequence and its chronology were provided by Mr Green.
191. Green H. J. M. 1975, 185; *Britannia* 1, (1970), 287; 2, (1971), 264; 3, (1972), 321; 6, (1975), 250.
192. *Britannia* 13, (1982), 363.
193. Inf. from Mr Green.
194. Green H. J. M. 1975, 185.
195. *Britannia* 3, (1972), 320; 6, (1975), 250.
196. *Britannia* 8, (1977), 398.
197. Inf. from Mr Green.
198. Inf. from Mr Green.
199. *Britannia* 8, (1977), 398.
200. *Britannia* 6, (1975), 250.
201. For general details, see Green H. J. M. 1975, 185 and 190; 1977, 7–9.
202. For the doubts, see Cleary 1987, 86 and Smith 1987, 67. For the villa and the 1975 trenching, see Green 1978, 107 and fig. 35.
203. For general details, see Green H. J. M. 1975, 191; 1977, 9. The function of corn-drying ovens has been questioned by experimental work, cf. Reynolds and Langley 1980.
204. For the construction of the *mansio* and related features, see Green H. J. M. 1975, 196, 198 and 201; 1977, 10 and 15–16.
205. For the extent of second-century occupation, see *Britannia* 6, (1975), 250; 8, (1977), 398; 10, (1979), 301.
206. Garrood 1937, 440 and 442; 1947, 105–6.
207. Tebbutt 1961.
208. Ladds 1930; Green 1973.
209. For the early third-century changes, see Green H. J. M. 1975, 202 and 204.
210. Inf. from Mr Green.
211. For the range of structures, see especially Green H. J. M. 1975, 196 and 201; 1977, 10.
212. Cf. *Britannia* 4, (1973), 288 (St Ann's Lane); 6, (1975), 250–1 (Post Street and Piper's Lane; Earning Street); 13, (1982), 363 (St Ann's Lane).
213. *Britannia* 8, (1977), 398 (Pinfold Lane); 6, (1975), 251 (Earning Street).
214. *Britannia* 3, (1972), 320; 10, (1979), 301.
215. *Britannia* 4, (1973), 289.
216. *Britannia* 10, (1979), 301.
217. Green H. J. M. 1975, 198; 1977, 13.
218. Green H. J. M. 1959; 1960b; 1961b; 1975, 198.
219. Green H. J. M. 1975, 202.
220. *Ibid.*, 196; 1977, 16–17.
221. Inf. on the bakery from Mr Green; for the metal-worker, see *Britannia* 4, (1973), 289.
222. *Britannia* 2, (1971), 264; 10, (1979), 301.
223. Green H. J. M. 1975, 201; *Britannia* 8, (1977), 398.
224. Evidence is conveniently collated in Green H. J. M. 1986; see also 1975, 201 and 207; 1977, 17.
225. *Britannia* 2, (1971), 264.

226. The sequence established in Green H. J. M. 1975, 204–7 has now been considerably revised; inf. from Mr Green.
227. Green 1961a.
228. *Britannia* 6, (1975), 251.
229. *J. Roman Studs.* 52, (1962), 174; *Britannia* 6, (1975), 251; Green H. J. M. 1975, 204.
230. *Britannia* 10, (1979), 301.
231. Inf. from Mr Green.
232. For the fire and its aftermath in the central area, see Green H. J. M. 1975, 206–7.
233. *Britannia* 13, (1982), 363.
234. Inf. from Mr Green.
235. For late details, see Green H. J. M. 1975, 207; 1977, 22.
236. *Britannia* 6, (1975), 250 (Post Street); 8, (1977), 398 (Park Lane); 10, (1979), 301.
237. Green H. J. M. 1977, 18.
238. Green H. J. M. 1975, 207 and 209; inf. from Mr Green.

Chapter 8 (pp. 130–164)
1. For details of earlier discoveries, cf. Corder 1951, 6.
2. Corder 1951; 1954; 1961.
3. Todd 1968.
4. For details of forts, see St Joseph 1961b, 13–17; Todd 1968; Todd 1973, 24–7.
5. Corder 1951, 8 and 14.
6. Corder 1961, 35.
7. *Ibid.*, 49–50.
8. *Ibid.*, 33–4.
9. *Ibid.*, 35–9.
10. Corder 1951, 8 and 10; 1954, 7–10; 1961, 24, 25 and 26.
11. For details, see Corder 1951, 6–8; 1954, 1–3; 1961, 26–7.
12. Corder 1951, 10.
13. Corder 1954, 3.
14. *Ibid.*
15. Corder 1961, 30–2.
16. *Ibid.*, 49–50.
17. *Ibid.*, 36–8.
18. *Ibid.*, 50–3; Whitwell and Dean 1966, 46.
19. Corder 1961, 36–7.
20. *Ibid.*, 37–8 and 47.
21. Corder 1954, 5; 1961, 20–6.
22. Corder 1954, 4.
23. Corder 1961, 33.
24. *Ibid.*, 27.
25. *Ibid.*, 59–60.

26. *Ibid.*, 50.
27. Whitwell and Dean 1966, 46.
28. Corder 1961, 72 and 75–6.
29. Stukeley 1776, 78–9.
30. Neville 1847; 1848; 1855; 1856; 1860; Smith 1849.
31. Brinson 1949; 1950; 1963.
32. Rodwell 1972; Collins 1978; 1980; 1981; *Britannia* 10, (1979), 309–11; 12, (1981), 348–9; 13, (1982), 371.
33. St Joseph 1953, 92; Wilson 1975, 10 and pls. 5a and b.
34. Brinson 1950, 146.
35. Brinson 1949, 13; 1963, 80.
36. Collins 1981, 51.
37. Webster 1958a, 80.
38. Brinson 1963, 72.
39. Rodwell 1972.
40. Collins 1980, 42–3.
41. Dunnett 1975, 87.
42. Brinson 1949, 12; 1950, 147.
43. *Britannia* 12, (1981), 348.
44. Brinson 1950, 147; 1963, 78–9.
45. Brinson 1963, 80.
46. Rodwell 1975, 93.
47. *Britannia* 12, (1981), 350.
48. Brinson 1963, 82.
49. *Ibid.*
50. Neville 1848, 34 and 42; Oldham 1850; Brinson 1963, 86–7.
51. Wilson 1975, 10.
52. Smith 1849, 369; Brinson 1950, 147–8; 1963, 79.
53. Brinson 1950, 148; 1963, 80–1.
54. Brinson 1963, 72–6; *Britannia* 12, (1981), 350.
55. Brinson 1963, 76.
56. *Britannia* 12, (1981), 350.
57. *Ibid.*
58. Brinson 1963, 84; Neville 1856.
59. *Ibid.*, 83–4.
60. Neville 1855; Green 1976, 211.
61. Manning 1972, 246–9.
62. Brinson 1963, 83; *Britannia* 10, (1979), 309–11.
63. The evidence is usefully summarized by Brinson 1963, 86–8.
64. *Ibid.*, 83.
65. Rodwell 1975, 95.
66. Inf. from Dr W. Rodwell.
67. Morton 1712, 517.
68. Camden 1789, 179; 1806, 282.

69. Baker 1875; 1879; 1882; for a summary, see also Haverfield 1902, 178–84.

70. *J. Roman Studs.* 16, (1926), 223.

71. Hall and Nickerson 1968; Knight 1968; *Britannia* 13, (1982), 366; 16, (1985), 288 and 291; Windell 1984.

72. St Joseph 1966, 26 and pl. V; Wilson 1975, 11 and pl. VIA; Frere and St Joseph 1983, 170–3 and pl. 104.

73. For a summary and a plan, see R.C.H.M. 1979, 91–6 and fig. 89.

74. Hall and Nickerson 1968, 72 and fig. 5.

75. R.C.H.M. 1979, 92.

76. Knight 1968, 114.

77. Kenyon 1948, 31; for revised date, see Wacher 1975a, 342, n. 132.

78. Cf. Frere and St Joseph 1983, pl. 104.

79. Knight 1968, 107–9; R.C.H.M. 1979, 92.

80. Hall and Nickerson 1968, 75–8; these three ditches were subsequently confirmed in 1981–2, cf. Windell 1984, 36 and 41.

81. Knight 1968, 110.

82. *Ibid.*, 109–110; R.C.H.M. 1979, 92–4.

83. Knight 1968, 110–11.

84. Baker 1879, 50 and 52; R.C.H.M. 1979, 92.

85. Knight 1968, 107.

86. Cullen 1970, 227.

87. Wilson 1975, 11, confirming the conjectures by Haverfield 1902, 180 and Lewis 1966, 2.

88. Baker 1879, 50–1 and 54.

89. Körber 1906, 54–63.

90. *J. Roman Studs.* 50, (1960), pl. XXII 2, 218.

91. Haverfield 1920, pls. IX-X, 190.

92. Baker 1879, 54 and pl. II; Haverfield 1902, 181; Woodfield P. 1978, 81–2.

93. Baker 1875.

94. R.I.B. 233.

95. Hall and Nickerson 1968, 72–4; Knight 1968, 103–5; Windell 1984.

96. Knight 1968, 105.

97. *Ibid.*

98. Hall and Nickerson 1968, 78.

99. Woods and Hastings 1984.

100. Selkirk 1972; Woods 1974.

101. Johnston 1969.

102. Neal 1987.

103. Agache 1978, *passim.*

104. R.C.H.M. 1979, 91, quoting Knight 1968, 111.

105. Knight 1968, 111–13.

106. Hawkes 1961, 189; Kennet 1969.

107. Knight 1968, 116–17; see also Thomas 1981, 310–13.

108. Mackreth 1978.

109. Antonine Itinerary 486.5 (Iter XIV); Rivet and Smith 1979, 328–9. For a summary of discoveries up to the 1950s, see Grinsell 1957, 88–9.

110. Thomas 1956, 242.

111. St Joseph 1953, 90–1 and pl. XIII 2; 1966, 24–5; Wilson 1975, 12 and pls. 8A and B; Frere and St Joseph 1983, 166–8 and pls. 101–2.

112. Interim notes appear in Thomas 1956; Annable 1960; 1966; Anon. 1961; 1962; 1964 and 1965.

113. Swan 1975, 43; Annable 1976; Griffiths 1983, 53–5.

114. Anon. 1964; Annable 1966; the date proposed by the original excavator (Annable 1966, 13) has since been revised by Swan 1975, 44.

115. Griffiths 1983, 53.

116. Wilson 1975, 12; Frere and St Joseph 1983, 168.

117. Margary 1973, 135.

118. *Ibid.*, 99.

119. Frere and St Joseph 1983, 168.

120. Thomas 1956; Annable 1960. Additional information was kindly provided by Messrs K. F. Annable and A. J. Clark.

121. In both trenches E and J where the later wall apparently had deep and massive foundations, cf. Annable 1960, 235 and Anon. 1962, 245. Comparable evidence was not located in other trenches on the north and east, suggesting that the two phases are not coincident throughout their length.

122. Annable 1960, 235.

123. Anon. 1965.

124. Wilson 1975, 12.

125. Anon. 1961.

126. St Joseph 1953, 90–1; Anon. 1962.

127. Frere and St Joseph 1983, 167 and pl. 101.

128. Besley and Bland 1983.

129. Annable 1980.

130. Brooke 1920.

131. Brown *et al.* 1983, fig. 1.

132. Antonine Itinerary 470.6 (Iter II); 476.11 (Iter VI); Ravenna Cosmography, 106.49.

133. Rivet and Smith 1979, 382–3. Literally the name means 'hard milk' = cheese? Perhaps the earliest Stilton?
134. Camden 1610, 430.
135. Bridges 1791, 272.
136. Baker 1841, 318 and 320.
137. Haverfield 1902, 184–6.
138. Lambrick et al. 1980; Brown and Alexander 1982; Brown et al. 1983.
139. Lambrick et al. 1980, 39 and 113–14.
140. Ibid., 60–1.
141. Britannia 16, (1985), 288.
142. Lambrick et al. 1980, 39–40 and 114.
143. Britannia 15, (1984), 300.
144. Brown and Alexander 1982, 29.
145. Britannia 16, (1985), 288.
146. See R.C.H.M. 1982, 151–3 for a recent survey; it should be noted, though, that this conflicts with other sources.
147. Britannia 17, (1986), 399.
148. Both lines are shown in Brown and Alexander 1982, fig. 1; Brown et al. 1983, 46 revert to the line taken by Haverfield 1902, 185, while R.C.H.M. 1982, 152 favour the alternative.
149. Excavated in 1954; Brown and Alexander 1982, 24–9.
150. Woodfield C. 1978.
151. As at Cirencester: Wacher 1961, pl. XVII.
152. Brown et al. 1983.
153. Architectural masonry from Northants. has been collected and published by P. Woodfield 1978.
154. Brown et al. 1983, 130–1; for the lamp see p.104 and M. Green 1975; 1981, 258–60.
155. Summary of cemeteries in R.C.H.M. 1982, 156.
156. Toynbee 1962, 148.
157. Woods 1974.
158. Turland 1977.
159. Brown and Alexander 1982, 29–30.
160. Antonine Itinerary 485.5 (Iter XIII). See also Rivet 1970, 58 and 73, but with reservations in Rivet and Smith 1979, 350.
161. Aubrey and Jackson 1862, 194; Colt Hoare 1821, 94–5; Passmore 1922.
162. Phillips and Walters 1977, pl. XIVB.
163. Greenfield 1967; 1968; cf. J. Roman Studs. 57, (1967), 196; 58, (1968), 201; 59, (1969), 230.
164. Cooke and Wacher 1970; Wacher 1970; 1971c; 1975c; cf. Britannia 1, (1970), 300;

2, (1971), 282; D.O.E. Arch. Excavations 1969, 24.
165. Britannia 8, (1977), 416; see also Anderson and Wacher 1980.
166. Anderson and Wacher 1980, 116–17.
167. Ibid.
168. Wacher and McWhirr 1982, 58–9.
169. Phillips and Walters 1977, 225–7.
170. Ibid., 227.
171. Cf. Britannia 16, (1985), 308 and fig. 30.
172. Wacher 1971c, 188–9.
173. Britannia 8, (1977), 416; Anderson and Wacher 1980, 119.
174. Anderson and Wacher 1980, 119–21; see also Wacher 1975c, 233.
175. Swan 1975.
176. Young 1977.
177. Walters, Phillips and Greene 1973; Greene 1974; Swan 1977; Anderson 1978.
178. Conveniently collected in McWhirr and Viner 1978.
179. McWhirr 1979, 181–2, fig. 6.1.
180. Anderson and Wacher 1980, 119.
181. Rea 1972.
182. Greene 1974, 65, fig. 7.
183. Phillips and Walters 1977, 225.
184. Britannia 8, (1977), 416.

Chapter 9 (pp. 165–202)
1. Englefield 1792; Lysons 1813; Irvine 1873; Davis 1881.
2. Haverfield 1906.
3. Knowles 1926.
4. The principal reports include Cunliffe 1966, 1969, 1976a, 1980 and 1988; Cunliffe and Davenport 1985.
5. Wedlake 1966; Cunliffe 1979; O'Leary 1981.
6. R.I.B. 138–78; Cunliffe and Fulford 1982.
7. For a useful general summary of the site, see Cunliffe 1984.
8. Antonine Itinerary 486.3 (Iter XIV); see Rivet and Smith 1979, 255–6.
9. Cunliffe 1988, 1; Lynwood, in Cunliffe 1988, 279–80.
10. For details, see Cunliffe 1969, 1–3; 1979, 137; 1984, 179.
11. Cunliffe and Davenport 1985, 9–10.
12. Ibid., 38–42.
13. Temple Period 1: Cunliffe 1984, 38–48; Cunliffe and Davenport 1985, 33–4 and 178–9.

14. Lysons 1813, pl. V; Cunliffe 1969, 10–16; Cunliffe and Davenport 1985, 26–9.
15. Richmond and Toynbee 1955; Cunliffe and Davenport 1985, 115–17.
16. Cunliffe and Davenport 1985, 35–7.
17. Blagg 1979.
18. Baths Period 1: Cunliffe 1969, 95–8 and 100–1; 1976a, 4–5; 1984, 109–21.
19. Cunliffe and Davenport 1985, 179.
20. Baths Period 2: Cunliffe 1969, 113; 1976a, 6–8; 1984, 123–9.
21. Baths Period 3, reroofing: Cunliffe 1969, 98–9, 102 and 105–6; 1984, 129–39.
22. West end: Cunliffe 1976a, 8–11; East end: Cunliffe 1969, 113–14.
23. Cunliffe and Davenport 1985, 42–3 and 49–52.
24. Temple Period 2: Cunliffe 1984, 48–50; Cunliffe and Davenport 1985, 34–5 and 179–80.
25. Cunliffe 1969, 148–9; 1984, 149–50.
26. Cunliffe 1969, 151–4; 1984, 154–7; R.I.B. 138, 150 and 153.
27. Cunliffe 1969, 154; 1984, 157; R.I.B. 146. Inf. on recent work from Prof. B. W. Cunliffe.
28. Cunliffe 1969, 149–50.
29. Inner Precinct Period 3: Cunliffe 1984, 68–73; Cunliffe and Davenport 1985, 55–61 and 180–1.
30. Cunliffe 1969, 29–33; Cunliffe and Davenport 1985, 123–9.
31. Baths Period 4: Cunliffe 1969, 114–15; 1976a, 11–16; 1984, 139–44.
32. Cunliffe 1969, 166–73; O'Leary 1981.
33. Cunliffe 1984, 169–72.
34. *Ibid.*, 177.
35. Haverfield 1906, 264–7; Norton, in Cunliffe 1969, 212–18.
36. R.I.B. 156 and 165.
37. R.I.B. 155.
38. R.I.B. 155; Cunliffe 1969, 189 and 205.
39. Cunliffe 1969, 206.
40. R.I.B. 149 and 163.
41. Cunliffe 1988.
42. R.I.B. 141.
43. Cf. Branigan 1976, fig. 5; Cunliffe 1984, 181.
44. Greene, in Cunliffe 1979, 9.
45. Ambrose, in Cunliffe 1979, 115–22.
46. Greene, in Cunliffe 1979, 72.
47. R.I.B. 151.

48. R.I.B. 152.
49. Inner Precinct Period 4: Cunliffe 1984, 73–4; Cunliffe and Davenport 1985, 61–5 and 181.
50. Temple Period 3: Cunliffe and Davenport 1985, 35.
51. Baths Period 5: West end: Cunliffe 1976a, 16–19; East end: Cunliffe 1969, 115.
52. Cunliffe and Davenport 1985, 184.
53. Inner Precinct Period 5: Cunliffe 1984, 209–13; Cunliffe and Davenport 1985, 66–72 and 184–5.
54. Inner Precinct Period 6: Cunliffe and Davenport 1985, 72–5.
55. Cunliffe 1983.
56. Cunliffe 1969, 159.
57. Alcock 1973a, 118.
58. Ravenna Cosmography, 106.57.
59. Rivet and Smith 1979, 254.
60. Conveniently summarized in Haverfield 1905, 222–7.
61. R.I.B. 2243.
62. Jones 1975, 134.
63. Haverfield 1905, 223–4.
64. Rooke 1789, 137–8; Haverfield 1905, 225.
65. Rolleston 1869; 1880; Dudley Buxton 1921.
66. Bradford and Goodchild 1939.
67. Harding 1972, 62; 1987.
68. Hingley 1982; 1985.
69. Site C, Bradford and Goodchild 1939, 11–15.
70. Harding 1987, 11.
71. *Ibid.*, 11–12.
72. Site B, Bradford and Goodchild 1939, 6–8.
73. Site A, *ibid.*, 8–11.
74. Harding 1987, 5–9.
75. *Ibid.*, 13.
76. Harding 1972, 123; 1987, 16; Hingley 1985, 209.
77. Stevens 1940; Picard 1970.
78. For the relevant details, see Hingley 1985.
79. Bradford and Goodchild 1939, 27–35.
80. Harding 1987, 13–15.
81. Bradford and Goodchild 1939, 36–7.
82. Hingley 1982, 306–9; 1985, 205–7.
83. Fulford 1985, 68–9.
84. Site C, Bradford and Goodchild 1939, 37; Site A, *ibid.*, 32 and 35.
85. Sutherland, in Bradford and Goodchild 1939, 63.

86. Rolleston 1869; 1880; Dudley Buxton 1921; Bradford and Goodchild 1939, 54–7.
87. Bradford and Goodchild 1939, 65–6 and fig. 12.
88. Inf. from Dr R. Hingley.
89. Wheeler 1928.
90. France and Gobel 1968; 1985; Bartlett 1988a and b.
91. Hull 1963, 139–43; Davison 1973.
92. 1970–1: D.O.E. *Arch. Excavations* 1970, 60–1; *Britannia* 2, (1971), 272–3, 289; Conlon 1973. 1980–1: *Britannia* 12, (1981), 350; 13, (1982), 371–2.
93. 1962: *J. Roman Studs.* 53, (1963), 138. 1972–5: D.O.E. *Arch. Excavations* 1972, 49; *Britannia* 4, (1973), 304 and 325; 5, (1974), 442. 1979–80: *Britannia* 12, (1981), 350.
94. France and Gobel 1985, 21–3.
95. Fitzpatrick, in France and Gobel 1985, 56–8.
96. Bartlett 1988a and b.
97. France and Gobel 1985, 82 and 104.
98. Conlon 1973, 41–6.
99. For the temple sequence, see France and Gobel 1985, 23–48.
100. See for example Wacher 1975a and Frere 1983.
101. Wheeler 1928, 304–5.
102. Hull 1963, 139–41; France and Gobel 1985, 17.
103. For the inscription, see France and Gobel 1985, 101; for the head, Bartlett 1988a, 6.
104. Conlon 1973, 37–8.
105. *Britannia* 4, (1973), 304.
106. Conlon 1973, 38.
107. Inf. from Mr R. Bartlett.
108. *Britannia* 11, (1980), 378.
109. Hull 1963, 141.
110. Conlon 1973, 34.
111. *Ibid.*, 34 and 38.
112. *J. Roman Studs.* 53, (1963), 138.
113. For the weights and coins, see Conlon 1973, 38; for the leather finds, *Britannia* 12, (1981), 350.
114. *Britannia* 13, (1982), 371–2.
115. Inf. from Mr R. Bartlett.
116. *Britannia* 4, (1973), 304; 5, (1974), 442.
117. Hull 1963, 142.
118. France and Gobel 1985, 48; Bartlett 1988a, 3.
119. France and Gobel 1985, 48.
120. Inf. from Mr R. Bartlett.
121. Wedlake 1982, fig. 2.
122. The finds from these excavations, apart from the statue which is in the Bristol Museum, are in Devizes Museum: Anon. 1958, 104.
123. Wedlake 1982.
124. *Ibid.*, 4.
125. *Ibid.*, 6–7.
126. *Ibid.*, 7–14; for inscriptions and other objects associated with religion, see pp.135–50.
127. Wedlake 1982, 7.
128. *Ibid.*, 8, 112–18.
129. *Ibid.*, 36.
130. *Ibid.*, 104.
131. *Ibid.*, fig. 5.
132. *Ibid.*, 99–100.
133. *Ibid.*, 94.
134. *Ibid.*, 54–7.
135. *Ibid.*, 67–75.
136. *Ibid.*, 95–8.
137. *Ibid.*, 90–3.
138. Green 1982.
139. Wedlake 1982, 84–6, 179–80.
140. Scrope 1862, 59; Grinsell 1957, 92.
141. Antonine Itinerary 472.2 (Iter II).
142. Rivet and Smith 1979, 485.
143. Harker 1980, 286.
144. Penn 1966, 113.
145. *Ibid.*, 116; Harker 1980, 286.
146. Hull 1958, 263–4.
147. Penn 1966, 109.
148. Harker 1980, 286.
149. Penn 1959, 81.
150. Penn 1968a, 109.
151. Penn 1960.
152. Penn 1963, 110–16.
153. Penn 1961.
154. Penn 1963, 116–32.
155. Harker 1974.
156. Harker 1971–3.
157. Penn 1959, 83–9.
158. Blagg 1980.
159. Penn 1959, 79–81.
160. Penn 1969a, 164–71.
161. *Ibid.*, 171–6.
162. Penn 1966, 112.
163. Penn 1958.
164. Penn 1966, 111.
165. Wheeler and Wheeler 1932, 44–9.

166. Penn 1966, 110; Harker 1980, 286.
167. Jessup 1928, 339.
168. Penn 1969b, 257.
169. Wheeler *et al.* 1932, 91.
170. Rashleigh 1803; Jessup 1959, 14 and 29–30.
171. Penn 1967, LXIII.
172. Penn 1968b.
173. Penn 1960, 11.
174. Penn 1963.
175. Gelling 1967, 95.
176. Brief accounts appear in Lawrence 1863 and 1864a and b.
177. Rawes 1973; 1976; 1980.
178. St Joseph 1969, 128, pl. VI, 1; Wilson 1975, 13. For a useful summary of the site, see R.C.H.M. 1976, 125–6.
179. Lewis 1966, 3 and 77; R.C.H.M. 1976, 126.
180. Toynbee 1964, 178.
181. Rawes 1976.
182. Toynbee 1964, 179.
183. Green 1976, 175.
184. R.C.H.M. 1976, 126.
185. I.e. not unlike the theatre at Gosbecks Farm, Colchester: Dunnett 1971.
186. Lawrence 1864a, 424.
187. R.C.H.M. 1976, 126.
188. Rawes 1980, 19.
189. R.C.H.M. 1976, 125.

Chapter 10 (pp. 203–34)

1. The principal accounts are those by Green, C. 1977 and Knowles 1977, summarizing research to 1976. Short notes on more recent work appear in *Britannia* 8, (1977), 403; 9, (1978), 448; 11, (1980), 375; 12, (1981), 347; 13, (1982), 369–70; 14, (1983), 307–8; 15, (1984), 305; 18, (1987), 330.
2. Edwards 1977, 230–2 and plates 19–22.
3. Considerable unpublished information was generously supplied by Dr and Mrs A. K. Knowles.
4. Knowles 1977, 211; information about the skillets from Dr Knowles.
5. For the area south-west of the river, see Edwards 1977, 232; the north-eastern suburb in the Oxnead area has only recently been defined from finds during fieldwork.
6. *Britannia* 11, (1980), 375.
7. *Britannia* 8, (1977), 403.
8. Knowles 1977, 211.
9. Green, C. 1977, 37.
10. Edwards 1977, 232.
11. Green, C. 1977, 37–47.
12. Knowles 1977, 213.
13. See summaries in *Britannia* 3, (1972), 330; 6, (1975), 260; 8, (1977), 403; 9, (1978), 448; 11, (1980), 375; 12, (1981), 347; 13, (1982), 369–70; 14, (1983), 307–8; 15, (1984), 305; 18, (1987), 330.
14. Green, C. 1977, 44–8.
15. E.g. *Britannia* 6, (1975), 260; 11, (1980), 375.
16. Knowles 1977, 213–15.
17. *Britannia* 8, (1977), 403.
18. *Britannia* 6, (1975), 260; 7, (1976), 341; Knowles 1977, 211–13.
19. Knowles 1977, 216–20.
20. Green, C. 1977, 93.
21. Knowles 1977, 211.
22. Biek, in Green, C. 1977, 54–5.
23. For brief details, see Knowles 1977, 213.
24. *Britannia* 5, (1974), 438.
25. Inf. from Dr A. K. Knowles.
26. For the Venus figures, see Green, C. 1977, 87; *Britannia* 13, (1982), 369–70; for the other objects, see Green 1976, 205.
27. Details from Dr A. K. Knowles; see also *Britannia* 13, (1982), 369–70; 14, (1983), 307–8.
28. Knowles 1977, 215.
29. *Britannia* 8, (1977), 403; 9, (1978), 448.
30. Green, C. 1977, 47–8.
31. *Britannia* 8, (1977), 403; 11, (1980), 375.
32. For nineteenth-century discoveries, see especially Scarth 1874–6 and Haverfield 1906, 334–9. A detailed bibliography appears in Budge *et al.* 1974, 345–7.
33. For the amphitheatre, see Anon. 1909 and Gray 1910; for more recent work and a summary of the lead pigs, see Boon 1951, *Britannia* 2, (1971), 278 and fig. 12, Budge *et al.* 1974 and Elkington 1976, Appendix 4, 230–4.
34. Bulleid and Gray 1911, 241.
35. *Britannia* 2, (1971), 278.
36. Elkington 1976, 230 Nos. 1 and 5; Clement-Whittick 1982.
37. Elkington 1976, 231 No. 7.
38. *Britannia* 2, (1971), 278.
39. Haverfield 1906, 335–7; Budge *et al.* 1974.

40. Haverfield 1906, 335.
41. Anon. 1909; Gray 1910.
42. Donovan 1949, 80–1.
43. Haverfield 1906, 337.
44. Jones and Lewis 1974, 136–7, fig. 2.
45. Pliny, *Historia Naturalis* XXXIV, 17, 164.
46. Elkington 1976, 231–3 Nos. 6,8,14 and 16–17.
47. Frere 1987, 278.
48. Haverfield 1906, 338.
49. Ravenna Cosmography, 106.31 and 106.46.
50. Ptolemy, *Geography* II, 3, 11.
51. Rivet and Smith 1979, 120 and 451.
52. Rivet 1964, 168.
53. Berry 1975; Simmons 1979, 188; 1980, 69.
54. For a summary of early finds, see Haverfield 1901, 208–10.
55. For a general treatment of the site, see Freezer 1979, 1–8.
56. St Joseph 1943; 1946, 39–40.
57. Whitehouse 1962; *Britannia* 9, (1978), 439.
58. Hunt 1975; *Britannia* 8, (1977), 396–7.
59. Sawle 1978; *Britannia* 10, (1979), 299.
60. Gelling 1959a, 2–3.
61. *Britannia* 3, (1972), 317; 4, (1973), 288.
62. Gelling 1959a, 3–7.
63. Haverfield 1901, 208.
64. Hodgkinson 1928; 1930b; St Joseph 1946, 42.
65. Tomlinson 1967; Barfield and Tomlinson 1971; *J. Roman Studs.* 58, (1968), 187; Freezer 1979, 5–7.
66. Barfield and Tomlinson 1971, 18; *Britannia* 3, (1972), 317.
67. *Britannia* 5, (1974), 430; Barfield 1974, 49.
68. *Britannia* 3, (1972), 317.
69. Barfield 1976; 1977; *Britannia* 8, (1977), 396–7; 9, (1978), 439.
70. Sawle 1978; *Britannia* 10, (1979), 299.
71. *Britannia* 3, (1972), 317.
72. *Britannia* 19, (1988), 448.
73. Gelling 1959a, 21.
74. Pape 1934 and Bemrose 1958.
75. Goodyear 1970 and 1976.
76. Charlton 1961 and 1962.
77. *Britannia* 2, (1971), 259–60.
78. Goodyear 1976.
79. Cf. Charlton 1961, 31; 1962, 61.
80. Goodyear 1976, 14.
81. Charlton 1961, 31; somewhat larger figures are quoted in Charlton 1962, 64, but these seem excessive on current published evidence.
82. Charlton 1961, 34.
83. *Ibid.*, 30 and 34–8.
84. Charlton 1962, 62 and 65–6.
85. Charlton 1961, 30–1.
86. *Ibid.*, 32.
87. *Ibid.*, 34–8; Charlton 1962, 64.
88. Charlton 1961, 38.
89. *Ibid.*, 39–41.
90. *Ibid.*, 46; Charlton 1962, 64.
91. Charlton 1961, 36 and 37; 1962, 62 and 64.
92. Charlton 1961, 31.
93. *Ibid.*, 28 and 32.
94. Ravenna Cosmography, 106.46.
95. Rivet and Smith 1979, 334.
96. Stukeley 1776, I, 85.
97. Webster 1961; Brassington 1967; Todd 1967; Brassington 1969.
98. Now conveniently summarized in a series of articles edited by Dool, Wheeler *et al.* 1986. See also Brassington 1971; 1980; 1982a; Dool 1972.
99. *Britannia* 19, (1988), 446.
100. Forrest 1967; Brassington 1970; Dool 1986a.
101. *Britannia* 4, (1973), 285.
102. *Britannia* 1, (1970), 283.
103. For a summary of this military sequence, see Wheeler 1986c, 300–3.
104. Brassington 1971.
105. Wheeler 1986a; Dool 1986b.
106. Cf. Brassington 1981; Birss and Wheeler 1986.
107. Brassington 1982b.
108. Wheeler 1986c, 303.
109. *Britannia* 19, (1988), 446.
110. Wheeler 1986b, 222–7 and 248–50.
111. Cockerton 1959.
112. Wheeler 1986b, 229–48 and 250–2.
113. For details, see Watkin 1886, 243–51 and Thompson 1965, 91–7.
114. Anon. 1960.
115. For interim reports see Bestwick 1972; 1974; 1975a; 1975b. Shorter notes appear in *J. Roman Studs.* 57, (1967), 181; 59, (1969), 210–11; *Britannia* 1, (1970), 282; 2, (1971), 255; 3, (1972), 314; 4, (1973),

284; 5, (1974), 419; 6, (1975), 242; 7, (1976), 321. For a recent summary of evidence see Petch 1987, 202–8.

116. Bestwick 1975a, 50; 1975b, 66–7 and 68.
117. *J. Roman Studs.* 59, (1969), 210–11; Bestwick 1972, 3–4; 1975a, 49.
118. Jones 1975, 168.
119. *Britannia* 1, (1970), 282.
120. Margary 1973, 302–4, routes 40a and b.
121. Thompson 1965, 93; its course, however, must run east of the known buildings on Sites B, C and J and west of those on Site G; inf. from Dr D. J. Bestwick.
122. Watkin 1886, 246.
123. Bestwick 1975a, 50.
124. Bestwick 1974, 30; 1975a, 49.
125. *J. Roman Studs.* 59, (1969), 210–11; *Britannia* 1, (1970), 282; Bestwick 1972, 4; 1975b, 66–8.
126. Bestwick 1975a, 50.
127. Bestwick 1974, 30.
128. Ravenna Cosmography, 106.46; Rivet and Smith 1979, 451.
129. Bestwick 1975a, 50; 1975b, 67 and 68.
130. *Britannia* 1, (1970), 282; Bestwick 1975b, 67–8.
131. *Britannia* 1, (1970), 313.
132. Bestwick 1975b, 70; for the individual examples, see pp. 66, 67 and 68 respectively. The function of the circular kilns still remains uncertain.
133. *Britannia* 4, (1973), 284; 5, (1974), 419; Bestwick 1974, 30; Bestwick and Cleland 1974, 147.
134. *Britannia* 6, (1975), 242; 7, (1976), 321; Bestwick 1975a, 49.
135. *J. Roman Studs.* 59, (1969), 210–11.
136. *Britannia* 2, (1971), 255.
137. Inf. from Dr D.J. Bestwick.
138. For these early discoveries, see Watkin 1886, 260–73.
139. May 1897; 1900; 1902; 1904; 1905; 1907.
140. Interim summaries in *J. Roman Studs.* 57, (1967), 179; 58, (1968), 182; *Britannia* 1, (1970), 281–2; D.O.E. *Arch. Excavations* 1974, 50–1; 1976, 36–7. For a recent summary of evidence see Petch 1987, 194–8.
141. Thompson 1965, 18–19.
142. Cf. *J. Roman Studs.* 57, (1967), 179; 58, (1968), 182; *Britannia* 1, (1970), 281–2.
143. Hartley and Webster 1973.

144. Thompson 1965, 80; Hartley and Webster 1973, 103; Webster 1975; Petch 1987, 197.
145. Petch 1987, 197–8.
146. Hartley and Webster 1973, 103.
147. For a summary of the main buildings excavated by May, see Thompson 1965, 72.
148. For these and other industrial aspects, cf. Thompson 1965, 73–8.
149. Hartley and Webster 1973; Thompson 1965, 78.
150. D.O.E. *Arch. Excavations* 1974, 50–7; 1976, 36–7.
151. Petch 1987, 198.
152. Camden 1695, 519.
153. Antonine Itinerary 484.8.
154. The alternative reading of Ptolemy and the Ravenna list – *Branogenium* – is preferred by Rivet and Smith 1979, 275.
155. Ravenna Cosmography, 106.30.
156. Rivet and Smith 1979, 496.
157. *Britannia* 8, (1977), 397.
158. Barker 1970, 16.
159. *Ibid.*, 14–15 and 48.
160. *Ibid.*, 16.
161. *Ibid.*, 48.
162. *Britannia* 9, (1978), 439.
163. Barker 1970, 16 and 50.
164. Gelling 1959b.
165. Barker 1970, 16.
166. *Ibid.*, 18.
167. Haverfield 1901, 205.
168. Sawle 1977; *Britannia* 9, (1978), 439.
169. *Britannia* 8, (1977), 397.
170. Barker 1970, 18 and 63–4.
171. Carver 1980, 26.
172. Carver 1976; *Britannia* 8, (1977), 397.

Chapter 11 (pp. 235–78)

1. Trollope 1870.
2. Work on the defences has been published in full by Todd 1981. Interim accounts on the other excavations include Barley 1964, Wilson and May 1965, Whitwell *et al.* 1966 and Barley *et al.* 1974.
3. For general syntheses, see Whitwell 1970, 65–7 and Todd 1975.
4. Todd 1981, 2–4.
5. Todd 1975, 215; May 1976, 165–8.
6. Wilson and May 1965, 13; Whitwell *et al.* 1966, 13; Barley *et al.* 1974, 16; Todd 1975, 215.

7. Todd 1981, 15, 17–18, 21 and 22.
8. Whitwell *et al.* 1966, 10 and 12.
9. Todd 1981, 92. A possible street running west, excavated in 1960 (*J. Roman Studs.* 51, (1961), 171), has been assigned by Todd 1981, 94 to a medieval or later date.
10. Todd 1981, 29.
11. *Ibid.*, 92–5.
12. *Ibid.*, 14.
13. Whitwell *et al.* 1966, 12.
14. For details of the defensive sequence, see Todd 1981, 10–46.
15. Trollope 1870, 8–9.
16. Frere 1961.
17. Whitwell 1970, 124–6; *J. Roman Studs.* 52, (1962), 192, No. 7.
18. Trollope 1870, 11; *Britannia* 2, (1971), 257.
19. Todd 1981, 93 and fig. 25.
20. Hawkes 1946, 20.
21. Barley 1964, 9; Wilson and May 1965, 13; Whitwell *et al.* 1966, 13; Barley *et al.* 1974, 16; Wilson 1968; Todd 1975, 221.
22. Wilson and May 1965, 13; *J. Roman Studs.* 56, (1966), 203.
23. Trollope 1870, 3–4.
24. Todd 1975, 223.
25. Ravenna Cosmography, 106.55; Rivet and Smith 1979, 265–6.
26. Stukeley 1724, 28 and 96–7.
27. Hawkes 1946.
28. Caistor: Rahtz 1960; Horncastle: Field and Hurst 1983.
29. *Britannia* 18, (1987), 322.
30. Field and Hurst 1983, 76–84.
31. Whitwell 1970, 7.
32. Rahtz 1960, 178–87; Field and Hurst 1983, 49–59.
33. Corder and Romans 1936.
34. Field and Hurst 1983, 59–62.
35. C.I.L. VII 1267; Hawkes 1946, 23–4; Toynbee 1964, 355; for the Christian significance, see Thomas 1981, 125.
36. Field and Hurst 1983, 76–82.
37. Ramm 1971, 187–9.
38. Radford 1946, 89–91 and 95–9. It has been suggested that Caistor, renamed Sidnacester, became the centre of the episcopal see of Lindsey.
39. For a summary of earlier discoveries, see R.C.H.M. 1959, XXXVI ff. and the gazeteer of finds in Browne 1974; the latter also contains a useful list of references.
40. The main accounts are those in Alexander 1975, Pullinger 1978 and Wilkes and Elrington 1978, 39–43. Interim summaries include Alexander 1964, and Alexander *et al.* 1967. Short notes appear in *J. Roman Studs.* 54, (1964), 167–8; 55, (1965), 213; 58, (1968), 194; *Britannia* 1, (1970), 290; 4, (1973), 300; 5, (1974), 438; 7, (1976), 340–1; 15, (1984), 296. Dr J. Alexander and Mrs J. Pullinger kindly allowed access to their unpublished manuscript as well as generously providing much additional information.
41. Alexander 1975, 104.
42. Inf. from Dr J. Alexander.
43. For the coins, see Alexander 1975, 104; for the enclosure see *Britannia* 7, (1976), 340–1 and Pullinger 1978, 59, though any religious association is now discounted.
44. R.C.H.M. 1959, XXXVI; Wilkes and Elrington 1978, 39.
45. Inf. from Mrs J. Pullinger.
46. Alexander 1975, 106; Pullinger 1978, 59; Wilkes and Elrington 1978, 39–41; *Britannia* 7, (1976), 340–1.
47. Wilkes and Elrington 1978, 41; inf. from Dr J. Alexander.
48. *Britannia* 15, (1984), 296.
49. Inf. from Mrs J. Pullinger.
50. *Britannia* 7, (1976), 340–1.
51. Browne 1974, 19–20 and Map 2.
52. For details see Wilkes and Elrington 1978, 41.
53. *Britannia* 19, (1988), 450; inf. from Mrs J. Pullinger.
54. R.C.H.M. 1959, LXII.
55. Wilkes and Elrington 1978, 41–2; inf. from Dr J. Alexander.
56. Alexander 1975, 106 and 108; inf. on kilns from Mrs J. Pullinger.
57. Browne 1974, 20.
58. Pullinger 1978, 57–8.
59. *Ibid.*, 58–9; *Britannia* 7, (1976), 340–1; additional inf. from Mrs J. Pullinger.
60. Alexander 1975, 108; Wilkes and Elrington 1978, 42; inf. on most recent work from Mrs J. Pullinger.
61. South-west gate, Alexander *et al.* 1967; *J. Roman Studs.* 58, (1968), 194; *Britannia* 1,

(1970), 290. North-west and north-east gates, inf. from Mrs J. Pullinger.

62. Alexander 1975, 108; Wilkes and Elrington 1978, 42–3; inf. from Dr J. Alexander.

63. The evidence is summarized in Liversidge 1977.

64. Inf. from Dr J. Alexander and Mrs J. Pullinger.

65. Pullinger 1978, 60.

66. St Joseph 1973, 245; Wilson 1975, 14, pl. 13A.

67. Andrews 1926.

68. *Ibid.*; R.I.B. 243.

69. *J. Roman Studs.* 52, (1962), 171.

70. *J. Roman Studs.* 58, (1968), 188.

71. *Ibid.*

72. Haverfield 1904, 234–5.

73. For a summary of current knowledge, see R.C.H.M. 1976, 12–13 and McWhirr 1981, 60–2.

74. Oswald 1964, 21.

75. For those along Watling Street, see Webster 1971.

76. St Joseph 1961a, 133 and pl. X 2.

77. Oswald 1964.

78. Haverfield 1901, 221.

79. *Ibid.*

80. Taylor 1963.

81. Morcom 1938.

82. Webster 1971.

83. Antonine Itinerary 470.3 (Iter II).

84. See Haverfield 1904, 233–4.

85. Scott 1973; 1981; *Britannia* 15, (1984), 295.

86. Webster 1978, 97.

87. Hartley 1973a; Fulford 1977.

88. For principal kilns, see Hemsley 1961; Hartley 1973b; Swan 1984, 98–101.

89. *J. Roman Studs.* 56, (1966), 206.

90. *Britannia* 3, (1972), 319; Hartley 1971; *Britannia* 9, (1978), 440.

91. Vose 1980, 132–3.

92. O'Neil 1931.

93. Oswald and Gathercole 1958.

94. Mahany 1971.

95. *Ibid.*, 24–5.

96. Oswald and Gathercole 1958, 39.

97. The site's name is well established from the Antonine Itinerary 477.6 (Iter VI) and 479.1 (Iter VIII), see Rivet and Smith 1979, 413–14.

98. For a summary of early references, see Standish 1909 and Walters 1910, 15–17.

99. Pryce 1912; Oswald and Pryce 1914.

100. The principal summaries appear in Oswald 1928; 1941; 1948a and 1952. Various pottery reports were also issued by Oswald (1923; 1926; 1948b), but these need to be used with extreme caution.

101. Todd 1966; 1969. For a brief summary of all the evidence, see Todd 1975, 211–14.

102. Cf. Todd 1969, 17. For the military metalwork, see Webster 1958a, 88.

103. Oswald 1952, 3–6.

104. For details, see Todd 1969, 22–7.

105. *Ibid.*, 17.

106. For discussions of the site's internal morphology, see Todd 1969, 70–1 and 1975, 211.

107. For H, I and J, as well as other structures excavated in 1966–8, see Todd 1969, 59–63.

108. For F see Oswald 1952, 6; for G see Oswald 1948a, 3–6.

109. Todd 1969, 63–5.

110. Oswald 1941, 44–5; Todd 1969, 57.

111. Oswald 1941, 34–41; Todd 1969, 57.

112. Oswald 1941, 42–4; Todd 1969, 58.

113. Oswald 1941, figs. 5–6.

114. Todd 1966; 1969, 42–55.

115. Todd 1969, 70–1.

116. *Ibid.*, 61–2.

117. For the *Deae Nutrices*, see Todd 1969, 93. The relief is illustrated in Green 1976, pl. IIIa, but is not certainly from Margidunum; cf. Todd 1971.

118. Todd 1969, 73–7.

119. Walters 1910, 16.

120. Todd 1969, 78.

121. Clarke 1959, 88.

122. Millett 1975; Graham and Millett 1980; Millett and Graham 1986 (this latter contains a full bibliography of earlier interims and forms the basis of the current account).

123. For a discussion of the main roads and the associated side-streets, see Millett and Graham 1986, 151.

124. Area A: *ibid.*, 13–21.

125. Area F burials: *ibid.*, 61.

126. Area B: *ibid.*, 27.

127. Area D: *ibid.*, 46–8.

128. For a discussion of the site's layout, see Millett and Graham 1986, 151–3.

129. *Ibid.*, 21–3.
130. Areas E and F: *ibid.*, 49–54.
131. For general comments on buildings, see Millett and Graham 1986, 151.
132. *Ibid.*, 33–6.
133. *Ibid.*, 158.
134. *Ibid.*, 157.
135. Millett 1975, 216; 1979, 133.
136. Area C: Millett and Graham 1986, 43–6.
137. *Ibid.*, 158.
138. *Ibid.*, 159.
139. *Ibid.*, 56–61.
140. *Ibid.*, 33 and 37.
141. Antonine Itinerary 477.7 (Iter VI); Rivet and Smith 1979, 241.
142. Variously published: St Joseph 1953, 91; 1958a, 98, pl. XV, 1; 1966, 28–9, pl. VI; *J. Roman Studs.* 54, (1964), pl. XIII, 1; Webster 1958a, pl. IXA; and most recently Frere and St Joseph 1983, 177, pl. 108. It should be noted that the plan of the enclosure on fig. 17 repeats an earlier error by showing an entrance into the annexe. Excavations have shown that it does not exist.
143. The excavations by A. Oswald, M. W. Barley and K. D. M. Dauncey down to those in 1952 are usefully summarized in Inskeep 1966. See also Oswald 1939 and *J. Roman Studs.* 51, (1961), 177 for the excavations by C. Green in 1955 and 1960.
144. *J. Roman Studs.* 54, (1964), 159; 56, (1966), 203.
145. Inskeep 1966.
146. *J. Roman Studs.* 54, (1964), 159.
147. *J. Roman Studs.* 56, (1966), 203.
148. Toynbee 1962, 156 and pl. 78.
149. Webster 1971.
150. Antonine Itinerary 470 (Iter II).
151. Ravenna Cosmography, 106.48.
152. Stukeley 1724, I, 58.
153. For details see Blay 1925.
154. Lynam 1913; 1915; Webster 1958b; Round 1971b; 1974b; 1975.
155. St Joseph 1953, 83.
156. Principal details in Lyon and Gould 1961; 1964, 7–11; Gould 1964; 1968; Round 1971a; 1983.
157. Oswald 1968.
158. Webster 1958b.
159. Lynam 1913; Webster 1958b; Round 1974a and b; 1975.
160. Webster 1959; Gould 1964, 2–7.
161. Cunliffe 1975, 65–8.
162. Webster 1971, 44–5.
163. Round 1976; 1977; Round *et al.* 1980; *Britannia* 8, (1977), 393–4; 9, (1978), 435–6; 10, (1979), 296; 11, (1980), 367.
164. Jackson 1927.
165. Blay 1925; Hodgkinson 1930a.

Chapter 12 (pp. 279–313)

1. Hadman and Upex 1975, fig. 4.
2. Hadman and Upex 1977, 9.
3. Hartshorne 1847, 13.
4. Summarized successively in Hadman 1967; Hadman and Upex 1972; 1975; 1977; 1979; Dix 1983; and in *Britannia* 6, (1975), 253; 8, (1977), 399; 9, (1978), 442; 10, (1979), 302; 12, (1981), 341; 14, (1983), 305–6; 15, (1984), 300–1; 16, (1985), 288; 17, (1986), 397.
5. Cf. Hadman and Upex 1975, 13–15.
6. Guy 1977.
7. Guy 1981.
8. *Britannia* 15, (1984), 300; 16, (1985), 288.
9. Painter 1977.
10. Westell 1932a and b; Westell and Applebaum 1932; Applebaum 1933.
11. Stead 1975; Stead and Rigby 1986.
12. For interim summaries, see Burleigh 1982 and Selkirk 1983; short notes also appear in *Britannia* 12, (1981), 345; 13, (1982), 369; 15, (1984), 304; 17, (1986), 401–2; 18, (1987), 327. Additional information was provided by Mr G. Burleigh.
13. Stead and Rigby 1986, 51–61.
14. Burleigh 1982, 7–14; Selkirk 1983, 71–2.
15. *Britannia* 17, (1986), 401.
16. Stead and Rigby 1986, 61.
17. For details, see Stead 1975, 127; Stead and Rigby 1986, 84–5; Burleigh 1982, 14.
18. Rigby, in Stead and Rigby 1986, 224.
19. Inf. on the roads from Mr G. Burleigh.
20. *Britannia* 17, (1986), 401.
21. Stead 1975, 127 and 128; Stead and Rigby 1986, 43–4 and 84–5, and figs. 3–5.
22. Burleigh 1982, 10 and 15.
23. Stead and Rigby 1986, 44 and 86.
24. *Ibid.*, 44–50.
25. For the general range of buildings, see Stead 1975, 127–8 and Stead and Rigby 1986, 32–42.
26. Burleigh 1982, 14.

27. Buildings 5–7, Stead and Rigby 1986, 36–8.
28. *Ibid.*, 86; *Britannia* 17, (1986), 401.
29. Buildings 10 and 11, *ibid.*, 40–2; another possible large building has also been suggested by the geophysical survey in the area south-west of the Romano-Celtic temple.
30. *Ibid.*, 43; Burleigh 1982, 8–9.
31. Burleigh 1982, 14 and 15.
32. Foster, in Stead and Rigby 1986, 143.
33. *Ibid.*, 86.
34. For the Venus figurine, see Stead and Rigby 1986, 168; for the lead curse, Westell 1932b, 290–2.
35. Stead and Rigby 1986, 167–8.
36. Westell 1932a and b.
37. Stead and Rigby 1986, 61–75.
38. Selkirk 1983, 73; *Britannia* 15, (1984), 304.
39. Stead and Rigby 1986, 75–8; *Britannia* 18, (1987), 327 and additional inf. from Mr G. Burleigh.
40. *Britannia* 17, (1986), 401.
41. Stead and Rigby 1986, 78; inf. from Mr G. Burleigh.
42. Stead and Rigby 1986, 34, 38 and 87.
43. *Ibid.*, 44 and 86.
44. *Ibid.*, 259.
45. *Ibid.*, 87; Burleigh 1982, 8.
46. Selkirk 1983, 74.
47. Witts 1881, 56; Anon. 1882–3; 1886; Donovan 1935.
48. Dunning 1976.
49. Usefully summarized down to 1976 in R.C.H.M. 1976, 17–19.
50. *Ibid.*, 20–1; Donovan 1935; O'Neil 1969; 1973.
51. Witts 1881, 56; O'Neil 1969, 30.
52. *Ibid.*, 35–9.
53. *Ibid.*, 39–42.
54. *Ibid.*, 34–5.
55. Donovan 1934.
56. *Britannia* 10, (1979), 318; 13, (1982), 377.
57. R.C.H.M. 1976, 79–80.
58. O'Neil and Toynbee 1958, 52–5; Toynbee 1964, 161 and 177–8.
59. Herdman 1933; Donovan 1934, 115–17; Guy 1981.
60. Donovan 1935, 243.
61. Hull 1963, 55–6; Drury 1976, 3–86; Eddy 1984. Short notes appear in *Britannia* 12,

(1981), 348; 15, (1984), 307; 16, (1985), 295 and Hope 1983.
62. Drury 1976, 86–120.
63. For details and a tentative chronology, see Drury 1976, 121–3.
64. Pratt, in Drury 1976, 6 and 63.
65. Drury 1978, 37 and 134–5.
66. Drury 1976, 104–8 and 123.
67. Eddy 1984.
68. *Britannia* 16, (1985), 295.
69. Hope 1983, 163; *Britannia* 15, (1984), 307; Drury 1976, 109–10 and 113.
70. For details, see Drury 1976, 124–5.
71. Pratt, in Drury 1976, 6–8 and 63.
72. *Ibid.*, 41.
73. Drury 1976, 92 and 124.
74. For the property boundaries and buildings, see Pratt in Drury 1976, 63–4.
75. *Britannia* 15, (1984), 307.
76. Pratt, in Drury 1976, 26 and 64; Tylecote, Bayley and Biek, *ibid.*, 94–6.
77. Pratt, in Drury 1976, 64.
78. Drury 1976, 103.
79. Pratt, in Drury 1976, 23.
80. For Sites 8–12, see Drury 1976, 91–6; for the other possible cemeteries, *ibid.*, 99 and 114.
81. *Ibid.*, 112.
82. Rodwell 1975, 93; Drury 1976, 42.
83. Pratt, in Drury 1976, 46.
84. Drury 1976, 127.
85. Collinson 1791.
86. Skinner (n.d.). He made the extraordinary claim that Camerton was the 'true' *Camulodunum*, not Colchester.
87. Scarth 1863.
88. Haverfield 1906, 289–94.
89. Horne 1929; 1934.
90. The work from 1946–56 was published in Wedlake 1958.
91. Wedlake 1958, 37–41.
92. Rivet and Smith 1979, 121.
93. Wedlake 1958, 7.
94. *Ibid.*, 48–52.
95. Branigan 1977.
96. Leech 1982; Ellis 1984.
97. Wedlake 1958, 54–63.
98. *Ibid.*, 79–82.
99. *Ibid.*, 82–7. Another mould was found in 1958; *J. Roman Studs.* 49, (1959), 129.
100. Wedlake 1958, 58 and 60.
101. *Ibid.*, 63–7.

102. *Ibid.*, 52–4.
103. R.I.B. 180.
104. R.I.B. 179.
105. Wedlake 1958, 98–101.
106. *Ibid.*, 235–42.
107. *Ibid.*, 96–7.
108. Antonine Itinerary 484.3; for discussion, see Rivet and Smith 1979, 273. Early knowledge of the site is summarized in James and Francis 1979, 13–19 and Robinson 1980, 19–26.
109. For geophysical surveys, see Thomas 1980 and Chamberlain 1983.
110. The principal interims include Anon. 1978; Evans 1983; 1984; Parkhouse 1981a, b and c; 1982a and c; *Britannia* 13, (1982), 333–4; 15, (1983), 282.
111. Anon. 1978, 21; Parkhouse 1981b, 309.
112. Parkhouse 1982a, 15–16 and 18–19.
113. Davies 1967; R.C.A.H.M. 1976, 40–1; Robinson 1980, 12–13.
114. Anon. 1978, 17–18.
115. James and Francis 1979, 17; Parkhouse 1982a, 9–10.
116. No. 75, Anon. 1978, 18–19; No. 77, Parkhouse 1981a, 24–6; No. 83, Parkhouse 1982a, 16.
117. Thomas 1980.
118. Parkhouse 1982a, 11–12.
119. Chamberlain 1983.
120. Parkhouse 1983; Evans 1983 and 1984.
121. Parkhouse 1981a, 15–19; 1982a, 7–8; *Britannia* 13, (1982), 333–4; Inf. on the revised dating from Mr J. Parkhouse.
122. Parkhouse 1982a, 11.
123. Evans 1983, 28–30.
124. For inhumations in the bath-house area, see Parkhouse 1981a, 17; 1982a, 7; for an isolated cremation, Evans 1984, 64.
125. Parkhouse 1982b.
126. Parkhouse 1982a, 8; Evans 1984, 63.
127. Parkhouse 1982a, 10.
128. Phillips 1934, 111; Dudley 1949, 158–60; Loughlin and Miller 1979, 199–200.
129. Only the west side could be adequately excavated: *Britannia* 7, (1976), 324; 8, (1977), 389; 9, (1978), 433; 11, (1980), 366; Smith 1976–78; 1980–1. The most detailed account so far is Smith 1987, 188–98.
130. Cf. Smith 1987, 25–9.
131. *Ibid.*, 192–3.
132. *Britannia* 8, (1977), 390.
133. Smith 1987, 193.
134. *Ibid.*, 191–2; Pitts 1983.
135. *Ibid.*, 194.
136. Rudkin 1933, 225.
137. Interim notes appear in *Britannia* 7, (1976), 326; 8, (1977), 391; 9, (1978), 434; 10, (1979), 295; 12, (1981), 336; 13, (1982), 356; 17, (1986), 390; 18, (1987), 322; 19, (1988), 447. See also Simmons 1976; 1985; Oetgen 1986; 1987.
138. *Britannia* 8, (1977), 391; 10, (1979), 295; Simmons 1985, 17.
139. *Ibid.*, 18.
140. *Britannia* 7, (1976), 326; Simmons 1985, 18.
141. Oetgen 1987, 13.
142. *Britannia* 19, (1988), 447; Oetgen 1987, 14.
143. Simmons 1985, 18; Oetgen 1987, 15.
144. Simmons 1985, 18.
145. Oetgen 1987, 13–14; *Britannia* 19, (1988), 447.
146. *Britannia* 7, (1976), 326.
147. Oetgen 1987, 15.
148. Antonine Itinerary 478.4; Rivet and Smith 1979, 441; Sharpe 1913 and 1932.
149. Rendell 1970.
150. Elmsleigh, Crouch 1976a; FBG, Crouch and Shanks 1984. Interim accounts of the other sites include Crouch 1976b and 1978; short notes on most recent work appear in *Britannia* 7, (1976), 374; 8, (1977), 409; 9, (1978), 468; 11, (1980), 400; 13, (1982), 393. Much of this material is currently being revised for publication and so interim sequences and conclusions must be used with caution. Considerable advice and unpublished information was generously provided by Dr D. G. Bird and Mr P. Jones.
151. Crouch 1976b, 364 and map.
152. Inf. from Mr P. Jones.
153. For the cheek-piece, see Crouch 1976a, 77–80; inf. on the pottery from Mr P. Jones. The early road mentioned by Rendell 1970, 162 seems doubtful and was certainly not located to east or west.
154. *Britannia* 8, (1977), 409.
155. Inf. on the revised sequence from Mr P. Jones, replacing Crouch 1978, 180.
156. Crouch and Shanks 1984, 9–11 and 125–6.

157. Inf. from Mr P. Jones, supplementing and revising Crouch 1978, 180.
158. *Britannia* 8, (1977), 409.
159. Crouch and Shanks 1984, 13–17 and 126–7.
160. *Britannia* 13, (1982), 393.
161. Crouch 1978, 180.
162. Inf. from Mr P. Jones.
163. Rendell 1970, 162.
164. Crouch 1978, 180, confirmed by Mr P. Jones; Rendell 1970, 162.
165. *Britannia* 13, (1982), 393; inf. from Mr P. Jones.
166. For the flooding, see Crouch and Shanks 1984, 18.
167. Sheldon and Schaaf 1978, 67.
168. Elmsleigh, Crouch 1976a, 85–6; CAD, Crouch 1978, 180.
169. Crouch and Shanks 1984, 13 and 126; Bayley, *ibid.*, 114.
170. *Ibid.*, 17.
171. *Ibid.*, 18.
172. Jenkins, in Crouch and Shanks 1984, 82–4; *Britannia* 13, (1982), 393.
173. Sharpe 1932, 115.
174. Crouch 1976a, 86; the pottery from the fills of the beam slots must post-date the demolition of the building, cf. Jones 1982, 193.
175. Jones 1982, 188.
176. CAD, Crouch 1978, 180; Market Square, *Britannia* 13, (1982), 393; FBG, Crouch and Shanks 1984, 18.
177. Inf. from Mr P. Jones.
178. For discussion of the whole late Roman and Saxon sequence, see Jones 1982, esp. 193–8 and 209–10. Additional inf. from Mr P. Jones.
179. Jones 1982, 209.
180. Fieldhouse, May and Wellstood 1931.
181. For a summary of earlier work, see Slater and Wilson 1977.
182. For the initial geophysical survey and trial work, see Aspinall *et al.* 1979, Mather 1980 and Palmer 1980. For subsequent interims, see Palmer 1981 and 1983.
183. Palmer 1981, 19–21.
184. Palmer 1983, 37–9.
185. *Ibid.*, 43.
186. Palmer 1981, 21.
187. Palmer 1983, 41.
188. *Ibid.*, 39; *Britannia* 14, (1983), 303.
189. Palmer 1981, 22.

190. *Ibid.*, and 1983, 41.
191. Palmer 1981, 21.
192. For the known buildings, see Palmer 1981, 21 and 1983, 39.
193. Palmer 1981, 21 and 23.
194. *Ibid.*, 21 and 1983, 39.
195. Fieldhouse, May and Wellstood 1931, 8; Palmer 1981, 23 and 1983, 39.
196. Webster 1974, 53.
197. Slater and Wilson 1977, 22.
198. Palmer 1981, 17 and 22 and 1983, 41.
199. Slater and Wilson 1977, 29.

Chapter 13 (pp. 314–19)

1. For the flooding, see Crouch and Shanks 1984, 18; for decline elsewhere, cf. Crouch 1978, 180 and *Britannia* 13, (1982), 393.
2. Eddy 1982, 17 and 20; Rodwell 1987, 136.
3. Rodwell 1987, 135 (Kelvedon); Drury 1975, 170–1 (Chelmsford).
4. Crickmore 1984b, 105.
5. Palmer 1983, 41.
6. Cunliffe 1984, 48–50; 68–73; 129–144.
7. France and Gobel 1985, 35–48.
8. Penn 1960; 1963, 110–16.
9. Harding 1987, 13–15.
10. Green H. J. M. 1975, 202.
11. Freezer 1979, 5–7.
12. Booth 1979; *Britannia* 11, (1980), 368–9.
13. Green H. J. M. 1977, 18.
14. Wedlake 1958, 47ff.
15. *Britannia* 12, (1981), 348–9.
16. Smith 1987, 189–94.
17. *J. Roman Studs.* 48, (1958), 139–40; Dannell 1974; Frere *et al.* 1987, pl. 5.
18. Booth 1980, 12–13 (Alcester); *J. Roman Studs.* 50, (1960), 218 (Catterick); Leach 1982, 24–30, 65–82 (Ilchester).
19. Cf. Branigan 1976; Frere 1987, 272.
20. Daniels 1978, 97 (Corbridge); McCarthy 1984 (Carlisle).
21. Wacher 1971a, 171; Wilson 1984.
22. Frere 1987, 242–4; Crickmore 1984a.
23. Young 1975, 138–52.
24. Todd 1981, 10–34.
25. *J. Roman Studs.* 48, (1958), 139.
26. Alexander 1975, 108.
27. Webster 1971.
28. See for example Frere 1966; Wacher 1975a, ch. 10; Biddle 1976, 103–12; Reece 1980; Cleary 1987, 197–200.

29. Rahtz 1960, 178–87.
30. Field and Hurst 1983, 49–59.
31. Thomas 1956; Annable 1960.
32. Cf. Crickmore 1984b, fig. 3.
33. Heys and Thomas 1959, 102–7.
34. Contrast Frere 1987, 346 with Casey 1983.
35. Todd 1975, 221.
36. Green H. J. M. 1977, 18.
37. Brinson 1963, 86–8.
38. Leach 1982, 82–8.
39. Dannell and Wild 1969, 7.
40. Green H. J. M. 1975, 207.
41. Drury 1975, 165.
42. Drury 1976, 46 and 125.
43. Rogerson 1977, 120–1.
44. Partridge 1975, 150.
45. Cunliffe and Davenport 1985, 184.
46. Holmes 1955, 106.
47. France and Gobel 1985, 48; Bartlett 1988a, 3.
48. Penn 1960, 11.
49. Wacher 1971a, 171–2.
50. Frere 1966, 93; Reece, in Frere 1985, 135.
51. Drury and Wickenden 1982.
52. Pullinger 1978, 60.
53. Millett and Graham 1986, 33 and 37.
54. Rodwell 1975, 95; Rodwell K. 1987, 136–7.
55. Brinson 1963, 88; Rodwell 1975, 95.
56. Trollope 1870, 3–4; Todd 1975, 221–3.
57. Liversidge 1977, 11.
58. Rolleston 1869; 1880; Dudley Buxton 1921.
59. Whitwell and Dean 1966, 46; Todd 1973, 135.
60. Jones 1982, 193–8 and 209–10.
61. Frere 1962, 121–8; Rowley 1974.
62. *J. Roman Studs.* 48, (1958), 140; Dannell 1974, 8.
63. Drury 1972, 24–5.
64. Green H. J. M. 1977, 23–4.
65. Frere 1987, 368–9.
66. Bede, *Vita Sancti Cuthberti*, 4.
67. Cunliffe and Davenport 1985, 66–75.
68. Heys and Thomas 1963, 156–8.
69. Leach 1982, 12.
70. Hildyard 1953; Wilson 1984, 75.

Chapter 14 (pp. 320–3)
1. Based perhaps on: The Roman Society, 1985; Jones and Wacher 1987, 42.
2. Atkinson 1957; Barker 1977, 117–21.
3. Barker 1977, *passim*.
4. Information from Prof. Alan Ponter, Dept. of Engineering, University of Leicester.

BIBLIOGRAPHY

AGACHE, R. 1978 *La Somme Pré-Romaine et Romaine*

ALCOCK, J. P. 1966 'Celtic Water Cults in Roman Britain', *Arch. J.* 122, (1966), 1–12

ALCOCK, L. 1973a *Arthur's Britain*

ALCOCK, L. 1973b *By South Cadbury, is that Camelot . .*

ALCOCK, L. 1983 'Gwŷr y Gogledd: an archaeological appraisal', *Arch. Cambrensis* 132, (1983), 1–18

ALEXANDER, J. 1964 'Early Cambridge. An Interim Report on the Excavations at Castle Hill, Cambridge, 1956–1962,' *Archaeological News Letter* 7, No.10 (March 1964), 222–6

ALEXANDER, J. 1975 'The development of urban communities: the evidence from Cambridge and Great Chesterford', in Rodwell and Rowley 1975, 103–9

ALEXANDER, J., TRUMP, D., FARRAR, R. and HALL, R. 1967 *Excavations in Cambridge 1964–7. A Preliminary Report on Excavations at Mount Pleasant and Arbury Road* Board of Extra-Mural Studies, Cambridge and London

ALFÖLDY, G. 1974 *Noricum*

ALLEN, G. W. G. 1938 'Marks seen from the air in the crops near Dorchester, Oxon.', *Oxoniensia* 3, (1938), 169–71.

ANDERSON, A. S. 1978 'Wiltshire Fine Wares', in Arthur, P. and Marsh, G. (Eds.) *Early Fine Wares in Roman Britain*, B.A.R. 57, 373–92

ANDERSON, A. S. and WACHER, J. S. 1980 'Excavations at Wanborough, Wiltshire: An Interim Report', *Britannia* 11, (1980), 115–26

ANDREWS, F. B. 1926 'The earthworks of Chesterton, Warwickshire', *Trans. Birmingham Arch. Soc.* 49, (1923), 58–60

ANNABLE, K. F. 1960 'Black Field, Mildenhall: a Romano-British walled township', *Wilts. Arch. Mag.* 57, (1958–60), 233–5, 397

ANNABLE, K. F. 1966 'A late first-century well at Cunetio', *Wilts. Arch. Mag.* 61, (1966), 9–24

ANNABLE, K. F. 1976 'A Bronze Apron Mount from Cunetio', *Wilts. Arch. Mag.* 69, (1974), 176–9

ANNABLE, K. F. 1980 'A Coffined Burial of Roman Date from Cunetio', *Wilts. Arch. Mag.* 72/3, (1977/8), 187–91

ANON. 1882–3 'Notes', *Trans. Bristol and Gloucester Arch. Soc.* 7, (1882–83), 16, 36.

ANON. 1886 'Notes', *Proc. Cotteswold Natur. Field Club* 8, (1881–2), 71–2.

ANON. 1909 'Excavations at Charterhouse on Mendip', *J. Brit. Archaeol. Assn.* NS 15, (1909), 112–14

ANON. 1958 'Curator's Report', *Wilts. Arch. Mag.* 57, (1958), 99–107

ANON. 1960 'Fragment of Roman Military Diploma from Middlewich', *J. Chester Arch. Soc.* 47, (1960), 23–4

ANON. 1961 'Black Field, Mildenhall: Cunetio: Romano-British Walled Township', *Wilts. Arch. Mag.* 58, (1961–3), 35

ANON. 1962 'Black Field, Mildenhall: Cunetio', *Wilts. Arch. Mag.* 58, (1961–3), 245

ANON. 1964 'Mildenhall: Black Field (Cunetio)', *Wilts. Arch. Mag.* 59, (1964), 187

ANON. 1965 'Mildenhall: Black Field (Cunetio)', *Wilts. Arch. Mag.* 60, (1965), 137

ANON. 1978 'High Street, Cowbridge', *Annual Report, Glamorgan-Gwent Arch. Trust* 1977–8, 16–22

ANTONINE ITINERARY = Cuntz, O. (Ed.) 1929, in *Itineraria Romana I* Leipzig

APPLEBAUM, E. S. 1933 'Excavations at Baldock in 1932', *StAlban's Archit. and Arch. Soc. Trans.* (1932), 244–58

ARNOLD, A. A. 1921 'The Earliest Roman Bridge; was it built by the Romans?' *Arch. Cantiana* 35, (1921), 127–38

ARTIS, E. T. 1828 *The Durobrivae of Antonius Identified and Illustrated*

ASPINALL, A. and P., and HEATHCOTE, C. 1979 'Tiddington, Stratford-upon-Avon, Warks.', *West Midlands Arch. News Sheet* 22, (1979), 45

ATKINSON, D. 1931 *Caistor Excavations 1931*

ATKINSON, D. 1942 *Report on Excavations at Wroxeter 1923–1927*

ATKINSON, R. J. C. 1957 'Worms and Weathering', *Antiquity* 31, (1957), 219–33

AUBREY, J. and JACKSON, J. E. 1862 *Wiltshire: Topographical Collections*

BAKER, A. 1966 'Aerial reconnaissance over the Romano-British Town of Magna (Kenchester)', *Trans. Woolhope Nat. Field. Club* 38, (1964–6), 192–5

BAKER, G. 1841 *The History and Antiquities of Northamptonshire* Vol.II

BAKER, R. S. 1875 'Roman Discoveries at Irchester', *Ass. Archit. Soc. Rpts.* 13, (1875), 88–118

BAKER, R. S. 1879 'Roman Exploration at Irchester', *Ass. Archit. Soc. Rpts.* 15, (1879), 49–59

BAKER, R. S. 1882 'Notes on Archaeological Discoveries at Irchester', *Proc. Soc. Antiquaries* 9, (1882), 85–9

BARFIELD, L. 1974 'Excavations at Bays Meadow, Droitwich', *West Midlands Arch. News Sheet* 17, (1974), 49–50

BARFIELD, L. 1975 'Bays Meadow, Droitwich', *West Midlands Arch. News Sheet* 18, (1975), 48

BARFIELD, L. 1976 'Bays Meadow, Droitwich', *West Midlands Arch. News Sheet* 19, (1976), 42–4

BARFIELD, L. 1977 'Bays Meadow, Droitwich', *West Midlands Arch. News Sheet* 20, (1977), 52

BARFIELD, L. and TOMLINSON, R. 1971 'Droitwich: Bays Meadow enclosure', *West Midlands Arch. News Sheet* 14, (1971), 17–19

BARKER, P. A. 1970 'The Origins of Worcester', *Trans. Worcs. Arch. Soc. 2*, (1969), 1–116

BARKER, P. A. 1977 *Techniques of Archaeological Excavation*

BARLEY, M. W. 1964 'Ancaster, Causennae', *East Midlands Arch. Bull.* 7, (1964), 9

BARLEY, M. W., MAY, J., TODD, M. and WILSON, D. R. 1974 'Ancaster – miscellaneous excavations', *East Midlands Arch. Bull.* 10, (1974), 16–17

BARR, B. and GILLAM, G. R. 1964 'Excavation and fieldwork on the Roman roads at Braughing, Herts.', *East Herts. Arch. Soc. Trans.* 14, (1964), 108–16

BARTLETT, R. 1988a *Harlow Temple Excavations 1985–87 : An Interim Report* Typescript, Harlow Museum

BARTLETT, R. 1988b 'The Harlow Celtic Temple', *Current Arch.* 112, 163–66

BARTON, I. M. 1958 'Further excavations at Pennocrucium, near Stretton Bridge 1953–4', *Trans. Birmingham Arch. Soc.* 74, (1956), 6–9

BEMROSE, G. J. V. 1958 'Trial Excavation at Chesterton, Staffs.', *North Staffs. Field Club Trans.* 91 (1956–7), 96–102

BERRY, E. K. 1975 'Medieval Droitwich and the Salt Trade', in de Brisay and Evans 1975, 76–80

BESLEY, E. and BLAND, R. 1983 *The Cunetio Treasure : Roman Coinage of the third century* AD

BESTWICK, D. J. 1972 'Excavations at the Roman Town of Middlewich (Salinae) 1964–1971', *Middlewich Arch. Soc. News Letter* 1, (1972), 3–4

BESTWICK, D. J. 1974 'Middlewich, Excavation of Site J, 1973–4', *Cheshire Arch. Bull.* 2, (1974), 29–30

BESTWICK, D. J. 1975a 'Middlewich, Excavation of Site J and Site K', *Cheshire Arch. Bull.* 3, (1975), 49–51

BESTWICK, D. J. 1975b 'Romano-British Inland Salting at Middlewich (Salinae), Cheshire', in de Brisay and Evans 1975, 66–70

BESTWICK, D. J. and CLELAND, J. H. 1974 'Metal-working in the North-West', in Jones, G. D. B. and Grealy, S. (Eds.) *Roman Manchester*, 143–57

BIDDLE, M. 1976 'Towns', in Wilson, D. M. (Ed.) *The Archaeology of Anglo-Saxon England*, 99–150

BIRLEY, E. 1954 *Corbridge Roman Station* H. M. S. O.

BIRLEY, R. 1977 *Vindolanda: A Roman Frontier Post on Hadrian's Wall*

BIRSS, R. and WHEELER, H. 1986 'Introduction', in Dool, Wheeler *et al.* 1986, 7–14

BISHOP, M. C. and DORE, J. N. 1988 *Corbridge: Excavations of the Roman Fort and Town 1947–1980*

BLAGG, T. F. C. 1979 'The Date of the Temple of Sulis Minerva at Bath', *Britannia* 10, (1979), 101–7

BLAGG, T. F. C. 1980 'The Votive Column from the Roman Temple Precinct at Springhead', *Arch. Cantiana* 95, (1979), 223–9

BLAY, W. F. 1925 *Letocetum, Wall* Walsall Hist. Society

BOON, G. C. 1951 'A Roman Field-System at Charterhouse-on-Mendip', *Proc. Univ. Bristol Spelaeol. Soc.* VI, 3, (1951), 201–4

BOON, G. C. 1974 *Silchester: The Roman Town of Calleva*

BOOTH, P. 1976 '1 Bleachfield Street (Alcester)', *West Midlands Arch. News Sheet* 19, (1976), 49–52

BOOTH, P. 1977 '1 Bleachfield Street: excavations (Alcester)', *West Midlands Arch. News Sheet* 20, (1977), 59–62

BOOTH, P. 1979 'Alcester, Priory Row, Coulter's Grange', *West Midlands Arch. News Sheet* 22, (1979), 49–52

BOOTH, P. M. 1980 *Roman Alcester* Warwickshire Museum

BOWMAN, A. K. and THOMAS, J. D. 1983 *Vindolanda: the Latin Writing Tablets*

BRADFORD, J. S. P. and GOODCHILD, R. G. 1939 'Excavations at Frilford 1937–8', *Oxoniensia* 4, (1939), 1–70

BRADLEY, R. 1978 'Rescue excavation in Dorchester on Thames 1972', *Oxoniensia* 42, (1978), 17–39

BRANIGAN, K. 1976 *The Roman Villa in South West England*

BRANIGAN, K. 1977 *Gatcombe Roman Villa* B.A.R. 44

BRANIGAN, K. 1985 *The Catuvallauni*

BRASSINGTON, M. 1967 'Roman Material recovered from Littlechester, Derby 1965', *Derbyshire Arch. J.* 87, (1967), 39–69

BRASSINGTON, M. 1969 'Roman Wells at Littlechester', *Derbyshire Arch. J.* 89, (1969), 115–19

BRASSINGTON, M. 1970 '1st century Roman occupation at Strutt's Park, Derby', *Derbyshire Arch. J.* 90, (1970), 22–30

BRASSINGTON, M. 1971 'A Trajanic kiln complex near Littlechester, Derby 1968', *Antiquaries J.* 51, (1971), 36–69

BRASSINGTON, M. 1980 'Derby racecourse kiln excavations 1972–3', *Antiquaries J.* 60, (1980), 8–47

BRASSINGTON, M. 1981 'The Roman Roads of Derby', *Derbyshire Arch. J.* 101, (1981), 88–92

BRASSINGTON, M. 1982a 'Exploratory Excavations at Littlechester, Derby', *Derbyshire Arch. J.* 102, (1982), 74–83

BRASSINGTON, M. 1982b 'The Excavation of the Hypocaust on Parker's Piece, Littlechester, Derby 1924–6', *Derbyshire Arch. J.* 102, (1982), 84–6

BREEZE, D. J. 1982 *The Northern Frontier of Roman Britain*

BREEZE, D. J. and DOBSON, B. 1987 *Hadrian's Wall*

BRIDGES, J. 1791 *The History and Antiquities of Northamptonshire*, Vol. 1

BRIDGEWATER, N. P. 1967 'Excavations at Weston-under-Penyard', *Trans. Woolhope Nat. Field. Club* 38, (1964–6), 124–35

BRINSON, J. G. S. 1949 'Great Chesterford', *Arch. News Letter* 1, (1949), 12–13

BRINSON, J. G. S. 1950 'Great Chesterford', *Arch. News Letter* 2, (1950), 146–8

BRINSON, J. G. S. 1963 'Great Chesterford', in Hull 1963, 72–88

BROOKE, J. W. 1920 'The excavation of a late Roman well at Cunetio', *Wilts. Arch. Mag.* 41, (1920–22), 151–2

BROWN, A. E. and ALEXANDER, J. 1982 'Excavations at Towcester 1954: the Grammar School Site', *Northants. Arch.* 17, (1982), 24–59

BROWN, A. E., WOODFIELD, C. and MYNARD, D. C. 1983 'Excavations at Towcester, Northamptonshire : the Alchester Road Suburb', *Northants. Arch.* 18, (1983), 43–140

BROWNE, D. 1974 'Archaeological Gazetteer of the City of Cambridge', *Proc. Cambridge Antiq. Soc.* 65, (1974), 1–38

BUDGE, A. R., RUSSELL, J. R. and BOON, G. C. 1974 'Excavations and Fieldwork at Charterhouse-on-Mendip 1960–67', *Proc.*

Univ. Bristol Spelaeol. Soc. 13, 3, (1974), 327–47

BULLEID, A. and GRAY, H. St G. 1911 *The Glastonbury Lake Village* Vol.1

BURLEIGH, G. 1982 'Excavations at Baldock 1980–81: An Interim Report', *Hertfordshire's Past* 12, (1982), 3–18

BURNHAM, B. C. 1979 'Pre-Roman and Romano-British Urbanism? Problems and Possibilities', in Burnham and Johnson 1979, 255–72

BURNHAM, B. C. 1986 'The Origins of Romano-British "Small Towns"', *Oxford J. of Arch.* 5, (1986), 185–203

BURNHAM, B. C. 1988 'The Morphology of Romano-British "Small Towns"', *Arch. J.* 144, (1987), 156–90

BURNHAM, B. C. 1989 'A Survey of Building Types in Romano-British "Small Towns"', *J. British Arch. Assn.* 141, (1988), 35–59

BURNHAM, B. C. and JOHNSON, H. B. (Eds.) 1979 *Invasion and Response : the Case of Roman Britain* B.A.R. 73

BURROW, I. 1981 'A Mosaic from 17 Limington Road, Ilchester', *Somerset Arch. and Nat. Hist. Proc.* 125, (1980–1), 116–18

BURROW, I. 1984 'Ilchester, Northover and Limington Road', in Burrow, I., Minnitt, S. and Murless, B. (Eds.) 'Somerset Archaeology 1982', *Somerset Arch. and Nat. Hist. Proc.* 127, (1982–3), 21–2

BUSH, T. S. 1908 'Explorations . . . at the north end of Lansdown, Bath', *Proc. Soc. Antiqs.* 2s, 22, (1908), 34–8

BUTLER, R. M. (Ed.) 1971 *Soldier and Civilian in Roman Yorkshire*

CADE, J. 1789 'Some Observations on the Roman Station of Cataractonium', *Archaeologia* 9, (1789), 276–91

CADE, J. 1792 'Further Observations on Cataractonium', *Archaeologia* 10, (1792), 54–66

CADOUX, J. L. 1971 'Le Sanctuaire Gallo-Romain de Ribemont-sur-Ancre', *Bull. Trimestriel de la Société des Antiquaires de Picardie*, 1971, 43–70

CAMDEN, W. 1610; 1695 (Gibson Edn.); 1789 and 1806 (Gough Edns.) *Britannia*

CARUANA, I. 1983 'Carlisle', *Current Arch.* 86, 77–81

CARVER, M. 1976 'Worcester, Sidbury', *West Midlands Arch. News Sheet* 19, (1976), 42

CARVER, M. 1980 'Medieval Worcester: an archaeological framework', *Trans. Worcs. Arch. Soc.* 7, (1980), 1–335

CASEY, J. 1983 'Imperial campaigns and fourth century defences in Britain', in Maloney, J. and Hobley B. (Eds.) *Roman Urban Defences in the West*, C.B.A. Res. Rpt. 51, 121–4

CHAMBERLAIN, M. 1983 'Bear Field, Cowbridge: Magnetometer Survey of Roman Structures', *Annual Report, Glamorgan-Gwent Archaeological Trust* 1982–3, 14–26

CHAPLIN, R. E. 1963 'Excavations in Rochester, Winter 1961–2', *Arch. Cantiana* 77, (1962), 1

CHARLESWORTH, D. 1979 'Roman Carlisle', *Arch. J.* 135, (1978), 115–137

CHARLESWORTH, D. 1980 'The South Gate of a Flavian Fort at Carlisle', in Hanson and Keppie 1980, 201–10

CHARLTON, J. M. T. 1961 'Excavations at the Roman site of Holditch 1957– 1959', *North Staffs. J. of Field Studies* 1, (1961), 26–50

CHARLTON, J. M. T. 1962 'Excavations at the Roman site of Holditch 1960–1962', *North Staffs. J. of Field Studies* 2, (1962), 62–71

C.I.L. = *Corpus Inscriptionum Latinarum* (1863–)

CLARKE, A. 1959 'The Chichester-Silchester Roman Road', *Proc. Hampshire Field Club* 21, (1959), 82–97

CLEARY, S. E. 1987 *Extra-Mural Areas of Romano-British Towns* B.A.R. 169

CLEMENT WHITTICK, G. 1982 'Roman Lead-Mining on Mendip and in North Wales', *Britannia* 13, (1982), 113–24

COCKERTON, R. W. P. 1959 'Roman Pigs of Lead from Derbyshire – Recent Dating Evidence from the Mendips', *Derbyshire Arch. J.* 79, (1959), 88–96

COLLINS, A. 1978 'Great Chesterford', in Couchman, C. (Ed.) 'Excavations in Essex 1977', *Essex Arch.and Hist.* 10, (1978), 240–8

COLLINS, A. 1980 'Great Chesterford', in Eddy, M. R. (Ed.) 'Excavations in Essex 1979', *Essex Arch. and Hist.* 12, (1980), 39–50

COLLINS, A. 1981 'Great Chesterford', in Eddy, M. R. (Ed.) 'Excavations in Essex 1980', *Essex Arch. and Hist.* 13, (1981), 48–62

COLLINSON, J. 1791 *History of Somerset*

COLT HOARE, R. 1821 *Ancient Wiltshire II, Roman Aera*

CONLON, R. F. B. 1973 'Holbrooks – An Iron Age and Romano-British Settlement', *Essex J.* 8, No. 2, 30–50

COOKE, F. M. B. and WACHER, J. S. 1970 'Photogrammetric Survey at Wanborough, Wilts.', *Antiquity* 44, (1970), 214–16

CORDER, P. 1951 *The Roman Town and Villa at Great Casterton : 1st Interim Report* Univ. of Nottingham

CORDER, P. 1954 *The Roman Town and Villa at Great Casterton : 2nd Interim Report* Univ. of Nottingham

CORDER, P. 1955 'The reorganisation of the defences of Romano-British towns in the 4th century', *Arch. J.* 112, (1955), 20–42

CORDER, P. 1961 *The Roman Town and Villa at Great Casterton : 3rd Interim Report* Univ. of Nottingham

CORDER, P. and ROMANS, T. 1936 *Excavations at the Roman Town at Brough, E. Yorks 1935*

COWEN, J. D. 1936 'An inscribed openwork gold ring from Corstopitum', *Arch. Aeliana* 4s, 13, (1936), 310–19

COX, J. S. 1952 'The Roman Town of Ilchester', *Arch. J.* 107, (1950), 94–5

COX, J. S. 1982 *Ilchester and District Occasional Papers No. 32* Guernsey

CRICKMORE, J. 1984a *Romano-British Urban Defences* B.A.R. 126

CRICKMORE, J. 1984b *Romano-British Urban Settlements in the West Midlands* B.A.R. 127

CROUCH, K. 1976a 'Excavation at Staines, a survey of recent work', *London Arch.* 2 No. 14, 362–5

CROUCH, K. 1976b 'The Archaeology of Staines and the Excavation at Elmsleigh House', *Trans. London and Middlesex Arch. Soc.* 27, (1976), 71–134

CROUCH, K. 1978 'New thoughts on Roman Staines', *London Arch.* 3 No. 7, 180–6

CROUCH, K. and SHANKS, S. 1984 *Excavations in Staines 1975–76 : The Friends' Burial Ground* Joint London and Middlesex Arch. Soc. and Surrey Arch. Soc. publication No. 2

CULLEN, P. R. 1970 'Cirencester: the Restoration of the Roman Town Wall', *Britannia* 1, (1970), 227–39

CUMING, H. S. 1856 'Antiquities found at Alchester, Oxfordshire', *J. British Arch. Assn.* 12, (1856), 176–8

CUNLIFFE, B. W. 1966 'The Temple of Sulis Minerva at Bath', *Antiquity* 40, (1966), 199–204

CUNLIFFE, B. W. 1969 *Roman Bath* Soc. of Antiq. Res. Rpt. 24

CUNLIFFE, B. W. 1975 *Excavations at Portchester Vol. 1* Soc. of Antiqs. Res. Rpt. 32

CUNLIFFE, B. W. 1976a 'The Roman Baths at Bath : Excavations 1969–75', *Britannia* 7, (1976), 1–32

CUNLIFFE, B. W. 1976b 'The Origins of Urbanisation in Britain', in Cunliffe and Rowley 1976, 135–62

CUNLIFFE, B. W. 1978 *Iron Age Communities in Britain*

CUNLIFFE, B. W. (Ed.) 1979 *Excavations in Bath 1950–1975* C.R.A.A.G.S. Exc. Rpt. No.1

CUNLIFFE, B. W. 1980 'The Excavation of the Roman Spring at Bath 1979 : A Preliminary Description', *Antiquaries J.* 60, (1980), 187–206

CUNLIFFE, B. W. 1983 'Earth's Grip Holds Them', in Hartley, B. R. and Wacher, J. S. (Eds.) *Rome and Her Northern Provinces*, 67–83

CUNLIFFE, B. W. 1984 *Roman Bath Discovered* (2nd edn.)

CUNLIFFE, B. W. 1985 'Aspects of urbanisation in northern Europe', in Grew and Hobley 1985, 1–5

CUNLIFFE, B. W. 1988 *The Temple of Sulis Minerva at Bath Vol. 2 : The Finds from the Sacred Spring* O. U. C. A. Monograph 16

CUNLIFFE, B. W. and DAVENPORT, P. 1985 *The Temple of Sulis Minerva at Bath Vol. 1 : The Site* O.U.C.A. Monograph 7

CUNLIFFE, B. W. and FULFORD, M. 1982 *Corpus Signorum Imperii Romani Vol. 1 Fasc. 2 : Bath and the Rest of Wessex*

CUNLIFFE, B. W. and ROWLEY, T. (Eds.) 1976 *Oppida : the Beginnings of Urbanisation in Barbarian Europe* B.A.R. s11

CURLE, J. 1911 *A Roman Frontier Post and its People*

DANIELS, C. (Ed.) 1978 *Handbook to the Roman Wall* (J. Collingwood Bruce 13th edition)

DANNELL, G. 1974 'Roman Industry in Normangate Field, Castor', *Durobrivae* 2, (1974), 7–9

DANNELL, G. and WILD, J. P. 1969 'Castor', *Bull. Northants. Fed. of Arch. Socs.* 3, (1969), 7–9

DANNELL, G. and WILD, J. P. 1971 'Castor, Normangate Field 1969 and 1970', *Bull. Northants. Fed. of Arch. Socs.* 5, (1971), 7–15

DANNELL, G. and WILD, J. P. 1974 'Castor, Normangate Field 1973', *Bull. Northants. Fed. of Arch. Socs.* 9, (1974), 86–8

DANNELL, G. and WILD, J. P. 1976 'Castor, Normangate Field 1974', *Bull. Northants. Fed. of Arch. Socs.* 11, (1976), 186–91

DANNELL, G. and WILD, J. P. 1987 *Longthorpe II, The Military Works-Depot : An Episode in Landscape History* Britannia Monograph 8

DAVIES, J. 1967 'Excavations at Caer Dynnaf, Llanblethian, Glam. 1965–67', *Morgannwg* 11, (1967), 77–8

DAVIES, J. 1980 'Roman Military Deployment in Wales and the Marches from Claudius to the Antonines', in Hanson and Keppie 1980, 255–77

DAVIS, B. W. 1930 'Excavations in Malt Mill Lane (Alcester)', *Trans. Birmingham Arch. Soc.* 54, (1929), 76–7

DAVIS, C. E. 1881 'Excavations at the Baths', *Bath Field Club* 4, (1881), 357–60

DAVISON, K. 1973 'Ancient Harlow', *Essex J.* 8, No.2, 26–9

DE BRISAY, K. W. and EVANS, K. A. (Eds.) 1975 *Salt. The Study of an Ancient Industry*

DETSICAS, A. (Ed.) 1973 *Current Research in Romano-British Coarse Pottery*

DILKE, O. A. W. 1971 *The Roman Land Surveyors*

DIX, B. 1983 'Ashton Roman Town', *South Midlands Arch.* 13, (1983), 18–20

DONOVAN, D. T. 1949 'A Revised Account of the Earthworks between Shipham and Charterhouse', *Proc. Univ. Bristol Spelaeol. Soc.* 6, 1, (1949), 80–3

DONOVAN, H. E. 1934 'Excavation of a Romano-British Building at Bourton on the Water, Gloucestershire', *Trans. Bristol and Gloucs. Arch. Soc.* 56, (1934), 99–128

DONOVAN, H. E. 1935 'Roman finds in Bourton on the Water, Gloucestershire', *Trans. Bristol and Gloucs. Arch. Soc.* 57, (1935), 234–59

DOOL, J. 1972 'An Excavation in Darley Playing Fields, Littlechester, Derby', *Derbyshire Arch. J.* 92, (1972), 5–14

DOOL, J. 1986a 'Excavations at Strutt's Park, Derby 1974', in Dool, Wheeler *et al.* 1986, 15–32

DOOL, J. 1986b 'Derby Racecourse: Excavations on the Roman Industrial Settlement in 1970', in Dool, Wheeler *et al.* 1986, 155–221

DOOL, J., WHEELER, H. *et al.* (Eds.) 1986 'Roman Derby: Excavations 1968–1983', *Derbyshire Arch. J.* 105, (1985), 1–348.

DORE, J. and GREENE, K. (Eds.) 1977 *Roman Pottery Studies in Britain and Beyond* B.A.R. s30

DRURY, P. J. 1972 'Preliminary Report on the Romano-British Settlement at Chelmsford, Essex', *Essex Arch. and Hist.* 4, (1972), 3–29

DRURY, P. J. 1975 'Roman Chelmsford – Caesaromagus', in Rodwell and Rowley 1975, 159–73

DRURY, P. J. 1976 'Braintree : Excavations and Research 1971–1976 and an Archaeological Gazeteer', *Essex Arch. and Hist.* 8, (1976), 1–143

DRURY, P. J. 1978 *Excavations at Little Waltham 1970–71* C.B.A. Res. Rpt. 26

DRURY, P. J. 1988 *The Mansio and other sites in the South-Eastern sector of Caesaromagus* C.B.A. Res. Rpt. 66

DRURY, P. J. and RODWELL, W. R. 1980 'Settlements in the Later Iron Age and Roman Periods', in Buckley, D. G. (Ed.) *Archaeology in Essex to AD 1500* C.B.A. Res. Rpt. 34, 59–75

DRURY, P. J. and WICKENDEN, N. P. 1982 'An Early Saxon settlement within the Romano-British Small Town at Heybridge, Essex', *Mediaeval Arch.* 26, (1982), 1–40

DUDLEY, H. 1949 *Early Days in North-West Lincolnshire*

DUDLEY BUXTON, L. 1921 'Excavations at Frilford', *Antiquaries J.* 1, (1921), 87–97

DUNCAN-JONES, R. P. 1974 *The Economy of the Roman Empire*

DUNNETT, R. 1971 'The Excavation of the Roman Theatre at Gosbecks', *Britannia* 2, (1971), 27–47

DUNNETT, R. 1975 *The Trinovantes*

DUNNING, G. C. 1976 'Salmonsbury, Bourton on the Water, Gloucestershire', in Harding, D. W. (Ed.) 1976 *Hillforts : Later Prehistoric Earthworks in Britain and Ireland*, 75–118

DURHAM, B. and ROWLEY, T. 1972 'A Cemetery Site at Queensford Mill, Dorchester', *Oxoniensia* 37, (1972), 32–7

EDDY, M. R. 1982 *Kelvedon : The Origins and Development of a Roman Small Town* Essex County Council Occasional Paper 3

EDDY, M. R. 1984 'Excavations on the Braintree Earthworks 1976 and 1979', *Essex Arch. J.* 15, (1983), 36–53

EDWARDS, D. 1977 'The Air Photographs Collection of the Norfolk Archaeological Unit : Second Report', *East Anglian Arch.* 5, (1977), 225–37

ELBE, J. von 1977 *Roman Germany. A Guide to Sites and Museums*

ELKINGTON, H. D. H. 1976 'The Mendip Lead Industry', in Branigan, K. and Fowler, P. J. (Eds.) *The Roman West Country: Classical Culture and Celtic Society*, 183–197 and Appendix IV, 230–4

ELLIS, P. 1984 *Catsgore 1979; Further Excavation of the Romano-British Village*

ELLIS, P. 1987 'Sea Mills, Bristol: the 1965–8 Excavations in the Roman Town of Abonae', *Trans. Bristol and Gloucs. Arch. Soc.* 105, (1987), 15–108

ELLISON, J. A. 1962 'Excavations at Caister-on-Sea 1961–1962', *Norfolk Arch.* 33, (1962), 94–107

ENGLEFIELD, H. 1792 'Account of Antiquities Discovered in Bath 1790', *Archaeologia* 10, (1792), 325–33

ESPÉRANDIEU, E. 1913 *Receuil général des bas relief, statues et bustes de la Gaule Romaine* Vol.5

EVANS, E. M. 1983 'Excavations on the Bear Field, Cowbridge', *Annual Report, Glamorgan-Gwent Arch. Trust* 1982–3, 27–30

EVANS, E. M. 1984 'Excavations on the Bear Field, Cowbridge', *Annual Report, Glamorgan-Gwent Arch. Trust* 1983–4, 59–65

FIELD, N. and HURST, H. 1983 'Roman Horncastle', *Lincs. Hist. and Arch.* 18, (1983), 47–88

FIELDHOUSE, W. J., MAY, T. and WELLSTOOD, F. C. 1931 *A Romano-British Settlement near Tiddington, Stratford upon Avon*

FINLEY, M. I. 1973 *The Ancient Economy*

FLIGHT, C. and HARRISON, A. C. 1979 'Rochester Castle 1976' *Arch. Cantiana* 94, (1978), 27–60

FLIGHT, C. and HARRISON, A. C. 1987 'The Southern Defences of Medieval Rochester', *Arch. Cantiana* 103, (1986), 1–26

FOREMAN, M. and RAHTZ, S. 1984 'Excavations at Faccenda Chicken Farm, near Alchester, 1983', *Oxoniensia* 49, (1984), 24–46

FORMIGÉ, J. 1944 'Le Sanctuaire de Sanxay', *Gallia* 2, (1944), 43–97

FORREST, M. 1967 'Recent Work at Strutt's Park, Derby', *Derbyshire Arch. J.* 87, (1967), 162–5

FORSTER, R. H. 1908 'Corstopitum: Report of the excavations of 1907', *Arch. Aeliana* 3s, 4, (1908), 205–303

FORSTER, R. H. 1915 'Corstopitum: Report on the excavations in 1914', *Arch. Aeliana* 3s, 12, (1915), 226–86

FORSTER, R. H. and KNOWLES, W. H. 1914 'Corstopitum: Report of the excavations in 1913', *Arch. Aeliana* 3s, 11, (1914), 279–310

FRANCE, N. E. and GOBEL, B. M. 1968 'Harlow Roman Temple', *Current Arch.* 11, 287–90

FRANCE, N. E. and GOBEL, B. M. 1985 *The Romano-British Temple at Harlow*

FREEZER, D. F. 1979 *From Saltings to Spa Town. The Archaeology of Droitwich*

FRERE, S. S. 1961 'Some Romano-British sculptures from Ancaster and Wilsford, Lincs.', *Antiquaries J.* 41, (1961), 229–31

FRERE, S. S. 1962 'Excavations at Dorchester on Thames 1962', *Arch. J.* 119, (1962), 114–49

FRERE, S. S. 1966 'The End of Towns in Roman Britain', in Wacher 1966b, 87–100

FRERE, S. S. 1975 'The origin of "Small Towns"', in Rodwell and Rowley 1975, 4–7

FRERE, S. S. 1983 *Verulamium Excavations Vol. II* Soc. of Antiqs. Res. Rpt. 41

FRERE, S. S. 1984 'British Urban Defences in Earthwork', *Britannia* 15, (1984), 63–74

FRERE, S. S. 1985 'Excavations at Dorchester on Thames 1963', *Arch. J.* 141, (1984), 91–174

FRERE, S. S. 1987 *Britannia : A History of Roman Britain*

FRERE, S. S., RIVET, A. L. F. and SITWELL, N. H. H. (Eds.) 1987 *Tabula Imperii Romani: Britannia Septentrionalis*

FRERE, S. S. and ST JOSEPH, J. K. S. 1974 'The Roman Fortress at Longthorpe', *Britannia* 5, (1974), 1–129

FRERE, S. S. and ST JOSEPH, J. K. S. 1983 *Roman Britain from the Air*

FULFORD, M. G. 1975 *New Forest Roman Pottery* B.A.R. 17

FULFORD, M. G. 1977 'The location of Romano-British pottery kilns – institutional trade and the market', in Dore and Greene 1977, 301–16

FULFORD, M. G. 1982 'Town and Country in Roman Britain – a Parasitical Relationship?' in Miles, D. (Ed.) *The Romano-British Countryside: Studies in Rural Settlement and Economy*, B.A.R. 103 (i and ii), 403–19

FULFORD, M. G. 1984 *Silchester Defences 1974–1980* Britannia Monograph 5

FULFORD, M. G. 1985 'Excavations on the sites of the Amphitheatre and the Forum-Basilica at Silchester, Hampshire : An Interim Report', *Antiquaries J.* 65, (1985), 39–81

GARNSEY, P., HOPKINS, K. and WHITTAKER, C. R. 1983 *Trade in the Ancient Economy*

GARROOD, J. R. 1927 'Discoveries at Godmanchester', *Antiquaries J.* 7, (1927), 315–19

GARROOD, J. R. 1937 'Roman Godmanchester', *Trans. Cambs. and Hunts. Antiq. Soc.* 5, (1937), 439–58

GARROOD, J. R. 1947 'Cremation Burial Group from Godmanchester', *Trans. Cambs. and Hunts. Antiq. Soc.* 6, (1938–1947), 105–6

GELLING, M. 1967 'English Place-Names derived from the compound *Wīchām*', *Mediaeval Arch.* 11, (1967), 87–104

GELLING, P. S. 1959a 'Report on excavations in Bays Meadow, Droitwich, Worcestershire', *Trans. Birmingham Arch. Soc.* 75, (1957), 1–23

GELLING, P. S. 1959b 'Excavation by Little Fish Street, Worcester, 1957', *Trans. Worcs. Arch. Soc.* 3, (1958), 67–70

GERISH, W. B. 1900 'The Roman Station at Braughing', *East Herts. Arch. Soc. Trans.* 1, (1900), 173–9

GILLAM, J. P. and DANIELS, C. M. 1961 'The Roman Mausoleum on Shorden Brae, Beaufront, Corbridge, Northumberland', *Arch. Aeliana* 4s, 39, (1961), 37–61

GOODYEAR, F. 1970 'The Roman Fort at Chesterton, Newcastle under Lyme', *North Staffs. J. of Field Studies* 10, (1970), 103–5

GOODYEAR, F. 1976 'The Roman Fort at Chesterton, Newcastle under Lyme : Report on Excavations 1969–1971', *North Staffs. J. of Field Studies* 16, (1976), 1–15

GORDON, A. 1726–7 *Itinerarium Septentrionale*

GOULD, J. 1964 'Excavations at Wall 1961–3', *Trans. Lichfield and South Staffs. Arch. and Hist. Soc.* 5, (1964), 1–50

GOULD, J. 1968 'Excavations at Wall 1964–6 on the site of the Roman Forts', *Trans. Lichfield and South Staffs. Arch. and Hist. Soc.* 8, (1966–7), 1–38

GRAHAM, D. and MILLETT, M. 1980 *Neatham : A Roman Town and its Setting* Farnham and District Museum Soc.

GRAY, H. St G. 1910 'Excavation at the "amphitheatre", Charterhouse-on-Mendip', *Proc. Somerset Arch. Soc.* 55, (1909), 118–37

GRAY, H. St G. 1934 'Roman Coffins found at Ilchester', *Proc. Somerset Arch. Soc.* 79, (1933), 101–8

GREEN, C. 1977 'Excavation in the Roman Kiln Field at Brampton 1973–4', *East Anglian Arch.* 5, (1977), 31–95

GREEN, C. J. S. 1982 'The Cemetery of a Romano-British Community at Poundbury, Dorchester, Dorset', in Pearce, S. M. (Ed.) *The Early Church in Western Britain and Ireland*, 61–76

GREEN, H. J. M. 1959 'An architectural survey of the Roman Baths at Godmanchester, Part 1', *Arch. News Letter* 6, no.10, 223–9

GREEN, H. J. M. 1960a 'Roman Godmanchester Part I: An Early Dwelling', *Proc. Cambridge Antiq. Soc.* 53, (1960), 8–22

GREEN, H. J. M. 1960b 'An architectural survey of the Roman Baths at Godmanchester, Part 2', *Arch. News Letter* 6, no.11, 252–58

GREEN, H. J. M. 1961a 'Roman Godmanchester Part II: The Town Defences', *Proc. Cambridge Antiq. Soc.* 54, (1961), 68–82

GREEN, H. J. M. 1961b 'An architectural survey of the Roman Baths at Godmanchester, Part 3', *Arch. News Letter* 6, no. 12, 276–81

GREEN, H. J. M. 1969 'Godmanchester', *Current Arch.* 16, 133–38

GREEN, H. J. M. 1973 'Roman Godmanchester Part III: Emmanuel Knoll', *Proc. Cambridge Antiq. Soc.* 64, (1973), 15–23

GREEN, H. J. M. 1975 'Roman Godmanchester', in Rodwell and Rowley 1975, 183–210

GREEN, H. J. M. 1977 *Godmanchester* Oleander Press

GREEN, H. J. M. 1978 'A villa estate at Godmanchester', in Todd 1978, 103–116

GREEN, H. J. M. 1986 'Religious Cults at Roman Godmanchester', in Henig, M. and King, A. (Eds.) *Pagan Gods and Shrines of the Roman World*, 29–56

GREEN, M. 1975 'Romano-British non-ceramic model objects in south-east Britain', *Arch. J.* 132, (1975), 54–70

GREEN, M. 1976 *The Religions of Civilian Roman Britain* B.A.R. 24

GREEN, M. 1981 'Model Objects from Military Areas of Roman Britain', *Britannia* 12, (1981), 253–70

GREENE, K. T. 1974 'A Group of Roman Pottery from Wanborough, Wilts.', *Wilts. Arch. Mag.* 69, (1974), 51–66

GREENE, K. T. 1986 *The Archaeology of the Roman Economy*

GREENFIELD, E. 1967 'Excavations at Wanborough', *Wilts. Arch. Mag.* 62, (1967), 125–6

GREENFIELD, E. 1968 'Wanborough, Romano-British Settlement', *Wilts. Arch. Mag.* 63, (1968), 109–10

GREENFIELD, E. and WEBSTER, G. 1965 'Excavation at High Cross 1955', *Trans. Leics. Arch. Soc.* 40, (1964–5), 3–41

GRENIER A. 1958 *Manuel d'Archéologie gallo-romaine, III, L'Architecture* Paris

GRENIER A. 1960 *Manuel d'Archéologie gallo-romaine, IV, Les Monuments des Eaux* Paris

GRIFFITHS, N. 1983 'Early Roman Metalwork from Wiltshire', *Wilts. Arch. Mag.* 77, (1983), 49–59

GRINSELL, L. V. 1957 'Romano-British Wiltshire', *Victoria County History : Wiltshire vol. 1*

GUY, C. J. 1977 'The Lead Tank from Ashton', *Durobrivae* 5, (1977), 10–11

GUY, C. J. 1981 'Roman Circular Lead Tanks in Britain', *Britannia* 12, (1981), 271–6

HADMAN, J. 1967 'Oundle', *Bull. Northants. Fed. of Arch. Socs.* 2, (1967), 17

HADMAN, J. and UPEX, S. 1972 'Ashton', *Bull. Northants. Fed. of Arch. Socs.* 7, (1972), 12

HADMAN, J. and UPEX, S. 1975 'The Roman Settlement at Ashton near Oundle', *Durobrivae* 3, (1975), 12ff.

HADMAN, J. and UPEX, S. 1977 'Ashton 1976', *Durobrivae* 5, (1977), 6–9

HADMAN, J. and UPEX, S. 1979 'Ashton 1977–8', *Durobrivae* 7, (1979), 29–30

HALL, D. N. and NICKERSON, N. 1968 'Excavations at Irchester 1962–3', *Arch. J.* 124, (1967), 65–99

HANSON, W. S. and KEPPIE, L. J. F. (Eds.) 1980 *Roman Frontier Studies 1979* B.A.R. s71 (i)

HARDEN, D. B. 1937 'Excavations at Chesterton Lane, Alchester 1937', *Oxford Arch. Soc. Report* 83, (1937), 23–39

HARDEN, D. B. 1939 'Romano-British Oxfordshire', *Victoria County History : Oxfordshire vol. 1*, 271–303

HARDING, D. W. 1972 *The Iron Age in the Upper Thames Basin*

HARDING, D. W. 1987 *Excavations in Oxfordshire 1964–66* Univ. of Edinburgh, Dept. of Archaeology Occ. Pap. 15

HARKER, S. R. 1971 'Springhead : The Well F19', *Arch. Cantiana* 85, (1970), 139–48; 190

HARKER, S. R. 1972 'Interim Report : Temple 7 (Summary)', *Arch. Cantiana* 86, (1971), 236–7

HARKER, S. R. 1973 'Interim Report : Temple 7. Wooden structures', *Arch. Cantiana* 87, (1972), 229–30

HARKER, S. R. 1974 'Interim Report : Road (R1)', *Arch. Cantiana* 88, (1973), 225–6

HARKER, S. R. 1980 'Springhead – a brief re-appraisal', in Rodwell, W. R. (Ed.) *Temples, Churches and Religion in Roman Britain*, B.A.R. 77 (i), 285–288

HARMAN, M., LAMBRICK, G., MILES, D. and ROWLEY, T. 1978 'Roman Burials around Dorchester-on-Thames', *Oxoniensia* 43, (1978), 1–16

HARPER, G. M. 1928 'Village Administration in the Roman Province of Syria', *Yale Classical Studs.* 1, (1928), 117–21

HARRISON, A. C. 1971 'Excavation in Rochester', *Arch. Cantiana* 85, (1970), 95–112

HARRISON, A. C. 1973 'Rochester East Gate 1969', *Arch. Cantiana* 87, (1972), 121–57

HARRISON, A. C. 1982 'Rochester 1974–75', *Arch. Cantiana* 97, (1981), 95–136

HARRISON, A. C. 1986 'Rochester Priory', *Arch. Cantiana* 102, (1985), 265–6

HARRISON, A. C. and FLIGHT, C. 1969 'The Roman and Medieval defences at Rochester in the light of recent excavations', *Arch. Cantiana* 83, (1968), 55–104

HARRISON, A. C. and WILLIAMS, D. 1980 'Excavations at Prior's Gate House, Rochester 1976–7', *Arch. Cantiana* 95, (1979), 19–36

HARTLEY, B. R. 1972 *Notes on the Roman Pottery Industry in the Nene Valley* Peterborough Museum Soc. Occ. Pap. 2

HARTLEY, B. R. and KAINE, K. F. 1954 'Roman Dock and Buildings', *J. Chester and North Wales Arch. Soc.* 41, (1954), 15–37

HARTLEY, K. F. 1971 'Mancetter SP326967', *West Midlands Arch. News Sheet* 14, (1971), 15–16

HARTLEY, K. F. 1973a 'The Marketing and Distribution of Mortaria', in Detsicas 1973, 39–51

HARTLEY, K. F. 1973b 'The Kilns at Mancetter and Hartshill', in Detsicas 1973, 143–7

HARTLEY, K. F. and WEBSTER, P. V. 1973 'Romano-British Pottery Kilns near Wilderspool', *Arch. J.* 130, (1973), 77–103

HARTSHORNE, C. H. 1847 'Description of a statue of Minerva Custos and other Roman antiquities recently discovered . . . at Sibson and Bedford Purlieus in the county of Northampton', *Archaeologia* 32, (1847), 1–15

HASELGROVE, C. 1984 'The later pre-Roman Iron Age between the Humber and the Tyne', in Wilson *et al.* 1984, 9–25

HAVERFIELD, F. J. 1901 'Romano-British Worcestershire', *Victoria County History : Worcestershire vol. 1*, 199–221

HAVERFIELD, F. J. 1902 'Romano-British Northamptonshire', *Victoria County History : Northants. vol. 1*, 157–222

HAVERFIELD, F. J. 1904 'Romano-British Warwickshire', *Victoria County History : Warwickshire vol. 1*, 223–49

HAVERFIELD, F. J. 1905 'Romano-British Derbyshire', *Victoria County History : Derbyshire vol. 1*, 191–263

HAVERFIELD, F. J. 1906 'Romano-British Somerset', *Victoria County History : Somerset vol. 1*, 206–371

HAVERFIELD, F. J. 1916 'Roman Notes', *Trans. Cumberland and Westmorland Antiq. and Arch. Soc.* 16, (1915–16), 282–6

HAVERFIELD, F. J. 1920 'Roman Cirencester', *Archaeologia* 69, (1917–18), 161–200

HAWKES, C. F. C. 1927 'Excavations at Alchester 1926', *Antiquaries J.* 7, (1927), 155–84

HAWKES, C. F. C. 1939 'The Roman Camp-site near Castor on the Nene', *Antiquity* 13, (1939), 178–90

HAWKES, C. F. C. 1946 'Roman Ancaster, Horncastle and Caistor', *Arch. J.* 103, (1946), 17–25

HAWKES, C. F. C. 1947 'Britons, Romans and Saxons in Cranborne Chase', *Arch. J.* 104, (1947), 27–81

HAWKES, C. F. C. 1961 'Bronze-workers, Cauldrons and Bucket animals in Iron Age and Roman Britain', in Grimes, W. F. (Ed.) *Aspects of Archaeology in Britain and Beyond*, 172–199

HAWKES, S. C. and DUNNING, G. C. 1961 'Soldiers and Settlers in Britain, fourth to fifth century, with a catalogue of animal-ornamented buckles and related belt-fittings', *Mediaeval Arch.* 5, (1961), 1–70

HEBDITCH, M. and MELLOR, J. 1973 'The Forum and Basilica of Roman Leicester', *Britannia* 4, (1973), 1–83

HEMSLEY, R. 1961 'A Romano-British Kiln at Manduessedum', *Trans. Birmingham Arch. Soc.* 77, (1959), 5–17

HENDERSON, G. B. 1938 'Braughing : Belgic and Romano-British Settlements', *East Herts. Arch. Soc. Trans.* 10, (1938), 227–8

HERDMAN, D. W. 1933 'Excavations (lead vessels) at Bourton on the Water', *Trans. Bristol and Gloucs. Arch. Soc.* 55, (1933), 377–81

HEYS, F. G. and THOMAS, M. J. 1959 'Excavation on the defences of the Romano-British town of Kenchester', *Trans. Woolhope Nat. Field. Club* 36, (1958), 100–16

HEYS, F. G. and THOMAS, M. J. 1963 'Excavation on the defences of the Romano-British town of Kenchester: final report', *Trans. Woolhope Nat. Field. Club* 37, (1962), p. 2, 149–78

HIGHAM, N. and JONES, G. D. B. 1985 *The Carvetii*

HILDYARD, E. J. W. 1953 'A Roman and Saxon Site at Catterick', *Yorks. Arch. J.* 38, (1953), 241–5

HILDYARD, E. J. W. 1957 'Cataractonium, fort and town', *Yorks. Arch. J.* 39, (1957), 224–65

HILDYARD, E. J. W. and WADE, M. V. 1951a 'Trial Excavations at Catterick Bridge', *Yorks. Arch. J.* 37, (1950–1), 402–19

HILDYARD, E. J. W. and WADE, M. V. 1951b 'Catterick Bridge – A Roman Town', *Yorks. Arch. J.* 37, (1950–1), 521–2

HINGLEY, R. 1982 'Recent discoveries of the Roman Period at the Noah's Ark Inn, Frilford, South Oxfordshire', *Britannia* 13, (1982), 305–9

HINGLEY, R. 1985 'Location, function and status : a Romano-British "Religious Complex" at the Noah's Ark Inn, Frilford (Oxfordshire)', *Oxford J. of Arch.* 4, (1985), 201–14.

HODDER, I. 1972 'Locational models and the study of Romano-British settlement', in Clarke, D. L. (Ed.) *Models in Archaeology*, 887–909

HODDER, I. 1974a 'The Distribution of Savernake Ware', *Wilts. Arch. Mag.* 69, (1974), 67–84

HODDER, I. 1974b 'The distribution of two types of Romano-British coarse pottery', *Sussex Arch. Coll.* 112, (1974), 1–11

HODDER, I. 1974c 'Some Marketing Models for Romano-British Coarse Pottery', *Britannia* 5, (1974), 340–59

HODDER, I. 1975 'The spatial distribution of Romano-British Small Towns', in Rodwell and Rowley, 1975, 67–74

HODDER, I. 1979 'Pre-Roman and Romano-British Tribal Economies', in Burnham and Johnson 1979, 189–96

HODDER, I. and HASSALL, M. W. C. 1971 'The non-random spacing of Romano-British Walled Towns', *Man* 6, (1971), 391–407

HODGKINSON, H. R. 1928 'Note on Roman Buildings at Droitwich', *Trans. Birmingham Arch. Soc.* 51, (1925–6), 35–8

HODGKINSON, H. R. 1930a 'Note on Excavations in the Roman Cemetery at Wall, October 1927', *Trans. Birmingham Arch. Soc.* 52, (1927), 308–11

HODGKINSON, H. R. 1930b 'Roman Villa, Bays Meadow, Droitwich', *Trans. Birmingham Arch. Soc.* 52, (1927), 312–14

HOGG, A. H. A. and STEVENS, C. E. 1937 'The Defences of Roman Dorchester', *Oxoniensia* 2, (1937), 41–73

HOGG, R. 1956 'Excavations in Carlisle in 1953', *Trans. Cumberland and Westmorland Antiq. and Arch. Soc.* 55, (1955), 59–107

HOGG, R. 1964 'Excavations at Tullie House', *Trans. Cumberland and Westmorland Antiq. and Arch. Soc.* 64, (1964), 13–64

HOLMES, J. 1955 'Excavation and Fieldwork at Braughing', *East Herts. Arch. Soc. Trans.* 13, (1952–4), 93–127

HOPE, J. H. 1983 'The Fountain, Braintree', in Priddy, D. (Ed.) 'Excavations in Essex 1982', *Essex Arch. and Hist.* 15, (1983), 163–72

HOPE, W. St J. 1898 'The Architectural History of the Cathedral Church and Monastery of St Andrew at Rochester', *Arch. Cantiana* 23, (1898), 194–328

HORNE, E. 1929 'Saxon Cemetery at Camerton, Somerset', *Proc. Somerset Arch. Soc.* 74, (1928), 61–70

HORNE, E. 1934 'Anglo-Saxon Cemetery at Camerton, Somerset, Part II', *Proc. Somerset Arch. Soc.* 79, (1933), 39–63

HUGHES, H. V. 1960 'Recent work at Roman Alcester', *Trans. Birmingham Arch. Soc.* 76, (1958), 10–18

HULL, M. R. 1958 *Roman Colchester* Soc. of Antiqs. Res. Rpt. 20

HULL, M. R. 1963 'Romano-British Essex', *Victoria County History : Essex vol. 3*

HUNNYBUN, C. 1952 'Pinfold Lane, Godmanchester', *Trans. Cambs. and Hunts. Antiq. Soc.* 7, (1948–52), 72–3

HUNT, A. 1975 'Friar Street, Droitwich, Worcs.', *West Midlands Arch. News Sheet* 18, (1975), 40, 49

HUSSEY, R. 1841 *An Account of the Roman Road from Alchester to Dorchester, and other Roman Remains in the Neighbourhood*

ILIFFE, J. H. 1929 'Excavations at Alchester 1927', *Antiquaries J.* 9, (1929), 105–36

ILIFFE, J. H. 1932 'Excavations at Alchester 1928', *Antiquaries J.* 12, (1932), 35–67

INSKEEP, R. R. 1966 'Excavations at Ad Pontem, Thorpe Parish, Notts.', *Trans. Thoroton Soc.* 69, (1965), 19–39

IRVINE, J. T. 1873 'Remains of the Roman Temple and Entrance Hall to Roman Baths found at Bath in 1790', *J. British Arch. Assn.* 29, (1873), 379–94

JACK, G. H. 1916 *The Romano-British Town of Magna (Kenchester) Herefordshire : Excavations 1912–1913*

JACK, G. H. and HAYTER, A. G. K. 1926 *The Romano-British Town of Magna (Kenchester) Herefordshire : Excavations 1925–1926*

JACKSON, F. 1927 'A Roman Bronze Bowl', *Trans. Birmingham Arch. Soc.* 50, (1924), 50

JACKSON, K. 1939 'The Gododdin of Aneirin', *Antiquity* 13, (1939), 25–34

JAMES, B. and FRANCIS, D. J. 1979 *Cowbridge and Llanblethian, Past and Present*

JARRETT, M. G. 1976 'An Unnecessary War', *Britannia* 7, (1976), 145–51

JESSUP, R. F. 1928 'A Romano-British settlement at Springhead, Kent', *Antiquaries J.* 8, (1928), 337–43

JESSUP, R. F. 1959 'Barrows and Walled Cemeteries in Roman Britain', *J. British Arch. Assn.* 22, (1959), 1–32

JOHNS, C. and CARSON, R. 1975 'The Waternewton Hoard', *Durobrivae* 3, (1975), 10–12

JOHNSON, S. 1975 'Vici in Lowland Britain', in Rodwell and Rowley 1975, 75–83

JOHNSTON, D. E. 1969 'Romano-British Pottery Kilns near Northampton', *Antiquaries J.* 49, (1969), 75–97

JOHNSTON, D. E. 1974 'The Roman Settlement at Sandy, Bedfordshire', *Beds. Arch. J.* 9, (1974), 35–54

JONES, A. H. M. 1964 *The Later Roman Empire 284–602*

JONES, G. D. B. 1972 'Excavations at Northwich (Condate)', *Arch. J.* 128, (1971), 31–77

JONES, G. D. B. and LEWIS, P. 1974 'Ancient Mining and the Environment', in Rahtz, P. (Ed.) *Rescue Archaeology*, 130–49

JONES, G. D. B. and REYNOLDS, P. 1978 *Roman Manchester : the Deansgate Excavations 1978*

JONES, G. D. B. and REYNOLDS, P. 1983 'Northwich: Excavations at the Castle 1983', *Cheshire Arch. Bull.* 9, (1983), 82–5

JONES, G. D. B. and WEBSTER, P. V. 1968 'Mediolanum : excavation at Whitchurch 1965–6', *Arch. J.* 125, (1968), 193–254

JONES, M. 1975 *Roman Fort Defences to AD 117* B.A.R. 21

JONES, M. J. and WACHER, J. S. 1987 'The Roman Period', in Schofield, J. and Leech, R. (Eds.) *Urban Archaeology in Britain* C.B.A. Res. Rpt. 61, 27–45

JONES, P. 1982 'Saxon and Early Medieval Staines', *London and Middlesex Arch. Soc. Trans.* 33, (1982), 186–213

KENNET, D. H. 1969 'The Irchester Bowls', *J. Northants. Mus. and Art Gallery* 4, (1969), 5–39

KENYON, K. M. 1948 *Excavation at the Jewry Wall Site, Leicester* Soc. of Antiqs. Res. Rpt. 15

KIRK, J. R. and LEEDS, E. T. 1953 'Three Early Saxon Graves from Dorchester, Oxon.', *Oxoniensia* 17/18, (1952–3), 63–76

KLEISS, W. 1962 'Die Öffentlichen Banten von Cambodunum', *Materialhefte zur Bayerischen Vorgeschichte* 18, (1962), 55–64

KNIGHT, J. K. 1968 'Excavations at the

Roman Town of Irchester 1962–3', *Arch. J.* 124, (1967), 100–28

KNOWLES, A. K. 1977 'The Roman Settlement at Brampton, Norfolk : Interim Report', *Britannia* 8, (1977), 209–21

KNOWLES, W. H. 1926 'The Roman Baths at Bath with an account of the Excavations conducted during 1923', *Archaeologia* 78, (1926), 1–18

KÖRBER, K. 1906 'Die grosse Juppiter-Säule von Mainz', *Mainzer Zeitschrift* 1, (1906), 54–63

LA BAUME, P. n.d. (Eng. Edn.) *The Romans on the Rhine* Bonn

LADDS, S. I. 1930 'Excavation at Emmanuel Knoll, Godmanchester', *Trans. Cambs. and Hunts. Antiq. Soc.* 4, (1915–1932), 14–16

LAMBRICK, G. *et multi alii* 1980 'Excavations in Park Street, Towcester', *Northamptonshire Archaeology* 15, (1980), 35–118

LAWRENCE, W. L. 1863 'Wycomb', *Proc. Soc. Antiq.* 2, (1863–4), 302–7

LAWRENCE, W. L. 1864a 'Wycomb', *Proc. Soc. Antiq.* 2, (1863–4), 422–6

LAWRENCE, W. L. 1864b 'Antiquities and Works of Art Exhibited', *Arch. J.* 21, (1864), 96–97

LEACH, P. 1982 *Ilchester vol.1 : excavations 1974–1975*

LEACH, P. 1987 *Ilchester Great Yard 1987, an archaeological assessment* Birmingham University Field Arch. Unit

LEACH, P. and ELLIS, P. 1985 *Ilchester: Interim Report on Excavations 1985* Western Arch. Trust

LEACH, P. and THEW, N. 1985 *A late Iron Age "oppidum" at Ilchester, Somerset : an interim assessment 1984* Western Arch. Trust

LEECH, R. H. 1982 *Excavations at Catsgore 1970–1973 : A Romano-British Village*

LELAND, J. 1744 (2nd Edn.) *The Itinerary of John Leland, the Antiquary* 9 volumes

LEWIS, M. J. T. 1966 *Temples in Roman Britain*

LEWIS, P. R. 1977 'The Ogofau Roman Gold Mines at Dolaucothi', *National Trust Yearbook* 1976–7, 20–35

LEWIS, P. and JONES, G. D. B. 1969 'The Dolaucothi Gold Mines I : the Surface Evidence', *Antiquaries. J.* 49, (1969), 244–72

LIVERSIDGE, J. 1977 'Roman Burials in the Cambridge Area', *Proc. Cambridge Antiq. Soc.* 67, (1977), 11–38

LOUGHLIN, N. and MILLER, K. 1979 *A Survey of Archaeological Sites in Humberside*

LUCAS, J. 1981 'Tripontium, Third Interim Report', *Trans. Birmingham Arch. Soc.* 91, (1981), 25–54

LYNAM, C. 1913 'Notes on Excavations at Wall', *North Staffs. Nat. Club Ann. Rpt. and Trans.* 47, (1913), 139–43

LYNAM, C. 1915 'Excavation on the Site of Wall (Letocetum)', *North Staffs. Nat. Club Ann. Rpt. and Trans* 49, (1915), 132–44

LYNE, M. A. B. and JEFFERIES, R. S. 1979 *The Alice Holt / Farnham Roman Pottery Industry* C.B.A. Res. Rpt. 30

LYON, F. H. and GOULD, J. T. 1961 'Preliminary Report on the Excavation of the Defences of the Roman fort at Wall', *Trans. Lichfield and S. Staffs. Arch. and Hist. Soc.* 2, (1960–61), 31–7

LYON, F. H. and GOULD, J. T. 1964 'Section through the defences of the Roman forts at Wall', *Trans. Birmingham Arch. Soc.* 79, (1960–1), 11–23

LYSONS, S 1806 [Inscription found at Kenchester], *Archaeologia* 15, (1806), 391–2, pl. 27

LYSONS, S. 1813 *Reliquiae Britannico-Romanae I*

McCARTHY, M. R. 1979 'Carlisle', *Current Arch.* 68, 268–72

McCARTHY, M. R. 1980 *Carlisle, a frontier city*

McCARTHY, M. R. 1984 'Roman Carlisle', in Wilson *et al.* 1984, 65–74

McCARTHY, M. R. and DACRE, A. 1983 'Roman Timber Buildings at Castle Street, Carlisle', *Antiquaries J.* 63, (1983), 124–30

McCARTHY, M. R., PADLEY, T. G. and HENIG, M. 1982 'Excavations and finds from The Lanes, Carlisle', *Britannia* 13, (1982), 79–90

MACKRETH, D. 1978 'Orton Hall Farm, Peterborough: A Roman and Saxon Settlement', in Todd 1978, 217–23

MACKRETH, D. 1979 'Durobrivae', *Durobrivae* 7, (1979), 19–21

MACLAUGHLAN, H. 1849 'On the Roman roads, camps and other earthworks, between the Tees and the Swale, in the North Riding of the County of York', *Arch. J.* 6, (1849), 213–25

MACMULLEN, R. 1963 *Soldier and Civilian in the Later Roman Empire*

McWHIRR, A. 1979 'Roman Tile Kilns in Britain', in McWhirr, A. (Ed.) *Roman Brick and Tile: Studies in Manufacture, Distribution and Use in the Western Empire* B.A.R. s68

McWHIRR, A. 1981 *Roman Gloucestershire*

McWHIRR, A. and VINER, D. 1978 'The Production and Distribution of Tiles in Roman Britain with particular reference to the Cirencester Region', *Britannia* 9, (1978), 359–77

MAHANY, C. M. 1971' Excavation at Manduessedum 1964', *Trans. Birmingham Arch. Soc.* 84, (1967–70), 18–44

MAHANY, C. M. forthcoming *Excavations at Alcester 1964–66*

MANNING, W. H. 1972 'Ironwork Hoards in Iron Age and Roman Britain', *Britannia* 3, (1972), 224–50

MARGARY, I. D. 1935 'Roman Roads near Durobrivae (Castor, Northants)', *Antiquaries J.* 15, (1935), 113–18

MARGARY, I. D. 1939 'Roman Camp-site near Castor', *Antiquity* 13, (1939), 455–8

MARGARY, I. D. 1973 *Roman Roads in Britain*

MARSHALL, J. and BROWN, W. L. 1858 'Alchester', *Trans. Arch. Soc. North Oxfordshire* 5, (1857–8), 123–41

MATHER, C. 1980 'Tiddington, Warks. : Site evaluation of Roman settlement', *West Midlands Arch. News Sheet* 23, (1980), 119–21

MAY, J. 1970 'Dragonby : an interim report on excavations on an Iron Age and Romano-British site near Scunthorpe, Lincs, 1964–69', *Antiquaries J.* 50, (1970), 222–45

MAY, J. 1976 'The Growth of Settlements in the later Iron Age in Lincolnshire', in Cunliffe and Rowley 1976, 163–80

MAY, J. 1977 'Romano-British and Saxon sites near Dorchester, Oxon.', *Oxoniensia* 42, (1977), 42–79

MAY, T. 1897 'On the altar and other relics found during recent excavations, 1895–6', *Trans. Hist. Soc. Lancs. and Cheshire* 48, (1897), 1–28

MAY, T. 1900 'The Roman Fortifications recently discovered at Wilderspool', *Trans. Hist. Soc. Lancs. and Cheshire* 50, (1898), 1–40

MAY, T. 1902 'Excavations on the site of the Romano-British civitas at Wilderspool 1899–1900', *Trans. Hist. Soc. Lancs. and Cheshire* 52, (1900), 1–52

MAY, T. 1904 *Warrington's Roman Remains*

MAY, T. 1905 'The Excavations on the Romano-British site at Wilderspool and Stockton Heath 1901–4', *Trans. Hist. Soc. Lancs. and Cheshire* 55/56, (1903–4), 209–37

MAY, T. 1907 'The Excavations on the Romano-British site at Warrington during 1905', *Trans. Hist. Soc. Lancs. and Cheshire* 58, (1906), 15–40

MERTENS, J. and BRULET, R. 1974 'Le Castellum du Bas-Empire Romain de Brunehaut-Liberchies', *Arch. Belgica* 163, (1974), 9–15

MEYERS, W. 1964 'L'Administration de la Province Romaine de Belgique', *Dissertationes Archaeologicae Gandenses* 8, (1964).

MILES, A. 1975 'Salt Panning in Romano-British Kent', in de Brisay and Evans 1975, 26–31

MILLETT, M. 1975 'Recent work on the Romano-British settlement at Neatham, Hampshire', *Britannia* 6, (1975), 213–16

MILLETT, M. 1979 'The Dating of Farnham Pottery', *Britannia* 10, (1979), 121–138

MILLETT, M. and GRAHAM, D. 1986 *Excavations on the Romano-British Small Town at Neatham, Hampshire, 1969–1979* Hampshire Field Club Monograph 3

MONAGHAN, J. 1987 *Upchurch and Thameside Roman Pottery*

MORCOM, R. K. 1938 'Roman Steelyards found in Worcestershire', *The Engineer* Jan 7th 1938, 26 and Jan 21st 1938

MORTON, J. 1712 *Natural History of Northamptonshire*

MYLIUS, H. 1936 'Die Ostthermen von Nida und ihr Prätorium', *Bonner Jahrbuch* 140/41, (1936), 299–324

MYRES, J. L. 1892 'On Excavations at Alchester, Oxon.', *Proc. Oxford Archit. and Hist. Soc.* 5, (1892), 355

MYRES, J. N. L. 1969 *Anglo-Saxon Pottery and the Settlement of England*

NEAL, D. 1987 'Stanwick', *Current Arch.* 106, 334–36

NEVILLE, R. C. 1847 *Antiqua Explorata*

NEVILLE, R. C. 1848 *Sepulchra Exposita*

NEVILLE, R. C. 1855 'Notices of certain shafts, containing remains of the Roman period, discovered at Great Chesterford, Essex', *Arch. J.* 12, (1855), 109–25

NEVILLE, R. C. 1856 'Description of a remarkable deposit of Roman antiquities of iron, discovered at Great Chesterford, Essex', *Arch. J.* 13, (1856), 1–13

NEVILLE, R. C. 1860 'Account of recent discoveries of Roman remains at Great Chesterford, Essex', *Arch. J.* 17, (1860), 117–27

NIGHTINGALE, M. D. 1952 'Roman Land Settlement near Rochester', *Arch. Cantiana* 65, (1952), 150–9

OETGEN, J. M. 1986 'Sapperton Roman Town', *Arch. in Lincolnshire* 1985–86, 10–12

OETGEN, J. M. 1987 'Sapperton Roman Town', *Arch. in Lincolnshire* 1986–87, 13–15

OLDHAM, J. L. 1850 'Account of Roman Urns . . . at . . . Chesterford', *Arch. J.* 7, (1850), 139–41

O'LEARY, T. J. 1981 'Excavations at Upper Borough Walls, Bath, 1980', *Mediaeval Arch.* 25, (1981), 1–30

O'LEARY, T. J. and DAVEY, P. J. 1977 'Excavations at Pentre Farm, Flint 1976–7', *Flints. Hist. Soc. Pub.* 27, (1976), 138–51

O'NEIL, B. H. St J. 1931 'Excavations at Mancetter 1927', *Trans. Birmingham Arch. Soc.* 53, (1928), 173–95

O'NEIL, B. H. St J. 1944 'The Silchester region in the fifth and sixth centuries AD', *Antiquity* 18, (1944), 113–22

O'NEIL, H. E. 1969 'The Roman Settlement on the Fosse Way at Bourton Bridge, Bourton on the Water, Glos.', *Trans. Bristol and Gloucs. Arch. Soc.* 87, (1968), 29–55

O'NEIL, H. E. 1973 'Bourton Bridge Posting House, Bourton on the Water. Part II : Pottery and Finds', *Trans. Bristol and Gloucs. Arch. Soc.* 91, (1972), 92–116

O'NEIL, H. E. and TOYNBEE, J. M. C. 1958 'Sculptures from a Romano-British Well in Gloucestershire', *J. Roman Studs.* 48, (1958), 52–55

ORDNANCE SURVEY 1956 *Map of Roman Britain* (3rd Edn.)

ORDNANCE SURVEY 1979 *Map of Roman Britain* (4th Edn.)

OSWALD, A. 1939 'Excavations at Ad Pontem, 1937–8', *Trans. Thoroton Soc.* 42, (1938), 1–14

OSWALD, A. 1964 'Roman Material from Dorn, Glos.', *Trans. Bristol and Gloucs. Arch. Soc.* 82, (1963), 18–24

OSWALD, A. 1968 'Observation on the construction of the bypass road at Wall, Staffs.', *Trans. Lichfield and S. Staffs. Arch and Hist. Soc.* 8, (1966), 39–41

OSWALD, A. and GATHERCOLE, P. W. 1958 'Observation and excavation at Manduessedum, 1954–56', *Trans. Birmingham Arch. Soc.* 74, (1956), 30–52

OSWALD, F. 1923 'The Pottery of a Claudian Well at Margidunum', *J. Roman Studs.* 13, (1923), 114–26

OSWALD, F. 1926 'The Pottery of a Third Century Well at Margidunum', *J. Roman Studs.* 16, (1926), 36–44

OSWALD, F. 1928 'Margidunum', *Trans. Thoroton Soc.* 31, (1927), 54–84

OSWALD, F. 1941 'Margidunum', *J. Roman Studs.* 31, (1941), 32–62

OSWALD, F. 1948a *The Commandant's House at Margidunum* Univ. of Nottingham

OSWALD, F. 1948b *The Terra Sigillata of Margidunum* Univ. of Nottingham

OSWALD, F. 1952 *Excavation of a Traverse of Margidunum* Univ. of Nottingham

OSWALD, F. and PRYCE, T. D. 1914 'Margidunum : a Roman fortified post on the Fosse Way : Excavation in 1913', *Antiquary* 50, (1914), 477–52

PAGE, W. and TAYLOR, M. V. 1912 'Romano-British Hertfordshire', *Victoria County History : Hertfordshire* vol. 4, 119–72

PAINTER, K. 1977 *The Waternewton Early Christian Silver* Brit. Mus. Publications

PALMER, N. 1980 'Excavation of a Roman Settlement at SP219557', *West Midlands Arch. News Sheet* 23, (1980), 121

PALMER, N. 1981 'Tiddington Roman

Settlement : an Interim Report', *West Midlands Arch. News Sheet* 24, (1981), 17–24

PALMER, N. 1983 'Tiddington Roman Settlement : second Interim Report', *West Midlands Arch. News Sheet* 26, (1983), 37–47

PAPE, T. 1934 'Roman Finds at Chesterton', *North Staffs. Field Club Trans.* 68, (1934), 159–62

PARKHOUSE, J. 1981a 'Excavations in Cowbridge', *Annual Report, Glamorgan-Gwent Arch. Trust* 1980–1, 15–26

PARKHOUSE, J. 1981b 'Cowbridge', *Current Arch.* 81, 308–9

PARKHOUSE, J. 1981c 'Cowbridge', *Arch. in Wales* 21, (1981), 46–50

PARKHOUSE, J. 1982a 'Excavations in Cowbridge', *Annual Report, Glamorgan-Gwent Arch. Trust* 1981–2, 7–21

PARKHOUSE, J. 1982b 'The Cowbridge Lion : a preliminary report', *Annual Report, Glamorgan-Gwent Arch. Trust* 1981–2, 87–90

PARKHOUSE, J. 1982c 'Cowbridge', *Arch. in Wales* 22, (1982), 23–4

PARKHOUSE, J. 1983 'Cowbridge, Bear Field', *Arch. in Wales* 23, (1983), 36

PARTRIDGE, C. R. 1975 'Braughing', in Rodwell and Rowley 1975, 139–57

PARTRIDGE, C. R. 1978 'Excavations and Fieldwork at Braughing 1968–73', *Herts. Arch.* 5, (1977), 22–108

PARTRIDGE, C. R. 1980 'Excavations at Puckeridge and Braughing 1975–9', *Herts. Arch.* 7, (1979), 28–132

PARTRIDGE, C. R. 1981 *Skeleton Green : a late Iron Age and Romano-British Site* Britannia Monograph No. 2

PARTRIDGE, C. R. 1982 'Braughing, Wickham Kennels 1982', *Hertfordshire Arch.* 8, (1980–2), 40–59

PASSMORE, A. D. 1922 'Roman Wanborough', *Wilts. Arch. Mag.* 41, (1920–2), 272–80

PATTEN, T. 1974 'The Roman Cemetery on the London Road, Carlisle', *Trans. Cumberland and Westmorland Antiq. and Arch. Soc.* 74, (1974), 8–13

PAYNE, G. 1895 'Roman Rochester', *Arch. Cantiana* 21, (1895), 1–16

PENN, W. S. 1958 'Excavation of the Bakery, Site A', *Arch. Cantiana* 71, (1957), 53–105

PENN, W. S. 1959 'Excavation of the Watling Street, shop and pedestal, Site B', *Arch. Cantiana* 72, (1958), 77–110

PENN, W. S. 1960 'Excavation of Temple 1, Site CI', *Arch. Cantiana* 73, (1959), 1–61

PENN, W. S. 1961 'Springhead : Temples 3 and 4', *Arch. Cantiana* 74, (1960), 113–40

PENN, W. S. 1963 'Temples 2 and 5', *Arch. Cantiana* 77, (1962), 110–32

PENN, W. S. 1966 'Springhead : Map of Discoveries', *Arch. Cantiana* 80, (1965), 107–17

PENN, W. S. 1967 'Springhead', *Arch. Cantiana* 81, (1966), lxii–lxiii

PENN, W. S. 1968a 'Springhead : Temple 6 / Gateway', *Arch. Cantiana* 82, (1967), 105–23

PENN, W. S. 1968b 'Possible Evidence from Springhead for the Great Plague of AD 166', *Arch. Cantiana* 82, (1967), 263–71

PENN, W. S. 1969a 'Springhead : miscellaneous excavations', *Arch. Cantiana* 83, (1968), 163–92

PENN, W. S. 1969b 'Springhead', *Arch. Cantiana* 83, (1968), 257

PETCH, D. F. 1987 'The Roman Period', in *Victoria County History: Cheshire Vol. 1*, 115–236

PETCH, J. A. 1928 'Excavations at Benwell (Condercum)', *Arch. Aeliana* 4s, 5, (1928), 52–7

PHILLIPS, B. and WALTERS, B. 1977 'A *mansio* at Lower Wanborough, Wiltshire', *Britannia* 8, (1977), 223–7

PHILLIPS, C. W. 1934 'The Present State of Archaeology in Lincolnshire', *Arch. J.* 91, (1934), 97–187

PHILLIPS, E. J. 1976 'A workshop of Roman Sculptors at Carlisle', *Britannia* 7, (1976), 101–8

PICARD, G. 1970 'Les Théatres ruraux de Gaule', *Revue Archéologique* (1970), 185–92

PITTS, L. F. 1983 'A Bronze Jupiter', *Oxford J. of Arch.* 2, (1983), 119–21

POTTER, T. W. and TROW, S. D. 1988 'Puckeridge-Braughing, Herts: The Ermine Street Excavations, 1971–1972', *Hertfordshire Arch.* 10, (1988), 1–191

PRYCE, T. D. 1912 'Margidunum : a Roman fortified post on the Fosse Way : excavations of 1910–11', *J. British Arch. Assn.* NS18, (1912), 177–210

PULLINGER, J. 1978 'The Cambridge Shrine', *Current Arch.* 61, 57–60

RADFORD, C. A. R. 1946 'A lost inscription of pre-Danish Age from Caistor', *Arch. J.* 103, (1946), 95–99

RAHTZ, P. 1960 'Caistor, Lincolnshire 1959', *Antiquaries J.* 40, (1960), 175–187

RAHTZ, P. 1977 'Kenchester 1977 : Interim Report on Excavations', *West Midlands Arch. News Sheet* 20, (1977), 33–36

RAMM, H. 1971 'The End of Roman York', in Butler 1971, 179–99

RAMM, H. 1978 *The Parisi*

RASHLEIGH, P. 1803 'An account of antiquities discovered at Southfleet in Kent', *Archaeologia* 14, (1803), 37–39 and 221–23

RAVENNA COSMOGRAPHY = Schnetz, J. (Ed.) 1940, in *Itineraria Romana II* Leipzig

RAWES, B. 1973 'Wycomb, Andoversford', *Glevensis* 7, (1973), 12–13

RAWES, B. 1976 'Wycomb, Andoversford', *Glevensis* 10, (1976).

RAWES, B. 1980 'The Romano-British site at Wycomb, Andoversford 1969– 1970', *Trans. Bristol and Gloucs. Arch. Soc.* 98, (1980), 11–55

R.C.A.H.M. Wales 1976 *Glamorgan vol.1, pt.2 : Iron Age and Roman Occupation*

R.C.H.M. 1926 *Inventory of Huntingdonshire*

R.C.H.M. 1959 *City of Cambridge vol. 1*

R.C.H.M. 1969 *Peterborough New Town : A Survey of the Antiquities in the Areas of Development*

R.C.H.M. 1975 *Historical Monuments in the County of Dorset. Volume V : East*

R.C.H.M. 1976 *Iron Age and Romano-British Monuments in the Gloucestershire Cotswolds*

R.C.H.M. 1979 *An Inventory of Archaeological Sites in Central Northamptonshire*

R.C.H.M. 1982 *An Inventory of Archaeological Sites in South-West Northamptonshire*

REA, J. 1972 'A Lead Tablet from Wanborough', *Britannia* 3, (1972), 363–7

REECE, R. 1980 'Town and Country : the End of Roman Britain', *World Arch.* 12, (1980), 77–92

RENDELL, M. 1970 'Roman Staines', *London Arch.* 1, No. 7, 161–2

REYNOLDS, P. J. and LANGLEY, J. K. 1980 'Romano-British Corn-Drying Oven : an Experiment', *Arch. J.* 136, (1979), 27–42

R. I. B. = Collingwood, R. G. and Wright, R. P. 1965 *The Roman Inscriptions of Britain, I, Inscriptions on Stone*

RICHMOND, I. A. 1943 'Roman Legionaries at Corbridge, their supply base, temples and religious cults', *Arch. Aeliana* 4S 21, (1943), 127–224

RICHMOND, I. A. 1966 'Industry in Roman Britain', in Wacher 1966b, 76–86

RICHMOND, I. A. and CRAWFORD, O. G. S. 1949 'The British Section of the Ravenna Cosmography', *Archaeologia* 93, (1949), 1–50

RICHMOND, I. A. and TOYNBEE, J. M. C. 1955 'The Temple of Sulis Minerva at Bath', *J. Roman Studs.* 45, (1955), 97–105

RILEY, D. N. 1977 'Roman Defended Sites at Kirmington, S. Humberside and Farnsfield, Notts., Recently Found from the Air', *Britannia* 8, (1977), 189–192

RIVET, A. L. F. 1955 'Conference on Romano-British Villas 1955', *Arch. News Letter* 6, no. 2, (1955), 29–55

RIVET, A. L. F. 1964 *Town and Country in Roman Britain*

RIVET, A. L. F. 1969a 'Social and economic aspects', in Rivet 1969b, 173–216

RIVET, A. L. F. (Ed.) 1969b *The Roman Villa in Britain*

RIVET, A. L. F. 1970 'The British Section of the Antonine Itinerary', *Britannia* 1, (1970), 34–82

RIVET, A. L. F. 1975 'Summing Up : the classification of Minor Towns and related settlements', in Rodwell and Rowley 1975, 111–14

RIVET, A. L. F. 1977 'The Origins of Cities in Roman Britain', in Duval, P. M. and Frezouls, E. (Eds.) *Thème de Recherches sur les Villes Antiques d'Occident* Colloques internationaux du C.N.R.S. no. 542, 161–72

RIVET, A. L. F. and SMITH, C. 1979 *The Place-Names of Roman Britain*

ROBINSON, D. M. 1980 *Cowbridge : The Archaeology and Topography of a Small Market Town in the Vale of Glamorgan*

ROBSON, J. R. 1921 'Rochester Bridge: The Roman Bridge in Masonry', *Arch. Cantiana* 35, (1921), 139–44

RODWELL, K. 1987 *The Prehistoric and Roman Settlement at Kelvedon, Essex* C.B.A. Res. Rpt. 63

RODWELL, W. 1972 'The Roman Fort at Great Chesterford, Essex', *Britannia* 3, (1972), 290–93

RODWELL, W. 1975 'Trinovantian towns and their setting : a case study', in Rodwell and Rowley 1975, 85–101

RODWELL, W. and ROWLEY, T. (Eds.) 1975 *The 'Small Towns' of Roman Britain* B.A.R. 15

ROGERSON, A. 1977 'Excavation at Scole, 1973', *East Anglian Arch.* 5, (1977), 97–224

ROLLESTON, G. 1869 'Researches and Excavations carried on in an Ancient Cemetery at Frilford, near Abingdon, Berkshire in the years 1867–1868', *Archaeologia* 42, (1869), 417–85

ROLLESTON, G. 1880 'Further researches in an Anglo-Saxon Cemetery at Frilford', *Archaeologia* 45, (1880), 405–10

ROMAN SOCIETY (The) 1985 *Priorities for the Preservation and Excavation of Romano-British Sites*

ROOKE, H. 1789 'Account of Roman Building and Camp discovered at Buxton', *Archaeologia* 9, (1789), 137–40.

ROUND, A. A. 1971a 'Excavations at Wall 1966–67 on the site of the forts', *Trans. Lichfield and S. Staffs. Arch. and Hist. Soc.* 11, (1969–70), 7–30

ROUND, A. A. 1971b 'Excavation at Wall 1971', *West Midlands Arch. News Sheet* 14, (1971), 13

ROUND, A. A. 1972 'Excavation at Wall 1972', *West Midlands Arch. News Sheet* 15, (1972), 13–14

ROUND, A. A. 1974a 'The Bath-House at Wall, Staffs: Excavations in 1971', *Trans. Lichfield and S. Staffs. Arch. and Hist. Soc.* 15, (1973–74), 13–28

ROUND, A. A. 1974b 'Excavation at Wall 1974', *West Midlands Arch. News Sheet* 17, (1974), 54–5

ROUND, A. A. 1975 'Excavation at Wall 1975', *West Midlands Arch. News Sheet* 18, (1975), 50–1

ROUND, A. A. 1976 'Excavation at Wall 1976', *West Midlands Arch. News Sheet* 19, (1976), 39

ROUND, A. A. 1977 'Excavation at Wall 1977', *West Midlands Arch. News Sheet* 20, (1977), 55–9

ROUND, A. A. 1983 'Excavations at Wall (Staffs.) 1968–1972, on the site of the Roman Forts', *Trans. Lichfield and S. Staffs. Arch. and Hist. Soc.* 23, (1981–2), 1–67

ROUND, A. A., ROSS, A. and HENIG, M. 1980 'Eleventh Report of Excavations at Wall, Staffs.', *Trans. South Staffs. Arch. and Hist. Soc.* 21, (1979–80), 1–14

ROWLEY, R. T. 1974 'Early Saxon Settlement in Dorchester', in Rowley, R. T. (Ed.) *Anglo-Saxon Settlement and Landscape*, 42–50

ROWLEY, R. T. 1975 'The Roman Towns of Oxfordshire', in Rodwell and Rowley 1975, 115–24

ROWLEY, R. T. and BROWN, L. 1981 'Excavations at Beech House Hotel, Dorchester on Thames 1972', *Oxoniensia* 46, (1981), 1–55

RUDKIN, E. H. 1933 'Roman Sites North of Lincoln', *The Lincolnshire Magazine* 1, (1933), 224–8

ST JOSEPH, J. K. S. 1943 'The Roman Fort at Dodderhill, Droitwich : Interim Report', *Trans. Birmingham Arch. Soc.* 62, (1938), 27–31

ST JOSEPH, J. K. S. 1946 'Roman Droitwich', *Trans. Birmingham Arch. Soc.* 64, (1941–2), 39–52

ST JOSEPH, J. K. S. 1953 'Air Reconnaissance of Southern Britain', *J. Roman Studs.* 43, (1953), 81–97, pls. 8–16

ST JOSEPH, J. K. S. 1958a 'Air Reconnaissance in Britain, 1955–57', *J. Roman Studs.* 48, (1958), 86–101, pls. 11–16

ST JOSEPH, J. K. S. 1958a 'Air reconnaissance in Britain, 1955–57', *J. Roman Studs.* 48, (1958), 86–101, pls. 11–16

ST JOSEPH, J. K. S. 1958b 'The Roman Site near Stretton Bridge, the ancient Pennocrucium', *Trans. Birmingham Arch. Soc.* 74, (1956), 1–5

ST JOSEPH, J. K. S. 1961a 'Air Reconnaissance in Britain, 1958–1960', *J. Roman Studs.* 51, (1961), 119–35, pls. 8–12

ST JOSEPH, J. K. S. 1961b 'The Roman Fort at Great Casterton : discovery and situation', in Corder 1961, 13–17

ST JOSEPH, J. K. S. 1965 'Air Reconnaissance in Britain, 1961–64', *J. Roman Studs.* 55, (1965), 74–89, pls. 9–13

ST JOSEPH, J. K. S. 1966 'The contribution of aerial photography', in Wacher 1966b, 21–30

ST JOSEPH, J. K. S. 1969 'Air Reconnaissance in Britain, 1965–8', *J. Roman Studs.* 59, (1969), 104–28, pls. 2–6

ST JOSEPH, J. K. S. 1973 'Air Reconnaissance in Britain, 1969–72', *J. Roman Studs.* 63, (1973), 214–46, pls. 15–18

SALWAY, P. 1965 *Frontier People of Roman Britain*

SAWLE, J. 1977 'HWCM 117, Sidbury (Worcester)', *West Midlands Arch. News Sheet* 20, (1977), 43–5

SAWLE, J. 1978 'Excavation of the Old Bowling Green, Ricketts Lane, Droitwich', *West Midlands Arch. News Sheet* 21, (1978), 76–8

SCARTH, H. M. 1863 'On Roman Remains discovered at Camerton', *Proc. Somerset Arch. Soc.* 11, (1861–2), 174–86

SCARTH, H. M. 1874 'Roman Remains at Charterhouse-on-Mendip', *Proc. Soc. Antiquaries* 25, 6, (1874), 187–91

SCARTH, H. M. 1875 'Notes on the Roads, Camps and Mining Operations of the Romans in the Mendip Hills', *J. British Arch. Assn.* 31, (1875), 129–42

SCARTH, H. M. 1876 'Further Gleanings in the Mendips and its Valleys', *Proc. Bath Field Club* 3, (1874), 334–41

SCOTT, K. 1973 'A Section across the Defences of a Roman Fort at Mancetter, Warwickshire', *Trans. Birmingham Arch. Soc.* 85, (1971–73), 211–13

SCOTT, K. 1981 'Mancetter Village: a first century fort?' *Trans. Birmingham Arch. Soc.* 91, (1981), 1–24

SCROPE, G. P. 1862 'Roman Villa at North Wraxhall, discovered in 1859', *Wilts Arch. Mag.* 7, (1862), 59–74

SELKIRK, A. 1972 'Rushden', *Current Arch.* 31, 204–5

SELKIRK, A. 1981 'Carsington', *Current Arch.* 75, 125–6

SELKIRK, A. 1983 'Baldock', *Current Arch.* 86, 70–4

SHARPE, M. 1913 *The Middlesex District in Roman Times*

SHARPE, M. 1932 *Middlesex in British, Roman and Saxon Times*

SHAW, R. C. 1924 'Romano-British Carlisle: its structural remains', *Trans. Cumberland and Westmorland Antiq. and Arch. Soc.* 24, (1924), 95–109

SHELDON, H. L. and SCHAAF, L. 1978 'A Survey of sites in Greater London', in Bird, J., Chapman, H. and Clark, J. (Eds.) *Collectanea Londiniensia : essays presented to Ralph Merrifield*, 59–88

SHOESMITH, R. 1969 'Excavations at Weston-under-Penyard', *Trans. Woolhope Nat. Field Club* 39, (1967–9), 157–9

SHORTT, H. de S. 1959 'A provincial Roman spur from Longstock, Hants., and other spurs from Roman Britain', *Antiquaries J.* 39, (1959), 61–76

SHORTT, H. de S. 1964 'Another spur of the first century from Suffolk', *Antiquaries J.* 44, (1964), 60–1

SHORTT, H. de S. 1976 *Old Sarum* H.M.S.O.

SIMMONS, B. B. 1976 'Sapperton, an Interim Report', *Lincs. Hist. and Arch.* 11, (1976), 5–11

SIMMONS, B. B. 1979 'The Lincolnshire Car Dyke : Navigation or Drainage?', *Britannia* 10, (1979), 183–96

SIMMONS, B. B. 1980 'Iron-Age and Roman Coasts around the Wash', in Thompson, F. H. (Ed.) *Archaeology and Coastal Change*, 56–73

SIMMONS, B. B. 1985 'Sapperton', *Arch. in Lincs.* 1984–5, 16–20

SIMPSON, F. G. 1976 *Watermills and Military Works on Hadrian's Wall* (ed. G. Simpson)

SKINNER, J. n.d. *The Diary of the Rev. J. Skinner, Rector of Camerton 1800–37* British Museum Add. MSS. 28793–28795, 33633–33730; and Egerton MS 3099–3123

SLATER, T. R. and WILSON, C. 1977 *Archaeology and Development in Stratford-upon-Avon* Univ. of Birmingham

SMITH, C. R. 1849 'Recent Discoveries made at Ickleton and Chesterford', *J. British Arch. Assn.* 4, (1849), 356–78

SMITH, D. J. 1969 'The Mosaic Pavements', in Rivet 1969b, 71–126

SMITH, R. F. 1976 'Hibaldstow: Staniwells Farm', *Lincs. Hist. and Arch.* 11, (1976), 58

SMITH, R. F. 1977 'Hibaldstow: Staniwells Farm', *Lincs. Hist. and Arch.* 12, (1977), 74

SMITH, R. F. 1978 'Hibaldstow: Staniwells Farm', *Lincs. Hist. and Arch.* 13, (1978), 78

SMITH, R. F. 1980 'Hibaldstow: Staniwells Farm', *Lincs. Hist. and Arch.* 15, (1980), 71–2

SMITH, R. F. 1981 'Hibaldstow', *Current Arch.* 77, 168–71

SMITH, R. F. 1987 *Roadside Settlements in Lowland Roman Britain* B.A.R. 157

SOMMER, C. S. 1984 *The Military Vici in Roman Britain: aspects of their origins, their location and layout, administration, function and end* B.A.R. 129

SPAIN, R. J. 1984 'Romano-British Watermills', *Arch. Cantiana* 100, (1984), 101–28

STANDISH, J. 1909 'Margidunum', *Trans. Thoroton Soc.* 12, (1908), 38–46

STANFORD, S. C. 1970 'Credenhill Camp, Herefordshire : An Iron Age Hill-fort Capital', *Arch. J.* 127, (1970), 82–129

STANFORD, S. C. 1980 *The Welsh Marches*

STANLEY, C. 1979 'Thames Valley', *Aerial Archaeology* 4, (1979), 105–6

STEAD, I. M. 1970 'Trial Excavation at Braughing', *Hertfordshire Arch.* 2, (1970), 37–47

STEAD, I. M. 1975 'Baldock', in Rodwell and Rowley 1975, 125–9

STEAD, I. M. and RIGBY, V. 1986 *Baldock: The Excavation of a Roman and pre-Roman Settlement, 1968–1972* Britannia Monograph No.7

STENTON, F. 1971 (3rd Edn.) *Anglo-Saxon England*

STEVENS, C. E. 1940 'The Frilford Site : a Postscript', *Oxoniensia* 5, (1940), 166–7

STEVENS, C. E. 1952 'The Roman Name of Ilchester', *Proc. Somerset Arch. Soc.* 96, (1951), 188–92

STUKELEY, W. 1724 (1st Edn.); 1776 (2nd Edn.) *Itinerarium Curiosum*

SWAN, V. G. 1975 'Oare reconsidered and the origins of Savernake Ware in Wiltshire', *Britannia* 6, (1975), 36–61

SWAN, V. G. 1977 'Relief decorated imitation samian cups from Wanborough, Wilts.', in Dore and Greene 1977, 263–8

SWAN, V. G. 1984 *The Pottery Kilns of Roman Britain*

TAYLOR, C. C. 1983 *Village and Farmstead : A History of Rural Settlement in England*

TAYLOR, M. V. 1926 'Romano-British Huntingdonshire', *Victoria County History : Huntingdonshire vol. 1*, 219–69

TAYLOR, M. V. 1963 'Romano-British Sculpture from Dorn', *Trans. Bristol and Gloucs. Arch. Soc.* 81, (1962), 194–5

TAYLOR, S. 1969 'Alcester, Warwickshire. No. 27–33 Bleachfield Street SP088572', *West Midlands Arch. News Sheet* 11, (1969), 21–2

TEBBUTT, C. F. 1961 'Roman Cremation Groups from Godmanchester', *Proc. Cambridge Antiq. Soc.* 54, (1960), 83–4

THOMAS, A. C. 1981 *Christianity in Roman Britain to AD 500*

THOMAS, J. 1980 'A Magnetometer Survey of the Bear Field, Cowbridge', *Annual Report, Glamorgan-Gwent Arch. Trust* 1979–80, 35–7

THOMAS, N. 1956 'Note on excavations at Mildenhall', *Wilts. Arch. Mag.* 56, (1955–6), 241–5

THOMPSON, F. H. 1965 *Roman Cheshire*

THORNHILL, P. 1977 'A Lower Thames Ford and the Campaigns of 54BC and AD43', *Arch. Cantiana* 92, (1976), 119–28

THORNHILL, P. 1979 'Second Thoughts on Strood's "Causeway"', *Arch. Cantiana* 94, (1978), 249–54

TODD, M. 1966 'East Bridgeford, Margidunum', *East Midlands Arch. Bull.* 9, (1966), 38–40

TODD, M. 1967 'Excavations at Littlechester, Derby in 1966', *Derbyshire Arch. J.* 86, (1966), 103–4

TODD, M. 1968 *The Roman Fort at Great Casterton, Rutland : excavations of 1960 and 1962* Univ. of Nottingham

TODD, M. 1969 'The Roman Settlement at Margidunum : the excavation of 1966–8', *Trans. Thoroton Soc.* 73, (1969), 6–104

TODD, M. 1970 'The Small Towns of Roman Britain', *Britannia* 1, (1970), 114–30

TODD, M. 1971 'A relief of a Romano-British Warrior God', *Britannia* 2, (1971), 238

TODD, M. 1973 *The Coritani*

TODD, M. 1975 'Margidunum and Ancaster', in Rodwell and Rowley 1975, 211–23

TODD M. (Ed.) 1978 *Studies in the Romano-British Villa*

TODD, M. 1981 *The Roman Town at Ancaster, Lincolnshire : The excavations of 1955–1971*

TOMLINSON, R. 1967 'Droitwich, Bays Meadow 1967', *West Midlands Arch. News Sheet* 10, (1967), 7

TOYNBEE, J. M. C. 1962 *Art in Roman Britain*

TOYNBEE, J. M. C. 1964 *Art in Britain under the Romans*

TRIBBICK, R. C. 1974 'Evidence of iron-working at Braughing', *J. Hist. Metallurgy Society* 8, (1974), 112–15

TROLLOPE, E. 1870 'Ancaster, the Roman Causennae', *Arch. J.* 27, (1870), 1–15

TROLLOPE, E. 1873 'Durobrivae', *Arch. J.* 30, (1873), 127–40

TURLAND, R. E. 1977 'Towcester, Wood Burcote', *Northants. Arch.* 12, (1977), 218–23

VAILLAT, C. 1932 *Le Culte des Sources dans la Gaule Antique* Paris

VOSE, R. H. 1980 *Glass*

WACHER, J. S. 1961 'Cirencester 1960, First Interim Report', *Antiquaries J.* 41, (1961), 63–71

WACHER, J. S. 1966a 'Earthwork Defences of the second century', in Wacher 1966b, 60–9

WACHER, J. S. (Ed.) 1966b *The Civitas Capitals of Roman Britain*

WACHER, J. S. 1969 *Excavations at Brough-on-Humber 1958–1961* Soc. Antiq. Res. Rpt. 25

WACHER, J. S. 1970 'Wanborough, Romano-British settlement at Durocornovium', *Wilts. Arch. Mag.* 65, (1970), 204–5

WACHER, J. S. 1971a 'Yorkshire Towns in the 4th century', in Butler 1971, 165–77

WACHER, J. S. 1971b 'Roman Iron Beams', *Britannia* 2, (1971), 200–2

WACHER, J. S. 1971c 'Wanborough, Romano-British settlement', *Wilts. Arch. Mag.* 66, (1971), 188–9

WACHER, J. S. 1974 'Villae in Urbibus?', *Britannia* 5, (1974), 282–4

WACHER, J. S. 1975a *The Towns of Roman Britain*

WACHER, J. S. 1975b 'Village Fortifications', in Rodwell and Rowley 1975, 51–2

WACHER, J. S. 1975c 'Wanborough', in Rodwell and Rowley 1975, 233–6

WACHER, J. S. 1978 *Roman Britain*

WACHER, J. S. and McWHIRR, A. 1982 *Cirencester Excavations I: Early Roman Occupation at Cirencester*

WALTERS, B., PHILLIPS, B. and GREENE, K. T. 1973 'Some Romano-British Material salvaged from Wanborough, Wilts.', *Wilts. Arch. Mag.* 68, (1973), 64–70

WALTERS, H. B. 1908 'Romano-British Herefordshire', *Victoria County History : Herefordshire vol. 1*, 167–97

WALTERS, H. B. 1910 'Romano-British Nottinghamshire', *Victoria County History : Nottinghamshire vol. 2*, 1–36

WATKIN, W. T. 1886 *Roman Cheshire*

WEBSTER, G. 1957 'Excavations on the defences of the Romano-British town of Kenchester, 1956', *Trans. Woolhope Nat. Field Club* 35, (1956), 138–45

WEBSTER, G. 1958a 'The Roman Military Advance under Ostorius Scapula', *Arch. J.* 115, (1958), 49–98

WEBSTER, G. 1958b 'The bath-house at Wall, Staffs.: excavation in 1956', *Trans. Birmingham Arch. Soc.* 74, (1956), 12–25

WEBSTER, G. 1959 'A section through the defences at Wall, Staffs', *Trans. Birmingham Arch. Soc.* 75, (1957), 24–9

WEBSTER, G. 1961 'An excavation on the Roman site at Littlechester, Derby 1960', *Derbyshire Arch. J.* 81, (1961), 85–110

WEBSTER, G. 1966 'Fort and Town in Early Roman Britain', in Wacher 1966b, 31–45

WEBSTER, G. 1971 'A Roman System of Fortified Posts along Watling Street, Britain', in S. Applebaum (Ed.) *Roman Frontier Studies 1967*, 38–45

WEBSTER, G. 1974 'The West Midlands in the Roman Period', *Trans. Birmingham Arch. Soc.* 86, (1974), 49–59

WEBSTER, G. 1978 *Boudica: the British Revolt against Rome, AD 60*

WEBSTER, G. 1981 *Rome against Caratacus*

WEBSTER, P. V. 1975 'The late Roman Occupation at Wilderspool', *J. Chester and North Wales Arch. Soc.* 58, (1975), 91–2

WEDLAKE, W. J. 1958 *Excavations at Camerton, Somerset, 1926–56*

WEDLAKE, W. J. 1966 'The City Walls of Bath', *Proc. Somerset Arch. Soc.* 110, (1966), 85–107

WEDLAKE, W. J. 1982 *The Excavation of the Shrine of Apollo at Nettleton, Wiltshire, 1956–1971* Soc. of Antiqs. Res. Rpt. 40

WESTELL, W. P. 1932a 'Notes on a Romano-British Cemetery in Hertfordshire', *Proc. Soc. Antiquaries Scotland* 66, (1932), 105–13

WESTELL, W. P. 1932b 'A Romano-British Cemetery at Baldock, Herts.', *Arch. J.* 88, (1931), 247–301

WESTELL, W. P. 1936 [Finds at Braughing in 1936], *East Herts. Arch. Soc. Trans.* 9, (1936), 362–3

WESTELL, W. P. and APPLEBAUM, E. S. 1932 'Romano-British Baldock : past discoveries and future problems', *J. British Arch. Assn.* 38, (1932), 235–77

WHEELER, H. 1986a 'The Racecourse Industrial Area 1969 and 1973', in Dool, Wheeler *et al.* 1986, 154

WHEELER, H. 1986b 'The Racecourse Cemetery', in Dool, Wheeler *et al.* 1986, 222–80

WHEELER, H. 1986c 'Conclusion: The Development of Roman Derby', in Dool, Wheeler *et al.* 1986, 300–4

WHEELER, R. E. M. 1926 'The Roman Fort at Brecon', *Y Cymmrodor* 37, (1926), 1–260

WHEELER, R. E. M. 1928 'A Romano-Celtic Temple near Harlow, Essex', *Antiquaries J.* 8, (1928), 300–26

WHEELER, R. E. M. 1932 with Haverfield, F. J. and Taylor, M. V. 'Romano-British Kent', *Victoria County History : Kent vol. 3*, 1–176

WHEELER, R. E. M. 1954 *The Stanwick Fortifications, North Riding of Yorkshire* Soc. of Antiqs. Res. Rpt. 17

WHEELER, R. E. M. and WHEELER, T. V. 1932 *Report on the Excavation of the Prehistoric, Roman and Post Roman Site in Lydney Park* Soc. of Antiqs. Res. Rpt. 9

WHITAKER, T. D. 1822 *A History of Richmondshire*

WHITEHOUSE, D. B. 1962 'A note on excavation of the Roman fort at Dodderhill, Droitwich, 1961–2', *Trans. Worcs. Arch. Soc.* 39, (1962), 55–58

WHITWELL, J. B. 1970 *Roman Lincolnshire* History of Lincolnshire, vol. II

WHITWELL, J. B. and DEAN, M. J. 1966 'Great Casterton', *East Midlands Arch. Bull.* 8, (1966), 46

WHITWELL, J. B., TODD, M., PONSFORD, M. and WILSON, D. R. 1966 'Ancaster – miscellaneous excavations', *East Midlands Arch. Bull.* 9, (1966), 10–13

WIGHTMAN, E. M. 1985 *Gallia Belgica*

WILD, J. P. 1974 'Roman Settlement in the Lower Nene Valley', *Arch. J.* 131, (1974), 140–70

WILD, J. P. 1976 'A Roman Farm at Castor, 1975', *Durobrivae* 4, (1976), 26

WILD, J. P. 1978 'Villas in the Lower Nene Valley', in Todd 1978, 59–70

WILKES, J. J. and ELRINGTON, C. R. (Eds.) 1978 'Roman Cambridgeshire', *Victoria County History : Cambridgeshire and the Isle of Ely vol. 7*

WILLIAMS, A. 1947 *Roman Canterbury No. 2* (Medici Society)

WILLIAMS, I. 1938 *Canu Aneirin*

WILMOTT, A. 1978 'Kenchester : Interim Report on Excavations', *West Midlands Arch. News Sheet* 21, (1978), 69–74

WILMOTT, A. 1980 'Kenchester (Magnis) : a Reconsideration', *Trans. Woolhope Nat. Field Club* 43, (1980), 117–33

WILMOTT, A. and RAHTZ, S. 1985 'An Iron Age and Roman Settlement outside Kenchester (Magnis), Herefordshire. Excavations 1977–9', *Trans. Woolhope. Nat. Field Club* 45, (1985), 36–185

WILSON, D. R. 1968 'An Early Christian Cemetery at Ancaster', in Barley, M. W. and Hanson, R. P. C. (Eds.) *Christianity in Roman Britain*, 197–9

WILSON, D. R. 1975 'The "Small Towns" of Roman Britain from the air', in Rodwell and Rowley 1975, 9–49

WILSON, D. R. and MAY, J. 1965 'Ancaster', *East Midlands Arch. Bull.* 8, (1965), 13–14

WILSON, P. R. 1984 'Recent Work at Catterick', in Wilson *et al.* 1984, 75–82

WILSON, P. R., JONES, R. F. J. and EVANS, D. M. (Eds.) 1984 *Settlement and Society in the Roman North*

WINDELL, D. 1984 'Irchester Roman Town : Excavations 1981–82', *Northants. Arch.* 19, (1984), 31–51

WITTS, G. B. 1881 *Archaeological Handbook of Gloucestershire*

WOODFIELD, C. 1978 'Towcester SP690481', *Northants Arch.* 13 (1978), 182–4

WOODFIELD, P. 1978 'Roman Architectural Masonry from Northamptonshire', *Northants. Arch.* 13, (1978), 67–86

WOODS, P. J. 1974 'Types of Late Belgic and Early Romano-British Pottery Kilns in the Nene Valley', *Britannia* 5, (1974), 262–81

WOODS, P. and HASTINGS, S. 1984 *Rushden : the early fine wares* Northamptonshire County Council

WOOLLEY, C. L. 1907 'Corstopitum: Provisional Report of the Excavations in 1906', *Arch. Aeliana* 3s, 3, (1907), 161–86

WRIGHT, R. P. 1976 'Tile-stamps of the Sixth Legion found in Britain', *Britannia* 7, (1976), 224–35

YOUNG, C. J. 1975 'The Defences of Alchester', *Oxoniensia* 40, (1975), 136ff.

YOUNG, C. J. 1977 *Oxfordshire Roman Pottery* B.A.R. 43

YOUNG, C. J. 1981 'The late Roman Water-Mill at Ickham, Kent and the Saxon Shore', in Detsicas, A. (Ed.) *Collectanea Historica*, Essays in memory of Stuart Rigold, 32–9

Index

Note: page numbers in **bold type** indicate illustrations